THE ESOTERIC SUBSTANCE
OF VOLTAIRIAN THOUGHT

THE ESOTERIC SUBSTANCE
OF VOLTAIRIAN THOUGHT

by

DENISE BONHOMME

PHILOSOPHICAL LIBRARY

New York

Printed in the United States of America

CONTENTS

PREFACE

The task of presenting Voltaire as an adept, a mystic, and a possible emissary from extra-terrestrial regions is not altogether enviable. Such is the task undertaken by the writer of the present book.

The esoteric or hidden core of texts surveyed in this study has long been known to a relatively small number of persons. But the material in question remains generally unperceived and untaught. The chief purpose of the present work is to expose to the scrutiny of all the veiled bequest of Voltaire.

The philosophy disclosed is not the monopoly of one man. Similar findings are accessible elsewhere in Western literature. Rabelais, Vigny, Shelley, Saint Exupéry, Céline and Proust are but a few others whose lives and writings were dedicated to the same "smuggling" enterprise. The second purpose of the present work is to encourage the esoteric study of numerous literary texts.

The choice of writings analyzed is intended to gather essentials. Voltaire seems to have designed several of his short stories as compact esoteric vehicles of his philosophy. Such are *Zadig, Micromégas, Memnon, Candide,* and *L'Ingénu.* Other Voltairian texts which seem to belie most strongly the possibility of mystical inspiration are likely to be invoked in refutation of the present thesis. Such are *Le Mondain* and the *Poem on the Disaster of Lisbon.* They are examined also.

Numerals frequently convey arcane secrets of secret lore. The full meaning of Voltairian numbers is probably inscrutable to all but the initiate. The chapter devoted to numbers is therefore limited. An effort is made, however, to relate certain figures to corresponding veiled substance.

The exoteric surface of Voltairian writings is too well known to justify much comment. It is mentioned only in relation — and contrast — to esoteric substance.

Esoteric study is comparative in nature. The fundamental question which is raised is the following: Did Voltaire — and many others — conceal in their works the ancient body of knowledge designated as the Secret Doctrine? The question must necessarily be answered by reference to the works of Mme H. P. Blavatsky, founder of the modern Theosophical Society. It was through publication of her works that the previously *Secret* Doctrine was partially released to the general public for the first

7

time in recorded history. In the words of the author, the same material had formerly been restricted to "secret Scriptural records."*

The most widely known books of Mme Blavatsky, *Isis Unveiled and The Secret Doctrine*, were published in 1877 and 1888 respectively. The chronology involved does not rule out kindred inspiration on the part of Voltaire. "Theosophy" — with a small "*t*" — is no recent production of any individual or group. The modern Theosophical Society claims to be no more than the transmitter of ancient science. The identity and continuity of views derived from the Secret Doctrine transcends the barriers of earthly time and space. Separated as they are in time and otherwise, Voltaire, Mme Blavatsky, and many other writers "drank" from the same ancient well of archaic lore. In the words of the author of *The Secret Doctrine*, the set of beliefs commonly designated — and little known — as "Theosophy" is as old as thinking man.**

The non-initiate who wishes to study Voltaire — or other writers — in the light of the Secret Doctrine must turn to the only published form of the Doctrine available to him. The present study therefore relies heavily on the works of Mme Blavatsky. Quotations are generally taken from the "Verbatim" edition of *The Secret Doctrine* which follows most closely the oral teachings of Mme Blavatsky. A few exceptions are made in the case of references which can be found only in the Adyar edition of the same work.

The plan of the present work generally follows the appearance of esoteric material as it presents itself in the writings of Voltaire. Logical veiled sequences underlie each short story. Such hidden architectures are exposed individually and collectively. *Micromégas* is a commentary on the embryonic nature of human knowledge and a positive hint of the full dimensions of cosmos, man, and matter. *Micromégas* is a supplement to the trilogy composed of *Zadig, Candide*, and *L'Ingénu*, a deceptively fragmented unit devoted to the fate of Truth in various times and places. The evolutionary thread running through the trilogy is the main guide of interpretation.

Veiled material is also found in the form of scattered nuggets. The initial paragraph of Chapter II of *L'Ingénu* is a good example of esoteric concentration. Within a short passage are locked symbols involving a Day of Brahma, individual and general evolution, the solitude of spiritual striving, initiation rites, voluntary reincarnation and the esoteric concept of "good company." Esoteric symbolism may have as many as seven keys

---

The Secret Doctrine, p. 797, Vol. II.
**The Secret Doctrine*, p. xxxvi, Vol. I.

or levels of meaning.* The wealth of hidden substance which may be released from one word or expression is often dizzying even to the apprentice using only a few "keys." The multiple inter-connecting reflections defy conventional pigeon-holes and pre-fabricated structures. Presentation is complicated by the novelty aspect of esoteric symbolism. The general public is unfamiliar with the Secret Doctrine and with the special value of such words as "necessity," "silence," "pleasure," "amusement," "usefulness," "inaction," "strength" and "sunrise." The reader must be made aware and reminded of the consistent esoteric "algebra" constituted by such terms which must be "translated" if light is to be shed on certain texts. Some amount of repetition is unavoidable. Some "disgressions" are worthwhile in establishing the consistency of the "underground" literary network. In view of the traditional image of Voltaire, the "unbeliever," the "infidel," the "materialist," the man who understood "nothing about faith or mysticism," the burden of proof inherent to this study is enormous. Full use must be made of the abundance of proof.

The presentation of quoted French texts is generally limited to English translation. But an exception is made in deference to the rich beauty of esoteric poetry. Some prose passages which cannot be adequately studied in translation are presented in both French and English.

What is the *raison d'être* of esoteric literature? Why was some material concealed in certain texts? Why was it not written clearly or openly? One answer lies in the protection of esoteric writers. Persecution, unflattering diagnoses, and sneers have been — and to some extent continue to be — the lot of declared occultists. Secrecy is the necessary shield of esoteric writers, their relatives, and associates. The same rules of prudence apply to Initiates and to literary transmitters of the Secret Doctrine:

> "Several cases could be cited, and well-known names brought forward but for the fact that such publicity might annoy the surviving relatives of the said late Initiates." (*The Secret Doctrine*, pp. xxxv-xxxvi, Vol. I).

Vigny stresses the necessity of esoteric practice in his autobiographical poem, *La Flûte*. Having reported the experimentation of a "beggar" — whose "music" goes "unheard" — with the doctrine of Buddha, the poet then notes that the modern era is "wary of smugglers." The Diary of the same author covertly refers to the destruction of external evidence capable of revealing the true sense of his evolution: "— why this condemnation? You will never know that. . . . The documents of the great trial are burnt, it is insane to look for them."** It is a well known fact

---

*Ibid., p. 22 fn., p. 335, Vol. II.
**Diary, 1833.

of literary history that the testamentary executor of the poet faithfully carried out certain instructions. To the enduring spite of many puzzled critics, various papers about which we can only speculate were kept out of circulation.

The ultimate goal of esoteric writers is to be understood fully and generally in due course of time. Their courtship of the sensitive reader tends to promote spiritual experience. It is intended to prove that certain insights may be gained through use of subjective faculties and through such means only. Rational "bookeeping" is not equal to the task. Another brand of "Reason" is required. Convenient documents neatly laid out in affidavit form will not be found to state: "I am an esoteric writer." "My secret brother X is an esoteric writer." Nor will the key to veiled substance be found in such sources. External evidence of mystical inspiration is far from lacking. But it is of unconventional nature. It must be sought in the texts of the secret literary community and in the comments of esoterically enlightened critics.

The consistency of the esoteric algebra which has already been mentioned is illuminating in many ways. The steady value of esoteric terms used by many writers and the concealed identity of views transmitted by the timeless esoteric network amount to a weighty form of external evidence. Time and repeated testing will be needed to make their reality tangible to a large number or readers.

Considerable insight can be derived from the occasional criticism of one author by another. Certain comments of Vigny on Voltaire are examined in this study. We have much to learn from a deceptive type of fraternal "castigation" which is the veiled tribute of one "smuggler" to another.

Various critics seem to have perceived the esoteric substance of certain texts. Vigny found such commentators in the persons of J. Barbey d'Aurevilly and F. Baldensperger. The following statements give virtual recognition to the concealed essence of the works of Vigny.

> "It is about soul and the highest labor of a soul. A fearsome riddle for all mediocre minds. In that respect, for the minds, the rare minds, who will make sense out of it, nothing so beautiful or nothing so poignant as this book . . . since Pascal!" (J. Barbey d'Aurevilly, *Poésie et poètes*, 1906.)

> "One is prompt to infer from the Silence of Vigny, a haughty sterility, from certain disapprovals a total pessimism, and above all from his reserve and dignity an impersonal and icy rigidity. Fortunately, the true sense of his life and work continues to inspire a few scattered readers. — The work and the person of Vigny become something like the rallying word of an indiscernible community, often scorned by the victors of the day, ignored by the turbulent consecrations of publicity; that community which upholds the reincarnations of pure spirit, intelligence, devotion, self-denial,

10

dignity, the given word; immune to injury and dereliction." (F. Balden-sperger, *Alfred de Vigny*, Essais Critiques, 1929.)

It is stated by both critics that appearance and reality are two different things where the message of Vigny is concerned. It is felt by both that the thought of the poet is not generally understood. Only a few "rare minds" — or an "indiscernible community" — are expected to grasp the essence of texts under study. The term "reincarnations" is used by Baldensperger openly and provocatively — though in appearance figuratively. General contempt and low visibility suggest that the "indiscernible community" mentioned by the latter critic may be a secret society. The common verdict of both commentators seems to be aimed at the superficial judgment of the majority of readers. The grievance voiced by many esoteric writers and especially by Proust seems to be expressed here. The Western or Judaeo-Christian world "knows" people in general and writers in particular "without knowing them."*

Sinclair Lewis refers to a certain type of cultured person who "knows all about literature except maybe how to read."** Ionesco writes in a critical essay that Proust is not generally understood. Proust himself invites his reader to try various kinds of "optics" and see how he "reads" best. Sartre refers in *Les Mots* to the days of his youth when he *believed* that he fully grasped the message of Rabelais and Vigny. The same work of Sartre contains a candid admission: the author confesses that he has had to use his own writings to "deceive" his "blind orphan:" mankind. Louis Pauwels and Jacques Bergier — who blandly label Rabelais as the "great initiate"*** — speculate on the possible existence of a "code" in literary works. William Braden observes that the works of many great writers lend themselves to esoteric interpretation. English literature is surmised to be remarkably rich in hidden substance.**** Thoreau suggests in his chapter of *Walden* devoted to *Reading* that the same is true of great classics in general.

The reader is left to his own devices where positive enlightenment is concerned. Sinclair Lewis makes no statement on how one should "read" literature. Ionesco does not say what a correct interpretation of Proust might be. Proust does not designate the optical "glasses" which might be most helpful in the study of his writings. Sartre does not tell us what is difficult to perceive in the works of Rabelais or Vigny. Nor does he hint in what manner he deceives his own readers. Neither Pauwels nor

---

A la Recherche du temps perdu, p. 382, Vol. II.
**Arrowsmith*, Ch. V, III.
***The Morning of the Magicians*, p. 224.
****The Private Sea — LSD and the Search for God*, Ch. XI.

11

Bergier specify the character of the "code" about which they "speculate" or the nature of what it might disclose. Braden does not choose to shed positive light on the nature of the esoteric mystery. The reader might as well be told again and again: "Seek, you may find." He is therefore justified in seeking boldly. The many hints of perceptive critics — often illustrious in their own right — are valuable guides of the explorer of esoteric literature. In this respect also time and repeated testing will be needed before the solid reality of the veiled message and the consistency of the "code" become tangible to many readers.

The raison d'être of esoteric practice involves more than the safety and tranquillity of certain persons. Occult science is viewed by its believers as a source of awesome power. Dangerous knowledge must be withheld from the amateurs and from the irresponsible. In the words of Mme Blavatsky, "to impart to the unprepared multitude secrets of such tremendous importance," is "equivalent to giving a child a lighted candle in a powder magazine."*

Esoteric practice also reflects evolutionary belief. The veiled message is fated to emerge in due course of human progress and at that time only. It is often stated by Mme Blavatsky that so much information and no more could be given on certain topics at the time of writing. Additional knowledge was then — as always — available to initiates. But it could not be released for general consumption. Evolutionary timing is a major preoccupation of all esoteric writers. (The same concern may shed light on the allegorical role of a Proustian character: Mme Bontemps. The name of the incorruptible lady may be translated as "Mrs. Right Time.") The importance of the "right time" is repeatedly stressed in the Secret Doctrine:

> "The Secret Doctrine was the universally diffused religion of the ancient and prehistoric world. Proofs of its diffusion, authentic records of its history, a complete chain of documents, showing its character and presence in every land, together with the teaching of its great adepts, exist to this day in the secret crypts of libraries belonging to the Occult Fraternity.
>
> This statement is rendered more credible by a consideration of the following facts: the tradition of the thousands of ancient parchments saved when the Alexandrian library was destroyed; the thousands of Sanskrit works which disappeared in India in the reign of Akbar; the universal tradition in China and Japan that the true old texts with the commentaries, which alone make them comprehensible — amounting to many thousands of volumes — have long passed out of the reach of profane hands; the disappearance of the vast sacred and occult literature of Babylon; the loss of those keys which alone could solve the thousand riddles of the Egyptian

*The Secret Doctrine, p. xxxv, I.

hieroglyphic records; the tradition in India that the real secret commentaries which alone make the Veda intelligible, though no longer visible to profane eyes, still remain for the initiate, hidden in secret caves and crypts; and an identical belief among the Buddhists, with regard to their secret books.

The Occultists assert that all these exist, safe from Western spoliating hands, to re-appear in some more enlightened age, for which in the words of the late Swami Dayanand Sarasvati, 'the Mlechchas (outcasts, savages, those beyond the pale of Aryan civilization) will have to wait.'" (*The Secret Doctrine,* p. xxxiv, Vol. I.)

Does our era qualify as the "right time" for the emergence of secret knowledge long withheld from the profane? Some facts and trends suggest that it may.

Strongly established in its own right, Science can afford to survey previously delicate domains. The stigma of theological and other superstition is less readily attached to certain studies than it used to be. Various tenets of the Secret Doctrine such as the existence of submerged continents may now be examined with relative impunity — as long as the precedence of occult philosophy and occult philosophy itself remain unmentioned. The probable existence of Lemuria was already recognized by some representatives of official Science during the lifetime of Mme Blavatsky (1831-1891). The recent work of Immanuel Velikovsky tends to give considerable support to the occult belief in the periodic tilting of the axis of earth. While the tendency remains to smile indulgently at ancient knowledge, there is a certain willingness to compare some of its aspects with current findings. The rills and "mascons" detected on the lunar surface a few years ago constitute a case in point:

"Paul L. Muller, a mathematician at Caltech's Propulsion Laboratory, reached this conclusion by studying the moon's 'mascons,' — mass concentrations of very dense material below the lunar surface. 'In two months, two U.S. astronauts are scheduled to land on the moon and gather samples of the soil in a mare.' 'If the samples reveal an unusually high percentage of iron,' Muller said, 'I think it would support the theory that there once was water on the moon. It would be ironic if the ancient astronomers should prove to have been right when they called the dark areas of the moon 'seas.' And if the seas were real, then the inevitable next question is: did life exist in those areas?'" (NEWSWEEK, *Science and Space, Moon Rivers?,* May 12, 1969.)

The "ironic" possibility considered by Paul Muller represents a tenet of the Secret Doctrine. Occult Science has held from time immemorial that life once existed on our satellite and that it is related to life on our planet.

Medical research has found some "old wives' remedies" to have scien-

13

tific value. The once derided belief in the therapeutic power of certain fungi was vindicated when penicillin was "discovered." Magnetism, hypnotism, and electricity are now taken for granted though imperfectly understood. The ABC of modern science would have smacked of the faggot not too many years ago had it then been offered to public scrutiny. The accepted truths of our era frequently reflect no more than the restated occult lore of ancient times. There seems to be no reason why the same gradual re-evaluation of knowledge should stop abruptly in our age. The separation of valid occult science from superstition may be in order in all areas of human learning.

What fantastic domains may soon be annexed by the ever-expanding field of human inquiry is anyone's guess. Famous voices are heard to advocate "new" ventures. The proposed undertakings are closely related to the Voltairian "conveyances of up there" or intuitive flights. The recent apotheosis of space rocketry has aroused deserved enthusiasm. It has also resurrected an old dilemma. Does the key to knowledge and progress lie in more and more sophisticated machines? Is a scientific dead end any less of a dead end for the material distance traveled by space capsules? Must our explorations reach beyond the trodden path of matter-bound science into new dimensions?

It is suggested by some contemporary writers that the latter query should be answered in the affirmative. One observation made by Mr. Norman Mailer at the time of the first manned moon-landing is provocative. Having wistfully baptized himself "Aquarius," the author asks the weighty question of the Aquarian age:

"Are we poised for a philosophical launch? It is possible there is no way to settle for less." (LIFE, *A Fire on the Moon*, August 29, 1969.)

In a letter addressed to LIFE magazine and released by the same publication, an illustrious colleague and a possible kindred spirit of Saint Exupéry — Charles Lindbergh — points to vast horizons now open to man. They are non-technological horizons. Lindbergh can hardly be accused of scorning the exploits of scientists, engineers, or astronauts — least of all those of pilots. But he recognizes the limitations of matter-bound knowledge. His convictions, those of Voltaire, Saint Exupéry, and Norman Mailer may echo the same basic belief.

The Voltairian concept of a "philosophical launch" seems to transcend the plane of lumbering "vehicles:"

"Those who travel by stagecoach and carriage only will no doubt be surprised at the conveyances of up there; for we, on our little heap of mud, conceive nothing beyond our ways." (*Micromégas*, Ch. I.)

Saint Exupéry has a similar comment on XXth Century flying machines:

"He nodded gently as he looked at my airplane. — 'It's true that on that, you could not have come from very far.'" (*The Little Prince,* Ch. III.)

Lindbergh expresses himself as follows:

"If we can combine our knowledge of science with the wisdom of wildness, if we can nurture civilization through roots in the primitive, man's potentialities appear to be unbounded. Through his evolving awareness; he can merge with the miraculous — to which we can attach what better name than 'God?' And in this merging, as long sensed by intuition but still only vaguely perceived by rationality, experience may travel without need for accompanying life.

"Will we then find life to be only a stage, though an essential one, in a cosmic evolution of which our evolving awareness is beginning to become aware? Will we discover that only *without* spaceships can we reach the galaxies; that only *without* cyclotrons can we know the interior of the atom? To venture beyond the fantastic accomplishments of this physically fantastic age, sensory perception must combine with the extra-sensory, and I suspect that the two will prove to be different faces of each other. I believe it is through sensing and thinking about such concepts that great adventures of the future will be found." (LIFE, *Forty-two years after another historic flight. A Letter from Lindbergh,* September 15, 1969.)

A qualitative shifting of gears seems to be advocated in our approach to knowledge.

Movement is perceptible within some churches. Its course frequently parallels the trends noted above. Oblique though it be, "return to the source" of being and knowledge is the goal of many current religious quests. The alleged divinity of the anthropomorphic Biblical God is increasingly questioned. Catechisms tend to designate God as Pure Spirit. The ecumenical movement — which makes strange bed-fellows — is a transparent attempt of the spiritual establishment to survive at any price. But its pragmatic necessity is in itself significant and rich in attractive possibilities. The same urge to perform a spiritual synthesis is felt by a meaningful number of sincere individuals. Obscure but dedicated Christians voice occasional belief in original virtue — not original sin. Such prominent men as Teilhard de Chardin and the late Bishop Pike give us abundant food for thought. The abyss commonly separating Christian preaching from Christian practice is bravely denounced by a few men of the cloth. The pleas of such priests and clergymen are usually hushed by the executive bolts or the thunderous silence of hierarchs. But the force of generous indignation is uncrushed.

The Jehovic God dies hard. "Pozzo"* lives on with baneful semi-

---

*Samuel Beckett, *Waiting for Godot.*

15

subtlety in the general attitudes and institutions of the Judaeo-Christian world. Self-righteous materialism and warmongering, social injustice, calculated "indifference" to the population bomb, thinly disguised hatred of woman, debased masculine mystiques continue to plague mankind. But the poorly camouflaged tangle of entrenched evils does not go undetected. Nor does the truncated, tortured dogma from which it stems. The heartening "scandal" caused within some churches by a few militants tends to restore to Christians the integrity of the true word of Christ. Whether the courageous dissenters know it or not, whether or not they covet the title, they are "Voltairian" soldiers.

The veiled message of Voltaire is the true message of Buddha and Christ. It is the same as the teaching of great spiritual leaders of all times. Christ, the arch-agitator of incurable subversives, would find his most fanatical devotees ready to crucify him again in the name of Christian values were he to return. But he would find no shortage of youthful followers of all ages, weary of dog-eat-dog mystiques and Pharisaic blindness. Our world may be ready for the Voltairian re-statement of his Word.

Interest in occult science is at an all-time high. It is inseparable from multiple news items ranging from the amusing to the gruesome. Karma, Sutratma, "The Great Wall of Skin," "Nothing is Real," "Release," are upon us in a psychedelic wave of sense and mind-blowing symphonies. Magic finds its way into popular magazines and Sunday papers. All is fish that comes to the net of sensationalism. Magic is the sensational topic par excellence. Facts suffer accordingly in the reporting process. The Secret Doctrine is rarely mentioned as such when it should be mentioned. The word "Theosophy" is put to strange use. The majority of articles dwell upon thriller-type horror stories connected with black magic. The expert definition of occultism which is given by Mme Blavatsky — "Occultism is altruism" — is too "dull" for a profitable "scoop." It is seldom — if ever — quoted. But the prejudice of some and the ignorance of many does not alter one fact: general interest is there. Truth will probably emerge some day from the current welter of misconceptions.

The present study demonstrates the identity of substance linking Voltairian thought and the Secret Doctrine. Similar work remains to be done on a large number of authors who lived in widely separated times and places. The texts of such writers are occasionally quoted in the course of the present analysis. But the general scope of esoteric literature can only be suggested within the narrow confines of one book. The field of literary research which now lies open is too plentiful and too precious to be hoarded by any one person. It is neither possible nor desirable that the task be performed by one individual. It is all too easy to dismiss a personal interpretation as "subjective" or pathological. It will be less easy to lavish such convenient labels if and when similar discoveries are made by numerous readers. There is reason to believe that the present findings will not be welcome in all quarters and that the above-mentioned labels — perhaps a few others — will be used. It is therefore hoped that the vast amount and impressive quality of research to be done will attract many dedicated seekers. The elements of esotericism which are now gathered from the works of Rabelais, Proust, Saint Exupéry, Céline, and others can be no more than introductions to future studies.

It is hoped that the esoteric equivalences now presented will be tested by many readers against the background of many texts. It is hoped that one hypothesis will be kept in mind: Could the Secret Doctrine form the hidden core of numerous writings? Many persons are currently interested in mystical literature such as the works of Hermann Hesse. They will readily grasp the concealed message of Voltaire which is only one link in a spectacular chain. They will learn to speculate on their own where other great writers are concerned. They will detect "Voltairian" philosophy under all kinds of garbs — or "veils" — in an impressive number of places.

The present study contains a reference to an old popular French song. Other unorthodox media of esoteric expression are examined. Eclecticism is an old tradition with transmitters of the Secret Doctrine. The divine sense of humor possessed by "smugglers" is bound to a vision of the world which is all-embracing. Esoteric writers capitalize on the fact that spirit is present on all planes of existence. They know that truth may be found — and conveyed — on least exalted levels. They are grandly unafraid of what is commonly termed "common." We should not be surprised if their unbridled flights lead us anywhere in time, space, or other dimensions. We may find ourselves studying the Book of Dzyan, the latest paperback, "children's" books and fairy tales. We may speculate on certain movies, perhaps even comic strips. We will assuredly travel where timid minds fear to venture.

The present work contains a section on prophecy. Also featured are passages dealing with the probable mission and cosmic origin of Voltaire. Voltairian texts strongly suggest that their author appeared on earth as a result of voluntary reincarnation. Such unorthodox material is not presented for the sake of sensationalism. Voltaire is too sensational in his exoteric personality alone to need embellishment. The inclusion of such findings is dictated by the essence of texts analyzed.

17

What is here perceived of the Voltairian esoteric iceberg may not extend very far beyond the water-line. But it is presented without cowardice. Voltaire hoped that his veiled message would be faced squarely when found. This study is an attempt to respect his sacred wish.

INTRODUCTION

The legendary fame of Voltaire no longer seems newsworthy. The popular image of François-Marie Arouet is firmly established. His figure dominates an age. His name lives on in language. The terms "Voltairian spirit," "Voltairian philosophy" rival venerable clichés of comparable origin: "Platonic love" and "Machiavelic intent." No erudition is required to make them negotiable in everyday exchange. They are the joint property of scholars and the man on the street.

For all their practicality — perhaps because of it — such characterizations as the word "Voltairian" are uneasy à peu près. Texts defy and mock them with galling irreverence. Complexity and seeming paradox stand unresolved and untouched by compact formulae. Thought in general, Voltairian thought in particular, resists tidy labels and their narrow confines. While the adjective "Voltairian" generally brings to mind the idea of religious doubt or even unbelief, while it is associated with the famous imprecation: "Crush the infamous!", positive grasp of the underlying system is no easy task. Voltairian commentators give evidence of acute puzzlement:

"— one must make no mistake about the deism of Voltaire. No one ever was more profoundly irreligious. His philosophical God is an affirmation which seemed necessary to his mind, but which did not touch his heart. Belief in a real and tangible God seemed to him to be foolishness and the believer who loves and hopes a dupe. He limited his thoughts to earthy life." (*Histoire de la Littérature Française*, G. Lanson and P. Truffau, p. 414.)

"But there is also a basic conflict between Voltaire and Christianity; and one can only grasp it in his commentary on the *Thoughts* of Pascal. A person who has not read them cannot know to what extent the contradiction is impossible to resolve. Voltaire does not accept the idea that man is *wretched* and he proves it by showing that civilization develops from day to day, that the streets of Paris are lit, that beautiful carriages are seen there, etc. One would easily believe in paradox or in a prank if all the other writings of Voltaire did not support the seriousness of these arguments." (*Histoire Illustrée de la Littérature Française*, Ch. M. Des Granges, p. 503.)

"He cannot be respectful, he can't help it. God himself, about whom he has written (*Philosophical Dictionary*) such beautiful pages, is subjected at random to his irreverence. He believes in the immortality of the soul and in a future life but vaguely; and on that score also contradiction abounds."

In short, it is very difficult to precise the philosophy of Voltaire which appears to us today to be contained in these few words: moral and civic freedom, material progress of society, tolerance, deism." (*Histoire Illustrée de la Littérature Française,* Ch. M. Des Granges, p. 604.)

"His skepticism prepared him poorly for an objective study of religious. He understands nothing about faith or mysticism. For him religious minds are divided into two categories: the "rogues" who do not believe in their religion but who consider it as a means of domination, and the "imbeciles," credulous and enthusiastic who become fanatics." (*Dialogues,* XXV.) This amounts, obviously, to underrating what is profound in religious feelings." (*Lagarde et Michard,* XVIIIe Siècle, p. 115.)

"Is it true that this thought (Voltairian thought) is not sufficiently bold and is satisfied with partial criticisms without posing the true social problem? — In the face of those who will construct systems at all costs, oracles and fortune-tellers who interpret the providences and inescapable decrees of History — the *Tales* invite us to modestly limit ourselves to facts." (*Voltaire, Romans et contes,* Classiques Garnier, Edition de H. Bénac, pp. XI-XII.)

Confusion and contradiction are obviously not limited to Voltaire. Hesitant statements and further questioning are frequent products of Voltairian study. "Paradox," "pranks," "a philosophy difficult to define," occasional reverence, blasphemous tendencies, metaphysical interests and rank materialism are all noted with legitimate perplexity.

The "basic conflict between Voltaire and Christianity" which is noted by Mr. Ch. Des Granges does exist, as any reader of Voltairian texts well knows. But the next statement of the commentator is open to question. It is not from the isolated survey of Pascal which is made by Voltaire that light may be gathered or shed on the nature of the conflict. The present study will show that it is from the trilogy represented by *Zadig, Candide,* and *L'Ingénu* that insight may be gained on the matter. The important distinction which should be made between the true message of Christ and "Christianity" will also clarify puzzling aspects of Voltairian philosophy. It will explain — among other things — the Voltairian evaluation of Pascal.

The "materialism" of Voltaire is genuine. But it should be carefully defined in terms of the Voltairian concept of "matter." "Micromégas" suggests — with some insistence — that matter is the external manifestation of Spirit on the lowest plane of existence. Such hints should be heeded. The dedication of Voltaire to material progress includes but mostly transcends such conveniences as street-lights and carriages. Voltaire recognized — as does any reasonable person — that a certain level of physical well-being favors intellectual and spiritual development. He knew that the average Western man is ill-equipped to transcend a suffering body. But his ultimate objective was the superior potential of Man.

M. Des Granges is partially correct when he speculates on the likelihood of Voltairian "pranks." But he seems to overlook the symbolic possibilities of "light" and the symbolic possibilities of "wheels" of evolution.

The irreverent or disrespectful attitude of Voltaire toward the Deity should give us food for thought rather than a basis for summary judgment. How does one explain the numerous and vibrant professions of faith which may be found in his writings if the charge has substance? Should we not speculate that one inferior version of God — anthropomorphic Jehovah for instance — may be rejected while the Unknowable Supreme Being is ardently worshipped?

The skepticism of Voltaire is a prime target of critics. It is, as shown above, usually felt to be opposed to "the objective study of religions." It is commonly viewed as a form of systematic and negative bias.

Skepticism demands and *examines* evidence — as etymology suggests. (Greek: skopein, to examine) — One may briefly note that "bishops" — whose titles have the same linguistic origin — may be unqualified for "the objective study of religions" if skepticism is deemed a handicap in the performance of such work. Skepticism is linked to the generally respected requirements of impartiality and burden of proof. Far from being opposed to "objective" thinking, it is an indispensable aspect of such thinking. Descartes once wrote that "he who seeks the truth must as far as possible, doubt everything." Diderot once defined skepticism as the first step toward truth:

> "What one has never questioned has not been proven. What one has not examined without prejudice has never been well examined. Skepticism is therefore the first step toward truth." (Denis Diderot, *Pensées Philosophiques,* XXXI).

No author should be deemed unfit for "the objective study of religions" because of our failure to use words correctly. The fact that "skepticism" has practically become synonymous with negative bias does not alter the value of pure skepticism. We sorely need to approach the writings of Voltaire — and of many others — with a careful definition of terms.

The commentary of *Lagarde et Michard* seems to postulate a special "objectivity" applicable to religions only: perhaps an objectivity of subjective nature. The present study submits that Voltaire himself wholeheartedly endorsed such a view where a specific plane of belief is concerned. With respect to "faith," "mysticism," and "depth of religious feelings," all areas in which Voltaire is summarily found wanting, the present work will show that the alleged infidel "understood" them to an impressive degree.

There is an element of sad irony in the judgment of *Lagarde et Michard*. The same subjective type of objectivity which seems to be advocated would perform wonders if the authors of certain manuals could apply it to some writers — such as Voltaire.

The question raised by Henri Bénac is answered by the esoteric message of Voltaire. Voltairian thought *is* daring enough whether "the true social problem" or other matters be concerned. The *Tales* do stress the realm of fact. But the Voltairian definition of "fact" which is conveyed by the said short stories involves "the reverse side of a fine picture." No one worked harder to make us "lift the veil" of appearance or gaze on "the other side" than did the Sage of Ferney.

Let us ponder the exquisite *Epître Dédicatoire à la Sultane Sheraa* which is affixed to *Zadig*. In Voltaire's own words, the story "says more than it seems to say." Could this statement refer to a creed more dangerous to proclaim than his already explosive socio-political views? Could the discreet observation point to occult philosophy? What unbreakable golden thread of unsuspected logic might emerge if one responds to the above plea for understanding with the occult hypothesis in mind? Let us attempt the daring venture, remembering another Voltairian exhortation: "Don't be surprised at anything, and follow me!"*

Zadig, L'Ermite.

22

ACKNOWLEDGMENT

This writer wishes to thank all persons from whom she received moral support during the difficult and rewarding years which were primarily devoted to the preparation of this book.

No person engaged in such work needs any great amount of sustenance other than the work itself. But the "slings and arrows" which are expected and received are many and sources of support are all the more precious.

I wish to thank my foul-weather friends who followed and encouraged my slow progress. I wish to thank my son, Norman, who shared the experience. I wish to thank my daughter Claire — and her husband Leo — who also gave me loving, understanding, spirited support.

I wish to most specially thank my loyal students. Their loyalty was not primarily directed at a person. The young people knew well that, if the teacher was sometimes "inspiring," it was only because of that certain something other and infinitely bigger than herself.

The students did not care if the teacher was more than thirty. They did not care whether she was "straight" or "non-straight." They did not care which kind of "coat of skin" she wore. They did not care whether she was known or unknown. They pursued knowledge for its own sake. Their sole concerns were the nature of the new field of study and its potential value to mankind.

The teacher watched the attentive young faces brighten with unfakable light. She took those faces home. The faces were there at night, when physical exhaustion threatened, when the right words would not come. They reminded the teacher and writer that the task must be done for them and for other "children" of all ages who would be heartened by the esoteric message of great men. The teacher watched the students come to class "loaded to the gunwales" — as Céline would have it — with the happy burden of their own findings.

To those who claim — as has been claimed from time immemorial — that young people have "gone to the dogs," this teacher will never cease to say: "Give them something truly pure and truly beautiful. And watch them go!"

ZADIG

The portrait of the title character lends itself to allegorical interpretation from the very beginning of the story.

The young man lives in ancient Babylon or Babel, a symbol of Pagan knowledge. He is well acquainted with the philosophy of Zoroaster, a doctrine which guides his thinking, his words, and his actions. In spite of his paganistic background — perhaps because of it — he is endowed with remarkable wisdom and attains a rare degree of virtue:

> "Du temps du roi Moabdar, il y avait à Babylone un jeune homme nommé Zadig, né avec un beau naturel, fortifié par l'éducation. Quoique riche et jeune, il savait modérer ses passions, il n'affectait rien; il ne voulait point toujours avoir raison, et savait respecter la faiblesse des hommes. On était étonné de voir qu'avec beaucoup d'esprit il n'insultât jamais par des railleries à ces propos si vagues, si rompus et tumultueux, à ces médisances téméraires, à ces décisions ignorantes, à ces turlupinades grossières, à ce vain bruit de paroles, qu'on appelait *conversation* dans Babylone. Il avait appris, dans le premier livre de Zoroastre, que l'amour-propre est un ballon gonflé de vent, dont il sort des tempêtes quand on lui a fait une piqûre. Zadig surtout ne se vantait pas de mépriser les femmes et de les subjuguer. Il était généreux; il ne craignait point d'obliger les ingrats, suivant ce grand précepte de Zoroastre: *Quand tu manges, donne à manger aux chiens, dussent-ils te mordre.* Il était aussi sage qu'on peut l'être, car il cherchait à vivre avec des sages. Instruit dans les sciences des anciens Chaldéens, il n'ignorait pas les principes physiques de la nature tels qu'on les connaissait alors, et savait de la métaphysique ce qu'on en a su dans tous les âges, c'est-à-dire fort peu de chose." (*Le Borgne*, p. 11).

("In the days of King Moabdar, there was in Babylon a young man named Zadig, born with fine natural gifts fortified by upbringing. Although rich and young, he knew how to control his passions; he was without affectation; he did not want to always have the last word, and knew how to respect the weakness of men. People were surprised to see that, with a great deal of wit, he never attacked by means of mockery those exchanges which are so vague, so broken, so loud, those summary pronouncements, those crude comedies, that vain noise of words which were called *conversation* in Babylon. He had learned, in the first book of Zoroaster, that pride is a balloon inflated with wind, from which storms are released when it is punctured. Zadig, above all, did not boast of scorning women or of subjugating them. He was generous; he did not fear to oblige the ungrateful, following this great precept of Zoroaster: *When you eat, feed the dogs, even if they are to bite you.* He was as wise as one can be, for he sought to live with wise men. Learned in the sciences of the ancient Chaldees, he was not ignorant about the physical principles of nature as they were known in those days, and knew about metaphysics what has been known about them in all ages, which is to say very little.")

Judged by its fruit — or remarkable human product — the tree of Chaldean knowledge seems to deserve respect. Lack of vanity; respectful, uncalculating, and compassionate treatment of all fellow-beings are prized and demonstrated by Zadig. The injunction set off by italics amounts to the well-known exhortation to "turn the other cheek" or kill hatred with goodness. While the precept brings to mind the teachings of Christ, it is an indirect reflection of Far Eastern thought on Good and Evil, Cause and Effect, and impersonal Divine Retribution. Within such a system revenge is not only pointless but harmful to the person who seeks it. Vicious circles of wickedness must be arrested through lack of retaliation. In one respect at least, the lofty ethics practiced by the disciple of Zoroaster resembles the ethics of Buddha and Christ.

The importance of knowledge is stressed. Zadig is familiar with the "physical principles of nature as they were known in those days," a concept likely to embrace occult science. The spiritual aspect of ancient learning is frequently noted in theosophical and related publications.

> "The third degree of the Pythagoricians was that of the 'Physikoi,' not of physicists in the modern sense of the word, but of students of the inner life, who learned to recognize divine life under all its veils, and were thus able to understand its evolution. A life of the greatest purity was required of all those students." (*La Sorcellerie des campagnes*, Charles Lancelin, p. 13).

The quality of Zoroastrian ethics reminiscent of both Buddha and Christ suggests universal values representing the finest traditions of both East and West. The possible existence — and practice — of such a system was a well-known preoccupation of Voltaire. While the reference to Chaldean culture as it was known in those days may bring to mind obsolete beliefs incompatible with modern progress, it may also suggest lost or concealed treasures of science. The secrecy surrounding such lore is due to the awesome power which is said to be the product of advanced occult knowledge. As we should know in our era of nuclear fission, superior learning can destroy its possessors — and itself — through scorn of ethics. What applies to the atomic age is said to have applied to ancient traditions. The vital necessity of fusing Knowledge-and-Ethics is repeatedly stressed in theosophical and esoteric texts.

> " — religion and science were closer knit than twins in days of old — they were one in two and two in one from the very moment of their conception. With mutually convertible attributes, science was spiritual and religion was scientific." (*Isis Unveiled*, p. 263, Vol. 2).
>
> "It is not the pure at heart, and he who studies but with a view to perfecting himself and so more easily acquiring the promised immortality, who need

have any fear; but rather he who makes of the science of sciences a sinful pretext for worldly motives, who should tremble." (*Isis Unveiled*, p. 119, Vol. 2).

The fact that the ethics of Zadig are stressed *first* and his knowledge *second* suggests the precedence of the former. Ethics belong to the very foundation of "Zoroastrian" philosophy which is itself reported to have its origin in India.* Voltaire seems to have deliberately placed first things first, combining science and spirituality and in effect subordinating the former to the latter.

The final observation on metaphysics seems to imply the folly of any speculation beyond sensory experience and related intellectual inquiry. But the apparent innuendo does not necessarily extend to Chaldean lore except through more or less conscious projection on the part of the reader. Voltaire's use of the indefinite pronoun *on* leaves room for valid metaphysical knowledge restricted to a few persons. What "people in general" have known about metaphysics throughout recorded history does not rule out the existence of valuable, carefully guarded metaphysical learning. The keen interest of Zadig in an élite of "wise men" tends to support the possibility.

The "physical" sciences of Antiquity in general — and Chaldea in particular — were transcendental, metaphysical, and psychic:

> "Sciences which remain unknown in our days were, it has been ascertained, thoroughly studied and practiced in the sacred crypts of the ancient East, and other areas of knowledge which now seem to us absolutely outside of nature because they are based upon natural laws which escape us — such as occult experimentation, psychic and in general hyperphysical experimentation — were common in most ancient times, in the temples of India, Egypt, Thracia, Gaul, etc." (*La Sorcellerie des Campagnes*, Charles Lancelin, p. 20).

It is suggested in *L'Ingénu* that the Voltairian concept of "physics" does not shun the realm of the "psychic." "My son — everything is physical within us, any secretion benefits the body and everything which relieves it relieves the soul." If all is physical within us, the soul — the existence of which seems to be beyond doubt — must be physical itself. The alert reader has reason to conclude that the Voltairian view of "physics" is identical to that of the Ancients.

If the "physical" sciences of the Ancients in general — and Chaldea in particular — were permeated with spirituality, it may follow that the popular metaphysics mentioned by Voltaire are mere constructions of the unspiritualized intellect. Zadig does not "ignore" the former, spiritualized

---

Isis Unveiled, pp. 142-43, Vol. 2.

variety of science which is restricted to a few sages. But he knows very little about the other type of speculation. The metaphysical physics of old and the metaphysics known to the modern world may therefore be different things. The distinction seems to have allowed Voltaire to aim a deceptive barb at metaphysical speculation while remaining faithful to metaphysical revelation. If such a contrastive judgment was intended by the author of *Zadig*, it is identical to corresponding theosophical views:

"The highest flights of modern (Western) metaphysics have fallen far short of the truth. Much of current agnostic speculation on the existence of the 'First Cause' is little better than veiled materialism — the terminology alone being different. — " (*The Secret Doctrine*, p. 327, Vol. I).

The transcendental capacity of Man is recognized and stressed in the Secret Doctrine. Man is regarded as potentially "omniscient."* The qualities of Zadig — both natural and acquired — tend to support that view. The wisdom of the young man represents a rare degree of knowledge, sensitivity and reason which is esoterically and otherwise apparent at an early stage of the story. The transcendental potential of less advanced human beings is also stressed — with typical Voltairian humor and lucidity. Psychological "storms" are viewed as likely development whenever misguided self-love, selfishness and vanity — "l'amour-propre" — prevail. The suggested parallel between unnamed cataclysmic forces and the explosive capacities of Man is intriguing. For better or for worse, "homo sapiens" carries within himself in more or less latent state an awesome reserve of power.

The "naturalism" of Antiquity — which may be worth comparing with the Rabelaisian "physis" — embraced what we now regard as the "supernatural." The physical principles of nature as they were known in those days may reflect the same concept in *Zadig*. The philosophy of Zoroaster is regarded by occultists as a version of the Far Eastern Secret Doctrine. The Voltairian hero is therefore likely to conceive "Nature" in a manner which leaves abundant room for unknown "wonders" and no room whatsoever for the "supernatural."

" 'I do not like the supernatural,' said Zadig — " (*The Dance*, p. 83).

" — There is no miracle. Everything that happens is the result of law — eternal, immutable, ever active. — Apparent miracle is but the operation of forces antagonistic to what Dr. W. F. Carpenter, F.R.S. — a man of great learning but little knowledge — calls 'the well-ascertained laws of nature.' Like many of his class, Dr. Carpenter ignores the fact that there

The Key to Theosophy, p. 23.

may be laws once 'known,' now unknown to science." (*Isis Unveiled*, **p.** 587, Vol. 2).

The Voltairian designation of "the physical principles of Nature" is etymologically pleonastic. It is doubly redundant on the esoteric plane. The exploitation of terms "physics," "metaphysics" and "Nature" which is suggested may have been intended to achieve two ends: to place a barrier in the path of the majority of readers and to induce critical meditation in others. It will be found frequently in the course of the present study that such "killing of two birds with one stone" is a favorite technique of esoteric writers.

The natural heritage of uncommon virtue enjoyed by Zadig suggests a harvest prepared in previous incarnations. The effect of Divine Justice, Unfailing Retribution, or Karma, is perceptible in various aspects of birth such as physical, intellectual, and spiritual endowment. Etymologically at least, the "fine *nature*" of the young man — "un beau naturel" — (c.f., Latin *natus*) may be related to birth, and in the present case, to rebirth.

Elements of esoteric vocabulary are found in the first chapter of *Zadig*. "Strength," "force," "energy" all represent spirituality in the Secret Doctrine.* The native temperament of Zadig, "fortified" by upbringing and personal effort suggests a spiritual orientation. The adjective "sage" and the noun "sages" — "wise," "wise men" — also convey the idea of superior wisdom.

Wisdom is demonstrated in the encounter opposing the young man and the priests:

> "Il était fermement persuadé que l'année était de trois cent soixante et cinq jours et un quart, malgré la nouvelle philosophie de son temps, et que le soleil était au centre du monde; et quand les principaux mages lui disaient, avec une hauteur insutante; qu'il avait de mauvais sentiments et que c'était être ennemi de l'Etat que de croire que le soleil tournait sur lui-même et que l'année avait douze mois, il se taisait, sans colère et sans dédain." (*Le Borgne*, p. 11).

> ("He was firmly convinced that the year had three hundred and sixty and five days and one quarter, in spite of the new philosophy of his time, and that the sun was in the center of the world; and when the chief magi said to him, with insulting arrogance, that he was holding evil views and that one was the enemy of the State if one thought that the sun revolved on its axis and that the year had twelve months, he remained quiet without anger and without scorn.")

The Secret Doctrine, p. 731, Vol. II.

The disciple of Zoroaster has impressive astronomical knowledge. Long before the era of Galileo he is aware of the heliocentric structure of our universe. The young man apparently believes the sun to be "a central star relatively motionless, turning only on its axis."* His precise estimate of the length of a year gives further evidence of learning. Such beliefs — which are the boast of modern science — are actually far from new. Voltaire seems to pay tribute to ancient knowledge as does Mme Blvatsky. Perhaps for the same reasons.

"How few of our recent alleged discoveries are in reality new, and how many belong to the ancients, is again most fairly and eloquently though but in part stated by our eminent philosophical writer, Professor John W. Draper. His *Conflict between Religion and Science* — a great book with a very bad title — swarms with such facts. At page 13, he cites a few of the achievements of ancient philosophers, which excited the admiration of Greece. In Babylon was a series of Chaldean astronomical observations, ranging back through nineteen hundred and three years, which Callisthenes sent to Aristotle. Ptolemy. the Egyptian king-astronomer possessed a Babylonian record of eclipses going back seven hundred and forty-seven years before our era. As Prof. Draper truly remarks: 'Long-continued and close observations were necessary before some of these astronomical results that have reached our times could have been ascertained. Thus, the Babylonians had fixed the length of a tropical year within twenty-five seconds of the truth, their estimate of the sidereal year was barely two minutes in excess. They had detected the precession of the equinoxes. They knew the causes of eclipses, and by the aid of their cycle, called *saros,* could predict them. Their estimate of the value of that cycle, which is more than 6,585 days, was within nineteen and a half minutes of the truth."
'Such facts furnish incontrovertible proof of the patience and skill with which astronomy had been cultivated in Mesopotamia, and that, with very inadequate instrumental means, it had reached no inconsiderable perfection. These old observers had made a catalogue of the stars, had divided the zodiac into twelve signs; they had parted the day into twelve hours, the night into twelve. They had, as Aristotle says, for a long time devoted themselves to observation of star-occultations by the moon. They had correct views of the structure of the solar system, and knew the order of emplacement of the planets. They constructed sundials, clepsydras, astrolabes, gnomons.'
Speaking of the world of eternal truths that lies 'within the world of transient delusions and unrealities,' Professor Draper says: 'That world is not to be discovered through the vain traditions that have brought down to us the opinion of men who lived in the morning of civilization, nor in the *dreams of mystics* who thought they were inspired. It is to be discovered by the investigations of *geometry, and by the practical interrogations of nature.'*
Precisely. The issue could not be better stated. This eloquent writer tells us a profound truth. He does not, however, tell us *the whole* truth, because

---

*The Secret Doctrine, p. 100, Vol. I.

he does not know it. He has not described the nature or extent of the knowledge imparted in the Mysteries. No subsequent people has been so proficient in geometry as the builders of the Pyramids and other Titanic monuments, antediluvian and post-diluvian. On the other hand, none has ever equalled them in the practical interrogation of nature." (*Isis Unveiled*, pp. 21-22, Vol. 1).

The tolerant attitude and the learning of Zadig are contrasted to the repressive propaganda of the priests. The prostitution of knowledge to a socio-religious system is evident in the veiled threats of the magi. Any person upholding "heretical" beliefs on the nature of the universe is "the enemy of the State." The "new philosophy" — which cannot be forced upon Zadig — is the exact opposite of progress. The implied degradation of science suggests a "fall" from enlightenment into "obscurantism." The same theme of an evolutionary "fall" underlies the entire story of Zadig. It will have illuminating prolongations in *Candide* and *L'Ingénu*. Its importance is manifest at an early stage of *Zadig* in the repression of Zoroastrian or Pagan ideas and in the increasing prevalence of Judaeo-Christian myths. The name of King *Moabdar* — the presumptive fountainhead of power and thought-control — contains the term *Moab*. The latter word is the name of a portion of ancient Syria located East of the Dead Sea. The Moabites of Biblical tradition are said to have formed a warlike tribe which caused great fear among the Israelites until it was defeated by David and Saul. Their legendary origin is connected with an initial battle against "aboriginal giants"* and with their eventual defeat suffered at the hands of the Israelites. Such a history suggests a possible esoteric function of King Moabdar; the personified stage of transition from legendary to historical times. The relevance of another transition from superior Pagan knowledge to truncated Mosaic dogma may also be inferred. Subsequent chapters of *Zadig* will support the probability.

The behavior of the hero caught in a Babylonian "conflict between Religion and Science" is that of a sage. The young man seems to be aware of the futility — and danger — of any discussion with the priests. Zadig may also think that no real conflict exists between the "separated twins:" Religion and Science. The arrogance and the threats of the magi are endured in silence. "Silence" and related terms such as "se taire," "ne dire mot," etc. — "to hush," "to say not a single word" — commonly symbolize occult secrecy, the meditation of the sage, and the development of latent spiritual powers. While "silence" seems to be passive, perhaps even cowardly to the exoteric reader of *Zadig*, it is the auxiliary of spiritual effort and a sign of true strength. The Voltairian hero is a likely

---

Encyclopaedia Brittanica, Moab.

31

candidate to adeptship and the Pagan counterpart of certain "stoics" praised by Alfred de Vigny in the XIXth Century. "Silence," "strength," and "solitude are aspects of the same transcendental quest:

> "Seul le silence est grand; tout le reste est faiblesse."
> (*La Mort du loup*).
>
> ("Alone silence is great; all the rest is weakness.")
>
> "Le vrai Dieu, le Dieu fort, est le Dieu des idées.
> Sur nos fronts où le germe est jeté par le sort,
> Répandons le Savoir en fécondes ondées;
> Puis recueillant le fruit tel que de l'âme il sort,
> Tout empreint du parfum des saintes solitudes;
> Jetons l'oeuvre à la mer, la mer des multitudes;
> — Dieu la prendra du doigt pour la conduire au port."
> (*La Bouteille à la mer*).
>
> ("The true God, the strong God, is the God of ideas.
> On our brows where the seed has been cast by fate,
> Let us spread Knowledge in fruitful showers;
> Then gathering the fruit such as it issues from the soul,
> All filled with the perfume of holy solitudes,
> Let us cast the work to the sea, the sea of multitudes.
> God will take it in hand and will guide it to port.")

Non-silence amounts to "weakness" in the esoteric systems of both Vigny and Voltaire. The "weakness' of the majority of men is associated with a "vain noise of words" from the very first lines of Zadig. "Silence" is a characteristic attitude of persons spiritually gifted from birth who become "fortified" by upbringing and personal effort. Zadig is such a person. The same natural endowment and the same spiritual quest are stressed by Vigny in his reference to the "seed cast by fate" and in his glorification of Knowledge. To the team-work of "silence" and "strength" is opposed the alliance of vain displays and "weakness." The same equivalences are consistently found in the works of esoteric writers. It may be noted again in this connection that the *Silence* of Vigny, a stanza affixed to *Le Mont des Oliviers*, is generally misunderstood if F. Baldensperger is correct. The following passage of the writings of Rabelais links "silence," "sure oracles," and a tradition so secret as to be transmitted without written or spoken words:

> "The fiendish spirit deceives you; but listen. I have read that in gone-by days the most authentic and sure oracles were not those which were handed down in writing, or were uttered by word. Many times were thus misled even those who were esteemed to be astute and clever, because of the ambiguities, subtleties, and obscurities of words and because of the brevity of

32

formulae: — Let us use that manner, and through signs, without speaking, do take counsel from some mute." (Rabelais, *Tiers Livre*, Ch. XIX).

It will be found in due course of *Zadig* that the main characters created by Voltaire do take occasional "counsel from a" little "mute."

A fox who wishes to be "tamed" — perhaps understood — also believes in the value of Rabelaisian and Voltairian "silence:"

> " — if you want a friend, tame me!
> — What must one do? said the little prince.
> — One must be very patient, replied the fox. First of all you will sit a little bit far from me, like that, in the grass. I shall look at you from the corner of my eye and you will say nothing. Language is a source of misunderstanding. But, each day, you will be able to sit a bit closer.' " (Antoine de Saint Exupéry, *Le Petit Prince*, Ch. XXI).

The Rabelaisian reference to "ambiguities," subtleties, and obscurities of words is provocative. The statement of Saint Exupéry: "Language is a source of misunderstandings" is a virtual definition of esotericism.

"Silence" pervades the experience of a literary character who finds himself under the spell of great writers. The intuitive faculties of the entranced reader are challenged. His everyday, personal existence recedes into nothingness. Hours dissolve in magical fashion. A major clue is given to the esoteric treatment of Time in Proustian literature. Time is simultaneously compressed, expanded, and transcended. As was the case in the stanza of *The Bottle to the Sea* which is quoted above, perfume, solitude, and silence are in conjunction. The hours of mystical communion with great minds are "silent, vibrant, perfumed, and limpid."*

The first part of *Zadig* takes place in Babylon. The choice of site seems to serve three purposes. It satisfies XVIIIth Century taste for exotic literature. It favors socio-political satire comparable to the substance of Montesquieu's *Lettres Persanes*. The emptiness of conversations evoked brings to mind a community of Parisian "beaux esprits." The general atmosphere tends to suggest French society garbed in a thin veneer of Orientalism. Attention is thus diverted from such esoteric themes as the scientific achievements and the noble ethics of early Pagan civilizations. The name Babylon or Babel — which has become a symbol of vanity, madness and confusion — may have been used by Voltaire in its probable etymological sense of "gate to the Highest God." More than an exotic veil covering a satire of Parisian and French mores, Babylon may be a doubly misleading front concealing its own occult reality.

---

*A la Recherche du temps perdu, p. 88, Vol. I.

Occult philosophy teaches that the Babylonian tradition is closely connected with the Secret Doctrine.

> "The tower of Babel was built as much by the direct descendants of Shem as by those of the 'accursed' Ham and Canaan, for the people in those days were 'one,' and the whole earth was one of language: Babel was simply an astrological tower, and its builders were astrologers and adepts of the primitive Wisdom-Religion or again what we term Secret Doctrine." (*Isis Unveiled*, p. 217, Vol. 2).

The philosophy of Zoroaster is regarded as a reflection of the Secret Doctrine:

> " — that Zarathustra and his followers, the Zoroastrians, 'had been settled in India before they immigrated into Persia' is also proved by Max Muller, 'That the Zoroastrians and their ancestors started from India,' he says, 'during the Vaidik period, can be proved as distinctly as that the inhabitants of Massilia started from Greece.' " (*Isis Unveiled*, pp. 142-143, Vol. 2).

> " — Many of the gods of the Zoroastrians come out — as mere reflections and deflections of the primitive and authentic gods of the *Veda*.
> — all these gods, whether of the Zoroastrians or the *Veda*, are but so many personated occult powers of nature, — " (*Isis Unveiled*, p. 143, Vol. 2).

Voltaire may have courted an esoteric connection between his hero — a disciple of Zoroaster — and "the primitive Wisdom-Religion" or Secret Doctrine. The philosophy which guided and inspired the learned élite of Antiquity at a time when "the people — were 'one,' and the whole earth was one of language —" may have appealed to the modern thinker whose preoccupation with universal values is well known. The Zoroastrian doctrine — which is polytheistic in appearance yet monotheistic in reality — is compatible with the Voltairian concept of a Supreme Being. The unmatched spirit of tolerance promoted by THE UNIVERSAL WRIT* is reminiscent of the *Traité sur la Tolérance*. The following passage is an expression of views not basically different from those expressed in *Zaïre*.

> "Sri Ramakrishna, the great nineteenth century saint, followed many a devotional and ecstatic path but he allowed no narrowness, no ignorant denunciation or exclusion of other paths. He said: 'The eternal religion, the religion of the Rishis, has existed from time out of mind and will exist eternally. This *sanatana dharma* contains all forms of worship — worship of God with form and worship of the Impersonal as well. It contains all paths, the path of Knowledge, the path of devotion, and so on.' He also said: 'I ask a Vaishnava (worshipper of Vishnu) to hold to his cult and a Sakta (worshipper of Sakti or Divine Mother) to his. But this I also say to them: 'Never feel that your path alone is right and that the paths of others are wrong and full of errors. Hindus, Muslims, and Christians are going to the

---

*Alfred de Vigny, *L'Esprit pur*.

same goal through different paths.' " (Arthur Osborne, *Buddhism and Christianity in the Light of Hinduism*, p. 52).

The first chapter of *Zadig* seems to stress the comprehension gap separating exoteric appearance from esoteric reality. The ironic surface of the text favors satirical interpretation of semi-esoteric nature. The exotic veneer of the story is blatantly artificial. Voltaire exploits with a playful appearance of candor the conventional props of the fictionalized Orient immortalized by Molière, Montesquieu, and Diderot. The verbal alchemy of terms such as Moabdar, magi, Zadig and Zoroaster promotes the amusement and the "dépaysement" of the reader. But the general tone of airy banter may serve to conceal serious allusions to the Secret Doctrine. Superficial irony vies with esoteric earnestness if not reverence. The rare degree of wisdom and virtue possessed by Zadig may arouse an admiring as well as a skeptical reaction. The doctrine of Zoroaster which has produced such a rare type of human being may be viewed with irony or with respect. The choice is left to the reader whose vision is all-important. Voltaire may have wished to hint as much when he entitled the first chapter of *Zadig*: *The One-Eyed Man*.

Many suggestions are made under the guise of amazement. The acquaintances of Zadig marvel at his virtue. The too-good-to-be-true quality of the young man's wisdom is in itself an invitation to reflect. Zadig is characterized in terms of what he is expected to be but *is not*. Wealth and youth seem to decree that he should pursue romantic conquests. Zadig shows little interest in such endeavors. Social prominence suggests that he should take part in conversational displays. Zadig does not care for such empty pastimes. Material well-being could easily produce religious indifference and unconcern with the lot of others. Such is not the case. Superior knowledge could deal devastating blows to the arrogance of the priests. If used it serves better ends. The reader is left to fathom the silent serenity of the young man.

Two interpretations are possible. The easy course points to one conclusion: Such virtue is not of this world. The reader tends to see in Zadig a human counterpart of the balloon filled with self-esteem which is mentioned in the first paragraph. Perfection is slightly suspect, a likely disguise for intellectual if not spiritual pride. The hero is expected to be quickly punctured by experience. Such views are partially confirmed — on an unsuspected plane — in the course of the story. Zadig proves to be far more than an ordinary human being. Life has a way of molesting unorthodox goodness. The easy path of inquiry leads to certain truths. The second path lies in reluctance to judge hastily and in consideration of one possibility: Could such a remarkable intellectual and moral attain-

35

ment — subject to human frailty though it be — reflect genuinely superior character based on solid values?

Esoteric reading is a test administered to the reader. Major requirements include "a small fund of philosophy" (*Epître Dédicatoire à la Sultane Sheraa*) and an ability to resist appearance. "Philosophy" supplies the meaning of important esoteric terms and underlying concepts. Distrust of external attributes serves to solve riddles and to dissolve paradox. The striking antagonism of general expectation vs. fact which is stressed in the portrayal of Zadig may be a prime example of Maya or Illusion incarnate in literature. The same theme — which is often developed by esoteric writers — is insistently featured in the works of Marcel Proust. Pondering the "contradictions" of his friend "Legrandin," the narrator perceives on one occasion the importance of a certain type of "intermediate work" essential to understanding.* It may well be that the same type of "intermediate work" must be performed in the case of Voltaire.

Zadig is a declared enemy of falsehood who prefers in all things "being to appearance." The conceited self-righteousness of which he is innocent may be expressed by the word "vanity." Avoidance of the latter sin is prescribed by most religions, notably Christianity. But "vanity" in a far broader sense has crucial significance in Oriental philosophy. It is the ever-present, formidable obstacle to spiritual perfection. It is the sum of base aspects of selfhood, the illusion of separate existence, the imprisonment of spirit in matter or incarnation. It is *Maya*, a term frequently rendered as "that which does not exist," the bondage of material human condition, the network of ignoble drives, captive thinking, and partial perception.

> "The profoundest and most transcendental speculations of the ancient metaphysicians of India and other countries are all based on that great Buddhistic and Brahmanical principle underlying the whole of their religious metaphysics — illusion of the senses. — Everything that is finite is illusion, all that which is eternal and infinite is reality. Form, color, that which we hear and feel, or see with our mortal eyes, exists only so far as it can be conveyed to each of us through our senses. The universe for a man born blind does not exist in either form or color, but it exists in its privation (in the Aristotelean sense) and is a reality for the spiritual senses of the blind man. Alone the highest and invisible *originals* emanated from the thought of the Unknown are real and permanent beings, forms, and ideas; on earth, we see but their reflections: more or less correct, and ever depedent on the physical and mental organization of the person who beholds them.

---

*A la Recherche du temps perdu, p. 129, Vol. I.

Ages untold before our era, the Hindu Mystic Kapila, who is considered by many scientists as a skeptic, because they judge him with their habitual superficiality expressed this idea in the following terms:
'Man (physical man) counts for so little, that hardly anything can demonstrate to him his proper existence and that of nature. Perhaps that which we regard as the universe, and the diverse beings which seem to compose it, have nothing real, and are but the product of continued illusion — *maya* — of our senses.' " (*Isis Unveiled,* pp. 157-58, Vol. 2).

The Hindu mystic Kapila seems to share a few traits with Voltaire. His legacy remains generally misunderstood. Skepticism and mysticism blend harmoniously in his philosophy. The former approach to knowledge transcends material appearance. The latter mode of being is achieved as true Science or oneness with non-contingent reality. In the case of the Hindu sage as in the case of the great modern, honest doubt is a high form of belief.

Purely sensory experience is a divorce from true reality. Such is the teaching of many great writers who may be inspired by the Secret Doctrine. "The invisible is real" says Alfred de Vigny.* That the visible is unreal is stressed by Saint Exupéry: "The essential is invisible to the eyes." "One sees well only with the heart."** "The visible world — is not the real world,"*** writes Proust. The inverse relationship which exists between purely sensory experience and true insight is illustrated with particular vigor in the *Recherche.* The condition of an ailing person — which has not been detected in the course of personal contact — is instantly perceived during a telephone conversation with the invalid. Heightened consciousness resuls from the non-involvement of all senses but one.**** The suffering of a theoretical patient described in a medical textbook produces intense compassion in Françoise, the servant. But the visible, audible, tangible, and identical torment of an associate arouses only callousness in the same person. Compassion is a partial transcendence of the Lower Self. It is an aspect of true insight. True insight is shown to be best achieved in a state of sensory abstraction.

Maya — the illusion of the senses — seems to be the major theme of the first chapters of *Zadig.* The experience of the hero with two women — Sémire and Azora — marks the beginning of a series of disillusioning experiences. The adventures in question will prove to involve inferior planes of consciousness or faulty "vision."

Women are often used as allegorical representations of Maya. Powerful

---

*La Maison du berger.
**The Little Prince, Ch. XXI.
***A la Recherche du temps perdu, p. 248, Vol. I.
****Ibid., pp. 133-34, Vol. II.

means of seduction and biological aspects of incarnation combine to give substance to such allegory. The biblical story of Samson and Delilah is a confrontation of spirituality or "strength" — Samson — with treacherours, inferior powers personified by Delilah. The same biblical episode is the subject of a well known work of Vigny, *La Colère de Samson.* The poem is an esoteric description of the eternal battle waged by the superior "strength" or spirituality of Man against base material impulses such as sensuality. The internal nature of the struggle is suggested in the following lines:

> "Vient un autre combat plus secret, traître et lâche;
> Sous son bras, sur son coeur se livre celui-là;
> Et, plus ou moins, la Femme est toujours DALILA."

> ("Comes another combat more secret, treacherous and cowardly;
> Under his arm, on his heart that battle is waged;
> And, more or less, Woman is always DELILAH.")

The proclaimed equivalence of "Woman" and "Delilah" raises the question of another esoteric value. If Delilah is always Woman, what is Delilah in the first place? The riddle is answered in a verse which seems to be a masterpiece of calculated poetic gaucherie. Delilah is "that which does not exist." In a word: Maya. The awkward line conveys a major clue to the allegory of a great "smuggler:"

> " 'Donc, ce que j'ai voulu, Seigneur, n'existe pas!' "

> (" 'Thus, what I have desired, o Lord, does not exist!' ")

Maya is eventually defeated at the cost of physical sight and physical life. The exoteric disaster represented by physical blindness and death is an esoteric triumph over the bondage of sensory consciousness and incarnation. The fallacy of Maya is shown by the fact that Samson, the apparent loser, is the actual victor. His liberation is logically marked by the collapse of the temple representing a false creed or false values. As the last lines of the poem clearly suggest, Delilah-Maya finally perceives that her apparent victory is a defeat. The "pale prostitute" understands that her power is lost.

> "Et près de la génisse aux pieds du Dieu tuée (ils)
> Placèrent Dalila, pâle prostituée,
> Couronnée, adorée, et reine du repas,
> Mais tremblante et disant: " 'IL NE ME VERRA PAS!' "

> ("And near the heifer killed at the feet of the God (they)
> Placed Delilah, the pale prostitute,

Crowned, adored, and queen of the feast,
But trembling and saying: 'HE WILL NOT SEE ME!'")

The same transition from spiritual blindness to spiritual vision is an element of the story of Paul's Way to Damascus. The latter episode is used by Vigny in his autobiographical poem *La Flûte*. The "twenty years of silence" mentioned in *L'Esprit pur* refer back to the year during which *La Flûte* was written. The accession of the "beggar" and "smuggler" to superior vision is described as follows:

"L'idée à l'horizon est à peine entrevue,
Que sa lumière écrase et fait ployer ma vue,
Je vois grossir l'obstacle en invincible amas,
Je tombe ainsi que Paul en marchant vers Damas.

———

Et le rayon me trouble et la voix m'étourdit,
Et je demeure aveugle et je me sens maudit."

("Hardly is the idea glimpsed on the horizon
When its light crushes and forces down my sight.
I see the obstacle grow into an invincible mass.
I fall, as did Paul on the Way to Damascus.

———

And the beam of light confuses me and the voice dizzies me
And I remain blind and I feel cursed.")

It should be noted briefly that the word "cursed" may have the opposite meaning of "blessed" in occult philosophy.*

The same antagonism of two mutually exclusive types of vision is illustrated in many texts. The strong case made by Saint Exupéry in favor of the inner eye has already been noted. *La Nausée* seems to convey a similar message which is dramatized by a violent impulse of the narrator. Sickened by the amiable clichés of the Self-Taught Man — whose dedication and independence he respects — Roquentin feels the urge to put out the eyes of his acquaintance. The criminal movement which is barely repressed may stem from the desire to perform an act of mercy. The Self-Taught Man needs to wrench his vision from inferior planes of platitudes. He must learn to "see" beyond fronts and surfaces as does his friend.

The uneasy co-existence of two types of vision — one Mayavic the other spiritual — is recognized and commented as follows in theosophical writings:

———

Isis Unveiled, p. 309, Vol. I.

"'Mere intellectual enlightenment cannot recognize the spiritual. As the sun puts out a fire, so spirit puts out the eyes of mere intellect.'" (*Isis Unveiled*, p. 409, Vol. 1).

The first experience of Zadig with "women" is connected with "vision."

The young man is jilted by his fiancée, Sémire, when he faces the probable loss of one eye. "The powerful dominion" of physical charm — or lack of charm — is irresistible. Not only does the lady abandon her faithful lover, but she literally throws herself into the arms of Orcan, the vain and brutal suitor who caused the injury of Zadig.

"She had an overwhelming aversion to one-eyed men. "
(*Le Borgne*, p. 13).

The rejection of Zadig by the young woman is caused by the unfavorable prognosis of a famous doctor. The representative of official science is a human gold-mine to Voltairian satire.

Having arrived on the scene with a spectacular cortège of medical "satellites," Hermes predicts the day and the hour when the injured eye will be lost. His learning and skill are praised throughout Babylon. But the wounded eye heals naturally in spite of authority and public relations. The damaged ego of Hermes does not recover as well.

Conceit is evident in the professional "mise en scène" of the physician. True knowledge would scorn such props as the convoy of "satellites." True knowledge would either avoid spectacular prediction or ascertain its value. True knowledge would recognize its own limitations and the possibility of unprecedented developments such as natural healing of a left eye. The dogmatic showmanship of Hermes suggests a fraudulent mixture of science and religion which is also suggested by the doctor's name.

The name *Hermes* brings to mind the Hermetic tradition which is an aspect of the Secret Doctrine. The exoteric reader of *Zadig* is unlikely to conclude that Voltaire was partial to the said tradition. But the multiple signs of quackery which surround Hermes may be more relevant to the character than to the Hermetic doctrine. The name of the doctor may have been intended to act as a decoy placed in the path of exoteric readers and as a stimulant offered to others. The latter possibility seems to be confirmed by one fact. The name of the physician suggests imposture. "Hermes" is a generic term designating a tradition, not an individual. Any person using it as his private property is automatically suspect:

"Hermes was a generic *nom de plume* used by a series of generations of mystics of every shade — " (*The Secret Doctrine*, p. 286, Vol. I).

40

The "shade" of the "mystic" portrayed by Voltaire is clearly open to question.

The itinerary of the doctor may also be revealing. Hermes is summoned from Memphis to Babylon, a considerable distance. It is observed in a perceptive footnote of the Bénac edition that the geography of Voltaire is rather fanciful. It might be more appropriate to comment on the geography of Hermes. The unlikely trip suggests imposture as does the dishonest use of a prestigious name.

The professional stock in trade of Hermes includes a physical approach — "he visited the patient" — and a type of prognosis akin to prophecy. Voltaire seems to take a dim view of the total formula of Science and Religion In One which is upheld by occultists. But the character of Hermes suggests that the "separated twins" are amalgamated and exploited by an ignorant and unethical person. No sound mind would reject mathematics as worthless because some men cannot add. The same objectivity may apply to all bodies of knowledge, unorthodox as some may seem. The unflattering portrayal of one physician does not necessarily mean rejection of the science which he claims to represent, in this case Hermetic philosophy. It may even constitute a cleverly veiled endorsement. If such be the case, interpretation must hinge on two factors. The "small fund of philosophy" which may or may not be possessed by the reader is all important. The proneness — or reluctance — of the reader to generalize and project ignorantly is also crucial. The prospects of esoteric understanding are intimately bound to one question: What is Hermetic philosophy?

The connection which exists between the said philosophy and the Secret Doctrine amounts to identity. In the words of Mme Blavatsky, "—our work is a plea for recognition of the Hermetic philosophy, the anciently universal Wisdom-Religion."* The present study will show that the undying contempt of Voltaire went to those persons who debased the said Wisdom-Religion, not to the rare beings who upheld it in pure form. Hermes belongs to the despised category of minds which promote the degradation of the occult concept of Science.

The inferior brand of knowledge sold by the physician reflects little credit on official Science which Hermes represents. The partly materialistic, partly "mystical" approach of the doctor might constitute a superior form of insight were it used on a higher plane. If such were the case, it might approximate the familiarity of Zadig with the "physical sciences as they were known in those days" or the Zoroastrian concept of Knowledge. But the assets of Hermes fall short of such standards. Voltaire may

---

*Isis Unveiled, p. vii, Vol. I.

have used the deficits of the doctor to represent and criticize a fundamental weakness of "exact science" which is often denounced in occult
and esoteric writings. The modern accumulation of learning which is
claimed to rest on the sole *terra firma* of matter is — in the opinion of
occultists — doomed to peripheral success and frequent error. Matter
is believed to be spirit on the lowest plane of existence. Matter cannot
be fully known unless its spiritual component is recognized as real.
Overtly or otherwise; consciously or otherwise, Science is bound to
postulate metaphysical supports for its empirical structure. In the words
of Mme Blavatsky, "materialistic, physical science is honey-combed with
metaphysics."* The same basic insecurity is noted by Voltaire in *Micromégas*. A representative of materialistic science is forced to admit that
he perceives only a few external attributes of matter and that he does
not know what matter is. Voltaire agrees with occult philosophy on one
important point at least. Exact science is admittedly ignorant of its own
foundation. It is an impressive growth. It is also a "rootless tree."

The power of official science tends to function as a tyrannical religion
in modern societies. It is frequently questioned in esoteric texts. Medicine,
the lionized profession par excellence, is presented in critical light. The
resultant satire which may be traced as far back as medieval fabliaux
is generally connected by critics with the old Gallic tradition of buffoonery focused on the medical profession. The connection is legitimate.
But we may have simplistic views of the intent of such writings when
we proclaim it to be purely — and naively — farcical. The same question
might be raised with reference to the medical satire contained in Mo-
lieresque literature.

A passage of *The Nausea* may amount to the indictment of a modern
counterpart of Hermes. A prestigious doctor, one of a few pillars of
society who believe they know men "as if they had created them," selects
a less exalted mortal as a target of verbal abuse. One might easily
compare the unequal protagonists to a lion and a mouse. The victim —
whose name is Achille — swallows all indignities in cowardly silence. It
is a rare soul which has the courage to defy the wielder of pigeon-holes
through which men may be categorized and manipulated without appeal.
It is a rare person who can challenge the Jehovic figure deified by the
almighty mystery of modern Science. One needs the vision of Roquentin
— who sees beyond the surface of oceans and beyond the surface of many
other things — to perceive that the formidable doctor is dying of an
incurable disease. M. Achille is unlikely ever to learn that *he* is the lion
and that his tormentor is the mouse. But his fellow-victims may some

---

The Secret Doctrine, p. 485, Vol. I.

day realize that the ordinary man — whose name is that of a demi-god — carries within himself a latent spark capable of establishing another order of things. The god-like medical man who tries to palliate hidden fears with comforting thoughts of his impressive *Experience* may represent the Judaeo-Christian or Western concept of Science based on the sacrosanct *experimental* method. The incurable disease from which he suffers may reflect the limitations of the purely materialistic approach to Knowledge. Whatever the case may be, the tyrannical physician described by Sartre is a worthy fellow of Hermes whose dubious knowledge suffices to alter several destinies.

Esoteric writers are as prompt to praise enlightened physicians as they are to denounce the false gods of medicine. Proust pays tribute to the Rabelaisian doctor named Cottard. Uncouth appearance to the contrary, the practitioner is an intuitive diagnostician of rare distinction. The same famous "medicine-man" is probably represented in Chapter XXIII of *The Little Prince*. The latter physician combines suggestions of the "Dive Bouteille" — "perfected pills which allay thirst" — and of the Thelemite motto: "Do as you please." Voltaire salutes an open-minded surgeon in a significant chapter of *Candide*. The occult and esoteric view of official science is often expressed by reference to medicine. In the words of Marcel Proust, medical science ignores "the secret of healing."[*] "To believe in medicine would be the supreme folly if not believing in it were not a greater folly, for, out of that accumulation of errors, a few truths have emerged in the end."[**]

The Voltairian view of exact science which is suggested by the portrayal of Hermes seems to be shared by many likewise inspired writers.

The second courtship of Zadig is no more felicitous than the first. Azora prolongs the experience with "vanity" — or Maya — which was begun with Sémire. Zadig soon finds the virtue of his new love to be of negative nature. It is a personally advertised product consisting chiefly of contempt for others. The obsession of Azora with surrounding worthlessness is compounded by inability to see the self as it is. Her cult of physical beauty is reminiscent of Sémire. Hers is another case of impaired "vision." Zadig detects in her "a bit of frivolity and a marked tendency to find that the most handsome young men were those who had the greatest amount of wit and virtue."

The French word "esprit" which means "wit" also means "mind" and "spirit." The *triple*-edged term is a precious tool and a source of delight to French esoteric writers. The "wit" — or spiritual "insight" —

---

[*]*A la Recherche du temps perdu*, p. 183, Vol. III.
[**]*Ibid.*, pp. 298-99, Vol. II.

of Azora equates physical beauty with "virtue," "strength," or esoteric "superior attainment." Faulty vision is evident.

Similar error may result from hasty reading of the French word "esprit." The esoteric warning of Saint Exupéry "language is a source of misunderstanding" is supplemented by suggestive handling of the misleading term. The following passage of *The Little Prince* is a virtual definition of esotericism:

> "Quand on veut faire de l'esprit, il arrive que l'on mente un peu." (Ch. XVII).

> ("When one wishes to be witty — or spiritual — one may chance to lie a bit.")

The inferior concept of "wit" formed by Azora is an esoteric hint aimed at the reader of *Zadig*.

Vanity — in the popular sense of the term — is the least imperfection of Azora. The self-appointed arbiter of universal vice and virtue becomes a willing party to a revolting act. Believing Zadig to be dead, she decides to amputate his nose for the sake of another man. The strange operation is intended to relieve the ailment of a prospective suitor. The practice smacks of superstition and black magic. Azora and her moral "repoussoir" — Widow Cosrou — are judged with equal severity. The plan of cutting off a man's nose is found "about as worthy as that of diverting a stream."

The engineering project of Widow Cosrou has aroused the indignation of Azora. The misdeed which seems childish and rather harmless on the surface is a cardinal sin in esoteric terms. Wishing to disguise her vanity and fickleness, the publicity-seeker has altered the course of a stream. Water is associated with all major religions as a symbolic source of physical and spiritual life. Baptismal rites, initiation, holy rivers, the esoteric expressions "fountain of knowledge," "well of knowledge," and "going back to the source" all link the vital element to dogma and sacrament. The camouflage of personal frailty performed by Mme Cosrou serves to dramatize a major grievance of occultists and esoteric writers: deliberate distortion of living, spiritual truth.

The name *Cosrou* was probably derived from two words: Cosmos and *Rupa*. The latter term is defined in the Secret Doctrine as visible or physical form. The suggested theme of cosmic vision subordinated to false sensory values is consistent with the character of the lady and with the dominant themes of the beginning of *Zadig*. The distorted self-concept and the general dishonesty of the Widow affect more than her own person. Esoterically at least, cosmic truth is disfigured by her act.

44

The names of Sémire and Azora seem to be rich in meaning. Sémire uses love as if it were a mirror, for ego gratification ("se mire" — "looks at herself in a mirror"). Voltaire may also have wished to suggest the idea of a "self" — French "se" — dominated by false knowledge or Science such as the dubious lore of Hermes. The word "mire" which means "physcian" in medieval literature appears in the title of a well-known fabliau: Le vilain mire. Finally, the word Sémire resembles Sémite — "semitic" a term embracing Hebrews and Arabs. The latter ethnic connection will prove relevant to the veiled architecture of Zadig in due course of the story. The name of the second woman is also suggestive. Azora brings to mind the present tense form of the Greek verb meaning "to see" — orao. The name also contains the first and last letters of the alphabet. It will be shown in connection with Zadig that the combination of both letters in reversed order was probably meant to reflect the idea of "going back to the source" of knowledge and being. The alphabetical sequence featured in the name Azora is therefore suggestive of an ordinary, poorly spiritualized order of things. The total formula of uninspired "vision" seems consistent with the outlook and the behavior of the young woman. Her name was probably calculated to convey a second, savory meaning. Azor is to Frenchmen the equivalent of the American term Fido. Voltaire is known — and often criticized — for having called a spade a spade on the exoteric plane. In view of his penchant for vigorous expression, in view of the international value of certain concepts, the feminized form Azora — which leaves little to imagination — is a stern though humorous verdict.

The dubious "love" of Azora for Zadig is tested by a strange method. The young woman is told that her husband has died suddenly. A theatrical display of grief follows. It is quickly over. A mourning period of two days blossoms into romance. Azora does not suspect that she is in the process of being tested by her new suitor, Cador, the wise and loyal friend of Zadig. Her decision to amputate the nose of the "dead" spouse is frustrated when the "dead" man objects to the proposed surgery and climbs out of the grave. The false demise and the false resurrection of Zadig may suggest that the tomb is no more than a passage to new life and — truth. The carefully planned act of literally leaving the sepulcher is reminiscent of Christ or at least of a Christ-figure. It may also suggest voluntary rebirth. The present study will show in due course that Bodhisattva — voluntary reincarnation, or the "Great Sacrifice" — is closely linked to more than one title character of the Voltairian trilogy. The phonetic identity existing between the French words "né" — "born" — and "nez" — "nose" — tends to support the view that the opportunity to make such a connection is hopefully extended to the reader of Zadig.

45

If such is the case, Voltaire announces the statement which will appear at a later date in another story: "— resurrection — is the simplest thing in the world. It is no more amazing to be born twice than once." If such is the case, Voltaire echoes the frequently expressed tenet of occult philosophy that death is true life, thereby inverting the poles of vision of the average Western man.

The theme of imperfect vision is insistently called to attention. Sight and presumed loss of sight change several human destinies. The beauty of Sémire is noted to have quasi-magical effect. The *sight* of her is capable of softening the heart of Himalayan tigers. The geographical reference may suggest that custodians of occult knowledge — traditionally linked to the "roof of the World" — are not entirely immune to the seductions of Maya. Zadig wishes to have *eyes* for his beloved only. Terrestrial love can easily result in impaired vision and is commonly believed to be "blind." Regaining consciousness after the battle between Orcan and Zadig, Sémire is overcome by the *sight* of her wounded suitor. Passionate effusions to the contrary she proves to be overcome in unexpected manner: she cannot abide the *sight* of a one-*eyed* man. The loss of attractiveness with which Zadig is threatened is only one consideration. His presumed inability to *see* spells the end of the powers of the young woman, a fact indicative of her "vanity" or lack of true substance. The reaction of the fickle lady to the visual handicap of Zadig is identical to the reaction of Delilah facing similar disaster in *La Colère de Samson*. The exclamation: HE SHALL NOT SEE ME! might equally well be voiced by Sémire or by Delilah. The young woman is described anxiously "awaiting the moment when Zadig would enjoy the sight of her." The seeming hopelessness of her expectation spells the doom of her "love." The same type of inferior vision is stressed in the case of Azora. Her susceptibility to *looks* is noted as is her obsession with a flattering self-image inevitably constructed at the expense of others. The type of human being represented by Sémire and Azora brings to mind certain thoughts of Pascal which seem to be echoed in existential writings. Many persons exist only in the eyes of others. Voltaire is one of many great authors who regard the quality of vision as inseparable from the quality of essence.

The sense of hearing is important also. Sémire does not wait to observe the evolution of the wound of Zadig. It is on the basis of prestigious — but false — *hearsay* evidence that she abandons her lover. Obsessed as she is with sensory values, the girl fails to make use of the one valid form of knowledge available to her: personal recognition of visible fact. Sensory perception itself is shown to suffer when a purely materialistic outlooks prevails. Another aspect of Maya is exposed: unquestioning submission to false authority. The latter weakness has far-reaching effects.

"Infamous" establishments thrive on popular refusal to see and think for oneself. The guilt of impostors is inseparable from the guilt of human sheep who follow them.

The sense of smell is not overlooked. The projected surgery to be performed on the nose of Zadig tends to confirm the general esoteric impression of purely sensory values. The Secret Doctrine places on the same low plane of evolution and existence the senses of smell, touch and taste* which correspond to deep materiality. The survey of a purely physical outlook seems complete from the very beginning of *Zadig*.

Many persons are prisoners of inferior modes of existence. The love of Orcan for Sémire is no love at all. It is a manifestation of vanity and jealousy aroused by the "virtue" and the "graces" of Zadig. The unprovoked attack launched by the young bully is prompted and aided by "courtiers" and "satellites" who seem to represent forces external to the self. The inferiority of such "forces" is clearly shown by the outcome of the fight. Aided by only two slaves, Zadig routs the aggressors. The reader may compare with profit the "satellites" of Hermes and the acolytes of Orcan. The same lack of true substance characterizes the brutal young man and the false medical god. The fact that Orcan is the nephew of a politically mighty person — a minister of State — tends to connect the executive power with the same absence of genuine values which is noted in regard to Science — Hermes — and Religion — the priests. The "separated twins" seem to go hand in hand with insecure and tyrannical social "forces" which are poor substitutes for genuine "strength."

The "courtiers" and "satellites" of shaky power suggest disembodied entities of the kind commonly attracted in the course of inferior mediumnic or spiritualistic experimentation. To the spurious substance of Hermes and Orcan — a substance which consists mainly of external props — is added a suggestion of amateurish occult ventures. A diametrical opposition is hinted to exist between the nascent mastery of Zadig and the inferior pursuits of his adversaries. Such an opposition — if suggested by Voltaire — is identical to the view of occultists who regard adepts and mediums as being poles apart. The same important distinction will be made and extensively developed in a subsequent chapter of *Zadig*.

Arbitrary as it may seem, the above interpretation of the words "courtiers" and "satellites" is supported by the texts of numerous esoteric writers. The esoteric meaning of "courtiers," "slaves," "servants," "satellites," and "familiars" frequently illuminates the hidden substance of innocent-looking writings. Counterparts of Voltairian "satellites" are found in various "séides" mentioned in the works of Vigny. The occult concept of

---

*The Secret Doctrine, p. 107, Vol. II.

"seidism" carries mediumnic as well as psychological and socio-political implications. We may wonder about the possible esoteric value of "servants" portrayed by Marcel Proust, particularly the immortal Françoise. The esoteric equivalence of "servants" is given in falsely casual manner in the *Recherche*. "Servants" are "witty" or "spiritual" persons.* Magic is suggested to dwell in the kitchen of Françoise — and in her cooking. Her ability to discern hidden truths is uncanny. Her devotion to established religion is as instinctive as are her paganistic — etymologically "peasant" — traits. A popular syncretism of intriguing variety seems to be the key to her character and to the tradition of Saint André des Champs, "a tradition at once ancient and direct, unbroken, oral, distorted, unrecognizable, and alive.** We may also wonder about the fairly common theme of the "servant" who becomes the "master" in the writings of Diderot and Beaumarchais.

Little doubt is possible where the meaning of Rabelaisian "familiars" is concerned. Some persons "summon devils by name and surname. And not only do they summon them but declare themselves friends and familiars thereof."*** The definition of the same term which is given by John Steinbeck in connection with an unfriendly cat named George is equally clear:

> ". . . the unseen presence of George was everywhere. In a more enlightened day when witches and familiars were better understood, George would have found his or rather her, end in a bonfire, because if ever there was a familiar, and envoy of the devil, a consorter with evil spirits, George is it." (John Steinbeck, *Travels with Charley*).

"Courtiers" and "satellites" — or inferior powers — are controlled by the adept. But they usually control the sorcerer's apprentice and may drive him to madness and destruction. The two slaves of Zadig — who may represent the "separated twins," Science and Religion In One, probably also represent the alliance of superior Knowledge and lofty ethics. Such "slaves" work loyally and effectively for their "master." The initial chapters of *Zadig* convey the suggestion of significant alignments. Inferior "force" is connected with the realm of sensory illusion. Superior "force" is on the side of the disciple of Zoroaster. The main character is a likely devotee of the Secret Doctrine.

The experience of Zadig with inferior forms of religion, science and "love" is rich in social implications. A common factor of "vanity" and

---

*A la Recherche du temps perdu, p. 567, Vol. III.
**Ibid., p. 151, Vol. I.
***Cinquième Livre, Ch. X.

base selfhood is present in all individuals — Zadig and his friend Cador excepted. The same sordid orientation seems to prevail on a collective plane. The "romantic" victory of Orcan tends to promote brutality as a way of life. The credulity of Sémire tends to perpetuate the reign of impostors. The callousness of Azora contributes to the degradation of sacred values such as Love. The face-saving project of Widow Cosrou disfigures certain aspects of eternal verities. The book written by Hermes to vindicate his untenable theory will probably be hailed as gospel truth. Born of wounded pride, lust for power, and disregard of fact, it will deal a major blow to an already battered body of knowledge. The collusion of Church and State — which is apparent in the threats of the priests — is likely to sanctify the burning of genius conveniently labeled as "heresy." No sin against Truth — however venial it may seem — fails to generate a socio-political mystique of criminal whitewash.

The disciple of Zoroaster who seeks "to live with wise men" and who prefers in all things "being to appearance" does not belong in such a society. The young hero departs from the scene of painful experience, a scene which appears to represent the low plane of Maya.

Zadig returns to the pursuit of knowledge, "seeking happiness in the study of nature," acquiring soon "a wisdom which revealed to him a thousand differences where other men saw nothing but uniformity." Liberated from previous handicaps — which were mostly products of Illusion — the hero accedes to a state blessed with genuine vision. The "one-eyed man" becomes a seer. Sensory limitations are transcended. While he has never "seen" them through physical sight, Zadig is able to describe in amazing detail the missing animals sought by royal emissaries.

The young man pays the penalty incurred by spiritually advanced mortals. His truthfulness and "wit" barely allow him to survive. He is accused and convicted of sorcery by jealous priests. The occult establishment does not favor competition. It is unsafe to poach on the sacred preserves of professionals. Voltaire transmits the ageless warning given to daring persons who seek superior knowledge. "Zadig soon saw how dangerous it was sometimes to have too much learning and earnestly resolved, next time, not to tell what he had seen." The same exhortation to prudence underlies a scriptural injunction which is often quoted by occultists:

> "'Give not that which is holy unto the dogs, neither cast ye your pearls before swine; lest they trample them under their feet, and turn again and rend you.'" (*Matthew*, Ch. vii, 6).

The monopolistic attitude of Babylonian priests is noted. Similarly inspired and controlled practices — such as exorcism — are mentioned in *Le Siècle de Louis XIV*. "Infamous" spiritual structures are ever the same. The author of *Zadig* and the author of *Isis Unveiled* seem to agree once more on an important point:

> "The occult knowledge gleaned by the Roman Church from the once fat fields of theurgy she sedulously guarded for her own use, and sent to the stake only those practitioners who "poached" on her lands of the Scientia Scientiarum, and those whose sins could not be concealed by the friar's frock. The proof of it lies in the records of history." (*Isis Unveiled*, p. 58, Vol. 2).

The grim experience of Zadig does not go unheeded. A second chance to bear witness finds the young man unwilling to speak. He is therefore convicted of withholding information. Prudence itself is no guarantee of safety in the case of persons presumed guilty of superior knowledge. Only one safeguard exists: the systematic concealment of transcendental learning. The episode justifies secrecy — and esoteric practice — on the basis of self-preservation.

The "sorcery" imputed to Zadig would not disgrace Sherlock Holmes or a modern crime lab. Findings involve material facts such as tracks, angles, measurements, pressures, and the specific qualities of metals. Keen intelligence and considerable knowledge are displayed by the hero. One mystery remains. How did the young man chance to note — and interpret — the given facts of a problem in anticipation of the formulated problem? What caused the brilliant synthesis of scattered evidence to be made if not habitual alertness to objectively perceived data? The former question hinges on probable kinship between immaterial reality and material proof. The second question may be answered by the existence of a sixth sense capable of transmuting the findings of the five others.

The episode is conducive to respect of ancient lore. If one agrees with Professor Draper that scientific achievement involves "geometry" and "the practical interrogations of Nature," one must admit that the Voltairian disciple of Zoroaster is proficient in those domains. One may also concede that the theosophical and the Voltairian view of ancient knowledge are not incompatible with each other.

The cruelty of the priests who wish to burn Zadig alive cannot be justified. The stake, the favorite tool of spiritual law and order, is abhorrent to all decent beings. But the suspicion of witchcraft is understandable. The faculties of Zadig do seem uncanny until they are explained by the hero himself. Weird appearance and deep logic are sides of the same occult coin: full understanding of "Nature." Such seems to be a major theme of the chapter entitled *The Dog and the Horse*.

Also suggested is belief in the existence of superior human attributes. Man can acquire extraordinary powers by cultivating the spiritualized intellect. The alertness and the ability to synthesize which are displayed by Zadig transcend the limits of cold intelligence. While the resulting vision seems akin to sorcery, the hero has simply and wisely developed natural faculties which are latent in all men. Miraculous though they seem, such faculties belong to the realm of Natural, Universal Law:

> "We assert that the divine spark in man being one and identical in its essence with the Universal Spirit, our 'Spiritual Self' is practically omniscient, but that it cannot manifest its knowledge owing to the impediments of matter." (*The Key to Theosophy*, p. 23).

"The impediments of matter" were viewed in similar manner and like spirit by Alfred de Vigny:

> "Tout homme a vu le mur qui borne son esprit.
> Du corps et non de l'âme accusons l'indigence.
> Des organes mauvais servent l'intelligence."
> (*La Flûte*).

> ("Every man has seen the wall which limits his mind (or spirit)
> Of the body, not the soul, let us accuse the poverty.
> Poor organs serve the intelligence.")

Omniscience is a dominant preoccupation in Proustian literature. The emphasis placed by Marcel on intuition and total recall should suffice to encourage esoteric study of the *Recherche*. Many characters are shown seeking "the whole truth" on widely separated planes of endeavor: through sealed envelopes, through closed doors and windows, with the help of spies, in art and literature. A transient form of omniscience is occasionally granted. The divine flash embracing the entire universe bound to past experience is vastly superior to the partial memory of the intelligence. The narrator finds that mysterious domains await reclamation from the "lost past."* Literature teems with echoes of the inner-most self. Marcel discovers — via the works of "Bergotte" — a deeper region of his being, "more unified, broader, from which obstacles and separations" seem to have been removed."** What obstacles? What separations? The handicap of sensory perception? The bondage of separate being? "The impediments of matter" perhaps?

Not unlike "grace" or "charity," knowledge begins at home. The Proustian theme of heightened consciousness — or sensory perception in abeyance — resembles the fugue of Zadig earning freedom from Maya. The path to mysterious regions of Cosmos begins in corresponding regions of the Self where the data of the senses are fully used but essentially transcended. The case of Zadig suggests that the resulting vision involves knowledge of all kingdoms of existence from the mineral to the

---

*A la Recherche du temps perdu, p. 67, Vol. I.
**Ibid., p. 94, Vol. I.

human. The occult axiom: "Man is a microcosm in a macrocosm" — which is embodied in the title of *Micromégas* — is virtually present in the first chapters of *Zadig*. The hero must — and does — develop the superior faculties latent in the Self before he can penetrate the secrets of the universe which surrounds him. The unvarying inspiration of esoteric writers of all times is the Delphic injunction: "Know Thyself!" The study of Nature pursued by the hero is true to the ancient precept:

> " 'Nothing is happier,' he said, 'than a philosopher who reads in that great book which God has placed under our eyes. The truths which he discovers are his; he nourishes and elevates his soul; — ' " (*The Dog and the Horse*, p. 16).

> "Man must know *himself* before he can hope to know the ultimate genesis even of beings and powers less developed in their inner nature than himself." (*Isis Unveiled*, p. 264, Vol. 2).

The ultimate mastery in Self-Knowledge is claimed by Vigny in his testamentary poem *L'Esprit pur*. Reference is made to that certain "mirror" in which the Self may be known. Two "broken chains" are mentioned — the chain of terrestrial genealogy and the chain of rebirth. The poet celebrates the approaching release from the bondage of incarnation. "Past labors" — the entire chain of existence of a human spirit — are "seen" and judged through the vision of the "perfect."

Rabelaisian "good company" is likewise dedicated to the attainment of Self-Knowledge. "It is a beautiful thing to meet good company" — "in Delphi on the front part of the temple of Apollo was found this divinely written maxim: KNOW THYSELF."*

The next chapter contains the story of an envious man who tries to cause the ruin of Zadig. Envy is a major symptom of Mayavic vision, divisiveness, or selfhood at its worst. It is an implacable destroyer of intrinsic values such as true happiness. It is the malignant potency of a perverted concept of success. One may have every reason to feel fortunate. But the fact that another person seems more fortunate is intolerable. Tangible blessings become meaningless as soon as they fail to arouse the jealousy — which is to say the suffering — of others. The capacity for joy is obliterated. The ability to "satisfy" and to arouse envy is a major element of motivation in Western societies. One strives to surpass certain fellow-men, to "keep up with" others, and to look down on the rest. The sacrosanct ideal of comparative, "competitive" effort is all too often a nice name concealing sordid things. The same ideal

---

Quart Livre, XLIX.

would perform wonders on a loftier plane of preoccupation. But the prevalence of materialistic, basely selfish values degrades the crucial factor of *level*. The debased concept of success and selfhood which is promoted in the modern Western world is generally traced to the Judaeo-Christian tradition of the Old Testament by esoteric writers.

The Jehovic God is emphatically "jealous" and divisive. The anthropomorphic Deity thrives on sibling rivalries among his creatures, promotes hatred between individuals and nations, manipulates favorites and torments whipping-boys. The same God commands the humiliation, spoliation, and extermination of the "accursed" by the "chosen." One may say that the example of glorified envy and resulting strife comes from high quarters since the Bible continues to be read literally by numerous persons.

Vigny is one of many authors who connect the omnipotence of envy with the Old Testament. The condemned daughter of Jephté laments the fact that her exalted status of wife and mother will not arouse the envy of other women. Moses dwells — in somewhat morbid fashion — on the penalties entailed by his greatness. Greatness is defined in part by the envy of angels whose powers do not equal his own.

The name of the envious man portrayed by Voltaire — *Arimaze* — resembles *Ahriman*, the "Angel of Darkness" of Zoroastrian philosophy.* The Secret Doctrine places on the same level "the primal twins Osiris-Typhon, Ormazd-Ahriman, and finally Cain-Abel and the *tutti quanti* of contraries."** The occult equivalence of Cain-Abel and Jehovah*** suggests a possible interpretation of Arimaze-Ahriman as the Biblical God. Voltaire seems to have included in his survey of Mayavic realms the divisiveness which prevails in the material universe and which is the necessary companion of faulty "vision." All is One on the plane of Absolute Reality. All is division and chaos on the phenomenal plane of existence. Arimaze seems to be assimilated to the host of mythological "adversaries" which are personated powers of Nature and which are designated in the Secret Doctrine as "strife-makers."**** The envious man seems to announce two additional appearances of the "jealous" Biblical God which will be made in *Zadig*. The apparent assimilation of Ahriman to Jehovah tends to convey two major themes of occult and esoteric literature. "Jehovah has ever been in antiquity only 'a god *among*

The Secret Doctrine, p. 577, Vol. I.
**Ibid.,* p. 412, Vol. I.
***Ibid.,* p. 126, Vol. II.
****Ibid.,* p. 413, Vol. I.

other *Gods.*' "[*] The Judaeo-Christian tradition is the ungrateful daughter of Pagan mythologies.

Zadig is an object of envy for persons and institutions lacking true substance. He must fear the jealousy of priests, the resentment of pseudo-scientists such as Hermes, and the ignorance of common men. He must also fear envious scholars who sense a threat in his superiority. The young hero prefers in all things "being to appearance" or True Reality to Maya. But the pontiffs of Academe with whom he has contact care only for their image and for the preservation of their careers. They are more or less conscious cogs of a powerful machine bent on the maintenance of the status quo. Their worldly success is achieved through drawing-room and bedroom politics.

A scholar has written thirteen erudite books on the properties of a non-existent animal, the griffin. The related discussion is an exercise in futility and buffoonery. But the scholar is noted to be "a great theurgist" or person versed in secret lore.

The mythical character of the griffin is a subtle exoteric reflection on the "substance" of many scholarly works which contribute little to the advancement of knowledge. But the esoteric symbolism of the griffin is important. The griffin — or serpent in a circle — represents eternity and evolution.[**] The snake, dragon, or reptile biting its own tail or putting its tail into its mouth is the emblem of esoteric literature inspired by the Secret Doctrine. It is designated by Mme Blavatsky as "the theosophical Serpent of Eternity."[***] It is generally found in the final portion of a literary work which is often written toward the end of an author's career.

The griffin appears in the *Cinquième Livre* of the works of Rabelais, a fact strongly suggesting — if not proving — that Rabelais was indeed the author of the contested text. (" — un dragon soy mordant la queue —" " — a dragon biting its own tail —")[****] The circular snake is humorously featured in *Le Taureau blanc,* a story produced by Voltaire in 1774. It is mentioned in the poetry of Shelley (*Queen Mab*). It is present in *Les Oracles,* a poem written by Vigny in 1862. It is also suggested in the *Diary* of the same author. The significant emblem is part of a doomed demonstration of fireworks in *Madame Bovary.* It appears in the form of a ruby-eyed snake ring in *La Bête Humaine* — as it does in James Baldwin's *Another Country.* The ring plays a meaningful role in the

---

[*]*Ibid.,* p. 508, Vol. II.
[**]*The Secret Doctrine,* p. 364, fn., Vol. I.
[***]*Ibid.,* p. 377, Vol. II.
[****]Ch. XI.

novel of Zola. It is the instrument of *revelation* of a sad *truth*. "Love" — esoteric spirituality — should have been sacred and pure. But Love has been tainted by a Jehovic figure: President Grandmorin. The snake is cleverly yet transparently veiled in the final portion of the *Recherche*: "— le progrès — finit par se manger la queue," — "progress (evolution or the symbolic serpent) finally ended up eating its own tail."* Sartre refers in *La Nausée* to the futility of "trying to catch time by the tail." It is suggested more than once in the same book through reference to "the bottom of time" that Eternity — the "serpent" — is cyclic in design. The snake forms a live, loving ankle-bracelet in *The Little Prince*. The same emblem appears in Genêt's *Notre Dame des Fleurs*. As final revisions are being made to the present work, a novel by Doris Lessing has been published which also contains the significant serpent. *Briefing for a Descent Into Hell*. Such are but a few examples of the dissemination of the "griffin" in literature.

The Voltairian scholar and theurgist can hardly be accused of ignorance. The subject of the griffin which, in the words of an expert, "would require a volume"** to be fully studied, has inspired him to write thirteen volumes. The political zeal of the savant is equal to his knowledge. He quickly denounces Zadig to the arch-priest Yebor. The learned author belongs to an academic minority held in equally low esteem by Voltaire and by occultists: "Men of letters, and various *authorities*, who hide their real belief in deference to popular prejudice.*** He is a pawn of the social system in general and a flunky of the Church in particular. To the unholy team-teaching of official science — Hermes — and perverted religion — the priests — is added the presence of lucid but voluntarily prostituted scholarship. The primary villain pulling strings back-stage is ever the same. It is the state-supported religion which cannot co-exist with truth.

The name of the arch-priest — *Yebor* — is occasionally believed to be the anagram of *Boyer* designating a contemporary of Voltaire. Esoterically, however, one may regard it as the modified anagram of *Horeb*, a biblical site openly and meaningfully mentioned at a subsequent stage of *Zadig*. Voltaire seems to have substituted one letter to another in a manner doubly suggestive of HAVEH-YAVEH or JEHOVAH. Mt. Horeb is the mountain peak where Moses is said to have been initiated and where the Judaeo-Christian tradition had its official beginning. The scholarly stool-pigeon featured in *Zadig* is the devoted servant of Mosaic power.

A la Recherche du temps perdu, p. 731, Vol. III.
**The Secret Doctrine,* p. 505, Vol. II.
***Isis Unveiled,* p. viii, Vol. I.

The prosecution of Zadig is ended for a fee. The transaction involves bartered Love or the services of a girl of easy virtue. The theme of prostituted sacred values which is prominent throughout Voltairian texts is apparent at an early stage of *Zadig.*

Voltaire evaluates sycophantic scholars by means of a subtle distinction. Zadig segregates "scholars" from "good company:"

> "In the morning his library was open to all scholars, at night his table was open to good company; but he soon found how dangerous scholars are." (*L'Envieux,* p. 20).

> "He cursed the scholars, and decided to live with good company only forever after."

Many counterparts of the griffin specialist are found in literature. The learned geographer of *The Little Prince* is more interested in the personalities of "explorers" — genuine discoverers — than he is in their discoveries. He is especially wary of the findings of esoteric "drunkards" or persons addicted to "spirit." Such dipsomaniacs occasionally see double — or have second sight. Their work is suspect and unwanted. Another devastating parable is found in the same book on the same subject. A Turkish astronomer has discovered an asteroid. He presents his findings. No one believes him — he wears the wrong clothes. The scientist exchanges his Oriental garb for reassuring Western finery. The conical hat which smacked of sorcery and Paganism is abandoned. Emphasis is placed on phallic regions through dignified "tails." The demonstration is made a second time. Everyone is convinced. For the discoverer — and the discovery — now look "orthodox," "civilized," "modern," and above all Western. One may safely conclude that the advancement of knowledge is not always welcome in our enlightened age. The sacred cow of XXth Century Judaeo-Christian superiority resents being kicked around.

The Voltairian distinction between "scholars" and "good company" has autobiographical overtones. Voltaire was — and remains — the target of many scholarly barbs. Learning did not suffice to establish between him and others the bond of "good company." Even in the absence of declared hostility, communication was probably difficult between the daring seeker of truth and his spiritually inhibited colleagues. In all likelihood, the "good company" cherished by the author consisted of a small group sharing special interests. Mme Denis, the beloved niece of the "sage who amused himself" by writing *Zadig,* seems to have been a member in good standing:

> "C'est à vous s'il vous plait, ma nièce,
> Vous femme d'esprit sans travers,

56

Philosophe de mon espèce,
Vous qui comme moi du Permesse
Connaissez les sentiers divers;
C'est à vous qu'en courant j'adresse
Ce fatras de prose et de vers — "
(*Voyage à Berlin, à Madame Denis, à Clèves,* Juillet 1750).

("It is to you, if you please, my niece,
You woman of wit (spirit) and faultless,
A philosopher of my specie,
To you, who like myself of Parnassus
Do know the diverse paths —
It is to you that, on the run, I despatch
This medley of prose and of verse — ")

Mt. Parnassus was once regarded as a sacred mountain and was the site of ancient initiation rites.* The allusion to the famous peak reflects more than superficial interest in mythology or the necessity of finding a rhyme. "Philosophers" of the Voltairian "specie," persons gifted with "wit" — or "spirit" — individuals familiar with certain "paths," seem to have been students and practitioners of the Secret Doctrine. The cheerful complicity reflected by the delightful "fatras de prose et de vers" is the complicity of a secret kinship transcending the bonds of flesh.

The following passage of the chapter devoted to the envious man likewise seems autobiographical. Voltaire the poet may be involved:

"Zadig did not pride himself upon being a good poet."
(*L'Envieux*, p. 23).

While the wording is non-committal, conveying an opinion rather than a fact, Voltaire seems to recognize the superiority of his prose over his poetry. Poetic quality, though desirable and generally achieved by the author of *Zadig,* may not have been a primary goal. The Muse may have been the mere servant of a concelead message. Esoteric poetry is defined by Mme Blavatsky as "poetised truth."** The poetry of Voltaire will be shown to fit the label.

The death sentence received by Zadig results from the fragmentary condition of poetry which he has written. A mutilated text is used as evidence of subversion. Partial understanding and injustice follow. An *innocent* is condemned. The substance of the episode is consistent with many Voltairian outcries against arbitrary legal practice. The fraudulent use of mutilated religious "scriptures" also seems to be attacked. The crimes of inquisitors are under indictment. It was on the alleged basis of mangled

---

The Secret Doctrine, p. 494, Vol. II.
**Ibid.,* p. 7, Vol. II.

scriptural authority that thousands of persons were sent to the torture chamber and to the stake.

Many pages of *Isis Unveiled* are devoted to the atrocities committed by the Inquisition. The militant indignation of Voltaire — a commitment born of the same concern — is common knowledge.

> " — in the brief space of fourteen years, Tomas de Torquemada, the confessor of Queen Isabella, burned over ten thousand persons, and sentenced to the torture eighty thousand more." (*Isis Unveiled,* p. 59, Vol. 2).

The chain of events which bring Zadig to fame — and to grief — involves two animals: a dog and a horse. One specific burning is described as follows by *Isis Unveiled*:

> "Granger tells the story, describing it as having occurred in his time. The poor animal 'had been taught to tell the spots upon cards, and the hour of the day by the watch. Horse and owner were both indicted by the sacred office for dealing with the Devil, and both were burned, with a great ceremony of auto-da-fé at Lisbon in 1601 as wizards!'" (*Isis Unveiled,* p. 59, Vol. 2).

The reference to the horse which is made in *Zadig* and the coverage of " a fine auto-da-fé" performed in Lisbon and reported in *Candide* suggest awareness of the burning described by Granger. Brief reference is also made to a similar trial "began in 1610 in Paris" in *Le Siècle de Louis XIV.** The same religion which denies that any animal can have a soul may on occasion tacitly recognize the existence of the said soul without which it is impossible to deal with the Devil. It cannot be ascertained from the text of *Zadig* whether or not an allusion was made to the story of Granger. But the *Siècle de Louis XIV* and Chapter VI of *Candide* show that the same caliber of absurdity and fiendishness is attacked by Voltaire and by Mme Blavatsky.

The incriminating portion of the poem written by Zadig contains a precious clue to the presence of esoteric material. The subject of the verse is the King. The text has a nursery-rhyme-like, crippled quality:

> "Par les plus grands forfaits
> Sur le trône affermi,
> Dans la publique paix,
> C'est le seul ennemi."
>
> ("Through the greatest misdeeds
> Firmly established on the throne

---

*Ch. II.

Within the public peace
He is the lone foe.")

Rhymes are crude approximation. Prosody and pronunciation are in conflict. The juggling of a few cumbersome mute *e*'s is required to rescue the stanza from total disaster. The general effect is grotesque.

The completed version of the poem has an adequate dignity of form:

"Par les plus grands forfaits j'ai vu troubler la terre.
Sur le trône affermi le roi sait tout dompter.
Dans la publique paix l'amour seul fait la guerre;
C'est le seul ennemi qui soit à redouter."

("Through the greatest misdeeds I saw the earth disturbed.
Firmly established on the throne the King knows how to conquer all.
Within the public peace love alone is at war;
He is the lone foe to be feared.")

Voltaire uses contrast to "say more than" he "seems to say." He points to common practices of esoteric writers such as deliberate "accidents" of form and calculated "slips" of knowledge. Such failings are designed to draw attention to veiled substance. The reader is subtly invited to practice objective alertness — and ethics. He is asked in the present case to meditate on a rewarding question: Could Zadig — alias Voltaire — have produced such lame verse as the fragmentary stanza without special reason? The previously quoted observation on the poetic skill of Zadig suggests that he did not. The reader is warned against certain obstacles to full comprehension which lie within himself. Mechanical acceptance of any and all printed matter, casual reading, and overly low esteem for the ability of an author are equally blinding.

The complete stanza — which seems to praise the King — may be read in two ways. The monarch's ability to overcome all obstacles may be seen as the extension of "the greatest misdeeds," or as a manifestation of despotism. No structural consideration rules out a connection between the King and the final line. Within the framework provided by the connection — as in the exoteric version of the poem — love remains the only warring element. It may be love of mankind, the sole surviving and subversive decency in the midst of universal oppression. It may be mystical love or commitment to superior knowledge. It may be the esoteric concept of "Eros, the Divine Will or Desire of manifesting — through visible creation,"* in other words the dynamic principle of evolution. Love may

---

*The Secret Doctrine, p. 65, Vol. II.

then be regarded as a second possible antecedent to "he is the only foe to be feared." The person endangered by such universal love then becomes the King or human symbol of the establishment. Whether or not one reads into the text praise of the monarch is determined by preceding paragraphs of the chapter and by the attitude of the reader. Assuming Zadig to be innocent of "lèse-majesté," assuming a basic conflict to exist between the fragmentary and the integral versions of the poem, one tends to project into the stanza a substance favorable to the sovereign. The double-edged character of the completed quatrain invites reflection on the "trial" of the author himself. Fragmentary perception of his message is hinted. Zadig *is* subversive after all, in grand manner, on an unsuspected plane. Zadig is also probably "innocent" in the esoteric sense of the term which will be shown to mean "initiate," in due course of this study.

The poetic quality of the completed stanza meets the requirements of metrics. One may even argue that it meets them too well. The unrelieved thumping rhythm of the basic alexandrin is combined with ringing tones. The total trumpeting effect is about as poetic as the sound of a brass band. The Voltairian emphasis on fanfare may have been calculated to arouse skepticism where the greatness of the King is concerned. It may represent — among other things — an invitation to carefully read *Le Siècle de Louis XIV*.

The amusing stanza is a playful though fervent nudge aimed an potential esoteric readers. It is a plea for comprehension and a proof of the misleading nature of casual reading.

> "In spite of the progress of the human mind (or spirit) people read very little; and, among those who sometimes wish to gain instruction, most persons read very badly." (*L'Homme aux quarante écus, Des proportions*).

The poetic efforts of Zadig are rewarded by a death sentence. The young man is condemned without true hearing. The procedure is a one-way street. The prosecution is given *carte blanche*. Zadig is "not allowed to speak because his tablets spoke for themselves." While judicial abuse is attacked in typical Voltairian fashion, another view of altogether different nature is expressed in the brief statement. It is radically opposed to the traditional image of the writer. Recognition is given to occult forces which animate matter through non-physical means. The tablets *spoke* literally!

> "Speaking of Kashmere, Marco Polo observes that they have an astonishing acquaintance with the *devilries* of enchantment inasmuch that they make their idols to speak." (*Isis Unveiled*, p. 505, Vol. 1).

"The same knowledge and control of occult forces, inccluding the vital force which enables the fakir, temporarily to leave and then re-enter his body, and Jesus, Apollonius, and Elisha to recall their several subjects to life, made it possible for the ancient hierophants to animate statues, and cause them to act and speak like living creatures." (*Isis Unveiled*, p. 505, Vol. I.).

Louis Pauwels and Jacques Bergier cite the case of an interesting bronze head:

"There was . . . the extraordinary case of one of the most mysterious figures in Western history: the Pope Sylvester II, known also by the name of Gerbert d'Aurillac. Born in the Auvergne in 920 (d. 1003) Gerbert was a Benedictine monk, professor at the University of Rheims, Archbishop of Ravenna and Pope by the grace of Otho III. He is supposed to have spent some time in Spain, after which a mysterious voyage brought him to India where he is reputed to have acquired various kinds of skills which stupefied his entourage. For example, he possessed in his palace a bronze head which answered YES or NO to questions put to it on politics or the general position of Christianity. According to Sylvester II* this was a perfectly simple operation corresponding to a two-figure calculation, and was performed by an automaton similar to our modern binary machines. This "magic" head was destroyed when Sylvester died, and all the information it imparted carefully concealed. No doubt an authorized research worker would come across some surprising things in the Vatican Library." (*The Morning of the Magicians*, p. 68).

The tablets of Zadig spoke! Feeling amply protected by the weird implications of the literal statement, knowing himself to be well shielded by his reputation of "skeptic" and unbeliever, Voltaire was able to plant the startling statement in the text without benefit of veils. We can only speculate about his thoughts — and his smile — as the pen outlined the preposterous words. We may be helped in the task by remembering that the "sage" who wrote Zadig admittedly "amused himself."

The execution of Zadig is miraculously prevented. The young man is exonerated by a strange chain of events involving a parrot, a peach, and the missing portion of the incriminating tablets. Disaster and salvation seem to be the work of a Providence which is consistent in absurdity only. One may note, however, the heartening symbolism of a message finally perceived in its entirety. "Parrotting" can bear strange fruit in due course of time. The theme of eventual vindication obtained by the poetry of "Zadig" may also apply to the works of Voltaire.

Zadig is awarded the possessions of his denunciator by royal judgment. But the wealth is returned to the original owner. Legitimate as it may seem to the majority of men, revenge is rejected as unworthy. Earthly

---

*See Vol. CXXXIX of *Migne's Patrologie Latine*.

riches are scorned. Buddha and Paul — who were likewise endowed with disdained affluence — have a kindred spirit in the person of the young Zoroastrian.

Criticism of modern Western morality is transparently implied in the chapter entitled *Les Généreux*. The world of Antiquity is not presented as perfect. The beginning of the story contains abundant evidence of corrupt forces at work. But the promotion and reward of good deeds remains the concern of powerful élites. A comparison is difficult to avoid. Such is not the case in times and places which will come under the designation of modern "Westphalia" in *Candide*. In one respect at least the world of Paganism is superior to the environment in which Voltaire lived. Rather than a forced posture, virtue is a positive force:

The "tournament" described in the chapter has little to do with physical prowess. Virtue is the sole criterion of excellence.

> "Ce jour mémorable venu, le roi parut sur son trône, environné des grands, des mages, et des députés de toutes les nations qui venaient à ces jeux, où la gloire s'acquérait non par la légèreté des chevaux, non par la force du corps, mais par la vertu." (*Les Généreux*, pp. 24-25).

> ("The memorable day having come, the King appeared on his throne surrounded by the great, the magi, and the deputies of all nations who came to those games in which glory was acquired not through the speed of horses, nor through the strength of the body, but through virtue.")

The passage contains two esoteric equations. The word "virtue" is used in its etymological sense of "strength." Esoteric "strength" is spirituality. Brute force is openly declared irrelevant to the occasion. The general setting of the event — which resembles that of a medieval tournament — suggests that a symbolic interpretation of future jousts may be in order. Such will be the "battle" which will eventually oppose Otame, Itobad, and Zadig.

The top-ranking contestants are ethical supermen. Among them are a judge and a soldier. The judge has offered his entire fortune to compensate a citizen for a judicial error. The soldier has sacrificed his love life in order to save his mother. The bereaved lover — who contemplates suicide — finally consents to live for the sake of his aged parent. The bonds of flesh or incarnation are shown to be as meaningful as human beings make them. The will to live or to "endure life" — "il eut le courage de souffrir la vie" — "he found the courage to endure life" — is as noble or ignoble as human dedication. Voltaire may have had in mind the famous soliloquy of Hamlet when he wrote the passage. Whatever the case may be, the unbelievable judge and the sublime soldier seem to reflect the lingering influence of a Golden Age which is a far cry from XVIIIth Century France.

Zadig becomes a Babylonian Solomon whose wisdom is made manifest in judgments. A selfless son is preferred to another who has won public acclaim by building an expensive monument dedicated to the memory for his father. A strange paternity suit shows ethics to be more important than physical fatherhood. The righteous path is determined by scorn of false values. Various aspects of Maya are consistently rejected. Such are physical force, material wealth, social prestige and the purely biological attributes of incarnation.

The same rejection of "vanity" is evident in the attitude of Zadig. "He impressed upon everyone the sacred power of the laws and impressed upon no one the weight of his office." Sacred values are paramount. Human dignity is no more than the measure of human dedication to *them*.

The theme of pagan virtue based on a universal religion and on a universal system of ethics is a major element of occult philosophy. It is often stated that pagan culture is generally misunderstood — if not deliberately distorted — by modern mankind. An entire chapter of *Isis Unveiled* is entitled "Christian Crimes and Heathen Virtues." The Voltairian reprimand addressed to ignorant detractors of the Ancients: "You who cast slurs upon Antiquity without knowing it—"* may have the same secret source as the following statement of Mme Blavatsky:

> "*There were no Atheists in those days of old; no disbelievers or materialists in the modern sense of the word, as there were no bigoted detractors.* He who judges the ancient philosophies by their external phraseology, and quotes from ancient writings sentences *seemingly* atheistical, is unfit to be trusted as a critic, for he is unable to penetrate into the inner sense of their metaphysics."

It is noted by the author of *Isis Unveiled* that the philosophy of the Ancients held all things to be "illusion — save the Great Unknown and His direct essence." It is also stated that the same philosophy was upheld by "the whole pre-Christian world:"

> "Those philosophical beliefs extended like a net-work over the whole pre-Christian world; and surviving persecution and misrepresentations, form the corner-stone of every now existing religion outside Christianity." (*Isis Unveiled*, pp. 530-31, Vol. 2).

The universal character of pagan philosophy is suggested by Voltaire. The "tournament" described in *Les Génereux* is attended by "deputies from all the nations."

Poèmes et discours en vers, Oeuvres Complètes de Voltaire, de l'imprimerie de la Société Littéraire Typographique, 1785, Tome dousième.

The judiciary flair of Zadig is demonstrated in a dispute opposing right to left-foot advocates. Each group wishes to impose upon the faithful its own way of entering the temple. Arbitrarily contrived religious ritual is treated with contempt. Among other divisive aspects of Maya, such spiritual etiquettes are major sources of tension and strife. The same idea is expressed in the famous *Traité sur la Tolérance*: "Permit it to be so that — those who light tapers at high noon in order to glorify you may tolerate those who content themselves with the light of the sun."

The above passage of he *Prayer to God* addresses its plea for tolerance primarily to Christians. Christians are urged to bear the fact of the existence of faiths other than their own. It is suggested — with bleeding irony — that the sun may deserve the same religious consideration as man-made candles symbolically and materially cancelled by noon-day light. An appeal is made to common sense as well as decency. The latter part of the sentence: "those who content themselves with the light of the sun" brings to mind sun-worshippers or exoteric segments of mono-theistic Pagan faith. The admonition is aimed at one side, clearly showing where the need of tolerance is greatest.

Zadig solves the delicate problem of entry into sanctuaries by jumping into the temple with both feet joined. The procedure — which seems to lack reverence and decorum-may convey unexpected symbolism. Faith is no half-hearted venture. Faith is total commitment to be embraced with one's entire being.

The nature of spirited wisdom is suggested with typical esoteric humor. Zadig is willing to heed views differing from his own. He does not discourage the influence of "the voices of the divan." The latter Persian term suggests the relevance of literature. "Poetry is the register (divan) of the Arabs," says a proverb.* The term *divan* eventually came to designate all the government bureaus of Persia. "The divan of the Sublime Porte was for long the council of the empire, presided over by the grand vizier."* Voltaire seems to use the exotic term to bring to mind the combined forces of poetry — or literature — and political power. It is noted in *Zadig* that "there is always hope with princes who love verse." The divan is also a probable allusion to the "sofa" or couch used in ancient initiation rites, an object which is mentioned in *Candide* — with some insistence — and which is also featured in *L'Ingénu*. The trance-like state experienced on the said divan or couch involves travel in invisible realms and the hearing of "voices." Zadig apparently listens to the views

---

Encyclopaedia Britannica, Divan.

of initiates. In Voltaire's own words: "His principal talent was the ability to extricate the truth."

Zadig is admired by many persons. But he is severely criticized by others. He fails to meet certain popular requirements of religious showmanship. Some elements of the community feel cheated of their due. No spectacular wonders are offered — in rhetoric or otherwise — by the wise young man.

> "The envious man and his wife claimed that in his address he did not have enough symbols, that he had not caused the mountains or the hills to heave sufficiently. 'He is dry and without genius,' they said, "one does not see with him the sea in flight, the stars falling, or the sun melting like wax; he does not have the good oriental style.' Zadig contented himself with having the style of reason. Everyone was on his side, not because he was in the right path, not because he was sensible, not because he was kind, but because he was prime minister." (*Les Disputes et les Audiences*, p. 29).

The catalogue of desired and denied wonders seems to ridicule all aspects of the supernatural. Such was the intent of Voltaire. Cataclysms of the variety described in world mythology and scriptural texts do not belong to the realm of "miracles." They are manifestations of cyclic cosmic change. They are the work of impersonal, mathematical, universal law.

The opposition which seems to exist between "good Oriental style" and "the style of reason" has esoteric usefulness. Voltaire appears to reject Oriental "myths" in particular and related "superstition" in general. His belief in the veiled core of world mythology — which is covertly expressed in many of his works — is all the better concealed for the episode. The reference to "good Oriental style" may also have been designed to convey the idea that no single portion of earth has a monopoly on truth.

The antagonism which seems to exist between Faith and Reason is dissolved on the esoteric plane. Zadig's avoidance of certain displays is due to reason, not to lack of faith. His mode of entry into the temple suggests both attitudes to be compatible with each other. As was previously noted, the act of jumping into the sanctuary with both feet joined may symbolize total commitment to Faith. Common sense prompts Zadig to prevent further dissension and possible bloodshed between right and left-foot advocates. The same wisdom makes him shun "miracles" in which he does not believe anyway. "Figures" or symbols lend themselves to falsification and murderous debate. The young man sees no reason to invoke those which are already in existence or to invent new ones. Knowledge of their inflammatory potential is probably matched by knowledge of their deep essence.

The disciple of Zoroaster does "not ignore physical sciences as they were known in those days" or separate Faith from Reason. A serene fusion of spirituality and science dwells at the core of his being. The same blend is the essence of his deserved prestige. Zadig is regarded — by scientists — as an "oracle." His knowledge is recognized — by priests — to exceed the learning of Yebor, the able "thaumaturgist." A philosophical circle is squared in which Faith and Reason are One. The joined feet of the hero symbolize among other things a meaningful set of "separated twins." The twins are overshadowed and guided by a lofty sense of Ethics. Zadig is "sensible" and "kind." The occult trinity of Knowledge, Spirit and Goodness could hardly be more perfectly represented.

The envious man and his wife do not understand the criticized prime minister. "Zadig" is too "reasonable" to shout cosmic views from pulpits or rooftops. The era in which he lives is that of lingering but threatened Ancient Wisdom. The science of the hero is wisely kept secret. But the science in question would surprise the critics if its nature and scope were revealed. Heaving "mountains" or traveling mountains which are linked to the periodical tilting of the axis of earth belong to the veiled substance of the works of "Zadig." It will be shown in the course of the present study that the Voltairian trilogy contains references to shifting poles, displaced oceans, sunken continents and cataclysms. Other topics of staggering character are covered by the allegedly "dry" and uninspired public figure. The Mayavic insight which can be expected from "envy" or divisiveness personified points to numerous criticisms of Voltaire by various commentators. Voltaire had abundant opportunity to sample such commentaries during his lifetime. He had more than sufficient vision to foresee the learned litanies of the future which would be devoted to the works of "Zadig." "He is dry and without genius" says Arimaze. "He lacks depth and strength" says Des Granges.* "He does not have the sense of mystery. He does not have the sense of the past" says Lanson.** "He understands nothing about faith or mysticism" says Lagarde et Michard. "The envious man" has much to learn. The esoteric grin of Zadig-Voltaire underlies the passage.

Zadig solves another quarrel opposing white and black magic. He rules that one may turn equally well toward East or West when praying. Reason and tolerance are again prescribed to men of good will. The central message of the parable is identical in spirit to the statement of Sri Ramakrishna which has already been quoted: "Hindus, Muslims, and Christians are going to the same goal through different paths." The theme of

---

*Op. cit., p. 581.
**G. Lanson et P. Truffau, Histoire de la Littérature Française, p. 396.

universal values is once more in evidence. East and West are never divorced in the minds of "good company."

Zadig consistently plays the role of a unifying force bravely countering endemic strife. The Mayavic significance of the beginning of the story which places heavy stress on sensory values and/or divisiveness is prolonged in the next chapter which is meaningfully entitled *Jealousy*.

The popularity of Zadig with the royal couple leads to a dangerous attachment between the young man and the Queen. The jealousy of King Moabdar is aroused. Death is decreed for Zadig and for Queen Astarté. The hero and the Queen are ambushed by Cupid who wears the reassuring garb of social success, esteem, sympathy, and common interests. A parallel but casual adventure with a chambermaid is also reported. But it is never fully known whether Babylonian "annals" relative to the escapade are reliable. Whether the woman involved be Queen or servant, the spiritual progress of Zadig is threatened. The hero is tempted by forbidden love. The blue garter is ever the same on all social and emotional levels. The episode illustrates the powers stubbornly retained by Maya over persons who have advanced in the path of knowledge. Constant vigilance is the only effective safeguard against ever-present, insidious weakness. The importance of Self-Knowledge is implicitly stressed. The spiritual seeker must scrutinize his own motives. There lies the crucial — and often hazy — borderline between Good and Evil. There also lies the dividing line between white and black magic. In the words of Mme Blavatsky which have already been quoted, "— he who makes of the science of sciences a sinful pretext for worldly motives, — should tremble."

The symbolic parting of the ways faced by Zadig and Astarté seems to be announced in the preceding chapter featuring white and black magic. The amorous venture reported to involve a "servant" may also have been designed to suggest inferior occult pursuits. The fact that the "familiarity" of contacts between Zadig and the Queen produces forbidden love also seems meaningful. The couple appears to be swayed by powers of false innocence representing wicked entities. Such inferior spirits are characterized as follows in *Isis Unveiled*:

> " 'Their abode is in the neighborhood of the earth — and when they can escape the vigilance of the good daemons, there is no mischief they will not dare commit. One day they will employ brute force; another cunning — '
> It is a child's play for them to arouse in us vile passions, to impart to societies and nations turbulent doctrines, provoking wars, seditions, and other public calamities, and then tell you 'that all this is the work of the gods.' "
> (*Isis Unveiled*, pp. 332-33, Vol. 1).

The esoteric meaning of "love" is a major element of esoteric algebra.

Cupid is a logical and an excellent "blind." The mystery of physical life has a mystical counterpart in the mystery of spiritual Being. The theme of *union* — which is the very essence of the words "yogi," "yoga," "yoke," and the French "joug" — is as relevant to the fusion with the Higher Self and with the Absolute as it is to the oneness of earthly love. As was previously noted in connection with the subversive poetry of "Zadig," Eros is the vital principle underlying the universe on all planes of existence. It is only on the plane of gross matter that he becomes a physical — or phallic — aspect of cosmic energy.

> "Eros was connected in early Greek mythology with the world's creation, and only afterwards became the sexual Cupid." (*The Secret Doctrine*, p. 176, Vol. II).

The esoteric equivalence of sex or love is also given by an expert symbologist. The pansexualism of Freud is somewhat damaged by the following statement:

> "In ancient times the feeling of being "penetrated" by or "receiving" the god was allegorised by the sexual act. But it would be a gross misunderstanding to interpret a genuine religious experience as a 'repressed' sexual fantasy on account of a mere metaphor. The 'penetration' can also be expressed by a sword, spear, or arrow."

> The phallus is not a sign that indicates the penis. It is a "symbol because it has so many other meanings." (C. G. Jung, *Flying Saucers*, Ch. II).

Many a literary text commonly regarded as "risqué" or "obscene" contains an invitation to raise one's sight "beyond terrestrial thoughts in lofty contemplation of the marvels of Nature."* The magnificent pornography of Rabelais and Céline has no other raison d'être. The love tryst which is proposed in *La Maison du berger* is a mystical trip into regions of "poetised truth." The portrayal of Eloa — which is rather heavy with poetic "cheesecake" — conveys a message of infinite mercy and voluntary reincarnation. The house of ill-fame is the frequent esoteric facade of mysticism. The divine sense of humor of great "smugglers" is at its best in the exploitation of erotic substance.

> "Keep this Cupid and place it in some monastery. Those who will see it will turn their hearts toward God, for Love naturally knows how to rise to celestial thoughts." (Anatole France, *Thaïs, Le Papyrus*).

Western culture — from Moses to Freud — tends to represent the sex act as the ultimate experience in life. It is therefore not surprising that our interpretation of literary texts usually remains as phallic as does our

---

*Rabelais, *Tiers Livre,* Ch. XVIII.

interpretation of other scriptures. Sexual allusions are eagerly pounced upon and meticulously distilled. Meanwhile, as we salivate in Pavlovian fashion at the sound of the magic bell of SEX, the divine quintessence goes unnoticed — in spite of many warnings.

"We waste a precious time on an absurd track and pass, unsuspecting, by the truth." (*A la Recherche du temps perdu*, p. 100, Vol. III).

" — it is for the woman herself, were she not supplemented by those occult forces, that we would take such pains, — " (*A la Recherche du temps perdu*, p. 1127, Vol. II).

The suggestions of inferior love which are connected with Sémire, Azora, and the "servant" seem to represent inferior spiritual ventures. The impression tends to be confirmed by one fact. Zadig is reported to utter the name of the Queen at a most unexpected moment of his embrace with the chambermaid. It is noted that the same supreme instant finds the majority of men "silent" or voicing "sacred words." The reaction of the lady is likewise eloquent: "That man must have prodigious matters on his mind when he makes love." The grin of the "smuggler" is perceptible.

Astarté is clearly superior to Sémire and Azora in beauty, intelligence, and ethics. While she is subject to the tyranny of Maya — guilty passion — she is endowed with insight and kindness. Her name which designates the goddess of the moon, suggests her to correspond allegorically to the soul, the intermediate component of the human triad.

"Man, who is the microcosm of the macrocosm, or of the archetypal heavenly man, Adam Kadmon, is likewise a trinity; for he is body, soul and spirit." (*Isis Unveiled*, pp. 222-23, Vol 2).

The correspondence between soul and moon — or Astarté — is established by Plutarch, a famous initiate:

" '— the earth has given the body, the moon the soul, and the sun, the understanding to the generation of man.' " (*Isis Unveiled*, pp. 283-84, Vol. 2).

The proposed execution of Zadig and Astarté is prevented by the warning of a little mute. The dwarf — who is deeply devoted to the Queen — is the habitual "witness of most secret transactions as a domestic animal" might be. The word "witness" — which is the etymological equivalent of "martyr" (Greek: martur uros) is often used in a spiritual sense. The French word "domestique" often means "servant." The total combination of "silence," secrecy, "domesticity," and spirituality tends to suggest the occult character of events witnessed.

The written message sent by Astarté to Zadig suggests more to be at stake than a banal romantic involvement:

> " 'Fuyez, dans l'instant même où l'on va vous arracher la vie. Fuyez, Zadig, je vous l'ordonne, au nom de notre amour et de mes rubans jaunes. Je n'étais point coupable; mais je sens que je vais mourir criminelle.' "

> (" 'Take flight, in this very instant when life is about to be wrested from you, I order it, in the name of our love and of my yellow ribbons. I was not guilty but I feel that I am going to die a criminal.' ")

Two common esoteric devices are used. The presence of italics is calculated to attract attention to the concealed substance of the message. The indefinite meaning of the pronoun *on* leaves room for the desired interpretation. The Queen seems to realize that *she* is endangering — in effect "wresting" — the life of Zadig. The "life" which is threatened is suggested to be spiritual by the feeling of criminal guilt expressed at the end of the message. The heroine begs her lover to take flight in the name of purity and soul. The mystical significance of the allegorical couple is also hinted by the exoterically amusing yellow ribbons.

"Gold — most brilliant and precious — symbol of purity."
(*The Secret Doctrine*, p. 271, Vol. II).

"The thrice purified Gold is — *Manas* — the Conscious Soul."
(*The Secret Doctrine*, p. 520, Vol. II).

The melodramatic surface of the episode conceals the attainment of a significant degree of Self-Knowledge. The message of Astarté gives evidence of insight and compassion. The awakening of the "Conscious Soul" is suggested. Unjust suspicion and common peril fail to impel the lovers to take flight together, a step which might be expected of less noble persons. The renunciation of forbidden love marks a transcendence of the plane of "blindness," sensuousness, or Maya.

The gross disproportion which exists between the "offense" of the platonic lovers and the death sentence invites certain thoughts on the character of Moabdar. The record of the inflammable King is less than brilliant. His suspicions are aroused by certain signs of emotion shown by the Queen in the presence of Zadig: -'The King believed all that he saw and imagined all that he did not see." The low "vision" of the monarch is also suggested by the nature of "material evidence" of the alleged crime. A blue garter which is irrelevant to Zadig and Astarté is regarded as proof of their misconduct. Zadig and the Queen are noted to wear ribbons and slippers of the same color. "Those were terrible signs for a delicate prince. Suspicion turned to certainty in his embittered mind." The King is guilty of summary judgment and reckless cruelty. Insight and compassion are nil where the "delicate prince" is concerned.

The obtuse, jealous, and vengeful King has much in common with the occult view of the Biblical God. As was previously noted, occult philosophy teaches that Jehovah is merely a god among other gods and a third-rate figure of world mythology. His mediocre status as a God is matched by his man-like inhumanity. "Christian theology has evolved its self-created human and personal God, the monstrous Head from whence flow in two streams the dogmas of Salvation and Damnation."* The previously suggested biblical connotation of *Moab* seems consistent with the "embittered mind" — or "spirit" — of Moabdar. The final portion of his name is the German word *rad* "wheel" — in reverse. The same German word will be found to be significant in connection with the name of Jes*rad*, a hermit who will be featured in *Zadig*. The reversed "wheel" of evolution which is linked to the biblical element of *Moabdar* strongly suggests a reactionary force of Judaeo-Christian character. Moabdar is one of three unsavory representations of the biblical "vice-God" which appear in the story.

The young hero takes flight, steering his course by the stars. His path is charted by Sirius and Canopus. The reference to Sirius suggests the concealed identity of Zadig.

"Sirius was called the dog-star. It was the star of Mercury, or Buddha, called the great instructor of mankind, before other Buddhas." (*The Secret Doctrine*, p. 374, Vol. II).

The "Dog-Star" may be connected with the previous chapter of *Zadig* entitled *The Dog and the Horse*. A famous mythological horse is represented in heavens by the constellation Pegasus. According to ancient tradition, Pegasus opened the ground of the slopes of Mt. Helicon, releasing the Hippocrene Fountain which is the source of poetic inspiration. The conjunction of poetry — "poetised truth" — or literature — Pegasus — and of an instructor of mankind — Sirius — may fit the occult raison d'être of Zadig. The transparently concealed co-essence of hero and writer is once more suggested. Zadig wrote poetry of controversial and enlightening nature which was generally misconstrued. Voltaire used literature to promote intellectual and spiritual progress in a manner which is not generally understood. The choice of animals featured in the second chapter of *Zadig* seems to have its source in the secret biography of the "Sage" who "amused himself by writing *Zadig*." Sirius is also linked to the

---

The Secret Doctrine, p. 613, Vol. I.

71

origin of "Micromégas" and to the origin of the celestial visitor of *Memnon.*

The name of the star *Canopus* is also the name of a port of ancient Egypt located a few miles East of Alexandria. The keen interest of Voltaire in Canopus is expressed in *La Princesse de Babylone.* It is humorously observed that one does not "know whether the god Canopus had founded the port, or whether the inhabitants had fabricated the god, or whether the star Canopus had given its name to the city, or whether the city had given its name to the star."* Voltaire may have wished to call attention to the interesting ruins which have been found on the site of Canopus and which may contain enlightening inscriptions — as ancient monuments often do. Whatever the case may be, Canopus, one of the guiding lights of Zadig, is a very brilliant star of whitish-yellow color located in the *Carina* group of the Southern Hemisphere. The latter constellation is a modern subdivision of a much larger formation known to the Ancient as *Argo Navis.* The names *Carina* and *Argo Navis* involve the same concept of a ship which may be related to the sacred *Argha* or *Ark* of universal mythology. The vessel in question is itself connected with Astarté or Isis:

> "The Ark is the sacred *Argha* of the Hindus, and thus, the relation in which it stands to Noah's Ark may be easily inferred, when we learn that the Argha was an oblong vessel, used by the high priests as a sacrificial chalice in the worship of Isis, Astarté, and Venus-Aphrodite, all of whom were goddesses of the generative powers of nature, or of matter — hence, representing symbolically the Ark containing the germ of all living things." (*Isis Unveiled,* p. 256, Vol. 2).

The Argha or "ship running before the wind" is also connected with the Messiah, a figure frequently designated as DAG:

> "The Messiah is very often designated as "DAG" or the Fish. This is an inheritance from the Chaldees, and relates — as the very name indicates — to the Babylonian Dagon, the man-fish, who was the instructor and interpreter of the people, to whom he appeared." (*Isis Unveiled,* p. 256, Vol. 2).

The concept of an "Instructor of mankind" or of an "Instructor of the people" is a common factor in the background of Sirius and Canopus. It is also the concept of a Savior which will reappear on the exoteric plane of a subsequent chapter of *Zadig:* the Fisherman.

One may ask how Canopus, which is located in the heavens of the Southern hemisphere, can be seen from Babylonian or neighboring latitudes. The apparent visibility of the star may represent another proof of the superior vision of Zadig, a vision transcending the scope of the

---

*Ch. XI.

physical senses. Such a vision is consistent with the spiritual status of the suggested Savior or Instructor of Mankind. Zadig follows a path of superior insight traveled by great spiritual leaders. The same visibility of Canopus may be designed to convey the idea that the periodic tilting of the axis of earth changes the constellations which may be seen in each hemisphere. Southern constellations of modern days may once have been visible in Northern skies. The esoteric substance of *L'Ingénu* will be found to stress the importance of the same planetary movement.

Zadig becomes absorbed in contemplation of the stars. A "sublime philosophy" — and a sublime passage — are unexpected products of despair:

> "Il admirait ces vastes globes de lumière qui ne paraissent que de faibles étincelles à nos yeux, tandis que la terre, qui n'est en effet qu'un point imperceptible dans la nature, parait à notre cupidité quelque chose de si grand et de si noble. Il se figurait alors les hommes tels qu'ils sont en effet, des insectes se dévorant les uns les autres sur un petit atome de boue. Cette image vraie semblait anéantir ses malheurs en lui retraçant le néant de son être et celui de Babylone. Son âme s'élançait jusque dans l'infini, et contemplait, détachée de ses sens, l'ordre immuable de l'univers. Mais lorsque ensuite, rendu à lui-même et rentrant dans son coeur, il pensait qu'Astarté était peut-être morte pour lui, l'univers disparaissait à ses yeux, et il ne voyait dans la nature entière qu'Astarté mourante et Zadig infortuné."(*La Femme battue*, pp. 36-37).

> ("He was admiring those huge globes of light which seem only feeble sparks to our eyes, whereas the earth which is in fact only one imperceptible point in nature, seems to our greed something so great and so noble. He then imagined men such as they are indeed, insects devouring one another on a small atom of mud. This true image seemed to annihilate his misfortunes by representing to him the nothingness of his being and that of Babylon. His soul soared into infinity, and beheld, detached from his senses, the immutable order of the universe. But when, later, restored to the self and having re-entered his heart, he thought that Astarté was perhaps dead for him, the universe disappeared from his sight, and he only saw in the entirety of nature Astarté dying and Zadig grief-stricken.")

Meditation and cosmic awareness open the path to mysticism. The contemplation of Zadig which is "detached" from the "senses" clearly transcends the scope of the physical eye which is incapable of beholding "the immutable order of the universe." Intense suffering illuminates the true perspective of life. The cup of anguish is drained in a manner reminiscent of traditional saints and existential thinkers. A solid core of selfhood is revealed by the ultimate test. Despondency alternates with exaltation and becomes one with it. The transcended Lower Self gives way to true Being. The bondage of separate existence yields to oneness with suffering mankind. The Higher Self knows itself in the Absolute. The soul "soars into infinity" beyond the realm of earthly passion and sensory experience. Heartfelt humility exults.

The *cupidité* or "greed" which is the cause of ordinary, imperfect vision is a valuable clue to the deep sense of the passage. It is the false, materialistic conception of the dynamic essence of the universe — Eros made phallic *Cupid* — which turns a large number of men into blind, self-centered, and vicious "insects." The eternal tug-of-war between Illusion — or Maya — and reality is everywhere in evidence: ("appear," "appears," "imagined," "seemed," "disappeared," "true image," "saw," "indeed," "in fact"). The "ebb and flow" of spiritual striving receives stylistic energy from pre-Lamartinian rhythms and tones. Beyond the theme of relativity which is often expounded in XVIIIth Century writings, the passage contains numerous elements of cosmic vision and an echo of the "music of the spheres:"

> "It becomes patent why we could not perceive, even with the help of the best earthly telescopes, that which is outside our world of matter. Those alone, whom we call adepts, who know how to direct their mental vision and to transfer their consciousness — physical and psychic both — to other planes of being, are able to speak with authority on such subjects. And they tell us plainly:

> 'Lead the life necessary for the acquisition of such knowledge and powers, and Wisdom will come to you naturally. Whenever you are able to attune your consciousness to any of the seven chords of 'Universal Consciousness,' those chords that run along the sounding board of Komos, vibrating from one Eternity to another; when you have studied thoroughly 'the music of the Spheres,' then only will you become quite free to share your knowledge with those with whom it is safe to do so. Meanwhile be prudent.'" (*The Secret Doctrine*, pp. 166-67, Vol. I).

The mystical experience of Zadig marks a culminating point of his escape from Mayavic planes of existence. Limited insight is replaced by cosmic illumination. Divisiveness becomes unity with all living creatures. Transition has been made from nether depths of materialistic experience to the opposite pole of Being.

The vacillation of the young man between the "music of the spheres" and earthly concern suggests that his spirituality remains fitful. The impression is partially correct. Unalloyed spirituality is not of earth. Love for Astarté remains strong and seems opposed to transcendental yearning. It will become apparent, however, in due course of the story that conflict needs not exist between love of Astarté and love of Truth.

The encounter of Zadig with the beaten woman shows the need of the hero for improved judgment. Compassion, as well as knowledge, must be applied "prudently." The impulsive intervention of Zadig does honor to his heart. But it is a source of lasting hardship endured for the sake of a hopeless cause. No sooner is the lady in distress rescued from her tormentor than she laments her freedom and mourns the departed tyrant. The knight in shining armor is cursed for his pains. An ancient warning comes to mind: unfit recipients of "pearls" — wisdom and goodness — are apt to "turn again and rend you."

The beaten woman is a pathetic mixture of wile and masochism. A common esoteric theme is present: the degradation of "all that is divine in woman — Crucified twixt a smile and a whimper."* Tarnished remnants of human dignity and servile womanhood are chief characteristics of Missouf. The former attributes are connected by Voltaire with the striking resemblance borne by Missouf to Astarté. The latter trait can easily be traced to the personality of the tormentor: a jealous, brutal male. The woman-beater is a Jehovic figure created in the image of the Biblical God.

A key to the esoteric substance of *The Beaten Woman* may well lie in the following text:

> "When the Theosophists and Occultists say that God is no BEING, for IT is nothing, *No-Thing,* they are more reverential and religiously respectful to the Deity than those who call God a HE, and thus make of Him a gigantic MALE.
>
> He who studies the Kabala will soon find the same idea in the ultimate thought of its authors, the earlier and great Hebrew Initiates, who got this secret Wisdom at Babylonia from the Chaldean Hierophants, while Moses got his in Egypt." (*The Secret Doctrine,* p. 352, Vol. I).

A second key may lie in the itinerary of Zadig which coincides with the general expansion route of Far Eastern culture. The Zoroastrian — a legatee of the Primitive Wisdom-Religion which originated in India — travels from "Babylonia" to Egypt where Moses, an "ex-Egyptian priest," obtained his "wisdom" or "knowledge." The confrontation of Babylon and Egypt featured in *Zadig* tends to connect the uncouth *ménage* formed by Missouf and her tormentor with various phases of the bondage of the Jews. The propagation and the mistreatment of the Secret Doctrine seems to be allegorically recorded in the story of the "beaten woman." The degrading process seems to be traced to Moses — the "Egyptian". The latter impression will be confirmed by a subsequent passage of the story.

The lineage of the Judaeo-Christian tradition is outlined as follows in occult philosophy:

---

*Percy B. Shelley, *Peter Bell the Third.*

"Strictly speaking, it is difficult to view the Jewish *Book* of *Genesis* otherwise than as a chip from the trunk of the mundane tree of universal Cosmogony, rendered in Oriental allegories. As cycle succeeded cycle, and one nation after another came upon the world's stage to play its brief part in the majestic drama of human life, each new people evolved from ancestral traditions its own religion, giving it a local color and stamping it with its individual characteristics. While each of these religions had its distinguishing traits by which, were there no other archaic vestiges, the physical and psychological status of its creators could be estimated, all preserved a common likeness to one prototype. This parent cult was none other than the primitive Wisdom-Religion. The Israelitish *Scriptures* are no exception. The national history of the Israelites — if they can claim any autonomy before the return from Babylon, and were anything more than migratory septs of Hindu pariahs — cannot be carried back a day beyond Moses; and if this ex-Egyptian priest must from theological necessity be transformed into a Hebrew patriarch, we must insist that the Jewish nation was lifted with that smiling infant out of the bulrushes of Lake Moeris. Abraham, their alleged father belongs to the universal mythology. Most likely, he is but one of the numerous aliases of Zeruan (Saturn), the king of the golden age, who is also called the old man (emblem of time). (*Isis Unveiled*, p. 216, Vol. 2)."

The Judaeo-Christian tradition is viewed by occultists and esoteric writers as a plagiarized and distorted version of one "parent cult:" the Primitive Wisdom-Religion. The resemblance borne by "Missouf" to Astarté seems to be the "common likeness" shared by major religions and their superior "prototype" — in the present case the "Queen of Babylon."

The allegorical value of Missouf is also suggested by other details. Etymologically at least, her "capricious" character brings to mind a goat which should probably be read as the Jewish scapegoat. Her name tends to confirm that she is the inferior version of a superior prototype. The prefix *mis* conveys the idea of falsehood, perversion, or deformity. The Judaeo-Christian tradition is regarded as such by occult and esoteric writers. It is observed by Mme Blavatsky that the Nazarenes commonly likened the Jewish tradition to an abortion or a body "born out of time."* The remaining part of the name "Missouf" suggests derivation from *Sophia* or Wisdom. The pathetic, masochistic victim of the "Egyptian" is a falsified and abused version of Ancient Pagan Truth.

"With the Ophites and other Gnostics who took their models direct from more ancient originals, the unrevealed Bythos and her male counterpart produce Ennoia, and the three in their turn produce Sophia, thus completing the Tetratkys, which will emanate Christos, the very essence of the Father Spirit. — Sophia is the higher prototype of woman — the first

---

Isis Unveiled, p. 171, Vol. 2.

spiritual Eve. In the Bible the system is reversed and the intervening emanation being omitted. Eve is degraded to simple humanity." (*Isis Unveiled,* p. 171, Vol. 2).

The wilful degradation of woman is a major trait of the Judaeo-Christian tradition. The rejection of Christ by the Jews seems to have a counterpart in the behavior of Missouf toward her would-be "Savior." Estrangement from divine reality is evident in the curse formulated by the "beaten woman" against her defender.

The esoteric theme of an atrophied or injured body of knowledge is present in numerous literary texts. It is highly developed in those portions of the *Recherche* which are devoted to Jews and Jewish institutions. The violent anti-Semitism of Mr. de Charlus is directed at a doctrine, not at a race. The "vehicle" of a Jewish family or community is described by the forceful nobleman as a "cut and recut — a redundant cut."* The controversial *Silence* of Vigny contains a similar allusion to mutilated and adulterated Scriptures. Strong doubts are expressed about the veracity of scriptural texts in the first two lines of the stanza. Bearing in mind the esoteric value of certain "abortions" and the transcendental value of "silence," the reader may discover a transfigured message diametrically opposed to appearance.

LE SILENCE

"S'il est vrai qu'au Jardin sacré des Ecritures,
Le Fils de l'Homme ait dit ce qu'on voit rapporté;
Muet, aveugle et sourd au cri des créatures,
Si le Ciel nous laissa comme un monde avorté,
Le juste opposera le dédain à l'absence,
Et ne répondra plus que par un froid silence,
Au silence éternel de la Divinité."
(*Le Mont des oliviers*).

("If it be true that in the sacred Garden of the Scriptures,
The Son of Man did say what one sees reported;
Mute, blind and deaf to the outcry of creatures,
If Heaven abandoned us like an aborted world,
(Esoterically: if Heaven left to us some aborted vision of the world
                or: some aborted body of knowledge)
The just will oppose scorn to default**
And will only respond with cold silence
To the eternal silence of the Deity.")

The esoteric meaning of the fight between Zadig and the Egyptian is suggested by the different tactics and the different personalities of the

---

A la Recherche du temps perdu, p. 1107, Vol. II.
**C.f. "privation" — Maya — .

opponents. Brute force faces Divine Wisdom. Egotistical rage faces impersonal "strength."

> "The Egyptian was more robust than his adversary; Zadig was more skilled. The latter man fought like a person whose arm is commanded by the mind, and the former like an uncontrolled person whose movements were guided by chance and blind wrath." (*La Femme battue,* p. 38).

Physical force — or terror — is the chief asset of the Biblical God. The Mosaic Lord reigns through fire and brimstone, thunderbolts, indiscriminate destruction of innocence and guilt, and cataclysms. The "blind wrath" of the Egyptian which has been aroused by the "unfaithfulness" of Missouf seems to represent the reckless jealousy and vengefulness of Jehovah. The reported "blindness" is comparable to the limited insight of such other "envious" or "jealous" men as Arimaze and Moabdar. Mayavic divisiveness is again connected with the low vision of a Jehovah-related figure. The same divisiveness is linked to irrationality. The Egyptian behaves like an instrument of *chance,* a concept which has no substance in the Secret Doctrine or in Voltairian philosophy. One might as well regard the tormentor as a non-entity.

The mythological figure to which Voltaire occasionally referred as the "Vice-God"* is held in equally low esteem by occultists and esoteric writers. It is only "a God among other Gods." It is a mediocre potency of universal tradition.

> "Would Christians still maintain the identity of the 'Father' of Jesus and Jehovah, if evidence sufficiently clear could be adduced that the 'Lord God' was no other than the Pagan Bacchus, Dionysou. Well, this identity of the Jehovah at Mount Sinai with the god Bacchus is hardly disputable. The name is Yava, or Yao according to Diodorus and Lydus, and *Iao* is the secret name of the Phoenician Mystery-God; it was actually adopted from the Chaldeans with whom it was also the secret name of the creator. Wherever Bacchus was worshipped, there was a tradition of a place called Nysa, and a cave where he was reared. Beth-Sam or Scythopolis in Palestine once had that designation; so had a spot on Mount Parnassus. But Diodorus declares that Nysa was between Phoenicia and Egypt; Euripides states that Dionysos came to Greece from India, and Diodorus adds his testimony: 'Osiris was brought up in Nysa, in Arabia. the Happy; he was the son of Zeus, and was named from his father (Nominative Zeus — genitive Dios) and the place Dio-Nysos — the Zeus or Jove of Nysa —. This identity of name or title is very significant. In Greece Dionysos was second only to Zeus, and Pindar says:
> 'So Father Zeus governs all things, and
> Bacchus governs also.'
> But outside of Greece, Bacchus was the all-powerful 'Zagreus, the highest of Gods.' Moses seems to have worshipped him personally and together

---

*Voltaire, *Lettres d'Amabed,* Septième Lettre.

78

with the populace at Mount Sinai; unless we admit that Moses was an *initiated* priest, an adept, who knew how to lift the veil which hangs behind all such exoteric worship, but kept the secret. 'And Moses built an altar, and called the name of it Jehovah-NISSI!' What better evidence is required to show that the Sinaitic god was indifferently Bacchus, Osiris, and Jehovah?" (*Isis Unveiled*, p. 165, Vol. 2).

The "Egyptian" is defeated by the Zoroastrian. The devotee of Divine Wisdom is clearly superior to Jehovic force personified. The ethical superiority of Zadig is noted — as are other aspects of his mastery. The hero fights in purely defensive manner until the compound treachery of his enemy forces him to kill in self-defense. Zadig and the Egyptian personify the profound divergence which exists between the Oriental reverence of life and the Mosaic love of gore. The Old and the New Testaments seem to be in confrontation as are the Primitive Wisdom-Religion and its Judaeo-Christian copy. The Old Testament preaches the *lex talionis*. The New Testament is a doctrine of brotherhood and love.

> "If the Mosaic 'Lord God' was the only living God, and Jesus His only Son, how account for the rebellious language of the latter? Without hesitation or qualification he sweeps away the Jewish *lex talionis* and substitutes for it the law of charity and self-denial. If the Old Testament is a divine revelation, how can the New Testament be? Are we required to believe and worship a Deity who contradicts himself every few hundred years?" (*Isis Unveiled*, pp. 165-66, Vol. 2).

The significance of the Savior — unrecognized and cursed by "Missouf" —, the importance of his true message, and the sublime quality of his ethics are major elements of theosophical thought. Great spiritual leaders are said to incarnate in times of severe need. Jesus is regarded as one such leader. He is also viewed under the name of Christos or Chrestos as the manifestation of the divine spark in Man: "Christos, the very essence of the Father Spirit:"

> " — the term Christos, which to us represents the Higher Self." (*The Key to Theosophy*, p. 63).

> " — all the civilized portion of the Pagans who knew of Jesus honored him as a philosopher, an *adept* whom they placed on the same level with Pythagoras and Apollonius. Whence such a veneration on their part for a man, were he simply, as represented by the Synoptics, a poor, unknown Jewish carpenter from Nazareth? As an incarnated God there is no single record of him on this earth capable of withstanding the critical examination of science; as one of the greatest reformers, an inveterate enemy of every theological dogmatism, an opponent of bigotry, a teacher of one of the most sublime codes of ethics, Jesus is one of the grandest and most clearly defined figures on the panorama of human history. His age may, with

79

every day, be receding farther and farther back into the gloomy and hazy mists of the past, and the (Christian) theology — based on human fancy and supported by untenable dogmas — may, nay must with every day lose more of its unmerited prestige; alone the grand figure of the philosopher and moral reformer instead of growing paler will become with every century more pronounced and more clearly defined. It will reign supreme and universal only on that day when the whole of humanity recognizes but one father — the UNKNOWN ONE above — and one brother — the whole of mankind below." (*Isis Unveiled*, pp. 150-51, Vol. 2).

The Jehovic adversary of Zadig goes down in defeat. But the power of the *lex talionis* is far from dead.

Zadig is captured and sold into slavery. Biblical law and order come under scrutiny. Arbitrary "legal" practice is once more denounced. But the esoteric plane of the episode concerns a specific act of spoliation sanctified by the Scriptures:

> "It was recognized that Zadig was no assassin, but he was guilty of the blood of a man; the law sentenced him to be a slave. His two camels were sold to the benefit of the village; all the gold which he had brought was distributed to the inhabitants; his person was placed on the auction block in the public place as was that of his travel companion." (*L'Esclavage*, p. 40).

The "gold" of the disciple of Zoroaster may represent the treasure — or secret lore — of the Primitive Wisdom-Religion. The transmitter of the Secret Doctrine is stripped of his freedom and of his possessions. The underlying theme of "privation" may again be connected with the Mayavic values which dominate the realm of the defunct "Egyptian." Mankind enters the period of obscuration of Truth coinciding with and resulting from the establishment of the Judaeo-Christian tradition. The suggested theme of Mosaic spoliation of Pagan knowledge will be further developed in subsequent episodes of *Zadig* dealing with five hundred ounces of "borrowed silver" and with the "borrowed robe" — or suit or armor — paraded by Itobad. The chapter devoted to *Slavery* is part of a Voltairian indictment identical to a major grievance of occultists. The fraudulent appropriation of Pagan lore by Christians is denounced.

> " 'How can a god," inquired Marcion, 'break his own commandments? How could he consistently prohibit idolatry and image-worship and still cause Moses to set up the brazen serpent? How command: 'Thou shalt not steal,' and then order the Israelites to *spoil* the Egyptians of their gold and silver?' " (*Isis Unveiled*, p. 166, Vol. 2).

The death of the "Egyptian" symbolically defeated by a Savior does not spell the end of biblical slavery. Paradoxically in appearance, it is the beginning of centuries of bondage. Old gods never die. They live on in cruel hearts and cruel practice. But eternal Truth has a capacity of its own for survival as long as it is cherished by a few good men. The disciple of Zoroaster is such a person.

The sale of the valet brings a higher price than does the sale of Zadig. The poles of genuine values are inverted. Inferior spirituality is suggested by the predilection of the despoilers for "servants" and by phallic body-worship. Muscle is the ultimate good and the ultimate glamor in the Mosaic realm of brute force. The theme of brutishness — incidentally — conveys among other things the etymological flavor of "stupidity." The retail value of wisdom represented by Zadig is low. But the true worth of the hero finally compels recognition. It is noticed and rewarded by Sétoc, the slave-master. Kindness seems to be least of the businessman's concerns. But practicality and the prospect of increased profit naturally appeal to the representative of commerce. Zadig distinguishes himself in the management of "slaves" and is prized accordingly:

> "Sétoc began to laugh when he saw all his slaves bent as they walked. Zadig took the liberty of explaining the reason for it, and taught him the laws of balance." (*L'Esclavage*, p. 41).

Unlike Hermes and Orcan who are swayed by "courtiers" and "satellites," Sétoc is in control of his subordinates. The fact suggests that the latent spirituality of the merchant rests on genuine inner "strength," not on external props. The new owner of Zadig will eventually develop the superior attributes of an esoteric "master." Decency is one of his qualities. Reason is another. Sétoc has a rudimentary endowment of insight and ethics. The title character soon discovers in him "a nature leaning toward goodness, rectitude, and common sense."

The *rectitude* of *Sétoc* is suggested by his name which is the anagram of the French fencing term "estoc." The latter word designates the *straight* thrust of a sword. The symbolism of "that excellent sword — knowledge (secret wisdom)"* seems to be present. It is consistent with mastery over "slaves." The word *esoteric* is also suggested by the name of Sétoc. The slave-owner is as likely to succeed in a spiritual quest as any merchant can be in Judaeo-Christian regions. His kindness is initially the mere by-product of shrewd management. But it is better than nothing. The oneness of mastery and ethics is subtly brought to bear by Zadig acting as an efficiency expert. The merchant must indeed "treat his slaves decently if he wants to receive services from them."

A popular myth is implicitly and humorously exploded. "Zadig"

The Secret Doctrine, p. 536, Vol. I.

proves that superior knowledge can be far from inept in practical matters. The fact is suggested to apply to Voltaire. The author of *Zadig* is known to have been an outstanding businessman. The instruction of Sétoc seems to convey among other things an autobiographical smile.

The esoteric value of "commerce" which is introduced into the text by the profession of Sétoc is a standard tool of "smugglers." The exchange of goods is likely to promote an exchange of ideas and cultural insights which is favorable to the discovery of universal truth. The fact is especially true of international trade such as the ventures of Sétoc. The same esoteric concept of "commerce" is used by Voltaire in *Le Mondain* to celebrate the dissemination of "new goods, born at the springs of Ganges."

The mystical concept of "commerce" has its own deep logic as does the esoteric concept of "love." The terrestrial expression of love becomes a mystical union with the Higher Self and with Absolute Reality on the metaphysical plane. The trade of earthly "goods" becomes the possession of spiritual "goods." "Commerce" with the Higher Self and with Absolute Reality is achieved. Esoteric "commerce" is synonymous with esoteric "love." All is One on the plane of True Being.

The double-edged potency of "commerce" is illustrated by Vigny:

"Blessed be Commerce with its bold caduceus, — " (*La Maison du berger*).

Two equally valid meanings are conveyed by the above line. The verse may be read as a commentary on money-minded, mercenary practice in which case the exoteric "blessing" is sarcastic indeed. Vigny might as well have written in plain language: "Anything goes for the sake of money." Esoterically, however, the veiled sense of "commerce" and the rich occult symbolism of the caduceus* fill the line with reverence and fervor. Vigny might as well thank Heaven for the most sublime "commerce" accessible to Man — or for what he termed in his Diary — "joys worthy of Heaven".** The innocent-looking word "commerce" is an illuminating element of esoteric algebra. It is with the help of such double-edged concepts that one may — in the words of Proust — gaze beyond a veil of "superimposed symbols."***

The education of Sétoc begins with teachings on the "laws of balance." Cosmic harmony and equilibrium are brought to mind as are their countless manifestations on all planes of existence. Numerous allusions of like nature are found in numerous texts. The traditional view of gravity seems

---

The Secret Doctrine, p. 550, Vol. I.
**Diary*, 1832.
****A la Recherche du temps perdu*, p. 260, Vol. II.

to be broadened into "laws of attraction and repulsion" in *Micromégas*. The *Recherche* contains several references to the same laws. The space occupied by the smallest puff of alder can be explained by "laws of attraction and repulsion which govern far greater worlds."* What appears to be "inertia" in a human body is the resultant of the same generally unknown forces.** The salutations of the family of Guermantes reveal masterful control of opposite impulses or esoteric "equilibrium." Levitation — a form of balance — is suggested by the quick movements of "Saint Loup" and by his "flying" exercise in a "drinking-place" or *café*. Vigny celebrates cosmic harmony in *La Maison du berger*. "The accustomed route" of Nature is the "harmonious axis of divine balancing-poles." Rabelais uses "lenders" and "borrowers" to represent the same universal give-and-take.

The instruction of Sétoc has a transcendental aspect which involves the source and the distribution of universal energy. The laws of attraction and repulsion to which reference is made in *Micromégas* are regarded by occultists as manifestations of cosmic magnetism. Gravitation is one of their effects.

> "That such magnetism exists in nature, is as certain as that gravitation does not; not at any rate, in the way in which it is taught by Science, which never took into consideration the different modes in which the dual Force — that Occultism calls attraction and repulsion — may act within our solar system, the earth's atmosphere, and *beyond* in the Kosmos." (*The Secret Doctrine*, p. 497, Vol. I).

The burden of the slaves is lightened through wise handling of the "laws of balance." Voltaire seems to allude to the art of levitation which is based on control of electrical polarities. Such polarities are aspects of cosmic magnetism.*** Human levitation may result from the striving of the astral body — also called perisprit and astral soul — which ever yearns to escape from the physical body. The perisprit is the intermediate component of Man. It is bound to matter as well as spirit. It is far more ethereal than its prison of flesh.

> "It (the perisprit) is the prisoner, not the voluntary tenant, of the body. It has an attraction so powerful to the exernal universal force, that after wearing out its casing it finally escapes to it. — The astral soul, when the barriers are once opened, is so powerfully attracted by the universal, astral magnet, that it sometimes lifts its encasement with it and keeps it suspended in mid-air, until the gravity of matter reasserts its supremacy, and the body re-descends again to earth.

*Ibid., p. 213, Vol. III.
**Ibid., p. 315, Vol. II.
***Isis Unveiled p. xxiv, Vol. 1.

Every objective manifestation, whether it be the motion of a living limb, or the movement of some inorganic body, requires two conditions: will and force — plus *matter*, or that which makes the object so moved visible to our eye; and these three are all convertible forces, or the force-correlation of the scientists. In their turn they are directed or rather over-shadowed by Divine Intelligence which these men so studiously leave out of the account, but without which not even the crawling of the smallest earth-worm could ever take place." (*Isis Unveiled*, p. 198, Vol. 1).

Levitation seems to be involved in the following passage of the *Diary of a Country Priest*:

"Oh, of course, nothing is easier sometimes than climbing up there: God carries you there. It is only a matter of really wanting it, and, in some cases, of knowing how to get back down. You will observe that the saints, the true ones, showed great embarrassment upon returning. Once surprised in their works of balance, they began by begging that the secret be kept: 'Speak to no one of what you have seen. . .'" They were a bit ashamed, you understand? Ashamed of being the spoilt children of the Father, of having drunk from the cup of beatitude before everybody!" (Georges Bernanos, *Journal d'un curé de campagne*, Ch. I).

The "shame" of the experimenters mentioned in the above text is comparable to the feeling of the "drunkard" featured in Chapter XII of *The Little Prince*. The person in question drinks to forget that he is "ashamed" of drinking. A vicious circle indeed esoterically and otherwise. His misery may be caused by the attitude of a society which generally frowns on spritual pursuits.

That certain "works of balance" or the ability to "rise" are connected with "drinking from the cup of beatitude" is suggested by Rabelais. A man who seems to scorn *canon* law is reported to "rise" when he drinks of the spirit. "He had neither inhibition nor law in drinking, for he said that the bounds and limits of drinking were when, the person drinking, the cork of his slippers rose vertically one half-foot.* One may note briefly that the word *canon* is used to this day in some French provinces to designate a small amount of wine.

The Zoroastrian "Instructor of mankind" performs an important synthesis. The revelations of Zadig on various forces and the laws governing such forces tend to bridge a vitally important gap between the phenomenal and the noumenal worlds. The abyss in question is the realm of occult science, the *terra ignota* linking mysterious cause and visible effect. The synthesis performed by Zadig is designed to enrich and fuse harmoniously the glimmers of superior consciousness which are innate in the merchant.

Gargantua, Ch. XXI.

The instruction received by Sétoc will eventually transform scattered partial insights into an integrated whole. Such is the function of Atma-Vidya or Divine wisdom.

> "Of the four Vidyas, out of the seven branches of Knowledge mentioned in the *Pûranas,* — it is only the last one, 'Atma-Vidya,' or the true Spiritual and *Divine wisdom,* which can throw absolute and final light upon the teachings of the three first named. Without the help of Atma-Vidya, the other three remain no better than *surface* sciences, geometrical magnitudes having length and breadth, but no thickness. They are like the soul, limbs, and mind of a sleeping man: capable of mechanical motions, of chaotic dreams and even sleep-walking, of producing visible effects, but stimulated by instinctual not intellectual causes, least of all by fully conscious spiritual impulses. A good deal can be given out and explained from the three first-named sciences. But unless the key to their teachings is furnished by Atma-Vidya, they will remain for ever like the fragments of a mangled text-book, like the adumbrations of great truths, dimly perceived by the most spiritual, but distorted out of all proportion by those who would nail every shadow to the wall." (*The Secret Doctrine,* pp. 168-69, Vol. I).

The assistance of Zadig is required in connection with the theft committed by a dishonest Jew. The accused has failed to repay a "loan." Five hundred ounces of silver are at stake. The witnesses of the transaction have died. Exploiting their absence, the Hebrew feels justified in keeping the money. He thanks God "who gave him the means of swindling an Arab."

The Mosaic spoliation of Egyptian "goods" is again suggested by the nationality and righteous posture of the offender. The alleged sanction of "God" is also significant. The site of "borrowing," the vicinity of Mount Horeb, confirms the above interpretation. It was on Mount Horeb that Moses was initiated and received the powers which altered the history of mankind. The swindle — which is eventually exposed by "the Great Instructor of Mankind" — is weightier by far than the appropriation of any amount of silver. It is the crime committed against decency and truth through fraudulent establishment of the Mosaic tradition.

The swindler feels protected by the death of "witnesses" — a word often used in the etymological sense of "martyr". The theft of the five hundred ounces of silver is connected with a bloodbath of religious persecutions which is a matter of historical record and of exoteric Voltairian indignation.

The esoteric value of the number *five hundred* should probably be linked to our current sub-cycle of evolution, the *Fifth* Race. Mankind — as we know it — belongs to an evolutionary system of Rounds and Races — major and lesser cycles. "We have spoken of seven Races" says Mme

85

Blavatsky "five of which have nearly completed their earthly career."* Secret numbers are often veiled by added — or removed — zeros which are used as esoteric "blinds."** The figure *five* hundred may refer to universal treasures of occult lore covering five races, a treasure temporarily stolen and concealed by the Mosaic faith and its various branches.

The large stone which is used when the "loan" is made — presumably as a table — probably represents a bitter allusion to the "tables of the law" which proclaim among other things: "Thou shalt not steal." The said tables are tainted from the very beginning by the shady transaction.

It is suggested by Zadig that the stone should be brought to the site of the trial so that it may "give testimony" or "bear witness." Careful examination of the basis of the new faith seems to be advocated. The recommended transfer of the stone is also meaningful on the literal plane. The possibility of animating matter through non-physical means is again hinted. The stone which is expected to "speak" or "bear witness" — as did the tablets of Zadig — is also expected to "come."

> " — il reste une large pierre sur laquelle l'argent fut compté; et, s'il plait à Votre Grandeur d'ordonner qu'on aille chercher la pierre, j'espère qu'elle portera témoignage; nous resterons ici, l'Hébreu et moi, en attendant que la pierre vienne; je l'enverrai chercher aux dépens de Sétoc mon maitre." (*L'Esclavage*, p. 42).

> ("There remains a large stone upon which the money was counted — and if it pleases your Greatness to order that the stone be brought, I hope that it will bear witness; we shall remain here, the Hebrew and I, waiting for the stone to come; I will send for it at the expense of Sétoc, my master.")

The stone fails to travel as originally planned. Transfer is made unnecessary by the intelligence of Zadig. "The right path" is once again perceptible in the avoidance of spectacular wonders. Weapons supplied by dishonesty against itself are equally effective — and less troublesome. Liars in general, spiritual frauds in particular, are prone to become enmeshed in traps of their own making. The theft is exposed in cross-examination. No transcendental faculties are used or needed. The latter fact is a wry commentary on the crude manner in which Pagan lore was annexed by the Judaeo-Christian tradition.

It will be shown in connection with a subsequent episode of *Zadig* that the word *Petra* or "stone" carries the secret meaning of "Interpreter of the Secret Doctrine." The expected arrival of the stone may therefore be construed as the arrival of an interpreter of Divine Wisdom. Such a figure is likely to be connected with the "Great Instructor of Mankind."

The Secret Doctrine, p. 443, Vol. II.
**Ibid.*, p. 307, fn., Vol. II.

Zadig and the thieving Jew are expected to remain where they are until the arrival of the all-important stone or interpreter. Mankind and the Judaeo-Christian despoiler are expected to be relatively static — in a spiritual sense — until the predicted event takes place.

The final restitution of stolen goods belongs to a series of prophetic episodes which are insistently featured in the Voltairian trilogy. The eventual triumph of the Primitive Wisdom-Religion is contemplated in *Candide* and comes to pass in *L'Ingénu*. Within the time setting of *Zadig*, the esoteric value of the event may announce the coming of Christ whose true message is identical to the teachings of Buddha, Zoroaster, and other "Interpreters." As was previously noted, the message of Christ constitudes a radical departure from the Mosaic tradition.

The episode may also point to such subsequent developments as the intellectual and spiritual apocalypse which is prophesied in numerous esoteric texts — notably in the Book of Saint John. Vigny refers to such an imminent happening in *Paris*. A huge "stone" — usually compared by commentators with the "stone" of the Apocalypse — looms over the capital city which it may or may not threaten. It is "seen" within a fantastic context suggesting a synthesis of world cultures and the possible coming of an "animated form" or incarnate Savior who will "lead the human family" to its destiny. The destiny of mankind is universal salvation. *"All will be called, and all will be chosen."* The theme of impending apocalypse may also be perceived in the *Recherche* beyond the veil of World War I. It is present in *Flight to Arras (Pilote de Guerre)* beyond the veil of World War II. It is a recurring motif in *Death on the Installment Plan*. It is the probable raison d'être of the "Jeandieusards" of Samuel Beckett. It is developed in deceptive and nightmarish fashion in the final pages of *La Nausée*.

The "stone" may also be connected with the spiritual structure allegedly built by *Peter*. "'Thou art Peter; and upon this rock will I build my church —'" "On those little sentences have been built up the mighty edifice of the Church of Rome; in them lie the authority for the imperial power of the popes over temporal affairs and their godlike power to curse a soul or wash it white from sin."* The "stone" representing in *Zadig* the theft of Pagan knowledge perpetrated by Moses and by his successors involves Paganism, the dishonest "Jew" of Mount Horeb, Peter, and a certain apocalypse. It is one link of a chain which is the history of Truth.

The fame of Zadig and the story of the tainted transaction quickly reach the most remote regions of Arabia. A somewhat similar legend

---

*Mark Twain, *The Innocents Abroad*, Ch. 45.

featured in the *Toledoth Yeshu* may have partially inspired the Voltairian account of Mosaic larceny. The Jewish version of a similar spiritual swindle is summarized and commented as follows in *Isis Unveiled*:

> " 'There exists, in the sanctuary of the living God, a cubical stone, on which are sculptured the holy characters, the combination of which gives the explanation of the attributes and powers of the incommunicable name. The explanation is the secret key of all the occult sciences and forces in nature — Jesus, who had learned in Egypt the great secrets at the initiation, forged himself invisible keys, and thus was enabled to penetrate into the sanctuary unseen — He copied the characters on the cubical stone, and hid them in his thigh; after which, emerging from the temple, he went abroad and began astounding people with miracles — '
> Further the same Talmudist says in substance, the following: 'Jesus was thrown in prison, and kept there forty days; then flogged as a seditious rebel; then stoned as a blasphemer in a place called Lud, and finally allowed to expire upon a cross." All this explains Levi 'because he revealed to the people the truths which they (the Pharisees) wished to bury for their own use. He had divined the occult theology of Israel, had compared it with the wisdom of Egypt, and found thereby the reason for a universal religious synthesis.' " (*Isis Unveiled*, p. 202, Vol. 2).

The subversive revelations and unitarian leanings of Christ were naturally feared by Jewish despoilers of the Primitive Wisdom-Religion as they were feared by inquisitors of all times.

Voltaire seems to have known of the existence and meaning of ancient monuments which are repositories of occult science. His charming "medley of prose and of verse" — the *Voyage à Berlin* — contains a reference to an ancient grave capable of producing ecstasy in certain viewers. The present study will show that Voltaire also knew of the existence of Petra — an ancient city officially undiscovered in his times — where numerous kabalistic inscriptions were found in the XIXth Century. The heritage of Pagan lore consigned to stone by ancient and modern craftsmen seems to have aroused the same interest in the author of *Zadig* as it earned from occultists and esoteric writers of all times. The pages devoted by Rabelais to the architecture and pavement of the temple of the "Dive Bouteille" seem to have no other raison d'être. It is believed by many persons that alchemical and other symbols of major importance are embodied in the stones of medieval churches and cathedrals. Proustian writings dedicated to great cathedrals and to structures such as the church of Balbec suggest similar beliefs. It is only through the vision of the instructed artist —Elstir — that the wealth of meaning conveyed by certain inscriptions and sculptures can be grasped. The commentary of the painter on the esoteric beauties of the church of Balbec is as significant as the profound quality of his own work. The church of Balbec is likened to " a whole theological and symbolic poem."* The production of the discriminating artist is itself compared to "those mirrors of the world" which may be and are occasionally studied by means of a technique resembling astrological reading** Elstir seems to belong to a small minority of persons who recognize — and possibly decipher — the silent message of certain monuments. What is suggested by the friend of Marcel is openly claimed by occultists. The key to many scientific mysteries is said to be inscribed in stone in secret caves and on certain ruins.

> "The answers are there. They may be found on the time-worn granite pages of cave-temples, on sphinxes, propylons, and obelisks. They have stood there for untold ages, and neither the rude assault of time nor the still ruder assault of Christian hands, have succeeded in obliterating their records. — And so stand these monuments like mute forgotten sentinels on the threshhold of that unseen world, whose gates are thrown open but to a few elect." (*Isis Unveiled*, p. 573, Vol. 1).

The stone mentioned by Voltaire may represent among other things an allusion to the "mute, forgotten sentinels" evoked in *Isis Unveiled*. Whatever the case may be; whatever symbolic value may be attributed to the important object, the stone is an instrument of retribution. The basis of a shady transaction becomes the Nemesis of the Mosaic thief. The acquisitive Hebrew might have spared his race a great deal of misery had he respected one commandment of the tables of the law: "Thou shalt not steal." He might have gained immensely more from the stone than he gained from the five hundred ounces of stolen silver. The physical presence of the object is not required to expose the fraud. The facts of the case are disclosed by the determined intelligence of Zadig. Truth is found on the immaterial plane of human mind and spirit.

The swindle is a source of incalculable harm. But the spiritual "gold" of Ancient Wisdom — which will be an important element of *Candide* — loses its value in the hands of the "uninstructed" and of the unworthy. The thief gains no more than temporary custody of inferior "silver" gleanings. The "lost key" to secret science, a key forever inaccessible to the churches as a result of their own wrongdoing, is a major theme of theosophical writings. It is vigorously developed in a Voltairian parable contained in *Candide*. The same theme seems to be present in *Zadig*.

The stone which proves useful to Zadig "in absentia" is employed in pragmatic yet self-defeating manner by the Jew. The object which may contain the key to ethical — if not scientific — wisdom is turned into a mere physical utensil by the thief. The Judaeo-Christian use of important

---

A la Recherche du temps perdu, p. 841, Vol. I.
**Ibid.*, p. 126, Vol. II.

symbols is suggested to be blindly literal. The latter impression will be confirmed by other passages of the Voltairian trilogy. The "phallic" or literal interpretation of symbols and allegories which is generally made by Western commentators of ancient texts and cultures is often denounced by occultists.

Jews are portrayed in unflattering manner — and shown to come to grief — in various parts of Voltairian writings. A Jew is killed by Candide — along with an Inquisitor. Jews are presented as incorrigible swindlers. The last material remnant of the treasure acquired in Eldorado by Candide falls into their hands. The exoteric reader might easily conclude to the anti-Semitism of Voltaire. The same allegorical "prejudice" — which seems to be shared by many writers — should be carefully studied.

Céline is commonly regarded as an anti-Semitic writer. But his apparent hatred of Jews may represent the same denunciation of an institutionalized "swindle" as does the "prejudice" of Voltaire. The dominant esoteric theme of *Mort à Crédit* is the corruption and decline of the Judaeo-Christian tradition. The habitat of the family of the narrator — Ferdinand — is designated as "the Passage." "The Passage" may represent a certain segment of time in the course of human evolution. It may also connect the novel with the Jewish Passover or with the Judaeo-Christian tradition. The esoteric identity of the Jehovic father — "Auguste" — is repeatedly suggested. The mother is a shrewish and whiny cripple — literally "on her last leg" — who represents the Church. The allegorical couple operates a dingy shop, a symbolic flea-market, which once had valuable "antiques" — esoterically remnants of ancient Pagan knowledge. But the business which is headed for disaster has come to resemble "a filthy museum."* The "father" and "mother" of Ferdinand live in dread of the "World Fair," esoterically the inevitable "universal exposure" — "l'Exposition Universelle" — which is a terrifying threat to their shabby "commerce." The "Passage" — or Judaeo-Christian domain — is stifling, deprived of light, filled with disease, misery, hatred and violence. The family barely survives on a monotonous diet of noodles — a term which connotes litle intelligence in French slang. The inferior fare is slightly relieved by the limited availability of cheap "wine" or "spirit." General misery may be measured by two facts. Children of the squalid "Passage" cannot stand unpolluted spirit. "Fresh air" kills them.** The Oriental God of Happiness — a symbolic statuette made of authentic "gold" — can only be stolen in such a den of vice.

Marcel Proust conceals a similar indictment under a less sordid veil.

---

*Death on the Installment Plan, p. 57, Ralph Manheim Translation.
**c.f. Pneuma — "wind," "breath," "spirit." The Secret Doctrine, p. 113, Vol. II.

The Grand Hotel of Balbec is a transparent symbol of the Judaeo-Christian world filled with "servants" — and male chauvinism — especially on "low" echelons:

> "Downstairs, it was the male element which prevailed and which turned that hotel, because of the extreme and idle youth of servants, into something resembling a sort of Judaeo-Christian tragedy, having acquired substance and perpetually represented." (*A la Recherche du temps perdu*, p. 774, Vol. II).

Self-knowledge is absent from the grand establishment of "Balbec." No one seems to be aware of the possibility of a link with the occult tradition of Baalbek, Lebanon, the site of enormous and puzzling ruins. No one has heard of the mysterious terraces found on the said location which, according to Louis Pauwels and Jacques Bergier "may be remains of a landing ground constructed" in ancient times "by astronauts arriving from the Cosmos."* Such thoughts could open disturbing vistas in time and space and prove damaging to the unquestioned myth of modern Western superiority if entertained. But they are inconceivable to the majority of smug, snobbish residents. It is only in learned company that "the overseas Balbec"** is indirectly mentioned. Limited self-knowledge is matched by poor understanding of one's associates. One rubs elbows with others "without knowing them." The Grand Hôtel — which is "grand" in appearance only — is the haunt of synthetically glamorous demi-gods. The "Manager" is an incorrigible butcher of "language" whose every utterance must be "translated" to have meaning. The garbled "word" of Judaeo-Christian scriptures is suggested. Formidable in appearance, the Director is actually afraid of higher deities of the hotel hierarchy. The mediocre status of Jehovah in world mythologies is hinted. The phonetic identity which exists between the French terms "hôtel" and "autel" — "altar" — seems calculated to convey the esoteric meaning of the symbolic establishment and of its unattractive master. The "patron" seems to be none other than the biblical "Vice-God."

Stress is placed on specific traits of the Judaeo-Christian tradition in the Proustian description of a Jewish family. Bloch — a typical young "Jew" — is fond of playfully addressing his sisters as "bitches." Their adoration for him is undiminished. The boorish father figure is slavishly worshipped. Phallic obsession is suggested along with its unfailing companion: servile, degraded womanhood. The Proustian version of "Missouf" is not physically beaten. She is insidiously conditioned from infancy to play the role of a white "Uncle Tom."

The Morning of the Magicians, p. 307.
**A la Recherche du temps perdu*, p. 936, Vol. II.

A strange outburst of M. de Charlus suggests the true nature of esoteric antisemitism. The irascible nobleman delights in a morbid description of imaginary tortures to be inflicted on the mother of "Bloch." The fact that the latter person is "dead" has no effect on his wrath. "Blindness" is connected with the Jewish family. The blindfolded Synagogue evoked by Elstir — "the reign of which is over"* if the artist must be believed — seems to be viewed in the same light by M. de Charlus. The end of the strange dialogue between Marcel and his anti-Semitic friend is reported as follows:

> "I informed him that in any case, Mme. Bloch was no longer alive, and that where M. Bloch was concerned, I wondered to what extent he would relish a game which could very well put his eyes out. M. de Charlus seemed angry. 'That is,' he said 'a woman who made a great mistake when she died. As for eyes being put out, precisely, the Synagogue is blind, it does not see the truths of the Gospel.' " (*A la Recherche du temps perdu*, p. 289, Vol. II).

The esoteric equivalence of "Jews" is hinted at an early stage of the *Recherche*. Young Bloch is a typical Judaeo-Christian scholar: pedantic and plagiarism-prone who consistently stumbles over hidden truths unseeing. One of his wordy tirades — the significant "first" of many such displays — combines allusions to well-known writers, to the *Bhagavat Gita*, and to the Delphic oracle. The young man flippantly comments on the many failings and occasional virtues of authors whom he does not fully understand.** He might do well to ponder the Delphic oracle to which he glibly refers. There are certain connections to be made between the teachings of the *Bhagavat Gita*, modern literary genius, and the ancient precept: "Know Thyself!" The Judaeo-Christian — or Western — reader of Proust should himself bear in mind the same admonition as he notes and judges the refined blunders of "Bloch."

The same young scholar follows the developments of the "Dreyfus case" with keen interest. But he does not realize to what extent the "trial" and controversial "revision" concerns him. The cause célèbre involves an esoteric collectivity consisting of such persons as Voltaire, Vigny, and Proust.

There is reason to question the exact nature of "anti-Semitism" in the works of many great writers. Beyond the exoteric appearance of "Jews" we should probably read in numerous instances the esoteric reality of our Judaeo-Christian or Western civilization. In a word: ourselves.

Ibid., p. 841, Vol. I.
**A la Recherche du temps perdu*, p. 90, Vol. I.

The same basic theme of sectarian blindness is esoteric in the first chapters of *Zadig*. It becomes exoteric in *Le Souper*.

The chapter describes a gathering of persons representing various faiths. A heated argument is under way. Zadig decides to participate in the discussion. Acting as the lone apostle of positive thought and unity, he reconciles all present, temporarily at least. Scorning illusive divisions wrought by dogma and ritual, he compels all in attendance to recognize common belief in a "First Cause" or "initial principle." The First Cause is a fundamental concept of occult philosophy. It is essentially bound to the doctrine of Emanation. First Cause and Emanation correspond — and are opposed — to the Judaeo-Christian dogmas of a personal deity and personal creation.

> "Never have the Jews in their Bible (a purely esoteric, symbolical work) degraded so profoundly their metaphorical deity as have the Christians, by accepting Jehovah as their own living yet *personal* God.
> This first, or rather ONE, principle was called 'the circle of Heaven,' symbolized by the hierogram of a point within a circle or equilateral triangle, the point being the LOGOS. Thus, in the Rig Veda, wherein Brahmâ is not even named, Cosmogony is preluded with the Hiranya gharba, 'the Golden Egg,' and Prajâpati (Brahmâ later on), from whom emanate all the hierarchies of 'Creators.' The Monad, or point, is the original and is the unit from which follows the entire numeral system. This Point is the First Cause, but THAT from which it emanates, or of which, rather, it is the expression, the Logos, is passed over in silence." (*The Secret Doctrine*, p. 426, Vol. I).

Many topics are discussed at the "ecumenical" supper. Food is among them. An Indian opposes the consumption of any kind of meat. An Egyptian sees no contradiction in the practice of his fellow-countrymen who worship the ox while eating oxen. Fish-eating is regarded as sacrilegious by a Chaldean. Scythians recognize that they are cannibalism-prone but nevertheless feel entitled to general respect. Beast-eating and man-eating seem to receive the same treatment from Voltaire. Little if any indications is given that one may be less reprehensible than the other. The discussion on meat-eating virtually conveys vegetarian views which are more clearly expressed by Voltaire in works produced toward the end of his life. The general climate of controversy and the evocation of cannibalism are consistent with the Voltairian view of mankind: a collectivity of insects devouring one another on a small atom of mud.

Metempsychosis is mentioned in jocular fashion. A guest is warned against the dangers of chicken-eating. The soul of his departed aunt may have migrated into the main course. The grotesque suggestion is an effective esoteric blind. The reader is unlikely to regard Voltaire as a rein-

carnationist. A popular misconception is exploited to veil belief in rebirth. The same erroneous view of metempsychosis is ridiculed by Voltaire
and rejected by occultists. In the words of Mme Blavatsky, Man "can
never become an animal except morally — hence *metaphorically*."* In
the words of Voltaire, reincarnation is "the simplest thing in the world:"

> " 'The resurrection, Madam, said the Phoenix, is the simplest thing in the
> world. It is no more surprising to be born twice than once." (*La Princesse
> de Babylone*, Ch. **IV**).

Zadig solves a dangerous religious controversy. Thanks to his intervention — and to it only — the turbulent gathering is restored to unity.
The "large family" rent by spiritual strife becomes a harmonious comun-
ity. Unanimous recognition of an "initial principle" comes close to recognition of one universal truth. The spirit generated by Zadig reflects an
ideal which is also expressed by the motto of the Theosophical Society:

> "There is no religion higher than truth."**

The enlightened arbitration of the young hero transforms an age-old
dream into reality:

> "The chief aim of the Founders of the Eclectic Theosophical School was
> one of the three objects of its modern successor, the Theosophical Society,
> namely, to reconcile all religions, sects, and nations, under a common
> system of ethics, based on eternal verities." (*The Key to Theosophy*, p. 8).

The short-lived state of harmony is a preview of distant future eras.
The time has not arrived for lasting, general enlightenment. Perverted
forms of religions continue to exist and to victimize mankind. India, the
fountainhead of knowledge, is not immune to such abuse. The practice
of *suttee* demonstrates the existence of "infamous" spiritual establishments in various parts of the world. The case of a young widow doomed
by custom to the funeral pyre comes to the attention of Zadig.

The origin of *suttee* may be traced to corrupt priests and adulterated
scriptures. Greed is clearly involved:

> "The precious stones and ornaments of the young widows sent by them to
> the stake belonged to them by right. — " (*Les Rendez-vous*, p. 49).

The criminal alteration of ancient scriptures is suggested in the following dialogue:

Isis Unveiled, Appendix, p. 36, Vol. 2.
**The Secret Doctrine*, p. 798, Vol. II.

> "For more than one thousand years, women have been possessed with the urge of burning themselves. Who among us will dare change a law consecrated by time? Is there anything more respectable than ancient abuse? — Reason is more ancient, replied Zadig." (*Le Bûcher*, p. 44).

The subversive nature of the passage is apparent on the exoteric plane itself. The Ancient Régime — which condoned countless burnings by no means limited to widows — fits the designation of "ancient abuse." The sacred cows of "antiquity" and precedent need not prevail in that case or any other. Corrective change is not only desirable but possible. The change must begin in minds which are prone to slavish worship of old impunities. An intellectual revolution is needed to establish the reign of "Reason." A political revolution may be necessary as well.

The word "possessed" suggests "possession" or influence exerted by occult means. The satanic malpractice of priests which is frequently denounced by Voltaire seems to be involved. Meaningful proximity exists between the reported act of "changing the law" and the expression "ancient abuse." *Suttee* is in fact the result of a change of law effected through abuse. The principle of "antiquity" invoked by its defenders is untenable. Man is by definition a thinking creature. "Reason" is as ancient as its its first glimmer in a human mind. Voltaire seems to court a connection between human ability to think and the Code of Manu which was adulterated to justify widow-burning. The same connection is made in occult philosophy:

> "The direct connection, moreover, between the 'Manus' and 'Mahat' is easy to see. *Manu* is from the root *man*, 'to think'; and thinking proceeds from the mind." (*The Secret Doctrine*, p. 452, Vol. I).

The antiquity and the falsification of Hindu scriptures are commented as follows in *Isis Unveiled*:

> "While every sect holds the *Vedas* as the direct word of God — *sruti* — (revelation) — the *Code of Manu* is designated by them simply as *smriti*, a collection of oral traditions. Still these traditions or 'recollections' are among the oldest as well as the most revered in the land. But perhaps the strongest argument in favor of its antiquity, and the general esteem in which it is held, lies in the following fact. The Brahmans have undeniably remodelled these traditions at some distant period, and made many of the actual laws, as they now stand in the *Code of Manu*, to answer their ambitious views. Therefore, they *must have done it at a time when the burning of widows (suttee) was neither practiced nor intended to be*, which it has been for nearly 2,500 years. No more than in the Vedas is there any such atrocious law mentioned in the *Code of Manu!* — The Brahmans appealed to a verse from the *Rig-Veda* which commanded it. But this verse has been recently proved to have been falsified." (*Isis Unveiled*, pp. 588-89, Vol. 1).

> "The Hindu laws were codified by Manu more than 3,000 years before
> the Christian era, copied by the whole of antiquity, and notably by Rome,
> which alone has left us a written law — the *Code of Justinian* — which has
> been adopted as the basis of all modern legislation." (*Isis Unveiled*, p.
> 586, Vol. 1).

The looting of Pagan culture by the modern West which is the joint
concern of occultists and esoteric writers involves legislation as well as
science and religious dogma.

Rabelais calls attention to the falsification of the *Pandects* — or Justinian Code in Chapter XLIV of the *Tiers Livre*. Steinbeck may have referred
esoterically to the same "ancient abuse" when he wrote the following
observations on corrupt officials of "*Wessex*" County:

> "There it came — the Town Manager, the council, the magistrates, the works.
> I listened without hearing — sad and heavy — Maybe they had been doing
> what they were charged with, but they'd been doing it so long they didn't
> think it was wrong." (*The Winter of Our Discontent,* Ch. XIV).

"Ancient abuse" has multiple prolongations in modern times. Michel
Servète, the XVIth Century physician who discovered the pulmonary circulation of the blood was condemned by the Catholic Church and later
sent to the stake by Calvin. Swiss law did not stipulate the ultimate
penalty for religious offenses. Calvin therefore had the Justinian Code
revived for the needs of his cause. Michel Servète was found guilty of
discovery. He was burnt alive in Champel, near Geneva, in 1553.

The fraudulent basis of *suttee* is matched by the artificial quality of
its rites. Voltaire suggests an atmosphere reminiscent of a carnival or
tea-party complete with fanfare and invitations. The sacred character of
the ceremony is far from evident:

> "An Arab belonging to the tribe of Sétoc having died, his widow, named
> Almona, who was very religious, announced the day and the hour when
> she would throw herself into the fire to the sound of drums and trumpets."
> (*Le Bûcher,* p. 44).

The ironic reference to musical instruments likely to induce a trance-
like state is a probable allusion to drugs and other pain-killing devices
which were occasionally used in India in the course of *suttee*:

> "The widow, bent on the self-sacrifice of concremation, called *Suhama-
> rana,* has no dread of suffering the least pain for the fiercest flames will
> consume her, without one pang of agony being experienced. The holy plants
> which crown her brow, as she is conducted in ceremony to the funeral
> pile, the sacred root culled at the midnight hour on the spot where the
> Ganges and the Yuma mingle their waters; and the process of anointing

96

the body of the self-appointed victim with *ghee* and sacred oils, after she has been bathed in all her clothes and finery, are so many *magical* anaesthetics."

. . . .

"No such thing if the sacred ceremony is only conducted strictly after the prescribed rites. The widows are never drugged in the sense we are accustomed to understand the word — (The widow)'s mind is as free and clear as ever, and even more so. Firmly believing in the promises of a future life, her whole mind is absorbed in contemplation of approaching bliss — the beatitude of 'freedom,' which she is about to attain. She generally dies with the smile of heavenly rapture on her countenance; and if someone is to suffer at the hour of retribution, it is not the honest devotee of her faith, but the crafty Brahmans who know well enough that no such ferocious rite was ever prescribed. As to the victim, after having been consumed, she becomes a *sati,* transcendent purity — and is canonized after death." (*Isis Unveiled,* pp. 540-41, Vol. 1).

The Voltairian allusion to *suttee* is an eloquent commentary on established religions. If division and strife prevail in the marketing of dogma, impressive uniformity exists where the handling of the flock is concerned. Whatever differences there may be between auto-da-fés and *suttee,* sordid motives and practical results are the same. Perverted dogmas promote the same inhumanity in all ages under all latitudes.

The commentary of Zadig on widow-burning serves as an esoteric blind. Voltairian partiality to Eastern creeds seems unlikely in the light of the cruel custom. The reader must be aware of the illegal basis of *suttee* to remain undeterred in his pursuit of esoteric substance. The decoy technique employed in this instance — and in many others — postulates general ignorance. The guidance techniques postulates "a small fund of philosophy" or a little knowledge of the Secret Doctrine.

The spiritual progress of Sétoc is unsteady. The path of Knowledge is an arduous one. Caught in the act of worshipping stars, the merchant receives remedial instruction from Zadig. He is urged to regard celestial bodies as "bodies like others." Neither distance nor brilliance can alter the fact that stars and suns belong to Maya in their material aspect as do all material things. They are remote, imperfect reflections of the First Cause which is alone entitled to worship. Zadig promotes and guides the transition made by Sétoc from polytheistic belief to monotheistic faith.

An effective device is used to open the eyes of the merchant. Zadig pretends to worship a series of candles. His mimicry ridicules devotional practice which tends to lose sight of the Supreme Being. The effect is instantaneous. The absurd conduct of another person is quickly perceived. Sétoc is warned against another aspect of Maya: double standards which lead one to find fault with all creeds and attitudes except one's own. The power of egocentric illusion is demonstrated.

97

Intellectual progress is accompanied by improved ethics. The importance of love, compassion and humanity is stressed. But it is stressed indirectly. Initially, the prospect of local *suttee* fails to arouse deep sentiment in the merchant. Apparently satisfied with the respectability of "ancient abuse," the slave-master needs and receives enlightenment from his slave. Zadig deplores the sinful waste resulting from widow-burning. It is argued that the victims if alive could produce valuable subjects for the State or at least raise those subjects who are already produced. Demography is invoked rather than sentiment. The instruction of the merchant is designed to appeal to his pragmatic outlook. The moral of the story applies to the general scheme of human evolution. Truth should be revealed carefully with a view to the degree of development of persons receiving it.

The instruction of Sétoc is in part a process of un-learning. The merchant is cautioned against man-made obstacles to his mental and spiritual development. His blind acceptance of precedent, dubious dogma, and cruel practice is overcome. Candle-burners and widow-burners are suggested to have the same origin. Perverted religion is based on "abuse." Power-crazed priests are unwilling and unable to dispense truth.

General cruelty is lessened by the influence of Zadig. The over-burdened slaves of Sétoc and the young widow benefit. But the exploitation of slavery from which the merchant derives wealth and status is nowhere questioned. The biblical realm is slavery itself. The Judaeo-Christian businessman does progress. But he is not ready for teachings which threaten his privileged condition. Nor is he ready to question the fundamental "bias" implicit in suttee. Zadig — who does not "scorn women" and who does "not boast of subjugating them" — might ask why widowers do not receive the same benefit of instant sainthood as do widows. Such speculations would probably tax to the danger point the imagination and good will of Sétoc. The beneficiary of bondage and the product of ancient brain-washing will not change overnight.

The positive teachings of Zadig are connected with India and indirectly with Egypt. "Commerce" with the river-bank dwellers of Ganges brings certain "goods" or benefits to the merchant *via* the Red Sea: The land of Buddha may deserve the same worship as the stars:

> " 'You receive more benefits,' replied Zadig, 'from the waters of the Red Sea, which carry your merchandise to India. Why should it not be as ancient as the stars? And if you must worship what is remote from you, you must worship the land of the river-bank dwellers of Ganges which is at the extremities of the earth!' " (*Le Bûcher*, p. 43).

Worship of "what is remote" is a specific trait of the Judaeo-Chris-

tian tradition. The transcendent biblical Deity maintains a safe vertical distance between himself and his suffering creatures. The rare avenues of contact connecting divine and human planes tend to be the one-way paths of multiple "Thou Shalt nots" and chastising thunderbolts. Sétoc is encouraged to direct his worship beyond the plane of the supposedly transcendent, personal God. The truly transcendent "first principle" is infinitely distant from terrestrial regions. But it has graduated reflections on all levels of existence. It is inseparable from the divine spark which is present in more or less latent state in every human being. The observation of Zadig on the worship of "what is remote" tends to oppose the concept of the Unknowable to the concept of the biblical God. It is also an invitation to recognize and cultivate the superior attributes of Man. The Pagan teaching of the Delphic oracle is virtually fused with the statement of the Christian Savior: "The kingdom of heaven is within you."

The suggested co-essence of divine and terrestrial components in Man tends to abolish material distance on the plane of legitimate worship. The parallel between star and land cult invites an analogy. If it is absurd to revere celestial bodies rather than their immaterial Creator, it may also be absurd to revere the land of India rather than its spiritual message. Earthly space and matter must be transcended if true progress is to be made. Other dimensions must be conceived and explored.

The ships which ply the Red Sea as they carry the merchandise of Sétoc may be presumed to return from India with more than empty holds. The connection which can be made between the land of Ganges, worship, and "benefits" unnamed yet actualy received tends to dissolve the exoteric irony which accompanies the reference to India. The Far Eastern custodian of the Primitive Wisdom-Religion may deserve reverent thought.

Earthly Time is critically examined as is earthly Space. Misguided worship tends to place undue stress on age. What is true of "ancient abuse" applies to the age of the Red Sea and to the age of the stars. Misused chronologies may serve to veil crimes — such as the burning of widows. They also serve to obscure ancient realities of cosmogenesis and human history.

The conjunction of Red Sea and stars suggests an allusion to the secret meaning and dwarfed chronology of *Exodus*. It is believed by occultists that the portion of *Exodus* relating the famous parting of the waters is the allegorical description of a cosmic catastrophe caused by extra-terrestrial forces. "Stars (meteors) showered on the land of the black Faces —" says the Secret Commentary.* The upheaval is regarded as one

---

The Secret Doctrine, p. 428, Vol. II.

of several planetary convulsions involving the submersion and raising of Atlantis. The memory of the event lingers in universal mythology and folklore. Some of the Atlanteans who survived the "flood" are believed to have migrated to Egypt. They are viewed as remote ancestors of the pyramid-builders.* Moses, the initiated Egyptian priest — whose esoteric relevance to *Zadig* can hardly be doubted — may therefore be regarded as a distant heir of Atlantean knowledge. The enormous time span connecting and separating cosmic happenings, Atlantis, and Egypt seems to be glimpsed and made part of the instruction of Sétoc. The unsuspecting "Arab" is made aware of the fantastic background of his homeland. India, where the secret tradition of cosmogenesis is carefully preserved, is logically mentioned along with "benefits."

The cosmic event which eems to underlie the brief passage of *Zadig* explodes the limits of exoteric Time and Space. The geographical horizons which are opened by reference to Near and Far East are vast. But they are dwarfed by the perspective of interplanetary upheavals. The time span represented by the age of the Red Sea and the age of the stars is open to speculation. But the general esoteric background of *Zadig* suggests that one of many reassessments to be made concerns the exoteric chronology of the Bible.

Occult science teaches that the chronology of the Bible was drastically compressed by ecclesiastical editors:

> "From Bede downwards all the chronologists of the Church have differed among themselves, and contradicted each other. 'The chronology of the Hebrew text has been grossly altered, especially in the inverval next after the Deluge' — says Whiston (*Old Test.*, p. 20). (*The Secret Doctrine*, p. 395, f., Vol. II).

The story related in *Exodus* is also said to have been "built many hundred thousands of years"** after the catastrophe described in the Secret Commentary.

The shrinking of scriptural chronology continues to be felt in our own age. The controversial work of Immanuel Velikovsky, *Worlds in Collision*, is based on belief in the periodic tilting of the axis of earth. The same belief is a major tenet of the Secret Doctrine. The book of Dr. Velikovsky contains a wealth of mythological substance collected from all parts of the world showing the same cataclysmic events to have been universally recorded. According to the author, the episode related in *Exodus* is one veiled recollection among many of a world conflagration caused by the passage of Venus — then a comet — in the vicinity of our globe. The daring vision of the writer seems to be hampered by a literal

---

Ibid., pp. 429-30, Vol. II.
**Ibid.*, p. 428, Vol. II.

approach to chronology. The esoteric concepts of "day" and "age" —
which may cover thousands and, millions of years — are interpreted exoterically. The Bible itself states that a thousand years in the sight of the
Lord is but as one day. A provocative passage of the *Psalms* contains
the following verse: "So teach *us* to number our days that we may apply
our hearts unto wisdom."* The Secret Doctrine contains similar indications of the esoteric value of "days," "weeks," and "years." But the
Western world generally shuns recognition of a hoary past which cannot be reconciled with scientific or religious dogmas of the Judaeo-Christian tradition. The otherwise bold thesis of Dr. Velikovsky does not
challenge the chronological myopia of Western knowledge.

The instruction of Sétoc is calculated to stress the relative value of
Mayavic Time and Space. The path to divine reality in suggested to
lie in other dimensions. But there is a great deal to be learned from
terrestrial aspects of contingency which are dwarfed by official science
and established religion. Voltaire seems to agree with the occult view of
the Judaeo-Christian tradition: "a body born out of time." Voltaire also
suggests that the spatial outlook of the same tradition tends to divorce
mankind from its cosmic background. The "body born out of time" is
also truncated with reference to Space in its literal aspect.

The instruction of Sétoc is paralleled by the instruction of his future
wife, the young widow rescued from the funeral pyre by Zadig. The
evolution of the young woman is as meaningful as the progress of the
merchant.

The name of *Almona* seems significant. Read in reverse it may suggest
anomaly, monstrosity, lack of legitimacy — all qualities applicable to her
plight as she faces the stake. Her name also suggests a connection with
the word *monad*, an important concept of occult philosophy. The monad
is associated with the peregrinations of spirit through various forms of
existence from the mineral kingdom to perfected human form. It is the
reincarnating principle — which Proust may have had in mind when he
referred to "the only gift the good Lord never makes twice."** The pilgrimage of the monad is outlined in *Isis Unveiled*:

> "When the Central Invisible (the lord Ferho) saw the efforts of the divine
> Scintilla, unwilling to be draggged lower down into the degradation of mat-
> ter, to liberate itself, he permitted it to shoot out from itself a *monad*,
> over which, attached to it as by the finest thread, the Divine Scintilla
> (the soul) had to watch during its ceaseless peregrinations from one form
> to another. Thus the monad was shot down into the first form of matter
> and became encased in stone; then; in course of time, through the combined

---

*Psalms, 90, 4, 12.
**A la Recherche du temps perdu p. 88, Vol. I.

efforts of *living fire* and *living water,* both of which shone their *reflection* upon the stone, the monad crept out of its prison to sunlight, as a lichen. From change to change it went higher and higher; the monad, with every new transformation borrowing more of the radiance of its parent, Scintilla, which approached it nearer at every transmigration. For the 'First Cause had willed it to proceed in this order;' and destined it to creep on higher until its physical form became, once more the Adam *of dust,* shaped in the image of the Adam Kadmon. Before undergoing its last earthly transformation, the external covering of the monad, from the moment of its conception as an embryo, passes in turn, once more, through the phases of the several kingdoms. In its fluidic prison it assumes a vague resemblance at various periods of the gestation to plant, reptile, bird and animal, until it becomes a human embryo. At the birth of the future man, the monad, radiating with all the glory of its immortal parent which watches it from the seventh sphere, becomes *senseless.* It loses all recollection of the past, and returns to consciousness but gradually, when the instinct of childhood gives way to reason and intelligence. After the separation between the life-principle (astral spirit) and the body takes place, the liberated soul — Monad — exultingly rejoins the mother and father spirit, the radiant Augoeides, and the two, merged into one, forever form, with a glory proportioned to the spiritual purity of the past earth-life, the Adam who has completed the circle of necessity, and is freed from the last vestige of his physical encasement. Henceforth, growing more and more radiant at each step of his upward progress, he mounts the shining path that ends at the point from which he started around the GRAND CYCLE." (*Isis Unveiled,* pp. 302-03, Vol. 1).

Several basic tenets of occult philosophy are expounded in the above text. They will appear repeatedly in the Voltairian trilogy and in *Micromégas.* 1) All that exists in Nature follows the descending curve of evolution into deep materiality. Eventual return to original spirituality is gradually achieved. "A stone becomes a plant, a plant an animal, an animal a man, a man a spirit, and a spirit a god."* 2) Every human being undergoes multiple rebirths until perfection or total liberation from matter is attained. 3) The memory of previous existence is lost at the time of birth.

The concept of esoteric "necessity" or evolution is repeatedly suggested in Voltairian texts by words such as "nécessaire," "nécessairement," and "il faut;" — "necessary," "necessarily" and "it is necessary." Similar expressions of "necessity" are found in countless esoteric writings. The concept of esoteric "perfection" is suggested in like manner by such terms as the adverb "perfectly." The concealed value of the latter word is frequently hinted in the *Recherche.*

The liberation of Almona arouses the predictable fury of the priests. "Zoroastrian" free thought and free agency canot be tolerated in the

---

Isis Unveiled, p. xxvii, Vol. 1.

realm of venerable abuse. A few words of "reason" suffice to threaten the prosperous — yet — vulnerable — empire of widow-burning thieves. Several priests join forces to get rid of Zadig. The young emancipator is sentenced to death.

Almona becomes the liberator of Zadig — her savior. Exposing the corruption of the priests, the young woman succeeds in thwarting their designs. Her courage and intelligence bring about the undoing of villains. The episode is reminiscent of the trial of the Jew who did not wish to part with five hundred ounces of "borrowed" silver. Criminal lies are turned against their users with spectacular success. Poetic justice seems to exist after all.

Priests can be caught at their own games when confronted with their own shabby tricks. The detective work performed by Almona is especially fruitful in the area of "sacred writings." Evidence of sacerdotal corruption is obtained in "scriptural" or written form. The substance of the parable represented by the triumph of Almona is identical to the substance of a statement of Mme Blavatsky. The "infamous" can be "crushed" by appropriate comparative studies.

> "The Roman Catholic Church has two far mightier enemies than the "heretics' and the 'infidels,' and these are — Comparative Mythology and Philology." (*Isis Unveiled,* p. 30, Vol. 2).

The lust of the priests which is aroused by beautiful Almona proves self-defeating. The fact is esoterically meaningful. Each priest takes his own carnal drives for granted but is shocked to find their counterpart in his colleagues. Each religion takes sexual imagery for granted within its own system while judging it obscene and fiendish in others. A favorite grievance of Pagan-haters — obscene symbolism and ritual — is commented as follows in *Isis Unveiled*. The investigation of Almona invites the same conclusions:

> "Our modern demonologists conveniently overlook a few insignificant details, among which is the undeniable presence of heathen phallicism in the Christian symbols. A strong element of this worship may be easily demonstrated in the dogma of the Immaculate Conception of the Virgin Mother of God; and a physical element equally proved in the fetish-worship of the holy *limbs* of Sts. Cosmo and Damiano, at Isernia, near Naples; a successful traffic in which *ex-voto* in wax was carried on by the clergy, annually, until barely a half century ago.
>
> ---
>
> We find it rather unwise on the part of Catholic writers to pour out their vials of wrath in such sentences as these: 'in a multitude of pagodas, the phallic stone, ever and ever assuming, like the Grecian batylos, the brutally indecent form of the lingham — the Maha Deva.' Before casting slurs

on a symbol whose profound metaphysical meaning is too much for the modern champions of that religion of sensualism par excellence, Roman Catholicism, to grasp, they are in duty bound to destroy their oldest churches, and change the form of the cupolas of their own temples." (*Isis Unveiled*, p. 5, Vol. 2).

The "profound metaphysical meaning" of phallic symbolism extends from the plane of emanating Cosmos to the plane of individual spirituality. The sex-fiends of established religion portrayed by Voltaire neglect the one aspect of "sex" which could insure their survival: the key to Pagan sexual symbolism. Their interests and faculties are limited to the exoteric and phallic worship which is one and the same in occult philosophy.* The admirers of Almona do not possess the insight necessary to see beyond the immediate surface of their "sexual" ventures. Blinded by materiality and lust, they remain oblivious to their own professional raison d'être. The disastrous effect of their dead-letter phallicism becomes apparent to them when it is too late. Phallicism means impotence where spiritual insight and power are concerned. The relevance of doubtful "potency" is ably stressed by Almona in a statement made to a priest. The presence of the word "servant" further suggests the idea of inferior experimentation:

> " ' — vous en userez comme vous pourrez avec votre servante." (*Les Randez-vous*, p. 51).

> (" ' — you will use your servant whichever way you can.' ")

The recurring theme of the "lost key" to Knowledge — a theme dear to occultists and esoteric writers — is present in *Les Rendez-vous*.

Retribution comes to the priests under the form of a woman. The perfection of Karma or Divine Justice — could hardly be better illustrated. From the remote days when the *Code of Manu* was altered to legitimize the burning of widows to subsequent eras of mealy-mouthed hypocrisy, religion has been and remains a major instrument of the oppression of the "second sex." The Spiritual Eve of universal tradition — so deftly spirited from Judaeo-Christian scriptures — still serves the designs of "venerable abuse." The triumph of Almona may represent — among others things — a symbolic return of Sophia. The evolution of the young woman conveys a common belief of occultists and esoteric writers. The superior faculties of mind and spirit are sexless.

The description of beautiful Almona is a parody of many portraits founds in literature. Black eyes, a milky-white complexion, crimson cheeks,

---

*The Secret Doctrine, p. 361, Vol. II.

lips of coral, pearl-like teeth, a snowy-white bosom are all included in the sketch of the friend of Zadig. The conventional inventory of fairness is complete and amusing. The nose of the young woman clashes with other elements of her beauty. It is compared to an object which it does *not* resemble.

> " — her nose, which was not like the tower of Mount Lebanon. — " (*Les Rendez-vous*, p. 51).

While it is common to compare the neck of a beautiful woman to an art object — such as a tower — made of ivory or alabaster, the comparison involving the nose of Almona — whether positive or negative — demands an effort on the part of the reader. One is tempted to dismiss with a smile another example of Voltairian "espièglerie."

Isis Unveiled supplies information on Lebanese mountains and towers. Their unimpressive appearance often conceals sites of secret rites performed by Syrian Druzes:

> "Whoever desires to aassure himself that there now exists a religion which has baffled for centuries the impudent inquisitiveness of missionaries, and the persevering inquiry of science, let him violate, if he can, the seclusion of the Syrian Druzes. He will find them numbering over 80,000 warriors, scattered from the plain east of Damascus to the Western coast. They covet no proselytes, shun notoriety, keep friendly — as far as possible — with both Christians and Mohammedans, respect the religion of every other sect or people, but will never disclose their own secrets.
>
> Once in a certain period of time a solemn ceremony takes place, during which all the elders and the initiates of the highest two degrees start out for a pilgrimage of several days to a certain place in the mountains. They meet within the safe precincts of a monastery said to have been erected during the earliest times of the Christian era. Outwardly one sees but old ruins of a once grand edifice, used says the legend, by some Gnostic sects as a place of worship during the religious persecutions. The ruins above ground, are but a convenient mask; the subterranean chapel, halls and cells, covering an area of ground far greater than the upper building; while the richness of ornamentation, the beauty of the ancient sculptures, and the gold and silver vessels in this sacred resort, appear like 'a dream of glory,' according to the expression of an initiate. As the lamaseries of Mongolia and Tibet are visited upon grand occasions by the holy shadow of 'Lord Buddha,' so here, during the ceremonial, appears the resplendent ethereal form of Hamsa, the Blessed, which instructs the faithful. The most extraordinary feats of what would be termed magic take place during the several nights that the convocation lasts; and one of the greatest mysteries — faithful copy of the past — is accomplished within the discreet bosom of our mother earth; not an echo, nor the faintest sound, not a glimmer of light betrays without the grand secret of the initiates." (*Isis Unveiled*, p. 312, Vol. 2).

105

It is interesting to learn that the nose of Almona was not in ruins. It is far more interesting to note Voltaire's interest in Lebanese towers. While the existence of the Druzes, a tribe which has "baffled" investigators for centuries, was known at the time of writing of *Zadig*, the few words of irony aimed in passing at the face of a beautiful woman suggest possible confederacy between Voltaire and representatives of a secret tradition. The hypothesis of occult complicity is strongly supported by the esoteric content of *La Danse*, one of the final chapters of *Zadig*.

Almona is the esoteric transmitter of a few articles of faith. The interview resulting in her escape from the funeral pyre contains the following dialogue between Zadig and herself:

> " 'Il faut,' dit Zadig, 'qu'il y ait apparemment un plaisir bien délicieux à être brûlée vive.'
> — 'Ah! cela fait frémir la nature,' dit la dame, 'mais il faut en passer par là.' " (*Le Bûcher*, p. 45).

> (" 'It must be, said Zadig, 'that there apparently is a most delicious pleasure in being burned alive.'
> — 'Ah! it makes nature shudder,' said the lady, 'but there is no other way out.' ")

The symbolism of mystical flames is a standard element of esoteric texts from the mythological tradition of Prometheus and his divine fire to the tongues of the flames of the Holy Ghost. The same symbolism imparts unexpected meaning to the question of Zadig and to the reply of his friend. Blissful omniscience or mystical ardor is the ultimate, destiny of all. Such is the immutable decree of the law of "necessity" which is made part of the text by the expression "il faut." The presence of the word "pleasure" — which is tinged with irony on the exoteric plane — is consistent with the esoteric interpretation of mysticism. It will be found in due course of the present study that "pleasures lead to God" in the words of Voltaire himself.

The shudder which is aroused by the prospect of "burning" is a physical repercussion of spiritual experience. Trembling hands attend the discovery of an unsuspected scheme of life in *Micromégas*. Candide is described — with double-edged irony — "trembling like a philosopher." Trembling — and loss of sensory consciousness — accompany the symbolic "lifting of the veil" or first glimpse beyond Mayavic illusion in several episodes of the Voltairian trilogy. The final observation of Almona: "There is no other way out" is consistent with the occult view of evolution. Return to the source of Being is the destiny of mankind. Or, in the words of Vigny which have already been quoted: *All will be called, and all will be chosen!*"

106

The vanity and transient character of physical beauty are noted by Almona in a manner suggesting pious, hypocritical drivel. Her statement seems to be contradicted by the admiration of the priests and by the irony of Voltaire. But the passage is designed for literal esoteric consumption. Flesh, one of the most power seductions of Maya, is a mere attribute of illusory being.

> " 'I greatly fear that I committed an enormous sin by not burning myself on the funeral pyre of my dear husband. Indeed, what did I have to preserve? a perishable flesh, and which is already all wilted.' " (*Les Rendez-vous*, p. 40).

The edifying statement of Almona is made to one of her would-be seducers. An interesting situation is called to the attention of the esoteric reader. The supposed representative of ascetic holiness is told of the vanity of the flesh by a glamorous daughter of Eve. Two conclusions may be drawn. Genuine spirituality is more likely to be found in laymen than in priests. Woman, the scape-goat of the Judaeo-Christian tradition in general and the much-abused "vase of impurity" of the Church Fathers in particular may teach valuable lessons on purity to the Church Fathers themselves.

Almona is a "sex-symbol" in the exoteric sense of the expression. She is also the personification of highest Love. Her efforts on behalf of Zadig are partially prompted by sexual attraction. But the enduring devotion of the hero to another woman fails to arouse a spiteful reaction in the young widow. The new friend of Zadig can and does transcend amorous inclination. Personal gratitude and general compassion take precedence over other concerns. Having been sentenced herself, the intended victim of priests feels instinctive sympathy with her doomed savior. Her reaction to cruel injustice shows her to be closely bound to a suffering fellow-creature. Almona is well on the way to recognizing as "one brother" — "the whole of mankind" struggling in the earthly vale of tears.

Mystical love implies — among other things — reverence of life:

> "Almona, who had regained much taste for life, and who was obligated for it to Zadig, resolved to rescue him from the pyre the abuse of which he had disclosed to her." (*Les Rendez-vous*, p. 50).

The sacredness and the joyful challenge of life are recognized by the young woman. Imperfection is inherent to the human condition. But the dignity of existence lies in that very fact. It is from the plane of incarnate bondage and strife that noble aspiration and noble endeavor can and do rise. Life is not always wonderful. But it is always filled with wonder for devotees of Divine Wisdom.

The progress of Almona represents a transition from terrestrial to divine Love. It is consistent with the monadic element of evolution suggested by her name. The interplay of Knowledge and Love which is promoted by Zadig reflects the influence of Science-Religion-In-One. Science is imparted by the discipline of Zoroaster and by his exposure of "ancient abuse." Mystical "love" is latent in Almona. Its development is favored by the acquisition of Knowledge. The compassionate nature of the woman reflects an innate sense of Ethics. The pupil of Zadig begins to meet the requirements of spiritual growth. Tangible results are soon apparent. The former slave of religious fashion, the superficial merry widow, proves capable of independent and effective action. Frivolity is replaced by intelligent, spirited, and selfless commitment. The Monad — or "liberated soul" of occult philosophy — is perceptible in the evolution of a truly beautiful woman.

The instruction of Sétoc involves the same interplay of intellectual and spiritual faculties. To the practical quality of enlightened "commerce" which is a natural trait of the merchant is added a spark of sensitivity. In his case also valuable knowledge is imparted by Zadig. The sorely needed inspiration of Love comes to the slave-master under the form of Almona.

The pragmatic outlook of Sétoc is cleverly exploited by Zadig. The initial sentimental frailty of Almona is also used as an asset. Embryonic and earthbound as they may be, insight and love are equally susceptible to the appeal of the carrier of Truth.

Great "fortunes" are anticipated by the three friends. "Fortune" is related to the concept of "fate" and to the esoteric substance of spiritual treasures. The combination of meanings underlying the following passage amounts to a restatement of the fact established by Almona: "There is no other way out." The acquisition of spiritual wealth is the ultimate destiny of all. Superficial differences existing among men merely reflect stages of evolutionary progress. It is all a matter of who is "first" to acquire a large fortune:

> "Zadig took leave after having thrown himself at the feet of his beautiful liberator. He and Sétoc left each other with tears, swearing eternal friendship, and promising that the first one of them who would acquire a large fortune would notify the other." (*Les Rendez-vous*, p. 52).

The perfectibility of Man is proclaimed esoterically in those portions of *Zadig* which involve Sétoc and Almona. Voltairian optimism is no less genuine for being lucid — and veiled.

The human ability to endure and overcome the worst aspects of human condition is a major theme of the bondage of Zadig. Slavery itself can be turned into freedom. Crass practicality can be used to noble ends. Frivolous egotism can be raised to the plane of the Higher Self. Slight relief is brought to slaves as Sétoc is enticed to try efficient slave-driving techniques. No transmission of wisdom — in however small amount — goes without some general benefit. The continuity of "venerable abuse" is shaken by the liberation of Almona and by the exposure of a corrupt priesthood. The myth of invulnerable spiritual establishments is irreparably damaged. Freedom can be sought — if not fully attained — in the very realm of "slavery." Most important of all, the joint power of Knowledge and Ethics (or Love) is everywhere in evidence. It is allegorized by the marriage of Sétoc and Almona.

The "Great Instructor of Mankind" is well served by superior faculties and genuine humility. Zadig holds an accurate view of his person within the general scheme of existence. The Lower Self is judged with lucidity. The Higher Self is duly prized. No conflict lies in the co-existence of heartfelt modesty and self-conscious personal worth. The fact of being "a man like another" holds challenge and promise:

"'I am a man like another.'" (L'Esclavage, p. 41).

Sanity, integrity — even optimism — survive the worst hours of adversity. Divine Wisdom sees its faithful through the trials of life.

The esoteric concept of "a man like another" is a fine example of misleading honesty. Zadig obviously partakes of the same human condition as do other mortals. The "ebb and flow" of his spiritual consciousness which has already been noted gives evidence of human imperfection. The statement quoted above is therefore correct. But the full truth is not expressed. Zadig is also a "Great Instructor of Mankind" whose identity will emerge at a later stage of the story.

The dual viewpoint of the "ordinary man" and superior being united in One is a favorite device of esoteric writers. It is used to illustrate the feeling of oneness with suffering mankind which inspires every true spiritual seeker. It is occasionally used to suggest the ultimate expression of the latter feeling: voluntary reincarnation. It is used most effectively to veil esoteric substance. No sooner is a set of clues given to what a text may conceal — the viewpoint of the superior being — than the opposite viewpoint shatters the budding hypothesis. Confusion reigns. The attempt to explore hidden posibilities is abandoned. No more powerful obstacle could possibly be placed in the path of the casual researcher.

One may cite as example the pilot of The Little Prince. The flier represents the ordinary man or modern mankind. He is proud of the aircraft which is the symbol of XXth Century technology. He is primarily concerned with "reasonable," practical matters such as physical survival.

He has only limited time, patience, and understanding to bestow on the "poetry" which is the great love of the Little Prince. But he eventually listens to the "small voice" of his strange friend, a voice which is the echo of his own dormant spirit. The pilot is also a being who "flies" beyond contingency. He is a guide who can open the path of spirit to others. He is the initiate — probably Saint-Exupéry himself — a man capable of assisting a fellow-creature to the Well of Knowledge. He knows which "part" is missing from the stranded machine of Western civilization. The esoteric pilot and the "impractical" advocate of "poetry" are committed to the same cause of human survival and progress.

No contradiction is implied by the co-existence of such seemingly opposite components. Their fusion is the essence of human condition divided between material necessity and indestructible spirit. The superior being who frequently plays the role of narrator has attained an omniscience which embraces the outlook of the less advanced mortal. But the less advanced mortal himself is a "diamond-hearted" or "perfected" creature in latent state.

Many dual narrators may be found in literature. We may wonder about Roquentin, and his double-edged "nausea." We may wonder about Proustian "Marcel" who carries within himself an "extra-temporal being."*

Zadig resumes his search for Astarté. He comes to the borders of Rocky Arabia and Syria. The reference to "Rocky Arabia" — "l'Arabie Pétrée" — is geographically and phonetically compatible with an allusion to Petra, a city of ancient Edom, located in a mountainous area approximately 50 miles South of the Dead Sea. The town is surrounded by cliffs which are lined with tombs cut out of solid rock. Strange rock carvings abound. Among numerous ruins are a large theater capable of seating 3,000 spectators and a Nabathean temple. Nabathean groups are known to have belonged to sects of early Christians who were, in the words of Mme Blavatsky, "more or less kabalistic."** The ruins of Petra which were unknown to the Western world during the lifetime of Voltaire were not discovered until 1812.

The word *Petra* is a subject of extensive comment in *Isis Unveiled*:

> "Jesus says: 'Upon this *petra* I will build my Church, and the gates, or rulers of Hades, shall not prevail against it'; meaning by *petra* the rock-temple, and by metaphor the Christian Mysteries; — " (*Isis Unveiled*, p. 30, Vol. 2).

The same word is linked to an inscription found on the coffin of Queen Menthuhetep (2872 B.C.) which reads in part PTR. The three letters are

---

A la Recherche du temps perdu, p. 871, Vol. III.
**Isis Unveiled*, p. 127, Vol. 2.

connected with an open eye, a symbol of superior knowledge. They also form the structure of the old Aramaic and Hebraic term "Patar," which, in the words of Mme Blavatsky, "occurs" in the history of Joseph as the specific word for *interpreting*. Finally, a Graeco-Demotic manuscript of the first century mentions a hero frequently designated as the "Judaean Illuminator" who "communicates with his *Patar;* the latter term being written in Chaldaic characters."

> "But whether the 'illuminator' of the Graeco-Demotic manuscript is identical with Jesus or not, the fact remains that we find the latter selecting a 'mystery' appellation for one who is made to appear later by the Catholic Church as the janitor of the Kingdom of Heaven and the interpreter of Christ's will. The word Patar or Peter locates both master and disciple in the circle of initiation, and connects them with the 'Secret Doctrine.' " (*Isis Unveiled,* pp. 92-93, Vol. 2).

The reference to Rocky Arabia may have been intended to evoke the ancient city and its mysterious ruins. The occult Nabathean tradition may well have interested the author of *Zadig*. The word designating an initiated interpreter of the Secret Doctrine probably prompted the apparent allusion. As was previously noted, the title character of *Zadig*, a Great Instructor of Mankind, fits the designation. The relevance of Jesus and Peter to the chronology of *Zadig* is likely in view of the historical outline of the Judaeo-Christian tradition which forms the hidden architecture of the story. The word *Petra* may convey — among other things — the idea of an era of transition from impersonal Pagan worship to anthropocentric Christianity, in other words from Chrestos to Christ. Whatever the intent of Voltaire may have been, the probable allusion to the then undiscovered city is significant. Petra the city is openly and specifically mentioned in Chapter XXII of *Candide*. The previous reference to Lebanese towers suggests that the sage who wrote *Zadig* had access to an underground tradition independent of modern discovery. Voltaire's interest in Petra points to the same probability. Occult knowledge seems to be flaunted.

Unwittingly trespassing on the domain of an Arabian bandit, Zadig is taken prisoner but receives the treatment of an honored guest. In contrast to the priests of preceding chapters, the thief seems almost wholesome. His wickedness is refreshingly forthright.

> "The lord of the castle was one of those Arabs who are called *'thieves;'* but he sometimes performed good deeds in a multitude of bad deeds; he stole with furious greed and gave freely; was intrepid in action, fairly gentle in social contact, reckless at table, cheerful in debauchery, and above all full of frankness." (*Le Brigand,* p. 53).

Arbogad has done well in life, rising from the condition of valet to the exalted rank of feudal lord and Arabian "fermier général." His castle serves as headquarters from which the strategy of his "bandits" is directed. He has become the collaborator and partner in crime of the government which can no longer control him. His lifelong ambition: "to change from a grain of sand into a diamond" seems to have been achieved in terms of worldly success. But the spiritual symbolism of the "diamond" can hardly apply to him. The former valet remains an esoteric "servant."

> "The term Anupadaka, 'parentless,' or without progenitors, is a mystical designation having several meanings in the philosophy. By this name celestial beings, the Dhyan-Chohans or Dhyani-Buddhas, are generally meant. But as these correspond mystically to the human Buddhas and Bodhisattvas, known as the 'Manushi (or human) Buddhas,' the latter are also designated 'Anupadaka,' once that their whole personality is merged in their compound sixth and seventh principles — or Atma — Buddhi, and that they have become the 'diamond-souled' (Vajra-sattvas) the full Mahatmas. — even every Soul-endowed man is an Anupadaka in a latent state." (*The Secret Doctrine,* p. 52, Vol. I).

Diamonds are widely used symbols of superior spiritual attainment. Their esoteric significance can easily be perceived in *Micromégas, Candide, and L'Ingénu.* Crystal and diamonds are regarded by Vigny as "the vision and the purity of the JUST."* The ambition of Arbogad therefore lies in the realm of "perfection." But the factor of *level* militates against success. The only perfection which Arbogad has achieved is perfection in evil. As was previously noted, there are many "degrees" of occult pursuits ranging from passive mediumship to adeptship. Such "degrees" are determined to a large extent by the quality of motivation of the spiritual seeker. The activities of Arbogad and of his shady host clearly belong to low planes of spiritual "banditry."

The spiritual case history of Arbogad is in part a mystery. No indication is given as to how the intelligent and dynamic thief came into being. Two possibilities may be examined. "Diamonds" are frequently misunderstood as a result of literal interpretation. Arbogad may be the victim of the dead-letter approach which regards the precious stones simply as good investments. The "bandit" is "intrepid" in practical ventures. But he seems incapable of grasping the true significance of "daring" or pure spirituality. The influence of the literal, spoliation-prone Judaeo-Christian outlook may be to blame.

Arbogad may deliberately disregard perceived essence. The appeal of worldly success may outweigh all other considerations. Chronically and triumphantly breaking human law, the thief may somehow expect to by-

---

Les Oracles.

pass Divine Justice. Whatever the case may be, the ideal represented by spiritual "diamonds" is obscured and debased by the thief.

The "fairly strong stronghold"—"un château assez fort"—of the bandit represents more than a delightful pun. The dubious "strength" or spirituality of Arbogad is a menace to himself as well as to others. As is often the case, the self-made man has developed the lowest attributes of selfhood and manhood. The acts of the thieving community are exoterically "sinister." They are also "sinister" in the esoteric sense which implies use of black magic. The subordination of "force"—or spirit—to worldly benefit is the very definition of "left-handed magic." The impossible mixture of desired diamond-like attainment and actual rapine and gore is symbolically self-defeating. The theme of the sorcerer's apprentice is introduced into the text by the plight of the government which has lost control of its "servant." Arbogad may eventually face like adversity in confrontation with his own "bandits." Such is the rather common destiny of experimenters in inferior magic—and Mafia-ridden powers.

Psychologically—if not otherwise—Arbogad is insecure and lonely. He makes desperate efforts to retain the company and services of Zadig. He is instinctively aware of the "strength" of his young guest. But he is unable to benefit by the influence of the potential savior. The dim spiritual prospects of the thief bring to mind another character of *Zadig*. Missouf is the victim of the biblical God. Arbogad is the victim of the Lower Self. Debased spiritual essence—divine and human—is the nemesis of both persons. The *Arab* is also the likely personification of a warlike branch of World Religion: Islam. The masochistic "souffre-douleur" of Jehovah and the brutal predator of Allah share certain common traits.

Gluttony and reckless drinking deflect and impair the faculties of Arbogad:

> "As he spoke thus, he drank with such courage, he confused all ideas so thoroughly, that Zadig was unable to get any clarifications from him." (*Le Brigand*, p. 55).

"Drinking" should be prudently guided and controlled. The amateurish handling of occult forces is a dangerous game. The thief does not lack the "courage" or "daring" required to seek the benefits of "spirit." But he is doomed to inferior and perilous ventures by the limited insight which is an inevitable companion of tainted ethics. The "diamond" which he desires to be is, in the words of Voltaire, a selfless, "intrepid philosopher,"* not a self-seeking adventurer. Arbogad needs to recognize the

---

*L'Ingénu, Ch. XX.

113

practical value of ethics in spiritual pursuits. The bandit has at one time counted Queen Astarté among his captives. But his inability to see further than a good sale has blinded him to the unique value of his prisoner. The unrecognized Queen who might have helped the thief realize his main ambition has been promptly sold. Arbogad is unlikely to have another chance to "lift the veil" of Astarté — or Isis.

The dim prospects of the bandit are not limited to wasted opportunity. The confusion of ideas which results from his reckless "drinking" suggests incipient madness. Untrained mediumship and other inferior occult experimentation may cause physical and mental deterioration. King Moabdar will be the victim of such imprudence. The case of Arbogad is another example of poor spiritual hygiene.

The gluttony of the thief does not favor the development of a spiritual gem. The importance of eating habits is stressed in occult philosophy. The diets of "earnest students" should be wisely determined:

> " — we advise really earnest students to eat such food as will least clog and weight their brains and bodies, and will have the smallest effect in hampering and retarding the development of their intuition, their inner faculties and powers." (*The Key to Theosophy*, pp. 226-27).

Worldly success brings boredom in the absence of knowledge and virtue. Arbogad — who proclaims himself "the happiest of men" does protest too much. His search for bliss culminates in bestial living which must be flaunted to yield gratification. The thief is one of many characters of *Zadig* who exist mainly in the eyes of others. He personifies the large segment of mankind which is dedicated to vain appearance and materialism against its own superior interest.

The name of the bandit resembles the name of *Arbogast,* a barbarian soldier of the Roman Empire who died in A.D. 394. Arbogast is believed by some historians to have been of Frankish nationality. The latter fact may have been hinted in *Zadig* by the emphatic reference to the "frankness" of Arbogad, — "et surtout plein de franchise." Arbogast had a turbulent military and political career and is generally known as a great general and energetic statesman. But the quality of his "greatness" and "energy" seems to have belonged to the same plane of ethics as do corresponding assets of Arbogad. Arbogast is known to have played the role of an assassin. Voltaire may have used his bandit to allude to such gifted adventurers as Arbogast. Such men knew worldly success, scorned ethics, and usually came to tragic ends. Arbogast was eventually defeated by Theodosius and committed suicide. Voltaire may also have wished to draw attention to the religious convictions of Arbogast who tried to restore Paganism. The ambition of Arbogad to attain the status of "diamond" is clearly inspired by the Far Eastern legend of the grain of sand which become "the finest ornament of the crown of the King of India." The probable allusion to Arbogast is consistent with the time setting of *Zadig*: Paganism on the decline. It is also consistent with a transition to the modern era. Arbogad is — among other things — a typical feudal lord.

Read in reverse the name *Arbogad* strongly resembles *Dagobert*, the name of a *Frankish* King who was immortalized by a popular and rather ludicrous song. The frankness of the Voltairian character may have been designed to suggest the Merovingian monarch. Arbogad and Dagobert share certain traits. The historical sovereign is regarded as a man of genuine capacity in legislation and administration. He is also notorious for his cruelty and polygamy. The bandit of *Zadig* who sells kidnaped women as well as other ill-acquired possessions seems to qualify as a kindred soul of the Frankish King. The thief who needs the emotional support of Zadig is as dependent on external strength as was Dagobert if the famous song must be believed. The King of the song is repeatedly shown to have sought reassurance from Saint Eloi. The vestimentary quirk which caused the Dagobert of lyrics to wear his pants wrong side out may suggest inverted values. Materialistic Arbogad suffers from the same moral disease.

It is difficult to determine the date when the famous song began to circulate widely. But the possibility of a Voltairian allusion to its legendary content cannot be ruled out in view of the name, personality, and "frankness" of the thief.

The amusing lyrics of the well-known song are as follows:

"Le bon roi Dagobert
A mis sa culotte à l'envers.
Le bon Saint Eloi
Lui dit: 'o mon Roi,
Votre Majesté
Est mal culottée.'
— 'C'est vrai,' lui dit le Roi.
'Je vais la remettre à l'endroit.'

Le bon roi Dagobert
Chassait dans la plaine d'Anvers.
Le bon Saint Eloi
Lui dit: 'O mon Roi,
Votre Majesté
Est bien essoufflée.'
— 'C'est vrai,' lui dit le Roi,
'Un lapin courait après moi.'

("Good King Dagobert
Put on his pants wrong side out.
The good Saint Eloi
Said to him, 'O my King,
Your Majesty is badly trousered.'
— 'It's true,' the King said to him,
'I will put the pants back on
   right side out.'

Good King Dagobert
Was hunting on the plain of Antwerp.
The good Saint Eloi
Said to him, O my King,
Your Majesty
Is quite out of breath.'
— 'It's true,' the King said to him
'A rabbit was chasing me.'

115

Quand Dagobert mourut,	When Dagobert died,
Le Diable aussitôt accourut.	The Devil immediately rushed in.
Le bon Saint Eloi	The good Saint Eloi
Lui dit, 'O mon Roi,	Said to him, O my King,
Satan va passer.	Satan is on his way.
Faut vous confessor.'	You must go to confession.'
— 'Hélas!' lui dit le Roi,	— 'Alas!' said the King to him,
'Ne pourrais-tu mourir pour moi?' "	'Couldn't you die in my place?' ")

Dagobert is connected with fanciful magic in popular tradition:

" — one also has a tested recipe to be safe from evil spells, it is that of King Dagobert: put on your clothes wrong side out and the most skilled sorcerers will be powerless against you." (Charles Lancelin, *La Sorcellerie des campagnes*, p. 63).

The legendary background of Saint Eloi is mentioned in the *Recherche*. According to the priest of Combray, the saint is — among other things — a Burgundian mutation of a woman, Sainte Eulalie. The local Church which is dedicated to the same "Saint Hilaire" has a lurid history. It has been involved in bloody dynastic struggles and completely destroyed in the days of Charles le Bègue — Charles the Stutterer. Only the crypt — etymologically and esoterically the "hidden," underground, or occult foundation — remains of the original building. The Church of Combray seems to be one of many comparable structures built on what is called by Mme Blavatsky "the mangled remains" of a primitive, Pagan structure. The razing of the original edifice was the work of a violent prince whose character resembles that of the biblical God. The literal theme of Sodom and Gomorrah and the esoteric theme of "inversion" play an important part in the *Recherche*. They are present in the following passage:

"The brother of Gilbert, Charles the Stutterer, a pious prince but who, having lost his father, Pépin the Mad, at an early age, his father having died from the results of mental illness — wielded the supreme power with all the presumption of a youth lacking discipline as soon as he did not like the looks of a private citizen of a city, had everyone slaughtered down to the last inhabitant." (*A la Recherche du temps perdu*, p. 105, Vol. I).

The general picture of Dagobert and Saint Eloi which is presented by various elements of popular tradition is consistent in connecting the Throne and Altar with "inversion." "Inverted" clothes are associated with the monarch and with sorcery in the folklore mentioned by Charles Lancelin. "Inverted" trousers — which may be symbolic — are attributed to the King of the song who quakes with satanic fear. Inverted "sex" is the major trait of Hilaire-Eloi-Eulalie in the *Recherche*. The Proustian description of the Church dedicated to the same saint is tinged with evocations

116

of "hidden" — perhaps occult — structures. The esoteric theme of ambiguous sexuality or spirituality is everywhere present.

The corresponding "inversion" of Arbogad is suggested by Voltaire. The bandit speaks of certain disproportions initially existing between "men" and himself. No further information is given openly. But the nature of the "disproportions" seems to be revealed by the thief himself. Arbogad is a dispassionate merchant of kidnaped women who remains unaffected by his most beautiful captives. As was previously noted, the sole meaning of their loveliness in that of a good sale. The apparent polygamy of the bandit barely conceals the absence of a normal "love life." The failure of Arbogad to become a "diamond" is due to poor ethics and accordingly defective insight. It is also due to deviant "sexuality." The esoteric equivalence of "inversion" — tainted spirituality — which will be crucial in *Candide* is present in the chapter featuring the thief. It may finally be observed that the last syllable of the name Arbo-*gad* denotes the exact opposite of DAG the Savior: a person incapable of saving the Self, let alone others.

The general view of the Throne and Altar which is presented by popular tradition and by History itself is unflattering. The dynasty evoked by Proust has a spectacular record of cruelty and mental illness. The Dagobert of the song is a cowardly dullard. The lyricized Saint Eloi, mechanically stating the obvious does not seem exceedingly bright. The spiritual and temporal rulers who should be guided by superior insight and superior ethics leave much to be desired. The power structure is consistently characterized by "inversion" of sacred values. Voltaire was not alone in regarding the establishment as "infamous" exoterically and otherwise.

The historical scope of the chapter devoted to the Arabian bandit extends beyond the limits of Antiquity. Voltaire seems to have used Arbogad to trace the "ideology" of feudalism to ancient times — esoterically to the decadence of Paganism which was a factor at the origin of the Judaeo-Christian tradition. The tax-collecting sideline of the thief and his fortified castle suggest the exactions of the Ancient Régime in general and medieval society in particular. The self-righteous larceny of the Mosaic tradition which is recorded in preceding chapters and the "raubritter" mystique of Islam which is connected with Arbogad are presented as successive links in a long chain of "venerable abuse."

The esoteric dimension of History forming the background of *Zadig* seems to be additionally conveyed by a second sequence. The name of the brutal "Egyptian" killed by Zadig in a preceding chapter is *Clétofis*. The words "Clé au fils" — "key (belonging) to the son" — may be phonetically suggested. The possible meaning of a "key" — to ancient knowledge — which is in the possession of the Son — Chrestos, the

117

Higher Self, and Christ the Savior — is consistent with the esoteric content of *Zadig*. The fact that the said key belongs to the Savior has been demonstrated by the defeat inflicted on Clétofis by Zadig. Clétofis may also be linked phonetically to *Clovis*, the first Frankish King to receive baptism and to place France under the spiritual and temporal aegis of the Church. The esoteric sequence from ancient knowledge to Christ, Clovis, and Dagobert (d. 639) is consistent with the exoteric sequence from Babylon to the "Arab" or the beginning of Islam. (VII Century)

Voltaire reports on the final prospects of Arbogad at the end of *Zadig*. The bandit is in a difficult situation. He is bluntly advised to set himself straight. Two alternatives are offered to him.

> "He (Zadig) sent for the bandit Arbogad, to whom he gave an honorable rank in his army, with a promise to elevate him to the highest dignities if he behaved as a true warrior, and to have him hanged if he practiced the trade of bandit." (*Les Enigmes*, pp. 80-81).

The Voltairian view of "warrior" and "bandit" is clearly expressed in *Candide* and elsewhere. There is no reason to believe that the author sees any difference between the former and the latter concepts on the exoteric plane. The exoteric choice offered to Arbogad is no choice at all. Esoterically, however, a "true warrior" is a person dedicated to true "force" or spirit. Arbogad is given an opportunity to fulfill his ambition. An esoteric "true warrior" may become an esoteric "diamond". The offer of a regular rank in a regular "army" suggests the hierarchies and "degrees" of secret societies. The "highest dignities" are probably those of initiation.

The same equivalence of "rank" and "degree" serves numerous esoteric writers. "Degrees" are frequently suggested — with typical esoteric humor — by the steps of a stairway. But it is within the context of military hierarchies and spiritual weaponry that they seem to be used most effectively. Voltaire's *History of Charles XII* deserves a brief comment in this conection.

The Voltairian biography of Charles is a diptych. The Swedish King is shown — esoterically — to have possessed impressive spiritual gifts which he used erratically. The same use — and occasional misuse — of natural faculties is contrasted to the "instruction" received by Peter the Great of Russia. The preparation of the czar is noted to have proceeded "by degrees" in accordance with certain rules:

> "He (Peter the Great) became an officer by degrees. He created new regiments little by little; and finally feeling himself to be the master of disciplined troops, he dissolved the strelitz, who did not dare disobey." (*Pierre le Grand*).

118

The expression "little by little" may have been intended to suggest the esoteric concept of a "little one" or initiate.* The word "master" may suggest spiritual mastery. The reference to the "well disciplined troops" is often mentioned and questioned by Voltairian commentators. It is noted that the "well disciplined troops" mutinied in 1682, 1689, and 1697 and that their last mutiny was drowned in blood. Voltaire may have used the flagrant discrepancy between his own report and fact to steer attention to a symbolic or esoteric plane. The rebellious strelitz and the "well disciplined troops" of which Peter was unquestioned master may actually represent different units. The latter possibility is also suggested by a reference made in the same chapter to a new company created by the czar. The company in question was composed of "foreigners" — a term which may have the esoteric meaning of "heretic," "Protestant," or "occultist."** Peter the Great may have created companies of men who could be used to further activities of occult nature.

The Swedish King — and rival of Peter — is reported to have had little "instruction." It is difficult to reconcile such a statement with the fact that Charles knew French and was able to converse in Latin. The defective "instruction" seems to concern secret lore. Charles is also noted not to have known society. One may ask what kind of "society" was on the mind of Voltaire. The answer may well lie in the concept of *secret society*. The combination of "degrees," religion and absolute "power" which is found in the following text seems most suggestive:

> "The Moscovites learned by degrees what society is. Superstition itself was abolished; the religious rank of patriarch was discarded; the czar declared himself the head of religion, and the latter enterprise which would have cost a less absolute monarch his throne, succeeded almost without opposition, and insured his success in regard to other novelties." (*Peter the Great*).

The two royal figures forming the diptych mentioned above are compared as follows:

> "The czar had the same views as he (Charles XII) did on religion and on destiny, but he spoke of them more often for he used to converse familiarly about everything with his favorites, and had over Charles the advantage of the study of philosophy and the gift of eloquence." (*Mort de Charles* XII).

The word "familiarly" suggests involvement with occult forces as does the word "favorites" which frequently conveys the idea of subaltern powers. The term "everything," a practical equivalent of "All," expresses

---

The Secret Doctrine, p. 504, fn., Vol. II.
**Isis Unveiled*, p. 62, Vol. II.

119

the idea of Oneness which pervades the Secret Doctrine and which represents Ultimate Reality. The unique advantage derived from integrated "philosophical" knowledge is stressed in a manner reminiscent of the "instruction" of Sétoc. The difference in "degrees" of development which seems to have existed between Charles and Peter is comparable to the difference which exists between amateurish psychic experimentation and Atma-Vidya respectively. The long path to be traveled by Arbogad before he can reasonably aspire to become a "diamond" belongs to the same scale of multiple "degrees" which cannot be by-passed by any spiritual seeker. The "unveiling of Isis" — the Cypric goddess — should proceed in accordance with certain rules of secrecy and gradual preparation. In the words of Rabelais, "The act, performed on the sly, between two doors, through the degrees, behind the tapestry, discreetly — pleases the Cypric goddess more — than performed in the sight of the sun, in cynical fashion."*

The Voltairian comparison of Charles and Peter — and the probable allusion to Dagobert — suggest the unorthodox view of History which is shared by occultists and esoteric writers. "History itself is dealt with by the so-called historians as unscrupulously as legendary lore" says Mme Blavatsky. The latter view is generally supported by literary "smugglers" of the Secret Doctrine. Popular legend is regarded as a frequent refuge of buried or distorted historical fact. Official records are believed to be frequent products of manipulations designed to promote the same general ignorance as the dishonest handling of religious Scriptures. Flaubert notes that Bouvard and Pécuchet learned to distrust historians.** Proust states that the key to numerous historical myths and mysteries lies in secret meetings connected with "drinking" at fashionable "spas." J. Barbey D'Aurevilly contrasts "veritable history — the oral history — the living tradition —" to "the history of records and chanceries."*** Sartre refers to "our rigged history" in *Situations*. The skepticism of occultists toward official history does not lack distinguished support.

The modern Western mind is generally reluctant to devote serious thought to "legendary" prehistoric civilizations which may have equalled — perhaps surpassed — our own era in scientific achievement. The Darwinian view of man slowly evolving from the ape in a steadily rising pattern appeals to the natural and to the culturally induced vanity of the average modern Western mind. Darwinism tends to support the gratifying view of the present human specie: the end product and the crown-

*Tiers Livre, XVIII.
**Bouvard et Pécuchet, Ch. III.
***L'Ensorcelée, Ch. II.

ing glory of far less gifted historical periods. The thought of future mankinds looking on our naiveté with pitying disbelief is rarely considered.
It is as unsavory as the possibility of a brilliant, distant past. One must
grant that the existence of future mankinds is not guaranteed by the
present state of affairs. But our endemic inability to know ourselves
within the sobering perspective of time does not always stem from such
an awareness. The psychological residue of the Thomistic doctrine which
regards Earth — and by extension its residents — as the center of the
universe flatters egocentric weaknesses in relation to space as does Darwinism in relation to time. The effect of such ego-geocentric views is
still with us in modified, non-theological form. We are prone — and encouraged — to worship blindly and exclusively the worst aspects of the
Glorious Here And Now. We are prone — and encouraged — to do so at
the expense of the genuine grandeur of our era which is part of a timeless heritage.

We are culturally conditioned to live in a mental smog designed to
blur — if not obliterate — certain facts. Louis Pauwels and Jacques Bergier note the following:

"Now what do we find in Eskimo folklore? References to tribes being
transported to the Frozen North at the beginning of time by giant metallic
birds.

Nineteenth century archeologists have always scoffed at these "metallic"
birds. And what do we think?
— Optical lenses have been found in Iraq and Central Australia. The
question is: do they come from the same source, the same civilization? No
modern optician has yet been asked to give an opinion. All optical glasses
for the last twenty years, in our civilization, have been polished with ceria.
In a thousand years from now spectroscopic analysis will prove, from an
analysis of these glasses, the existence of a single civilization all over the
world. And that will be the truth.
Over vast areas in the desert of Gobi patches of vitrified soil have been
observed similar to those produced by an atomic explosion.
In a recent study published in the *Literaturnava Gazeta* (1959) Professor
Agrest, who accepts the hypothesis of the Earth having been visited long
ago by interplanetary travelers, relates his discovery among the first texts
introduced into the Bible by Jewish priests of references to beings from
another world who, like Enoch, disappeared into the heavens in mysterious
ark-like vessels. The sacred Hindu texts, such as the *Ramayana* and the
Maha Bharatra contain descriptions of airships appearing in the sky at the
very beginning of time and looking like 'blueish clouds in the shape of an
egg or a luminous globe.'
They could encircle the Earth several times, and were propelled by 'an
ethereal force which struck the ground as they rose,' or by 'a vibration
produced by an invisible force.'
In the *Mausola Purva* we find this singular description, which must have
been incomprehensible to nineteenth-century ethnologists though not to

121

us today: '. . . it was an unknown weapon, an iron thunderbolt, a gigantic messenger of death which reduced to ashes the entire race of the Vrishnis and the Andhakas. The corpses were so burned as to be unrecognizable. Their hair and nails fell out; pottery broke without any apparent cause, and the birds turned white. After a few hours, all foodstuffs were infected. The thunderbolt was reduced to a fine dust.'
And again: 'Cukra, flying on board a high-powered *vimana,* hurled on to the triple city a single projectile charged with all the power of the Universe. An incandescent column of smoke and flame as bright as ten thousand Suns, rose in all its splendor. . . . When the *vimana* returned to Earth, it looked like a splendid block of antimony resting on the ground. . . .' "
If a German engineer, Wilhelm König, had not paid a chance visit to the Museum at Baghdad, it might never have been discovered that some flat stones found in Iraq, and classified as such, were in reality electric batteries, that had been in use two thousand years before Galvani. The archaeological museums are full of objects classified as 'objects of worship,' or 'various' about which nothing is known." (*The Morning of the Magicians,* pp. 179-184).
"Professor Agrest — believes that Sodom and Gomorrah were destroyed by a thermo-nuclear explosion set off by space-travelers either wantonly, or because they considered it necessary to destroy their depots of energy before leaving for the Cosmos.
The Dead Sea scrolls contain the following description: 'A column of smoke and dust rose into the air like a column of smoke issuing from the bowels of the Earth. It rained sulphur and fire on Sodom and Gomorrah, and destroyed the town and the whole plain and all the inhabitants and every growing plant. And Lot's wife looked back and was turned into a pillar of salt. And Lot lived at Isoar, but afterwards went to the mountains because he was afraid to remain at Isoar. The people were warned that they must go away from the place of the future explosion and not stay in exposed places; nor should they look at the explosion but hide beneath the ground. . . .Those fugitives who looked back were blinded and died —' "
(*The Morning of the Magicians,* pp. 306-07).

The propulsion of air-vehicles described in the *Mahabhâratra* involves an "ethereal force which struck the ground as they rose." The said power seems to be the resultant of forces of attraction and repulsion. It is claimed in some occult writings that the air-vehicles of the Atlanteans were so propelled and therefore required no fuel. Voltaire may have alluded to the same type of engineering when he reported the interplanetary jaunt by Micromégas which was effected by similar means.

Speculation on the existence of brilliant prehistoric civilizations is generally unpopular in scientific circles.

"The Cyclic Law or Race-Evolution is most unwelcome to scientists. It is sufficient to mention the fact of "primeval civilization" to excite the frenzy of Darwinians; it being obvious that the further culture and science is pushed back, the more precarious becomes the basis of the ape-ancestor theory. But as Jacolliot says: — 'Whatever there may be in these traditions (submerged continents, etc.), and whatever may have been the place where a civilization more ancient than that of Rome, of Greece, of Egypt, and of

India, was developed, it *is certain that this civilization did exist,* and it is highly important for Science to recover its traces, however feeble and fugitive they be.' Donnelly has proved the fact from the clearest premises, but the Evolutionists will not listen. A *Miocene* civilization upsets the 'universal stone-age' theory, and that of a continuous ascent of man from animalism! And yet Egypt, at least, runs counter to current hypotheses. There is no stone-age visible there, but a more glorious culture is apparent the further back we are enabled to carry our retrospect." (*The Secret Doctrine,* p. 786 fn., Vol. II).

The same facts and beliefs could harly be welcome in political circles were they to come to the attention of a sufficient number of persons — political and other. Modern man is led to believe that he enjoys the quintessence of Civilization. He is accordingly conditioned to count his blessings and to ask a minimum of troublesome questions. Such questions might be asked if the "legend" of brilliant prehistoric civilizations ever proved to be true and to have been suppressed. The majority of XXth Century mankind follows the strategy of the ostrich where the possibility of nuclear and other scientific disaster is concerned. It is more reassuring to lull oneself into a false sense of security than it is to face the horrifying potentialities of modern science. It is easy to place blind faith in the professional father-figures of the political world with the hope that they know everytihng and that they can ward off the nightmare. It is easy to derive comfort from a vague belief that "it can't happen here." It is especially easy to rely on the "fact" that "it has not happened yet." Were the latter "fact" ever shown to be fiction, changes might well take place in the attitude of the average voter. Squarely faced danger might create a demand for a new type of leader. Rule by learned, ethical Men might supersede rule by Image. Questions might be raised by the average person about other facts which have been committed to quiet burial:

"Scientific knowledge is not objective. Like civilization, it is a conspiracy. Quantities of facts are rejected because they would upset preconceived ideas. We live under an inquisitional régime where the weapon most frequently employed against non-conformist reality is derision. Under such conditions, then, what can our knowledge amount to? —
What the world needs is an encyclopedia of rejected facts and realities that have been condemned." (*The Morning of the Magicians,* pp. 144-45).

The nature of destructive forces mentioned in the above texts seems to be defined in the Secret Doctrine as a vibratory "sidereal force" corresponding to certain states of matter. It is observed by Mme Blavatsky that the energy in question — which was discovered in modern times by John Worrell Keely — is none other than the "terrible sidereal force, known to and named by the Atlanteans MASH-MAK, and by the Aryan Rishis in their *Ashtar Vidya* by a name that we do not like to give." —

"It is this vibratory Force, which, when aimed at an army from an *Agni Rath* fixed on a flying vessel, a balloon, according to the instructions found in *Ashtar Vidya*, reduced to ashes 100,000 men and elephants, as easily as it would a dead rat. It is allegorized in the *Vishnu Pûrana*, in the Râmâyana and other works, in the fable about the sage Kapila whose *glance made* a mountain of ashes of King Sagara's 60,000 sons,' and which is explained in the esoteric works, and referred to as the Kapilaksha — 'Kapila's Eye.' "* The force in question is a manifestation of cosmic electricity. Terrestrial electricity is itself regarded as "a sort of atomic vibration." The exposé contains a tabulation of frequencies ranging from "Molecular vibrations" at the rate of 100,000,000 per second to "Inter Aetheric vibrations" at the rate of 24,300,000,000 per second.

The "black magic" which brought lasting fame — and disaster — ** to certain Atlanteans may therefore have involved misused atomic power as we know it, perhaps even a more devastating force emanating from planes of matter which are still unrecognized by official science in our day.

Voltaire may have had in mind more than the *Code of Manu* when he wrote certain pages of *Zadig* in which reference is made to "ancient abuse." The same abuse is known to have resulted in the consignment of many "charms" "to the fire." The "charms" in question may represent "magic" — or secret science — on one plane of interpretation. The "fire" which may have followed the said "abuse" of powers may have been a nuclear holocaust.

As was previously noted, the "legendary" background of *Zadig* is suggested from the very beginning of the story by the name of *Moabdar*. The tribe of Moab is traditionally believed to have displaced aboriginal giants. Similar stories of battles between giants and men are found in all world mythologies. Occult philosophy teaches that the Titans were Fourth Race Atlanteans.*** The name Moabdar may thus have been designed to serve as a link between the "aboriginal giants" or Fourth Race Atlanteans and Fifth Race mankind, particularly the Aryan races. The last two letters of the name — *ar* — may have been intended to suggest the Aryans with whom the last Atlanteans fought a long battle recorded in such Hindu Scriptures as the *Mahabârata*.**** Other meaningful details tend to situate the story within the same prehistoric vista. Zadig does not ignore "the physical sciences as they were known in" his "day." The disciple of Zoroaster or transmitter of the Secret Doc-

---

Ibid., p. 636, Vol. II.
**Ibid.*, p. 293, Vol. II.
***Ibid.*, p. 495, Vol. II.
****The Secret Doctrine*, p. 563, Vol. I.

trine — may be surmised to have knowledge of certain aspects of "physics" which would be termed "hyperphysical" in the modern age. Such knowledge is likely to involve those various states of matter which are potential sources of the "terrible sidereal Force" described above. A certain "balloon" filled with "wind" from which "storms" may be released is featured prominently in the very first lines of *Zadig*. The object in question — and the context within which it appears — suggest energies not usually regarded as "metaphysical."

The name of Almona which is significant on the plane of reincarnating human individuality is also meaningful on a limitless scale. The monad is intimately bound to the dynamic metaphysical principle underlying and guiding universal evolution from the plane of galaxies to the plane of atoms.

The monad — which taxes ordinary powers of definition — seems to be the meeting ground of the subjective and of the objective planes of existence. In the words of Mme Blavatsky, "the term Monad" is one "which may apply equally to the vastest Solar System or the tiniest atom."* The "UNIVERSAL MONAD (collective Elohim) — radiates *from within himself all* those Cosmic Monads that become the centres of activity — progenitors of the numberless Solar systems as well as of every being thereon. Each Cosmic Monad is 'Swayambhûva,' the SELF-BORN, *which becomes the Centre of Force, from within which emerges a planetary chain* —"** Monads may also be designated as *atomic souls* before atoms descend into pure terrestrial form."*** The boundless range of Being which is reflected by the monadic universe seems to be suggested in *Zadig* by the beauty of Almona. One of the amorous priests seeking the favors of the young woman states that "the sun, the moon, and all the fires of heavens were only wills of the wisp when compared to her charms." The fact that the assignations are scheduled by Almona in synchronization with the rising of certain stars further tends to connect the allegorized monad with the cosmic scheme of Being. The first part of the name *Al*mona may be a modified "*El*," a word which means "Sun" in the Codex Nazareus.**** The metaphorical impact of the heroine on cosmic planes is matched by her obvious impact on the plane of flesh and materiality. Voltaire seems to consistently connect the personated monad, *Almona*, with the same vast range of existence as does the Secret

*The Secret Doctrine, p. 21, Vol. I.
**Ibid., p. 311, Vol. II.
***Ibid., p. 619, Vol. I.
****Ibid., p. 463, Vol. I.

Doctrine: from Solar Systems to tiny sparks — "wills of the wisp." The deep irony of the poetic tribute paid by the priests to the beauty of Almona lies in its esoteric substance. The Universal Monad *is* superior to the Monads of Solar Systems. The aspect of "Almona" which corresponds to the Universal Monad deserves the compliment.

The priests are logically situated within the esoteric scheme of monads, atoms — and possible catastrophy. Their leader is addressed by Almona in the following words:

> " 'Elder son of the Big bear, brother of the Bull, cousin of the Big Dog' (Such were the titles of that pontiff) — " (*Les Rendez-vous*, p. 50).

Occult philosophy teaches that Fifth Race Aryan races originated in Northern Regions commonly allegorized as Ursa Major.* The Aryans are believed to be "the descendants of the *yellow* Adams, the gigantic and highly civilized Atlanto-Aryan race."** The designation of the Big Bear as the progenitor of the priests implies the same connection with Atlanteans and Aryans as does the name of Moabdar. The Bull — or "brother" — of the pontiff — symbolizes Aryan races.*** The connection with the Big Dog — Canis Major — a constellation of which Sirius is a part — involves a lesser degree of kinship with the Instructor of Mankind. The admirer of Almona is an esoteric compound representing Atlantean and Aryan races and secret knowledge. His determination to consign certain "charms" to the "fire" is worthy of Atlantean sorcerers. The "charms" or the secret science pertaining to the monad may include sidereal forces and nuclear power.

The emancipation of Almona results from an interview with Zadig during which several levels of knowledge are imparted to the young woman. The text contains a veiled reference to the "ancient abuse" perpetrated against the *Code of Manu* in order to legitimize the burning of widows. The adulteration of other Scriptures and the burning of other heretics is suggested to belong to the same order of crime. The scheme of individual reincarnation is hinted by the monadic quality of the name of Almona, by her projected rounds "from star to star," and by her final status of "liberated soul." Mystical ardor is the ultimate destiny of all. In the words of the young woman, "There is no other way out." The fundamental concept of the "circle of necessity" is present. But "necessity" does not require that the collective human monad follow the path of destruction to serve the greed and the good pleasure of criminal priests. The scheme of evolution will best be served by avoidance of a holocaust

---

*Ibid., p. 463, Vol. I.
**Ibid., p. 768, Vol. II.
***Ibid., p. 426, Vol. II.

the prospect of which does "cause Nature to shudder." The "shudder" of Nature which corresponds to the scientific level of the passage is the "vibratory Force" of sidereal or atomic nature which has long been known to occultists and which seems to have been "abused" in a distant past. The demographic considerations invoked by Zadig in his instruction of Sétoc involve far more than the children of a few widows who may or may not be born or raised. Humanity is in danger of being led into a scientific disaster which is not unprecedented. Humanity can be saved from such a disaster by the diffusion of knowledge long suppressed. The "Great Instructor of Mankind" is more than a metaphysical Messiah dealing in "idealistic nonsense." He is a Savior whose mission concerns the physical — as well as the spiritual — survival of men.

The scientific "instruction" of Almona is esoterically similar to the "instruction" of Sétoc. The benefits received by the merchant from the Red Sea and from India; the age of continents, oceans and stars; the monadic design of evolution embracing and linking galaxies and atoms all belong to the same secret tradition. The five hundred ounces of stolen "silver" and the "jewels" robbed from condemned vidows belong to the same scheme of Judaeo-Christian spoliation which is exposed and frustrated by a disciple of Zoroaster or transmitter of the Secret Doctrine:

> "It is from the Fourth Race that the early Aryans got their knowledge of 'the bundle of wonderful things,' the *Sabha* and *Mayasabha*, mentioned in the Mahabhârata, the gift of Baysâur to the Pándavas. It is from them that they learnt Aëronautics, *Viwân Vidya*, (the 'knowledge of flying in air-vehicles') and, therefore, their great arts of meteorography and meteorology. It is from them, again, that the Aryans inherited their most valuabble science of the hidden virtues of precious and other stones, of chemistry, rather alchemy, of mineralogy, geology, physics and astronomy.
>
> Several times the writer has put to herself the question: 'Is the story of Exodus — in its details at least — as narrated in the Old Testament, original? Or is it, like the story of Moses himself and many others, simply another version of the legends told of the Atlanteans?' For who, upon hearing the story told of the latter, will fail to perceive the great similarity of the fundamental features? The anger of 'God' at the obduracy of Pharaoh, his command to the 'chosen' ones, to spoil the Egyptians, before departing, of their 'jewels of silver' and 'jewels of gold' (Exod. xi.); and finally the Egyptians and their Pharaoh drowned in the Red Sea (xiv.)." (*The Secret Doctrine*, p. 426, Vol. II).

The initial chapters of *Zadig* stress the limitations of Maya: the Illusion of the senses and the Illusion of Divisiveness or separate Being. The veiled substance of the same chapters boldly transcends the Mayavic concepts formed by the average Western Man where Space, Matter and Time are concerned. Humanity is situated within a monadic Universe of dynamic nature and dizzy dimension. Matter is suggested to act as the vehicle of Universal Force or Spirit. History overflows orthodox boundaries reclaiming in the process the "legend" of brilliant prehistoric civilizations. The "jewels of gold" of Ancient Tradition are not inaccessible to the esoteric reader of Voltaire.

The chapter of *Zadig* which is entitled *The Fisherman* prolongs the theme of salvation which dominates other passages of the story. An unnamed, kindly merchant has been deserted by his wife and stripped of his possessions by her wicked associates. The destitute man tries unsuccessfully to obtain food by fishing. Zadig arrives providentially as the frustrated angler prepares to jump into the river.

The personal heartbreak of Zadig who mourns the reported death of Astarté is temporarily forgotten. Solace is found in aiding an unfortunate. Voltaire reveals the vibrant depth of his own compassion in the following passage:

> "It is claimed that one feels less miserable when one is not alone. But according to Zoroaster, it is not out of wickedness, it is out of need. One then feels attracted to a wretched creature as to one's fellow man. The joy of a happy man would be an insult; but two unfortunates are like two weak small trees which, supporting each other, strengthen each other against the storm." (*The Fisherman*, p. 56).

One might easily conclude that misery loves company. But the popular axiom is clearly rejected by the disciple of Zoroaster. The Pascalian "thinking reed" is also a suffering "reed" capable of transcending its own misery. Concern with the plight of others yields more than comparative relief. It is an important step toward defeating the illusion of separate existence. It is an indispensable stage of growth of future "trees" of knowledge. It is positive fulfillment. The well-known precept: "Love thy neighbor as thyself" reflects the Far Eastern concept of Universal Oneness. On the plane of true being, the neighbor *is* oneself. As is indicated by the words "strengthen each other," compassion is a source as well as a requirement of spiritual "strength."

> "The doctrine of Buddha is entirely based on practical works. A general love of all beings, human and animal, is its nucleus." (*Isis Unveiled*, p. 288, Vol. 2).

> "We see that the Golden Rule did not originate with Jesus; that its birthplace was India. Do what we may, we cannot deny *Sakya-Muni-Buddha* a less remote antiquity than several centuries before the birth of Jesus. In seeking a model for his system of ethics why should Jesus have gone to the foot of the Himalayas rather than to the foot of Sinai, but that the doctrines of Manu and Gautama harmonized exactly with his own philosophy, while those of Jehovah were to him abhorrent and terrifying. The

Hindus taught to return *good for evil,* but the Jehovistic command was 'an eye for an eye' and 'a tooth for a tooth.' " (*Isis Unveiled,* pp. 164-65, Vol. 2).

Zadig and the fisherman are affected by similar sets of forces. Oppressed by evil, they are nevertheless guided by compassion. The former merchant forgets his misfortune as he becomes aware of the grief of Zadig. The hero has experienced the ruthlessness of the Mosaic realm. The fisherman has experienced the ruthlessness of Orcan. Orcan is none other than the aggressive and successful suitor of Sémire. His name, his violence, and his polygamous mores suggest the Coran—Koran—of Islam. The victim of one perverted religion has much in common with the victim of another.

The sensitivity of the two friends is not limited to humans. The frustrated angler learns a valuable lesson. True life should not be sought in destruction of other life. The vegetarian views which were clearly expressed by Voltaire in subsequent works may be inferred from *The Fisherman* as they may be inferred from *The Supper.* Voltaire notes in *La Princesse de Babylone* that the "riverbank dwellers of Ganges" ate nothing which had "received from the gods the celestial gift of life" and that a good meal is one in which one does not see any "disguised corpses." The superficial irony of the following plea — made by animals — does not conceal the earnestness of Voltaire the vegetarian:

"Men finally acquired the habit of eating us; instead of conversing with and learning from us. The barbarians! Should they not be convinced that having the same organs as they do, the same feelings, the same needs, the same desires, we had what is called *a soul* just as they do; that we were their brothers, and that only the wicked should be cooked and eaten? We are your brothers to such an extent that the Great Being, the Eternal Being and the Source of Form, having made an agreement with men, included us expressly in the covenant. He forbade you to feed on our blood, and forbade us to suck yours." (*La Princesse de Babylone,* Ch. III).

Reverence of life is manifest in the prevention of suicide which is achieved by Zadig. The despondency of the young hero who believes that Astarté is lost to him forever equals and may surpass the despair of the destitute fisherman. But the disciple of Zoroaster never contemplates the illusive "escape" of physical death. Nor does he condone such an "escape" in the case of another person. Occult philosophy teaches that severe penalties are incurred by suicides. Evil and wretched entities are believed to be products of self-inflicted death:

"Porphyry presents to us some hideous facts whose verity is substantiated in the experience of every student of magic. 'The *soul*,' says he, 'having even after death a certain affection for its body, an affection proportioned to the violence with which their union was broken, we see many spirits hovering in despair about their earthly remains; we even see them eagerly seeking the putrid remains of other bodies; but above all, freshly spilled blood, which seems to impart to them for the moment some of the faculties of life.' " (*Isis Unveiled*, p. 344, Vol. 1).

The intended grave of the fisherman adds a meaningful element of symbolism to the chapter. The river — or eternal stream of life — cannot be ignored or altered with impunity. Zadig is a "fisher of men" who transforms waters of death into waters of life. The fisherman regains hope and joy. The "fellow" is a neophyte or "twice-born."

The role of the young hero is openly defined by the grateful fisherman. Zadig is hailed as a *Savior*:

"As he spoke thus he gave to the fisherman half of all the money which he had brought from Arabia, and the fisherman, overwhelmed and delighted, kissed the feet of the friend of Cador and said: 'You are a saving angel!' " (*Le Pêcheur*, pp. 58-59).

The appellation of "saving angel" contains the answer to a question asked by the fisherman himself. Puzzling as it may seem, the sadness of a Savior can be explained:

" 'But how can it be,' said the fellow, 'that the one who gives may be more pitiable than the one who receives?' " (*Le Pêcheur*, p. 59).

Saviors are voluntary expatriates from Nirvânic bliss. They are "diamond-hearted" beings who consent the great sacrifice of incarnation out of love of mankind. The idea of voluntary reincarnation which is connected with the concept of "Savior" seems to be conveyed by the reply of Zadig:

" 'Your greatest misfortune,' Zadig went on, 'was need — I am grieving in my heart.' " (*Le Pêcheur*, p. 59).

Material "need" is esoteric "necessity." "Necessity" is the cycle of evolution through which all life must proceed to ultimate release. The heartache of the Savior which is emphatically distinct from "need" adds to the probability of his being on earth by choice. The "angelic" component of the expression "Saving angel" is also significant. The word "angel" has the etymological meaning of "messenger," a concept clearly compatible with the concept of "Savior" and "Instructor of Mankind." The grieving heart of Zadig which is exoterically wounded by the arrows of Cupid is tormented by another form of Love on the esoteric plane of the text. It may be compared without blasphemy with another Sacred Heart.

"Fishing" is surprisingly successful in the end. Zadig himself is the miraculous "catch" of the candidate to suicide. The "Fish" — or DAG — which is a Messiah in world mythology has attained his goal. He has reached a "fellow." He has been "caught."

The same kind of "fishing" is celebrated by numerous "smugglers" of the Secret Doctrine.

THE BAIT

"Come live with me, and be my love,
And we will some new pleasures prove
Of golden sands, and crystal brooks,
With silken lines, and silver hooks.

There will the river whispering run
Warm'd by thy eyes, more than the Sun;
And there the enamour'd fish will stay,
Begging themselves they may betray.

When thou wilt swim in that live bath,
Each fish, which every channel hath,
Will amorously to thee swim,
Gladder to catch thee, than thou him. — "
(John Donne).

The Bottle to the sea — the esoteric message of countless ages — is also caught by a poor, baffled, dazzled fisherman:

"Un soir enfin, les vents qui soufflent des Florides
L'entraînent vers la France et ses bords pluvieux.
Un pêcheur accroupi sous des rochers arides
Tire dans ses filets le flacon précieux.
Il court, cherche un savant et lui montre sa prise,
Et, sans oser l'ouvrir, demande qu'on lui dise
Quel est cet élixir noir et mystérieux.

Quel est cet élixir? Pêcheur c'est la science,
C'est l'élixir divin que boivent les esprits,
Trésor de la pensée et de l'expérience,
Et si tes lourds filets, ô pêcheur, avaient pris,
L'or qui toujours serpente aux veines du Mexique,
Les diamants de l'Inde et les perles d'Afrique,
Ton labeur de ce jour aurait eu moins de prix."

("One evening at last, the winds blowing from the Floridas
Carry it toward France and her rainy shores.

131

A fisherman, hunched under arid rocks
Draws in his nets the precious flask.
He runs, finds a scholar and shows his catch to him,
And, not daring open it, asks to be told
What that black and mysterious elixir is.

What is that elixir? Fisherman it is science,
It is the divine elixir drunk by the spirits,
Treasure of thought and experience,
And if your heavy nets, o fisherman had caught
The gold ever winding in the lodes of Mexico,
The diamonds of India and the African pearls,
Your labor of this day would have had less worth.")

The full value of the miraculous "catch" defies terrestrial calculation. No one — least of all a Sage or Savior — can expect its boundless worth to be perceived instantly. The angler will need time to become fully aware of the size of the treasure which came with the person of "Zadig."

The neophyte is quick to apply the teachings of the master. Wishing to receive his due only, the victim of spoliation does not seek revenge when his property is returned. Having "become wise," he rejects the advances of his treacherous and faithless wife. The fisherman is engaged in "the right path." Like Almona and Sétoc he is receptive to the influence of a superior guide. His responsiveness to the Savior is another proof of human capacity for progress.

The episode itself is a delightful example of esoteric "angling." The fisherman expresses hope that "the famous minister Zadig" will compensate him for his original loss. The new friend of the hero seems unaware of an important fact. He is speaking to the minister Zadig himself. The identity of the Savior remains exoterically unrevealed — and unasked. Zadig simply states that he knows the minister in question and that the minister is an honest man. The reader tends to smile at the naiveté and lack of curiosity of the fisherman. The same reader would do well to ask himself the following questions: Who is the intriguing "fisher of men?" Who — or what — is "Zadig?" The value of an inquisitive turn of mind is stressed by default. The esoteric "hook" is in full view. Voltaire — and his fishing brothers — are not miserly where the amount or quality of "bait" is concerned. The masterful angling of esoteric writers is designed to produce direct communication between author and reader. The spirit which is captive in their works can abolish time, space, death, and the illusion of separate being when true contact is established. Such "tablets" as those of "Zadig" do speak to him who can "listen."

The exoteric mystery of the identity of Zadig is paralleled by the nameless status of the fisherman. The new friend of the hero is simply designated as "the fellow" — "le bonhomme." Both men function on a "nameless" or spiritual plane where the lower self is transcended. The expression "fellow' or literally "good man" is shown to be the esoteric equivalent of the Higher human Principle in *The Key to Theosophy*. The namelessness which it conveys is consistent with the general tenor of the chapter relating a transition from Mayavic to spiritual planes. The fisherman — and the reader — are insistently reminded to lift their sights beyond personal concern and terrestrial vision. Physical misery is suggested to be of less moment than the misery of the heart. Each man forgets his own misfortune in awareness of the grief of the other. Material destitution is overcome by spiritual wealth. The need of food becomes subordinated to need of superior nourishment. Literal fish proves less meaningful than does symbolic "Fish" and its incalculable treasure. The "nameless' element of *The Fisherman* belongs to the non-contingent spark to which the entire works and life of Voltaire are dedicated: the Truth-Loving Principle which somehow survives and grows in the heart of every man through darkest periods of human evolution.

The historical meaning of the chapter logically follows the experience of Zadig in Babylon, "Egypt," and "Arabia." As was previously noted, the oppressors of the fisherman seem to represent a certain branch of World Religion: Islam. The "fellow" has been betrayed by a wife who shares certain character traits with Missouf. The beaten Jewess rejects and curses a potential Savior. The fisherman's wife deserts and wrongs her kind husband. Goodness is scorned and abused in each case. But the masochism of Missouf is paralleled in seemingly opposite direction by the sadism of the latter woman. Vanity, greed, and lust for power drive her into the arms of Orcan who combines the same traits in his own personality. Masochism and sadism are two aspects of the same worship of brute force. The historical meaning of the encounter of Zadig with the fisherman may therefore be summarized as follows: Already wronged and diverted from its westerly course by the Mosaic tradition (Moabdar, the "Egyptian," "Missouf"), the carrier of the Primitive Wisdom-Religion (Zadig) comes into indirect contact with aggressive representatives of Moslem faith. The mystique of theft and violence of which Arbogad, the "Arab," has given a preview, is prolonged by the actions of "Orcan." The fragmentation of the original doctrine upheld by the disciple of Zoroaster results in the appearance of two sado-masochistic creeds.

The word "Orcan" — or anagram of "Coran" — resembles the name of *Orkhan,* a Turkish Sultan who lived in the XIVth Century and who created the famous corps of warring monks known as "Janissaries." The probable allusion to the sultan seems to stand in the same semi-esoteric relationship to Orcan as Arbogast does to Arbogad. The achievements of the sultan may easily be connected with the exoteric surface of *Zadig*, a story featuring many violent events taking place in the Near East at the instigation of various "janissaries." But the apparent allusion to Orkhan may lead the reader no further than the historical personage. It will be found in the course of the present study that Voltaire made frequent use of historically known persons whose names function as esoteric "decoys."

A certain pattern of Justice may be perceived in the story of the fisherman. It is consistent with the outcome of other acts of spoliation and abuse which are reported in preceding chapters of *Zadig*. The exposure of the thieving Jew and the fiasco suffered by the corrupt priests have a counterpart in the redress obtained by the fisherman. The victim of "Orcan" recovers his stolen property in the end. He also receives half of the money brought by Zadig from "Arabia." The finally righted wrong is suggestively linked to the gift — or message — of "Zadig," a "saving angel" or "messenger."

Another pattern may be perceived in the two salvations performed by the hero. Almona is saved from fire. The fisherman is saved from water. The presence of the two elements suggests correspondence to a tenet of the Secret Doctrine according to which the earth is periodically ravaged by cataclysms alternately involving fire and water. The same belief in cataclysmic floods and upheavals of volcanic character will be expressed in *Candide*. The Savior featured in *Zadig* is suggested to have the ability to prevent physical disasters which threaten the collective human monad or the man of good will.

Zadig resumes his wandering search for Astarté. He arrives in a meadow where several women are "looking for something with great application." The women are slaves who have been ordered to find a basilisk. The animal is needed to prepare a remedy for the ailing master of the domain: The situation is explained as follows by one of the women:

> "It is for our lord and master Ogul whose castle you see on the bank of this river, at the end of the meadow. We are his very humble slaves, his lordship Ogul is sick; his physician has ordered him to eat a basilisk cooked in rose water, and since it is a very rare animal, which never lets itself be caught except by women, his lordship Ogul has promised to choose as his beloved wife the one of us who would bring him a basilisk." (*Le Basilic*, p. 60).

The animal which can be caught by women only — and which is generally regarded as a mythical reptile — brings to mind the story of Eve and the serpent. That the said serpent is a myth in its official capacity of devil is promptly stated by Zadig:

134

" ' — learn that there is no basilisk in nature." (*Le Basilic,* p. 66).

The devil exists only in the minds of men. It is the fabrication of perverse beings impelled and compelled to reign through terror. The name of the "lord" who needs a basilisk in order to survive is suggestive of "ghouls" — Ogul, Fr. "goule" — and related vampirism. The sickness of the "lord" is viewed in identical manner by Voltaire and by occultists:

"We have already noticed the confession of an eminent prelate that the elimination of Satan from theology would be fatal to the perpetuity of the Church." (*Isis Unveiled,* p. 67, Vol. 2).

The theological genesis of much-abused Satan is traced as follows in the Secret Doctrine:

"Satan never assumed an anthropomorphic, individualized shape, until the creation by man, of a 'one *living* personal god,' had been accomplished; and then merely as a matter of prime necessity. A screen was needed: a scape-goat to explain the cruelty, blunders, and but too-evident injustice, perpetrated by him for whom absolute perfection, mercy and goodness were claimed." (*The Secret Doctrine,* p. 412, Vol. 1).

Satan is the personated form of one aspect of universal dualism:

"Everywhere the speculations of the Kabalists treat of Evil as a FORCE, which is antagonistic, but at the same time essential to Good, as giving it vitality and existence, which it could never have otherwise. There would be no *life possible* (in the *Mayavic* sense) without Death, nor regeneration and reconstruction without destruction. Plants would perish in eternal sunlight, and so would man, who would become an automaton without the exercise of his free will and aspirations after that sunlight, which would lose its being and value for him had he nothing but light. Good is infinite and eternal only in the eternally concealed from us, and this is why we imagine it eternal. On the manifested planes, one equilibrates the other." (*The Secret Doctrine,* pp. 415-16, Vol. I).

Satan belongs to the ill-acquired, degraded fund of Pagan allegory which forms the basis of Christian dogma:

"The serpent, the Tree of Knowledge of Good and Evil, and the Tree of Life, are all symbols transplanted from the soil of India." (*The Secret Doctrine,* p. 215, Vol. II).

Satan-Lucifer — whose latter name means "carrier of light" — has the merit of being the foe of ignorance. In the words of Mme Blavatsky,

"— ignorance is death, and knowledge alone gives immortality."* The Voltairian view of the serpent which is presented in *Le Taureau blanc* is identical to corresponding tenets of occult philosophy. The much-slandered scapegoat of the anthropomorphic God is its own able advocate. The suggestion which he gave to mankind in general and to Eve in particular is defended with logic and humor:

THE SERPENT

" 'I am being maligned: I gave her (Eve) the best advice in the world. She honored me with her trust. My opinion was that she and her husband should eat their fill of the fruit of the tree of science. I thought I was pleasing in this to the master of things. A tree so necessary to mankind did not seem to me to have been planted to be useless. Would the master have wished to be served by ignorants and by idiots? Is not the mind (or "spirit") made to gain enlightenment, to perfect itself? Must one not know good and evil in order to do one and to avoid the other? Certainly people should thank me." (*Le Taureau blanc,* Ch. III).

The acquisition of knowledge is "necessary" to mankind in the esoteric, evolutionary sense. The kind of "God" who "would wish to be served by ignorants and by idiots" is offered to the judgment of the reader. One may surmise that he would indeed have created man in his own image. Such a deity is unlikely to be the true "master of things."

The ailing "lord" of the castle is quickly cured by Zadig who prescribes a simple regimen of exercise and temperance. Common sense defeats the combination of basilisk and "rose-water" which amounts to theological superstition. The "rose-water" element of the remedy is a probable allusion to negotiable spiritual whitewash or penance and similar practices of Christian religions.

A passage seems to proclaim the folly of occult science:

" — one always enjoys good health with temperance and exercise — the art of reconciling intemperance and health is as futile as the philosopher's stone, judiciary astrology and the theology of the magi." (*Le Basilic,* p. 66).

Occult philosophy defines the philosopher's stone in the following terms:

"Man is the philosopher's stone spiritually — a triune or trinity in unity,' as Philaletes expresses it. But he is also that stone physically. The latter is but the effect of the cause, and the cause is the universal solvent of every-thing — divine spirit — . Man is a correlation of chemical physical forces, as well as a correlation of spiritual powers. The latter react on the physical powers of man in proportion to the development of the earthly man." (*Isis Unveiled,* p. 309, Vol. 1).

136

The barb directed at the philosopher's stone seems to be aimed at a misconception.

Astronomy and astrology are subjects of abundant comment in the Secret Doctrine. The Pythagorean or mathematical element of the Primitive Wisdom-Religion is closely bound to astrological and astronomical lore.

> "Astrology is a science as infallible as astronomy itself, with the condition, however, that its interpreters must be equally infallible; and it is this condition, *sine qua non,* so very difficult of realization, that has always proved a stumbling block to both. Astrology is to exact astronomy what psychology is to exact physiology." (*Isis Unveiled,* p. 259 , Vol. 1).

Voltaire seems to ridicule astrology and related beliefs in a passage of *Le Siècle de Louis XIV.* The fact that "astrologers were consulted and believed" in the XVIIth Century is noted. The general acceptance of predictions made in one particular case is regarded as a sign of "credulity" or "weakness:"

> "This credulity, the most unfailing sign of ignorance, was so generally accepted, that care was taken to have an astrologer hidden near the bedroom of the Queen of Anne of Austria, at the time of the birth of Louis XIV — The same weakness which made fashionable the absurd futility of judiciary astrology caused people to believe in possession and evil spells; it was all made into a point of religion; one saw nothing but priests casting out demons." (*Le Siècle de Louis XIV,* Ch. II).

Voltaire once wrote that chance does not exist and that the universe is governed by mathematical law. Such a statement is not easily reconciled with contempt for the correlation of forces forming the basis of astrology. The above verdict of "credulity" and "weakness" seems to be directed at the "stumbling block" mentioned by Mme Blavatsky: inadequate interpreters and deliberate quackery. The concealment of an astrologer "hidden near the bedroom of the Queen Ann of Austria" at the time of birth of Louis XIV suggests the hocus-pocus of a charlatan. Astrological calculations bearing on the destiny of a person are irrelevant to the whereabouts of anyone else at any given time. It should also be noted that the unfavorable judgment of Voltaire is openly connected with questionable "points of religion" and with general ignorance or "weakness." Two opposite interpretations are permissible. Astrology as a whole is unworthy of serious thought. Astrology requires considerable knowledge to be properly evaluated — and practiced.

Voltaire also reports in *Le Siècle de Louis XIV* that astrological predictions were made to Henry IV and that they were received "seriously" by the grave and severe duke of Sully.* It would be interesting to know

---

*Ch. II.

if the predictions referred in any way to the assassination which befell the King of France. The substance of prophecies remains intriguingly untold. Voltaire either scorned to expose their fallacy — or gave a silent grin to their truthfulness. The surprising attitude of the duke of Sully invites two lines of speculation. Learned and intelligent persons are occasionally found to believe in astrology. Are such persons mentally "weak?" Should an effort be made to understand the basis of their belief?

The combination of words: "credulity," "ignorance," and "weakness" — which are synonymous terms in the esoteric vocabulary — suggests that belief in astrology should rest on a firm basis of scientific knowledge. Occult lore is wrongly made into "a point of religion." One may conclude that it rightfully belongs to another realm which may be the realm of Natural Law as defined in the Secret Doctrine. Judiciary astrology is skillfully linked to possession and evils spells which fall into the category of dubious "points of religion." Popular misconceptions and general ignorance seem to be chief targets of the denunciation of Voltaire.

It is stated in the Secret Doctrine that "horoscopes and judiciary astrology are not quite based on a fiction."* But it is also stressed that modern astrology suffers from the same materialism as do other areas of modern knowledge. The great vertical distance representing the "fall" of astrology from ancient times to the XIXth Century is measured with eloquence:

> "Primitive astrology was as far above modern, judiciary astrology, so called, as the guides (the Planets and Zodiacal signs) are above the lampposts."
> (*The Secret Doctrine*, p. 332, Vol. V — Adyar Edition —).

Voltairian views of judiciary procedure used in his times are well known. Judiciary astrology may safely be assumed to be as corrupt as the rest. The "theology of the magi" or priests belongs to the same general enterprise of spiritual imposture which he consistently denounced.

The Basilisk contains misleading references to various superstitions which tend to be identified with occult science in the popular mind. Like other related barbs playfully scattered in Voltairian writings, such attacks do not resist careful examination. They are faithful echoes of corresponding views expressed in the Secret Doctrine.

Zadig is intrigued and attracted by one of the slaves. The woman is set apart from the pathetic sisterhood of hunters by her inaction. Unlike her companions, she is not looking for a basilisk. She is apparently aware of the futility of the search or of the fact that "there is no basilisk in

---

The Secret Doctrine, p. 647, Vol. I.

nature." She may also be aware of the dubious quality of the promised "reward." The slave is a veiled woman of majestic appearance. Zadig faces a startling experience:

> "When he was on the edge of a small stream, he found there another lady lying on the grass, and who was not looking for anything. Her figure appeared majestic, but her face was covered with a veil. She was leaning toward the stream; deep sighs were coming out of her mouth. She held in her hand a small rod with which she traced signs on a fine sand which was between the grass and the stream. Zadig had the urge to see what the woman was writing; he came near, he saw the letter Z, then an A; he was astounded; then appeared a D; he trembled. Never was surprise equal to his own when he saw the last two letters of his name." (*Le Basilic*, p. 60).

The symbolism of the waters of life — physical and spiritual — is conveyed by the presence of the stream. The grass probably represents an inferior form of life which is bound to earth, trapped in matter; in short to the realm of Maya. The lady reclining between water and lawn, true life and illusory being, is a link between both planes. The sand upon which the name of Zadig is traced is a substance frequently mentioned in esoteric texts. The coveted metamorphosis from a grain of sand to a diamond will be remembered from the chapter portraying Arbogad. The sandy deposits which constitute part of the Pineal Gland are believed by occultists to be closely bound to spiritual consciousness. Such deposits are regarded as remains of the now extinct Third Eye, the organ of immediate cognition once possessed by a semi-ethereal mankind.* The veiled woman is symbolically situated in a corresponding zone: a meeting-place of matter and spirit.

The amazement of the young man watching the appearance of "the last two letters of his name" suggests the possible alteration of one or perhaps two letters. It is hinted once more that the concealed identity of the hero is DAG, the Savior.

The first two letters of the name ZADIG are the last and first letters of the alphabet. They are commonly used to represent the Principle and the End of All Things:

> " 'I am the Alpha and Omega, the beginning and the ending — I am the first and the last,' says the Lord to John." (*Isis Unveiled*, p. 277, Vol. 2).

The reversal of the letters from the alphabetical order suggests the basic precept of all spiritual quests which is expressed in French by the

---

The Secret Doctrine, pp. 296-97, Vol. II.

terms: "remonter à la source" — "going back to the source." The goal of evolution is the return to the source of Being.

The Chaldean DAG and the Hindu god Vishnu are two versions of the same divine figure which is also represented by the mythological fish-man Oannes.

> " 'It is he' (Vishnu) says the sacred book, 'who taught men after the diluvium, all that was necessary for their happiness. One day he plunged into the water and returned no more, for the earth had covered itself again with vegetation, fruit, and cattle.
> But he had taught the Brahmanas the secret of all things.'
> So far, we see in this narrative the *double* of the story given by the Babylonian Berosus about Oannes, the fish-man who is no other than Vishnu — unless indeed we have to believe that it was Chaldea which civilized India." (*Isis Unveiled*, pp. 256-57, Vol. 2).

The fish-man Oannes-Vishnu is mentioned in an early chapter of *Zadig*. One of his vocal devotees attends the supper which brings together persons of various nationalities and creeds. The same religious exhibitionist speaks aggressively and dogmatically on behalf of his God:

> " 'You are mistaken,' said a Chaldean who was near him (Zadig), 'it is to the fish Oannes that one owes such great benefits, and it is just to pay tribute to him only. Everyone will tell you that he was a divine being, that he had a golden tail, with a handsome human head, and that he came out of the water to come and preach on the land three hours a day. He had several children who were kings as everyone knows. I have his portrait at home, which I venerate as I ought to.' " (*Le Souper*, p. 47).

The deep meaning of the passage is veiled by an element of misleading comedy. The "true believer" is smug, obtuse, and arrogant. The audience is expected to bow to the superiority of his faith, hence to his own personal excellence. Religion is popular myth divested of profound substance, what "everyone will tell you," and a conversation piece: a portrait of a divine being proudly kept and displayed at home. The Chaldean is obsessed with inferior aspects of faith: conformity, personal standing, and the exoteric facade of symbolism. By the same token he is blind to the presence facing him. Zadig is the much-vaunted messenger whose portrait he reveres while he cannot recognize the original.

The situation explodes the norms of ordinary humor. But it is filled with sad significance. The most aggressive spokesmen of a Savior are least able to grasp his true essence. Once again — as in the cases of Missouf and Arbogad — a divine presence remains unperceived. One may surmise that the same fate might befall Christ were he to return to earth.

The name ZADIG combines the idea of a Savior — DAG — and the idea of a return to the source. The title character is a "Great Instructor of Mankind" whose mission is intended to aid the scheme of human evolution.

The slave wistfully writing the name of the hero on the sand proves to be Queen Astarté. A significant detail can easily be overlooked by the reader who tends to concentrate on the emotional content of the "romantic" reunion. Hearing the familiar voice of the man she loves, the Queen raises her veil to look at the stranger:

> "Hearing that voice, hearing those words, the lady raised her veil with a trembling hand, looked at Zadig, exclaiming from emotion, from surprise, and from joy, and yielding to all the various impulses which beset her instantly, fell unconscious into his arms. It was Astarté herself, it was the Queen of Babylon, it was the one whom Zadig adored, and whom he felt guilty of adoring; it was the one whose destiny he had so lamented and feared. He was temporarily deprived of the use of his senses." (*Le Basilic*, pp. 60-61).

Astarté is a mythological counterpart of *Isis*. The reunion of the lovers therefore transcends the plane of ordinary romance. It is a crucial event in which "the dominion" of Mayavic or sensory "phantasy" is overcome by Pure Spirit. Metarialistic illusion is defeated. The symbolic veil of Isis is raised. Isis Unveiled equals Truth.

"Isis Unveiled" is found in various forms — ranging from grotesque comedy to loftiest lyricism — in the texts of esoteric writers. The unveiling experience — which supplied the title and the inspiration of a most important book — has ever been the goal of spiritual seekers. To be worthy of their own names, Science and Man must be willing and able to look beyond the *"veil"* of *matter*:

> "How is it that they who had so firmly believed, but a short time since, that matter was destructible and passed out of existence, and now have learned to believe as firmly that it does not, are unable to tell us more about it? Why are they forced in this case as in many others to return to a doctrine taught by Democritus twenty-four centuries ago? — And if they say that 'force is incapable of destruction, except, by the same power which created it,' then they tacitly admit the existence of such a *power*, and have therefore *no right* to throw obstacles in the way of those, who bolder than themselves, try to penetrate beyond, and find that they can only do so by lifting the *veil of Isis*." (*Isis Unveiled*, p. 408, Vol. 1).

A certain "boldness" or "daring" is required to "lift the veil." The same concept of spiritual "daring" may be tested with good results in numerous esoteric texts.

The reunion of the "lovers" features details commonly found in reports of mystical experience. Astarté faints. The young hero is for a moment "deprived of the use of his senses." Sensory perception is eclipsed by higher vision as the "veil" is "lifted." Or, in the words which have already been quoted, "As the sun puts out a fire, so spirit puts out the eyes of mere intellect." The same process is explained in *Isis Unveiled*:

> "In the Mysteries, the third part of the sacred rites was called *Epopteia*, or revelation, reception into the secrets. In substance it means that stage of divine clairvoyance when everything pertaining to this earth disappears, and earthly sight is paralysed, and the soul is united free and pure with its Spirit, or God. But the real significance of the word is "overseeing," from *optomai* — I see myself." (*Isis Unveiled*, p. 90, Vol. 2).

The lifting of the veil is accompanied by trembling. The sound of the voice of the beloved causes the hero to tremble. The lady raises her veil with a trembling hand. The esoteric reader is reminded of the words of Almona: mystical ardor causes Nature to "shudder." Trembling hands will be found in a corresponding passage of *Micromégas*. The modern mutation of Isis will be "a trembling woman of majestic proportions" in *Candide*. Candide himself will "tremble like a philosopher" in Chapter III of the story bearing his name. The physical repercussions of the first gaze beyond the veil usually involve a pounding heart and trembling.

The identity of Astarté and Isis is no esoteric mystery to students of mythology. It is confirmed in *Zadig* by two sets of correspondences. Isis is the feminine counterpart of Vishnu or DAG:

> "Lakmi, or Lakshmi, the passive or feminine counterpart of Vishnu, the creator and the preserver, is also called Adi-Maya. She is the Mother of the World,' Dhatri, the Venus- Aphrodite of the Greeks, also Isis and Eve." (*Isis Unveiled*, p. 259, Vol. 2).

Isis-Astarté is connected with the star of the "Great Instructor of Mankind:" Sirius.

> " 'I am the Queen of these regions,' says the Egyptian Isis; I was the first to reveal to mortals the mysteries of wheat and corn . . . I am she who rises in the constellation of the dog . . . (Dog-star) — ' " (*The Secret Doctrine*, p. 374, Vol. II).

Zadig and his beloved form a mystical couple united by an irrepressible force: the mutual attraction between Man and Truth. Any apparent conflict of the hero torn between spirituality and love dissolves on the esoteric plane. Knowledge, Truth, and Love are ONE.

The typical device of exoteric contradiction resolved on the esoteric level of meaning is frequently called to attention by its users. "Flowers" are noted to be "contradictory" until one learns to understand them. Such is an important finding of The Little Prince.* Proust — another lover of deceptive "flowers" — has the following comment on the same subject: "— the 'althoughs' are always unrecognized 'becauses.'—"***Voltaire calls attention in *Micromégas* to the concealed harmony which underlies the "profusion of varieties" of the manifest universe. Chaos prevails on the surface of things. Oneness may be perceived beyond the veil of differentiated matter. Esoteric literature — which is the mirror of the universe — reflects the same dualism of phenomenal confusion or contradiction and noumenal Unity.

Truth is allegorized as woman in countless esoteric works. The human symbol of incarnation and Maya is far more than a representation of the nether pole of being. She is the carrier of an intuitive spark which is all the greater for its struggle on material planes. The dual esoteric potency of female figures is suggested by the person and by the evolution of Almona. It is illustrated by the evolution of Astarté and by her situation on the sand — between matter and spirit. It is allegorized by the opposite and complementary figures of Delilah and Eva in the work of Vigny. The debased Eve of Christian tradition is no more — and no less — than the vehicle of spiritual Sophia. The poles of human existence and aspiration are fused in eternal Eve. We must learn to take with a sizable grain of salt the apparent misogyny of numerous esoteric writers. Their female images of Maya are etched without indulgence. But the divine Being in Eva receives magnificent equal time.

Intermediate planes exist between opposite poles of feminine allegory: Maya and Eva. The same scale of "degrees" may explain the following remark of Marcel Proust:

"There exist between the merits of the different women of the world only insignificant degrees." (*A la Recherche du temps perdu*, p. 276, Vol. III).

The above statement may constitute a clue to the concealed identity of female Proustian characters. There is — to be sure — "not a single character" in the *Recherche* who can be understood or identified by means of "a key."*** But the occult attributes of women to which reference is made by the author invite speculation. "Not a single character" could easily mean "many."

The reunion of Zadig and Astarté is followed by a review of their adventures. Much has happened to the lovers since the time of their separation. The tribulations of the young man have been equalled — if not surpassed — by the misfortunes of the Queen.

---

*The Little Prince, Ch. VIII.
**A la Recherche du temps perdu, p. 438, Vol. I.
***The Secret Doctrine, p. 281, Vol. III.

143

Missouf occupies an important place in the conversation. Her resemblance to Astarté has brought her to the attention of Moabdar. She has become his tyrannical consort. Her accession to power has brought chaos to the kingdom. Hidden in a colossal statue, Astarté has observed the decay wrought on her former realm by the false and erratic double who represents the Judaeo-Christian tradition. Using a concealed — occult — vantage point, Astarté renders an oracle which terrifies the King and drives him insane. The undoing and death of Moabdar are followed by the downfall of Missouf.

A dim view is again conveyed of the "supernatural." The statue which is located in a temple seems to be connected with sacerdotal trickery. But a staggering Truth is concealed beyond appearance. Were Moabdar prepared to gaze beyond the veil, he would perceive a rationally understandable presence. He would know that speaking statues can be manifestations of Natural Law. But the influence of "Missouf" produces a fit of superstitious terror. The short-lived reign of the capricious Jewess marks the decline from Pagan Knowledge — Truth-Astarté — to Judaism. The same general trend of decline is recorded in the Secret Doctrine which shows Science degenerating "into Sorcery, taking later on the shape of exoteric religions, of idolatry full of superstitions, and man, or hero-worship."*

The theme of Truth too simple and too fantastic to be believed is once more present. It is often exploited by esoteric writers who can safely present unbelievable offerings without benefit of veils and without fear of literal interpretation. In the words of Marcel Proust, "The infinite field of the possible stretches wide open, and if, by chance reality offered itself to our eyes, it would be so far beyond the possible that, in sudden dizziness, stumbling into that abruptly erected wall, we would fall over backwards."**

The parallel meetings of Truth — Astarté — with Zadig and Moabdar deserve comparison. The Queen raises her veil upon meeting her devotee. Such an encounter is favored by the goddess. But a "wall" of impenetrable matter stands between her and the unworthy. Moabdar perceives only a terrifying voice. Fortified by sustained efforts in the path of virtue, dedicated to Truth and to her only, Zadig is prepared to gaze at unveiled Nature. Impelled by base passions, subjugated by an inferior version of Truth, Moabdar is unfit to "lift the veil." The King incurs the penalty suffered by those who approach sacred mysteries without due preparation.

---

*The Secret Doctrine, p. 281, Vol. III.
**A la Recherche du temps perdu, p. 92, Vol. III.

"The *Talmud* gives the story of the four *Tanaïm* who are made in allegorical terms, to enter into the *garden of delights*, i.e., to be initiated into the occult and final science:

'According to the teaching of our holy masters the names of the four who entered the garden of delight are: Ben Azai, Ben Zoma, A'her, and Rabbi A'qibah —

Ben Azai looked and — lost his sight —

Ben Zoma looked and — lost his reason —

A'her made depredations in the plantation (mixed up the whole and failed). But A'qibah, who had entered in peace, came out of it in peace, for the saint, whose name be blessed, had said, 'This old man is worthy of serving us with glory.' " (*Isis Unveiled,* p. 119, Vol. 2).

The experience of Moabdar seems to reflect the same level of inadequacy as does the performance of Ben Zoma, the unsuccessful candidate who "looked and lost his reason." The "depredations" of A'her are reminiscent of the "confusion" of Abogad, the result of unethical uncontrolled "drinking." The adherence of Moabdar to a false version of Truth — Missouf — causes his undoing. Inadequate knowledge and shady motives cause the failure of the brigand. The Judaeo-Christian realm of Moabdar and the Moslem world of the Arab are culturally ill-equipped to till a certain spiritual "garden." The latter fact seems to echo the belief of occultists according to which the study of magic is "almost impracticable" in the modern Western world.*

The disastrous influence of "Missouf" on Babylon reflects ravages caused by the emergence of the Judaeo-Christian tradition and by its clash with purer forms of Truth. The end of *Zadig* finds the dangerous misfit — "*la belle capricieuse*" — roaming all over the world, a sad personification of the Wandering Jew.

Pursued by the wrath of insecure and vicious minds, Zadig must take flight again. The age of persecution continues to unfold. The death of the hero is prevented by a warning of Queen Astarté. The unfailing saving grace of the beloved is an occasion for exoteric merriment and esoteric depth. The quoted authority of Zoroaster transcends the boundaries of humor and gallant appearance:

" 'When one is loved by a beautiful woman,' says the great Zoroaster, 'one always gets by in this world.' " (*Le Basilic,* p. 67).

Divine Wisdom imparts to her faithful strength and resilience which cannot be obtained from any other source. The devotee of Truth should not be too surprised to find his "trace" or name written on certain "sands." The devotee of Truth receives from the goddess the benefit of high protection.

Isis Unveiled, p. 635, Vol. II.

The Basilisk serves several esoteric purposes. The chapter identifies the devil — a degraded concept of the serpent of Knowledge — with the theological superstitions of Christianity. The same equivalence is stressed in a subsequent portion of *Zadig* with special reference to the Jehovic God. *The Basilisk* opposes true Knowledge to scientific and religious dogma. True Knowledge can only be gained by "lifting the veil" of matter. The chapter featuring Isis Unveiled confirms the repeatedly suggested identity of the allegorical couple formed by Zadig and Astarté: Man In Search of Truth and his Love. The disciple of Zoroaster is the spiritual seeker in the era of Pagan decline. He is a Savior of the Higher Self as is every human being. He is also a Savior in the exoteric sense of the term. Isis-Astarté is the version of Eternal Truth corresponding to the transition period from Paganism to the Christian era.

We have much to learn from numerous love stories created by great writers. Many such "romances" are esoteric versions of the same basic allegory: Man irresistibly drawn to Truth. The Divine Mistress of Paracelsus, Voltaire — and countless others — hides under an infinite variety of "veils" ranging from rags to sumptuous finery. It is the privileged duty of our XXth Century to "unveil" her wherever she may be found.

> "I went in search of my art, often in danger of my life. I have not been ashamed to learn those things which to me have seemed useful — even from vagabonds, barbers, and executioners. For we know how a lover will go a long way to meet the woman that he loves. How much more, then, will the lover of wisdom be tempted to go in search of his divine mistress!" (Paracelsus)*

Zadig becomes a contestant in an important tournament. The victor is to marry the widowed Queen Astarté and to replace Moabdar as King of Babylon. The event resembles a medieval joust. Ladies watch the exploits of their knights. The arena, the spears, the horses, and the general nature of the contest seem to belong to a tradition which glorifies physical skill and physical strength. But the mystical symbolism of sand,** "penetrating" spears, and Pegasus seems to be present. The stress which is placed on "valor" and "wisdom" and the political importance of the occasion show more to be at stake than a spectacular clash of muscle.

> "One did not permit the first position in the world, which was to be that of husband of Astarté and King of Babylon, to be determined by intrigues and conspiracies. They swore to recognize as King the most courageous and the wisest man." (*Les Combats*, p. 67).

---

*Epigraph to the novel by Frank G. Slaughter, *Divine Mistress*.
**The word "arena" means "sand" in Spanish.

146

The passage invites comparison between ancient Babylon and modern Western Europe. As was the case in *Les Généreux,* certain traits of the Pagan world are praised at the apparent expense of XVIIIth Century "Westphalia." The King of Babylon who is chosen on the basis of merit may be an *elect* in the spiritual sense. Modern Western concepts of "nobility" and "divine right" have no bearing on his credentials. The élite of Antiquity world is as wary of politcal intrigue as it is wary of other forms of Mayavic division. The implied comparison does not favor modern Europe.

The presence of the word "cabales" which represents conspiracies suggests an allusion to the Kabala or occult tradition of the Jews. Babylon is too familiar with the chaos and strife which marked the short-lived supremacy of "Missouf" to welcome any "kabalas" or twisted fragments of Truth.

> "Very few Christians understand, if indeed they know anything at all, of the Jewish Theology. The *Talmud* is the darkest of enigmas even for most Jews, while those Hebrew scholars who do comprehend it do not boast of their knowledge. Their kabalistic books are still less understood by them; for in our days more Christian than Jewish students are engrossed in the elimination of their great truths. How much less is definitely known of the Oriental, or the universal Kabala! Its adepts are few; but these heirs elect of the sages who first discovered 'the starry truths which shone on the great Shemaïa of the Chaldean lore' have solved the 'absolute' and are now resting from their grand labor. (*Isis Unveiled,* p. 17, Vol. 1).

The symbolism of "sand," "spears," and "horses" which is noted above may have been intended to bring to mind the elements of truth which may be found under the exoteric surface of the Bible and other Judaeo-Christian Scriptures. Voltaire may have wished to evoke the "heirs elect of the sages who first discovered 'the starry truths which shone on the great Shemaïa of the Chaldean lore,'" when he referred to the elective status of the King of Babylon. The theosophical distinction made between the Oriental or Universal Kabala and its Judaic outgrowth may also have contributed to the inspiration of *Les Combats.* The general picture of Babylon which is presented in *Zadig* is that of a collectivity firmly committed to universal values in the face of increasingly sectarian trends. The Voltairian Babel has not forgotten the age in which the "whole" human race — was 'of one language and of one lip.'"* — esoterically "of one faith."

The tournament begins. Two contestants are introduced. Their names and performances reflect various levels of spirituality. Contained in the name *Itobad* are the letters which from the word *Obi* or *Ob.* The plane of *Ob* is the inferior and dangerous realm of passive mediumship. Cor-

---

*The Secret Doctrine, p.   8, Vol. II.

responding to the name *Otame;* perhaps to the monadic aspect of *atome* —"atom"—and *atma* is the plane of soul contemplation. While the term *atma* is known to numerous Westerners who are more or less familiar with the concept of *mahatma* or "great soul," the area represented by *Ob* requires clarification. It is defined in *Isis Unveiled:*

> "It is undeniable that there must have been some good reasons why the ancients persecuted *unregulated* mediums. Otherwise, why at the time of Moses and David and Samuel, should they have encouraged prophecy and divination, astrology and soothsaying, and maintained schools and colleges, in which these natural gifts were strengthened and developed, while witches and those who divined by the spirit of *Ob* were put to death? Even at the time of Christ the poor oppressed mediums were driven to the tombs and waste places without the city walls. Why should banishment, persecution, and death be the portion of the physical mediums of those days, and whole communities of thaumaturgists — like the Essenes — be not merely tolerated but revered? It is because the ancients, unlike ourselves, could 'try' the 'spirits' and discern the difference between the good and the evil ones, the human and the elemental. They also knew that unregulated spirit intercourse brought ruin upon the individual and disaster to the community." (*Isis Unveiled,* pp. 489-90, Vol. 1).

The personality and performance of Itobad denote less than noble goals and less than superior skills. The uncouth candidate is "vain, lacking in courage, very clumsy, and without wit" — or "spirit." He has been led to seek the hand of the Queen and the throne of Babylon by the pressure of his "servants." Genuine stature and independent strength are lacking. Itobad is the instrument of inferior beings similar to the "satellites" and "bandits" of Orcan, Hermes, and Arbogad. He is no match for such gifted contestants as Otame and Zadig who excel in "skill" and "grace." Babylon is prompt to recognize in Itobad a quality of spirit consistent with the level of *Ob.* The unworthy candidate is "booed and removed to his quarters." He is heard to repeat, as he barely manages to walk: "What an adventure for a man like me!"

The sportsmanship and the ethics of Itobad are of the same order as his skills. The defeated aspirant to the hand of Astarté and to the crown resorts to treachery: theft of the white suit of armor belonging to Zadig, a symbol of pure mastery and adeptship.

Otame is outstanding in skill and grace. But he is destined to lose. Zadig has received from Isis-Astarté the "arms" of mastery conferred upon those who look beyond the veil: a white suit of armor and "the finest horse in Persia."

The fight opposing Zadig and Otame features a significant progression. The equestrian battle of the beginning becomes a duel waged on foot. The gradual elimination of all external aids other than a saber —

or "sword of knowledge" — points to the supremacy of inner strength. The importance of occult "skill" is stressed by "feints" or hidden maneuvers. The equestrian batle is won by a movement to the "rear." The duel is won by a "feint." Finally, the victory of Zadig is determined by a recovery of "wits" or "spirit."

> "Finally, their horses being tired, and their spears broken, Zadig used the following trick: he passes behind the blue prince, jumps onto the rear of his horse, takes him by the middle of the body, throws him on the ground, gets into the saddle in his place, and rides briskly around Otame lying on the ground." (*Les Combats*, p. 69).

> "Finally Zadig, having regained his spirits for a moment, stops, makes a feint, passes over Otame, makes him fall, disarms him, — " (*Les Combats*, p. 70).

The outcome of the battle is determined by near-abandonment of the physical panoply and strife of war. It is a pause giving free rein to "spirits" which finally tips the scales in favor of Zadig. The esoteric equivalence of "arms" is virtually given.

The physical aspect of the fight is itself open to question. The maneuver of Zadig taking Otame "by the middle of the body" may refer to an action directed at the *astral body* of the blue knight. As was previously noted, the astral body — or astral soul or perisprit or "doppelganger" — is the intermediate or "middle body of Man: a component far more ethereal than the physical shell yet removed from the absolute immateriality of Spirit. The esoteric meaning of the French word "corps" seems to be that of "astral body."

Similar use of the word "corps" is made in the *Recherche*. A tirade of Saint Loup on the esthetic value of military strategy contains an invitation to read on two — or more — levels. The question of the "name" and nature of certain "corps" is called to attention:

> " ' — all that you read, I suppose, in the report of a military narrator, the smallest facts, the smallest events, are only signs of an idea which must be extracted and which often is superimposed on others, as in a palimpsest. So that you have a whole as intellectual as any science or any art, and which is satisfying to the mind — (or "spirit")
> — Examples, please if I am not asking too much.
> — It is difficult to tell you like that, Saint Loup interrupted. You read for instance that such and such a corps has attempted — before going any further, the name of the corps, its composition, are not without meaning.' " (*A la Recherche du temps perdu*, p. 109, Vol. II).

The rest of the spirited exposé contains a wealth of esoteric gems designed to suggest the concealed value of "arms" and the general nature of the scheme of evolution. The spiritual orientation of the text is hinted by an unexpected reference to a chalice. "Final annihilation" is the eventual dissolution of the astral body which is not immortal.[*] Spiritual "paths" are represented by "highways" and "railroads." Spiritual substance comes under the designation of "supplies." "Defensive" works, "feints," and the difficulty of understanding certain maneuvers are all thrown exuberantly at the unsuspecting exoteric reader. The importance of doctrines is stressed. Truth and "regulations" — Universal Law — are mentioned. The "sectarian" tendencies of each "army" are noted against a general background of analogy. The abuse to which Truth and "regulations" are subjected by the "high command" is not overlooked.

> " — it is likely that truth must be sought in regulations, not in the mouthings of the high command. And there is more than the regulations of each army. There are also their traditions, their habits, their doctrines." (*A la Recherche du temps perdu*, p. 110, Vol. II).

The discourse of Saint Loup is punctuated by irrepressible — and somewhat puzzling — laughter which is understandable and easy to share in the light of esoteric content. The merry lyricism of the young officer dedicated to Military Grandeur and Servitude — and his general portrayal — raise an interesting question. Who is *Saint Loup?* Could he be in any way connected with the "saint" or adept who wrote *La Mort du loup?* Could he be Vigny in disguise?

The official image of Vigny is not easy to reconcile with the popular idea of holiness. But, as Barbey d'Aurevilly observes — and as the reading public will soon discover — the work and the life of the poet are "about soul and the highest labor of a soul —"

The esoteric meaning of the French word "corps" may also shed light on Voltaire's report of the death of Charles XII. The Swedish King is noted to have been exposed to enemy fire "almost from the waist up" — literally "exposé presque à demi-corps"— when he was felled before Frederickshall. The commonplace nature of such an occurrence on the battlefield is contradicted by many facts surrounding the death of Charles. The material findings of physicians, ballistics experts and the knowledge of historians produce only confusion. The death of the Swedish King remains a mystery. The puzzling set of known facts may not be insoluble. Voltaire notes the presence on the scene of a "man of execution" named Siquier. The latter person accused himself of having shot the King but eventually retracted his spontaneous confession. Charles had strange abilities. He could endure without harm murderously cold temperatures which

---

[*]*Isis Unveiled*, p. 432, Vol. II.

caused his men to die at their stations. He could anesthesize himself during a painful surgical operation. He scorned danger and narrowly escaped death on the battlefield an astonishing number of times as if he had known that his hour had not yet come. He had, in the words of Voltaire, a remarkable "sense of destiny" which is suggested to amount to knowledge of the future. It is not inconceivable that the King was on astral "trip" when he was shot. The exposed "demi-corps" mentioned by Voltaire may designate the intermediate "body" or astral soul which can be deliberately projected outside its physical shell. Occult philosophy teaches that a blow sustained by the exposed astral body may be re-verberated on the physical person with tangible injuries.* The strange possibility that the astral body of Charles was the first recipient of the fatal missile may some day be studied seriously by historians. The pre-science of the King may also explain why he stubbornly refused to speak French — a language which he knew well — during his entire lifetime. The Swedish King may have known that he would be murdered by a Frenchman.

The probable value of the word "corps" or "body" may be tested with interesting results in the works of many writers. Voltaire is one of many authors who seem to make occasional use of the term in the sense of "astral body."

The victory of Zadig is temporarily cancelled by the treachery of Itobad. The defeated contender steals the white suit of armor and the "white weapons" of the victor. The impostor is proclaimed King by the deceived Babylonian community. The theft is committed while the legitimate owner is "asleep." The adept must maintain constant vigilance against the inferior but active spirits of "Ob."

The former advantage of Zadig is lost. He cannot claim the white armor or weapons as his own for fear of "compromising" Isis-Astarté who gave them to him. Secrecy rules the champion of Truth who has "raised the veil." General discretion — and esoteric practice — are justi-fied in a few, barely noticeable words:

> "He could not see the Queen; he could not claim the white suit of armor which she had sent him; it would have compromised her; thus, while she was plunged in grief, he was overwhelmed with fury and anxiety." (*Les Combats,* p. 71).

Zadig is compelled to wear the despised garments of Itobad while the knave disgraces and flaunts the white vestments of the adept. The double masquerade dramatizes a joint grievance of occult and esoteric

---

The Secret Doctrine, p. 198, Vol. II.

writers. Genuine spirituality is caricatured as quackery. Truth is judged by the least exalted aspects of occult science and by false representatives. An inferior repertoire of mediumship, spiritism, and shabby tricks is exploited by practitioners of *Ob* who discredit authentic secret lore.

The imposture is specifically connected with the Judaeo-Christian tradition and with the Biblical God. The vowel content of the name *Itobad* adds to the idea of inferior occult arts designated by *Ob* the suggestion of a faith based on worship of a third-rate mythological figure: IAO-Jehovah. The latter correspondence is consistent with the illegal holding of "five hundred ounces of *silver*" by the allegorical "Jew" of a preceding chapter. Voltaire designates the Judaeo-Christian branch of World Religion as a market of quackery and inferior magic. The same identification is made by occultists:

> "In India it (vulgar magic) was the work of the lowest clergy; in Rome that of the highest Pontiffs." (*Isis Unveiled*, p. 70, Vol. 2).

The same affinity of high Christian clergy for the black arts is demonstrated by the interesting work of Pope Honorius. The anthology of magic spells written by the prelate contains edifying "recipes" such as the technique required to make a girl dance naked until she dies. The teamwork of "servants" or "valets" and high pontiffs is mentioned in the *Recherche*. The shady brotherhood evoked by Proust consists of "hypocritical priests, sanctimonious father confessors, and comic opera levites."*

The word "levite" — which is used in the description of the Judaeo-Christian establishment of Balbec designates "black" or "left-handed" magicians in the Secret Doctrine.** The practical skills of clerical sorcerers are frequently mentioned in esoteric literature. It will be found in the course of the present study that Voltaire consistently credits a "learned" ecclesiastical order— the Company of Jesus — with such pursuits. The same accusation is made by occultists. In the words of Mme Blavatsky, "Some of the early Popes were initiates, but the last fragments of their knowledge have now fallen into the power of the Jesuits, who have turned them into a system of sorcery."*** The same activities are a matter of historical and judicial record. Such cases as those of Louis Gaufridi and Father Girard are notorious examples of fairly common practice. The former priest was charged in 1611 with having be-

---

*A la Recherche du temps perdu, p. 165, Vol. II.
**The Secret Doctrine, pp. 211-12, Vol. II.
***Ibid., p. 311, Vol. I.

witched a young girl. According to Barbey d'Aurevilly, "the young girl was noble and was named Madelaine de la Palud. The procedure of the trial is on record. One finds there in detail facts of possession which are as numerous as they are extraordinary. Modern science, which is cognizant of those facts and which explains them or believes it is explaining them, will never find the secret of the influence exerted by one human being over another in such colossal proportions."* The trial of Father Girard which took place in 1731 — and which is related in *Isis Unveiled* — involved similar charges and circumstances. The Père Joseph portrayed by Vigny in *Cinq Mars* is a shadowy "servant" whose occult influence on Richelieu is clearly suggested. The dominance exerted by the Cardinal himself over the French King seems to be of like nature. Voltaire states in Chapter XIX of *L'Ingénu* that Richelieu and Mazarin had their "guards" who constituted companies of "satellites." The monk who converts Thais in the novel of Anatole France bearing the name of the famous courtesan finally sees himself in true light: as a vampire. The bizarre priest featured in *Mort à Crédit* performs a spectacular act of vampirism. The clerical Tartuffe engaged in left-handed occult practice is a fairly common element of History and Literature.

The Chief Executive of clerical sorcerers is a choice source of inspiration to esoteric writers. IAO-Jehovah makes several appearances in the Voltairian trilogy. His loutish character is an eloquent clue to his identity. The "Vice-God" may be found in the works of many authors hiding under various "coats of skin" generally ludicrous, hateful, and obscene. President Grandmorin, the socially prominent seducer of *La Bête Humaine,* is such a Jehovic figure. His identity is flaunted in a passage in which some persons note that the dead executive was the "Good Lord" of certain people. Zola seems to suggest that connections might be made between "the Human Beast," the "President," and the apocalypse which marks the end of the novel. M. Jacotin, the thundering, arrogant, and pitiful father figure created by Marcel Aymé** is another representative of the biblical God. The dreaded "père de famille" terrorizes and humiliates everyone within his small kingdom. But he is neither powerful nor secure in his professional hierarchy. His self-concept vacillates between the figure of the vengeful God and the figure of the benevolent Deity who should be loved — if not worshipped. M. Jacotin is strangely incapable of coping with one weapon: the *silence* of his victims. He is addicted to fraudulent writing of "scriptures" the creation of which makes him feel "rich, master of a magnificent and flowery domain."

*Barbery d'Aurevilly, *L'Ensorcelée,* Ch. IX.
**Marcel Aymé, *Le Proverbe.*

The weaknesses of the family God are discovered by his son "Lucien" — whose name conveys the idea of light. They are not exposed rashly to the rest of the suffering "family". But the reader may surmise that they will not be forgotten by the perceptive new generation when the day of maturity and independence arrives. Samuel Beckett portrays the Jehovic God and the corresponding social system as *Pozzo*. The second part of his novel *Molloy* contains the self-portrait of another Jehovic figure also tyrannical, insecure, and vulnerable to "silence." His pedagogy is based on two principles: the Lord giveth and the Lord taketh away and *Sollst entbehren* ("he must do without, he must be deprived"). The latter motto conveys the ideas of necessity and Maya — privation — exploited to oppress the progeny of Jehovah: mankind. The despotic "father" knows that he may well be abandoned by the "child" whom he has deliberately stultified and forced into restless submission. As was previously noted, the manager of the awesome Grand Hôtel of Balbec is a Proustian counterpart of Jehovah. But the most impressive portrayal of the "Vice-God" may belong to Céline. There is a beautiful study to be made on the esoteric personality of the father figure of *Mort à Crédit*. The woman-hating, death-fearing father of Ferdinand is connected with Bacchus by his chief claims to distinction: a Baccalauréat and frequent "Bacchanals" or violent scenes. His status of low-ranking deity is suggested by professional standing. Auguste vegetates as a petty employee in the dismal cosmogony of a fire-insurance company. The specialty of the firm is a transparent allusion to Christian religion in general and to Hell in particular. Like M. Jacotin Auguste has a certain talent in the art of writing "letters." But he does not seem to desire a good education for his son. Like the "Vice-God" of Voltaire who must "be served by ignorants and by idiots," Auguste cannot maintain his shaky rule in an intelligent world. Sensing imminent disaster, he is obsessed with the passage of time. His downfall comes with the emergence of a generation more learned than his own and with the fast-spreading use of a new method of processing "letters." The revolutionary method used by holders of advanced "degrees" seems to be esoteric.

A typical performance of the family Jehovah created by Céline is described in the following texts. It is enriched by the presence of "Heaven," — the destination of prayers and the "attic" of the father. The atmosphere of esoteric drama is intensified by the sure prospect of a "Deluge" and by the catastrophic motions of a vagrant "*piano*." Happy the reader who can savor the potent alchemy of the original *argot!*

"Ma mère rendait grâce au Ciel. Mon père voulait pas voir ça. Il remontait dans sa soupente, zyeutant sa montre à chaque pas, il requinquait toute sa

hantise. Il préparait l'autre panique, et le Déluge qui tarderait pas . . .
Il s'entraînait. . . ."

("My mother gave thanks to heaven. My father couldn't bear to witness
these scenes. He'd climb up to his attic, looking at his watch at every
step, refurbishing his obsession. He was building up to the next outburst,
the Deluge that wouldn't be long in coming . . . Getting into trim . . ."
(*Ralph Manheim Translation* pp. 64-65).

"Maman va dérouiller, c'est sûr. De mon côté je préfère personne. Pour
les gueulements et la connerie, je les trouve pareils . . . Elle cogne moins
fort, mais plus souvent. Lequel que j'aimerais mieux qu'on tue? Je crois
que c'est encore mon papa.
   On me laissera pas voir, 'Monte dans ta chambre, petit saligaud! Va te
coucher! . . . Fais ta prière! . . '
   Il mugit, il fonce, il explose, il va bombarder la cuistance. Après les
clous, il reste plus rien . . . Toute la quincaillerie est en bombe . . . ça fuse
. . . ça gicle . . . ça résonne . . . Ma mère à genoux implore le pardon du
Ciel. . . La table il la catapulte d'un seul grand coup de pompe. . . . Elle
se renverse sur elle.
   'Sauve-toi Ferdinand!' qu'elle a encore le temps de me crier. Je bondis.
Je passe à travers d'une cascade de verres et de débris . . . Il carambole
le piano, le gage d'une cliente . . . Il se connaît plus. Il rentre dedans du
talon, le clavier éclate. . . c'est le tour de ma mère, c'est elle qui prend à
présent . . . De ma chambre je l'entends qui hurle . . . 'Auguste! Auguste!
Laisse-moi! . . .' et puis des brefs étouffements . . .
   Je redescends un peu pour voir . . . Il la traîne le long de la rampe. Elle
se raccroche. Elle l'enserre au cou. C'est ça qui la sauve." (*Mort à Crédit*,
Livre de Poche etd., p. 53).

("My mother's going to get it, that's a safe bet. As far as I'm concerned I
have no preference. For yelling and assy stuff there's nothing to choose
between them. . . She doesn't hit so hard, but more often. Which one of
the two I'd rather see killed by someone? Well, all in all, my daddy I
think.
   They don't want me to see 'Get to your room, you little swine! . . . Go
to bed! . . . Say your prayers! . . .'
   He bellows, he rushes, he explodes, he's going to bomb the chow.
After the nails there's nothing left. . . . The whole batch of hardware explodes . . . it rockets . . . it squirts, it bangs . . . My mother on her knees
implores the mercy of Heaven . . . The table he propels it in one great
kick . . . It tips over on top of her.
   'Run Ferdinand!' she still has the time to yell to me. I jump. I pass
through a cascade of glass and of débris . . . he sends the piano careening
that a customer left us as security . . . he's beside himself. He bashes his
heel into it, the keyboard bursts . . . It's my mother's turn, she's the one
who's getting it now . . . From my room I hear her howling . . . 'Auguste!
Auguste! Let go! . . .' and then short, choking sounds.
   I come down a little to see. . . He's dragging her along the banister.
She hangs on. She clutches his neck. That's what saves her.")

Céline seems to invite a connection between his despicable "Auguste"

155

and Voltairian Itobad. The lament of the defeated contender of *Zadig*: "What an adventure for a man like me!" has a counterpart in the self-pity expressed by the father of Ferdinand: "What a humiliation for a man of his education!"* Frustrated aspiration to supremacy and less than divine character are similarly stressed in each case.

The word "p*iano*" contains — in proper sequence — the three letters designating Jehovah. It is a natural source of expression — and delight — to esoteric writers. The demolition of the instrument perpetrated by the Almighty Father "Auguste" suggests the self-destructing or contradictory quality of the biblical God. The alleged source of Ultimate Light and Goodness is noted for blind, bestial, and vicious outbursts. The "better half" of Jehovah, significantly named "Clémence" — "Clemency" — suffers accordingly. (A similar principle of internal contradiction may be found in the Voltairian expression "Vice-God".) A second piano is mentioned at another stage of *Death on the Installment* Plan. It is the proud possession of an English school representing Reformed Churches. The impoverished establishment vainly tries to avert disaster. It is plain to all that the end has come when the grand p*iano* is removed from the institution. The narrator of *Tropic of Capricorn* connects his ability to play the p*iano* with phallic triumphs. No woman can resist the spell of his artistic performance. But it is stressed toward the end of the book that there is a higher, nobler kind of music."

The masquerade of Itobad-IAO flaunting the "borrowed" suit of armor of Zadig is heavy with significance. The Judaeo-Christian tradition personified is shown to exploit undeserved prestige. It is found guilty of shameless plagiarism. The latter crime is a major grievance of occultists and esoteric writers. Many pages of *Isis Unveiled* are devoted to "borrowed robes" representing stolen Pagan lore. Numerous "discoveries" which are the pride of modern science were already known to the Ancients long before they were re-stated — without acknowledgment — by the moderns.

The theft of scientic knowledge is paralleled by the "borrowing" of religious dogma and ritual used by modern Churches against legitimate Pagan holders.

> "Zoroastrianism anticipated far more than has been imagined. The cross, the priestly robes and symbols, the sacraments, the Sabbath, the festivals, and anniversaries, are all anterior to the Christian era by thousands of years." (*Isis Unveiled*, p. 179, Vol. 2).

> "And so, above, below, outside, and inside, the Christian Church, in the priestly garments, and the religious rites we recognize the stamp of exo-

---

Ralph Manheim Translation, p. 75.

teric heathenism. On no subject within the wide range of human knowledge, has the world been more blinded or deceived with such persistent misrepresentation as on that of antiquity. Its hoary past and its religious faiths have been misrepresented and trampled under the feet of its successors. Its hierophants and prophets, mystae and epoptae, of the once sacred adyta of the temple shown as demoniacs and devil-worshippers. Donned in the despoiled garments of the victim, the Christian priest now anathematizes the latter with rites and ceremonies which he had learned from the theurgists themselves. The Mosaic Bible is used as a weapon against the people who furnished it. The heathen philosopher is cursed under the very roof which has witnessed his initiation; and the 'monkey of God' (i.e., the devil of Tertullian), the originator and founder of magical Theurgy, the science of illusions and lies, whose father and founder is the demon,' is exorcised with holy water by the hand which holds the identical *lituus* with which the ancient augur, after a solemn prayer, used to determine the regions of heavens, and evoke, in the name of the HIGHEST, the minor god (now termed the Devil), who unveiled to his eyes futurity, and enabled him to prophesy! — On the part of the scholars it is the same apprehension of the possible necessity of having to modify some of their erroneously established theories of science. 'Nothing but such pitiable prejudice,' says Gross, 'can have thus misrepresented the theology of heathenism and distorted — nay, caricatured — its forms of religious worship. It is time that posterity should raise its voice in vindication of violated truth, and that the present age should learn a little of that common sense of which it boasts with as much self-complacency as if the prerogative of reason was the birth-right only of modern times.' " (*Isis Unveiled,* pp. 96-97, Vol. 2).

The identity of ideas and expressions presented by Voltaire and by Mme Blavatsky is striking. "Donned in the despoiled garments of the victim," Itobad-IAO-Jehovah, the Judaeo-Christian tradition personified —tries to exploit the ill-gotten assets of the Zoroastrian or Pagan. But the stolen goods amount to no more than "exoteric heathenism." Itobad will eventually suffer the same disastrous exposure as the swindling Hebrew featured in a previous chapter.

Cheated of his victory by the impostor, Zadig resumes his wanderings. He deplores the cruelty and absurdity of Fate; Pessimism seems justified. Noble ethics, wisdom and courage have been rewarded by stubborn misfortune. Insult is added to injury.

The encounter of the hero with a strange hermit leaves the young man — and the exoteric reader — more convinced than ever of the irrational nature of human destiny. The bizarre sage claims to possess the key to the Book of Fate. But his conduct does not seem to be guided by wisdom or lofty ethics. He rewards generous hospitality by stealing from his host. He responds to miserly and humiliating treatment by giving a treasure. He thanks a charitable and virtuous widow by killing her nephew. The self-proclaimed representative of divine law seems to invalidate his

157

own propaganda at every turn. Reason and Justice seem totally irrelevant to the operation of human fate. It is difficult to believe that there can be a God worthy of the name. The very concept of "destiny" appears to lose meaning.

The objective mind of Zadig is understandably repelled. But his subjective being is attracted by the hermit who wears an indefinable aura. The overwhelming weight of fact has little effect on the spell cast by the stranger. Instinct unfailingly perceives the hidden truth which is beyond the scope of the unaided intellect. Instinct is vindicated when the elder suddenly transforms himself into a dazzling angel. He reveals how divine law is at work in each human life. The vain and wealthy host will become wiser for the theft of his property. The miser will learn to practice true hospitality. The slain lad would have become a murderer had he been allowed to live. The hidden link between cause and effect is exposed in each case. The basic credo of the Secret Doctrine is proclaimed: There is no such thing as chance.

> . " 'Chance does not exist.' "
> (*L'Ermite,* p. 77).

> "The ONE LIFE is closely related to *the one* law which governs the World of Being — KARMA — . Exoterically, this is simply and literally 'action,' or rather an 'effect-producing cause.' Esoterically, it is quite a different thing in its far-fetching moral effects. It is the unerring LAW OF RETRIBUTION." (*The Secret Doctrine,* p. 634, Vol. I).

> " — verily there is not an accident in our lives, not a mishappen day, or a misfortune, that could not be traced back to our own doings in this or in another life." (*The Secret Doctrine,* pp. 643-44, Vol. I).

> "Karma-Nemesis is no more than the (spiritual) dynamical effect of causes produced and forces awakened into activity by our own actions." (*The Secret Doctrine,* p. 644, Vol. I).

Revelations end abruptly as the angel takes flight toward the tenth sphere. Zadig is left to speculate on the mysteries of human destiny. A final question remains unanswered:

> "Weak mortal, stop arguing about what must be worshipped.' — 'But,' — said Zadig. As he was saying 'but,' the angel was taking flight toward the tenth sphere." (*L'Ermite,* pp. 77-78).

The final plea for inaccessible lights reflects the inscrutable essence of The Law which is the mainspring of the Universe. The "silence" of the angel is the only possible answer and the only possible approach to the UNKNOWABLE.

"Karma is that unseen and unknown law which adjusts wisely, intelligently, and equitably each effect to its cause, tracing the latter back to its producer. Though itself unknowable, its action is perceivable." (*The Key to Theosophy*, p. 152).

The inability of Zadig to obtain further enlightenment is noted with irony on the exoteric plane of the text. But the quality of irony is radically changed on the esoteric level of reading by the unfathomable depth of Karma. The inscrutable cornerstone of occult philosophy is approached, not actually touched or probed. The unknowable essence of The One Law is a prominent theme of all esoteric writings. It will again be rendered by abrupt breaks in *Candide*. It is stressed with special beauty in the poetry of Vigny:

"O sujet d'épouvante à troubler le plus brave!
Question sans réponse où vos saints se sont tus!
O mystère, o tourment de l'âme forte et grave!" (*Les Destinées*).

(O awesome subject which confounds the most brave!
Question without an answer upon which saints remain silent!
O mystery, o torment of the strong and deep soul!")

Jesrad and the "saints" are likewise "silent" on the eternal question.

Karma is generally symbolized by a circle or by a wheel. The name of the angel featured in *Zadig* suggests a fusion of the words "just," "justice," — in French "juste," "justice" — and possibly "Jesus" — a Just and Savior incarnate — with the German term meaning "wheel": *rad*. All four words are likely to have been factors in the selection of the name of the hermit. The angel personifies the cyclic "wheel" of cosmic evolution and the Law of Retribution on the human plane.

The sudden metamorphosis of the hermit dramatizes opposition between material appearance and immaterial reality. The chaotic quality and the ugliness of Maya dissolve as the scheme of life is illuminated by Karma. Divine Law stands in their place. The change occurs in the eyes of the beholder as his strange teacher speaks. Karmic insight results in radically altered vision.

The same transcendence of terrestrial illusion is the hinge of occult philosophy. The exoterically suspect refrains of Pangloss which deal with "cause and effect" and the strange optimism of the master facing one calamity after another will be found to make sense in the light of Karmic belief. The preceptor of Candide has the ability to see hidden links between cause and effect. The same ability defines the occultist.

A passage of *The Fisherman* illustrates the reversible quality of Voltairian "pessimism." The apparent impunity which is enjoyed by such characters as Orcan is commented by Zadig.

> "'Ah!' he said to the fisherman, 'Orcan deserves to be punished. But ordinarily, it is such people who are the favorites of destiny.'" (*Le Pêcheur*, p. 59).

Success is the monopoly of rogues. Rogues are "favorites" of Destiny. Little encouragement is afforded by such findings. But the statement of the hero is esoterically modified by the vowel content of the words "*favoris*" and "*ordinaire*." The quality of achievement which is suggested by IAO — the lowly plane of Jehovic belief and vulgar magic — is neither high nor happy. Debased spirituality condemns itself to mediocrity and failure. Arbogad is unlikely to have his wish and to become a "diamond." His career may well end on the gallows. "Favorites," "satellites," "bandits," "slave-driven" impostors and other such creatures deserve more pity than envy. Such case histories as those of Orcan, Azora, Sémire and Itobad reveal dim prospects. The collection of women wrongfully acquired by Orcan bodes little good where his safety and well-being are concerned. Egocentric Sémire is unlikely to find fulfillment in the harem of her seducer. Fickle and cruel Azora gains nothing but ridicule and repudiation from her lack of heart. The former wife of the fisherman is likewise rewarded. Itobad can expect lifelong enslavement to his "slaves." The law of retribution *is* perceptible. Evil itself — while never justifiable or unpunished on human planes — fits into the scheme of Divine Law:

> "'The wicked,' replied Jesrad, 'are always unhappy; they serve to test a small number of sages scattered on earth; and there is no evil out of which some good does not come.' But,' replied Zadig, 'if there were only Good and no Evil?' — 'Then,' Jesrad went on, 'this earth would be another earth; the chain of events would be another order of wisdom; and this other order, which would be perfect, can only be in the eternal abode of the Supreme Being, who cannot be approached by Evil.'" (*L'Ermite*, p. 77).

The passage is ablaze with Voltairian reverence. It is a veritable *credo* containing basic tenets of the Secret Doctrine.

The falsely negative axiom: "There is no such thing as chance" is supplemented by positive revelation. Having shown the hidden bonds between cause and effect on the plane of individual destiny, the sage shows that similar connections operate on cosmic planes. The human condition is geared to the administration of certain tests which constitute the raison d'être of our terrestrial world. The universe reflects a certain "order" or a certain "wisdom." Good and Evil are necessary catalysts of human evolution. "Perfection" is suggested to prevail on a non-contingent, immaterial plane which "cannot be approached by Evil" or by the attributes of materiality. Intermediate levels of Being may be inferred to exist — as *Micromégas* and other Voltairian writings will confirm. The Supreme Being is totally removed from Evil or material degradation. But the power emanating from Unknowable is dynamically involved in every aspect of universal existence. The combination of a "chain of events" and of "another earth" suggests an allusion to the occult view of planetary chains. The "chain" is also the symbol of reincarnation. The symbolic wheel and chain representing the cornerstone of occult philosophy dominate the passage.

The same crucial combination of symbols is found in countless esoteric texts, particularly in the stanza of *Les Destinées* which contains the key to the literary production, the philosophy, and the life of Vigny. The strangely capitalized COLLIER — yoke, collar, necklace — is the nearest possible approximation of an exoteric answer to the weighty question of Fate on which "saints remain silent."

> "Oh! dans quel désespoir nous sommes encor tous!
> Vous avez élargi le COLLIER qui nous lie,
> Mais qui donc tient la chaîne? — Ah! Dieu juste, est-ce vous?"

> (Oh! in what despair we all still are!
> You have loosened the YOKE which binds us,
> But who does hold the chain? — Ah! just God, is it you?")

The symbolism of the NECKLACE, YOKE — and chain — has an ancient origin:

> "In the Hindu sacred books it is said that that which undergoes periodical incarnation is the *sutratma*, which means literally 'the thread soul.' As man at the moment of death has a retrospective insight into the life he has led, so, at the moment he is reborn on earth, the ego awaking from the state of Devachan, has a prospective vision of the life which awaits him, and realizes all the causes that have led to it. He realizes them, and sees futurity, because it is between Devachan and rebirth that the Ego retains his full consciousness, and rebecomes for a short time the god he was, before, in compliance with karmic law, he first descended into matter and incarnated in the first man of flesh. The golden thread sees all of its 'pearls' and misses not one of them." (*The Key to Theosophy*, p. 114).

The symbolic thread, rope, or chain of rebirth — and evolution — makes frequent appearances in esoteric texts. The "chain of events" or "circumstances" which is repeatedly mentioned by aging M. de Charlus does not connote senility to the esoteric reader of Proust. The rope and pulley — wheel of Karma — belong to the Well of Knowledge of which mankind must "drink" if it is to survive, according to the Little Prince. The karmic symbolism of the neck and of neck-related objects is a source of great "amusement" to esoteric writers and a source of considerable light to esoteric readers. The "eternal golden muffler" of the Little Prince is absent from many illustrations of the book. It is accordingly suggested to be symbolic and karmic. The collar and "rope" strangling "Lucky" — mankind, the slave of "Pozzo" and non-existent chance — are one in *En Attendant Godot*. The celluloid collar worn by modern Western man "unto the death" is viewed as a painful yet "magic sign" by the genial author of *Mort à Crédit*.

> "Collars are important too, you mustn't go wrong . . . a wide collar can atone for a multitude of sins when you're young and scrawny. The only flight of fancy permitted was a frivolous snap-on bow tie. Naturally there had to be a watch-chain, but darkened too for mourning . . ." (*Ralph Manheim Translation*, p. 136).

The above passage of *Mort à Crédit* deserves detailed comment from the standpoint of esoteric concentration. The importance of "collars" is the importance of Karma. Karma is virtually identified with the atonement of sin. The "bow-tie" which is known in French as a "butterfly-knot" — "noeud papillon" — belongs to the symbolism of Man transcending his "chrysalitic shell" or physical body. The butterfly is prominently featured in the works of Rabelais and Saint Exupéry — to name but two authors. The time element of evolution is represented by the watch which is "necessary." The cosmic chain and the chain of individual rebirth are present. But they are "darkened" or obscured in a world which is "in mourning" — bereft of spirituality. The same karmic symbolism of the "neck" adds to the esoteric dimension of a passage previously quoted in the present study. The family Jehovah of *Mort à Crédit* is noted to be weak in that one area. The choking defense of his beaten wife is accordingly effective: "That's what saves her." One may also note that the M. Jacotin created by Marcel Aymé is helpless when faced by the *responsibility* — Karma — of commenting a proverb. His "personal creation" or writing is found to remain outside of the subject by a "master." The proverb deals with a well-known "race" between a tortoise and a hare. The allusion to the truncated and distorted Christian *Genesis* is clear. Jehovah is consistently and logically shown to be weak on Karma which is the very negation of his existence.

The revelations of Jesrad-Karma suggest the occult view of a multitude of worlds rationally and specifically designed as sites suited to various stages of evolution.

> "The evolution of man is not a process carried out on this planet alone. It is a result to which many worlds in different conditions of material and

spiritual development have contributed." (A. P. Sinnett, *Esoteric Buddhism*, pp. 75-76).

"Man lives on many earths before he reaches this. Myriads of worlds swarm in space where the soul in rudimental states performs its pilgrimages, ere he reaches the large and shining planet named the Earth, the glorious function of which is to confer *self-consciousness*. At this point only he is man; at every other stage of his vast, wild journey he is but an embryonic being, a fleeting, temporary shape of matter — a creature in which a part, but only a part, of the high, imprisoned soul shines forth, a rudimental shape, with rudimental functions, ever living, dying, sustaining a flitting spiritual existence as rudimental as the material shape from whence it emerged; a butterfly, springing up from the chrysalitic shell, but ever, as it onward rushes, in new births, new deaths, new incarnations, anon to die and live again, but still stretch upward, still strive onward, still rush on the giddy, dreadful, toilsome, rugged path, until it awakens once more — once more to live and be a material shape, a thing of dust, a creature of flesh and blood, but now — a man!" (*Art-Magic, Anonymous*, quoted in *Isis Unveiled*, p. 368, Vol. 1).

The pilgrimage of the soul through various kingdoms of Nature is represented in the conceptual nutshell of metempsychosis. Man is the product of a lengthy journey on "the giddy, dreadful, toilsome, rugged path" leading to "perfection." Samuel Beckett seems to have proffered the same view when he referred to "man — a vast block, kneaded out of all the kingdoms —" "L'homme aussi est là, quelque part, vaste bloc pétri de tous les règnes."* As was previously noted, metempsychosis is a much-misunderstood element of occult philosophy. It is defined as follows in the Secret Doctrine:

> *METEMPSYCHOSIS.* — The progress of the soul from one stage of existence to another. Symbolized and vulgarly believed to be rebirths in animal bodies. A term generally misunderstood by every class of Europeans and American society, including many scientists. The kabalistic axiom, 'A stone becomes a plant, a plant an animal, an animal a man, a man a spirit, and a spirit a god,' receives an explanation in Manu's Manava-Dharma Sastra, and other Brahmanical books." (*Isis Unveiled*, pp. xxxvi-xxxvii, Vol. 1).

The flight of Jesrad to the *tenth* sphere fits into the suggested cosmic design of multiple planes of Being. Occult philosophy teaches that the number *ten* or "'Decad' or sum of all, involves the entire cosmos. The universe is the combination of a thousand elements, and yet the expression of a single spirit — a chaos to the sense, a cosmos to the reason."** The revelations of Jesrad-Karma which transform "chaos" into "reason"

Molloy, p. 171, Ed. Minuit.
**Isis Unveiled*, p. xvi, Vol. I.

163

are consistent with the cosmic insight suggested by the number ten. The angel does reside in highest regions.

The number *ten* may also have been intended to serve as an esoteric "blind." Occult philosophy teaches that the entire universe — from galaxies to atoms — evolves in accordance with a septenary structure of time, space, and matter.

> "1. Everything in the metaphysical as in the physical Universe is septenary. Hence every Sidereal body, every planet, whether visible or invisible, is credited with six companion globes. The evolution of life proceeds on these seven bodies from the 1st to the 7th in Seven ROUNDS or Seven Cycles.
> 2. These globes are formed by a process which the Occultists call the 're-birth of planetary chains (or 'rings').' When the seventh and last Round of one of such rings has been entered upon, the highest or first globe 'A,' followed by all the others down to the last, instead of entering upon a certain time of rest — or 'obscuration,' as in their previous Rounds — be-gins to die out. The 'planetary' dissolution (*pralaya*) is at hand, and its hour has struck; each globe has to transfer its life and energy to another planet." (*The Secret Doctrine*, pp. 158-59, Vol. I).

The esoteric or magical character of the number *seven* is not entirely unknown to the general public. Seven and "sevening" appear frequently in Biblical texts, as they do appear in innocent-looking fairy-tales and naïve-sounding folklore. Voltaire may have avoided *seven* out of esoteric prudence.

The dim view of our planet which is expressed in Voltairian texts seems to coincide with occult estimates of our position in the universe. *Memnon* situates our globe in the neighborhood of the "madhouse" of our cosmic regions. A space traveler featured in *Micromégas* doubts that anyone in his right mind would wish to live there. Voltaire and Mr. A. P. Sinnett place our "small globe of mud" in the same spiritually undistinguished neighborhood:

> "Our own world presents us with conditions in which spirit and matter are, on the whole, evenly balanced in equilibrium. Let it not be supposed on that account that it is very highly elevated in the scale of perfection. On the contrary, it occupies a very low place in that scale. The worlds that are higher in the scale are those in which spirit largely predominates. There is another world attached to the chain, rather than forming a part of it, in which matter asserts itself even more decisively than on earth, but this may be spoken of later." (A. P. Sinnett, *Esoteric Buddhism*, p. 79).

Our "little globe of mud" may well have been connected with the "prolific slime" of occult philosophy in the mind of Voltaire.

> "In the ancient Eastern mythologies, the cosmogonic myth states that there was but water (the father) and the prolific slime (the mother *Ilus* or *Hylè*)

from which crept forth the mundane snake-matter." (*Isis Unveiled*, p. 146, Vol. 1).

The planetary progeny of "slime" or "mud" cannot be the realm of perfection. It is the evolutionary "garden" where the *self-consciousness* of Man is cultivated. Such a process of growth cannot unfold in the absence of Evil. Reason dwells in the very absurdity which seems to rule our world.

Zadig is comforted by the teachings of the strange hermit. The fact can hardly surprise the esoteric reader. Revelation has been as generous as it could be for the period of human evolution involved. Karmic insight on the human plane is supplemented by a glimpse of a rational Cosmos.

Having returned to the site of the tournament, the young hero promptly defeats Itobad, the usurper. The lover of Truth and pupil of Jesrad is bound to conquer.

Itobad performs as poorly in the field of riddles as he had performed in the arena. IAO-Jehovah is deficient in concept-formation and symbolic understanding. Such a weakness is fatal for "a man like him." It is symptomatic of deficient self-knowledge or spirituality. It is also symptomatic of poor intellect.

> "It was Itobad's turn to speak. He replied that a man like him knew nothing about riddles, and that it was enough to have won with great blows of the spear." (*Les Enigmes*, p. 79).

The impostor earns the contempt of the Pagan community. Babylon does not agree that "a man like him" should reign. The nation is primarily concerned with eternal values and general well-being, not with the "adventures" of "a man like" Itobad. Babylon insists that intellectual and spiritual requirements be met by its leadership. No violation of ancient Law will be tolerated, least of all for the sake of "a man like Itobad!"

The alleged victory of the unworthy contender typifies the truthfulness of the Judaeo-Christian tradition personified. Itobad has not "won with great blows of the spear." The victory of which he boasts is actually the victory of Zadig, the Pagan. The superior power of "speed," "strength," "skill," the white "arms" of mastery, and the "sword" of "excellent knowledge" are in the possession of the Zoroastrian or transmitter of the Secret Doctrine. The "phallic" or literal use of the "spear" — an instrument of fictitious triumph — demonstrates the inability of Itobad to rise beyond the lowest plane of vision and endeavor. The Pagan community is unimpressed by the choice weapon of Jehovah. IAO will have to wait for a less enlightened era — which will be the time setting of *Candide* — to force his cruel and shaky supremacy upon mankind. He will not have his day until blind, literal phallicism has obscured the meaning and the feeling of Truth in the majority of minds.

Physical combat confirms the superiority of occult mastery. The adept is a predictable victor in practical works. The control of inferior "force" is the hard-earned privilege of his advanced spiritual status.

> "Zadig sut parer le coup, en opposant ce qu'on appelle le fort de l'épée au faible de son adversaire, de façon que l'épée d'Itobad se rompît." (*Les Enigmes*, p. 80).

> ("Zadig knew how to parry the blow, opposing what is called the strong part of his sword to the weak part of his adversary, so that the sword of Itobad broke.")

The intellectual and spiritual "strength" of Zadig is contrasted to the intellectual and spiritual "weakness" of Itobad. The inferior weapon is symbolically broken. It is aptly connected with the "adversary" — a word often linked with the devil and his works in medieval literature. The "excellent sword of knowledge" is victorious.

Itobad returns home where he rightfully belongs. The only sovereignty accessible to him is of "domestic" character:

> "Itobad went to have himself called 'milord' in his own house." (*Les Enigmes*, p. 80).

The fiasco of the unsuccessful "Lord" completes the esoteric survey of defunct Mosaic wrath and foiled Judaic swindle. It is supplemented by a rapid glance at the hidden weaknesses of Islam. Orcan and Arbogad are not as secure as they seem to be. Their prospects are approximately the same as those of Itobad. The disciple of Zoroaster — or transmitter of the Secret Doctrine — is consistently victorious in his confrontations with sectarian impostors.

Zadig ends in deceptively naïve fairy-tale fashion. The young hero wins his fair lady. Man and Truth are symbolically wedded. The good are rewarded. The wicked are punished. Retribution comes to all in the form of well-earned felicity or self-inflicted woe. Justice reflects Karmic law, not the decision or whim of a personal God. Love and "Commerce" or Knowledge are united in the persons of Almona and Sétoc as they are joined in the mystical couple formed by Zadig and Astarté. Spectacular "fortunes" result. Zadig becomes King and knows happiness. Comparison is implicitly invited with XVIIIth Century "Westphalian" monarchies.

Happiness is not restricted to a few individuals. A golden age begins:

" — ce fut le plus beau siècle de la terre — " (*Les Enigmes,* p. 81).
(" — it was the most beautiful era on earth — ")

The surface of faintly suspect idyllic bliss conceals an article of faith of occult philosophy:

> "Even the four ages of the Hindu chronology contain a far more philosophical idea than appears on the surface. It defines them according to both the psychological or mental and the physical states of man during their period. Crita-yug, the golden age, the 'age of joy,' or spiritual innocence of man; Treta-yug, the age of silver, or that of fire — the period of supremacy of man and of giants and of the sons of God; Dwapara-yug, the age of bronze — a mixture already of purity and impurity (spirit and matter) the age of doubt; and at last our own, the Kali-yug or age of iron, or darkness, misery, and sorrow. In this age Vishnu had to incarnate himself in Christna, in order to save humanity from the goddess Kali, consort of Siva, the all-annihilating — the goddess of death, destruction, and human misery. Kali is the best emblem to represent the 'fall of man;' the falling of spirit into the degradation of matter, with all its terrible results. We have to rid ourselves of Kali before we can ever reach 'Moksha,' or Nirvâna. the abode of blessed Peace and Spirit." (*Isis Unveiled,* p. 275, Vol. 2).

The idyllic joy which marks the end of *Zadig* is genuine. It is the blissful omniscience of a perfected creature remembering "the grain of sand which became a diamond." It is the fulfillment of a Savior with mission accomplished.

The evolutionary background of the story embraces legendary times when "Babylon" — perhaps mankind — was of one "language," one "lip," and one faith. It is prolonged into an era in which five hundred ounces of "borrowed silver" are returned to their legitimate owners; when the message of a Savior is "caught," and when "Itobad," the Judaeo-Christian spiritual usurper, goes down in abject defeat.

The historical background of *Zadig* covers specifically the first fragmentations of the Primitive Wisdom-Religion. Ancient Truth begins to suffer from the confusion wrought by Mosaic faith — Missouf-the "Egyptian" — the thieving "Jew" and Itobad — and by the depredations of Islam — Orcan and Arbogad. The report on "ancient abuse" points to previous falsifications of Truth perpetrated in India for the sake of sectarian goals. The Mayavic "dominion of phantasy" grows more and more severe. Sensory consciousness rules an increasing segment of mankind. The divisive force of Maya which is manifest in sectarianism is also perceptible in the outlook of the average individual. Envy and jealousy torment many souls. Obsession with the Lower Self thwarts and deflects the exercise of higher faculties. The Chrestos which is latent in every human being tends to become atrophied. The Savior goes unrecognized by all but a few persons. Truth suffers a similar fate. But she re-

167

tains radiant beauty for those who can "lift the veil." The spiritual quest of her devotees in favored by the Goddess.

Sectarian chaos fails to affect the entire world. The élites ruling the Orient remain faithful to the Secret Doctrine in the face of the Age of Darkness.

What general conclusions may be drawn from the story viewed in exoteric and esoteric fullness?

Traditional interpretations of *Zadig* remain valid under certain conditions. To readers unacquainted with the general tenor of the Universal Writ, Voltaire offers little reason for optimism. To those who possess "a small fund of philosophy," a message radiant with faith and hope is conveyed. Man needs not be enslaved by fear of damnation or by fear of a mythical Devil. Man needs not tremble in dread of a vengeful personal God. Secure in the knowledge that he has had and will have many lives, Man needs not waste his time on earth seeking various forms of deceptive grantification. The fundamental axiom of materialistic misery: "You live only once" is exploded. While its manifestations are not immediately apparent, divine justice rules the world. Charity needs be no distasteful medicine to giver or receiver. True charity is the most exalted form of selfless self-interest. Far from being forbidden or futile, knowledge of the secrets of Nature is the noblest and happiest enterprise open to Man.

Joyful tomorrows are announced. Impostors are doomed to distant yet inevitable downfall. *Le Souper* foretells a future in which confusion, division, ignorance and hatred will decline. Progress will go hand in hand with full appreciation of ancient knowledge. The Kali-Yuga or Age of Iron is but one stepping stone to a new Golden Age richer than the first.

> " — But our own age, after having mimicked the ancients in everything possible, even to their very names, such as 'senates,' 'prefects,' and 'consuls,' etc.; and after admitting that Napoleon the Great conquered three-fourths of Europe by applying the principles of war taught by the Caesars and the Alexanders knows so much better than its preceptors about psychology, that it would vote every believer in 'animated tablets' into Bedlam.
> Be this as it may, *the religion of the ancients is the religion of the future.* A few centuries more, and there will linger no sectarian beliefs in any of the great religions of humanity. Brahmanism and Buddhism, Christianity and Mohammedanism will all disappear before the mighty rush of facts."
> (*Isis Unveiled*, pp. 612-13, Vol. 1).

The personal plenitude of Divine Wisdom is discreetly reflected. A small measure of Voltaire's own joy is conveyed. One certain sage, probably the same who "amused himself" by writing *Zadig*, has found the key to happiness:

"The master was a philosopher, secluded from society, who cultivated in peace wisdom and virtue, and who, nevertheless, did not suffer from boredom." (*L'Ermite,* p. 74).

The concessive essence of the word "nevertheless" is magically dissolved on the esoteric plane. No contradiction exists between "wisdom," "virtue," and "joy." Such terms define the nature of the "garden" to be "cultivated" at the end of *Candide*: a terrestrial "plot" which may be transformed into a "garden of delights." The understated message of the sentence last quoted is only one element of spiritual autobiography found in Voltairian texts. *Memnon, Micromégas, L'Ingénu,* and the *Poem on the Disaster of Lisbon* conceal material of like nature and astounding — yet perfectly rational — character.

Zadig announces and divests of irony the puzzling sparks of optimism which appear in *Candide* and other Voltairian works. The solid faith of the sage in the destiny of Man reflects wholehearted adherence to the Secret Doctrine.

The story does "say" "more than it seems to say."

LA DANSE — LES YEUX BLEUS

The two chapters of *Zadig* which are entitled *The Dance* and *The Blue Eyes* are not found in editions printed during the lifetime of Voltaire. Their exclusion is easily explained by the esoteric content of the texts.

A King wishes to test the honesty of a prospective treasurer. The same King wishes to test the faithfulness of a woman. Zadig designs certain trials likely to expose any disloyalty. Temptation is placed in the way of all persons investigated. Precious objects are used as "bait" in the case of prospective treasurers. Illicit love is offered to the ladies of the harem.

The proceedings which involve the women are watched through peepholes.

> "Le roi, par des jalousies qui avaient vue sur toutes les cellules, vit toutes ces épreuves, et fut émerveillé. De ses cent femmes, quatre-vingt-dix-neuf succombèrent à ses yeux." (*Les Yeux bleus,* p. 86).
> ("The King through openings which gave views of all cells, saw all those tests, and was dazzled. Of his one hundred wives, ninety-nine yielded under his very eyes.")

Concentrated irony and erotic content are consistent with the traditional view of XVIIIth Century "libertinism." The reader is treated to a glimpse of the seraglio. But the chapter invites second thoughts transcending the level of a "divertissement" or "Turquerie."

The following text, quoted from a letter written in the United States during the second half of the XIXth Century, reveals interesting similarities between the "trials" of the amorous ladies and other "trials" belonging to a different tradition:

> "'34 Bond St., New York,
> June 6, 1877
> "'Your note, asking me to give you an account of my initiation into a secret order among the people commonly known as Druzes, in Mount Lebanon, was received this morning. I took, as you are fully aware, an obligation at that time to conceal within my own memory the greater part of the 'mysteries,' with the most interesting parts of the 'instructions;' so that what is left may not be of any service to the public. Such information as I can rightfully give you are welcome to have and use as you may have occassion.

———.

The initiates include both women and men, and the ceremonies are of so peculiar a nature that both sexes are required to assist in the ritual and 'work.' — The day of initiation must be a continual fast from daylight to sunset in winter, or six o'clock in summer, and the ceremony is from beginning to end a series of trials and temptations, calculated to test the endurance of the candidate under physical and mental pressure.

Among other tests of the neophyte's self-control are the following: Choice pieces of cooked meat, savory soup, pilau, and other appetizing dishes, with sherbet, coffee, wine, and water are set as if accidentally in his way, and he is left alone for a time with the tempting things. To a hungry and fainting soul the trial is severe. But a more difficult ordeal is when the seven priestesses retire, all but one, the youngest and the prettiest, and the door is closed and barred on the outside, after warning the candidate that he will be left to his 'reflections' for half an hour. Wearied by the long-continued ceremonial, weak with hunger, parched with thirst, and a sweet reaction coming after the tremendous strain to keep his animal nature in subjection, this moment of privacy and temptation is brimful of peril. The beautiful young vestal timidly approaching, and with glances which lend a double magnetic allurement to her words, begs him in low tones to 'bless her.' Woe to him if he does! A hundred eyes see him from secret peepholes, and only to the ignorant neophyte is there the appearance of concealment and opportunity." (Prof. A. O. Rawson, letter quoted in *Isis Unveiled,* p. 314, Vol. 2).

The only difference which exists between the tests described by Voltaire and those described by Professor Rawson resides in one detail. Trial by greed is reported in *Zadig.* Treasures are left "as if accidentally" in the path of prospective treasurers. Trial by hunger is similarly arranged in the situation described by Professor Rawson. The ordeal of materialistic temptation is basically the same in each case. Trial by sex is identical in both texts. The "gallery of temptations" featured in *Zadig* serves the same purpose as the barred room mentioned in the above letter. *The Dance* and *The Blue eyes* contain a thinly veiled allusion to initiation rites.

The site of the ceremonies described by Professor Rawson is Mount Lebanon. The same site is openly mentioned by Voltaire in his "amusing" reference to the nose of beautiful Almona. An interesting conclusion seems to be in order. Voltaire was familiar with occult activities and secret rites carried out in the mysterious region of the Near East.

Whether such knowledge came from study, hearsay, direct experience, or from all those sources, cannot be inferred by this writer from *Zadig* alone. But the secrecy surrounding the proceedings suggests that Voltaire was an initiate.

The latter probability seems to be supported by a passage of *Isis Unveiled.* It is noted by Mme Blavatsky that "the great Revolution of

France" was "elaborately prepared by the league of the secret societies and their clever emissaries."* In view of the numerous activities, travels, and connections of the author of *Zadig*, it is difficult to imagine a more fervent or more dedicated "emissary" than Voltaire. It is likely that he was eager to use any and all means — occult means included — to bring about the downfall of the hated "infamous." A passage of *L'Homme aux quarante écus* suggests that the great upheaval was anticipated and prepared at the time of writing. The impulse of one character to "burn" a "convent" is restrained by the advice of another person.

> "A wiser musketeer remonstrated with him that the time had not yet come, and begged him to wait two or three more years."

The two or more years may represent two or more centuries on a certain plane. Voltaire may have pointed to the Revolution which began in 1789. He may also have pointed to an intellectual and spiritual upheaval which he did much to prepare and which he expected to take place in our own age.

Beautiful Falide overcomes all trials described in *Les Yeux Bleus*. Wealth, lust, and power are placed in her path in the form in rich men, handsome pages, and "intrepid" priests. Their seductions are powerless to alter the purity and dedication of the girl. She remains devoted to the King and to him onlv.

The name *Falide* may be the augmented anagram of the word "ideal" which is the same in French and English. It may also be linked to the Arabic term meaning "pearl." Falide is the one candidate among one hundred women to survive all tests. Uniqueness is added to the incorruptible quality of the suggested gem.

Inability to curtsey proves her to be no "courtisane." Prostitution to worldly goods and concerns is alien to her character. The inferior arts of "courtiers" — such as those gravitating around base schemes —, the left-handed skills of "intrepid" "levites" are far beneath her level of preoccupation. "The truth of the story" is the accession of Falide to ultimate Truth. Hers is the plane of untainted spirituality:

> "The truth of the story does not make it possible to conceal the fact that she curtseyed badly; but she danced like the fairies, sang like the mermaids, and spoke like the Graces." (*Les Yeux bleus*, p. 86).

The divine dance performed by Falide is exultant harmony between Cosmos and Self. It is inspired by the "music of the spheres." Her songs

---

Isis Unveiled, p. 22, Vol. 2.

are expressions of thanksgiving rendered by the initiate. Magic dominates the passage — "like the fairies, like the mermaids". It is the magic of highest spirituality. It is the magic of true Grace — "like the Graces". The symbolic seraglio or prison of flesh is ennobled by the human ability to transcend its plane.

The comprehension gap separating exoteric surface from deep substance is enhanced by merriment. Falide is far more than a scheming harem beauty capable of "psyching out" certain tests. Her lofty dedication is made manifest in one trait: she knows how to laugh. She is instinctively sensitive to the grotesquerie of her would-be seducers. Her precious brand of laughter is Divine Wisdom Itself. It rings the same through the ages from Homer to Rabelais, from Voltaire to Vigny, from Céline, Proust and Saint-Exupéry to our times. Falide — and her creator — are sublime proofs of one heartening fact: a mystic who cannot smile is bound to be a phony.

The unworthiness of unsmiling candidates is stressed:

> "When all the candidates had arrived in the drawing-room, His Majesty ordered that they be made to dance. Never did anyone dance more heavily and with less grace; they all had their heads down, their backs bent, their hands stuck against their sides. 'What rogues!' said Zadig under his breath." (*La Danse*, pp. 83-84).

The inverse relationship which exists between "grace" and the force of materialism — or materiality — is clearly stressed. The dishonest candidates who have filled their pockets are subject to certain laws of gravitation. Their efforts fall short of minimal contact with earth.

The importance of vision is indicated by the presence of the amusing word "boopie" which is used to draw attention to the blue eyes of Falide. The etymology of the term seems to convey the concept of "second sight." (Prefix "bi": two — Greek "opsis": vision, sight.) The distinctive color of the eyes of the young woman also carries occult meaning. The "blue ray" has special properties. Some delicate shades of blue are not perceptible to Westerners:

> "The varied influence of the prismatic colors on the growth of vegetation, and especially that of the 'blue ray', has been recognized but recently. The Academicians quarrelled over the unequal heating power of the prismatic rays until a series of experimental demonstrations by General Pleasanton proved that under the blue ray, the most electric of all, animal and vegetable growth was increased to magical proportion . . . Thus we are enabled to show that the latest experiments of science corroborate that which was known to the Hindu sages before any of the modern academies were founded." (*Isis Unveiled*, pp. 264-65, Vol. 1).
> "The French dyers of Lyons, whom no one can surpass in skill, — have

173

a theory that there is a certain delicate shade of blue that Europeans *cannot see.* And in Cashmere, where the girls make shawls worth $30,000, they will show him (the dyer of Lyons) three hundred distinct colors, which he not only cannot make, but cannot even distinguish." (*Isis Unveiled,* Vol. 1).

The importance of "vision" is also stressed by default in the final portion of *The Blue eyes.* A note appended to *Zadig* refers to other adventures of the hero which have been "faithfully recorded in writing." Specialists in Oriental language are requested to transmit the manuscripts if the latter "reach them."

> "At this point is the end of the manuscript which has been recorded on the story of Zadig. These two chapters must certainly be placed after the twelfth chapter, and before the arrival of Zadig in Syria. It is known that he has experienced many other adventures which have been faithfully recorded in writing. Mssrs. the interpreters of Oriental languages are requested to communicate them if they reach them." (*Les Yeux bleus,* p. 88).

Mock deference does not conceal a dim view of the myopic insight which can be expected of most Orientalists. Mme Blavatsky was destined to make similar comments on the peripheral nature of the same insight in her own age.

> "We need not go very deep into the literature of the Orientalists to become convinced that in most cases they do not even suspect that in the arcane philosophy of India there are depths which they have not sounded and *cannot* sound, for they pass on without perceiving them. There is a pervading tone of conscious superiority, a ring of contempt in the treatment of Hindu metaphysics, as though the European mind is alone enlightened enough to polish the rough diamond of the old Sanskrit writers, and separate right from wrong for the benefit of their descendants. We see them disputing over the external forms of expression without a conception of the great vital truths these hide from the profane view." (*Isis Unveiled,* pp. 102-03, Vol. 2).

Simple elements of Oriental thought are common stumbling blocks in the path of erudite Orientalists. The concept of Nirvâna — often misinterpreted as annihilation of the Self — was to arouse the indignation of Barthélemy Saint-Hilaire who found it symptomatic of atheism. "Inaction" — featured in Voltairian writings under the prosaic form of "doing nothing" — concealed in the works of various authors under such savory terms as "lazy one" — "fainéant" and "paresseux" — was to mislead numerous commentators who saw it as a chronic state of physical and mental inertia. Transmigration or metempsychosis is often believed to imply the possible regression of human beings to animal state. Most edifying of all is the attitude equating rejection of the Biblical God with atheism. One needs only see repeatedly branded as unbelievers and even atheists such men as Spinoza and Shelley to measure the sad truth of the prophecy of Voltaire.

What is true of Oriental manuscripts applies to Voltairian texts. The transparent invitation to be "reached" by certain writings is directed at the reader of *Zadig. The Dance* and *the Blue eyes* are situated in the realm of *Serendib*. The spiritual faculty known as "serendipity" is tacitly recommended by the author.

The ironic request which is made of Orientalists is followed by an allusion to "many other adventures" of Zadig which have been recorded in writing. Voltaire may have had in mind certain secret documents "to which none but the highest initiates have access" which are frequently mentioned in the Secret Doctrine.* Such an allusion — if it was intended — may explain the puzzling knowledge displayed by the author. Where and how did he secure information on Petra, Lebanese towers, and initiation rites?

The same passage may contain astounding elements of spiritual autobiography. The status of Savior which is the esoteric status of Zadig connects significantly with certain details of the paragraph. The term "adventures" may be related to the term "avatara" or periodic reincarnation of a spiritual messenger. The verb "essuyer" — *"on sait qu'il a essuyé bien d'autres aventures —"* — the primary meaning of which is that of wiping off a liquid — may be an additional reference to the amphibious nature of the fish-man DAG-OANNES-VISHNU. The allusion to *Syria* may represent a phonetic clue to *Sirius*, a star which is linked to the Instructor of Mankind and which carries heavy significance in *Micromégas* and *Memnon*. The fact that the paragraph in question is written in italics is also suggestive of important esoteric content. It is hinted in *Zadig* — and confirmed in other Voltairian writings — that the Sage who "amused himself" concealed in his works a partial sketch of his cycle of rebirth.

Voltaire did not expect to be fully understood by the general public until the second half of the XXth Century. But it is interesting to note that he regarded *The Dance* and *The Blue Eyes* as sufficiently explosive to be undesirable subjects of immediate publication. The esoteric reader can hardly be surprised.

The Secret Doctrine, p. 437, Vol. II.

MICROMEGAS

Directly or otherwise, the adventures of Zadig involve various parts of the Orient. Chaldea, Egypt, Syria, Scythia, Arabia, India and China are either featured or mentioned in connection with the spiritual pilgrimage of the hero.

Micromégas dwarfs continents into near-insignificance. The solar system forms the setting of the story. The title character is an astronaut without space-capsule who is engaged in the probe of various infinities. Inter-stellar regions are explored. Saturn, Jupiter, Mars, and Earth are either visited or by-passed. The occult view of life passing from one globe to another is suggested. Man appears to live "on many earths before he reaches this."

Micromégas is a giant who normally resides on a satellite of Sirius. His height is of the order of eight leagues. One of his travelling companions has a life expectancy of 15,000 years. The human element represented by the giants proves as taxing to terrestrial imagination as does the cosmic background. Man is suggested to have unsuspected dimensions which are best grasped in the light of a universal design. His relation to Time and Space seems capable of exceeding generally conceived norms.

The idea of relativity is conveyed by the habitat of earthlings and by the name of the hero. The planet Earth — which is regarded by many men as an impressive focus of the universe — is designated as "our little anthill." The diminutive physical stature of human creatures is stressed by the first part of the word *Micro*mégas which means "small" in Greek — *micros*. Greatness is another attribute of Man. The "insects" who reside on the "anthill" prove capable of impressive achievement. Their potential is suggested by the second part of the term Micro*mégas* which means "large" or "great" in Greek — *megas*. The name of the title character contains in a nutshell the occult view of the human creature situated within the framework of the universe. Man is a microcosm within a macrocosm.

> "Man is a microcosm, or a little world; he carries in him a fragment of the great All, in a chaotic state." (*Isis Unveiled*, p. 323, Vol. 1).

The greatness of a small being such as Man constitutes no paradox.

Intellectual ability is independent of physical appearance or stature. But the apparent "contradiction" seems designed to do more than state a well-known fact. Attention is drawn to the illusory nature of material data. One of the travelers featured in the story eventually learns to rise beyond the plane of the senses. The result of his new "vision" is a startling insight into unsuspected schemes of life. The desirable faculty of "rising" beyond certain levels is recommended to the reader from the very beginning of the story. "We" who "conceive nothing beyond our ways" are invited to explore unfamiliar realms where exoteric "paradox" may lead. It is in such generally unknown domains that the key to cosmic mysteries, the key to "Micromégas" the Man, and the key to "Micromégas" the author may be found.

The hidden rationality of cosmic structures is demonstrated by the existence of cosmic harmony. The planet of origin of the title character is enormous. The size of the satellite is inferred from the height of the "Sirian:" "M. Micromégas."

> "A few specialists of algebra, persons ever useful to the public, will immediately take their pen, and will find that, since M. Micromégas, a resident of the country of Sirius, is twenty-four thousand paces high from head to foot, which makes one hundred and twenty thousand feet, and since we, citizens of earth, are about five feet high and since our globe is nine thousand leagues around, they will find, I dare say, that the globe which produced him absolutely must have a circumference twenty one million six hundred thousand times greater than our little earth. Nothing is simpler or more ordinary in Nature." (Ch. I, p. 107).

Chaotic appearance to the contrary, "nothing is more simple or ordinary in Nature" than proportion and harmony. The latter statement is consistent with the previously noted beliefs of Voltaire that "chance does not exist" and that the universe is ruled by mathematical law. The Pythagorean aspect of the Secret Doctrine seems to underlie the passage. The law of analogy which is celebrated in a subsequent portion of the story is implicitly recognized. The same proportions which are valid on Sirius are also valid on our "little anthill." The idea of "absolute necessity" — or evolutionary law — is introduced into the text by means of the locution "il faut absolument." The passage expresses the fundamental Hermetic axiom: "As above, so below; as in heaven, so on earth."

It is observed in *Zadig* that our earth would have to be "another earth" in order to become free of evil or matter-related misery. Systematic — if mysterious — correspondences underlie the various planes of

177

existence which compose the universe. The "prodigious differences" which exist among various modes of being may therefore reflect various degrees of materiality. Such differences cannot be grasped through such contingent optics as terrestrial concepts of Space and Time:

> "The States of a few monarchs of Germany or Italy, the territories of which may be covered in one half hour, compared with the empire of Turkey, Russia, or China, are but a very weak representation of the prodigious differences placed by nature in all beings." (Ch. I, pp. 107-08).

The conjunction of hypotheses "beyond our ways" — a major theme of *Micromégas* — and "prodigious differences" suggests far more to be at stake than the material framework of time and space. Voltaire seem to be concerned with the occult scale of *quality* of-or approach to-knowledge. The presence of the adjective "weak" tends to underscore by default the spiritual orientation and nature of the "prodigious differences." As was previously noted, "strength" is spirit in the esoteric vocabulary. "Weakness" therefore amounts to lack of spirituality. The "very weak image" of "prodigious differences" not revealed by a materialistic outlook prepares the apology of "the conveyances of up there." The qualitative survey of "differences" which is recommended to the reader seems to point to the occult view of planetary chains geared to various material and spiritual "densities." The importance of extra-sensory perception is likewise stressed in Voltairian texts and in theosophical literature.

Space travel is achieved through skilled use of the "laws of gravitation." The "forces of attraction and repulsion" are utilized.

> "Our traveller knew in marvelous manner the laws of gravitation and all forces of attraction and repulsion." (Ch. I, p. 109).

The same combination of forces is the subject of various comments in *The Secret Doctrine*. Gravitation, attraction and repulsion are regarded as mere aspects of the same physical and hyperphysical law: universal magnetism. Newton is believed to have been the cautious interpreter of a theosophist: Jacob Boehme:

> "Thus Newton whose profound mind read easily between the lines, and fathomed the spiritual thought of the great Seer in its mystic rendering, owes his great discovery to Jacob Boehme, — " (*The Secret Doctrine*, p. 494, Vol. I).

> "The *Athenaeum* of Jan. 26, 1867, has some curious information upon this subject. It says that 'positive evidence can be adduced that Newton derived all his knowledge of gravitation and its laws from Boehme, with

178

whom gravitation or ATTRACTION is the first property of Nature.' . . . For with him 'his (Boehme's) system, shows us the inside of things, while modern physical science is content with looking at the outside.' " (*The Secret Doctrine*, p. 494, Vol. I.)

"Thus, supposing attraction or gravitation should be given up in favour of the Sun being a *huge magnet* — which is a theory already accepted by some physicists — a magnet that acts on the planets as attraction is now supposed to do, whereto, or how much farther would it lead the astronomers from where they are now? Not an inch farther. Kepler came to this 'curious hypothesis' nearly 300 years ago. He had not dicovered the theory of attraction and repulsion in Kosmos, for it was known from the days of Empedocles, the two opposite forces being called by him 'hate' and 'love' — which comes to the same thing. But Kepler gave a pretty fair description of cosmic magnetism. That such magnetism exists in nature, is as certain as that gravitation does not; not at any rate, in the way in which it is taught by Science, which never took into consideration the different modes in which the dual Force — that occultists call attraction and repulsion — may act within our solar system, the earth's atmosphere, and *beyond* in the Kosmos. This was proven by Newton himself; for there are many phenomena in our Solar system, which he confessed his inability to explain by the law of gravitation." (*The Secret Doctrine*, pp. 497-98, Vol. I).

The same forces of attraction and repulsion underlie universal harmony or "balance" from the pragmatic level of "equilibrium" dear to Sétoc to the exalted plane of the music of the spheres. The Voltairian traveler who knows them "in marvelous manner" is probably not deceived by their "marvelous" or magical quality. The mode of expression which is used suggests that "gravitation" on the one hand "*and* all forces of attraction and repulsion" on the other hand amount to the same thing. Voltaire seems to exploit the word "and" in typically esoteric manner: in order to fuse, not to separate.

The occult concept of "force" is equivalent to "spirit."

"What is the WILL? Can 'exact science' tell? What is the nature of that intelligent, intangible, and powerful something which reigns supreme over all inert matter? The great Universal Idea willed, and the cosmos sprang into existence. I *will,* and my limbs obey. I *will,* and my thought, traversing space, which does not exist for it, envelops the body of another individual who is not a part of myself, penetrates through his pores, and superseding his own faculties, if they are weaker, forces him to a predetermined action. It acts like the fluid of a galvanic battery on the limbs of a corpse. The mysterious effects of attraction and repulsion are the *unconscious* agents of that will; fascination, such as we see exercised by some animals, by serpents over birds, for instance, is a *conscious* action of it, and the result of thought . . . What is then this inexplicable power of attraction but an atomical portion of that essence that scientists and Kabalists equally recognize as 'the principle of life' — the *akasa?*" (*Isis Unveiled*, p. 144, Vol. 1).

179

"Power," "Force," and "spirit" are clearly shown to be one and the same; "that intelligent, intangible, and powerful something which reigns supreme over all inert matter." Comparable concepts of "attraction and repulsion" seem to be presented in identical terms and identical spirit by Voltaire and by Mme Blavatsky. A passage of *L'Ingénu* suggests the link between mind and matter to be none other than Spirit, "that unknown fluid the existence of which is certain."

The same view of forces of attraction and repulsion seems to be held by various writers. It is stated by Marcel Proust that "—the space occupied by the smallest puff of alder can be explained by the conflict or equilibrium of laws of attraction and repulsion which govern far greater worlds."*

Rabelais is sometimes accused of "incoherence." The alleged failure of the author to follow a rigorous plan is occasionally demonstrated by a survey of the beginning of the *Tiers Livre*. It is a stressed that the "ramblings" on debtors and borrowers which appear at that point have "nothing to do with the question of the marriage of Panurge."** The latter name is generally interpreted etymologically as a derivation from the Greek *Pan ergos* — "all work" — or, in this particular instance, "capable of anything." But the same etymology may also convey the idea of "a (human) particle of cosmic energy" — perhaps that same "intelligent intangible, and powerful something which reigns supreme over all inert matter." Panurge may then be viewed as a human projection of the "principle of life" following its toilsome course of cyclic evolution.

The Rabelaisian character in question is indeed capable of anything — as literary manuals are quick to point out. He is even capable of achieving the mystical "marriage" or "perfection." But the latter capacity of Panurge usually goes unnoticed.

The praise of "lending and borrowing" is openly linked by Rabelais to the maintenance of the universe. It is consistent with an openly declared "scorn of fortuitous things."*** It is connected with the "lofty contemplation of the wonders of Nature.**** It is therefore inseparable from knowledge of cosmic law "above and below." The "love" and "hate" — or cosmic give — and-take of Empedocles — has terrestrial and celestial correspondences in the *Tiers Livre*. Such is the theme of "lending and borrowing" which is far from irrelevant to the "marriage" of Panurge.

A la Recherche du temps perdu, p. 213, Vol. III.
**Classiques Garnier, *Rabelais,* Pierre Jourda, pp. xxxii-xxxviii, Vol. 1.
***Prologue, *Quart Livre.*
****Tiers Livre, Ch. XVIII.

Voltairian considerations on cosmic laws and cosmic harmony are connected with a critical view of "exact science." M. le Secrétaire de l'Académie de Saturne is the target of deep irony — not to say sarcasm.

> "Il lia una étroite amitié avec le secrétaire de l'Académie de Saturne, homme de beaucoup d'esprit qui n'avait à la vérité rien inventé, mais qui rendait un fort bon compte des inventions des autres et qui faisait passablement de petits vers et de grands calculs." (Ch. I, pp. 109-110).

> ("He formed a close friendship with the Secretary of the Academy of Saturn, a man of great wit, who had in truth invented nothing, but who gave a very good account of the inventions of others and who made passably some small verse and some great mathematical operations.")

The plagiaristic weakness of M. le Secrétaire is an allusion to the "discoveries" or "borrowed robes" of modern science. Voltaire calls attention to the same spoliation of scientific "gold" as does Mme Blavatsky. The specific origin of M. le Secrétaire points to the "péché mignon" of many Judaeo-Christian scholars: shameless theft of the findings of others and shameless appropriation of ancient Pagan lore. As was previously noted, Saturn is the mythological equivalent of Bacchus, Dionysos, and Jehovah. His representative in the present case is a worthy precursor of certain Proustian characters personified by "Bloch." Such individuals are fairly common in "Jewish" — Judaeo-Christian — communities and are aptly labeled by Françoise as "des copiateurs."* The quality of their ethics and the worth of their knowledge are pungently characterized by the author of *Micromégas*. The productions of M. le Secrétaire may be read as "little worms" and "great kidney-stones." Voltaire — who once compared parasitic detractors of great minds to "excrements of literature"** seems to have used the pun value of the "petits vers" and "grands calculs" in the same rank vein. Coarse sarcasm was deemed worthy of its mark: incurably phallic or literal insight, mediocre intellect, and contemptible character.

The subsequent evaluation of Pascal is less easy to understand. The faculties of the XVIIth Century philosopher are compared with those of M. Micromégas:

> "He had not yet reached the age of two hundred and fifty years, and he was studying, according to the custom, at the college of Jesuits of his planet, when he divined through the strength of his mind more than fifty Euclidian propositions. That is eighteen more than Blaise Pascal, who, having divined thirty-two as if in child's play, according to his sister, be-

---

*A la Recherche du temps perdu, p. 1034, Vol. III.
**L'Ingénu, Ch. XI.

came later a rather mediocre geometrician and a very poor metaphysician."
(Ch. I, p. 108).

The genius of Pascal is credited with having sensed certain scientific truths. The words "divined," "strength," and "mind" — esoterically "spirit" — plainly situate the text in the realm of divination and spiritual effort. Voltaire deplores poor use of precious natural gifts. What prompted his judgment, particularly where metaphysics are concerned? The question is promptly answered by a reference to certain "conveyances of up there." Such aids were apparently not accessible to Pascal.

"Those who travel by carriage or stagecoach only will doubtlessly be amazed at the conveyances of up there: for we, on our small heap of mud, conceive nothing beyond our ways." (Ch. I, p. 109).

The cosmic vistas which may be opened to a few explorers — relying on certain "laws of attraction and repulsion" — are infinitely more vast than the limited horizons revealed by earth-bound "trips." Voltaire seems to contrast the restricted range of the cold intellect and the all-embracing flash of intuition.

The Pascalian view of Man struggling between the infinitely great and the infinitely small strikingly resembles the perspective of Micromégas the man and *Micromégas* the story. Insignificance and greatness are major human attributes in Pascalian thought and Voltairian philosophy. But the "roseau pensant" of Pascal does not venture beyond materialistic bounds of inquiry except to postulate Divine Grace from the depth of despair. The impressive faculties of Pascal suffer from intellectual and spiritual deprivation. The personal God and personal Devil of Christian tradition, related dogma, and the confines of "exact science" are to blame. The criticism of Voltaire contains reverence for and sympathy with a kindred soul deprived of the liberating influence of Divine Wisdom. The same attitude will be found to color his general view of Jansenism in the course of the present work.

Alfred de Vigny returned a similar verdict:

"Pascal took a great deal from Montaigne, but his concise form and the isolation of his ideas, which gives them a sententious quality, like the word of an oracle, made his views which were born of the meditations and walks of another.
If Pascal says: 'I am afraid of death and of the devil, that is why I break my head for fear of thinking, that only proves his weakness and all his book of *Thoughts* seems to amount to that.
Morbid poltroonery in a powerful brain." (*Journal*, 1843).

The fear of death dominates the majority of mankind. The human mind naturally rebels against the thought of annihilation. The terror is particularly severe in the Western world where belief in reincarnation is either unknown or rejected. Christian belief in eternal life is rarely firm. It is poisoned by the twin dreads of devil and Hell. Spiritual anguish is most intense where Jansenistic predestination is involved — as in the case of Pascal. The pre-ordained "dance macabre" which merit itself is powerless to avert is understandably seen as a curse. The analysis of Pascalian "weakness" performed by Voltaire and Vigny is focused on identical factors. It is the indictment of a faith divorced from the grace of personal merit. It is the indictment of a "faith" based on fear. "Crush the infamous!" may easily be perceived in the common verdict of the two great writers. The "infamous" is the perverted dogma which can stunt the intellect — not to mention the spirit — of a most "powerful brain."

The limitations imposed by exact science are added to the atrophy resulting from religious fear. The "walks" which supplied Pascal with a great deal of his philosophical substance are — in the opinion of Vigny — the "trips" of another person. The allusion of Voltaire to the report of Mme Périer — the sister of Pascal — points to a similar deficit in the area of mathematics. According to Tallemand des Réaux — who seems to be more reliable than Mme Périer — Pascal finally confessed to his father that he had secretly read the six first books of Euclid rather than "divined" them.* Voltaire and Vigny stress the same lack of the same "conveyances" which are required to produce independent discovery in the realm of metaphysics, mathematics, and elsewhere.

The meaningful presence of such terms as "strength" and "weakness" should be noted in the texts of each commentator. Such Voltairian expressions as "strength of mind," "very bad metaphysician" — "fort mauvais métaphysicien"; — such locutions of Vigny as "weakness" and "powerful brain" underscore the importance of the same intuitive or spritual faculties. The isolation of ideas which is noted by Vigny seems to involve far more than the realm of stylistics. Pascal is apparently regarded as a sort of modern European Sétoc as yet untutored by the disciple of "Zoroaster." Pascal is naturally gifted with insights which need to be integrated into a coherent whole.

The handicaps of Pascal — which cannot be designated openly by Vigny or Voltaire — reflect the joint failures of dogmatic theology and "exact science." The damaging separation of the once united "twins" is involved.

What can only be suggested by Vigny and Voltaire is positively stated in the Secret Doctrine. The "conveyances of up there" — which remained

---

Historiettes, 188-89.

inacessible to Pascal in integrated philosophical form — are defined by Mme Blavatsky. The ability to "transcend the narrow limitations of sense, and transfer — consciousness into the region of noumena and the sphere of primal causes" is the theosophical counterpart of the "conveyances of up there."

> "So far as Science remains what in the words of Prof. Huxley it is, viz., 'organized common sense;' so far as its inferences are drawn from accurate premises — its generalizations resting on a purely inductive basis — every Theosophist and Occultist welcomes respectfully and with due admiration its contributions to the domain of cosmological law. There can be no possible conflict between the teachings of occult and so-called exact Science, where the conclusions of the latter are grounded on a substratum of unassailable fact. It is only when its more ardent exponents, over-stepping the limits of observed phenomena in order to penetrate into the arcana of Being, attempt to wrench the formation of Cosmos and its *living* Forces from Spirit, and attribute all to blind matter, that the Occultists claim the right to dispute and call in question their theories. Science cannot, owing to the very nature of things, unveil the mystery of the universe around us. Science can, it is true, collect, classify, and generalize upon phenomena; but the occultist, arguing from admitted metaphysical data, declares that the daring explorer, who would probe the inmost secrets of Nature, must transcend the narrow limitations of sense, and transfer his consciousness into the region of noumena and the sphere of primal causes. To effect this, he must develop faculties which are absolutely dormant — save in a few rare and exceptional cases — in the constitution of the off-shoots of our present Fifth Root-Race in Europe and America. He can in no other conceivable manner collect the facts on which to base his speculations. In this not apparent on the principles of Inductive Logic and Metaphysics alike?" (*The Secret Doctrine,* pp. 477-78, Vol. I).

The necessary transfer of consciousness into certain regions is a major concern of esoteric writers. It is only by means of such a "conveyance" that the full tenor of their works can be perceived. Such a result is — of course — devoutly awaited at an appropriate point of human evolution. "Smugglers" never fail to stress the *sine qua non* condition of esoteric insight. To the Voltairian "conveyances of up there" may be added the Proustian definition of intuition as "experimental faith." The same daring approach to knowledge is also designated by Louis Pauwels and Jacques Berger as "a transmutation of the intelligence."*

> " — intelligence is not the most subtle, .the most powerful, the most appropriate instrument to grasp truth, that is only one more reason to begin with intelligence, and not with a subconscious intuitivism, with a ready-made faith in premonitions. It is life, which, little by little, case by case. permits us to note that what is most important to our heart, mind, or

---

The Morning of the Magicians, p. xxi.

spirit, is not taught us by reasoning, but by powers of another nature. And then, it is intelligence itself which, realizing their superiority, abdicates, through reasoning, to them, and accepts to become their collaborator and their servant. Experimental faith." (*A la Recherche du temps perdu,* p. 423, Vol. III).

The "daring explorer" who can and does "transfer" his "consciousness" into certain regions is often contrasted to his earthbound counterpart by esoteric writers. The term "explorer" makes numerous appearances in many texts. The title character of *The Little Prince* is aptly designated as such by the terrene, desk-bound *geographer*. The latter person is the academic extension of the Jehovic businessman featured in the same book. The scholar is more interested in the character of the discoverer than in the nature of the discovery. He is aware of the explosive potential of certain findings born of the second sight of "dipsomaniacs" who "see double." And he is sore afraid. Like M. le Secrétaire de l'Académie de Saturne, he has "in truth invented nothing." But he can give a fair account of the inventions and discoveries of others. Such discoveries as he does not choose to steal are subject to his dedicated sabotage. The "geographer" and others of his kind are the greatest enemies of new knowledge which upsets their preconceptions and professional applecarts. "In every instance," writes Mme Blavatsky, "they have done their best to shipwreck the new discovery, together with the discoverer."*

The distinction made by Voltaire between "scholars" and "good company" has a correspondence of ancient origin in the distinction made by occultists between "geographers" and "explorers." According to the Secret Doctrine, "Geography was part of the mysteries in days of old. "Says the *Zohar* (iii., fol. 10a): These secrets,(of land and sea) were divulged *to the men of the secret science,* but not to the geographers."**

Literature is not overlooked. Symbolism and metaphors are found to be abused and misused. Their deep substance is underrated. Such is the gist of a lively discussion opposing Micromégas and M. le Secrétaire. The "Sirian" "explorer" believes in the "usefulness" of great literary works. He does not accept the idea that readers should be content with flowery futility. He rejects the "poetic" effusions of his companion. The Saturnian is a master in the art of evasion. But his metaphorical smokescreen does not resist the probes of Micromégas:

" 'Yes,' said the Saturnian, 'nature is like a flowerbed the flowers of which
. . .' 'Ah!' said the other, 'spare me your flowerbeds.' — 'It is,' the secretary went on, 'like a gathering of blondes and brunettes whose ornaments
. . .' — 'Eh! what do I care for your brunettes,' said the other . . . — 'It

*Isis Unveiled, p. 84, Vol. 1.
**The Secret Doctrine, p. 9, Vol. II.

is like a gallery of paintings the features of which . . .' — 'Eh! no,' said the traveller, 'I repeat, nature is like nature. Why should one seek comparisons for it?' — 'To please you,' replied the secretary.' — 'I do not want to be pleased,' the traveller replied, 'I want to be taught.' " (Ch. II, p. 110).

Symbols and metaphors have merit under certain conditions. They serve to elevate thought from material regions to the plane of pure Idea. They supply sensory and intellectual points of departure to higher faculties: "the conveyances of up there." The imagery of M. le Secrétaire has the opposite effect of forcing thought downwards. This can hardly surprise the esoteric reader. The academician belongs to a system which promotes "phallic" or low-altitude interpretations. The mental flight likely to produce esoteric take-offs is not encouraged by the Jehovic — or Judaeo-Christian — personage whether or not he be able to conceive such "trips."

Micromégas has equal respect for all-embracing Nature and for the infinite potential of Man. The Sirian takes a dim view of the mental attitude which separates and degrades — through debasing comparison and otherwise — the twin aspects of Divine Ideation. The title character of the story seems to endorse the occult view that nothing could possibly be outside of Nature.

The literary outpourings of M. le Secrétaire represent a caricature of true poetry. Poetry — and generally, Literature — often carry the message of the Secret Doctrine. Far more than a "divertissement" aimed at "pleasing," they are repositories of secret knowledge. Their ambitious goal is no less than the *instruction* of mankind. In the words of Alfred de Vigny, the Muse is far more than "the daughter of a lovely whim."* According to Mme Blavatsky mythology and literature are frequent carriers of "poetised truth."** The reader of *Micromégas* is discreetly urged to make an important distinction between empty technical displays and genuine inspiration. By the same token he is invited to examine attentively the genuine article.

The beginning of *Micromégas* is dominated by a significant conjunction of physics, metaphysics, mathematics, and literature. The emphasis placed on spatial exploration and on the "conveyances of up there" suggests that such areas of knowledge might be viewed with profit from a lofty, cosmic plane which can be reached through certain "flights" and through them only. The total message is an exhortation to use subjective faculties.

Diary 1843.
**The Secret Doctrine*, p. 7, Vol. II.

The task of the spiritual seeker and the work of the esoteric researcher require an approach to knowledge which is not popular in the Western world. The esoteric student of literature — when and *if* allowed to present his findings — is usually taxed with "extreme subjectivity" by academic supervisors and rated accordingly. The supervisors do not realize what a spectacular compliment they are paying to the bold inquirer. Their view of *subjectivity* — a dirty word in their vocabulary — is that of a vagrant and baseless intuitivism. One may cite to them — at one's risk and peril — the careful distinction made by Proust between a ready-made faith in premonitions and *experimental subjective* insight. One may invoke the statement of Saint Exupéry: "To know is not to prove, nor to explain. It is to accede to vision."* One may cite the crucial pronouncement of Mme Blavatsky — which inverts the poles of Western philosophy and terrifies "geographers": "It needs but the right perception of things objective to discover that the only world of reality is the subjective."** One may show that the occult view of reality is reflected with individual and collective consistency in the texts of numerous great writers. One may demonstrate that the right kind of subjective approach leads to rock-like solidity. One may quote — with bittersweet irony — the ancient axiom which is the motto of some universities: "Mens agitat molem!" All in vain. The apostles of objectivity — a magic word — remain stubbornly allergic to their own notion of objective proof. One can only reflect on the sad accuracy of "Voltairian" thought. Those who travel by earthbound conveyances only — and turn the study of literature into dreary bookeeping — conceive nothing beyond their ways.

The Voltairian survey of knowledge continues with a strange element of zoology. An intriguing book written by the title character is mentioned:

> " — it was a matter of knowing whether the substantial form of the fleas of Sirius was of the same nature as that of snails — The trial lasted two hundred and twenty years." (Ch. I, p. 108).

While the topic of the book invites exoteric ridicule, it will be shown — in a subsequent chapter — to veil prophetic insight.

Two conclusions may be drawn from the initial survey of human knowledge. "More things are possible than is generally thought."*** The dimensions, the variety, and the harmony of Cosmos suggest as much.

Flight to Arras, Ch. V.
**Isis Unveiled*, p. 639, Vol. 2.
***Micromégas*, Ch. VII.

So does human ability to use "the conveyances of up there." General insight and genuine Self-Knowledge require courageous use of intuitive faculties.

The importance of the physical senses is recognized. The senses are necessary tools of practical experience which provide a basis for intellectual inquiry. Micromégas wishes to receive information on the sensory system of Saturnians:

> " — first of all begin by telling me how many senses the men of your planet have." (Ch. II, p. 110).

The inhabitants of Saturn have seventy-two senses. But their impressive endowment fails to produce happiness. They complain of the inadequacy of their faculties. Their "imagination" goes "beyond their needs." The Sirian confesses that his fellow-creatures are subject to a similar restlessness in spite of their "approximately one thousand senses." There seem to be no mortals who do not have "more desires than genuine needs and more needs than satisfaction." The statements of the Sirian and Saturnian and the emphasis placed on "need" stress the esoteric concept of "necessity" reflected on various globes of a planetary chain. The recognized inadequacy of the senses and the universal, unsatisfied longing point to the probable existence of unknown faculties which have little or no opportunity to express themselves. The omnipresent yearning for a better mode of life gives evidence of the vitality of human spirit. Voltaire conveys the occult view of graduated Being evolved on graduated planetary systems. Also suggested are views which do not limit the number of senses to five.

> "The division of the physical senses into five, comes to us from great antiquity. But while adopting the number, no modern philosopher has asked himself how these senses could exist, *i.e.*, be perceived and used in a self-conscious way, unless there was the *sixth* sense, mental perception to register and record them, and (this for the Metaphysicians and Occultists) the SEVENTH to preserve the spiritual fruition and remembrance thereof, as in a Book of Life which belongs to Karma. The ancients divided the senses into five, simply because their teachers (the Initiates) stopped at the *hearing,* as being that sense which developed in the *physical* plane (got dwarfed rather, limited to this plane) only at the beginning of the Fifth Race. (The Fourth Race already had begun to lose the *spiritual* condition, so pre-eminently developed in the Third Race.)" (*The Secret Doctrine*, p. 535 fn., Vol. I).

The "book of Life which belongs to Karma" is reminiscent of Jesrad — Karma personified — and of his Book of Fate. Voltaire seems to have the same conception of the seventh sense as does Mme Blavatsky. It is the mysterious source of relentless yearning with can only be satisfied by "perfection."

It is observed in the first chapter of the story that Micromégas undertakes his cosmic journey in order to "form his *heart and mind* as people say." The irony conveyed by the end of the sentence and by the esoteric bait of italics suggests a dim view of incomplete classifications. Man is far more complex than the accepted aggregate of "mind" and "heart."

The latter phrase is probably meant to convey the esoteric equivalence of "spirit" and "heart" — Knowledge-and-Ethics — the inseparable "twins" of occult philosophy. The deceptive use of *and* may be compared with the Proustian use of *or* in a text which has already been quoted: — what is most important for our heart, or for our spirit. Voltaire and Proust similarly join the separated "twins" on the same lofty plane. The symbolic reunion is not only possible but inevitable in the realm of "the conveyances of up there" which is also the realm of "experimental faith."

Profound differences exist between Micromégas and M. le Secrétaire. But agreement is reached on one point. There is universal longing for a happier, more perfect state. Fulfillment seems to elude all modes of existence in any way connected with sensory experience. The "country where nothing lacks" is suggested to lie in the realm of pure immateriality.

" — dans notre globe nous avons près de mille sens, et il nous reste encore je ne sais quel désir vague, je ne sais qulle inquietude, qui nous avertit sans cesse que nous sommes peu de chose et qu'il y a des êtres beaucoup plus parfaits. J'ai un peu voyagé; j'ai vu des mortels fort au-dessous de nous; j'en ai vu de fort supérieurs; mais je n'en vu aucuns qui n'aient plus de besoins que de satisfactions. J'arriverai peut-être un jour au pays où il ne manque rien; mais jusques à présent, personne ne m'a donné de nouvelles positives de ce pays-là." (Ch. II, pp. 110-111).

(" — on our globe we have almost one thousand senses, and there still remains in us an indefinable vague desire, an indefinable restlessness, which warns us constantly that we are very little and that there are far more perfect beings. I have travelled a little; I have seen mortals quite inferior to us; I have seen some who are far superior to us; but I have seen none who did not have more needs than satisfaction. Perhaps, some day, I shall arrive in the country where nothing lacks, but so far no one has given me positive news of that country.")

The raison d'être of planetary sites corresponding to various planes of existence is insistently connected with more or less prevalent spirituality. The esoteric presence of "force" ("fort au-dessous de nous," "fort supérieurs") is linked to the esoteric concept of "need" or "necessity" which represents cyclic evolution. Spirit is shown to dwell on all planes of being from the lowest to the highest: yearning is universal. The blessed state of Nirvana — "the country where nothing lacks" because No-Thing is ALL — is not found on any material plane. It is reached at the end of a long voyage through multiple lives. The existence of a chain of rebirth is acknowledged by the deceptively bland words: "I have traveled a little." That life is a journey through Cosmos and reincarnation is repeatedly stated by esoteric writers from Anaxagoras to our days.

No mortal is satisfied with his life expectancy. The Saturnian who will probably live 15,000 years, is depressed by the brevity of his existence:

> "Hardly has one begun to acquire a little instruction when death arrives before one has gained experience. Personally, I dare make no plans; I find myself like a drop of water in an immense ocean. I am ashamed, especially in front of you, of the ridiculous appearance which I put in this world." (Ch. II, p. 111).

Lyricism and comedy mingle in the above confession. Truth finds an unexpected advocate in the person of the Saturnian. The moment of death is connected with the moment of truth. The comparison between Man and a drop of water lost in the ocean is used in the texts of Christian Kabalists to represent the ocean of reincarnation and the ocean of occult knowledge. The microcosm in the macrocosm is one ocean within another. The comparison of the Kabalists is explained by Mme Blavatsky:

> "They compared 'the spirit imprisoned within the soul to a drop of water enclosed within a capsule of gelatine and thrown in the ocean; so long as the capsule remains whole, the drop of water remains isolated; break the envelope, and the drop becomes a part of the ocean — its individual existence has ceased. — So it is with the spirit. As long as it is enclosed in its plastic mediator, or soul, it has an individual existence." (*Isis Unveiled*, p. 315, Vol. 1).

The *imagery* of Christian kabalists is *alone* regarded as valid. Belief in the loss of spiritual individuality is strongly denied in subsequent passage of *Isis Unveiled* — and elsewhere *

The kabalistic mode of expression of the Saturnian is interesting. The traveling companion of Micromégas does not seem to lack insight. But his esoteric imagery lends itself to distortion. The latter fact may explain the feared loss of "instruction" which is expected at the end of each life. The same fact may account for the pedestrian interpretation of symbolism which was previously noted. The Saturnian seems

---

The Secret Doctrine, p. 266, Vol. I.

to know — or to sense — enough to dread the results of an inspired approach to knowledge.

The profound meaning of the discourse is veiled by the presence of comical elements. The life expectancy of 15,000 years — an eternity by prevailing earthly standards — combines drollery with a serious suggestion of time cycles involved in universal and individual evolution. The general mood induced by the passage — a mixture of grotesquerie and depth — is symbolic of the mortal condition.

Two aspects of sensory illusion — terrestrial time and space — are discussed. Micromégas makes the following statement:

> "When the body must be returned to the elements and when nature must be revived under another form, a process called dying, when that time of metamorphosis has come, to have lived an eternity or to have lived one day, is precisely the same thing." (Ch. II, p. 111).

Reality knows no such contingency as earthly time. Moments and aeons are meaningless on the ultimate plane of Being. The cyclic scheme of life and death — evolution and involution of matter — the succession of Days and Nights of Brahma — involve periods difficult to conceive. The spectacular life expectancy of the Saturnian is dwarfed by the fantastic schedule of the Universe:

> "Throughout the whole immense period of progressive creation, covering 4,320,000,000 years, ether, air, water and fire (heat), are constantly forming matter under the never-ceasing impulse of the Spirit, or the *unrevealed* God who fills up the whole creation for he is in all, and all is in him." (*Isis Unveiled*, p. 272, Vol. 2).

The Voltairian view of death is identical to the "modern" view of continuous transformation of matter. The destruction of transient physical forms is suggested to be a mere step in the evolution of new existence. Voltaire might as well have written — as did Mme Blavatsky — that "there is no inorganic or *dead* matter in nature, the distinction between the two made by Science being as unfounded as it is arbitrary and devoid of reason.*

Saturnian belief in eternal life is weak. The Judaeo-Christian Secrétaire sees little reason to "make plans" in the face of what he regards as total and inevitable destruction. No such fear is expressed by Micromégas who surveys the life-and-death process with serenity. The contrast is an eloquent commentary on Christian faith: a religion conducive to unbelief and despair. The "Sirian" idea of "reviving nature under another

---

The Secret Doctrine, p. 280, Vol. I.

form" points to the productive continuity of a meaningful chain of life. The same "chain" assumes significance in a subsequent chapter of the story.

The spatial distribution of matter reflects cosmic harmony. The work of a divine intelligence made manifest by proportion can be perceived beyond the veil of chaotic appearance.

> "There are everywhere persons of good sense who know how to adjust to the order of things and how to thank the author of nature. He has spread over this universe a profusion of varieties, with an admirable kind of uniformity — matter is spatial everywhere but it has different properties on each globe." (Ch. II, p. 112).

The cosmic picture of "a profusion of varieties" combined with "admirable uniformity" is identical to the occult view of planetary chains geared to various material and spiritual densities. In the words of Mme Blavatsky: "— reality, in the manifested world is composed of a *unity of units*."* The same concealed prevalence of "unity" is stressed by Voltaire with reference to living creatures. "Prodigious differences" are believed to exist between various kinds of beings. Basic similarities exist as well.

> " — all thinking beings differ, and all resemble one another fundamentally in that they are gifted with thought and desire." (Ch. II, p. 112).

The common factor of "thought and desire" — which corresponds to the team of "Mind" and "Heart" — amounts to more or less latent "spirit" on the esoteric plane. Spirit is the solvent of apparent contradiction between manifest chaos and noumenal harmony.

The universal consistency of spiritual dynamics noted by Voltaire is a re-statement of the Hermetic axiom: "As above, so below; as in heaven, so on earth."

The Voltairian concept of universal harmony reflects the occult view of Cosmos. The esoteric content of the beginning of *Micromégas* — which is insistently suggested by cleverly scattered remarks — can be summarized by the following statement of a theosophical writer:

> "It will readily be supposed that the chain of worlds to which the earth belongs are not all prepared for a material existence, exactly, or even approximately resembling our own. There would be no meaning in an organized chain of worlds which were all alike, and might as well all have been amalgamated into one. In reality the worlds with which we are connected are very unlike each other, not merely in outward condi-

---

Ibid., p. 629, Vol. I.

tions, but in that supreme characteristic, the proportion in which spirit and matter are mingled in their constitution." (A.P. Sinnett, *Esoteric Buddhism*, p. 79).

Three modes of being are reported to exist on Saturn. A scale of ascending spirituality is outlined under a deceptive surface of exoteric irony. The "supreme characteristic" of spiritual — or material — density underlies the passage.

"He inquired how many essentially different substances were found on Saturn. He learned that only about thirty were counted, such as God, space, matter, spatial beings who feel, spatial beings who feel and who think, thinking beings who are non-spatial, those which interpenetrate, those which do not interpenetrate, and the rest." (Ch. II, pp. 112-13).

The importance of "essence" or Spirit is again stressed by the presence of the word "essentially." Mutually penetrating forms of existence involve more than one planet. The entire Cosmos may be viewed as an interpenetration of matter and spirit distributed in varying proportions. The presence of "penetrating" spirit in every particle of matter will be suggested by Micromégas in a subsequent chapter of the story. Occult philosophy teaches that the human body itself is subject to the penetration of more or less ethereal agents who "*can enter in us*; move our limbs and organs; and use us as they please."*

Special reference seems to be made to the occult view of seven planes of human consciousness. While major classifications are those of body, soul, and spirit, the occult scale of awareness has *seven* components. The dividing line separating lower levels from one another is often hazy, some of the strata being vehicles — *upadhis* — of the next higher plane. A similar relationship exists between the sixth principle — *Buddhi*, divine intuition — and *Atma* — the highest spiritual principle or innermost essence. The level upon which "penetration" occurs is the level of consciousness:

" — the sixth principle may be called the vehicle of the seventh, and the fourth the vehicle of the fifth; but yet another mode of dealing with the problem teaches us to regard each of the higher principles, from the fourth upwards, as a vehicle of what in Buddhist philosophy, is called the one life or Spirit. According to this view of the matter the one life is that which perfects, by inhabiting the various vehicles. In the animal the one life is concentrated in the *kama rupa*. In man it begins to penetrate the fifth principle as well. In perfected man it penetrates the sixth, and when it penetrates the seventh, man ceases to be man, and attains a wholly superior condition of existence." (*Esoteric Buddhism*, A. P. Sinnett, pp. 72-73).

---

*Baron du Potet, quoted in *Isis Unveiled*, p. 333, Vol. 1.

It will be found in due course of the present study that all seven planes of consciousness but one are personified in *Candide*. The seventh and highest — *Atma* — is symbolized by non-incarnate, adamantine purity. Such a mode of representation is consistent with the occult view according to which Atma is too pure to be tainted with contingent existence yet is indissolubly connected with each individual.

A flippant tone is used to lump together "about thirty substances," "God," "Space," and "matter." It is suggested that the number *thirty* denotes inferiority, an interesting hypothesis from non-Saturnian standpoints. It is also suggested by the same number that Saturnians hold trinitarian views and that the concept of a trinity — or Three-in-One — has concrete reflections in the entire universe. There are, incidentally, *three* hundred substances on Sirius. Micromégas claims to have discovered *three* thousand others. The glib enumeration of metaphysical concepts "and the rest" tends to equate related speculation and foolishness. The promiscuous handling of matter and Deity suggests certain lack of respect for the Supreme Being. Such an appearance is misleading. Belief in the omnipresence of the Deity does not imply irreverence. Micromégas comments on the "limited" scope of Saturnian substances. The exact opposite of irreverence is expressed.

> "Apparently, replied the traveller, this small number sufficed for the designs which the Creator had upon your small habitation. I admire his wisdom in all things; I see differences everywhere but I also see proportions." (Ch. II, p. 112).

The reverence of the Saturnian is as limited as his belief in eternal life. But the reverence of Micromégas is genuine.

The "thirty substances," "God," "space," "matter *and* the rest" are all regarded by the "Sirian" as aspects of the same Divine Reality. Two opposite views of the Deity — one transcendent one immanent — are held by the Saturnian and by Micromégas respectively. The concept of the immanent Deity is the same as that of the Kabalists:

> " — in the Kabala, as in India, the Deity was considered as the Universe, and was not, in his origin, the extra-cosmic God he is now." (*The Secret Doctrine*, p. 92 fn., Vol. I).

The Saturnian seems unaware of the profound and admirable uniformity which underlies the variety of his phenomenal world. The divisive — or Mayavic — nature of his perception is consistent with his Jehovic character.

Sexual humor is present. Such beings as "interpenetrate" — or procreate in the manner known to modern mankind — do not belong to highest planes of existence. The Secret Doctrine teaches that the first Races of men reproduced in a "non-penetrating" manner reflecting their ethereal nature. Sexual penetration was clearly irrelevant to sexless beings. Voltaire seems to connect the presence or absence of sex with corresponding degrees of materiality. Non-penetrating beings appear to be "thinking beings who are non-spatial" or immaterial. The latter suggestion is confirmed by the sexless and ethereal nature of the celestial visitor in *Memnon*. The Voltairian view of immaterial beings seems to coincide with the corresponding occult view.

"Penetration" of another kind is also involved. Persons who practice esoteric "penetration" — in the Jungian or mystical sense of the term — achieve a certain degree of spirituality. Those persons who "penetrate" the mysteries of Cosmos and Self belong to high levels of attainment. The same type of "penetration" inspires "erotic" passages of the Proustian *Recherche*. The passionate kisses exchanged by the narrator and by Albertine — Marcel and his "work"* — involve the mingling of "tongues" — "language." The same contact leads to "the mysterious sweetness of a penetration."** The "tongue" of the beloved is characterized as "maternal, incomestible, nutritious, and saintly."

Further information is sought and exchanged on the constitution of Cosmos. The color of various suns is discussed. The sun of the Saturnian is of a "very yellowish white." The sun of the Sirian is "close to red." Other suns are suggested to vary greatly in characteristics. Voltaire seems to draw attention to the occult view of the matter.

> " — the true colour of the Sun is blue, but it appears yellow only owing to the effect of the absorption of vapours (chiefly metallic) by its atmosphere. All is Maya on our Earth." (*The Secret Doctrine*, p. 441, Vol. V - Adyar edition).

The same belief seems to be suggested by Voltaire in a passage of *L'Ingénu*. The young hero of the story, Hercule de Kerkabon, has lodgings at the Inn of the Blue Sundial. ("le Cadran Bleu") Hercules represents — among other things — the Sun.*** The conjunction of Sun and blue strongly suggests as esoteric allusion to the occult belief stated above. It is also hinted in the Proustian *Recherche* that the sun which we see is not the true one.****

The space voyage continues. A profitable year is spent on Jupiter.

---

*A la Recherche du temps perdu, p. 129, Vol. III.
**Ibid., pp. 497-98, Vol. III.
***The Secret Doctrine, p. 353, Vol. I.
****A la Recherche du temps perdu, p. 439, Vol. III.

"Ils passèrent dans Jupiter même, et y restèrent une année, pendant laquelle ils apprirent de fort beaux secrets, qui seraient actuellement sous presse sans messieurs les inquisiteurs qui ont trouvé quelques propositions un peu dures. Mais j'en ai lu le manuscrit dans la bibliothèque de l'illustre archevêque de — qui m'a laissé voir ses livres avec cette générosité et cette bonté qu'on ne saurait assez louer." (Ch. III, p. 114).

("They stopped in Jupiter itself, and remained there one year during which they learned some most beautiful secrets, which would now be released without Mssrs. the Inquisitors who judged a few findings a bit hard to take. But I have read that manuscript in the library of the illustrious bishop of — who allowed me to see his books with a kindness and a generosity which can never be praised enough."

The "most beautiful" data gathered by the daring explorers are exoterically "secret" and may be regarded as exoterically "occult." Their connection with universal force or Spirit is suggested by means of the expression "*fort* beaux." The knowledge derived from the conveyances of up there is clearly superior to the expurgated offerings of spiritual middlemen. It is noted and stressed that various treasures of science are impounded in ecclesiastical archives and carefully kept under wraps. The spirited — and suspect — tribute paid to the "illustrious archbishop of—" thinly covers the venom of pure indignation. Truth is withheld and suppressed by the very persons who should be its servants. The monopolistic stance of the Church can easily be explained. Knowledge means wealth and power and must therefore be retained and controlled by spiritual money-changers. The passage may be compared to the chapter of *The Little Prince* which is devoted to the Jehovic businessman. The person in question keeps the stars — cosmic light and cosmic knowledge — under lock and key.

Blindness may also be involved. Because of the spiritual decay of the clergy, numerous monks, priests, and prelates are unable to understand the value of precious documents which are in their material possession. The passage may contain an allusion to specific writings such as the works of Celsus. Whatever the case may be, the Voltairian grievance relative to sequestered knowledge has an echo in the works of Mme Blavatsky:

"If no copy — has descended to our present generation of scientists, it is not because there is none extant at present, but for the simple reason that the monks of a certain Oriental Church on Mt. Athos will neither show nor confess they have one in their possession. Perhaps they themselves do not even know the value of the contents of their manuscripts, on account of their great ignorance." (*Isis Unveiled*, p. 52, Vol. 2).

The above passage is supplemented by a lengthy footnote relating the experience of a learned traveler who gained the confidence of the monks of Mt. Athos. The inquisitive guest was taken to a vault located in the monastery. The vault contained a large trunk in which numerous ancient manuscripts were kept. The traveler was allowed to study the documents until the monks became auspicious and withdrew the privilege of examination. Among other materials, a large number of which proved worthless, the learned reader found a half-destroyed manuscript which appeared to be a copy of the *True Doctrine*, the *Logos Alethes* of Celsus. No amount of money could persuade the monks to part with the document.

> "They did not know what the manuscript contained, not 'did they care,' they said — They were constantly quarrelling and fighting with the Catholic monks and among the whole 'heap,' they knew that there was a 'holy' relic which protected them. They did not know *which,* and so in their doubt abstained. It appears that the Superior, a shrewd Greek, understood his *bévue* and repented of his kindness, for first of all, he made the traveller give him his most sacred word of honor, strengthened by an oath he made him take on the image of the Holy Patroness of the Island, never to betray their secret, and never mention, at least, the name of their convent. And finally, when the anxious student who had passed a fortnight in reading all sort of antiquated trash before he happened to stumble over some precious manuscript, expressed the desire to have the key, to 'amuse himself' with the writings once more, he was very naively informed that the 'key had been lost,' and that they did not know where to look for it. And thus he was left to the few notes he had taken." (*Isis Unveiled*, p. 52, Vol. 2).

The "generosity" and "kindness" displayed by the archbishop of *Micromégas* resemble corresponding traits of the monks of Mt. Athos. While the traveler whose adventure is related in *Isis Unveiled* arrived at the monastery by steamship, a fact making his experience posterior to the lifetime of Voltaire, similar events may have occurred — and even been planned — before the time of writing of *Micromégas*. Such developments — if any — must have interested Voltaire. The same channels of information which made him aware of secret rites at Mount Lebanon may have guided his attention to Mt. Athos. The learned traveler mentioned by Mme Blavatsky who wished to "amuse himself" once more by studying manuscripts spoke in Voltairian style and may well have belonged to "good company." The publicity given to his adventure suggests that he was affiliated with the secret community. In spite of certain barriers of time and space, it is not inconceivable that Voltaire had in mind — "among other "buried" documents — the work of Celsus. Whatever the case may be, the smooth praise lavished on the archbishop has a typically Voltairian double-edged ring. It is strongly hinted that the admirable traits of the gracious prelate should be read as "ignorance" and "stupidity."

The obtuseness of one man is more than compensated by the alertness of others. Important areas of knowledge are "classified" by vigilant Inquisitors. The falsification of writings — or Scriptres — a crime denounced in *Zadig,* is compounded by hoarding of stolen goods or ill-acquired occult lore. Spoliation is not limited to the world of Antiquity.

The transparent excuse offered by the monks of Mt. Athos is — in part — an involuntary statement of Truth. As was previously noted, the theme of the "lost key" to ancient knowledge, a key forever inaccessible to the Church as a result of her own malpractice, is a frequent subject of theosophical and esoteric comment. It is relevant to the survey of human knowledge which is the core of *Micromégas.*

Continuing their voyage, Micromégas and his friend scorn Mars which offers little in the way of accommodations. But the planet does not go unnoticed.

> "Ils côtoyèrent la planète Mars, qui, comme on sait, est cinq fois plus petite que notre petit globe; ils virent deux lunes qui servent à cette planète; et qui ont échappé aux regards de nos astronomes. Je sais bien que le père Castel écrira, et même assez plaisamment, contre l'existence de ces deux lunes; mais je m'en rapporte à ceux qui raisonnent par analogie. Ces bons philosophes-là savent combien il serait difficile que Mars, qui est si loin du soleil, se passât à moins de deux lunes." (Ch. III, p. 114).

> ("They passed close to the planet Mars, which, as one knows, is five times smaller than our little globe; they saw two moons which serve that planet, and which have eluded the eyes of our astronomers. I know well that Father Castel will write, and even rather pleasantly, against the existence of those two moons; but I refer myself to those who reason by analogy. Those good philosophers know how difficult it would be for Mars which is so far from the sun, to do with less than two moons.")

The moons of Mars were discovered by representatives of exact science in 1877. How could Voltaire have gained knowledge of their existence more than one century before that date? The "good philosophers" who "reason by analogy" probably were his source of information. From days of remote antiquity, those who perceive universal harmony "above" and "below" have possessed scientific secrets some of which are now the pride of modern "discovery."

> "If the Pythagorean metempsychosis should be thoroughly explained and compared with the modern theory of evolution, it would be found to supply every 'missing link' in the chain of the latter. But who of our scientists would consent to lose his precious time over the vagaries of the ancients? Notwithstanding proofs to the contrary, they not only deny that the nations of the archaic periods, but even the ancient philosophers had any positive knowledge of the Heliocentric system. The 'Venerable Bedes,' the Augustines, and Lactantii appear to have smothered, with their dog-

matic ignorance, all faith in the more ancient theologists of-the pre-Christian centuries. But now philology and a closer acquaintance with Sanskrit literature have partially enabled us to vindicate them from these unmerited imputations. In the *Vedas*, for instance, we find postive proof that so long ago as 2000 B.C., the Hindu sages and scholars must have been acquainted with the rotundity of our globe and the Heliocentric system. Hence Pythagoras and Plato knew well this astronomical truth: for Pythagoras obtained his knowledge in India, or from men who had been there, and Plato faithfully echoed his teachings." (*Isis Unveiled*, pp. 9-10, Vol. I).

The planet *Mars* and its moons are subjects of guarded comments in *The Secret Doctrine*. The following statements were obtained by Mme Blavatsky from esoteric teachers. The same statements were regarded by her as "an authoritative version" of occult astronomy dealing with Mars and several other planets. Care was taken to reveal a few facts only. It seems clear from the particular brand of reserve surrounding Mars that the subject is viewed by occultists as a sensitive one.

> " — '*It is quite correct that Mars is in a state of obscuration at present, and Mercury just beginning to get out of it. You might add that Venus is in her last Round . . . If neither Mercury nor Venus have satellites, it is because of the reasons . . .* (vide footnote supra, where those reasons are given), *and also because Mars has two satellites to which he has no right. Phöbos, the supposed* INNER *satellite, is no satellite at all.'* " (*The Secret Doctrine*, p. 165, Vol. I).

The style used by Voltaire is worthy of attention. The "good philosophers who reason by analogy" know how difficult it would be for Mars — a planet so far removed from the sun — to manage with less than two moons. The French verb "se passât de" is generally interpreted as "se contentât de."* The explanatory footnote which is usually appended to the passage shows the expression "se passer à moins de" to be an uncommon one. The idiom "se passer de" means "to do without." It is frequently used in everyday French. It is never heard in combination with "à moins de." Voltaire seems to have wished to stress its significance of privation or subtraction in order to suggest the occult view of Phöbos. "Less than two moons" may amount esoterically to "one moon" or to no moon at all. The same expression may have been used to convey the idea of "passing away" — a meaning often attached to the French verbs "passer" and "trépasser" — or, in the case of a planet, the idea of obscuration. The cumbersome and bizarre phrase could have been avoided by simple use of the verb *to have* in the case of an ordinary text. But *Micromégas* — like *Zadig* — is a story which "says more than it seems to say." The tortuous mode of expression was probably calculated to attract the attention of esoteric readers.

*Edition Garnier-Bénac, p. 630.

Voltaire flaunts uncanny knowledge of the two moons of Mars which were officially undiscovered in his time. Not content to anticipate XIXth Century findings he suggests keen awareness of ancient astronomical knowledge. Once again he seems to have possessed very secret information — perhaps "cautiously given out" — gained from some mysterious source. In view of his occult interests, in view of his knowledge of secret cities and initiation rites, in view of the strange yet suggestive expression used in the passage last quoted above, it is likely that his commentary on Mars reflects classified intelligence derived from the Secret Doctrine.

Jonathan Swift — who is overtly mentioned by Voltaire in a subsequent passage of *Micromégas* — was interested in the same area of astronomy. According to Swift, the astronomers of Laputa had discovered the two moons of Mars. Rather than a gratuitous bit of whimsy the Spanish-sounding name *Laputa* may a racy, phonetic reference to Lahore. The latter city was once famous as a cultural center. Its library remains outstanding to this day. Swift may have believed — as did Mme — Blavatsky that "the Hindu sages and scholars must have been acquainted with the rotundity of our globe and the Heliocentric system." That Swift may have derived his insight from "good philosophers who reason by analogy" is an interesting possibility.

The occult view of Phöbos deserves comparison with certain hypotheses of XXth Century science:

> "Several eminent scientists think that Phobos, the satellite of Mars, may be hollow, and may be an artificial asteroid put into orbit around Mars by intelligent beings outside the Earth. This was the conclusion arrived at in a serious article in the review *Discovery* in November 1959 and the same hypothesis has been put forward by the Soviet Professor Chtlovski, an expert on radio-astronomy." (*The Morning of the Magicians,* Part III, Ch. I).

The "rather pleasant" writings of Father Castel, a contributor to the *Journal de Trévoux,* are not regarded as truthful by Voltaire. The occult meaning of the word "pleasure" suggests that Father Castel is far from ignorant. The probability is supported by the fact that the learned Father wrote about gravitation "and its relation to light in terms which, two centuries later, seem astonishingly similar to Einstein's ideas."* Father Castel seems to belong to the ranks of editorial inquisitors dedicated to the suppression of Truth.

The planet Earth is next on the itinerary of Micromégas. The last leg of the journey to the "small globe of mud" is enlivened by a few observations:

The Morning of the Magicians, The Example of Alchemy, Ch. II.

"As those strangers travel rather fast, they had gone around the globe in thirty-six hours, the sun in truth, or rather the earth, covers a like distance in one day; but it must be observed that one travels with far greater ease when revolving around one's axis than when walking on one's feet." (Ch. IV, p. 115).

"Strangers" appear frequently in the writings of Voltaire. They are persons of unorthodox faith or "heretics" in the sight of the Catholic Church. The same appellation is found by the author of *Isis Unveiled* in the hideous ledgers of some German municipalities. The documents show on record the rationale and volume of XVIth Century witch-burnings.

"One glance at this horrible catalog of murders in Christ's name is sufficient to show that out of 162 persons burned, more than one-half of them are designated as *strangers, (i.e.,* Protestants) in this hospitable town and of the other half we find *thirty-four children,* the oldest of whom was fourteen, the youngest *an infant* child of Dr. Schultz." (*Isis Unveiled,* p. 62, Vol. II).

The "daring explorers" of *Micromégas* are labeled as "heretics" or criminals. The independent pursuit of knowledge is a cardinal sin in the eyes of the Church. No further explanation is needed of the function of Inquisitors or of the raison d'être of learned falsehoods such as those of Father Castel.

Dizzy "speed" is an attribute of the conveyances of up there. Esoteric "speed — which is practically equivalent to esoteric "force" — reflects intuitive insight and spiritual power. The "rapidity" of "strangers" is often celebrated in esoteric texts:

"Mais notre esprit rapide en mouvements abonde;
Ouvrons tout l'arsenal de ses puissants ressorts.
L'invisible est réel. Les âmes ont leur monde
Où sont accumulés d'impalpables trésors."
(*La Maison du berger*)

("But our rapid mind (or spirit) abounds in impulses;
Let us release the whole arsenal of its powerful forces
The invisible is real. The souls have their domain
Where intangible treassures are accumulated.")

Voltaire contrasts axial revolution to prosaic use of one's feet. The superiority of the conveyances of up there is re-affirmed. Rotation around an axis is characteristic of heavenly bodies. Corresponding possibilities of divine equilibrium exist on the human plane. Man — the microcosm in a macrocrosm — can learn to partake of the "music of the spheres" if he will board the vertiginous — yet rational — vehicle of his own intuition.

A quickly corrected *faux pas* serves to emphasize two points: "The sun in truth, or rather the earth, makes a similar journey in one day." The passage constitutes a transparent allusion to Galileo, an unending source of embarrassment to the Church. The erroneous beginning of the sentence which suggests the existence of a geocentric universe also serves to illustrates esoteric "mistakes" made for a purpose.

The terrestrial habitat of men is designated as "the molehill," a fact reflecting little credit on the vision of residents. The limited insight prevailing on earth is a logical reflection of rather low standing in cosmic hierarchies. The same myopia is connected with the criminal suppression of knowledge by ecclesiastical thought-police.

The limited scope of sensory perception is demonstrated by the traveling companion of Micromégas. The "Saturnian" "dwarf" — a symbolically atrophied being — contends that no life can exist on earth. Having explored the planet by means of sight, hearing, and touch, he is unable to detect any sign of existence. The chaotic appearance of the "small globe of mud" further convinces him that "no people of good sense could possibly wish to dwell there."

The "dwarf" is partially right. "People of good sense" raise their sight to higher spheres. But they are the same rare individuals who perceive universal harmony and divine design under the disorderly surface of earthly phenomena. They are those who "thank the author of nature" for "profuse variety" and "admirable uniformity." They are persons who do not reduce the universe — or its Unknowable Cause — to the phantasy of rudimentary faculties such as the senses.

The following dialogue is reported:

"Le nain, qui jugeait quelquefois un peu trop vite, décida d'abord qu'il n'y avait personne sur la terre. Sa première raison était qu'il n'avait vu personne. Micromégas lui fit sentir poliment que c'était raisonner assez mal: 'Car,' disait-il, 'vous ne voyez pas avec vos petits yeux certaines étoiles de la cinquantième grandeur que j'aperçois très distinctement; concluez-vous de là que ces étoiles n'existent pas?' — 'Mais,' dit le nain, 'j'ai bien tâté.' — 'Mais,' répondit l'autre, 'vous avez mal senti.' " (Ch. IV, p. 116).

("The dwarf, who sometimes judged a little too fast, promptly decreed that there was no one on earth. His first reason was that he had seen no one. Micromégas politely impressed upon him that it was rather poor reasoning. 'For,' he said, 'you do not see with your small eyes some stars of fiftieth magnitude which I see very distinctly; do you conclude from that that those stars do not exist?' — 'But,' said the dwarf, 'I thoroughly searched with my hand.' — 'But,' replied the other, 'you perceived poorly.' ")

The last sentence is a thinly veiled invitation to seek a suitable approach to universal mysteries in general — and esoteric literature in particular. Purely sensory and intellectual data are not equal to the task.

The remonstrations of Micromégas have little effect. The Jehovic "dwarf" is determined to "dwarf" the universe. The protagonists grow more and more emotional. A diamond necklace worn by Micromégas is broken in the course of the heated argument.

The fortunate accident supports a fundamental Voltairian — and occult — axiom: "Chance does not exist." The "breaking of the chain" is doubly beneficial. Dangerous controversy is forgotten. Most important of all, the loose stones function as optical instruments through which earth-life and human life can be seen. An unsuspected universe, inaccessible to ordinary perception is revealed by the spiritual insight derived from the "diamond." The Saturnian is compelled to recognize that "the invisible is real." Beyond the concept of relativity which is stressed on the exoteric plane is the startling reality of the occult scheme of life.

The necklace represents the chain of universal evolution and individual rebirth (*sutratma*). The pearls or stones are cycles of evolution of matter (*Manvantaras*) on the cosmic plane. The intervals separating them are cycles of dissolution or latent state of matter (*Pralayas*). The necklace is equally meaningful on the plane of individual human existence. The pearls or stones represent multiple reincarnations. The intervals are those of Devachanic sleep or rest which separate two successive lives. The ultimate goal of the cosmic pilgrimage of spirit is the final "break" from the chain of material existence, the state of "perfection," "the country where nothing lacks," Nirvâna.

As was previously noted, the chain of evolution and rebirth is a standard element of esoteric symbolism. It is an integral part of the crucial NECKLACE in Vigny's *Destinées*. It is present in the celebration of approaching release which constitutes the finale of *L'Esprit pur*. It is the major theme of the refrain of M. de Charlus in the *Recherche*. It is also the refrain of a relative of the narrator. The grandfather of Marcel cunningly uses a song to urge "Israel" — the Judaeo-Christian world — to "break" its "chain."*

The Proustian necklace which is the intended gift of "Saint Loup" to Rachel deserves attention. The jewel seems to be the key-word of the *Destinies*. It is likened to a "trial" which appears to be the lengthy and tumultuous "trial" of Micromégas-Voltaire. The matter of influencing a famous jeweler is as heavy with consequence as the matter of winning

---

A la Recherche du temps perdu, p. 91, Vol. I.

a case in court. The question of the "trial" and "necklace" is an affair of "cosmic" dimension!

> "—, whether it be a matter of influencing Boucheron or of winning a trial before a tribunal, — Listen, you know, for me, everything which concerns her, that is immense, that assumes some cosmic quality." (*A la Recherche du temps perdu,* pp. 278-79, Vol. II).

The same cosmic vision — also supplied by a symbolic "necklace" — reveals the existence of unsuspected life to the Voltairian travelers. Improved insight causes a whale to be seen. The sequence faithfully reflects the sequence of *Genesis:*

> "We may, perhaps, throw addtional light upon the puzzling question of the fish-symbol by reminding the reader that according to *Genesis,* the first created of living beings, the first type of animal life was the fish. 'And the Elohim said 'Let the waters bring forth abundantly the moving creature that hath life. . .' And God created great whales.' " (*Isis Unveiled,* p. 258, Vol. 2).

Human life is next. Unspiritualized insight is again unable to discern an *objective* form of existence. The Voltairian and the theosophical view of "microscopes" seem to be identical:

> "No earthly microscope can be compared with the keenness of the spiritual perception." (*Isis Unveiled,* p. 14, Vol. I).

> "The microscope, which barely made visible a whale and a ship, had no hold on such an imperceptible being as men." (Ch. V, p. 118).

A subtle structural break should be noted between the singular quality of "an imperceptible being" and the plurality of "men." The stylistic flaw is probably not accidental. That man is a multiple or complex being is a major theme of *Micromégas.* That he is — in "perfected" form — the product of numerous lives or "men" is relevant to the story in general and to the symbolic "necklace" in particular.

Alternate cycles of incarnation and Devachanic repose are observed by the travelers. Devachan is defined as follows in theosophical texts:

> "We say that man suffers so much unmerited misery during his life, through the fault of others with whom he is associated, or because of his environment, that he is surely entitled to perfect rest and quiet, if not bliss, before taking up again the burden of life." (*The Key to Theosophy,* p. 29).

The tiny human creatures held in the hand of Micromégas "carry burdens," "go down," and "rise again." The heavy loads are those of Maya and Karma — incarnate life — which keep potentially divine beings in their prison of flesh. The ebb and flow of death and rebirth is represented by downward and upward motions:

> "I see them,' they both said at once; 'don't you see them who carry their burdens, who bend, who rise again?' As they spoke thus, their hands trembled from the pleasure of seeing such new objects and from fear of losing them." (Ch. V, p. 119).

The "pleasure" which accompanies the flash of superior vision was in all likelihood well known to Voltaire. Little imagination is required to believe that such "pleasures lead to God." The joy described in the passage is a modest preview of the bliss of the initiate or neophyte — man "born" to a new dimension of Cosmos and Self. Elation mingles with fear of losing the precious sight. The trembling hands of the travelers are reminiscent of the shudder mentioned by Almona, a shudder evoked by certain mystical flames. It will also be remembered that the reunion of Man and Truth — Zadig and Astarté — is attended by trembling. The episode of *Micromégas* featuring the "broken chain" of sensory perception is a partial "lifting of the veil."

Revelation fails to impart superior insight where the companion of Micromégas is concerned. Physical and intellectual consciousness still rule. The wayfarer is merely enjoying the flash of spiritual insight which is occasionally granted to all men. The Saturnian remains stubbornly literal — and phallic — in his interpretation of newly glimpsed wonders. Viewing the activities of tiny human creatures, the observer concludes that they are engaged in the propagation of the species:

> " '*Ah!*' he said, *I caught nature in the act.* But he was deceived by appearances, something which happens only too often, whether microscopes be used or not." (Ch. V, p. 119).

The frequent subtlety of esoteric substance is demonstrated by the error of the Saturnian "dwarf." The companion of Micromégas is misled by Mayavic "appearances." But he is unwittingly correct where reality is concerned. Men *are* engaged in "propagating" the species in the sense of promoting human evolution. Every single act of "carrying one's burden," "going down," and "rising again" is significant and fruitful within the perspective of cosmic and individual progress. The presence of italics serves to stress the truthful aspect of the statement which is inaccurate in one sense and valid in another.

Another discussion arises. Can such a microscopic "insect" as man have a soul? "Micromégas," a far better observer than his dwarf, thinks so. Blinded by vanity and materialistic prejudice — which are one and the same — the Saturnian holds the opposite view.

205

The misconceptions of M. le Secrétaire are promptly refuted by fact. Having established communication with the inhabitants of earth, Micromégas proves the existence of human souls and intellects. The moral of the story is edifying. If our eminently "real" world cannot be perceived by the unaided senses of Saturnians, there may be worlds equally "real" which are inaccessible to our terrestrial senses. The attitude limiting the universe to the narrow scope of a few faculties is absurd. It is therefore also absurd to regard one's species as the crowning glory of creation and sole possessor of superior attributes. The omnipresence of Spirit eludes the puny grasp of materially confined experience. It is stated by Micromégas that human beings are not the exclusive owners of "souls." His acquaintance with various "animals" residing in various regions of Cosmos supplies evidence to the contrary. The following passage seems to announce a comparable text written by Mme Blavatsky:

> "I see more than ever than one must swear to nothing on the basis of apparent size. O God who gave intelligence to beings who seem so contemptible, the infinitely small costs you as little as the infinitely great, and if it is possible that there exist beings smaller than these, they may still have a mind (or spirit) superior to those of the grand animals I saw in heavens, the foot of which would alone cover the globe where I have descended." (Ch. VI, p. 122).

> "If there is a developed immortal spirit in man; it must be in everything else, at least in a latent or germinal state; and it can only be a question of time for each of these germs to become fully developed. What a gross injustice it would be that an impenitent criminal, who perpetrates a brutal murder in the full exercise of his free will, should have an immortal spirit which may in due time be purged of its sin, and enjoy perfect happiness, while a poor horse, innocent of all crime, should toil and suffer under the merciless torture of his master's whip during its whole lifetime, and then be annihilated at death! Such a belief implies a brutal injustice, and is only possible among people taught in the dogma that everything is created for man, and that he alone is the sovereign of the universe — a sovereign so mighty that to save him from the consequences of his own misdeeds, it was not too much that the God of the universe should die to placate his own just wrath." (*Isis Unveiled, pp.* 330-31, Vol. 1).

The impersonal essence of the Supreme Being is stressed by the following words of Micromégas: "— the infinitely small costs you as little as the infinitely great." The recognized omnipresence of spirit which is implied in the reference to "grand animals" further tends to reject the concept of an anthropomorphic deity removed from his own creation yet emotionally involved with the same creation. ("vous coûte", costs you"). The degree of absurdity to which such a concept has driven Judaeo-Christian dogma is ably commented by Mme Blavatsky. A subsequent presentation of the same Thomistic view will be received with

Homeric laughter in the final chapter of *Micromégas*. More or less overtly, the same denial is present in both texts quoted above. Anthropocentric conceptions of the universe and Jehovic conceptions of the Deity are symptoms of the same disease: negation and degradation of spiritual essence.

The passionate invocation of Micromégas has Pascalian overtones. Man is viewed in relation to the dual abyss of the "infinitely great" and "infinitely small." Such is also the case in the writings of Pascal. But the wretchedness of human nature — and the correspondingly wretched nature of God — which are either proclaimed or implied by the author of the *Pensées* — are not endorsed by Voltaire. Human substance seems contemptible yet is not. "Good philosophers who reason by analogy" are likewise optimistic on the subject of genuine divine essence. The similarty which exists between the Pascalian definition of Man: "Glory and outcast of the universe" and the corresponding Voltairian concept of "Micro-mégas" fails to reduce the abyss separating the two writers. Voltaire once more seems to evoke the spiritually deprived greatness of a thinker who did not have access to certain philosophical "conveyances" or "resources."

The same passage also seems to contain an allusion to Descartes — whose philosophy is represented at a later stage of the story by a Cartesian thinker. The joint presence of the words "spirit" and "animals" suggests a reference to the animal spirit element of Cartesian thought.

The residents of Earth display amazing competence in geometry. Human insects are capable of spectacular insight. God geometrizes — according to Plato. So does man on his own modest scale. The Sirian "who scorns no one" is vindicated by the achievement of the tiny creatures.

The decisive test of geometric knowledge involves two different techniques designed to measure the visitors from outer space. A mathematician, significantly described as "a reasoner bolder than the others" trains his sight on a quarter of a circle, makes two stations, and gives a correct measurement. His method involves three phases which produce accurate findings. Suggested by the procedure is the occult concept of a trinity or Three In One completed by the quaternary.

"Everything in this world is a trinity completed by the quaternary and every element is divisible on this same principle. Physiology can divide man *ad infinitum,* as physical science has divided the four primal and principal elements into several dozens of others; she will not succeed either. Birth, life, and death will ever be a trinity completed only at the cyclic end. Even were science to change the longed for immortality into annihilation, it still will ever be a quaternary for God 'geometrizes!' " (*Isis Unveiled,* p. 508, Vol. 1).

The omnipresence of the "trinity" suggested in an earlier chapter of *Micromégas* tends to be confirmed by the successful technique of the "bold" "reasoner." The same trinitarian element — which is closely bound to the occult view of cosmic Creation — rather Emanation — and Evolution — is obviously "creative" on the human plane as well. One may note that the Voltairian view of "going down," "carrying burdens," and "rising again" corresponds to the thesophical ternary of "death," "life," and "birth." The "longed for immortality" of theosophists is none other than the Voltairian "country where nothing lacks."

The "bold" brand of "reason" — a pleonastic phrase in the Voltairian system — is related to the Pythagorean concept of mathematics. It is clearly superior to elaborate machinery. The procedure has the speed of the intuitive flash. No physical contact with the measured "object" is involved. The latter fact is quite a reflection on on fumbling, matter-bound approaches to knowledge. No discomfort is experienced by the person measured. The measurer is spared a great deal of physical toil. His energies are better spent on a more productive plane.

The second technique is neither painless nor simple:

> " 'Yes, I measured you,' said the physician, 'and I will also measure your
> tall companion.' The offer was accepted; His Excellency lay down full
> length, for, had he remained standing, his head would have been too
> far above the clouds. Our philosophers planted a big tree in a part of his
> anatomy which Dr. Swift would name, but which I will carefully avoid
> calling by its name because of the deep respect I have for the ladies. Then
> with a series of triangles bound together, they concluded that what they
> saw was indeed a young man one hundred and twenty thousand feet high."
> (Ch. VI, p. 122).

Considerable time, energy, equipment, and discomfort are involved. Some impressive visual props of "exact science" are satirized. The grand display seems to be a face-saving device. While the bizarre method seems to be successful, one conclusion could have been anticipated by the dullest intellect: "What they saw was indeed a young man."

The proliferating "scholarship" under which countless library shelves may be heard to groan is under scrutiny. Voltaire ridicules the elaborate documentation of the obvious. A good question remains unasked and therefore unanswered. Would the problem have been solved by means of the same approach without the previous finding of the "reasoner?"

A common element exists in both methods. The use which is made of "triangles" in the second case suggests the identity of a basic principle related to the trinitarian essence of all things. Whether the bustling engineers of the second technique know it or not, they are using the basic approach of the "bold reasoner" duly embellished and sanctified by machinery, manpower, blood, sweat, and tears.

The superior procedure is the work of a minority of one person. The second approach is the effort of a collectivity. The better method is not within reach of the general public. Ironically, it is the second experiment which erases general doubt and opens the way to belief. The grand display of men and material has irresistible eye appeal. The reassuring character of a community project leaves little room for threatening individualities. The second technique is intellectually and otherwise suited to fundamental popular values.

The technological superproduction must receive the benefit of the doubt. A correct solution seems to be reached with its aid. The legitimate worth of earth-bound or materialistic inquiry is recognized. It can and does lead to many truths. But the quality of those truths remains peripheral. The identity and the essence of the "visitor" transcend the realm of material "measure." Voltaire anticipates the statement of Mme Blavatsky which has already been quoted: "Science can, it is true, collect, classify, and generalize upon phenomena." But it usually fails to "trascend the narrow limitations of sense, and transfer" its "consciousness into the region of noumema and the sphere of primal causes."

What is measured in "pieds de roi" remains an inscrutable mystery the existence of which cannot even be conceived by the majority of men. The Sirian traveler who "must lie down" so that his "head" may not be "too far above the clouds" is far more than a gigantic physical body. He is a "King" or "Titan" in the esoteric or spiritual sense. His coming to earth is no ordinary jaunt The full significance of his arrival, a fact too staggering to be believed by most, is further suggested in a subsequent passage which is a masterpiece of esoteric understatement. Try as they may, the residents of earth are incapable of conceiving "who speaks to them."

The contrastive value of the episode is rich. The "conveyances of up there" are shown to be vastly superior to lumbering "stagecoaches" or matter-bound inquiry. The determination of exact science to "get to the bottom of things" is basically noble. But it is not well served by a "phallic" approach. The symbolic Tree of Knowledge is bound to be damaged in the uprooting process.

The esoteric substance of the passage is concealed by exoteric irony. The allusion to Dr. Swift and the self-defeating rejection of anal humor act as effective and delightful decoys. No better illustration could possibly be given of the double-edged value of esoteric "phallicism."

The appearance of the giants spreads panic among residents of Earth. Titans are terrifying by definition to insect-like passengers of the vessel of life. An interesting cross-section of mankind is observed in the grip of fear. The first greeting of Micromégas is received as follows:

"If anyone was ever surprised, it was the people who heard those words. They could not guess from where they came. The chaplain of the ship recited the prayers of exorcisms, the sailors swore, and the philosophers constructed a theory; but no matter what theory they constructed, they never could guess who was speaking to them."

Helplessness is general. But variety prevails. There is an ascending order in the enumeration of fear-related reflexes. The professional secretion of the chaplain places him at the bottom of the ladder. Occultists in general and Voltaire in particular take a dim view of exorcism, a practice all too profitable to the Church in terms of power and wealth. The control of evil spirits — for a consideration — implies recognition of the invisible world and exploitation of a monopoly. The case of Augustine, a saint admittedly well-versed in knowledge and management of spirits, earned vitriolic comments from Mme Blavatsky. Two questions are raised by the author of *Isis Unveiled*. Why is ecclesiastical intercourse with spirits beneficient and holy while other experimentation of like nature is ruthlessly condemned? Where and how does the clergy obtain technical data necessary to approach and control demons if not from demons themselves?

> " ' — how could one know had he not been taught by the demons themselves . . . the name which attracts, or that which forces them into obedience, 'asks Augustine.
> Useless to remark that we know the answer beforehand: 'revelation — divine gift — the Son of God; nay God himself, through His direct Spirit, who descended on the apostles as the Pentacostal fire,' and who is now alleged to overshadow every priest who sees fit to exorcise for either glory or a gift. Are we then to believe that the recent scandal of public exorcism, performed about the 14th of October 1876, by the Senior Priest of the Church of the Holy Spirit, at Barcelona, Spain, was also done under the direct superintendence of the Holy Ghost?" (*Isis Unveiled*, pp. 67-68, Vol. 2).

The exorcists mentioned by Voltaire in *Le Siècle de Louis XIV* have a counterpart in the chaplain of the ship. The appearance — and desired removal — of the giants is wrongly made into "a point of religion." The travelers from outer space do belong to a foreign world. But they do not necessarily qualify as "demons." The superstitious ignorance of the Church representative is noted. The worthlessness of his remedy is demonstrated by fact: the presumed "demons" fail to vanish in a puff of smoke.

Although lacking refinement, the crew's reaction to fear is more wholesome and harmless than the efforts of the chaplain. The sailors' oaths reflect a higher level of instinct, sincerity, and professional skill.

The emergency system evolved by the philosophers of the ship is futile.

No man-made theory can solve the mystery of non-terrestrial regions. No man-made theory can probe the connection of the same regions with our "small globe of mud." But the efforts of the thinkers carry the redeeming grace of intellectual striving.

Micromégas tries to control the wave of unavoidable panic. The Sirian softens his voice in order to "speak" to mankind. Spiritual "force" — a pleonastic concept in esoteric terms — must be subdued. The divine voice of Truth must be adjusted to the faculties of a non-spiritual age. The divine voice of Truth runs the risk of "deafening" without being "heard" or "understood." Esoteric practice is justified in the light of evolutionary belief.

The anatomy and physiology of the Inner Man are discussed. So thorny is the subject that Micromégas himself seems to be deceived by materialistic illusion. The small size of human "insects" prompts certain observations:

> " — having so little matter and seeming to be all mind (or spirit) you must spend your life loving and thinking, that it the true life of spirits. Nowhere have I seen true happiness but it is here no doubt. Whereupon all the philosophers shook their heads; and one of them who was more truthful than the rest, confessed in good faith that, with the exception of a small number of inhabitants held in very low esteem, all the rest was a collection cf madmen, wicked men, and wretched men." (Ch. VII, p. 123).

Spirituality is defined as the co-essence of Love — mysticism and Ethics — and Knowledge, a definition which agrees with the theosophical concept of occultism. "— true occultism is the 'Great Renunciation of SELF,' unconditionally and absolutely, in thought as in action. It is ALTRUISM. 'Not for himself, but for the world,' does the true occultist live.*

The "happiness" — or spirituality — which is believed to reign on earth is actually restricted to very few persons. The tiny minority which is immune to general wretchedness is scorned by the general public. The ostracized status of pure joy is a sad reflection on the state of human affairs.

An inverse relationship is noted to exist between matter on the one hand and spirit — or happiness — on the other. Because of his small size or small amount of matter, man is presumed to be spiritually inclined and happy. The assumption has a certain amount of logic. But it fails to consider the crucial factor of spiritual or material density which is independent of mass. The leading question asked by Micromégas in falsely naïve fashion is calculated to stress the importance of the same density.

---

*H. P. Blavatsky, *Studies in Occultism*.

The crucial factor is cautiously approached through the reassuring, familiar plane of matter. Material density is discussed. It is well known to the residents of Earth:

> "How much does your air weigh? He thought that he had them cornered but all told him that air weighs approximately nine hundred times less than a like volume of the lightest water, and nineteen thousand times less than ducat gold. The little dwarf from Saturn, amazed by their replies, was tempted to take for sorcerers those same people to whom he had denied a soul fifteen minutes earlier." (Ch. VII, p. 125).

The Judaeo-Christian tendency to swing abuptly from blind skepticism to boundless credulity is noted. The same Saturnian who previously believed that he had caught Nature in the act with his superior faculties tries to explain the unexpected knowledge of others as "sorcery." The egocentric illusion which sees the mote in a neighbor's eye while failing to see the beam in its own is present. The popular Western mind is unable to conceive the abyss which separates genuine occult knowledge from the lurid, overly publicized realm of witchcraft.

The expression "lightest water" suggests an allusion to *heavy water*. The connection which seems to be courted conveys praise of alchemical knowledge. Heavy water was not generally known to official Western science until the XIXth Century. But the occult view of hydrogen as the "Upadhi" or basis of both Air and Water suggests that it may have been known many centuries ago. The conjunction of physics, chemistry, mathematics, and alleged "sorcery" which sheds light on the passage points to Alchemy.

The theosophical view of Alchemy is expressed in the following texts:

> "Some people — nay, the great majority — have accused alchemists of charlatanry and false pretending. Surely such men as Roger Bacon, Agrippa, Henry Kunrath, and the Arabian Geber (the first to introduce into Europe some of the secrets of chemistry), can hardly be treated as impostors — least of all fools. Scientists who are reforming the science of physics upon the basis of the atomic theory of Demokritus, as restated by John Dalton, conveniently forget that Demokritus of Abdera, was an alchemist, and that the mind that was capable of penetrating so far into the secret operations of nature in one direction must have had good reasons to study and become a Hermetic philosopher." (*Isis Unveiled*, p. xxv, Vol. 1).
>
> "Among the great mass of peoples plunged deep in the superstitious ignorance of the medieval ages, there were but a few students of the Hermetic philosophy of old, who profiting by what it had taught them, were enabled to forecast discoveries which are the boast of our present age, while at the same time the ancestors of our modern high-priests of the temple of the Holy Molecule were yet discovering the hoof-tracks of Satan in the simplest natural phenomena." (*Isis Unveiled,* p. 413, Vol. 1).

Voltaire may have known of the existence and potential of heavy water which is used in our XXth Century for atomic research. His treatise on the nature of fire may some day prove relevant to the "last word" in nuclear physics. We are entitled to wonder just what experiments he performed in the scientific laboratory of Mme du Châtelet at Cirey.

Alchemical knowledge has interesting prolongations in XXth Century technology. Louis Pauwels and Jacques Bergier have the following information and comments:

> "The alchemists speak of the necessity of distilling water to be used in preparation of the elixir many thousands of times. We have heard an expert historian declare such an operation to be completely crazy. He knew nothing whatever about heavy water and the methods employed to convert ordinary water into heavy water. We have heard a learned scientist affirm that since endless repetitions of the process of refining and purifying metals and metalloids do not in any way alter their properties, the recommendations of the alchemists in this connection could only be considered as a kind of mystic lesson in patience, a ritual gesture, like telling the beads of a rosary. And yet it is by just such a refining process and the technique described by the alchemists known today as 'zone fusion,' that the germanium and silicon used in transistors is prepared. We know now, thanks to the work done on these transistors, that by purifying a metal very thoroughly and then introducing minute quantities, some millionths of a gram, of impurities carefully selected, the substance thus treated is endowed with new and revolutionary properties. It is unnecessary to go on citing examples indefinitely, but we wish to stress the desirability of undertaking a really methodical study of alchemist literature. This would be an immense task demanding many years of work and hundreds of research workers drawn from every branch of the sciences. Neither Bergier nor myself have been able even to draft the outline of such a study, but if our book ever inspired some Maecenas to sponsor this undertaking, we shall not have wasted our time completely." (*The Morning of the Magicians, The Example of Alchemy,* II).

It is interesting to find that one of the "boasts" — or mixed blessings — of our boastful age — the transistor — is in part a reflection of alchemical knowledge. It is even more interesting to note that, toward the end of World War II, some representatives of the U. S. Government "were paying fabulous prices for any manuscripts or documents dealing with alchemy"* while the "scientific press in the U.S.S.R. appears to be taking a great interest in alchemy, and is undertaking historical researches.'**

Rabelais may have had in mind the specific chromosome of the human female when he wrote Chapter XXXIII of the *Tiers Livre*. The passage

---

The Morning of the Magicians, p. 125.
**Ibid.,* p. 129.

in question contains an intriguing reference to Demokritus of Abdera, the atom-conscious physicist mentioned by Mme Blavatsky in the text reproduced above. The same chapter of the *Tiers Livre* links the "organ which is not found in men" — and remains unnamed — with certain "Bacchic" tendencies of women. The organ is said to impart to its owners a keen sensitivity to odors. (The esoteric concept of "odor" seems to commonly represent invisible beings. The latter meaning seems to be supported by at least one medieval fabliau to be examined in a subsequent chapter of this study.) Exoterically as well as otherwise, such a property is difficult to attribute to what is generally called "female organs." But it seems consistent with certain tenets of the Secret Docrine dealing with cell structure and cell formation. It is also consistent with the "Bacchic" or specific spiritual endowments of Eve. Some researcher of the future may shed unexpected light on the alleged misogyny of Rabelais, particularly where the said chapter is concerned.

We should not be surprised if numerous scientific findings of the modern age prove to be re-statements of ancient knowledge and to have been transmitted in esoteric form in the literature of many centuries. The amazement of the Saturnian facing uncanny learning may well be prophetic of what awaits us.

The cultural exchange continues between Micromégas, the Saturnian, and the inhabitants of Earth. An old enigma remains unanswered. What is the nature of that human soul the existence of which has been demonstrated by human insight? Various theories are offered. None seems valid. Confusion reigns. Most arduous to obey is the age-old injunction: "Know Thyself!"

A peripatetician speaks with assurance:

> "The soul is an entelechy, and a reason through which it has the faculty of being what it is." (Ch. VII, p. 125).

The soul is the subject of numerous statements made in the Secret Doctrine. Among authorities cited by Mme Blavatsky on the thorny question of its nature are Plato and . . . Voltaire:

> "How precise and true is Plato's expression, how profound and philosophical his remark on the (human) soul or EGO, when he defined it as 'a compound of the *same* and the *other*.' And yet how little this hint has been understood, since the world took it to mean that the soul was the breath of God, of Jehovah. It is 'the *same* and the *other*', as the great Initiate-Philosopher said: for the EGO (the 'Higher Self' when merged with and in the Divine Monad) is Man, and yet the *same* as the 'OTHER,' the Angel in him incarnated, as the same with the universal MAHAT. The great classics and philosophers felt this truth, when saying that 'there must be some-

214

thing within us which produces our thoughts. Something very subtle; it is fire; it is ether; it is quintessence; it is a slender likeness; it is an intellection; it is a number; it is harmony. . .'' (Voltaire)* (*The Secret Doctrine*, pp. 88-89, Vol. II).

Entelechy is a stumbling block in the path of many thinkers. Certain philosophers are mentioned in *Micromégas* in connection with the difficult subject. Among them are Aristotle — the authority quoted by the peripatetician — and Leibnitz. The pronouncement of Aristotle postulates the ability of the soul to exist within or without a contingent vehicle. While some characterization is achieved by the statement, the concept of entelechy remains hazy. The idea of independent dualism is conveyed by etymology and by the substance of the quotation. But the "very subtle" subject of discussion can be apprehended by the intellect to a certain degree only. Such seems to be the consensus of thinkers — ancient and modern. The essence of the soul is a mystery which cannot be solved by probes of the unaided mind.

The laborious nature of soulful speculation is noted with irony. Insecurity is apparent in the linguistic defense used by the "peripatetician" who speaks Greek.

"Je n'entends pas trop bien le grec, dit le géant. — Ni moi non plus, dit la mite philosophique. — Pourquoi donc, reprit le Sirien, citez-vous un certain Aristote en grec? — C'est répliqua le savant, qu'il faut bien citer ce qu'on ne comprend point du tout dans la langue qu'on entend le moins." (Ch. VII, p. 125).

("I don't understand Greek very well, said the giant — Neither do I, said the philosophical mite. — Why then, the Sirian went on, do you quote one certain Aristotle in Greek? — It is, the scholar replied, because one must certainly quote what one does not understand in the language which one understands least.")

Esoteric practice is justified once more. What is not understood at all (by the majority of men) is occult knowledge. It is a matter of survival for its possessor to express himself cautiously. It is a matter of respect for cyclic law to reveal such knowledge sparingly until mankind is ready for extensive information. The emphasis which is placed on the verb *entendre* is a reminder of the secondary meaning of the word — "to understand." The reader is reminded that the voice of Truth must be "softened" or veiled for the benefit of the general public at certain times. The stress which is placed on "necessity" — "il faut bien" — "one must certainly" — connects the "softening" process with the scheme of evolu-

---

*Exact reference not given in *The Secret Doctrine*.

tion. It is doubtful, however, that the peripatetician of *Micromégas* grasps the profound truth of his own statement. Voltaire designates him as a "scholar," not as a member of "good company" or "bold reasoner." The philosopher is using the favorite face-saving device of shaky knowledge: pedantic obscurity.

The matter or "esoteric language" is not the only one to receive attention. The question of why the peripatetician — a disciple of Plato — does not quote Plato himself is raised by Voltaire: "Why . . . do you quote one certain Aristotle?" A connection seems to exist between estrangement from primary sources and the insecurity of resultant systems. The Platonist suffers from a common Western ailment: inability and/or refusal to "go back to the source." It is suggested that all seekers of knowledge would do well to turn to the original, unadulterated fountainhead of learning. What is hinted in *Micromégas* is squarely stated in theosophical texts. "Aristotle was no trustworthy witness. He misrepresented Plato, and he almost caricatured the doctrines of Pythagoras."[*] Aristotlean writings themselves are said to have suffered from the ministrations of "too many hands."[**]

An interesting similarity of language should be noted between Rabelais and Voltaire. The author of *Micromégas* connects the soul — or "quintessence" — with the concept of entelechy. Rabelais relates the arrival of his heroes in the Kingdom of Quintessence named Entelechy.[***]

The Voltairian symposium on the soul continues. A Cartesian philosopher enunciates a strange theory:

> "The soul is a pure spirit which has received in the womb of its mother all metaphysical ideas and which, as it gets out of there, has to go to school and to learn all over again what it has known so well and no longer knows." (Ch. VII, pp. 125-26).

Buffoonery is present in bizarre substance and prosaic style. Embryos are not generally credited with knowledge — least of all metaphysical insight. But the Cartesian statement reported by Voltaire is compatible with various elements of occult belief. It is pervaded by the idea of a "pure spirit" subjected to "necessity." ("Has to go to school") The same "necessity" of "going to school" is the very purpose of the evolutionary process: the attainment of blissful omniscience: Nirvâna. The knowledge of pure spirituality prevails in the universal "womb" — *yoni*, one of two "creative cosmic agencies."[****] The same knowledge is present

---

[*]*Isis Unveiled,* p. xv, Vol. I.
[**]*Ibid.,* pp. 319-20, Vol. I.
[***]*Cinquième Livre,* Ch. XVIII.
[****]*The Secret Doctrine,* p. 391, Vol. I.

on the individual human plane at the time of birth and at the time of death. The only difference which exists between the Cartesian theory reported by Voltaire and corresponding theosophical statements is one of style:

"As the man at the moment of death has a retrospective insight into the life he has led, so at the moment he is reborn on earth, the Ego, awaking from the state of Devachan, has a prospective vision of the life which awaits him, and realizes all the causes that have led to it." (*The Key to Theosophy*, p. 114).

"At the birth of the future man, the monad, radiating with all the glory of its immortal parent which watches it from the seventh sphere, becomes senseless. It loses all recollection of the past and returns to consciousness but gradually, when the instinct of childhood gives way to reason and intelligence." (*Isis Unveiled*, p. 303, Vol. 1).

Voltaire uses unadorned words to conceal a startling concept of life and to give his reader a glimpse of the pilgrimage of the soul. Such expressions as "in its mother's belly" — or "womb"—, "as it gets out of there" and "has to go to school" create an atmosphere of naive drollery which is well calculated to veil profound substance. The same technique of prosaic understatement is demonstrated in such esoteric expressions as "amusing oneself," and "doing nothing." The relaxed, everyday quality of such phrases creates a psychological climate diametrically opposed to metaphysical flights. A question asked by the "Sirian" might serve as epigraph to all esoteric texts: "You see a few attributes; but the deep substance of the thing, do you know it?" The grin of the sage is perceptible indeed.

The same antagonism of appearance and reality dominates the question of the essence of matter. The nature and relationship of material and immaterial existence are surveyed. Both aspects of the universe seem to be mutually exclusive and definable only through externals. The following dialogue is reported between the Sirian and the Cartesian philosopher:

" ' — But what do you mean by spirit?' — 'What are you asking there?' said the reasoner, I have no idea of that. 'People say that it is not matter.' — 'But do you at least know what matter is?' — 'Very well, 'replied the man. 'For instance, this rock is gray and has such a shape, it has three dimensions, it has weight and is divisible.' — 'Well,' said the Sirian, 'this thing which seems to you divisible, heavy and gray, will you tell me what it is? You see a few attributes; but the deep essence of the thing, do you know it?" — 'No,' said the other. — 'Then, you don't know what matter is.' " (Ch. VII, p. 126).

217

A sobering conclusion is virtually drawn. It is identical to the theosophical view of exact science. "Modern physical science is content with looking at the outside" of things whereas it should aspire to explore "the inside."* Microscopes and other devices geared to and limited by matter cannot lift the veil of materialistic appearance. A non-materialistic approach must be used if science is ever to realize its full potential which is as boundless as Cosmos itself. As was pointed out by a student of this writer, man needs to discover the deep essence of his own "gray matter." He must learn to know himself in order to probe universal mysteries "above and below." He must be bold enough to board the "conveyances of up there'" which lie in the depths of his innermost being. The alternative is easy to judge on the basis of objective evidence: the prevailing state of affairs. What is the value of a scientific structure resting solely on matter and admittedly ignorant of the deep nature of matter?

The question of what is meant by Spirit is rather well answered in the negative. Spirit is NO-THING. It is understandable that the reasoner should have "no idea" of its nature which is unknowable to the unaided intellect. It is partially accurate to say that Spirit is not matter for it is incorruptible while matter is in a constant state of transformation. Attention is subtly drawn to the Western concept of "matter" which is narrowly restricted to the so-called "objective" plane. Spirit is not *matter* in the Western sense of the word "matter" although it is present in every particle of matter in the manifest universe.

"Spirit is matter on the seventh plane; matter is Spirit — on the lowest point of its cyclic activity; and both — are MAYA. — " (*The Secret Doctrine*, p. 633, Vol. 1).

The occult view of the close connection between matter and spirit is strongly suggested by Voltaire. The calculated vagueness of the expression "people say —" ("on dit") and the negative quality of the definition of Spirit invite critical appraisal of the stated popular creed. Spirit and matter are presented in meaningful promixity as "separated twins" might be which lend themselves to synthesis or reunion. The subsequent exchange on attributes vs. essence is another invitation to view the poles of being in the unifying light of the "conveyances of up there."

One seed of hope does exist. Man is aware of the fact that matter is divisible. Human knowledge is engaged on a promising track. Science is but a few evolutionary steps away from rediscovery of atomic structure. "Good philosophers who reason by analogy" know the atom for

---

The Secret Doctrine, p. 494, Vol. I.

what it is: "— the most metaphysical object in creation."* The realm of the infinitely great, the domain of the infinitely small, all that separates and joins them is about to be seen in the light of divine intelligence, co-essence, and harmony.

The philosophical discussion is enriched by the contribution of a disciple of Malebranche. His exposé is briefly — and deceptively — acknowledged by "the animal from Sirius."

> "Then, Mr. Micromégas, addressing another sage whom he was holding on his thumb, asked him what his soul was and what it was doing. 'Nothing at all,' replied the disciple of Malebranche, 'it is God who does every thing for me; I see all in him; it is he who does everything without my meddling with it.' — 'One might as well not be,' the sage from Sirius went on." (Ch. VII, p. 126).

The spirituality of the Malebranchiste reflects esoteric "inaction." "Doing nothing" is the logical — and productive — expression of his faith. The same deceptive "inertia" or detachment from Mayavic pursuits is abundantly featured in many literary works. The new friend of Micromégas anticipates the sly comment of Saint Exupéry: "One may be at the same time lazy and faithful."** The soul which is reported to be and to do "nothing at all" has been absorbed by the seventh principle of consciousness. According to the theosophical statement which has already been quoted, "Man then ceases to be man, and attains a wholly superior condition of existence." Or, in the words of "Micromégas,, "One might as well not be" or exist on the material plane. The personal god or Higher Self of the philosopher "does everything" without interference from the subjugated lower ego— "without my meddling with it." The liberated Spirit communes with the Absolute and sees "all" with Divine insight. The personal god is free and united with the Unknowable of which it is the reflection. The "inactive" sage and "the animal from Sirius" understand each other perfectly.

A disciple of Leibnitz offers the following information on his soul:

> " 'And you, my friend,' said (Micromégas) to a Leibnitzian who was there, 'what is your soul?' — 'It is,' replied the Leibnitzian, 'a hand which shows the hours while my body chimes; or else, if you will, it is my soul which chimes while my body shows the hour; or else my soul is the mirror of the universe, and my body is the molding of the mirror; that is clear.'" (Ch. VII, p. 126).

---

*The Secret Doctrine, p. 485, Vol. I.
**Le Petit Prince, Ch. XIV.

The vibrant soul of the philosopher belongs, to the atomic, monadic universe of Leibnitz in which — according to Mme Blavatsky — the "monads closely resemble the elementals of mystic philosophy — these monads are representative Beings. Every monad reflects every other. Every monad is a living mirror of the Universe within its own sphere. And mark this, for upon it depends the power possessed by these monads, and upon this depends the work they can do for us; in mirroring the world, the monads are not mere passive reflective agents, but *spontaneously self-active;* they produce the images spontaneously, as the soul does a dream. In every monad, therefore, the adept may read everything, even the future. Every monad or *Elemental* is a looking-glass that can speak."*

The soul of the disciple of Leibnitz featured by Voltaire is "the mirror of the universe." The same soul — or "hand" — which "shows the hours" may therefore have the ability to "read everything, even the future." The designation of the philosopher's body viewed as the "molding" or frame of the soul can also be explained. "For we, too, claim that it is the 'Soul,' or the *inner* man, that descends on Earth first, the psychic *astral,* the mould on which physical man is gradually built — his Spirit, intellectual and moral faculties awakening later on as that physical stature grows and develops."** It may therefore be said in occult philosophy — as it is said in *Micromégas* — that the physical body is the "molding," the "frame," or the "edge" of the soul. The similarities which exist between the philosophy of Leibnitz and the Secret Doctrine are often commented by Mme Blavatsky. They form the concealed basis of the strange statement found in *Micromégas.* In the light of certain comparisons the manifesto of the follower of Leibnitz is "clear" indeed.

A disciple of Locke is next. He believes in an omnipresent divine design. His profession of faith receives hearty — if discreet — endorsement from Micromégas-Voltaire.

> " 'I do not know,' he said, 'how I think, but I know that I have never thought except at the prompting of my senses. That there may be immaterial and intelligent substances is one thing I do not doubt; but that it be impossible to God to communicate thought to matter, that is what I greatly doubt. I revere the eternal power, it is not fitting that I should limit it; I affirm nothing, I content myself with thinking that more things are possible than one thinks.'
> The animal from Sirius smiled; he did not find that one to be the least wise." (Ch. VII, pp. 26-27).

---

*The Secret Doctrine, p. 631, Vol. I.
**Ibid., p. 728, Vol. II.

The mysterious mechanism of human thought is called to attention. The question of *how* one thinks is all-important. ("I do not know how I *think*.") The crucial *how* is generally determined by sensory data and by the intellect. But other planes of consciousness are believed to exist. The disciple of Locke does not doubt the reality of "immaterial and intelligent substances." Nor does he doubt divine ability to impregnate matter with "thought." His philosophical refusal to limit divine essence suggests an actively open mind and an unfettered brand of Reason. The credo of the follower of Locke is skillfully veiled by a skeptical tone in which negative terms abound and the word "doubt" dominates. Diderot and other apologists of skepticism come to mind: "Honest skepticism — is the first step toward truth."

> " 'When you doubt, abstain,' says the wise Zoroaster, whose prudent aphorism is found corroborated in every case by daily life and experience. Yet, like St. John the Baptist, this sage of the past Ages is found preaching in the desert, in company with a more modern philosopher, namely Bacon, who offers the same priceless bit of practical Wisdom. 'In contemplation,' he says (in any question of Knowledge, we add), 'if a man begin with certainties, he shall end in doubts; but *if he will be content to begin with doubts, he shall end in certainties.*' (*The Secret Doctrine*, pp. 442-43, Vol. II).

> " 'He who seeks the truth,' wrote Descartes, 'must, so far as possible, doubt everything.' This saying is well known, and it sounds very new. If, however, we look at the second book of Aristotle's *Metaphysics*, we find this: 'He who seeks to acquire knowledge must first know how to doubt, for intellectual doubt helps to establish the truth.' " (*The Morning of the Magicians, An Open Conspiracy*, Part III).

The philosophical discussion is far from sterile. The harvest of odd findings reaped by the seekers seems to have a common root. There may be truth in the statement that the soul is its own raison d'être. There may be truth in the strange theory of the Cartesian. The monadic universe of Leibnitz bears a striking resemblance to the monadic universe of occult philosophy. The candid skepticism of the disciple of Locke finds understandable favor with "the animal from Sirius." The deceptive quietism of the disciple of Malebranche is the No-Thingness of True Being. A soulful quest for knowledge pervades the variegated fabrics of several philosophers. The same spirit of uninhibited inquiry is the ineffable golden thread which runs through *Micromégas*. It is an awareness of cosmic chains of more or less ethereal matter. It is the faculty which can break "chains" of perception.

The philosophical discussion is dramatically entered by a proponent of the doctrine of Saint Thomas:

"There was in attendance, unfortunately, a small diminutive animal wearing a square bonnet, who interrupted all the philosophizing diminutive animals; he said that he knew the whole secret, that it could be found in the *Sum* of Saint Thomas; he looked the two celestial inhabitants up and down; he maintained to them that their persons, their worlds, their suns, their stars, all was made exclusively for the benefit of man." (Ch. VII, p. 127).

The arrogant evangelist is a long way from truth. The soul is nowhere mentioned in his dogmatic exposé, a fact suggesting estrangement from spiritual reality. His authority is suspect to members of "good company." St. Thomas is alleged to have manipulated various portions of Hindu scriptures for the greater glory of his own gospel.* The Thomistic manifesto broadcast in *Micromégas* is identical in substance to the anthropocentric view of the universe which is scornfully rejected by occultists. Voltaire may have intended to connect the sermon with the status of allegedly soulless creatures by repeated use of the word "animal." The "Sirian" and Mme Blavatsky seem to agree on the value of dogma teaching "that everything is created for man, and that he alone is the sovereign of the universe —" Homeric laughter greets the *credo* of the aggressive evangelist. But the comical confrontation has a serious aspect. Embraced by many theologians, the Thomistic doctrine affects the lives, minds, and sprits of countless persons. It is a killer of insight. It is a killer of joy.

Another burst of mixed laughter marks the end of the story. Micromégas promises to the inhabitants of Earth a book containing the key to universal mysteries — "the end of things." The promise is kept. The book is examined by the eager Secretary of the Academy of Sciences. The scholar sees only a blank. Unfailing expertise and professional habit come to the rescue. He saves face:

"*Ah!* he said, *just what I expected!*"

The book has the appearance of a hoax. It is suggested that any work alleged to reveal "the end of things" is a product of fraud; that no key to universal mysteries is accessible to Man, and that the entire Cosmos is the child of blind chance.

The Secrétaire is correct in one respect. The non-existent revelation which he expects is all he can receive. No enlightenment can possibly come to him from the book. Some modes of expression and some eternal verities are beyond reach of his literal approach. Blind scholars, "closed books," and "lost keys" belong to the realm of non-fiction. M. le Secrétaire has numerous flesh-and-blood counterparts whose limited vision is often

---

Isis Unveiled, p. 539, Vol. 2.

deplored by occultists and esoteric writers. Such representatives of knowledge "cover only half the ground. Lacking the true key of interpretation, they see the symbols only in a physical aspect. They have no password to cause the gates of mystery to swing open and ancient spiritual philosophy is to them a closed book."* The blank page is the crowning glory of blind erudition faced with esoteric material. It is the negative achievement of unspiritualized knowledge. The vision of the Secrétaire is on the same low plane as the insight of the gracious archbishop. Science and Religion are suggested to be "corpses without souls."

"The end of things" — Spirit, Nirvâna, No-Thingness, immaterial existence — is a "blank" to the average learned Western mind. But it is the Alpha and Omega, the dynamic thread and fabric of Being in occult philosophy. The same intangible radiance, coursing through Cosmos — and Literature — is the key to the thinking of Voltaire.

The reaction of the academician is a prophetic reflection on the fate of Voltairian writings. The italicized expression: "— *just what I expected!*" is more than the expression of the dead-letter insight which prevails to our day. It is the lament of an author long misunderstood. It is the triumphant shout of the esoteric "smuggler" finally viewed in splendid integrity. It is doubly prophetic. It is Voltaire's very own.

Micromégas conveys a veiled message which has to do with no less than "the end of things." The overall scheme of existence and evolution is viewed in the light of the Secret Doctrine. Man is situated within the universe of which he is the tiny and potentially boundless reflection. "Micromégas" is "below" as Cosmos is "above." "The country where nothing lacks," the realm of immaterial Being and blissful omniscience is the source, the goal and the raison d'être of all things.

Cosmos is the extension of Divine Essence and Divine Harmony. "God geometrizes." Man owns a special share of the spiritual spark rationally distributed from galaxies to atoms. Various alloys of the matter-spirit compound determine planes of existence "above" and "below;" from planetary chains to human consciousness. The scheme of life can be grasped in the light of the symbolic circle or "necklace" of Karma-Sutratma (Cause-Effect-Evolution-Retribution-Rebirth).

Cosmic vision is the framework and the essence of the story. Knowledge of universal and human mysteries is shown to be accessible to Man. Man must discover and use "the conveyances of up there." He must cultivate the ethics and the science of the "diamond-hearted." He must use his intellect and his other faculties to master the art of "flight."

The focus of the story is the status of human knowledge. The myopic outlook of the majority of mankind reflects *necessarily* a certain stage

Isis Unveiled, p. 120, Vol. 2.

of general evolution. But it is compounded by more or less criminal human influence. The Church — which has lost the key to universal mysteries — suppresses and distorts that learning which remains. "Exact science" is not above reproach. It is stubbornly wedded to a narrow conception of matter. Matter is materialized spirit and cannot be fully known without the insight of spirit. Exact science leaves out of account the most crucial element of its own foundation. Literary material is as incompletely known as the other kind of "matter." It is — in many cases — "materialized spirit" of which most academicians see only the surface. Universal harmony and unity are reflected in the works of many great writers taken individually and collectively. "A profusion of varieties with a kind of admirably uniformity" prevails there also. Concealed under deceptive veils of multiple fabrics and styles is the common denominator of genial inspiration: Spirit. Quite frequently and unmistakably the Secret Doctrine. Literature is a powder-keg of secret knowledge as the Martian views of Voltaire well show. The author of *Micromégas* and the author of the *Recherche* seem to agree on the nature of the "same beauty" refracted through "diverse media:" the literary echo of the music of the spheres:

"That unknown quality of a unique world — perhaps it was in that — that the most authentic proof of genius lay, far more than in the content of the work itself. 'Even in literature,' Albertine asked me. — 'Even in literature.' And — I explained to Albertine that the great writers have never done but one work, or rather, have refracted a same beauty through diverse media, which they bring to the world. 'Were it not so late, little one,' I said to her, ' I would show you the same identity as in Vinteuil. Those model phrases, which you are beginning to recognize as I do, my little Albertine, the same in the sonata, in the septuor, in the other works, they would be for instance if you wish, in Barbey d'Aurevilly, a concealed reality, revealed by a material sign,' — " (*A la Recherche du temps perdu*, p. 375, Vol. III)

Micromégas is a commentary on the status of modern knowledge. The story must be viewed within the evolutionary framework of the Voltairian trilogy — *Zadig, Candide, L'Ingénu,* — to be fully understood. The allegories of Man in Search of Truth from Antiquity to our days are supplemented by a key to the object of the search. *Micromégas* is the key, the quaternary emanated out of the ternary. The title of the story and the name of the principal character contains it all. It is in the essential identity of Cosmos and Man that the revelation of universal mysteries can be found. It is in the infinite smallness of the human "insect" and of other atoms that the infinitely great and the pathway to the stars will be discovered. *Micromégas* explains how and why the

224

high grade of Ethics and Knowledge which prevailed in Pagan days is almost completely lost in the nightmarish, modern setting of *Candide*. *Micromégas* paves the way for the re-discovery of the Primitive Wisdom-Religion which is firmly awaited in all parts of the trilogy but which is specifically envisioned in the era of *L'Ingénu*. *Micromégas* does in vertical depth what is done in the other three stories against the background of the horizon of Time.

CANDIDE

Candide returns the reader to terrestrial vistas. The story takes place in Westphalia, a location suggesting the Western world. The times are those of modern Christianity. One question arises. What is the meaning of the specific stopover in time and space within the general framework of Voltairian writings?

Zadig designates Eastern Antiquity as the historical source of Universal Knowledge. Fundamental aspects of the Secret Doctrine form the hidden core of the story. *Micromégas* prolongs and supplements the esoteric substance of *Zadig*. The sustained and dominant presence of the Secret Doctrine in both stories points to one possibility. Having traced the origin of the Primitive-Wisdom-Religion to the East and related its first fragmentations; having situated mankind within the cosmic scheme of evolution, could Voltaire have used *Candide* to outline the fate of the Secret Doctrine in a modern, "civilized" milieu corresponding approximately to the milieu in which he lived?

A young man and his beloved are the two main characters. Candide and Cunégonde live happily and ignorantly on what they regard as an idyllic domain. The castle of Thuder-ten Tronckh seems to them a modern version of the Garden of Eden.

> "There was once in Westphalia, in the castle of his lordship the baron of Thunder-ten Tronckh, a boy endowed by nature with the most gentle ways. His face mirrored his soul. He had fairly sound judgment, along with the simplest mind; it is, I believe for that reason that he was called Candide. The old servants of the household suspected that he was the son of the sister of his Lordship and of a good and honest nobleman of the neighborhood, whom that lady never consented to marry, because he had been able to show only seventy-one quarters of nobility, and because the rest of his genealogical tree had been lost through the injury of time.
>
> His Lordship was one of the most powerful lords in Westphalia, for his castle had a door and some windows. His great hall even boasted a tapestry. All the dogs of his barnyard made up a pack in case of need; his grooms were his hunting men; the village priest was his High Chaplain. They all called him Milord, and they laughed when he made up stories." (Ch. I, pp. 143-44).

The initial presentation of Candide deserves comparison with the corresponding portrayal of Zadig. The young Pagan seems to be superior to his modern counterpart. Zadig is endowed with a fine temperament fortified by instruction. Candide has "gentle ways" — a dubious asset in certain societies. The characterization of his mind evokes the popular concept of "simple-minded." The initial sketch of Zadig stresses freely embraced beliefs and attitudes. The first presentation of Candide stresses the influence of the environment. Zadig is mostly defined as a person of intellectual, moral, and spiritual substance. Candide is presented primarily as the resultant of materialistic values and social forces. His status is externally determined by a dubious family tie with dubious grandeur. The Westphalian realm of materialistic illusion seems to invite comparison with the ancient realm of solid values. The strong selfhood of Zadig the Pagan is opposed to the weak identity of Candide, the modern.

Numerous details suggest that the Westphalian paradise is an illusion totally indebted for its fame to the provincial blindness of the inhabitants. Various expedients are used by the lord and master of the household to ape genuine greatness. Dogs, servants, and priest in residence are called upon to perform duties for which they are not prepared by nature or training. Results are gratifying to residents of the fine castle. But the reader is aware of certain shortcomings. The flattery of "servants" who lionize the person and glorify the jokes of His Lordship brings to mind inferior forms of spirituality reminiscent of Itobad. The prestige of Thunder-ten-tronckh depends on cheap imitations, make-believe, and servility. The castle is a Mecca of smug materiality personified by the three hundred and fifty pounds of the much-admired baroness. The castle is also reported to have "a door" and "some windows." Such refinements may be viewed as taxable assets and status symbols. But the overall impression is one of pretentious and grotesque mediocrity. The "windows" of ego-centric illusion belong to the general picture of smug, obese materiality. The dogs add a pungent touch to the establishment of lowest "necessity." — "une meute dans le besoin." Céline may have been inspired by the latter detail when he created his own version of "Westphalia:" the "Passage."

The esoteric symbolism of "windows" — representing the physical senses — is found in numerous texts such as the writings of Rabelais:

"Fils trescher (dist Gargantua), je vous en croy, et loue Dieu de ce qu'à votre notice ne viennent que choses bonnes et louables, et que, par les fenetres de vos sens, rien n'est on domicile de vostre esprit entré fors liberal sçavoir." (*Tiers Livre*, Ch. XLVIII).

("Dearest son (said Gargantua), I do believe you and praise God that to your knowledge do come only good and laudable things, and that, through the windows of your senses nothing has entered to dwell in your mind except liberal learning.")

The tapestry which beautifies the great hall brings to mind another Rabelaisian symbol: the veil behind which secret ventures are concealed — "darrière la tapisserie, en tapinois."* The subject of the Westphalian objet d'art is not described by Voltaire. But it is likely to be mythological and esoteric. Great benefit might be derived from its study were it more than an ornament. The establishment of the mighty Lord seems blind to the value of its own heritage.

The name *Thunder-ten-tronckh* suggests a thundering force somehow connected with modified Rabelaisian "drinking." The oracle of the Dive Bouteille comes to mind. Drinking of the fountain of forbidden knowledge proves a risky venture in the "Westphalian" domain. The experimentation of Candide with certain laws of Nature — physical love — leads to his expulsion from the heavenly castle. The "romantic" episode takes place behind a screen — "derrière un paravent" — the concealment value of which is nil. Occult pursuits are neither practical — nor occult in "Westphalia." The search for "knowledge" — a natural aspiration of man — is savagely and selectively punished. The seat of guilt is the logical target of the vengeful lord. Candide is literally kicked out of the Garden of Eden. Cunégonde loses consciousness.

The fainting spell of the girl would do honor to a "roman larmoyant." But its most important function is esoteric — not "literary." The swooning episode is an abortive attempt to raise the veil of Nature or Isis.

The Westphalian Jehovah — a petty "baron" in spiritual hierarchies — tolerates no such subversion which could easily result in his downfall. His jealous and vengeful disposition is reminiscent of the "Egyptian" of Zadig. The Jehovic power of darkness is present in *Zadig* as well as in *Candide*. But the general attitudes of ancient and modern societies are radically different. The young disciple of Zoroaster lived in a world which resisted such forces of spiritual disintegration as "Missouf," "the Egyptian," and Itobad. Candide is not so fortunate. The Ancient tradition promoted and glorified Science. The "Westphalian" establishment cannot allow it to exist.

Marcel Proust may have had in mind "the most beautiful castle in the world" when he wrote a certain passage of the *Recherche*:

> "Such is aristocracy, in its heavy construction, endowed with few openings, letting in little light, showing the same lack of soaring impulse, but also the same massive and blinded might as does roman architecture; locking up, walling in, and darkening the expression of all history." (*A la Recherche du temps perdu*, p. 537, Vol. II).

A major clue is given in the "heavy construction" — or literal interpretation — of esoteric "aristocracy" — which is exclusively spiritual.

Tiers Livre, Ch. XVIII.

But the chief purpose of the text seems to be to characterize feudal "roman" structures and their repressive influence on historical truth. Proust seems to have made typical esoteric use of the word "roman" in the sense of "Roman Catholic." Massive materiality, lack of soaring or lofty aspiration, scarcity of light, blindness and an incurable allergy to human knowledge are meaningful negative findings. Voltaire, Proust — and numerous others — seem to share the same view of the same spiritually deprived and depraved establishment.

Candide goes from bad to worse. His expulsion from the phony paradise is followed by military induction. The "fall" seems to be complete. Adding insult to injury is the fact that divine truths are occasionally uttered by rogues — such as the recruiters — and used to promote base ends. Outrageous as their exploitation may be, such eternal verities retain strong appeal:

> " ' — men were created only to help one another.' " (Ch. II, p. 146).

The misused formula shows the effectiveness of a popular esoteric device. Conflict between pure substance and polluted source is exploited. The reader is induced to react negatively to a statement which he would normally endorse. More or less consciously, hostility is transferred from tainted mouthpiece to valid pronouncement. The same technique is used in *Paris* by Alfred de Vigny. An ugly, bloodthirsty mob utters an explosive paraphrase:

> " '*All will be called and all will be chosen!*' "

The exoteric call to anarchy serves to conceal a spiritual message. The war cry is the equivalent of the Voltairian "end of things." It is also a translation of the "end" of the "human family" which is contemplated in *Paris* itself. The hidden substance of the italicized expression is an affirmation of belief in universal salvation. Nirvâna is the ultimate destiny of all. The comprehension gap separating exoteric sarcasm from esoteric fervor is a significant measure of the power of illusion.

No spokesman of eternal verities seems to suffer more from the existence of the same comprehension gap than does Pangloss, the preceptor of Candide. The incurable optimism of the master is difficult to characterize in practical terms. Its lingering influence on the young hero may be seen alternately as a blessing and as a curse. Throughout a long series of distressing adventures, the young Westphalian will remember the teachings of the master: "There is no effect without cause." "All is arranged necessarily for the best." "Those who stated that all is well spoke ineptly; they should have said that all is for the best."

The veiled message of Pangloss—a name meaning "all languages" and therefore suggesting Universal Knowledge—belies its appearance of rank insanity. The Panglossian refrain: "There is no effect without cause" is a profession of Karmic faith. The "necessary chain of events" frequently invoked by the preceptor is a divine network of rational correlations underlying the chaos of the visible universe. It is also the symbol of the process of reincarnation which rules the destinies of men. The occult "circle of necessity"—and the entire body of philosophy which goes with it—is repeatedly brought to bear in the homilies of the master. The same "necessity" or evolutionary framework may explain how "all is for the best" in a specific phase of human progress.

The dialectics of Pangloss cry out for refutation:

> "All having been made to one end, all is necessarily designed to the best end. Do note that noses were made to wear glasses, therefore, we do have glasses. Legs were clearly devised to be breeched, and we have breeches. Stones were formed to be cut and to make into castles; so my Lord has a very handsome castle; the greatest baron in the province must have the best lodgings; and, pigs being made to be eaten, we eat pork all year round."

One may object that noses were made to smell—in French "to feel" —"sentir"—or that "sensitivity" is their major function. One may argue that glasses denote "poor vision." One may submit that legs were intended to promote "walking"—an activity which will not be encouraged in a subsequent chapter of *Candide*. One may note that fragmentary interpretations or truncated bodies of knowledge are suggested by "cut stones." One may speculate on the interesting proximity linking baron and swine. One may question that pigs—or other living creatures—were meant to be slaughtered or devoured. Such arguments might find favor with "the first philosopher in the province." The Panglossian eulogy of the status quo is double-edged indeed. Deflected "sensitivity," limited vision, prohibited exploration, fragmentary learning, cruelty to fellow-creatures; repetitive and toxic nourishment; such are the chief glories of Westphalia, the modern Western world.

No exoteric sign of rational divine law is discernible in the adventures of Candide. Absurdity and suffering seem to be the sole constants in his fate. The experience of Candide the soldier does not promote optimism. Having left quarters in order to take a walk, the young recruit finds himself quickly tried and convicted by military justice:

> "He followed his urge, one fine spring day, to go for a walk, walking straight ahead, believing that it was a privilege of the human species, as of the animal species, to use its legs for its pleasure." (Ch. II, p. 147).

The free exercise of one's ability to walk is punished by the power structure with the same savagery as was the pursuit of "love" by the Lord of Thunder-ten-tronckh. The independent use of human faculties finds little grace in the eyes of Westphalian hierarchies. Every natural aspiration of man seems to constitute a crime and a "forbidden fruit."

Candide is offered a "choice" between a deadly run of the gauntlet and a deadly shower of bullets. The disproportion existing between "crime" and punishment suggests more to be at stake than proverbial military insight and army regulations.

The young man wishes to use his legs for his "pleasure." The Voltairian value of the latter word suggests the "walk" or "walk abroad" to be spiritual in nature. The esoteric concept of "walk abroad" may be tested with profit in the works of numerous writers, particularly in English literature. It is frequently connected with conical hats suggesting the garb and the activity of the magician, "mirrors" of self-knowledge and other elements of esoteric symbolism. As was previously noted, Vigny found Pascal to owe a great deal to the "walks" of Montaigne. Such excursions which involve active minds and spirits promote far more than physical exercise.

> "Dear friends, there is no cause for so much sympathy I shall certainly manage from time to time to take my walks abroad. All that matters is an active mind, what is the use of feet? By land one can ride in a carrying chair; by water, be rowed in a boat." (Po-Chu-i, *Illness*, written circa A.D. 842, when he was paralyzed).

It should be noted briefly that Voltaire shunned the esoteric concept of "walks" in *Micromégas*. The fact is understandable in a text devoted to the difference existing between earthbound progress and "the conveyances of up there." The exoteric meaning of the word "walk" is too closely connected with the idea of earth in the majority of Western minds to lend itself to the interpretive flight which is courted in *Micromégas*. Such was the probable reason why the term was avoided. Having made himself as clear as was esoterically possible on the subject of spiritual transports in *Micromégas*, Voltaire reverts to the use of the standard occult concept of a "walk" in *Candide*.

The military structure of which the young Westphalian is a reluctant part is not only repressive. It is selectively and perversely regressive. Its idea of punishment — and self-preservation — is to try to turn back the clock of evolution. Candide is forced to run the gauntlet twice and begs to be "mercifully shot before the third race," "la troisième course." The esoteric concept of *Race* or evolutionary sub-cycle lends significant dimension to the episode.

Our era and the era in which Voltaire lived belong to the same Fifth Race of the Fourth Round of the present Grand Cycle. It is an age of deep materiality, therefore an age of refinement in evil. But it is also an age of transition. Having reached the nethermost point of a descending curve, mankind can only go upwards. Modern man is approaching a phase of spectacular intellectual and spiritual development.

> "In our present all-material Fifth Race, the earthly Spirit of the Fourth is still strong in us; but we are approaching the time when the pendulum of evolution will direct its swing decidedly upwards, bringing Humanity back on a parallel line with the primitive third Root-Race in Spirituality." (*The Secret Doctrine*, pp. 224-25, Vol. I).

The esoteric value of the forced "race" brings Candide to the borderline of ethereal, original mankind. How ethereal the establishment wishes him to be is demonstrated by the death sentence. The goal of the punishing tyrants is a return to good old days when the life expectancy of their system was greatest. The forces of oppression sense that time is running out.

Evil and Ignorance are one and the same in the esoteric mind. No better illustration of the fact could possibly be found than the misguided maneuvers of shaky tyrants in *Candide*. A general return to the ethereal and spiritual state of mankind would bring the very collapse of their domination which is rightly feared. No spiritually inclined humanity would tolerate — or even conceive — the existence of such devilish hosts. The self-defeating efforts of the mighty have interesting causes. Physical death and non-existence are regarded by them as the same thing. The fact is an edifying reflection on religions of state and their alleged belief in eternal life. Evolutionary insight seems totally absent.

The meaningful "runs" or "races" of Candide supplement the suggestion of materiality which is conveyed by the embonpoint of the baroness of Thunder-ten-tronckh. The bulk of the lady — "approximately *three* hundred and *fifty* pounds" — represents a probable allusion to the *fitfh* subrace of the *Third* Race, the time when the descent of Man into materiality became most dramatically manifest through the separation of the sexes.

> "The little ones of the earlier races were entirely sexless — shapeless even for all one knows; but those of the later races were born androgynous. It is in the Third Race that the separation of sexes occurred. From being previously a-sexual, Humanity became distinctly hermaphrodite or bi-sexual; and finally the man-bearing eggs began to give birth, gradually and almost imperceptibly in their evolutionary development, first to Beings in which one sex predominated over the other, and, finally, to distinct men and women." (*The Secret Doctrine*, p. 132, Vol. II).

> "Though we apply the term '*truly human*,' only to the Fourth Atlantean Root-Race, yet the Third Race is almost human in its latest portion, since

232

it is during its fifth sub-race that mankind *separated* sexually, and that the *first man was born* according to the now normal process. This 'first man' answers in the Bible (*Genesis*) to Enos, or Henoch, son of Seth (ch. iv)" (*The Secret Doctrine*, p. 715 fn., Vol. II).

The size of the baroness seems to also suggest the Fourth Race of Atlantean giants, "the earthly" — matter-bound — "Spirit" of which "is still strong in us." The voluminous consort of the Jehovic "Lord" is clearly connected with *matter* within the evolutionary frameworks of Time and Space.

The dominance of "flesh" is also suggested by the initial sketch of Cunégonde. The girl has oral as well as other appeal. The young lady, "aged seventeen, had a vivid complexion, was fresh-looking, chubby, appetizing." The sweetheart of Candide combines the powerful attractions of food and sex which represent ultimate fulfillment to countless Westerners. No such emphasis on sensuality may be found in the corresponding portrait of Pagan Astarté. The *seventeen* years of age of the Westphalian heroine tend to suggest the specific era of the seventeen hundreds. The XVIIIIth Century seems to be regarded by Voltaire as an age of bestiality. The latter hint will find a tragic abundance of support in subsequent chapters of *Candide*.

The young man is virtually crippled and flayed alive in the course of the disciplinary process. Some skin and ability to walk are eventually regained with the help of a kindly surgeon. The damaged "coat of skin" or physical body further tends to situate the second chapter of *Candide* within the perspective of occult evolution. The symbolic coat of skin represents the advent of corporeal mankind during the Third Race:

> " — primeval man, who contrary to the Darwinian theory was purer, wiser, and far more spiritual, as shown by the myths of the Scandinavian Bur, the Hindu Dejotas, and the Mosaic 'Sons of God,' — in short, of a far higher nature than the man of the present Adamic race, became de-spiritualized or tainted with matter, and then, for the first time, was given the *fleshly body,* which is typified in Genesis in that profoundly significant verse: 'Unto Adam also and to his wife did the Lord God make *coats of skin,* and clothed them.' Unless the commentators would make of the First Cause a *celestial tailor,* what else can the apparently absurd words mean, but that the spiritual man had reached, through the progress of involution, to that point where matter, predominating over and conquering spirit, had transformed him into the physical man, or the second Adam, of the second chapter of *Genesis?*" (*Isis Unveiled*, p. 149, Vol. I).

Divine Reason is conspicuously absent from the exoteric plane of *Candide*. But human consistency is admirable where the repression of knowledge is concerned. The target of oppressors is basically the same in the Jehovic castle of Thunder-ten-tronckh and in the military realm of "heroic butchery." It is the human faculty to desire and seek truth. The seat of guilty knowledge is damaged by the wrathful baron. The ability to "walk" is impaired by the military sadists. The loss of skin which is suffered needs no interpretation. The means of learning and the means of existence are threatened. Punishment is not determined by vagrant impulse. It is calculated to protect the vicious *status quo*. The experimentation of "lovers" who wish to unveil the mystery of Life and the "trips" of young metaphysicians are equally unwelcome in the modern Western world. The Jehovic power structure is vulnerable and opposed to knowledge.

Candide is rescued from execution by the King of the Bulgarians. The monarch chances to pass at an opportune time and also happens to be in a benevolent mood. The young hero is pardoned by divine right:

> "Candide, unable to stand any more, requested the mercy that they should be so kind as to crush his skull; he obtained that favor; he is blindfolded, he is made to kneel. The King of the Bulgarians passes by at this moment, inquires about the crime of the patient; and, that King having a great genius, he understood, from all that he learned of Candide, that he was a young metaphysician quite ignorant of things of this world, and granted him mercy with a clemency which will be praised in all the newspapers and in all ages to come." (Ch. II, p. 148).

Grace is granted by a personal *deus ex machina*, a worthy representative of Jehovic "justice" in the Jehovic domain of egocentric perversion. "As above — so below. As in heaven, so on earth!"

The praise lavished upon the King is of the same double-edged variety as the eulogy of the archbishop mentioned in *Micromégas*. Against a background of chronic spiritual and physical abuse, one decent act is observed in each case. The prelate who helps withhold knowledge from millions of spiritual victims, past, present, and future, allows one person to see certain documents briefly. The King who has ordered the massacre of thousands and will order the massacre of thousands more, feels compelled to display spectacular mercy toward one man. Both acts are motivated by whim and public relations. The terrestrial minions of Jehovah wish to be feared and idolized as does their Deity. Tyrannical power craves occasional love, The sycophants of the present and the flunkeys of the future will not fail to glorify the magnanimous figures. The Throne and the Altar have no better ally than the abysmal stupidity of the masses.

The King enjoys his role of omnipotent Savior. The occasion is a good one to gloat over the ignorance of metaphysical "eggheads" — a favorite sport of political clowns of all times. Divine Justice is far

234

from manifest in the person of the monarch. But it is manifest in the unknown "chain of events" which bring him on the scene and shape his royal pleasure. Beyond the appearance of personal, Jehovic agency lies the reality of impersonal and unknowable Decrees. The King is no more than an instrument of Karma.

The work of Retribution is obscured by the murderous tidal wave of war. The fate of Cunégonde, the destruction of the community of Thunder-ten-tronckh, and the subsequent reprisals are related by Pangloss. The biblical concept of justice: an eye for an eye, a tooth for a tooth, has yet to be rejected. Little has changed since the heroic days of the Old Testament:

"Cunégonde is dead! Ah! best of worlds where are you? But from what illness did she die? would it not be from having seen me expelled from the beautiful castle of her father by means of great kicks? — No, said Pangloss, she was disembowelled by Bulgarian soldiers, after having been raped as much as one can be, they crushed the head of his Lordship the baron, who tried to defend her; Her Ladyship the baroness has been cut into pieces; my poor pupil, treated exactly as his sister; and as for the castle, there do not remain two stones one on the other; there remains not one barn, not one sheep, not one duck, not one tree; but we were well avenged, for the Abares did the same thing in a nearby baronial domain which belonged to a Bulgarian lord." (Ch. IV, pp. 151-152).

The Nationalities of persons avenged — and of the avengers — seem to have esoteric significance. Exoteric commentators generally believe that the Bulgarians represent the Prussians while the Abares represent the French.* Such interpretations seem correct on the exoteric plane. But they fail to do justice to the deep substance of the text. The "vulgarization" or debasement of a once noble force — Spirit — may well be suggested by the word "Bulgarian." The machinery of war is viewed by Voltaire — and by many others — as the lowest possible form of degraded "strength." The transition from divine Breath or Spirit to brutality is a natural aspect of the evolutionary "fall" into materiality. The change is symptomatic of the cyclic nadir reached by "Westphalian" Faith Race mankind.

The word "Abare" seems intended to convey — among other things — the suggestion of "avare," or the idea of a miserly, selfish person. The stress which appears to be placed on selfishness is consistent with the evolutionary theme of an all-time low in the course of human progress. Mayavic values reign supreme in the domain of ethics and in the realm of insight. The same divisiveness is the essence of the sectarianism which is bound to the esoteric core of *Candide*.

Debased "force" and debased selfhood point to the same degrada-

*Garnier-Bénac edition, note, p. 633.

tion of Spirit. The apparent conflict between "Bulgares" and "Avares" is a virtual alliance of equally evil powers. The murderous strife promotes the interests of two ruthless dynasties. The restlessness of the masses which might otherwise take the form of internal uprisings is channeled into other directions. Potential revolutionaries are turned into cannon-fodder in the name of the motherland. The simultaneous singing of victorious *Te Deums* by the kings of both warring countries is an eloquent commentary on a sinister job well done by the Throne-Altar compound. The "infamous" is sole beneficiary of the pious carnage.

The common soldier takes for granted and condones his dual status of cannon-fodder and slave. The recruiters sing the praise of their glorious *alma mater*. The fellow-victims of Candide participate with gusto in the administration of his punishment. The sado-masochistic insanity of bellicose mystiques is exposed with special brilliance in a Voltairian short story entitled *Le Monde Comme il va. The World as it goes*. A soldier is asked to give the reason of the war in which he is fighting. His edifying reply is as follows: "That is not my business. I know nothing about that. My business is to kill and be killed to make a living." Mankind has clearly strayed to the antipodes of Ethics and Reason when major portions of the planet are laid waste by senseless carnage, when the sheep being led to slaughter find no better scapegoats than their fellows, and when "heroic butchery" is endorsed by the victims themseles.

The reference to the "Abares" seems to have historical dimensions. It is a probable allusion to an expedition carried out by a lieutenant of Charlemagne. The Avars were defeated in 795 by a Frankish chief named Eric. They were groups of Huns who had settled in the plains of Hungary. The "Bulgarians" of Voltaire may thus be linked more or less directly to the site of the battle — Hungary having once embraced vast territories. The Avar "ring" or circular camp was stormed by the Franks who found within its enclosures large quantities of gold, silver, jewels, and precious objects. The treasure was the product of multiple lootings. The symbolism of spoliated "wealth" derived from the Far East seems to be introduced by the "Abares." The impression tends to be confirmed by ethnic kindship. The Bulgarians share Asiatic origins with the Avars. Racially and symbolically a fratricidal struggle is suggested by Voltaire.

The shabby wealth of "Westphalia" is annihilated. "Not one barn, not one sheep, not one duck, not one tree" is spared. The contents of the barns may represent spiritual nourishment. The flocks are gone. They may represent dispersed congregations. The trees which did not escape destruction may have been divided remnants of the original One Tree of Knowledge. The ducks — is French "canards" — may convey through a play on words the idea of the propaganda of the defunct paradise. Little "strength" has been imparted to dishonest custodians by the five hundred ounces of "borrowed silver." The fact that the "borrowed" silver" is of Oriental origin adds a spiritual dimension to the fratricidal aspects of the war. The era of conciliatory "suppers" such as the gathering described in *Zadig* is long gone. Sectarian disputes over spiritual wealth are suggested to underlie national disputes over material holdings.

The theme of sectarian rivalry suggests an allusion to certain "crusades" waged by Christians against various sects. Mme Blavatsky calls attention to the persecutions endured by the Neo-Platonists and by "Christian sects whose theories were usually grouped under the generic name of *Gnosticism*:

> "These are those which appeared immediately after the alleged crucifixion, and lasted till they were nearly exterminated under the rigorous execution of the Constantinian law. The greatest guilt of these were their syncretic views, for at no other period of the world's history had truth a poorer prospect of triumph than in those days of forgery, lying, and deliberate falsification of facts.

> But before we are forced to believe the accusations, may we not be permitted to inquire into the historical characters of their accusers? Let us begin by asking, upon what ground does the Church of Rome build her claim of supremacy for her doctrines over those of the Gnostics? Apostolic succession, undoubtedly. The succession *traditionally* instituted by the direct Apostle Peter. But what if this prove a fiction? Clearly, the whole superstructure supported upon this one imaginary stilt would fall in a tremendous crash." (*Isis Unveiled*, p. 326, Vol. 2).

The syncretic tendencies of the Gnostics, the sectarian policies of their persecutors, and the dubious, "stilt" of apostolic succession seem to be allegorized in *Candide*. The "syncretic" aspirations of the title character are violently discouraged by the Westphalian "Lord" in the first chapter of the story. The corresponding desire of Cunégonde to become "learned" or to acquire knowledge — Greek *gnosis* — is likewise doomed by the jealous tyrant. The collapse of the finest castle in the world is a "tremendous crash" brought about by the onslaught of "foreigners" or "heretics." The wrathful baron is killed. His voluminous spouse is cut to pieces. The "spiritual" structure of Westphalia undergoes fragmentation or sectarian division. No two rocks of the castle remain standing: "Il n'est pas resté pierre sur pierre." The latter sentence is reminiscent of the destruction of Jerusalem, a likely symbol of the Judaeo-Christian tradition. It is also a transparent allusion to the famous statement: "Thou art Peter; and upon this rock will I build my church." The collapse of the "Westphalian" or Western edifice constituted by "Pierres" or Popes seems to be the "tremendous crash" ever threatening the shaky "stilt" or apostolic succession. One may also note that the Voltairian view of the Constantinian era bears a marked resemblance to the view of occultists. It is regarded as the origin of a "detestable and absurd" mode of government — modern monarchism. It is diseased by an spectacular over-supply of "monks."*

The structure built around Jerusalem and Peter is a subject of abundant theosophical comment. Among numerous arguments brought to bear against ecclesiastical tradition is the belief that Peter never was in Rome. The same belief is reflected in the writings of Voltaire.

> This tax was levied by Saint Peter upon Gaul from the very year when he came to Rome, and — I doubted that Saint Peter had ever made that trip —" (Garnier-Bénac, *Pot-Pourri*, p. 420.)
> "He used to read every morning, took notes, and in the evening consulted scholars to know: in what language the serpent had spoken to our good mother; whether the soul is in the corpus callosum or in the pineal gland; whether Saint Peter had dwelt in Rome for twenty-five years — " (*L'Homme aux 40 écus - de la vérole.*)

The Secret Doctrine teaches that Peter was not involved in the foundation of the Church. The apostle is regarded as a personification of spurious spiritual and temporal leadership:

> "As to Peter, biblical criticism has shown before now that he had probably no more to do with the foundation of the Latin Church at Rome, than to furnish the pretext so readily seized upon by the cunning Iraeneus to benefit his Church with the new name of the apostle — *Petra* or *Kiffa* — a name which allowed so readily, by an easy play upon words, to connect it with *Petroma*, the double set of stone tablets used by the hierophant at the initiations, during the final Mystery." (*Isis Unveiled*, pp. 91-92, Vol. 2).

The relevance of a medieval crusade is also suggested in *Candide* by the word "Bulgares." The Albigensian "heretics" who were savagely persecuted during the XIIIth Century were often designated as "les Bulgares" — also as "les bons hommes" and "les bons chrétiens." They believed in reincarnation and denounced the corruption of the Catholic clergy. The purity and goodness of their mode of life earned them the veneration of common people and the adherence of many noblemen. It is easy to see what a danger such "heretics" represented for the "Westphalian" Church and why they were practically exterminated.

"The finest castle in the world" bears a striking resemblance to the

---

*L'Homme aux 40 écus — Sur les moines —

structure built around Jerusalem and Peter. The vulnerable edifice cannot withstand confrontation with esoteric "strangers" or "heretics." The chief strength of the Westphalian citadel seems to lie in the blinders worn by its residents.

The system described in the first chapters of *Candide* remains appallingly strong throughout the story in spite of the destruction of one community. But the congenital weaknesses of Jehovic structures such as the Throne, the Altar and the Castle are clearly diagnosed in Chapter IV. They may be traced to a vulnerable foundation of stolen and falsified dogma. The long-term prognosis of the establishment is not good. The trend of sectarian division is likely to worsen. The "Abares" — esoterically suggesting "Arabes" or Moslems — will make appearances in subsequent chapters of *Candide*. The "Bulgares" and the related domain of the Greek Orthodox Church announce the "Great Schism" which will be an important element of the story of the old woman. The chapter dealing with the origin of Jesuitry is also prepared by the remarkable survival of the brother of Cunégonde. Dead or alive, the Jehovic Lord of Thunder-ten-tronckh will have imitators. He will also leave an heir dedicated to the maintenance of His oppressive realm.

The desolate regions of Westphalia are abandoned in search of more hospitable lands. Lured by the wealth and Christian background of the Dutch, Candide seeks help and charitable treatment in their country. The majority of the inhabitants is cold-hearted in all respect but one. Sectarian passion is the one fiery commitment. Far from heeding the precepts of the Savior who preached — and practiced — the brotherhood of Man, the Dutch citizens encountered by Candide treat as human beings only those persons who are "for the good cause:" their own.

The dogmatic ignorance of the reformed congregation is demonstrated in a brief dialogue. Candide is enjoined to state whether or not he is "for the good cause." The amusing exoteric malentendu resulting from the question covers a valid profession of Panglossian faith.

> "He then addressed a man who had just spoken by himself one hour and a half on charity in a large gathering. This orator, giving him a dirty look, said to him: 'What do you come here for? are you there for the good cause?' — 'There is no effect without cause,' replied Candide modestly, 'all is linked necessarily and arranged for the best.'" (Ch. III, pp. 149-50).

The Panglossian "cause" of multiple "effects" and "necessary" "chains of events" is the First Cause or the Supreme Being. The entire occult scheme of cosmic and human evolution is evoked in a minimum of words. The acrimonious preacher is unable to perceive the divine truth stated by Candide. The target of sectarian contempt is the true representative of the "good cause" par excellence: the First Cause.

One may ask how the orator can speak by — or to — himself in a large gathering. The character of the assembly and the subject matter of the talk solve the contradiction. No one really wants to hear any message of charity. The Dutch burghers of Voltaire have much in common with the English farmers of Samuel Butler who "would have been equally horrified at hearing the Christian religion doubted, and at seeing it practiced."*

Candide receives from a poor anabaptist all the help which the kindly man can offer. True Christian practice is found on the outside of the Church. Hypocrisy reigns inside. The Protestant community is found wanting in two essential requirements of spirituality: compassion — Love — and insight. It is as bitterly opposed to genuine Christian charity as the Jehovic God is opposed to general enlightenment and progress. Universal truth can expect poor treatment from such a society.

The unexpected reunion of Candide and Pangloss is marred by the condition of the master. Pangloss suffers from venereal disease. He is unrecognizable and — at first — unrecognized by his former student. The illness of the preceptor results from a dalliance with Paquette, a former lady-in-waiting at the castle of Thunder-ten-tronckh. The girl has been infected by a very learned monk who "has gone back to the source." The latter phrase is an unveiled clue to the occult nature of the friar's interests.

The scourge is. traced to persons of various social positions: ultimately to a jesuit who contracted the disease unnaturally. The second partner in the "original sin" is a companion of Christopher Columbus. The "strange genealogy" of the ailment has its polluted source in predatory politics and religious fanaticism. Columbus, the instrument of royal greed for material treasures and territorial conquests, paved the way for the physical and spiritual oppression of primitive races of the New World. Civilized American natives fared no better than their less advanced counterparts under the fiendish, genocidal frenzy of the invaders. The historical record of Philip and Isabella — the sponsors of Columbus — is well-known. The efficiency of their spiritual guide — Torquemada — is a matter of bloody historical record. The Jesuitic order which is involved in the corruption of sacred values is notorious for its learning — occult science included — and for its militaristic hierarchy and ways. The machinery of war — so vigorously indicted in preceding chapters of *Candide* — assumes a thoroughly sinister form: It is wedded to sick religion in unnatural col-

---

The Way of All Flesh, Ch. 15.

lage. The general formula of the poison is identical to the formula of black magic. The spiritual essence of Love and Knowledge which is degraded is manipulated to base ends. The Voltairian "pox" *is* a commentary on exoteric venereal disease. But it is also and above all a symbol of the spiritual disintegration plaguing the entire Western world. The equivalence is virtually given in *L'Homme aux Quarante Ecus*:

> "The Turks call the pox *the Christian disease,* and that redoubles the profound contempt which they have for our theology." (*De la vérole*).

The same symbolism is used in *Mort à Crédit*. The equivalence of venereal disease and of a certain type of religion is suggested.

> "Here is 'Case No. 34' the employee with dark glasses, the bashful one, the sly one, he goes and gets his dose on purpose, every six months, at the Cour d'Amsterdam, the better to expiate by the rod — that's his prayer, the way he calls it." (*Mort à Crédit,* p. 23, Ed. de Poche).

The disease described in *Candide* plagues an appalling cross-section of society including the aristocracy — a countess —; an officer — the army —; the Church — the learned monk and the Jesuit — ; and a page or "servant" representing the low classes as well as a low grade of spirituality. No one seems immune to the dread disease. The fact that Pangloss — a *master* — is affected reflects the "catholic" or "universal" quality of the scourge. The fact that he becomes unrecognizable as a result is also edifying. The era of the "pox" is the era of concealment for "masters." It is also an era of general blindness.

The pollution of sacred values which is reported in Chapter IV is a major source of fear of Panurge. The Rabelaisian hero, torn between desire to "marry" — "mystically" — and fear of cuckoldom, sees his misgivings confirmed by an oracle. Man — the potentially divine particle of universal energy — Pan-ergos — is told that his spiritual destiny is threatened by the adulterous intrusion of a monk or representative of the Church.

The Voltairian "pox" is linked to "controversy," division, or Maya; in short to a stage of deepest materiality in cyclic evolution.

> "— until our times, on our continent, this illness is peculiar to us, as is controversy. The Turks; the Indians, the Persians, the Chinese, the Siamese do not know it yet; but there exists a sufficient reason why they should know it in their turn in a few centuries." (Ch. IV, pp. 152-53).

The prophecy of Voltaire had already been fulfilled when Mme Blavatsky gave the theosophical opinion of sectarian "pox:"

> "Better a 'heathen' religion that can extort from a Francis Xavier such a tribute as he pays the Japanese, in saying that 'in virtue and probity they

241

surpassed all the nations he had ever seen;' than a Christianity whose advance over the face of the earth sweeps aboriginal nations out of existence as with a hurricane of fire. Disease, drunkness, and demoralization are the immediate results of apostasy from the faith of their fathers, and conversion into a religion of mere forms. — Yes, these are the 'blessings' that the modern Christian religion brings with its *Bibles* and *Catechisms* to the poor 'heathen.' Rum and bastardy to Hindustan, opium to China, rum and foul disorders to Tahiti; and, worst of all the example of hypocrisy in religion, and a practical skepticism and atheism, which, since it seems to be good enough for *civilized* people, may well in time be thought good enough for those whom theology has too often been holding under a very heavy yoke. On the other hand, everything that is noble, spiritual, elevating, in the old religion is denied, and even deliberately falsified." (*Isis Unveiled*, pp. 573-74, Vol. 2).

In contrast to unnatural love which is the source of the "pox," the dalliance of Pangloss and Paquette is natural and innocent. But their experiment with the forbidden fruit is dreadfully punished. The penalty is not inherent to the act of love itself. It is the result of pre-existing corruption. "Love" seems doomed to degradation in the sinister domain of "Westphalia."

The ecclesiastical dogma of original sin and the parallel belief in works of the devil are symbolically rejected by Pangloss:

"O, Pangloss, exclaimed Candide, that is a strange genealogy! Was it not the devil who was its progenitor? — Not at all, replied the great man; it was an indispensable thing in the best of worlds, a necessary ingredient: for if Columbus had not caught in an island of America that disease which poisons the source of generation, which frequently even prevents generation, and which is obviously the opposite of the great goal of nature, we would have neither cocoa nor cochineal." (Ch. IV, p. 152).

Esoterically proclaimed in the passage is the sacredness of the mystical union which is the "great goal" or design of nature and which is thwarted by the spiritual "pox" or perversion of divine values. "Generation," incarnation, evolution, all tend to fulfill the same need. Love of knowledge and fellow-creatures is the "necessary" ingredient of perfection. While it is never desirable, desired, or excusable — as far as Panglossian philosophers are concerned — the corruption of spirituality is itself "necessary," inherent to certain stages of the "circle of necessity." The same degradation is the inevitable corollary of a materialistic "faith" wedded to an anthropomorphic God. It is also consistent with the myth of an anthropomorphic Devil. In that sense and in that sense only, the Fiend, or his human projection, may be said to be at work. The scourge is ironically connected with "commerce" which is a powerful aid to human progress but which can be perverted by ignoble beings and goals.

The question of what other "goods" may come to Westphalia from American "commerce" — besides cocoa, cochineal, and the "pox" — is not asked. It is answered in a subsequent chapter devoted to Eldorado. It is also answered by the esoteric substance of *L'Ingénu*, a story in which the Primitive Wisdom-Religion is brought back to Europe from the so-called "New World."

Voltaire suggests that the existence of the plague will serve good purposes in the end. For, in the words of Jesrad, there is no evil out of which some good does not come. Future generations will understand the nature of the scourge and will fight it with adequate weapons. Surface sarcasm to the contrary, the praise of Love is genuine and vibrant on the esoteric plane:

> " — it is love, love, the consolation of mankind, the preserver of the universe, the soul of all sentient beings, tender love — " (Ch. IV, p. 152).

"Preserver of the universe" is the title of Vishnu, the creative principle of Cosmos. As was previously noted, Vishnu, or DAG, the Savior, is relevant to the works — perhaps to the life — of Voltaire. The "fish-man" is closely connected with the course of universal evolution.

The task of curing Pangloss of the "pox" raises difficult questions. Where will the necessary money be found?

> "I do not have any money, my friend, and, on the entire surface of this planet, it is impossible to either be bled or to have an enema without paying, or without having someone pay for us." Ch. IV, p. 153).

The suggested cure is a combination of "blood" — bleeding — and whitewash — "enema," a panacea available for a fee. The idea of "paying" for oneself or of having someone else pay brings to mind a perverted concept of "redemption." Sacrifices, indulgences, absolution and salvation on the installment plan are attacked in the passage. Such practices are logical aspects of a disease which treats spirituality as negotiable merchandise. The market is admirably arranged. Thriving retailers of "pox" are also merchants of cures.

No person guided by belief in an impersonal First Cause manifest in Karmic Law can accept the blood-whitewash foundation of Christian formalism. Esoteric writers unanimously reject the concept of spiritual bargaining. The theme of prostituted sacred values which is forcefully allegorized in *Candide* has numerous counterparts in literary texts. The Christ portrayed by Vigny in *Le Mont des oliviers* foretells and deplores the "false sense" which will be given to his redemption. The "harsh dominators escorted by false sages" who will preach that "It is permissible for all to kill the innocent" are equally relevant to the poem of Vigny and to *Candide*. The mystique of redemption by innocent blood is the wash-away philosophy condensed in the famous words: "Out, damned spot!" It is the philosophy which elects irresponsibility and ignorance as a way of life. It is the philosophy which dreads the day when a certain "forest" of knowledge will be on the march.

Rituals of propitiation and expiation have no bearing on Universal Law. Karma does not honor such spurious stonement of sin by any culprit much less by unrelated victims. "Bleeding," "enema," punishment, mortification, confession and penance are equally powerless to undo what has been done when universal harmony has been wilfully disturbed. The doctrine of negotiable redemption is the worthy prop of a fictitious flesh-and-blood deity and of a personal devil. It is the logical servant of a religion based on fear.

The same doctrine is symptomatic of an era of dire material "necessity" in which Mammon reigns supreme. It is the philosophy which places steep price tags on all God-given things: fresh air, light, the sight of tree, sea, and sky, and the drawing of every single breath. It is the philosophy of a society in which justice and respectability can be — and are — bought. It is the philosophy of a society which knows one capital offense only: the unforgivable crime of being poor.

The brief statement of Pangloss repudiates several articles of Christian faith such as original sin and the orthodox view of Redemption. The passage accordingly rejects the alleged value of certain Christian sacraments.

Candide, Pangloss, and their friend, Jacques, — the kindly anabaptist —sail for Lisbon. Their ship is overtaken by a violent storm which suddenly develops within sight of the Portuguese capital. Jacques tries to save the ship from destruction. He is rewarded for his efforts by the vicious assault of an enraged sailor. Saviors are not welcome in the modern Western world. Returning good for evil, Jacques rescues his attacker who is in danger of drowning. The Good Samaritan loses his life in the process. His death is viewed by the wretched sailor with crass indifference. Justice seems to be more mythical than ever. All passengers have perished except Candide, Pangloss, and the ingrate. Candide wishes to die. The exoteric absurdity of the "consolations" of Pangloss compound his grief.

> "He wants to throw himself into the sea; the philosopher Pangloss prevents him from doing so, by proving to him that the harbor of Lisbon had been created for the express purpose of having the anabaptist drown there." (Ch. V, pp. 154-55).

The raison d'être of the harbor of Lisbon involves more than the need of a site for the death of one man. But the destiny of Jacques does involve drowning in that locality. The "express purpose" of the watery grave does not exclude other functions. The decrees of fate cannot be eluded. The apparent change of heart of Candide who decides to live suggests that Pangloss proved his point.

The strange theory of the master is vindicated in one respect. The survivors of the shipwreck arrive in Lisbon at the beginning of a formidable earthquake. The disaster is followed by an auto-da-fé from which Candide and Pangloss escape by miracle. Drowning saves the anabaptist from probable death at the stake. The latter fact would not fail to be stressed by a celestial messenger such as the hermit of *Zadig*. But there seem to be no Jesrads in the grim lands of "Westphalia."

Pangloss speculates on the probable cause of the earthquake. A similar tremor is known to have occurred in Lima, Peru, during the preceding year. The master concludes that "an underground vein of sulphur runs from Lima to Lisbon." The deadly "fault" seems to be the fire and brimstone mystique of Christianity. Conquest has carried the bane from the Old World to the New. Pangloss seems to anticipate the comment of Mme Blavatsky which has already been quoted. The exportation of the "pox" into "heathen" lands has the effect of sweeping "aboriginal nations out of existence as with a hurricane of fire." The latter calamity and the fiery "fault" mentioned by the master seem to be one and the same.

The spiritual and temporal terror wrought by Christian faiths is called to attention. Fear of God, fear of Satan, fear of Hell, fear of the rack and stake all point to a foundation of dread which is abundantly manifest in *Candide*. Such are basic ingredients of the cement which holds together the oppressive yet flimsy spiritual citadel of "Westphalia."

Pangloss does not fail to stress that "all is well" with volcanos and earthquakes. His statement seems ridiculous. But it is defensible within the framework of the Secret Doctrine:

> " — all this — all this is the best. For, if there is a volcano at Lisbon, it could not be elsewhere. For it is impossible for things not to be where they are. For all is well." (Ch. V. p. 156).

Lisbon has tolerated and actively promoted the hideous spectator sport known as "auto-da-fé." No better proof of the degradation of sacred values could possibly be given than the euphemistic phrase "act of faith" which covers such horror. Lisbon is a chronic offender, guilty of aggravated assault on human bodies and spirits. A cause-effect relationship is suggested to exist between the habitual burning of live human beings and cataclysmic upheavals. The grotesque surface of the Panglossian oracle veils earnest Karmic belief. The devastated city seems to reap a harvest of deadly Retribution. The same judgment is rendered esoterically in the Poem on the Disaster of Lisbon which is analyzed in a subsequent chapter of the present study.

The Secret Doctrine teaches that collectivities are subject to Karma as are individuals. Man-made cataclysms can be predicted by means of mathematical calculation. The commentary of Pangloss on the Portuguese "volcano" may well amount to the substance of the following text:

> "In the prognostication of *such* future events, at any rate, all foretold on the authority of cyclic recurrences, there is no psychic phenomenon involved. It is neither *prevision*, nor *prophecy;* no more than is the signalling of a comet or star, several years before its appearance. It is simply knowledge and mathematically correct computations which enable the WISE MEN OF THE EAST to foretell, for instance, that England is on the eve of such or another catastrophe; France, nearing such a point of her cycle, and Europe in general threatened with. or rather, on the eve of, a cataclysm, which her own cycle of racial *Karma has led her to.*" (*The Secret Doctrine,* p. 646, Vol. I).

The ocean storm and the earthquake described by Voltaire are suggested to be different aspects of the same upheaval. The symmetry which exists between water and fire — sea and volcano — may reflect the occult view of periodic change in the anatomy of Earth:

> "At the close of each 'great year,' called by Aristotle, according to Censorinus, the *greatest*, and which consists of six *sars* our planet is subjected to a thorough physical revolution. The polar and equatorial climates gradually exchange places; the former moving slowly toward the Line, and the tropical zone, with its exuberant vegetation and swarming animal life, replacing the forbidding wastes of the icy poles. This change of climate is necessarily attended by cataclysms, earthquakes, and other cosmical throes. As the beds of the ocean are displaced, at the end of every deci-millennium and about one neros, a semi-universal deluge like the legendary Noachian flood is brought about. This year was called the *Heliacal* by the Greeks; but no one outside the sanctuary knew anything certain either as to its duration or particulars. The winter of this year was called the Cataclysm or the Deluge, — the Summer, the ecpyrosis. The popular traditions taught that at these alternate seasons the world was in turn burned and deluged." (*Isis Unveiled,* pp. 30-31, Vol. 1).

Various elements of Chapter V tend to place the reported episode within the perspective of cosmic and planetary "throes." The passage describing the behavior of the corrupt sailor contains significant esoteric clues:

> "Le matelot court incontinent au milieu des débris, affronte la mort pour trouver de l'argent, en trouve, s'en empare, s'enivre, et, ayant cuvé son

vin, achète les faveurs de la première fille de bonne volonté qu'il rencontre sur les ruines des maison détriutes et au milieu des mourants et des morts." (Ch. V p. 155).

("The sailor runs immediately into the midst of the débris, braves death in order to find money, finds some, appropriates it, gets drunk, and, having sobered up, buys the favors of the first willing wench he meets on the ruins of destroyed houses and in the midst of the dying and the dead."

The sailor is an edifying specimen of Voltairian "insects" devouring one another on a small globe of mud. His conceptions of "spirit" and "love" go no further than tainted and bartered commodities: lust, debauchery, and greed. The surrounding desolation, suffering, and death arouse no pity in him. Rather they serve to enhance his private good fortune. The wretch "never had it so good." The sailor personifies the general background of selfishness and bestiality which prevails in the Western world.

The word "incontinent" — which is rarely used in writing and almost never in conversation — suggests a reference to "continents." The conjunction of water, fire, cataclysms and land masses which is present in the passage seems to be meaningful.

Thirty thousand inhabitants of "all age and of all sex" are reported to have perished under the ruins of Lisbon. The concept of "age" may be linked to Root Races and to the concept of geological ages. The intriguing question of the existing number of sexes — "of all sex" — presumably two amalgamated into singular expression — is a probable reference to the first Adam or Adam Kadmon, the first physical man, who was bi-sexual. The number of victims — 30,000 — esoterically veiled by zeros — may point to the early portion of the Third Race, the period when androgynous men lived on earth. The location of Lisbon — and its predilection for auto-da-fés — combines the geographical presence of the Atlantic Ocean and the ultimate refinement of religious fanaticism. The submerged continent of Atlantis and the left-handed leanings of a portion of the Atlanteans seem to be called to attention.* The retort of the sailor to the reprimands of Pangloss points to the sunken continent of Lemuria which is said to have been connected with Atlantis at one time.** The fact of having been born in Batavia is stressed. Pangloss is observed to tug at the sleeve of the wicked sailor. The "Sleeve" — la Manche — is the French name of the English Channel. The latter reference to the Western world tends to complete a suggested background of global dimension. The passage seems calculated to bring to mind a

---

*The Secret Doctrine, p. 192fn., Vol. I.
**Ibid., p. 333, Vol. II.

mass of history, geography, geology and anthropology reflecting the occult view of those sciences.

The reprimands of Pangloss bear on two significants concepts: "universal reason" and "time." The ruthlessness and the bestiality of the sailor seem to belong to a dark age of the past — probably to the era of Atlantean body-worship and sorcery:

> "Pangloss le tirait cependant par la manche. "Mon ami,' lui disait-il, 'cela n'est pas bien vous manquez à la raison universelle, vous prenez mal votre temps.' — 'Tête et sang!' répondit l'autre,' je suis matelot et né à Batavia, j'ai marché quatre fois sur le crucifix dans quatre voyages au Japon; tu as bien trouvé ton homme avec ta rason universelle!' " (Ch. V, p. 155).
>
> ("Pangloss, meanwhile, was tugging at his sleeve. 'My friend,' he said to him, 'that is not good, you are derelict with respect to universal reason, your timing is poor.' — 'Head and blood!' the other replied, 'I am a sailor and I was born in Batavia; I have walked on the crucifix four times during four voyages to Japan, you found your man well with your universal reason!' ")

The emphasis which is placed on *four* further tends to suggest Atlantis, — the "*Fourth* Continent" of occultists — and its *Fourth* Race mankind. The crucifix or cross — which has *four* branches — symbolizes — among other things — spirit gradually descending into matter, a process illustrated in spectacular fashion by the base nature of the sailor.

The "cross of birth" — usually inscribed in a circle — is the occult symbol of human procreation or generation.** The cross acquires a markedly phallic significance when it is removed from the circle.*** The crucifix or material object of worship mentioned by the sailor is in all likelihood detached from its symbolic, circular background of spirituality. Dedicated phallicism is clearly relevant to the sad character. The bestiality of a portion of Fourth Race mankind — a trait which eventually led to interbreeding with animals and which is the subject of unveiled allusions at a latter stage of *Candide* — has found a devout practitioner in the person of the sailor. "The first willing wench" to come by is in all likelihood "subhuman." The skilled technicians of Atlantean black magic have been emulated by the defiler of the crucifix. The sacred symbol of love — human and divine — has been trampled underfoot. The oath of the wretch is unwittingly appropriate. "Head and blood" are meaningful acquisitions made by mankind at the time of its materialization — the Third Race. The loss of spiritual insight which is a "necessary" aspect of the "fall' is well demonstrated. The criminal does not perceive the profound verity conveyed by his

---

*Ibid., p. 8, Vol. II.
**Ibid., p. 5, Vol. I.
***Ibid.

profanity or by his sarcasm: "You found your man well with your universal reason!"

Man is found indeed — or situated — within the perspective of terrestrial evolution. The panoramic view of Third, Fourth, and Fifth Race mankind which is allegorized in Chapter V is a corrected version of the Christian "fall" of Man. Fifth Race humanity is little better than the worst segment of its Atlantean ancestry. It is difficult to imagine a more depraved creature than the heartless sailor. Voltaire seems to anticipate the characterization of modern-day Man which is made by Mme Blavatsky and which has already been quoted: "In our present all-material Fifth Race, the earthly Spirit of the Fourth is still strong in us; —"

The relevance of the "Fall" of Man to the chapter is exoterically apparent in the subsequent dialogue between Pangloss and a "familiar" or representative of the Inquisitition. The agent provocateur broaches the dangerous subjects of original sin, human fall, and divine chastisement:

> "A small black man, a familiar of the Inquisition, who was next to him, politely began to speak and said: 'It is apparent that monsieur does not believe in original sin; for, if all is for the best, there was, therefore, neither fall nor punishment.—' 'I very humbly beg the pardon of your Excellency, 'replied Pangloss even more politely, for the fall of man and the curse necessarily entered into the best of possible worlds." (Ch. V, pp. 156-57).

The clever reply of Pangloss places the "fall' and the "curse" within the occult framework of the Circle of Necessity — "necessarily". The fall is thus regarded as the gradual descent into materiality which takes place during the first half of a cycle, The process in question is the rational, impersonal manifestation of Universal Law. The "curse" is the resulting incarnate condition, Maya, or the "cross of birth" and rebirth. The Jehovic God has no place in such a scheme. The apparent agreement of Pangloss with the traditional Christian view of the "fall" is belied by the esoteric presence of the word "necessarily." The doctrine of the master is not what is called the "orthodox" line.

> "Man was intended from the first to be a being of both a progressive and retrogressive nature. Beginning at the apex of the divine cycle, he gradually began receding from the center of light, acquiring at every new and lower sphere of being (worlds each inhabited by a different race of human beings), a more solid physical form, and losing a portion of his *divine* faculties.
> In the "fall' of Adam we must see not the personal transgression of man, but simply the law of the dual evolution." (*Isis Unveiled*, p. 277, Vol. 2).

The persistent Inquisitor brings up the conflict which seems to exist between human freedom and predestination. An age-old source of frustration and despair to theologians and to their hapless flocks, the thorny question is expected to trap Pangloss into heretical statements. Pangloss proclaims free will and "absolute necessity" to be compatible with each other. The jansenistic dilemma is resolved by the essence of Karma. Predestination does exist in one sense: it is the expression of human commitment to either Good or Evil. The law of Retribution is inescapable, but its human mechanism can be activated by human beings only. "Karma-Nemesis predestines nothing and no one."* Man is predestined by nothing but himself. Appearances and theologists to the contrary, Divine Justice and free will not only co-exist but are inseparable from each other.

> " — free will can co-exist with absolute necessity; for it was necessary for us to be free; for after all, determined will — " (Ch. V, p. 157).

The doctrine of cyclic evolution is again brought to bear — with some insistence — by means of the words "necessary" and "necessity." "All is for the best" within the occult perspective of the Grand Cycle.

Pangloss is providentially saved from further explanation by an interruption. As was previously noted, Karma is frequently connected with meaningful silence representing the inscrutable quality of Divine Law. The unfinished sentence of Pangloss is reminiscent of the abrupt disappearance of Jesrad leaving Zadig to utter a feeble "mais —". The typical Karmic break again illustrates the presence of the unknowable. The mysterious essence of Karma has already been demonstrated by the fate of Jacques and by the death of other passengers of the ship.

The fortunate reference to Port wine ("vin de Porto," quickly rectified by the word *Oporto*) is an example of specialized esoteric devices generally known as *gematria* and *temura*:

> " — the familiar made a sign with his head to his footman who was serving to him some wine of Port or Oporto." (Ch. V, p. 157).

> "The kabalistic *gematria* — one of the methods for extracting the hidden meaning from letters, words, and sentences — is arithmetical. It consists in applying to the letters of a word the sense they bear in numbers; in *outward* shape as well as in their individual sense. Moreover, by the *Temura*, (another method used by the kabalists) any word could be made to yield its mystery out of its anagram —
> Ancient names were always consonant with the things they represented.'
> (*Isis Unveiled*, pp. 298-99, Vol. 2).

The Secret Doctrine, pp. 304-05, Vol. II.

The presence of the three *o*'s in the word *Oporto* — a presence stressed by the repetition and correction of equivalent terms — points to the symbolic circle or wheel of Karma which is an essential aspect of the chapter. The three *o*'s contained in the word *Oporto* represent the occult concept of the *Three in One*, "the first manifested unit"* in the doctrine of emanation. The latter detail completes the esoteric architecture of Chapter V which is placed under the triple sign of Karma-Emanation-Evolution. It is probably not by chance that the very number of the chapter corresponds to the occult genealogy of Fifth Race mankind.

The subsequent account of the "fine auto-da-fé" is too well known and too eloquent to need lengthy comment. Divine aspiration, the noblest impulse in man, sinks to the nadir of evil. Perverted religion is a sadistic sideshow of ritual, music, pathos, and horror. Energized by a striking sobriety of description, the Goya-like passage brings home the best at its corrupt worst. The Voltairian view of ecclesiastical "mercy" naturally coincides with the corresponding view of theosophists:

> "*Ecclesia non novit sanguinem!* meekly repeated the scarlet-robed cardinals. And to avoid the spilling of blood which horrified them, they instituted the Holy Inquisition. If, as the occultists maintain, and science half confirms, our most trifling acts and thoughts are indelibly impressed upon the eternal mirror of the astral ether, there must be somewhere, in the boundless realm of the unseen universe, the imprint of a curious picture. It is that of a gorgeous standard waving in the heavenly breeze at the foot of the great 'white throne' of the Almighty — on its crimson damask face a cross, symbol of 'the Son of God who died for mankind,' with an *olive* branch on one side, and a sword, stained to the hilt with human gore, on the other. A legend selected from the *Psalms* emblazoned in golden letters, reading thus: '*Exurge, Domine, et judica causam mean.*' For such appears the standard of the Inquisition, on a photograph in our possession, from an original procured at the Escurial of Madrid." (*Isis Unveiled*, p. 59, Vol. 2).

Ecclesiastical mercy — allegedly opposed to bloodshed, is a sinister farce. Blood is spilled in abundance in the course of hygienic burnings and in the course of other punishment. Candide emerges from his own "purification" "all bloody." Chastisement once more concentrates on the part of his anatomy corresponding to guilty knowledge. Candide is "spanked rhythmically" while a devout chorus chants.

Chapter V and VI of *Candide* contain a crushing indictment of Lisbon, the symbolic vanguard of Catholic "Westphalia." Natural cataclysms seem almost benign when compared to the refinements of Man's cruelty to Man.

It is senseless to look for a Savior is such a witches' caldron swarming with "familiars" of the Inquisition. The plight of Candide emerging from

---

Ibid., p. 599, Vol. II.

the first earthquake has collective significance. The young man is wounded by symbolic rock fragments — a reminder of the divided citadel of Peter. He begs in vain for oil and wine — substances once used by Christ the Savior.* The symbolic commodities are beyond reach in such a man-made hell. Candide is lucky to receive "a small amount of water." Chrestos, the Higher Self, is the sole possible savior. The selfishness which rules the modern Western world seems to rule spiritual planes. "Every man for himself" is the apparent key to survival in all domains.

Candide is helped by an unknown old woman. Her unexpected kindness acts as a soothing balm. Solace is found in the midst of despair. The existential anguish of Zadig and the subsequent spiritual flight come to mind.

Having done her best to repair the tortured body and broken spirit of the victim, the stranger takes the young man to a secluded house. The residence is surrounded by gardens and canals. The former are presumably tilled in the philosophical manner prescribed at the end of *Candide*, a pursuit likely to lead to the "garden of delights." Representing artificial, yet vital, arteries of life and "commerce," the canals seem to symbolize remote outposts of the living truth or Secret Doctrine operating far from the "source." The solitary and mysterious dwelling is such a retreat. The canals which seem to represent an allusion to the engineering feats of ancient Egypt, also play a supportive role in establishing the secret identity of Cunégonde.**

The strange guide makes two requests of her protégé:

"Come with me, she said, and do not say a word."
(Ch. VII, p. 159).

Candide obeys the double injunction. The exhortation to "silence" is suggestive of the occult. The young hero embarks on a spiritual venture. Silence is also protective. It is indispensable to secret undertakings, particularly in the hostile milieu of modern Western Europe. The mysterious old woman and the mysterious site belong to the invisible world.

An incredible reunion takes place. Cunégonde is found to be safe in the house of the old woman. The miraculous "resurrection" of the girl — one of several reappearances of persons presumed dead — suggests, among other things, the possibility of rebirth.

The reunion is a priceless occasion for parody of tearful melodramas. The very short phrases and sentences, the exclamations, and the crescendo movement sustain a breathless climate of thrills, chills, and sus-

---

*Isis Unveiled, p. 133, Vol. 2.
**Isis Unveiled, pp. 516-17, Vol. I.

pense. The roman larmoyant is undoubtedly ridiculed. But esoteric substance transcends the convenient facade of literary satire. The concealed focus of the episode is the "lifting of the veil." The surface irony is delightfully suggestive of Voltairian merriment at the time of writing.

> "The old woman reappeared soon; she was supporting with effort a trembling woman, of majestic build, shining with precious stones, and covered with a veil. 'Take off that veil,' said the old woman to Candide. The young man comes near; he lifts the veil with a timid hand. What a moment! what a surprise! he thinks that he sees Mlle Cunégonde; he was seeing her indeed, it was herself. Cunégonde falls on the sofa. The old woman lavishes spirits upon them; they regain their senses, they speak to each other; first of all there are halting words, questions and answers crossing one another, sighs, tears, exclamations." (Ch. VII, p. 159).

The climatic encounter bears an understanble resemblance to the reunion of Zadig and Astarté. In each case the hero sees a veiled woman of "majestic" build or "appearance." "Trembling" or "shuddering" is noted. The flames of Almona which cause "Nature to shudder" and the trembling hands of *Micromégas* also come to mind. The symbolic veil is lifted. Temporary loss of speech and sensory consciousness results. The same initial experience with the invisible world is described in all three stories.

The "spirits" administered by the old woman add a minor yet significant touch to the general tableau. The amusing evocation of boudoir furniture such as the sofa is a probable allusion to the Tau-shaped couch used for initiation rites in ancient Egypt.* The latter probability seems strengthened by the determination of Voltaire to mention again "that beautiful couch which we have already spoken of." — "ce beau canapé dont on a déjà parlé". The flexible use of tenses which is evident in the combination of present, *imperfect,* and *perfect,* suggests the relevance of imperfection and perfection. Also hinted is the timelessness of spiritual experience.

The hidden reality of the episode is poles apart from comical appearance. Cunégonde is the counterpart of Isis-Astarté transplanted — rather uprooted — into the modern Western world. The esoteric reader viewing the passage on two planes can only "laugh in tears" in Villonesque fashion.

The raising of the veil which points to the presence of Isis supplements the presumed connection made above between Egyptian waterways and "Westphalian" canals. The natural stream of "life" which belongs to

---

The Secret Doctrine, pp. 558-59, Vol. II.

the setting of the corresponding scene in *Zadig* has become symbolically artificial and stagnant. Spirituality has gained little in transit from the Pagan era to modern times. "Force" and purity have been lost.

Another clue to esoteric substance is supplied by the name of Cunégonde. The Secret Doctrine teaches that Diana, the mythological huntress, is the equivalent of Isis:

> "— Neith. Isis, Diana, by whatever name she was called, was a demiurgical Goddess, at once visible and invisible, having her place in Heaven, and helping on the generation of species." (*The Secret Doctrine,* p. 399, Vol. I).

The name of the Voltairian heroine is etymologically based on a Greek word meaning "hunter" or "huntress" —Kunêgos. Cunégonde Unveiled equals Truths as does Astarté Unveiled.

The esoteric identity of Cunégonde is confirmed by an "amusing" element of the situation. The heroine has become the joint property of a Jew and of an Inquisitor. No one seems to know who is entitled to have "commerce" with Truth during "the night from Saturday to Sunday." Controversy continues to arise on the question of precedence of "ancient" or "new law." The quarrel points to the unresolved question of the Sabbath.

The union of Man and Truth can only be brief and furtive in the realm of Westphalia. The blissful intercourse of Candide and Cunégonde is brutally interrupted by don Isaacar, the transparent representative of the Judaeo-Christian tradition. His irruption on the scene is followed by the arrival of a modern Inquisitor whose function is self-explanatory. Forced to defend himself against the aggressive co-owners of the beloved, Candide kills both men. Don Issacar does not realize that the "adversary" is "armed." But the lover of Cunégonde has received a "hidden" sword or weapon of "excellent knowledge." The useful gift of the old woman is comparable to the white suit of armor received by Zadig from Queen Astarté.

Zadig and Candide show the same reluctance to take human life. Lovers of Truth kill in self-defense only. The Jew and the Inquisitor show no such repugnance.

The preservation of Self and Truth requires use of violence. Passive resistance does not work in the realm of sanctified butchery. Incorrigible pacifists such as Candide find themselves compelled to assume murderous roles. The absolute perversion of prevailing values is evidenced by two facts. Self-defense is regarded as subversion. Drastic action and immediate flight are imperative.

The old woman is prudent and wise in planning the escape of the trio.

In her opinion, "it is a great pleasure to travel in the coolness of the night." The hasty retreat is a matter of survival to which considerations of "pleasure" seem irrelevant. But the joy of spiritual "trips" taken in protective darkness is consistent with the hidden substance of the story. The equivalence of "pleasure" and spirituality is again suggested.

The escape plan is temporarily thwarted by the theft of certain possessions of Cunégonde. The culprit is a monk belonging to the order of the Cordeliers. The parallel experiences of Paquette and Cunégonde with the same brotherhood show the friars' capacity for a certain type of give-and-take. Taking concerns itself with authentic treasures. Giving involves tainted blood and spirituality. The deprived monk is understandably lured by the wealth of Isis. The episode is a commentary on material — as well as spiritual — ecclesiastical thievery. Such practice was especially lucrative in the case of victims of the Inquisition such as Candide and his friends.

> "Of the multitudes of persons who perished at the stake in Germany during the first half of the seventeenth century for sorcery, the crime of many was their attachment to the religion of Luther, says T. Wright, and 'the petty princes were not unwilling to seize upon any pretense to fill their coffers — the persons most persecuted being those whose property was a matter of consideration." (*Isis Unveiled*, p. 61, Vol. 2).

The Code of *Manu* and the "respectability" of "ancient abuse" are indirectly brought to mind. The "Arabian" priests of *Zadig* who combine widow-burning and jewel-hoarding have worthy successors in the Inquisitors of *Candide*.

The property stolen from Cunégonde includes diamonds. The esoteric value of the symbolic gems — which is demonstrated in *Micromégas* — is reaffirmed. The precious stones represent occult knowledge, vision, and purity. Truth is robbed of her treasure by a representative of the Church. The same diamonds were given to Cunégonde by the Great Inquisitor. Readers are left to speculate about legitimate owners: liquidated heretics and Truth-seekers. Ecclesiastical larceny is eventually punished. The European Arbogad or amateur of diamonds ends on the gallows. The stones are finally acquired by a merchant or representative of "commerce." Karma is ever at work even in the sinister depths of "Westphalian" societies.

The stolen money consists of a number of *moyadors*. The Cluny edition of *Candide* contains the following comment:

> "On ne sait d'où Voltaire a tiré ce mot. Il s'agit sans doute des pistoles dont parle Cunégonde à la première ligne du chapitre suivant." (p. 32).

("It is not known from where Voltaire drew this word. It doubtlessly de-

255

signates the coins which are mentioned by Cunégonde in the first line of the following chapter.")

The first part of the intriguing word resembles "Maya." The second part coincides with the form of the French term "or" which means "gold." The combined presence of Illusion —Moya or Maya — and genuine value —gold, a symbol of advanced spirituality — seems to reflect the dual nature of earthly life and incarnate condition. Matter is materialized spirit on the seventh — or lowest — plane and the fusion of both is Maya. Gold is spirit on the esoteric level. The ambiguous quality of the word seems intended to stress the mixed nature of all that exists materially. Such a meaning is consistent with the secret identity of Cunégonde-Isis, a personated power of Nature, hence a carrier of both matter and spirit.

The esoteric role of the puzzling word "moyadors" seems to correspond to the esoteric function of the symbolic site where Astarté is found by Zadig, a realm partaking of both matter and spirit. The personification of Pagan truth reclines on the sand or border separating grass from water — matter from spirit — in a natural setting reflecting her dual essence and her spiritual potential. The personification of modern truth lives in closed quarters in apparent estrangement from the treasures of Nature. Her existence unfolds in a materialistic domain governed by money and the absence of money. The adoration of Mayavic treasures is suggested by moyadors. The spiritual potential of Maya which is closely connected with Nature in Zadig is represented by money and man-made devices in Candide. The latter difference between ancient and modern worlds tends to confirm a suggestion frequently made by Voltaire. Maya and Spiritual Reality are necessary poles of existence in each environment. But mankind has suffered a loss in transition from Pagan Nature to the so-called reality contrived by the modern Western world. The Rabelaisian concepts of "Physis" — Nature — and "Antiphysis" may not be irrelevant to the same change.

The word moyadors may also represent an allusion to Adi-Maya, a name which the term moyador resembles when the hyphenated segments of Adi-Maya are reversed. The significance of Adi-Maya is the same as the significance of Isis.

> "Lakmi or Lakshmi, the passive or feminine counterpart of Vishnu, the creator and the preserver, is also called Adi-Maya. She is 'the Mother of the World 'Dhatri, the Venus-Aphrodite of the Greeks, also Isis and Eve." (*The Secret Doctrine*, p. 399, Vol. I.)

The connection which exists between Adi-Maya and Vishnu is relevant to the esoteric substance of Voltairian writings. Vishnu or DAG is an important element of *Zadig*. He is a background figure in the dark set-

256

ting of Candide which admits no other Savior than the Chrestos in every man.

The intriguing word *moyadors* is the vehicle of multiple minor clues to the veiled identity of "Mlle Cunégonde."

Money supplies the substance of subversive comments. Candide remembers the views of Pangloss on the distribution of wealth. "Worldly goods are common to all men, each man has an equal right to them." The statement carries symbolic as well as literal implications. Equal opportunity to acquire spiritual "gold" and "diamonds" is afforded to all by the scheme of evolution.

Hounded by the authorities, Candide, Cunégonde, the old woman and two valets sail for Paraguay where Candide is expected to take charge of an infantry company. Grim experience in the Bulgarian army becomes a means of escape from certain death. A detestable cause has beneficient effect. It is suggested that the philosophy of Pangloss may not be entirely wrong. Also significant is the sense of values which uplifts the hero to the exalted rank of captain. The conscientious objector, the man who raised the veil of Isis, must make the best of a despised occupation. His worth is determined by his least commendable skills acquired in spite of himself. Voltaire seems to have exploited the irony of the military status of Candide to suggest the reluctant masquerade which is often used as a protective screen by Western European adepts. Such persons are compelled to adjust to an external way of life for which they have little taste. That the masquerade in question is often grotesque, obscene, and self-imposed is a probability which will be examined in another chapter.

As was previously noted, the word "captain" — etymologically "head," "chief," or "leader" — conveys specific meaning in occult hierarchies. The esoteric rank of the title character is consistent with the bearing of spiritual "arms" which has already been suggested in *Candide*.

The crossing of the Atlantic begins. The fugitives hope that life in the New World will be better than in the Old. The state of affairs prevailing in Europe leaves much to be desired. It is characterized by a gross understatement:

> "We are going to another universe, said Candide; it is in that one, no doubt, that all is well. For one must confess that one could complain a little about what takes place in ours in the physical and moral domains." (Ch. X, p. 166).

All men aspire to the best possible universe. The haven where "all is well" is the probable equivalent of the "country where nothing lacks" which is mentioned in *Micromégas*. "Westphalia" falls short of such an ideal state. The planet earth in general is far removed from "perfection,"

257

belonging as it does to inferior realm of contingency. The "physical" domain surveyed by Candide is blighted by gross materiality and related miseries. Human knowledge suffers accordingly. The majority of mankind sees no further than sensory illusion. The human herd ignores and scorns its own spiritual heritage. The "moral" element of observation made by Candide concerns rigid and arbitrary systems of ethics, rootless trees which have no support in eternal truth. The small measure of existing insight which could relieve general misery is savagely suppressed. The European establishment is alienated from knowledge and decency.

The sea-voyage is soothing. It is a sorely needed truce in the midst of bitter strife. The ocean is "more placid," the winds are more "constant" than they were in the Old World. Added to the blissful calm the spiritual symbolism of the wind evokes serene breaths from ethereal regions. The restful mood of the crossing is colored by memories of life in the Old World. The elderly woman compares her experience with the adventures of her friends. Her story is a long series of tragic events including, rape, mutilation, and slavery. But the recollection of past horror is softened by the tranquility of wind and sea. The most gruesome episodes of her existence — such as the murder of a lover and the rape of the speaker — are shrugged off as insignificant:

> "But that is only a trifling thing." (Ch. XI, p. 168).
> "But let us go on! Those are such common things that they are not worth talking about." (Ch. XI, p. 170).

The startling statements have validity on exoteric and esoteric planes. Tragedy is the common lot of most "passengers" of the vessel of life. Viewed against a timeless background of cosmic journeys and multiple rebirths, no hardship — however severe — can attain more than trivial dimension.

The restful lull of the crossing, the symbolic ocean of reincarnation, the symbolic "breath" of the wind or spirit and the subdued memory of previous life all suggest Devachanic sleep, "the state of Bliss, the reward for all the undeserved miseries of life"* which separates successive incarnations.

Numerous allusions to Devachanic sleep are found in esoteric texts. The theosophical view of death as a "door through which" Man "passes to another life on earth after a little rest on its threshold — Devachan —"** may shed light on many obscure episodes of the novels of Beckett some day. The symbolism of "strings" — sutratma — wind and ocean which is

---

*Isis Unveiled, p. A-34, Vol. 2.
**The Secret Doctrine, p. 39, Vol. I.

used by Shelley in *Queen Mab* is identical to the corresponding mode of expression of Voltaire.

> "Then dulcet music swelled
> Concordant with the life-strings of the soul;
> It throbbed in sweet and languid beatings there,
> Catching new life from transitory death,
> Like the vague sighings of a wind at even,
> That wakes the wavelets of the slumbering sea
> And dies on the creation of it breath,
> And sinks and rises, fails and swells by fits; —
>
> "Fear not then, Spirit, Death's disrobing hand,
> So welcome when the tyrant is awake,
> So welcome when the bigot's hell-torch burns;
> 'Tis but the voyage of a darksome hour
> The transient gulf-dream of a startling sleep."
> (Percy Bysshe Shelley, *Queen Mab*).

The Proustian *Recherche* contains a brief episode which may represent an esoteric allusion to Voltaire, the old woman, and a certain philosophical view of "trifling" events. The ailing grandmother of the narrator senses approaching death as she rides in a carriage on the Champs Elysées. Her failure to return the salute of a friend — "Legrandin" — is followed by a gesture signifying that the whole matter has no importance in her eyes. The esoteric meaning of the mythological Elysean Fields is that of the nether regions.* The arrival at the Champs Elysées on "wheels" seems significant. The unspoken message of the elderly woman: "What of it? that has no importance," may apply to death itself. The Voltairian personality of "Legrandin" further tends to suggest the sort of veiled allusion commonly made by an esoteric writer to another.

The story of Cunégonde and the story of the old woman are remarkably alike. The reader may easily forget which one of the women is speaking. The elderly person is of noble — but illegitimate — parentage. She is the daughter of a Pope. She was born to high status. She has known abject misery. As in the case of Cunégonde, rape and slavery have been endured. Harsh treatment has become part of the daily routine.

Presented as a libertine tribute to her own former beauty is the report of the crone of her own "unveiling" duly accompanied by ecstasy:

> "The women who dressed and undressed me fell into ecstasy looking at me from front and rear, and all the men would have wished to be in their place." (Ch. XI, p. 168).

The apparent reference to an "unveiling of Isis" is supplemented by

---

*A la Recherche du temps perdu, p. 315, Vol. II.

other elements of the story. It was first intended that the girl would marry the Prince of Massa-Carrara. By association with the Spanish word *mascara* meaning "mask," the name of the Prince may be linked to the concealment of occult activities. Taken in its entirety, the name is reminiscent of the word *Masra* formerly designating the city of Cairo, Egypt.

"Masra was the name of Cairo, — " (*Isis Unveiled*, p. 627, Vol. 1).

The combination of occultism and Egypt probably determined the selection of the name *Massa-Carrara*.

The girl is the daughter of a fictitious Pope and of the Princess of Palestrina. The latter word is a suggestive link to Palestine and to the city of Palestrina — ancient Praeneste.

In the words of Mme Blavatsky "strange traditions" are reported to survive in Palestine where "learned rabbis" — pass their lives in commenting upon the *Talmud*. According to those traditions, the priceless contents of the famous library of Alexandria were not entirely lost:

"They say that not all the rolls and manuscripts, reported in history to have been burned by Caesar, by the Christian mob, in 389, and by the Arab General Amru, perished as it is commonly believed; — all the librarians, aided by several hundred slaves attached to the museum, succeeded in saving the most precious of the rolls. — One of these manuscripts is alleged to be preserved till now in a Greek convent; and the person who narrated the tradition to us had seen it himself. He said that many more will see it and learn where to look for important documents, when a certain prophecy will be fulfilled; adding, that most of these works could be found in Tartary and India." (*Isis Unveiled*, p. 27, Vol. II).

Many of the texts contained in the library of Alexandria had Far Eastern origins.

" — the greater part of the literature included in the 200,000 volumes of the Alexandrian library was due to India, and her next neighbors — " (*Isis Unveiled*, p. 27, Vol. 2).

Palestine belongs to a portion of the world where the descendants of ancient sects survive to this day. Such are the Druzes of Mount Lebanon who were of considerable interest to Voltaire. In the words of Mme Blavatsky, "All these sects have an immediate connection with our subject for they are of kabalistic parentage and have once held to the secret Wisdom-Religion, recognizing as the One Supreme, the Mystery-God of the *Ineffable Name*."* The Far Eastern connections of such groups are corroborated by Pliny who reports the presence of "Brachmanical" settlements on the shores of the Dead Sea.**

Isis Unveiled, p. 288, Vol. 2.
**Ibid., p. 321, Vol. 2.

Palestrina — or Praeneste — is situated near Rome. The ancient city is famous for its "great temple of Fortune," "an immense complex probably by far the largest sanctuary in Italy," and for the oracles rendered on its site in days of old. "Considerable portions of the southern wall of the ancient citadel, built in very massive Cyclopean masonry of blocks of limestone, are to be seen." The sanctuary contains "a mosaic pavement" representing "a sea-scene — a temple of Poseidon on the shore, with various fish swimming in the sea."* The combination of oracular tradition, Cyclopean ruins, and worship of Poseidon — the occult symbol of Atlantis — ** is rich in significance. The suggested Atlantean connection is also present in the Palestine-related element of the name under study. The tradition of Ancient Egypt — which found a refuge in Palestine — is regarded by occultists as a surviving branch of a once brilliant Atlantean civilization. The Egyptian pyramids are said to have been built by the descendants of the Atlanteans. The esoteric connections of the Princess of Palestrina involve the Near East, Egypt, India, and even Atlantis. The maternal ancestry of the old woman represents a global cultural background extending back into pre-historic times.

The daughter of the fictitious Pope is the product of illicit ecclesiastical design on ancient Pagan lore. The Egyptian portion of her heritage suggests the Mosaic spoliation which is an important element of *Zadig* and the Jewish "borrower" of five hundred ounces of silver representing the same Mosaic larceny. The amorous Pope and father of the once young woman seems to be the modern successor of sanctimonious and sanctified Judaeo-Christian thieves. The prestigious sire has no legitimate status, actual identity, or substance. But the few glimpses of the mother which are afforded by the story show her to have been beautiful and good. Her outstanding and lasting qualities are reminiscent of the vitality and enduring appeal of Isis-Astarté, the heroine of *Zadig*. The ill-fated mother of the old woman is the probable esoteric aggregate of sects which were in existence in the early Christian era. Such groups as the Nazarenes, the Essenes and the Gnostics maintained spiritual allegiance to major tenets of the Secret Doctrine. Their beliefs were accordingly condemned as "heresies" and their members charged with "demonolatry, blasphemy, and licentiousness"*** by various representatives of the Church. The fictitious pontiff evoked by Voltaire seems to belong to the same early Christian era, a time when a few of the Popes were initiates.****

The early misfortunes of the old woman seem to be connected with

---

**Encyclopaedia Britannica,* Atahualpa.
***The Secret Doctrine,* p. 356, Vol. II.
****Isis Unveiled,* p. 289, Vol. 2.
*****The Secret Doctrine,* p. 311, Vol. I.

the Neo-Platonic School of Alexandria and with the persecution to which it was subjected. Mother and daughter are captured by a pirate as they sail for Gaeta, a city once ruled by hereditary *hypati* or consuls. The indirect reference to *hypati* was probably calculated to suggest the figure of Hypathia, the beautiful, learned, and ill-fated head of the Neo-Platonic School whose memory is revered by numerous esoteric writers.* The "very beautiful land" or property owned by the mother of the girl near Gaète suggests spiritual holdings akin to the heritage of the Neo-Platonists. The chronology of *Candide*, placing the capture at a time anterior to arrival in Morocco — a symbol of Islam — is consistent with the concealed historical element of Chapter XI.

The story of Hypathia is told and commented as follows by Mme Blavatsky:

> "At the beginning of the fourth century crowds began gathering at the door of the academy where the learned and unfortunate Hypathia expounded the doctrines of the divine Plato and Plotinus, and thereby impeded the progress of Christian proselytism. She too succesfully dispelled the mist hanging over the religious 'mysteries' invented by the Fathers, not to be considered dangerous." (*Isis Unveiled*, p. 252, Vol. 2).

> "During the life-time of the youthful Hypatia, her friendship and influence with Orestes, the governor of the city, had assured the philosophers securiy and protection against their murderous enemies. With her death they had lost their strongest friend — What would have been the feelings of this most noble and worthy of Christian bishops (***), who had surrendered family and children and happiness for the faith into which he had been attracted, had a prophetic vision disclosed to him that the only friend that had been left to him, his 'mother, sister, benefactor,' would soon become an unrecognizable mass of flesh and blood, pounded to jelly under the blows of Peter the Reader — that her youthful, innocent body would be cut to pieces, 'the flesh scraped from the bones,' by oyster shells and the rest of her cast into the fire, by order of the same Bishop Cyril he knew so well — Cyril, the CANONIZED Saint!!" (*Isis Unveiled*, pp. 52-53, Vol. 2).

The rich spiritual heritage of the old woman is supplemented by the wealth her intended spouse. The projected union with the representative of Ancient Egyptian tradition — the Prince of Massa-Carrara — would have re-established the original unity of the Primitive Wisdom-Religion had it been consummated. The fragmented bequest of the Near East, Egypt, India, and probably Atlantis, would have been restored to its integrity. Such a synthesis would have entailed the exposure of sectarian spiritual impostors. The tragic events related in Chapter XI of *Candide*

---

*A la Recherche du temps perdu, p. 639, Vol. I.

and the following comment of Mme Blavatsky seem to convey the same basic message:

"— the Church had to fight for her life, to say nothing of her future supremacy. Alone, the hated and erudite Pagan scholars, and the no less learned Gnostics, held in their doctrines the hitherto concealed wires of all these theological marionettes. Once the curtain should be lifted, the connection between the old Pagan and the new Christian religions would be exposed; and then, what would have become of the Mysteries into which it is sin and blasphmy to pry? With such a coincidence of the astronomical allegories of various Pagan myths with the dates adopted by Christianity for the nativity, crucifixion, and resurrection, and such an identity of rites and ceremonies, what would have been the fate of the new religion, had not the Church, under the pretext of serving Christ, got rid of the too-well informed philosophers? To guess what, if the *coup d'état* had then failed, might have been the prevailing religion in our own century would indeed, be a hard task. But, in all probability, the state of things which made of the middle ages a period of intellectual darkness, which degraded the nations of the Occident, and lowered the European of those days almost to the level of a Papuan savage — could not have occurred." (*Isi Unveiled*, p. 253, Vol. II).

The enduring beauty of the Primitive Wisdom-Religion dies with the mother of the old woman and with the short-lived beauty of the girl. No amount of adversity could disfigure the personification of Truth in the setting of Antiquity — *Zadig* — or in the early period of the Christian era. The old woman and Cunégonde face a different state of affairs in "the finest castle in the world." It will be the sad distinction of the modern Western world to mar and mutilate beyond recognition its legacy of Truth.

The line of allegorical women which is featured in *Candide* spans the period of transition from ever-young Paganism — Astarté — to increasingly battered Christianity — the old woman and Cunégonde.

Marcel Proust was apparently aware of the connection existing between such allegories, the course of human evolution, and certain deceptive "outfits" or "veils."

"And each era thus finds itself personified in new women, in a group of new women, who, deeply concerned with what heightens the newest curiosities, seem, in their outfits, to appear only at that time, as an unknown species born of the latest deluge." (*A la Recherche du temps perdu*, p. 743, Vol. II).

The death of the mother of the old woman is also linked to the origin and bloody expansion of Islam. Following capture by Mohammedan pirates who are as devout as they are evil, the girl, her mother, and several other women become involuntary causes of a deadly struggle:

263

"They fought with the fury of the lions, tigers, and snakes of that country to determine who would have us. One Moor seized my mother by her right arm, the lieutenant of my captain held her back by the left arm; a Moorish soldier took her by one leg, one of our pirates was holding her by the other. Practically all our girls found themselves thus pulled by four soldiers at that moment — I remained dying on a heap of corpses. Such scenes took place as one knows over an area of more than three hundred leagues, without the five daily prayers ordered by Mohammed ever being omitted." (Ch. XI, pp. 170-71).

The fiery North African pirates are compared to the tigers of the Atlas mountains. Tigers are found in Asia only. It is difficult to believe that Voltaire was ignorant of such a well-known fact. The reference to African tigers may have been used to sustain the general climate of macabre grotesquerie characterizing *Candide*. It may also be calculated to cover and stress esoteric substance. The occult meaning of Atlas — which is consistent with serious allusions to tigers — supports the latter probability.

"The myth of Atlas is an allegory easily understood. Atlas is the old continent of Lemuria and Atlantis, combined and personified in one symbol." (*The Secret Doctrine*, p. 762, Vol. II).

The use of black and white magic is suggested by reference to the left and right hands. The battle involves good and evil forces. The concealment of the girl *behind* the "captain" suggests powerful occult protection. All captives are killed with the exception of the future old woman who is left "dying on a heap of corpses."

The quartering process involving the women imperils and injures an already mistreated Christian version of Truth. The death of the mother seems to spell the end of the occult chain of living Truth. But the daughter remains to maintain the Presence in an increasingly hostile world. The Primitive Wisdom-Religion lives on in some form or other regardless of the destiny of any individual.

Four main rival limbs remain of the original body of Knowledge. "Westphalia" is spiritually divided between Judaism, Catholicism, Protestantism, and Islam. The era of the "Great Schism" is fast approaching.

Internal strife prevails in the kingdom of Morocco. The chaotic situation suggests an allusion to the "internecine war" which led to the ignition and spread of Islam:

"Morocco was in a bloodbath when we arrived. Fifty sons of the Emperor Muley-Ismael each had a political party: which produced in fact fifty civil wars, of blacks against blacks, of blacks against darks, of darks against darks, of mulattoes against mulattoes. There was a continuous slaughter in the entire territory of the empire." (Ch. XI, p. 170).

"Even the rapid spread of Mohammedanism before the conquering sword of the Islam prophet is a direct consequence of the bloody riots and fights

264

among Christians. It was the internecine war between the Nestorians and Cyrillians that engendered Islamism; and it is in the convent of Basra that the prolific seed was first sown by the Nestorian monk. Freely watered by rivers of blood, the tree of Mecca has grown till we find it in the present century, overshadowing nearly two hundred million people. The recent Bulgarian atrocities are but the natural outgrowth of the triumph of Cyril and the Mariolaters." (*Isis Unveiled*, p. 54, Vol. 2).

The fifty sons of Muley-Ismael do honor to the "prolific seed" of the "tree of Mecca." The Voltairian description of a fratricidal war and the "rivers of blood" mentioned in *Isis Unveiled* convey similar views of the same bellicose, phallic mystique.

The name of Muley-Ismael seems to place Chapter XI within a period contemporary with the life of Voltaire. A Moroccan sultan bearing that name lived from 1646 to 1727. The activities of his sons — if any — could therefore have coincided with the time of writing of *Candide* or with the second half of the XVIIIth Century. The same historical personage is mentioned in *Le Siècle de Louis XIV*. It is likely however, that the name was chosen as a convenient esoteric clue and "blind." Its latter portion: Ishmael or Ismael, is the name of a biblical character. Ishmael was the illegitimate son of Abraham and Hagar, the maid of Abraham's wife, Sarah. The jealousy of Sarah forced Ishmael to take flight into the wilderness where he lived as a hunter. The exile is regarded as the ancestor of the Ishmaelites or Arabian tribes. The Arabs consider Ishmael as the legendary father of their nation and as the author of their language. The name of the prolific sultan mentioned by Voltaire in *Candide* may designate a tradition rather than a man.

The love affair of Abraham and Hagar is rich in meaning. "Abraham and Saturn are identical in astro-symbology and he is the forefather of the Jehovistic Jews" says the Secret Doctrine.* As was previously noted, Saturn is an equivalent of Jehovah. The famed biblical romance which produced Ishmael therefore involves the "Vice-God." The union of the low-ranking figure of universal mythology with a "servant" — or inferior entity — is not devoid of logic. Voltaire probably was sensitive to the occasional candor of the Old Testament. The family feud of the biblical clan and the spectacular division of the tribe related in *Candide* seem to convey allusions to the legendary, esoteric character of "Ishmael" and an echo of the occult view of the origin of Islam. The broken home of Jehovah is connected with the mutilation and abuse of Truth — the old woman. The Islamic portion of the calvary of the victim fits into the general scheme of Jehovic oppression which forms the somber background of the entire story. Any "civilization" upholding the brutal, phallic mys-

---

The Secret Doctrine, p. 578, Vol. I.

tique of the "Vice-God" deals harshly with carriers of the Primitive Wisdom-Religion.

The color scheme stressed in the battle suggests tainted brands of spirituality. The entire spectrum of darkness is present in the affray. White is conspicuously absent in spite of the fact that numerous Arabs have light complexions. The amusing reference to "darks," "blacks," and "mulattoes" invites symbolic interpretation. Pure adeptship seems absent from the kingdom of "Ishmael."

A parallel theme of inferior spirituality proves sadly relevant to the next episode of *Candide*. Catholic outrage is added to Islamic abuse. In a bizarre episode following the battle, the girl lies abandoned on a heap of corpses. She is returned to consciousness by the unsuccessful efforts of a rapist. Using Italian, the native language of the intended victim, the offender bitterly deplores his inability to perform the sex act. In spite of the absence of linguistic barrier — an indication of occult kinship favorable to symbolic "love" — the girl remains as inaccessible as might a perfect stranger. She is fully protected by the incapacity of the assailant. Tortured and mutilated, degraded to the lowest possible level by various panders, Truth remains inviolable.

The aggressor is a musical *castratus* emasculated through affiliation with the Roman Catholic Church. The macabre ribaldry of the episode illustrates an important view of occultists. In spite of all their efforts to retain or extort ultimate secrets of Pagan lore, perverted branches of the original Wisdom-Religion have lost the key to the mysteries of Nature. Only the most inferior levels of occult performance are open to them. The impotent offender portrayed in *Candide* represents Western churches in general and the Roman Catholic Church in particular.

"If the study of Hermetic philosophy held out no other hope of reward, it would be more than enough to know that by it we may learn with what perfection of justice the world is governed. A sermon upon this text is preached by every page of history. Among all there is not one that conveys a deeper moral than the case of the Roman Church. The divine law of compensation (Karma) was never more strikingly exemplified than in the fact that by her own act she has deprived herself of the only possible key to her own religious mysteries. The assumption of Godfrey Higgins that there are two doctrines maintained in the Roman Church, one for the masses and the other — the esoteric — for the 'perfect,' or the initiates, as in the ancient mysteries, appears to us unwarranted, and rather fantastic. She has lost the key, we repeat. Otherwise, no terrestrial power could have prostrated her, and except as having a superficial knowledge of the means of producing 'miracles,' her clergy can in no way be compared in their wisdom with the hierophants of old.

In burning the works of the theurgists; in proscribing those who affect their study; in affixing the stigma of demonolatry to magic in general, Rome has left her exoteric worship and *Bible* to be helplessly riddled by every free-thinker, her sexual emblems to be identified with coarseness, and her priests to unwittingly turn magicians and even sorcerers in their exorcisms, which are but necromantic evocations. This retribution, by the exquisite adjustment of divine law, is made to overtake this scheme of cruelty, injustice, and bigotry, through her own suicidal acts." (*Isis Unveiled*, pp. 120-121, Vol. 2).

"The burnt works of the theurgists" — to which may be added the burnt theurgists themselves — represent the "lost key" forever inaccessible to the Church as a result of her own malpractice. The importance of the "key" which is repeatedly suggested in *Zadig* and *Micromégas* is vigorously dramatized in Chapters XI and XII of *Candide*. The thieving Jew portrayed in the former story failed to appropriate anything more than 500 ounces of "silver." Spiritual "gold" remained beyond his reach. The gracious archbishop and the Saturnian Secrétaire of *Micromégas* — representing state religion and state scholarship respectively — suffer from the same deprivation. The prelate seems to be blind to the value of certain documents placed in his custody. The uninspired scholar — apparently pressured to "publish or perish" — resorts to plagiarism. The reception of the book affording a view of the "end of things" gives evidence of the same lack of the crucial key.

The allegorical couple formed by the Princess of Palestrina and by the Prince of Massa-Carrara conveys the suggestion of a biblical event. The Egyptian connections of the lovers are added to the phonetic hint of a *massacre* — a word closely resembling the name *Massa-Carrara*. The massacre which is evoked may be linked to the slaying of Hypathia and other "innocents." It may also be linked to the slaughter ordered by Herod, an event which caused the flight of the Holy family to Egypt. All such killings were prompted by the same fear of carriers of knowledge. The massacre of "innocents" reported by Voltaire grows out of the same dread. The full significance of the episode related in the Bible is revealed by the esoteric value of the word "innocent" which means "initiate." The massacre of "Westphalian" or Western "innocents" seems calculated to stress the biblical event and the appalling record of "ancient abuse" which finds ultimate expression within the time setting of *Candide*.

The esoteric value of such words as "innocent," "child," and "little one" is given in the Secret Doctrine:

"So is the Dragon a mystery. 'Truly,' says Rabbi Simeon Ben-Iocahi, 'that to understand the meaning of the Dragon is not given to the 'Companions' (students, or *chelas*), but only to 'the little ones,' *i.e., the perfect Initiates.*[*]

---

[*]Such was the name given in ancient Judea to the Initiates, called also the 'Innocents' and the 'Infants,' *i.e.,* once more reborn. This *key* opens a vista into one of the New Testament mysteries, the slaughter by Herod of the 40,000 'Innocents.' — In the case of the N.T., Herod stands for Alexander Janneus (of Lyda), whose persecution and murder of hundreds and thousands of Initiates led to the adoption of the Bible story." (*The Secret Doctrine*, p. 504, Vol. II).

The esoteric concepts of "child," "little one," "infant," and "innocent" illuminate many literary texts. One may note in passing the distinction which is insistently made by Saint-Exupéry between "grown ups" and "children" in *The Little Prince*. "Grown ups" generally advocate the study of earth-bound geograhy, history, arithmetic, and grammar. Such topics — and the wholesome rationality which they seem to represent — are to "grown-ups" more "objective" and safe than the disturbing domain of esoteric boa constrictors — open and shut. "Grown-ups" favor the pursuit of what is called "education," a source of material well-being and prestige. But they are sore afraid of Knowledge. They cannot — or will not — realize that all areas of learning lead to the same dreaded realm of staggering insight when pursued in depth. Geography and History lead to the genesis and evolution of our world. Arithmetic leads to cosmic harmony or the "music of the spheres." Grammar paves the way to the non-mythical "garden of delights" which is Literature:

> "It is true that a sudden illumination may now and then light up a destiny and impel a man in a new direction. But illumination is vision, suddenly granted the spirit, at the end of a long and gradual preparation. Bit by bit I learnt my grammar. I was taught my syntax. My sentiments were awakened. And now suddenly a poem strikes me in heart." (*Antoine de Saint Exupéry, Flight to Arras*, Ch. VIII).

"Children" know that it is all a matter of levels. They never stop asking questions. They are unafraid of "going back to the source." "Children" avoid judging others lest they themselves be judged. Except perhaps where Jehovic "businessmen" are concerned who strive to keep stars and light for themselves — under lock and key.

The hoarding of stolen lights practiced by Christian churches in general — and by the Catholic Church in particular — fails to achieve its purpose in *Candide*. The sole key to spiritual supremacy has been lost by the offenders through their own misdeeds. The Panglossian jubilation of Voltaire is clearly perceptible: *"O che sciagura d'essere senza c. . . . .!"*

The rapist is a musician formerly attached to the chapel of the dead Princess of Palestrina. He is a native of Naples who was once included among the "two or three thousand children" castrated there every year. Some of the boys "die from the operation." Others "acquire a voice more beautiful than that of women." A few become governors of states. The criminal seems to belong to the second category of men — *castrati* — who were employed in Church choirs until the XIXth Century.

The musician was only a helpless child when the operation was forced upon him. But the former victim of the Church has become a dedicated predator, a peddler of "arms" used by certain Christians to exterminate other Christians. The same type of ethics which makes him thrive on the tragedy of others explains his atttempted rape of what seems to be a dying girl. The revealed identity of the intended victim fails to produce a genuine change of heart. The assailant feigns sympathy, promises help, and — sells the girl into Algerian slavery. The impotent candidate to symbolic fulfillment — the loser of the crucial key — can and will make the most of the mangled remains of Truth.

Subsequent ordeals of the then young lady include mutilation, resale to various owners, and forced wanderings. Anatomical consistency is remarkable. Impotent fury is ever localized on the same general area as was the punishment of *Candide*. The young man's labors of "love" never earned him anything but "one kiss and twenty kicks in the rear." The seat of guilty knowledge remains the choice target of various tormentors of Truth. Rape, mutilation of a buttock, and related cannibalism are reported as routine practice. The latter custom gives further evidence of a powerless desire to absorb all possible nourishment from the Secret of Secrets. But the coveted knowledge cannot be acquired through material dissection. It is accessible only to those who possess the required key or who can "lift the veil." It is suggested by the old woman that a view of her damaged posterior would cause second thoughts on the part of certain skeptics. The bizarre statement is correct. Diminished as she is, the ancient version of Truth retains astounding faculties of enlightenment.

Her spiritual genealogy is second to none:

> " 'Miss,' replied the old woman, 'you do not know what the rank of my birth is, and, if I showed you my behind, you would not speak as you do, and you would suspend your judgment." (Ch. X, p. 167).

The apparent obsession of Voltaire with sexual anatomy is uniquely heavy in *Candide*. References to "love — spiritual and other — are numerous in the works of the sage. But it is in the calvary of "Westphalian" Truth personified that the most stubborn concern with genitalia is found. The fact is a sad reflection on a culture symbolically, literally and viciously phallic: the much touted culture of "West*phalia*."

The racy quality of Voltairian humor is often regarded as a manifestation of XVIIIth Century "libertinism." The word "libertin" is interpreted as the virtual equivalent of the word "débauché." The surface of XVIIIth Century literature tends to support the common view of "libertine" writings. Pillars of respectability — such as Montesquieu — and controversial figures — such as Diderot — contributed in like manner to the erotic "amusement" of their contemporaries.

269

The exact nature of the "amusement" deserves careful study. We have a great deal to learn from "libertine" literature. The word which is generally connected with the idea of lust can also be connected with the idea of Free Thought. The "libertine" element of Western writings resembles a Proustian character who "plays dead" in the presence of typical Western scholars. Mme de Villeparisis, the controversial great lady with a past, has much is common with the spicy literary tradition. Her dislike of pedantic Bloch is easy to understand without esoteric insight. The deportment and the speech of the young man would try less sensitive constitutions than the "wit" or "spirit" of a Guermantes. Not only does Bloch fail to grasp the deep sense of his own plagiaristic mouthings. He is also oblivious to the reactions of others. Knowledge and ethics are equally faulty. Bloch's approach of another guest of the marquise shows him to be a master of blunder. "You must be a dreyfusard" ranks on the same plane of social flair and literary finesse as "you must be a homosexual," "you must be an occultist," or "you must be an esoteric writer." Such subtle probes reflect an obsessive desire to receive "objective" evidence or to "open windows." The final rebuff received by the young man from his hostess could be the kindest gift ever bestowed on him were he able to understand it. The closed eyes of the libertine great lady are a silent injunction to forget about "windows" and to search for inner lights. The wordless message is interpreted as one might expect. The marquise is conveniently diagnosed as senile.

The esoteric value of libertine presentation should be pondered in the case of "Legrandin." The puzzling Proustian "engineer" is a source of startling revelation to Marcel, the narrator of the *Recherche*. The urbane, learned, seemingly worldly — "mondain" — person, the man of "ingenuous" and "candid" expression, has an enlightening "backside" or veiled aspect. The behavior of "Legrandin" greeting a neighboring "châtelaine" is observed and commented as follows:

"The face of Legrandin expressed an extraordinary animation and zeal; he made a deep bow with secondary backward tilting, which abruptly returned his back to a position beyond the starting position and which must have been taught to him by the husband of his sister, Mme. de Cambremer. This quick straightening motion caused the rump of Legrandin to flow back in a sort of vigorous and muscular wave, a rump which I had not suspected of being fleshy; and I do not know why this undulating movement of pure matter, this all-carnal flux, devoid of an expression of sprituality, whipped into a storm by thoroughly base eagerness, suddenly awoke in my mind the possibiilty of a Legrandin entirely different from the one we knew." (*A la Recherche du temps perdu*, pp. 124-25, Vol. I).

The description of "Legrandin" — whose name suggests a giant —

270

seems calculated to evoke Voltaire in general and *Candide* in particular. The bowing and scraping which is performed for the benefit of the "châtelaine" brings to mind Mme du Châtelet and the aristocratic connections of a deceptive "snob." The "behind" which is prominently featured in *Candide* is very much in evidence. The movements of the engineer suggest the typical flirt of esoteric writers with potential new "contacts," a behavior alternately provocative and coy. The overtures of esoteric writers are generous. Clues abound. But esoteric ogling can only go so far without destroying esotericism itself. The inviting forward move is generally followed by marked withdrawal or return to esoteric reserve. Stumbling blocks are frequently thrown into the way of the courted researcher. One may cite as example of such esoteric "blinds" the passage of *Zadig* in which Voltaire lumps together — somewhat irreverently — the philosopher's stone, the theology of the magi, and judicial astrology. The enterprising reader sensing the presence of hidden material is likely to be deterred from his quest by the apparent rejection of all things occult. One of the final chapters of *Candide* contains a meaningful septenary classification of levels of consciousness. The sixth element of the series — which seems to break a smooth sequence of interpretation — is another sort of esoteric hurdle placed in the path of casual probers. The bawdy words of the old woman seem to apply to Voltaire, Proust, and numerous others. "— if I showed you my behind, you would not speak as you do, and you would suspend your judgment." Esoteric writings can suggest — not "show" — their "backsides" and must rely on readers for the devoutly wished unveiling: the "déjeuner sur l'herbe"* of the future.

The rest of the odyssey of the old woman is traced to various slave-markets of the Mediterranean area. Among her stations of the cross are Tunis, Alexandria, and Smyrna. Tunis, in antiquity Carthage, was the birthplace of Tertullian, one of the Fathers of the Church. Tertullian once expressed the fond hope of seeing all "philosophers" in the flames of Hell. Carthage was also the birthplace of Augustine, a saint who is no favorite of esoteric writers. Alexandria was the site of the famous book-burning and the site of the murder of Hypathia, a crime committed in accordance with the orders of Cyril. Smyrna was the birthplace of Iraeneus who built his church on the "mangled remains" of Pagan knowledge. The names Tertullian, Cyril, and Iraeneus are prominently featured in the rogues' gallery of theosophical and esoteric literature. The itinerary of the girl symbolically dragged through the realm of spiritual fraud and physical gore is a meaningful one.

The amputation of one buttock is performed during the siege of Azov.

A la Recherche du temps perdu, p. 1038, Vol. III.

Following the battle, the martyr becomes the property of a Russian "boyard." The "Great Schism" of the Orient is in geographical, historical, and anatomical evidence. What is left of ancient Truth becomes partially enslaved to the Greek Orthodox Church. The vowel content of the word "boyard" — which is spelled *boiard* in certain editions — leaves little doubt as to the identity of the oppressor. The girl has changed hands many times. The Jehovic source of her persecution is ever the same.

The amputation involves the planning of Moslems and the cooperation of Jews represented by a symbolic ointment:

> "We underwent the horrible operation. The Moslem priest applied on us the same ointment used on children who have just been circumcised." (Ch. XII, p. 173).

Literary commentators generally situate the episode in the year 1696, the time when the armies of Peter the Great stormed Azov. Such a date does not seem consistent with the gradual separation called "the Great Schism," a process which was completed in 1054.

It should be noted, however, that the Kipchak Turks overran the Crimean peninsula in 1050. The invasion — which coincided with the final stage of the Great Schism — presents the same general confrontation of Turks and Russians which was repeated in 1696 and which seems to be related in *Candide*. The story of the old woman shows the Russians to have landed in Azov from "flat boats." The latter detail seems to rule out the year 1696 in favor of a previous date. Peter the Great is known to have promoted the modernization — not to say the creation — of the Russian navy. The czar spent considerable time studying the latest English and Dutch ship-building techniques which he then introduced into his own country. The siege of 1696 was not implemented by a flottilla of flat boats. "Two warships, twenty three galleys, four fireships and numerous smaller craft"* participated in the blockade. The minor detail relative to primitive crafts was probably calculated to situate the episode of mutilation within the esoteric chronology of *Candide*: in the XIth Century.

Two rival branches of World Religion — the Judaic and the Moslem — welcome and promote the mutilation of Truth. The Voltairian Great Schism seems to have the endorsement of Jerusalem and Mecca. The timeless feud of Jews and Arabs is temporarily forgotten. The impossible dream of harmonious co-existence is compensated by unanimous hatred for the non-Semitic world.

The esoteric substance of Chapters XI and XII is a recital of woes

---

Encyclopaedia Britannica, Peter the Great.

272

endured by Universal Truth in modern Western Europe. The greatness of early Christianity is personified by the mother of the old woman. The separations of Islam and of the Greek Orthodox Church are added to edifying pictures of Catholic "Westphalia" and Protestant countries. The crippling process of sectarian division is complete.

Truth is tarnished, disfigured, and mutilated. But she cannot be destroyed. Karma seems to protect her person and the persons of her few devotees. The plague which follows one sale of the old woman to a new tormentor seems to symbolize the work of Retribution. It is compared by the heroine herself to an earthquake resembling the tremor of Lisbon. It is suggested once more than chance does not exist. The gruesome balance sheet of established religions is powerless to change two facts. The inexorable work of the wheel of evolution and the divine spark present in every man tend to further the same goal. The resultant force can and does thwart the powers of temporal and spiritual oppression. Countless living shrines exist which are susceptible to the strong appeal of Truth. Such temples are as enduring as mankind itself. The amazing survival of Cunégonde and the lasting vitality of the old woman convey a heartening message. The Truth which can withstand such hardship must triumph in the end.

"Enough has been given, it is believed, to show that the existence of a Secret Universal Doctrine, besides its practical methods of Magic is no wild romance or fiction. The fact was known to the whole ancient world, and the knowledge of it has survived in the East, in India especially. And if there be such a Science, there must be naturally, somewhere, professors of it, or Adepts. In any case it matters little whether the Guardians of the Sacred Lore are regarded as living, actually existing men, or are viewed as myths. It is their Philosophy that will have to stand or fall upon its own merits, apart from, and independent of any Adepts. For in the words of the wise Gamaliel, addressed by him to the Synedrion: 'If this doctrine is false it will perish, and fall of itself; but if true, then, — it *cannot be destroyed!*' " (*The Secret Doctrine,* p. 50, Vol. V — *Adyar Edition*).

Candide and his friends arrive in the New World. The blissful calm of the sea-voyage is shattered. The blurred, soothing memories coloring Devachanic sleep yield to harsh realities. Rumors of past misdeeds accompany the hero on the unknown shores. The authorities are in pursuit. Karma awaits man "at the threshold of his new incarnation."*

The small group faces the formidable person of the Governor of Buenos Aires.

_____

Isis Unveiled, p. 34-A, Vol. II.

"Cunégonde, Captain Candide and the old woman went to the residence of the governor Don Fernando d'Ibarra, y Fiigueroa, y Mascarenes, y Lampourdos, y Souza. This nobleman had a pride suitable for a man who wore so many names. He spoke to men with the most noble disdain, carrying his nose so high, raising his voice so ruthlessly, assuming such an imposing tone, displaying such a haughty gait, that all those who saluted him had a strong urge to beat him. He loved women madly." (Ch. XIII, pp. 175-76).

The arrogance of the nobleman is suitable indeed for a person of so many titles. The governor has a long way to go to attain the "nameless" state of spirituality. Voltaire may have intended an esoteric allusion to the "virgin men" or *Kumara* of occult tradition who are not to be mentioned by name.* The overbearing and lecherous official is the exact opposite of such "perfect" beings. Earthly prestige to the contrary, the governor can hardly be regarded as a spiritual aristocrat.

A delicate problem arises. Candide must account for the presence of Cunégonde. The nature of his connection with her must be explained. Any statement is potentially dangerous. The allegorical lover of Truth is incapable of lying. The dilemma faced by Candide is a thinly disguised riddle; an appeal to the reader to stop, think, and wonder. Who — or what — is Cunégonde?

"— he did not dare say that she was his wife because indeed she was not; he did not dare say that she was his sister, because she was not either; and although this officious lie was in the old days much in fashion among the ancients, and although it could be useful to the moderns, his soul was too pure to betray the truth." (Ch. XIII).

The officious lie suggestive of a false front used for a worthy cause invites speculation. Voltaire suggests the timeless esoteric dimension of the riddle by reference to the Ancients and the Moderns. The awesome power and the roving eye of the governor create an impasse. The impasse is the priceless vehicle of an equivalence. "Betrayal" of "truth" virtually amounts to betrayal of the girl. Voltaire literally dangles the veiled identity of Cunégonde under the nose of the reader.

Candide might truthfully reply that Cunégonde is his wife. For his mystical dedication — or wedding — to her has the indissoluble quality pertaining to spirit. He might truthfully state that she is his sister. For he carries a divine spark which is her reflection. Were the governor physically near-sighted — or partial to older women — Candide might even say that Cunégonde is his mother. For she nurtures his vital spiritual needs. Candide finally might add that Cunégonde is his child for Truth can only live in the yearning heart of Man.

---

*The Secret Doctrine, pp. 281-82, Vol. II.

Evidence is available to show that the "officious lie" was in vogue in the ancient world. Hypathia was addressed accordingly in the letters of Synesius. Certain fragments of the letters are said to have "reached" us. The bishop of Ptolemais expressed himself as follows:

> "My heart yearns for the presence of your divine spirit which more than anything else could alleviate the bitterness of my fortunes — Oh!, my mother, my sister, my teacher, my benefactress! —" (Quoted in *Isis Unveiled*, p. 53, Vol. 2).

The same "officious lie" seems to have found its way into modern texts:

> "Mon enfant, ma soeur,
> Songe à la douceur
> D'aller là-bas vivre ensemble!" —
> (Charles Baudelaire, *L'Invitation au voyage*).

> ("My child, my sister,
> Think of the sweet joy . .
> Of going there to live together.")

Albertine, the allegorical "work" or creation of a Proustian Pygmalion, is feared, and loved as an elusive "mistress," "sister," "daughter," and "mother."*

Spirit sublimates and joins the quintessence of all earthly Love. Cunégonde is one of many comparable allegories which may be found in literary texts.

The interplay of esoteric attraction and repulsion underlies the "useful" paragraph of *Candide*. Enticement is at a maximum. The counterweight of general exoteric substance remains undiminished. One is reminded of the exaggerated "advances" made by Legrandin which are followed by sudden withdrawal. The salutations of the "engineer" border on the obscene. The unmentionable is as close to the surface as it can be without rending the veil of overall appearance. No expression of spirituality is allowed to betray the Secret of Secrets to the "outsider." To the attentive observer — such as "Marcel" — there is, however, a disquieting suggestion; a practical certainty of things previously undreamed. Proust may well have had in mind — among other texts — the paragraph under present study when he described the provocative "flirt" and the intriguing "behind" of "Legrandin."

The same paragraph of *Candide* contains a fine example of massive esoteric understatement. How "useful" the officious lie might be — if per-

---

A la Recherche du temps perdu, p. 111, Vol. III.

ceived, remembered, and applied to general reading — is beyond means of expression. Homeric laughter is the only possible response to a full grasp of the bland little adjective.

The same innocent looking word is transparently connected with the amazing reaction of M. de Charlus when the Proustian narrator of the *Recherche* acknowledges the baron's desire to be "useful" to him.* We are told by Marcel Proust that the influence of "inversion" is so pervasive that the very vocabulary of its sufferers is altered. We are told by the same author that "Legrandin" is a notorious user of "delicate epithets."** We may thus wonder if such terms as "useful," "necessary," "silence," and other standard tools of esoteric algebra are not offered to our attention. If the Voltairian identity of "Legrandin" remains doubtful at this point, we may at least speculate on the possible meaning of Proustian "inversion."

The dilemma of Candide is basically similar to the problem once faced by Zadig. The young disciple of Zoroaster could not claim the stolen suit of armor for fear of "compromising" the Queen. The admirer of Cunégonde is likewise prevented from compromising his love. The scruples of esoteric secrecy are identical in each case.

A person presumed dead reappears. The brother of Cunégonde has escaped from the slaughter which overtook the residents to Thunder-ten-tronckh. He has become a provincial delegate of the Jesuits. Like his sister — and also Pangloss — the young nobleman has been "resurrected" in a manner suggesting either miracle or rebirth. The young baron relates the circumstances of his "death" and of his return to life.

> " — my mother, my father, and I were put into a tumbril with two servants and three little boys with slit throats, in order to go and bury us in a chapel of Jesuits, two leagues away from the castle of my forefathers." (Ch. XV, p. 181).

The delegate is left for dead on a heap of corpses. The occult symbolism of "mangled remains" of Truth is once more present. Another suggestion is made. Through repeated use of the same macabre situation, Voltaire seems to call esoteric attention to the occult view of death:

> " — it may not be out of place to inquire what assurance can any physician have, beyond *external* evidence, that the body is really dead? The best authorities agree in saying that there are none. Dr. Todd Thomson, of London, says most positively that 'the immobility of the body, even its cadaverous aspect, the coldness of the surface, the absence of respira-

---

*A la Recherche du temps perdu, p. 285, Vol. II.
**Ibid., p. 584, Vol. II.

tion, and pulsation, and the sunken state of the eye, are not unequivocal evidences that life is wholly extinct.' Nothing but total decomposition is an irrefutable proof that life has fled forever and that the tabernacle is tenantless. Democritus asserted that there existed no *certain* signs of real death. Pliny maintained the same, Asclepiades stopped the funeral of a man to him unknown, and restored him to life; and Pliny said assurance of death was more difficult in the case of women than in those of men." (*Isis Unveiled,* p. 479, Vol. 1).

Rabelais may be added to the list of authorities quoted in the above text. The unnamed feminine organ mentioned in the *Tiers Livre,* an organ related to the "Bacchic" or spiritual tendencies of its owners, has a dangerous property. Because of it women tend to offer deceptive appearance of death — "vraye resemblance de mort." The same belief may be connected with an undescribed — funerary rite which is regarded as important by the Duchess of Guermantes:

> "In the funeral chamber of a dead man of our times, Mme. de Guermantes would not have called attention to, but would have perceived immediately, all failures to observe the customs. She was shocked to see, at a funeral, women mingling with men, whereas there is a particular ceremony which must be performed for women." (*A la Recherche du temps perdu,* pp. 550-51, Vol. II).

The ceremony may be one in which completion of the death process is ascertained in the light of occult science.

The Secret Doctrine teaches that resurrection is impossible once dissolution of the vital link between various human components has occurred. It is asserted, however, that burial all too often takes place before the severance process has run its full course. In the words of Saint Exupéry, a man pronounced dead one day "will not die until to-morrow"* or the next day. Tragic cases are cited in *Isis Unveiled.* Many persons pronounced dead by physicians were later found to have been buried alive.** Voltaire is one esoteric writer among numerous others — such as Edgar Poe and Emile Zola — who warned the reading public against the all too real danger of premature burial.

The delegate miraculously "resurrected" by holy water seems to personify a false rebirth of historical character: the Counter-Reformation and the creation of the Jesuitic Order. The artificial character of the rebirth is suggested by two facts. The young nobleman was not dead in the first place. The Jesuitic establishment could not have been "resurrected" since it already existed under the form of the neighboring chapel. Voltaire may have wished to suggest the fact that the word "Jesuit" was already used

---

*Flight to Arras, Ch. II.
**Isis Unveiled, p. 479, Vol. 1.

prior to the formal creation of the Order in 1540, the term having its origin "in the preceding centuries."* He may also have implied that the seeds of Jesuitry to come were congenital defects of the religious structure fabricated around Peter. No Church supported by the "imaginary stilt" of apostolic succession; no Church erected on the "mangled remains" of other spiritual bodies could hope to survive without repressive agencies such as the "Holy Office" and the Company of Jesus. The false quality of the "rebirth" which was designed to check — if not cancel — the gains of Protestant "heresy" is also hinted. No punitive horde can legislate or enforce a state of mind or spirit.

Jesuitry is connected with the perversion of "love." The young baron has advanced rapidly in the Order. His remarkable rise is due to physical charm and to the homosexual weakness of his superior. The same tainted "genealogy" which is elsewhere linked to the epidemic of spiritual "pox" overshadows the beginning of the aggressive brotherhood.

The theme of Retribution is introduced by the "wheels" of the tumbril. A cause-effect relationship may exist between the surrounding abundance of death and the narrow escape of the Jesuit. The son and heir of the vengeful Lord of Thunder-ten-tronckh is already reaping a tragic harvest which condemns him to a lifetime of fear and strife. There is always the danger that Man and Truth may meet. The Jesuit will live in dread of the message of Jesus. He will disregard the warning of History. He will try to stop the progress of the wheel of evolution. He will prolong the tyranny wrought by his defunct Jehovic father.

The prophetic quality of imagery used by Voltaire deserves notice. Dead noblemen, dead servants, slit throats and tumbrils bring to mind bloody pictures of the Great Revolution. The missing guillotine may have been envisioned by the seer who wrote *Candide*.

Begun in joyful surprise, the reunion of Candide with the young baron ends in strife and death. The true character of the Jesuit is revealed when he suddenly passes from theatrical effusion to insult and violence. The significant mood swing calls attention to bellicose traits of the Company of Jesus, a reality ill concealed by a veneer of unction.

The attack of the baron is partially due to the naiveté of Candide. The young man is so presumptuous as to aspire to the hand of Cunégonde. Because of his controversial lineage such hopes are viewed as a crime of lèse-majesté. The obvious satire of aristocratic arrogance covers a condemnation of other nature. Perverted Truth — represented by the Jesuit — prides itself on the nobility of authentic Truth represented by Cunégonde. The alleged superiority of the line of Thunder-ten-tronckh is

---

Encyclopaedia Britannica, Society of Jesus.

278

open to question. The esoteric status of Candide — Man in Search of Truth — is as ancient as mankind itself. The Jesuit is unlikely to have enough "quarters" of match that precedence.

The esoteric reader is reminded of the discreet observation of Zadig which applies to man-made hierarchies as it applies to man-made laws: "Reason is more ancient."

The controversial ancestry of Candide which is mentioned at the beginning of the story is indirectly called to attention. The young hero is believed to be the nephew of the Lord of Thunder-ten-tronckh whose sister refused to marry a kindly gentleman of the neighborhood "because he could only prove seventy-one quarters and because the rest of his genealogical tree had become lost through the injury of time." It is observed in the Bénac edition that one quarter of nobility covers approximately one generation. The aristrocratic background of the scorned suitor extends over some 2,000 years. The rest of his genealogical tree recedes into disquieting vistas of by-gone eras. Such time perspectives can prove damaging to orthodox dogma where the date of Creation is concerned. The ancestry of the rejected lover might even be comparable to that of monuments dating back "to the fourth year of the World's creation agreeably with Bible chronology, and when Adam was in swaddling clothes."* No dedicated member of the family of Thunder-ten-tronckh can fail to dislike such implications. The myth of apostolic succession is not the only precarious "stilt" of the finest castle in the world. The dogma of personal Creation dating back to a mere few thousand years is equally vulnerable.

Equal doubt may be raised about the lineage of Candide and the lineage of Cunégonde. Equal status is revealed by esoteric reading. Precedence is irrelevant to the allegorical couple formed by Man and Truth. No mésalliance is possible between them. The Voltairian view of "nobility" is perceptible. The only aristocracy worthy of the name is the spiritual élite or "good company."

Much has been said and written about the "contradiction" which seems to exist between the revolutionary ideas of Voltaire and his dim view of the masses. If contradiction is implied, it is easily resolved by evolutionary belief. Voltaire saw all men as potential equals destined to make the same voyage through life. But he saw them proceeding in successive waves at more or less advanced stages of progress. No emotional ambivalence, certainly no hypocrisy, can be inferred from such views.

Similar comments are applicable to all esoteric writers. Vigny, the deceptive spokesman of "bluebloods" undoubtedly "amused himself" in

*The Secret Doctrine, p. 690, Vol. II.

the first stanza of *L'Esprit pur* when he celebrated the exclusive head-gear of the nobleman:

"J'ai mis sur le cimier doré du gentilhomme
Une plume de fer qui n'est pas sans beauté." (*L'Esprit pur*).

("I placed on the golden crest of the nobleman's helmet
An iron pen which is not without beauty."

The "iron pen" of inspired "poetry" — meaningfully placed above all else — meant infinitely more to the author than the false glamor of social aristocracy. No one was less impressed by the "trivial proud and unsubstantial rich" — "les orgueilleux méchants et les riches futiles" — than the writer of *L'Esprit pur*. Vigny overtly conceived the "least intolerable" form of possible government as a democracy patterned after the ideals of the U.S. Constitution. "The least harmful government is that which is seen the leasi, felt the least, and paid the least," says a passage of his *Diary* written in 1835. One may note briefly that the true nature of Vigny's political views seem to be acknowledged by Proust. The genuinely democratic convictions of "Saint Loup" are finally recognized after his death.*

The same view of a spiritual aristocracy is illustrated in the works of Rabelais. Admission to the Abbaye of Thélème carries one requirement. The candidates must be of "high rank." In view of the general state of XVIth Century society, the necessary condition of acceptance has literal validity on the exoteric plane itself. Social standing and freedom from poverty were practical musts of spiritual attainment. No great progress —intellectual or other — could be expected from persons totally absorbed by precarious and agonizing survival. Varying degrees of material security and well-being seem to have been bestowed on great "smugglers" of the past to enable them to complete their important task. But the esoteric meaning of "high rank" transcends the plane of social and economic considerations. The self-discipline displayed by the residents of Thélème in the face of the permissive motto: "Fay ce que voudras" — "do as you will" — is an indication of high character. "High birth" is the apparent harvest of Karmic merit destined to achieve the mystical union or "marriage" which awaits the candidates at the end of their stay. The esoteric "necessity" of "high birth" sheds interesting light on the well-known axiom: "Noblesse oblige."

The famous obsession of Saint-Simon with "precedence" may have the same spiritual basis. His view of "good company" seems to coincide with the corresponding view of Rabelais, Voltaire, and numerous others.

A la Recherche du temps perdu, p. 854, Vol. III.

The kinship of Cunégonde with the Lord of Thunder-ten-tronckh deserves close examination. The girl is initially designated as the daughter of Mme la Baronne — the esoteric daughter of materiality. The paternity of the heroine is less clearly traced to the vengeful "Lord." Such a fact is consistent with the hazy character of father figures linked to Voltairian allegories of Truth. Except for his abilities to fulminate and kick — which are negative skills — the father of Cunégonde lacks substance. The father of the old woman is a fictitious Pope or fictitious person. Corresponding mother-figures are vividly portrayed. The physique of the baroness is unforgettable. So are the briefly glimpsed beauty and goodness of the mother of the old woman. Loose paternal bonds and hazy father-figures contrast with well established maternal ties and tangible mothers. While Truth is self-existent and needs no sire — Minerva or Wisdom is fatherless — her vitality depends on the devotion of flesh-and-blood beings. Truth lives incarnate in the hearts of men. Such is the probable significance of the contrast. Such is also one probable meaning of the many-faceted note written by Voltaire on the father of the old woman:

> "See the extreme discretion of the author; there has never been until now, any Pope named Urbain X; he fears to give an illegitimate daughter to a known Pope. What prudence! What delicacy of conscience!"

The most compelling beauty of Cunégonde and of the old woman lies in the very imperfection of their mortal shells. Little is found to suggest the hidden identity of both characters at the time of their first appearance. Cunégonde seems to be just another sensuous, giddly lass. The old woman does not hesitate to describe herself as a pathetic crone. Seekers and carriers of Truth are ennobled by the very poignancy of human condition. One is reminded once more of the splendid Pascalian definition of Man: "Glory and outcast of the universe."

The Jesuit symbolically interposed between Man and Truth seems dimly aware of his inferiority — genealogical and other. He is regretfully dispatched by Candide. Self-defense and defense of Truth require his removal. The very close tie which exists between Cunégonde and the baron carries the danger of overwhelming family influence. One must choose between Jesuitry and Truth. The choice is quickly made by Candide. Truthseekers can no more co-exist with the Order of Loyola than they can come to terms with the Mosaic tradition or with Torquemada. The delegate is sent to the same limbo as were other oppressors of Cunégonde: the Jew and the Inquisitor. Candide is overwhelmed with grief:

> " 'Alas!' o God, 'he said, 'I have killed my former master, my friend, my brother-in-law; I am the best man in the world and there are already

three men whom I have killed; and out of those three, two are priests."
(Ch. XV, p. 183).

Another flight becomes imperative. Candide must leave Cunégonde
in order to escape. He is accompanied by a newly acquired valet, Cacambo. Racially, morally, and professionally, the servant is an interesting mixture. He is one-quarter Spanish. His father is a South American mulatto. He has held many positions such as those of choir-boy,
sexton, sailor, monk, soldier, and valet. It is suggested that he has had
many lives. His practical turn of mind seems to border on cynicism. But
Cacambo is devoted to his idealistic master. His name is a compound
of Greek, Latin, and French words jointly expressing ambivalence ("am-
bo"), imperfection (Gr. "kakos," "bad"), and goodness (Fr. "bon"
"good"). He is in short "good" and "bad", a combination of decency and
mischief commonly found in the ordinary man, a Voltairian counterpart
of Panurge. Most important of all, Cacambo represents the occasional
vacillations of his master. He acts "always as the interpreter of the doubts
of Candide."

Such doubts are freely expressed. Candide is overwhelmed with sorrow
at the thought of being separated from Cunégonde. Cacambo views the
state of things with apparent detachment. But his faith in feminine ability to survive suggests awareness of certain identities. In his considered
opinion, "women always manage." Some of his homespun maxims are
echoes of the wisdom of the old woman. Corresponding to her observations on the "pleasure" of nocturnal trips are his views of the pleasure of
seeing and doing new things. Prolonging the statement that "misfortunes
give rights" is a kindred axiom of the servant:
"When one does not find one's due in one world, one finds it in another." Cacambo seems to have unsophisticated yet valid notions on
the identity of Cunégonde and on the reliability of Karmic justice —
the law of compensation. The net product of his experience is a fund
of solid good sense and a beginning of insight.

A strange adventure awaits the fugitives. In a beautiful meadow
crossed by several streams are two naked girls pursued by apes. The
animals are biting the buttocks of the young ladies whose reaction
seems difficult to define. The "backside" of "Legrandin" is in evidence
once more:

> "The two lost travellers heard a few squeals which seemed to be uttered
> by women. They did not know if those squeals were prompted by pain
> or joy; but they rose hurriedly with the anxiety and the alarm inspired by
> everything in an unknown land. The outcry came from two stark naked
> girls who were running lightly at the edge of the meadow, while two apes
> were following them and biting their buttocks." (Ch. XVI, p. 184).

Candide kills the ferocious beasts and rescues their victims. But the girls loudly bemoan the death of their tormentors. As was demonstrated in *Zadig*, Good Samaritans are not always welcome. The nudity of the girls and the anatomical designs of the pursuers suggest Truth and Knowledge to be involved once more. The masochistic tendencies of the nymphs are noted.

The surprising love of the ladies for such caricatures of human beings prompts observations on the part of Candide:

> "I did not expect so much kindness of soul."
> (Ch. XVI, p. 184).

Some enlightenment is supplied in the subsequent dialogue. The strange occurrence is not without precedent. But the general mystery is not easily dispelled:

> " — 'why do you find it so strange that, in some countries, there might be apes which obtain the good graces of ladies? They are one-quarter human, as I am one-quarter Spanish.' — 'Alas!' Candide went on, 'I remember hearing master Pangloss say that in the old days such accidents had occurred, and that those mixtures had produced aegipans, fauns, satyrs; that several illustrious persons of Antiquity had seen some; but I took that to be fables." (Ch. XVI, pp. 184-85).

Weird tales of mythology seem to be ridiculed. But a major aspect of the occult theory of evolution is enunciated. Man is no descendent of the ape. The ape is a descendent of Man. As was previously noted, a stage of marked bestiality led a portion of Fourth Race mankind to interbreed with animals. Hybrid species were produced which are represented allegorically by the animal-men of mythology. Voltaire suggests the relevance of the *Fourth Race* through repeated reference to the number *four*: "one quarter human" — "one quarter Spanish". His view of certain "accidents" seems to coincide with corrresponding theosophical teachings.

> "The numberless traditions about Satyrs are no fables, but represent an extinct race of animal men." (*The Secret Doctrine*, p. 262, Vol. II).
> "The ape we know is not the product of natural evolution but an *accident*, a cross-breed between an animal being, or form, and man — This is how Occult Science explains the absence of any link between ape and man, and shows the former evolving from the latter." (*The Secret Doctrine*, pp. 262-63, Vol. II).

A page of modern history is also represented in Chapter XVI. The long and bitter struggle between Jesuits and Jansenists is evoked. The apemen or "Oreillons" have a fierce aversion to the Society of Jesus.

Mistaking Candide for a member of the despised congregation, they take immediate measures to boil or roast him alive. The hostile tribe is usually believed to represent the Orejones, "Indians of the rio Naya, an affluent of the upper Amazon."* But the intensity of their sectarian hatred and the very name of their community tends to suggest the Jansenists. A certain amount of phonetic resemblance exists between the word "Oreillons" and the last name of Duvergier de Hauranne, the Director of the nuns of Angélique Arnauld. The term "oreillons" is also the French word for "mumps," a disease capable of producing sterility. The symbolism of sickness — physical and spiritual — seems to be present in a manner reminiscent of the Voltairian concept of the "pox." Another variety of plague, also threatening the process of "generation" or evolution, is detected in the doctrine of Port Royal. Candide sadly notes that the projected cook-out is consistent with doctrines of predestination and eternal damnation:

> " 'Do not fail,' said Candide, 'to submit to them the hideous inhumanity of having human beings cooked, and how un-Christian that is.' " (Ch. XVI, p. 186).

The merciful message of Christ is sadly disfigured by the doctrine of Port Royal. Historical Jansenists did not boil or roast men alive as did other religious brotherhoods. But their belief in predestination and eternal damnation caused their flock to live in terror of the flames of Hell.

Candide and Cacambo leave the land of the Oreillons safely and without bloodshed. Sectarian as they are, the "natives" are open to reason and truth. The same approach would be suicidal with representatives of the Mosaic tradition, Inquisitors, or Jesuitic barons. The non-violent outcome of the encounter conveys the apparent sympathy of Voltaire toward certain aspects of Jansenism. Purity of mores, mysticism, lofty ethics, and generally non-aggressive pursuits characterize the followers of Jansen. Such traits compare favorably with the worldly and warlike leanings of the Jesuits. Port Royal is remotely close to the Secret Doctrine. The jansenistic view of Providence and predestination is a modified version of Karma. But the modification is an abysmal hair-breadth. Human free will is irrelevant to human destiny. Man is the helpless toy of a capricious and vengeful deity. Grace is no longer the reward of merit. It is the carrot and the stick of a personal "Vice-God." The obscuration of Karma which is the bane of Jansenism suffices to turn positive spirituality into despair.

---

*Edition Cluny, p. 54.

The Jansenists have lost a crucial element of their spiritual heritage. Such is the substance of the sympathetic words of Cacambo:

> " ' — you do not have the same resources as we do — you think that you are about to roast a Jesuit, and it is your defender, it is the enemy of your enemies whom you are about to roast. Personally, I was born in your country.' " (Ch. XVI, p. 186).

The theme of germane spiritual holdings is introduced by the observation: "I was born in your country." It is also conveyed by the community of "language." Cacambo acts as "interpreter" between "Westphalian" candor and tortured remnants of Primitive Wisdom. The theme of estrangement from the original fountainhead of Knowledge is discernible in the meaningful remark: "You do not have the same resources as we do." The word "resources" tends to suggest a much-needed "return to the source." The symbolic presence of several "streams" crossing the meadow tend to confirm the relevance of sectarian alienation from Truth.

Chapter XVI contains a valuable lesson on non-separated twins: Religion and Politics. The popular tendency to crucify potential saviors promotes the interests of genuine tyrants. It is the same in spiritual domains as it is in the "army." "Bulgarian" fellow-victims of Candide were prompt to beat him mercilessly. Religious fellow-victims are eager to roast him alive. The thought of turning jointly against true oppressors is hard to come by and requires the prompting of outside agitators. Divided and conquered mankind can no longer identify the real source of its man-made misery. Those persons who sense the identity of the culprits prefer to vent their frustrations of fellow-victims. The emotional outlet is effective. Things seem safer that way. Saboteurs of evolution are skilled in crushing the revolutions which they themselves produce. They need only turn one segment of the subjugated herd against the other and watch in smug contempt. If a bold "return to the source" is needed in spiritual realms, it is also needed in political affairs. Any such quest for Truth leads to the same doctrinal malady which plagues the whole spectrum of Western society and which has infected other portions of the world.

The value of "skepticism" is demonstrated. The personification of Doubt has no qualms about going straight "to the source." The common adversary of Truth-seekers and Jansenists is exposed by Cacambo. The general degragation of Truth and the advent of the Jesuitic Order are identified as "the enemy." The latter word — which is often used in medieval literature to designate the devil — is emphatically featured. The satanic foundation of the Church is the doctrinal price which must be paid for the promotion of an anthropomorphic Deity. A scapegoat must be found and programmed for the salvation of the "Vice-God." A faith which cannot withstand confrontation with "strangers" is doomed to reign through fiends — mythical and other. The satanic foundation of the Church is under indictment. The Jesuitic predilection for the black arts is noted. Esoterically and otherwise, "Crush the infamous!" rings through the passage.

Chapter XVI is overshadowed by the virtual image of various "missing links." The ape-like collectivity and its biological tie with the human race announce the phraseology — if not the views — of Darwin. Cacambo functions as a previously "missing link" between the Old World and the New — between modern and primitive societies. The divided streams of spirituality suffer from the absence of a crucial "missing link" — as do the "Oreillons." Jansenism is suggested to represent a "missing link" between the Primitive Wisdom-Religion and its sectarian, disfigured versions. Jansenism is a "missing link" in the pilgrimage to the "source" — Eldorado — which will be performed by Man in Search of Truth. Last but not least, Voltaire courts the connections which can be made with a few "missing links," a task to be performed by the source-conscious reader.

The team constituted by Candide and Cacambo is itself an invitation to establish a "missing link." The "interpreter" of the vacillations of the hero is part of Candide himself. Man, the incorrigible seeker of Truth, is torn — and occasionally enlightened — by Doubt. The primitive or Pagan element slumbering in every "civilized" Westphalian" is represented by the racially mixed servant. Doubt is also the product of a culture based on the mutilation of Truth and the persecution of Truth-Seekers. The existence of Doubt incarnate is not altogether unwholesome in such a setting. Skepticism may perform a constructive task comparable to the teamwork of Siva and Vishnu. It may be a destroyer of false creeds. It may be a creator and a preserver of Truth.

Candide and Cacambo arrive in the land of Eldorado at the end of a perilous journey. Courage, skill, and faith are required to reach the almost inaccessible country. The wealth of geographical details which is connected with the itinerary includes boulders, cliffs, "terrible obstacles," and a river which runs underground in certain spots. The dangerous path of the spiritual candidate is suggested at every turn. It is threatened by bandits representing evil occult forces.

The new country proves to be "the country where nothing lacks." Precious metals and stones are found in abundance. Lack of greed and vanity is the salient trait of all residents. Purity reigns. Kindness is shown to strangers. Laughter is heard. It is a scarce commodity in the somber realm of Thunder-ten-tronckh. While boundless wealth is everywhere, money might as well not exist. It is unnecessary in a domain where universal values prevail:

> " 'You undoubtedly do not have any currency of this country, but it is not necessary to have any to dine here." (Ch. XVII, p. 190).

Transcended "necessity" is an apt definition of the country where nothing lacks. It is consistent with the underlying theme of "room" — and board — generously given "at the inn."

Linguistic currency is also transcended. Communication retains full savor and significance when translated. "Spirit" rather than "wit" pervades the experience. "Wit" is not excluded.

> "Never was anyone treated to better food, and never did one have more wit at supper than did his Majesty. Cacambo explained the puns of the King to Candide, and although translated, they still seemed to remain puns." (Ch. XVIII, pp. 194-95).

Eldorado is the source and the destination of Being. It is the realm of the ineffable, omnipotent *Verbum*. Such Mayavic divisions as linguistic barriers do not apply in the happy land. The symbolic nourishment received by the guests is "necessarily" superior. The dinner with the King is an example of Voltairian "meals" which have the same spiritual essence as the "banquets" of Plato.

Faith possesses a universal quality. It is vibrantly alive in all individuals. No professional middlemen are tolerated — or required. Every man is his own priest and his own temple. Far from being a mercenary, bargaining venture, prayer is a spontaneous communion with the Supreme Being:

> " 'We worship God from evening to morning.' " (Ch. XVIII, p. 192).

The nocturnal quality of worship tends to suggest the blissful omniscience of Nirvâna or ultimate mode of Being which is attained by all at the term of a Grand Cycle during a Night of Brahma.

Only one religion exists: "The religion of the whole world," the Universal Doctrine:

> " 'Est-ce-qu'il peut y avoir deux religions? — nous avons, je crois, la religion de tout le monde.' " (Ch. XVIII, p. 192).

> (" 'Can there be two religions? — we have, I believe, the religion of everyone.")

The pursuit of knowledge is favored. Candide is prompt to notice the dedication to learning which is a distinction of Eldorado. One may surmise "mathematics" and transcendental physics to be "closer knit than twins."

"What surprised him more, and pleased him the most, was the palace of sciences, in which he saw a gallery two thousand paces long, all filled with mathematical instruments." (Ch. XVIII, p. 194).

"Commerce" is vigorously promoted by the supreme powers. Varying "degrees" of "wealth" are found in outlying regions of the Kingdom. The following explanation is offered to Candide and Cacambo for the "poor" fare which they received at the inn. The menu in question featured an abundance of meat.

" 'All inns which are established to facilitate commerce are supported by the government. You received poor fare here, because it is a poor village; but everywhere else you will be received as you deserve to be.' " (Ch. XVIII, p. 190).

The only currency which is honored in Eldorado — a currency which Candide and Cacambo do not yet possess — is the state of spiritual perfection. It is the abiilty to transact mystical "commerce" under proper conditions. Treatment is meaningfully connected with "merit." The skillful use of the words "as you deserve" tends to divert attention from Karmic substance and to suggest social distinction on the exoteric plane.

Governmental concern with "commerce" shows superior insight to prevail in high spheres. The democratic and "commercial" banquet given at the inn is attended by "merchants" apparently dedicated to fruitful exchange. There are also a few "carters" presumably relying on Karmic "wheels" in the exercise of their profession. The conjunction of science and ethics is stressed by the presence of seemingly prosaic figures. Elevated allegory wears deceptive, unadorned garb.

No repressive agencies are found in Eldorado. Bureaucracies, prisons, courts of justice, political structures do not exist. They are made unnecessary by individual and collective virtue. The power structure has the same positive orientation as does the "average" man. The comparative, *ecstatic* mood of Candide is understandable:

"Candide, hearing all those statements remained in ecstasy, and said within himself: 'This is quite different from Westphalia and from the castle of his Lordship the baron — " (Ch. XVIII, p. 193).

The site of Eldorado — a land where Peruvian is understood — brings to mind various legends relative to the mythical wealth of the region. The "gold rush" mystique of Ferdinand and Isabella which resulted in the accidental discovery of America was based on belief in fabulous wealth to be found in Cipangu — Japan — and India. Voltaire seems to use the fortuitous discovery of Eldorado by "Westphalians" to evoke the mis-

288

guided and righteous rapacity of European explorers. Candide and Cacambo can hardly be compared to the thieving crusaders and brutal conquerors of XVIth Century Spain. But they will prove unable to transcend the greed and vanity which dominate the average Western mind.

The Peruvian location of Eldorado may be intended to suggest the existence of non-mythical treasures. Under the sub-title "A Secret Now First Told," Mme Blavatsky describes at some length a secret underground network of passages located near Cuzco, Peru. The mysterious complex of tunnels has served as a repository for the treasures of the Incas since the days of Pizarro. The main passageway runs from Cuzco to Lima "and then, turning southward, extends into Bolivia."

> "We have in our possession an accurate plan of the tunnel, the sepulcher, and the doors, given to us at the time by the old Peruvian. If we had ever thought of profiting by the secret, it would have required the co-operation of the Peruvian and Bolivian governments on an extensive scale. To say nothing of physical obstacles, no one individual or small party could undertake such an exploration without encountering the army of smugglers and brigands with which the coast is infested; and which in fact, include nearly the whole population. The mere task of purifying the mephitic air of the tunnel, which had not been entered for centuries, would also be a serious one. There, however, the treasure lies, and there, the tradition says, it will lie till the last vestige of Spanish rule disappears from the whole of North and South America." (*Isis Unveiled,* p. 598, Vol. 1).

Common factors such as difficult terrain, bandits, underground passages — in the case of *Candide* underground segments of a river — all suggest that Voltaire and Mme Blavatsky deal with the same secret subject. The red sheep used by Candide as he leaves Eldorado are probable esoteric counterparts of South American pack animals or llamas. According to the Encyclopaedia Britannica the llama is found primarily in Southern Peru. Voltaire seems to use the "red sheep" — as well as the Peruvian language — to invite a geographical connection between Eldorado and a specific portion of the South American country. The setting of Chapter XVIIIth is further identified as "the former homeland of the Incas" by an elderly native. The same person refers to the extermination of the Incas which was systematically carried out by the Spaniards. Such members of the tribe who — in the words of the elder — "very imprudently" left their original territory — thereby losing their initial state of "innocence" and "bliss" — were put to death by the conquistadores. The biblical massacre of the "Innocents" or Initiates is suggested to have a South American counterpart.

The methodical annihilation of Indians by whites in both Americas is common knowledge. A specific act of murderous treachery is less well known to non-historians. The fate of an Inca chief slaughtered by order of Pizarro as his ransom was on the way to "Westphalian" bandits seems to have inspired Voltaire as well as Mme Blavatsky:

> " — who can tell what became of the primitive people who fled before the rapacious brigands of Cortez and Pizarro? Dr. Tschudi, in his work on Peru, tells us of an Indian legand that a train of 10,000 llamas, laden with gold to complete the unfortunate Inca's ransom, was arrested in the Andes by the tidings of his death, and the enormous treasure was so effectually concealed that not a trace of it has ever been found." (*Isis Unveiled*, p. 546, Vol. 1).

The above legend seems to deviate from historical records which state that the ransom — the equivalent of $4,000,000 in bullion — was actually received by Pizarro. But there is no divergence of opinion where the treacherous cruelty of the Spaniards is concerned. It is unanimously reported that the Spaniards were hospitably received by the Indians, that the native chief — Atahualpa — was captured by the invaders, initially sentenced to the stake, and eventually strangled. "With him died the Peruvian empire."* a fact which may be connected with the "amazing revolutions" of Peru mentioned in *Candide*. The exoteric chronology featured by Voltaire suggests an allusion to Atahualpa. The upheavals reported in Chapter XVIII are said to have been witnessed by the father of the elder. The latter person is 172 years old. The witness is likely to have lived at the time of the murder of Atahualpa if the date of writing of *Candide* is taken as a reference. Another detail tends to draw attention to the same events. The number of pack animals used by Candide as he leaves Eldorado totals 100. In view of the common esoteric practice of adding or removing zeros to secret numbers, we may speculate that the convoy mentioned in Chapter XVIII represents in part the legendary train of 10,000 llamas.

The fate "of the primitive people who fled before the rapacious brigands of Cortez and Pizarro" is a subject of interesting speculation in *Isis Unveiled*. Various reports of travelers and scholars point to the existence of secret cities located in various parts of the Americas.

> "He (Dr. Tschuddi), as well as Prescott and other writers, informs us that the Indians to this day perserve their ancient traditions and sacerdotal caste, and obey implicitly the orders of rulers chosen among themselves, while at the same time nominally Catholics and usually subject to the Peruvian authorities. Magical ceremonies practiced by their forefathers still prevail among them, and magical phenomena occur. So persistent are they in their loyalty to the past, that it seems impossible but that they should be in relations with some central source of authority which constantly sup-

---

Encyclopaedia Britannica, Atahualpa.

ports and strengthens their faith, keeping it alive. May it not be that the sources of his undying faith lie in this mysterious city, with which they are in secret communication? Or must we think that all of the above is again but a 'curious coincidence?'

The story of this mysterious city was told to Stephens by a Spanish Padre in 1838-39. The priest swore to him that he had seen it with his own eyes, and gave Stephens the following details, which the traveller firmly believed to be true. 'The Padre of the little village near the ruins of Santa Cruz del Quichè, had heard of the unknown city at the village of Chajul ... He was then young, and climbed with much labor to the naked summit of the topmost ridge of the sierra of the Cordillera. When arrived at a height of ten or twelve thousand feet, he looked over an immense plain extending to Yucatan and the Gulf of Mexico, and saw, at a great distance, a large city spread over a great space, and with turrets white and glittering in the sun. Tradition says that no white man has ever reached this city; that the inhabitants speak the Maya language, know that strangers have conquered their whole land, and murder any white men who attempts to enter their territory. . . . They have no coin; no horses, cattle, mules, or other domestic animals except fowls, and the cocks they keep underground to prevent their crowing being heard."

The report of another person is transmitted in the same portion of *Isis Unveiled*:

"He had travelled in his capacity of a *converted* native missionary, and had been at Santa Cruz, and, as he solemnly affirmed had been also to see some of his people by a 'subterranean passage' leading into the mysterious city. — Besides, we know of two other cities utterly unknown to European travellers; not that the inhabitants particularly desire to hide themselves; for people from Buddhistic countries come occasionally to visit them. But their towns are not set down on the European or Asiatic maps, and, on account of the too zealous and enterprising Christian missionaries, and perhaps for more mysterious reasons of their own, the few natives of other countries who are aware of the existence of these two cities never mention them. Nature has provided strange nooks and hiding places for her favorites; and unfortunately it is but far away from, so-called civilized countries that man is free to worship the Deity in the way that his fathers did." (*Isis Unveiled*, pp. 547-48, Vol. 1).

The absence of "coin" which prevails in the Central American city described above also prevails in Eldorado. The site which is surrounded by mountains "ten or twelve thousand feet" high resembles the "immense horizon, rimmed by inaccessible mountains" which is mentioned in *Candide*. Voltaire seems to have known the existence of secret American cities as he knew the existence of Petra, Lebanese towers, initiation rites, and Martian moons. The spiritual essence of Eldorado — a realm which is equated with "Innocence" and "bliss" — points to one of the "strange nooks and hiding-places" far removed from so-called civilization where "man is free to worship the Deity in the way that his fathers did."

The mythical appearance of Eldorado is a masterful combination of allegory and objective fact. The immaterial quality of the country where nothing lacks is stressed by its King:

> " 'Mon pays est peu de chose.' " (Ch. XVIII, p. 195).

> (" 'My country is very little.' ")

Literal translation of the French words "peu de chose" points to the absence of "things" or matter. The same spiritual essence is virtually defined by the indescribable construction material of the portal of the royal palace:

> "The portal was two hundred and twenty feet high and one hudred feet wide; it was impossibe to express what the construction material of it was. One sees well enough what a prodigious superiority it must have had over those pebbles and that sand which we name *gold* and *precious stones.*" (Ch. XVIII, p. 193).

Social symbolism is present. Negotiable gold and precious stones do not constitute the "cement" which holds together the community of Eldorado. The comparative observation of Candide which has validity on many planes is pertinent to the area of Western materialism: "This country is worth more than Westphalia."

The mixture of pebbles or rocks and sand which is absent from the superior architecture may well be read as "cement" or mortar. The latter detail further tends to suggest tangible South American architectures in which mortar was not used. Such are the ruins of Machu-Pichu — a city officially discovered in 1911 by Hiram Bingham.

> "Armies of masons built these walls, God knows how many centuries ago. They have cut and transported the stones themselves without the help of the wheel, of steel, or iron. Even greater multitudes of laborers have carried tons of arable land, probably taken from the valley, to create a productive soil which is still fertile in our days.
>
> ---
>
> Not one block of masonry is like another. Each one was cut with the design of having it occupy a precise space, with bizarre angles and meticulously made projections so that it might fit into its neighbors, as do the different pieces of a puzzle.
>
> The blocks of stone were cut carefully and so skillfully wedged that mortar was not needed." (Harland Manchester, *Voyages autour du monde,* Sélection du Reader's Digest, Paris-Montréal, 1968).

The size of the portal described in *Candide* is another suggestion of actual material structures of gigantic dimension remains of which have been found all over the world. Voltaire and Mme Blavatsky seem to have in mind the same cyclopean monuments of the archaic past.

"The Druidical circles, the Dolmen, the Temples of India, Egypt and Greece, the Towers and the 127 towns in Europe which were found "Cyclopean in origin" by the French Institute, are all the work of initiated Priest-Architects, the descendants of those primarily taught by the 'sons of God,' justly called 'The Builders.' This is what appreciative posterity says of those descendants.
'They used neither mortar nor cement, nor steel nor iron to cut the stones with; and yet they were so artfully wrought that in many places the joints are not seen, though many of the stones, as in Peru, are 18 ft. thick, and in the walls of the fortress of Cuzco there are stones of a still greater size.'" (Acosta, vi, 14). (*The Secret Doctrine,* p. 209 fn., Vol. I).

The ancient structures of Peru — which are relevant to *Candide* — bear a striking resemblance to monuments which have been found in various parts of the world, notably on Easter Island. "Identical glyphs, numbers and esoteric symbols are found in Egypt, Peru, Mexico, Easter Island, Indian, Chaldea, and Central Asia."* The exoteric architecture and the exoteric geography of *Candide* may be linked to a land mass overlapping a segment of ancient Lemuria.

" — our modern geologists are now being driven into admitting the evident existence of submerged continents. But to confess their presence is not to accept that there were men on them during the early geological periods — ay, men and civilized nations, not Paleolithic savages only; who, under the guidance of their *divine* Rulers, built large cities, cultivated arts and sciences, and knew astronomy, architecture and mathematics to perfection. This primeval civilization did not, as one may think, immediately follow their physiological transformation. Between the final evolution and the first city built, many hundred thousands of years had passed. Yet, we find the Lemurians in their sixth-sub-race building their first rock-cities out of stone and lava. One of such great cities of primitive structure was built entirely of lava, some thirty miles west from where Easter Island now stretches its narrow piece of sterile ground, and was entirely destroyed by a series of volcanic eruptions. The oldest remains of Cyclopean buildings were all the handiwork of the Lemurians of the last sub-races; and an occultist shows, therefore, no wonder on learning that the stone relics found on the small piece of land called Easter Island by Captain Cook, are 'very much like the walls of the Temple of Pachacamac, or the Ruins of Tia-Huanuco in Peru,' (*The Countries of the World,* by Robert Brown, Vol. 4, p. 43); 'and that they are in the CYCLOPEAN STYLE.'" (*The Secret Doctrine,* pp. 316-17, Vol. II).

The general picture of men — belonging to "civilized nations" — who, "under the guidance of their divine Rulers, built large cities, cultivated arts and sciences, and knew astronomy, architecture and mathematics

---

The Secret Doctrine, p. 323, Vol. I.

293

to perfection" clearly resembles the Voltairian presentation of Eldorado.

Esoteric "cities" frequently represent *doctrines* transmitted by "masons" or "builders."* The abundance of "good engineers" which is noted at the end of Chapter XVIII is equally meaningful on the level of doctrinal and cyclopean "construction." The genius of some "engineers" is not restricted to the immaterial plane which we tend to equate with baseless fancy. The fusion of Spirit and Matter which is effected through the medium of Eldorado is the splendid illustration of a startling fact. The heights of allegory which we regard as remote from our plane of "real life" have multiple, tangible reflections among and around ourselves.

The symbolic portal of the royal palace — the threshhold to spirituality — is a Time-Space compound of complex significance which will again be studied in chapters devoted to numbers and Prophecy. The esoteric vista afforded by Eldorado involves a massive portion of the globe and a dizzying span of centuries. The same suggestion of planetary perspective and lengthy time cycles forms the veiled background of the "fall" of the allegorical sailor of Chapter V. The veiled presence of Atlantis which is introduced at an early stage of *Candide* has a prolongation in "the islands" which appear at the end of the story. The Lemurian "cradle of sexual mankind"** — Batavia, the birthplace of the wicked sailor — is also mentioned in the final chapter. Voltaire seems to use Peru as a dual "missing link" to the submerged continents of Atlantis and Lemuria. Peru is also connected with the Universal Doctrine which produced their impressive civilizations. Chapter XVIII of Candide is the apex of a concealed Time-Space pyramidal structure the transparency of which dominates the entire story.

The return to the source of Being — or glimpse of Eldorado — which is granted to Man in Search of Truth is accompanied by an interesting phenomenon. Cacambo — the inferior — becomes the superior of his master. The bilingual valet or esoteric "amphibian" has an obvious advantage over Candide. The spiritual component represented by the "servant" naturally becomes dominant in the spiritual setting of Eldorado. The doubt which assails every thinking Western man — a feeling exoterically personified by Cacambo — gains ascendency in spiritual regions where the dividing line between Reality and Illusion must be questioned at every turn. The instinctual and primitive drive which is dormant in every "civilized" being — and which is not all bestial — logically asserts itself. The symbolic inversion of roles between Pagan servant and "Westphalian" master is the natural result of accession to lofty planes of consciousness. All that which is repressed — if not suppressed —

Ibid., pp. 795-96, Vol. II.
**The Secret Doctrine*, pp. 679-680, Vol. II.

in the average Western man finds expression and fulfillment. The meaningful inversion of "poles" is reported as follows:

"Candide ne jouait plus que le second personnge, et accompagnait son valet." (Ch. XVIII, p. 191).

("Candide was no longer playing more than the secondary part, and accompanied his valet.")

The word "accompanied" — "accompagnait" — was probably calculated to suggest the esoteric concept of "companion" or "student" or *chela* which must be distinguished from the concept of the *perfect Initiate*. The esoteric status of Candide is clearly that of a student.

Candide and Cacambo decide to return to Europe where the wealth acquired in Eldorado will surpass the riches of Kings. Scorning the spiritual values which prevail in the country where material gold is viewed as dirt, they wish to carry their treasure where it will set them apart from less fortunate men. Dazzled by negotiable metal and stones, blind to the wealth of True Being, seduced by the divisive vanity of Maya, they toy with thoughts of realms they may be able to purchase and turn their backs on the unrecognized Kingdom of Heaven. Little more can be expected from average products of "Westphalian" civilization.

A brief spiritual experience cannot undo the conditioning of a lifetime. Logically enough it is Candide — the "Westphalian" — who instigates the departure.

Extraordinary measures are required to leave the land of Eldorado. Having arrived in that country "by miracle," Candide and Cacambo cannot expect to depart in like manner. They are informed by the King that it is impossible to travel upstream, a fact which identifies the happy region as "the Source" on the exoteric plane itself. An ingenious machine designed and constructed by local "engineers" serves to transport the visitors beyond the impassible mountains which protect Eldorado. Voltaire may have wished to allude to the flying-machines which are believed to have been built by the Atlanteans.* He may have wished to refer to the art of levitation.

The treasure acquired in Eldorado by Candide and Cacambo is almost entirely lost at an early stage of the return trip to Europe. Various obstacles claim all but two of the red sheep laden with gold and precious stones:

"The first day of our two travellers was rather pleasant. They were heartened by the idea of seeing themselves owners of more treasures than Asia,

---

*The Secret Doctrine, pp. 426-28, Vol. II.

Europe, and Africa could all contain. Candide, filled with joy, wrote the name of Cunégonde on trees. On the second day, two of their sheep went down in swamps and sank there with their loads; two other sheep died from fatigue a few days later; seven or eight later died of hunger in a desert; others fell into precipices at the end of a few days. Finally, after one hundred days of travel, they had only two sheep left. Candide said to Cacambo: 'My friend, you see how perishable worldly goods are; nothing solid exists except virtue and the joy of seeing again Mlle Cunégonde.' " (Ch. XIX, p. 197).

The lesson which is learned sooner or later by all spiritual seekers is finally learned by Candide. Spiritual treasures cannot be retained in the absence of selfless motives. Spiritual wealth cannot survive stagnation or "swamps." It cannot co-exist with "weakness" or "fatigue." It is bound to die in the absence of proper nourishment — in a symbolic "desert" or wilderness. It is exposed to base impulses or fatal gravity — "precipices". It must have the "strength" or "virtue" necessary to counter such forces.

Diminished as it is, the treasure is not entirely lost. Two sheep remain with their precious cargo which exceeds the total wealth of the King of Spain. Such an affluence is difficult to reconcile with the material capacity of two animals. The symbolic value of "treasures" is confirmed. It is also stressed by Candide himself: "Worldly goods are perishable." Nothing solid exists save spirituality. Spirituality has two requirements: seeing Mlle Cunégonde — unveiling Isis — and practicing virtue. Human fulfillment lies in the union of Knowledge and Ethics.

The apparent conflict between desire for wealth and dedication to Cunégonde is thoroughly dissolved on the esoteric plane. Spiritual treasures and love of Truth are inseparable from each other.

The departure from Eldorado is aptly followed by encounter with "slavery."

Slavery is indicted on multiple counts in the chapter entitled *The Negro of Surinam*. The inhuman treatment of blacks is added to the extermination of Indians which is mentioned in a preceding passage of *Candide*. Black slaves are oppressed physically, intellectually, and spiritually. The Negro of Surinam is mutilated. His prospects of education and self-improvement are nil. He has been enticed to forswear his native tribal faith.

The owner of the captive is Dutch and presumably Protestant. More than a chance connection exists between his ruthless exploitation of human misery and the faith to which his slaves are "converted." The depraved justification of slavery which is commonly based on the authority of the Old Testament is implicitly condemned. The same vile rationalization is rejected by theosophical writers.

"It is upon the Old Testament, which panders to all their passions, that they base their laws of conquest, annexation, and tyranny over races which they call 'inferior.'" (*The Key to Theosophy*, p. 38).

The slave has lost his left leg and his right hand. The story of his mutilation is related:

"'When we work in the sugar-mills and when the millstone catches our finger, our hand is cut off; when we want to run away, our leg is cut off: I found myself in both situations. It is at that price that you are eating sugar in Europe.'" (Ch. XIX, p. 198).

The mutilation of the Negro is more than a crime. It is a blunder. The reader is indirectly reminded of another slave-master who was a Pagan. Sétoc tried to maintain minimal standards of humane treatment. If nothing else the heathen was guided by pragmatic concern with productivity and mortal investments. The outstanding abilities of the slave Zadig eventually earned him the position of associate and friend of the master. No such hope can be entertained by the slave of a "Christian." The implied comparison does not flatter modern Western man from the standpoint of kindness or intelligence.

One may explain — if not justify — the dim prospects of the slave by his apparent lack of skills comparable to those of Zadig. It is suggested, however, that the tribal background may not have been worthless. The slave remembers the last words of his mother as she sold him to the whites. The sordid role played by the mother may not invalidate her belief:

"'— bless our fetishes, worship them always, they will make you live happy; —'" (Ch. XIX, p. 198).

The captive does not lack intelligence. His attempts at exegesis produce sound and devastating conclusions. Disturbing lights are cast on scriptural weaknesses and self-righteous cruelty. Even an ignorant slave can detect "Christian" absurdity in dogma and hypocrisy in practice:

"'The Dutch witch-doctors who converted me say every Sunday that we are all children born of Adam, white and black. I am no genealogist; but if those preachers speak truly, we are all cousins in the first degree. Well, you must admit that one cannot treat one's relatives more horribly.'" (Ch. XIX, p. 198).

The "naive" lament of the slave is an edifying commentary on the literal interpretation of the Old Testament. The unnatural genealogy of the "first family" is candidly — if indirectly — exposed, the question of who married whom having always been an intriguing one. The uneducated black man seems to sense that biblical stories should be read in critical and symbolic light. His findings are identical to the view of occultists:

> "Without the esoteric explanation, the 'Old Testament' becomes an absurd jumble of meaningless tales — nay, worse than that, it must rank high with *immoral* books." (*Isis Unveiled*, p. 413, fn., Vol. II).

A conclusion of the slave has particular interest. If Dutch ministers are to be believed — a provocative thought in itself — "we are all children of Adam." The traditional dogma of monogenetic origin of Man is under scrutiny. The same dogma is rejected by occultists. The monogenetic theory of Professor A. Lefèvre is endorsed by Mme Blavatsky in the following text:

> " 'Does man descend from one single *couple* or from *several groups* — monogenism or polygenism? As far as one can venture to pronounce on what in the absence of witnesses (?) will never be known (?), the second hypothesis is far the most probable.' " (A. Lefèvre, *Philosophy*, p. 498, quoted in *The Secret Doctrine*, p. 169, Vol. II).

> " — the Secret Doctrine claims for man, (1) a polygenetic origin, (2) A variety of modes of procreation before humanity fell into the ordinary method of generation — " (*The Secret Doctrine*, p. 168).

The slave of Surinam is the semi-conscious interpreter of speculations on human origin. The same weighty matter and its corollary of familiar ties may have been used by Voltaire to suggest a certain "family likeness" between the upstart mythology of the Old Testament and its more ancient relatives:

> "Disfigured as the Old Testament is, yet in its symbolism is preserved enough of the original in its principal features to show the family likeness to the cosmogonies of older nations than the Jews." (*Isis Unveiled*, p. 265, Vol. 2).

The site of Chapter XIX belongs to a region where African occult traditions continue to survive.

> "According to the accounts of many travelers the negro women of Dutch Guiana, the Obeah women, excel in taming very large snakes called Amoditas or papa; they make them descend from the trees, follow and obey them by merely speaking to them." (J.C. Stedman, *Voyage in Surinam*, quoted in *Isis Unveiled*, p. 383, Vol. 1).

The Negro of Surinam probably lost a great deal through conversion to Christianity. Having abandoned a fund of ancestral tradition rich in occult awareness and power, he has received in exchange an obscure, useless, and tyrannical scriptural heritage.

Physical enslavement is manifest in the mutilation of two limbs which has been endured by the black man. The Negro of Surinam has lost his left leg and his right hand. Spiritual bondage is also suggested by the identity of limbs amputated. As was previously noted, legs and feet are commonly used by esoteric writers to symbolize physical and mental attachment to earth or a state of limited spirituality. Vigny once compared every "energetic" — spiritually oriented — man to the God Terme, a Roman deity usually represented without legs or feet.* The slave of Surinam is allowed to retain one lower limb: enough inferior support to remain in triple submission to earth, flesh, and master. He is denied the use of superior spiritual faculties commonly represented by the right hand. The occult concepts of "right" and "left-hand" magic — white and black magic respectively — shed sinister light on the spiritual effect of "right-hand" amputation. The slave is restricted to inferior forms of magic representing the less-than-golden spirituality of the Judaeo-Christian West. A vicious logic is reflected by the double mutilation. The welcome relief of death can come only through suicide. True life is inaccessible materially and otherwise.

The selective cruelty of the slave-master is comparable to corresponding traits of the "Westphalian Lord" which are emulated by "Bulgarian" subordinates. Mr. Vanderdendur — a worthy Protestant subdelegate of Jehovah — does not chastise half-heartedly or at random. His wrath tends to take the form of permanent and specific disability. The name of the slave-owner which suggests callousness — "dureté" — brings to mind the pathological harshness of the Old Testament.

Pangloss would not fail to note a cause-effect relationship were he present at this stage of the story. The genocide of Indians previously reported is the cause of the slavery of the blacks. So thorough was the extermination of American natives by the Spaniards that other sources of slave-labor had to be exploited. The spoliating, murdering "pox" which controls two hemispheres is felt in a third continent: Africa. No part of the world seems immune to the bane.

The spiritual blindness which is inseparable from the "pox" is an important element of the chapter. The sight of the slave fills Candide with compassion, a fact suggesting that the hero may yet fulfill his superior destiny. But the young man fails to perceive any similarity between his own situation and the plight of the mutilated man. The captive has been sold for a paltry sum of money paid to his parents.

---

*Alfred de Vigny, *La Maison du berger*.

Candide has forsaken the country where nothing lacks for vain gratification and material gain. In the light of spiritual values the ten Patagonian coins received for the slave and the gold-laden train of llamas come to like nothingness. A good deal of Voltairian "gardening" remains to be done before certain aspects of Truth are grasped. The selfless insight of compassion which is evidenced by the tears of Candide viewing the slave remains unmatched by corresponding insight regarding the Self-Analytical reason, the alleged foundation of Western thought, is itself impaired by lack of spiritual vision.

Mr. Vanderdendur suffers from the same disease. The greed which causes him to condone the multilation of slaves and to be blind to his own interests eventually prompts him to steal from Candide. The same greed causes his death.

The money-minded parents of the negro are infected by the same cupidity. The last homily of the mother to her son is as follows:

> " ' — you have the honor of being the slave of our lords the whites, and you thereby make the fortune of your father and mother.' " (Ch. XIX, p. 198).

The transaction has indeed "made the fortune" of the sellers who bear more than chance resemblance to Judas. The quality of Karma generated by their action is not enviable. But nothing can resist the powerful magic of Money.

The arrival of the hero in Dutch Guiana is a symbolic return to planes of low vision and crass materialism. The majority of men are shown to be blind builders of their own destinies. Varying degrees of submission to false values prevail. The Negro of Surinam is but one slave among several others.

Old insights are confirmed during the return crossing to Europe. Once again the "passengers" of the vessel of life swap tragic stories which are the stories of their own existence. Human passage on earth is judged agonizing. Optimism cannot be maintained without lunacy or transcendental vision. Candide remembers a statement of the old woman:

> " — there was no one on the ship who had not experienced very great misfortunes." (Ch. XIX, p. 201).

Also remembered are beliefs of the departed Pangloss:

> "He thought about Pangloss in connection with each adventure reported to him. 'That Pangloss,' he said, 'would have a difficult time supporting his system. I sure would like him to be here.' " (Ch. XIX, p. 201).

The preceptor, if present, would agree with certain findings of his pupil. All cannot be said to be well within the limited vista of terrestrial events. The overall perspective of cosmic design can alone justify the axiom: All is Well. ALL must be considered to vindicate Pangloss. The manifest universe reflecting a nadir of cyclic evolution is indeed "the best of possible worlds" — for a nadir of cyclic evolution. Which means a sad world — "in the opinion of "good company."

Some appearance of justice attends the undoing of Mr. Vandenderdur. The slave-shark and general swindler dies in a naval battle which is witnessed by Candide and a new friend Martin. But many innocent passengers are lost in the disaster which ends the life of the wicked man.

> " 'You see,' said Candide to Martin, 'that crime is punished sometimes; that wretched Dutch owner had the fate which he deserved.' — 'Yes,' said Martin, 'but was it necessary that the passengers who were on his ship perish also? God has punished that rogue, the devil drowned the others.' " (Ch. XX, p. 204).

No Jesrad is on hand to shed light on the unanswerable question: Why the death of the guiltless? The inscrutable essence of Karma which is generally dramatized in Voltairian texts by an abrupt break — or silence — is reaffirmed by an interruption:

> " 'Do you believe, said Candide, 'that men have always slaughtered one another as they do today? that they have always been liars, traitors, devious, treacherous, ingrates, bandits, weak, flightly cowardly, envious, greedy, slanderous. debauched. fanatical, hypocritical and dumb?' — 'Do you believe,' said Martin, 'that hawks have always eaten pigeons when they found some?' — 'Yes, certainly,' said Candide. — 'Well,' said Martin, 'if hawks have always had the same character, why do you want men to have changed theirs?' 'Oh!' said Candide, 'there is a considerable difference, for free will. . . .' As they were reasoning thus, they arrived in Bordeaux.' " (Ch. XXI, p. 206).

The comparison between men and birds of prey does not favor human cannibals. The rapacity of hawks reflects animal instinct and necessity. Man is alleged to be more than an aggregate of bestial impulses. In spite of his vaunted superiority, the crowning glory of the Thomistic universe behaves no better than a carnivorous fiend. Human guilt is compounded by perverted use of superior faculties which men do possess.

Candide firmly believes that the "necessity" ruling hawks differs from the "necessity" ruling men. The young hero has not forgotten the teachings of Pangloss. The importance of free will is affirmed. As was previously shown in connection with the "Oreillons," the obscuration of free will can radically distort an otherwise valid creed. Martin — an intelligent and kind person — may be likened to the Jansenists who did not have "the same resources" or Karmic knowledge as Candide. The case

301

of the Oreillons is indeed brought up. Martin finds nothing extraordinary in the strange story concerning the ape-men. The carrier of incomplete knowledge views absurdity as the sole consistent law of the Universe. If the Creation serves any purpose at all — a doubtful proposition to the friend of Candide — it must be to drive mankind to madness and distraction.

The theme of cosmic "necessity" or evolution is introduced into the dialogue. The reference to hawks and pigeons is rich in symbolic meaning. The hawk — which is commonly associated with Horus, the solar god of Ancient Egypt* — is connected with evolutionary cycles.** The poles are frequently represented as two "serpents with heads of hawks, one at each end."*** The pigeon or dove is a widely known symbol of the Holy Spirit. The eternal war between hawks and pigeons reflects the evolutionary interplay of "necessity" — related matter and spirit. It is interesting to note that the widely known Latin-American author, Ruben Darío, uses the same symbolism of hawk and dove in a poem entitled *Anankê* ("Necessity")

The polar symbolism of the hawk is connected with another element of occult lore. The occasional tilting of the axis of earth is believed to cause major geological changes. Such changes are mentioned by *Candide*:

> "'By the way,' said Candide, 'do you think that the earth was a sea originally, as is stated in that big book which belongs to the captain of the ship?'" (Ch. XXI, p. 206).

The esoteric reader is likely to meditate on the identity of the "captain" of the ship. The same reader is bound to relish the "à propos" of the question.

The spirited dialogue prolongs the veiled foundation of cosmogenesis which underlies preceding chapters of the story. The occult view of anthropogenesis is suggested by reference to the ape-men and by speculation on the perfectibility of mankind. The evolution of Man is logically connected with the evolution of his planet.

A major question seems to remain unanswered. Were men ever different from what they have become? Will they ever progress beyond their current wretched state? Such matters are almost impossible to consider in a world dominated by Jehovic figures, Inquisitors, Dutch-slave owners and Jesuitic barons. Only one certainty is accessible to the average person: Mankind in general and the "Westphalian" sugment of mankind in

*The Secret Doctrine, p. 366, Vol. I.
**Ibid., p. 359, Vol. I.
***Ibid., p. 360fn., Vol. II.

particular will long retain sordid traits. Karmic knowledge will have to be common knowledge before significant improvement takes place. Earth will have to be "another earth" before evil gradually fades away. Until that time humanity will remain subject to Mayavic aberrations which are "necessary" companions of deep materiality. In the words of François Villon:

"Nécessité fait gens méprendre
Et faim saillir le loup du bois."
(*Le Testament*, **XXI**).

("Necessity causes men to err
And the wolf to come out of the wood.")

Martin regards the drowning of Mr. Vanderdendur as a manifestation of Divine Justice. The character of the departed slave-owner tends to lend substance to the interpretation. But the death of other passengers is erroneously explained. God has punished a wicked man. The devil killed the innocent. Such a view of the supernatural division of labor — and belief in the supernatural itself — are ceaselessly challenged by theosophical writers as they are challenged by Voltaire.

Theologians regard occult power as their private stock in trade and oppose distribution of competitive brands. "Miracles" are credited to their personal "Vice-God." Other wonders are traced to the devil. The questions of supernatural happenings and of divine or guilty association elicit the following comment from Mme Blavatsky:

"Since the materialists deny the phenomena without investigation, and since the theologians in admitting them offer us the poor choice of two palpable absurdities — the Devil and miracles — we can lose little by applying to the theurgists, and they may actually help us to throw a great light upon a very dark subject." (*Isis Unveiled*, pp. 2-3, Vol. 2).

The matter of inextinguishable lamps is a case in point:

"Taking no account of exaggerations, and putting aside as mere unsupported negation the affirmation by modern science of the impossibility of such lamps, we would ask whether, in case these inextinguishable fires are found to have really existed in the ages of 'miracles,' the lamps burning at Christian shrines and those of Jupiter, Minerva, and other Pagan deities, ought to be differently regarded. According to certain theologians, it would appear that the former (for Christianity also claims such lamps), have burned by a *divine*, miraculous power, and that the light of the latter, made by 'heathen' art, was supported by the wiles of the devil." (*Isis Unveiled*, p. 277, Vol. 1).

Martin uses the Devil as the convenient explanation of a mystery and as a convenient scapegoat. His reasoning is typical of persons who lack the "resources" of Panglossian teachings. The dual theogony of Martin illustrates a misconception which is viewed in the same light by Voltaire and by Mme Blavatsky. As was previously noted, Satan is one victim of the overall degradation of ancient truth. The "fallen angel" is a product of the theological "fall" from the once universal Pantheistic philosophy into sectarian anthropomorphic creeds.

> "Satan never assumed an anthropomorphic, individualized shape, until the creation by man, of a 'one *living* personal god,' had been accomplished; and then merely as a matter of prime necessity. A screen was needed: a scape-goat to explain the cruelty, blunders, and but too-evident injustice, perpetrated by him for whom absolute perfection, mercy, and goodness were claimed. This was the first Karmic effect of abandoning a philosophical and logical Pantheism, to build, as a prop for lazy man, 'a merciful father in Heaven,' whose daily and hourly actions as *Natura naturans,* the 'comely mother but stone cold,' belie the assumption. This led to the primal twins, Osiris-Typhon, Ormazd-Ahriman, and finally Cain-Abel and the tutti-quanti of contraries." (*The Secret Doctrine,* p. 412, Vol. I).

The misconceptions of Martin can easily be traced to his cultural and spiritual background. Martin is first introduced as a rare kind of person: a scholar and a good man. The new friend of Candide has incurred the wrath — and heretical labels — of the preachers of Surinam, a fact suggestive of intellectual and spiritual distinction. The alleged Socinian is actually a disciple of Manes. His general outlook implies independence from dogma, a critical attitude toward scriptural texts, and an eclectic approach to knowledge. The Socinian "heresy" rejects orthodox concepts of original sin, the Trinity, and grace. Manichean belief in principles of good and evil needs relatively little enrichment to become Karmic belief. Manichean philosophy bears striking resemblance to the Secret Doctrine particularly where the meaning of Buddha and/or Christ is concerned.[*] Martin tends to see the triumph of evil in every aspect of human endeavor. The fact is easily explained by his personal experience of injustice and by the general state of human affairs. Martin is therefore unable to agree with Panglossian optimism. But he is not unwilling to recognize the existence of Good which is stubbornly proclaimed by Candide. Martin is a typical representative of Western doubt who will believe nothing without conclusive proof. Such honest skepticism is mentally healthy in the benighted realm of "Westphalia."

The first appearance of Martin in the story closely follows the separation of Candide and Cacambo. The latter event itself coincides with the

[*]*Isis Unveiled,* p. 286, Vol. II.

return of the title character to Europe. The cultural backgrounds represented by the servant and the scholar; the timing of their exit and entrance seem significant. The dominance of Cacambo which was a logical reflection of the stay in Eldorado subsides as Candide reenters the non-Pagan world. Western skepticism personified — Martin — regains ascendency. Man in Search of Truth — Candide — is the semiconscious carrier of two kinds of doubt: primitive sensitivity and "civilized" puzzlement. Both men — or attitudes — will finally co-exist in relative harmony in the last chapter of *Candide*. But the "separated twins" of Truth-seeking Doubt remain distinct within the "Westphalian" scope of *Candide*. Not until the advent of a subsequent age — envisioned in *L'Ingénu* — will they meet and fuse with spectacular success.

The first contact of Candide with France is the occasion of gloomy thoughts. National institutions in general, Parisian mores in particular, reflect a full spectrum of frivolity, absurdity, greed, wretchedness, and ennui. Not one of the epithets previously and generously used to characterize mankind is found baseless. Men are indeed "liars, traitors, débauchés, hypocritical, dumb," and more. Happiness is sought by all but remains generally absent. The human comedy enacted by gamblers, critics, swindlers, and Tartuffes of various sorts suggests a parade of puppets whose strings are pulled by Maya. Vast amounts of energy and ingenuity are devoted to sterile and destructive pursuits. The wealth of human resources which is misused and squandered could radically improve the world if nobler goals were set. The vanity of it all is brought into sharp focus by mention of a dead actress. The departed priestess of illusion is somehow more alive and real than are her survivors.

Mlle Monime is generally acknowledged as the transparent representative of Adrienne Lecouvreur, a famous actress who was a contemporary of Voltaire. Her ignominious funeral aroused the indignation of numerous persons notably that of the author of *Candide*. Because of her profession, Adrienne Lecouvreur was denied Christian burial.

> "— she was buried all alone of her group at the corner of the rue de Bourgogne, which must have caused her extreme grief, for she thought very nobly." (Ch. XXII, p. 209).

Voltaire's dim view of the privilege of Christian burial — a view which may have been shared by Adrienne Lecouvreur — in no way diminishes his sense of outrage. The disgraceful treatment of the dead woman reflects discredit on the entire nation. But it carries the strange virtue of thought-provoking abuse. Enhanced by persecution itself, Mlle Monime discreetly yet perceptibly dominates the Chapter. Beauty, artistic skill, dedication, and lofty thought are remembered. The fervent tribute of Voltaire imparts immortality. Having exchausted itself against the mortal shell, evil is powerless against the triumphant spirit which lives on in reverent memory. The "living" portrayed in the same passage are not expected to leave such monuments in the minds of posterity. In the midst of life they are in death. Theirs is a spectral quality. What is life? What is death? What is reality? What is illusion? Such are the eternal questions which the reader is invited to ponder. Meditation on the subject brings home the "unreal" quality of mortal existence.

> "The worship of the Vedic *pitris,* is fast becoming the worship of the spiritual portion of mankind. It needs but the right perception of things objective to discover that the only world of reality is the subjective." (*Isis Unveiled,* p. 639, Vol. 2).

The theme of objective subjectivity is conveyed in like spirit through like imagery in Voltairian texts and in theosophical literature:

> " '— a sage who since that time had the misfortune of being hanged, taught me that all that is grand; those are shadows on a beautiful picture.' 'Your hanged man was making fools of people,' said Martin, your shadows are horrible stains.' It is the men who make the stains,' said Candide, 'and they cannot help it.' 'Then,' it is not their fault,' said Martin."

> "The existences belonging to every plane of being, up to the highest Dhyan-Chohans, are, in degree, of the nature of shadows cast by a magic lantern on a colourless screen; but all things are relatively real, for the cogniser is also a reflection, and the things cognised are therefore as real to him as himself." (*The Secret Doctrine,* p. 39, Vol. I).

The magic lantern of occult symbology has a counterpart in the *Recherche.* The same type of object is prominently featured at the beginning of the work. The corresponding occult "inversion" of "realities" — objective and subjective — may shed light on the meaning of Proustian "optics" and Proustian "inverts." The author himself raises the question of the kind of "looking-glass" which must be used to "read" certain texts. What kind of looking-glass? The enigma may soon be answered for Proust — and for galaxies of others — in a few simple words: The Secret Doctrine. Intuition. Or, in Voltairian language: "A small fund of philosophy." The conveyances of up there."

> "Recognition within oneself, by the reader of what the book states, is the proof of truth of the latter, and *vice versa,* at least to a certain extent, the difference between both texts being often attributable not to the author, but to the reader. Moreover, the book may be too learned, too obscure for the naive reader, and thus offer him only a blurred lens with which he will not be able to read. But other peculiarities (such as inver-

sion) may cause the reader to need to read in a certain way in order to read well. The author should not take offense, but on the contrary should allow the reader maximum freedom and say to him: 'Look yourself and find out if you see better with this glass, with that one, or with that other.'" (*A la Recherche du temps perdu*, p. 911, Vol. III).

Proustian "inverts" are guilty of the same "offense" for which Pangloss is blamed by Martin. The hanged man did "make fun of the world" — se moquait du monde." He saw no more in its physical aspect than the reverse and seamy side of a "fine picture." "Marcel" takes the same view of the phenomenal universe when he states that "the visible world — is not the real world."

Maya is the dominant theme of the portion of *Candide* which is devoted to Parisian society. The queen of Western capitals suffers from spiritual deprivation. The city is the jail-like scene of a frantic rat-race. Comparison is invited with the serene vistas of Pagan Eldorado, a state blessed with true Wealth and with the reality of the "fine picture."

Limited optimism is opposed to limited pessimism in the lively discussion between Candide and Martin. Agreement seems to be reached on an important point. The sins of mankind are partially absolved by both men. Human beings "cannot help" their condition, says Candide. The general state of affairs is therefore "not their fault," says Martin. The apparent accord veils a thorny comprehension gap. The statement of the young hero reflects Panglossian teachings on cyclic evolution. Human beings "cannot help" a condition which is the inevitable or "necessary" lot of Fifth Race mankind. The conclusion of Martin — who does not have the same "resources" as Candide — constitutes an error. Men obviously cannot help the supremacy of Universal Law. But a great deal of what happens is their "fault" or the karmic harvest of their own actions.

Martin is the unconscious spokesman of partial truths. His last retort lends itself to byzantine comment. The scholar's belief that human condition is not the "fault" of men is compatible with the occult view of the "fault" or "fall." It may therefore be said that Candide and Martin agree on the exoteric surface, that they disagree on the first level of esoteric reading — because of Martin's lack of Karmic knowledge —, and that they agree on a second level of esoteric reading where the occult significance of the "fault" or "fall" is restored. The comical prominence of dissent born of agreement illustrates certain difficulties of communication. Students of "Panglossian" systems find it hard to make themselves clear to "uninstructed" persons. The "handicap" represented by Knowledge is similar to the perception gap mentioned by Proust. The problem is "attributable not to the author but to the reader." — or "listener." Martin is not fully equipped to "read" the statements of his friend.

The intuitive component of the young hero — enriched by contact with Pangloss and by "commerce" with Truth — struggles with a stubborn remnant of intellectual skepticism. The discussion between Candide and Martin is a vivid dramatization of inner conflicts which face the Western Seeker of Truth.

The arrival of Candide in Paris is followed by a strange episode: the impersonation of Cunégonde staged by a sinister team. Lured by a forged letter reporting the presence of the ailing beloved in the capital, Candide rushes to the bedside of the sick woman. The young hero is informed that the condition of the patient requires avoidance of light and avoidance of speech. "Light kills her — she cannot speak." The double disability identifies the impostor as a false version of Truth. The Voltairian parable of the photophobic deceiver anticipates the substance of the following statement of Mme Blavatsky:

> "True philosophy and divine truth are convertible terms. A religion which dreads the light cannot be a religion based on either truth or philosophy — hence it must be false." (*Isis Unveiled*, p. 121, Vol. 2).

Necessity — as well as choice — condemns fraudulent religions to dishonest use of mystery. Having lost the key to occult knowledge which should be their legitimate raison d'être, the impostors have little to reveal and much to hide. They are doomed to eternal masquerades and face-saving evasions. The perpetuity of the Church demands a protective veil of darkness and silence. The self-destructing potential of concealed ignorance is implicitly opposed to the explosive potential of genuine veiled knowledge.

The criminals have understandable designs on the spiritual "treasure" brought from Eldorado. A respectable quantity of gold and diamonds is extorted from Candide. Written communications of the authentic Cunégonde have the understandable interest of the Abbé Périgourdin. It is observed by the priest that the beloved of the young hero has a great deal of "wit" and writes "charming letters." Candide confesses that he has never "received" such messages. The abbot takes immediate steps to send the fraudulent "scriptures" which bring the seeker of Truth under his control. The coveted combination of "treasures" and "letters" from Truth tends to suggest the value of occult and esoteric literature. The allegorical representative of mankind has not yet "received" any such writings. The representative of the Church is prompt to offer less inspiring and less enlightening substitutes.

Voltaire once more denounces the impersonation of Truth by ecclesiastical looters — and losers — of occult knowledge. The attempted fraud is a re-enactment of the treachery and deceit of *Itobad*. The Abbé

Périgourdin and his partners in crime are no more successful than their predecessor. Their scheme is perceived and defeated.

A "faith" which must resort to such expedients is in poor condition. The feigned illness of the desperate impersonator is far more genuine than it is intended to be.

Not content to lie and extort, forces of phony truth must destroy their victims. Candide and Martin narrowly escape the horrors of a dungeon and the fate generally reserved to "heretics." The bizarre episode coincides with a wave of arrests of "strangers." The simultaneous timing of both events is no esoteric "coincidence." Doctrinal fraud and temporal abuse naturally go hand in hand.

The Parisian experience of Candide justifies somber thoughts. The "Westphalian" way of life leaves much to be desired. France, the symbolic and glamorous symbol of Western civilization, is in the grip of the powers of darkness.

There are nevertheless a few heartening gleams of light. Difficult as it is to perceive, the "fine picture" may be glimpsed beyond its sordid veil. The greatness of art survives in the cherished memory of a departed actress. The exertions of venomous critics pay unintended tribute to instinctively recognized, threatening brilliance. Lovers more or less consciously reach for a happier world. Gamblers yearn to rectify the "cruelties of fate," giving bizarre, yet irrefutable evidence of man's innate desire of justice. Persecution bares the Achilles' heel of corrupt bodies maintained by fear and steeped in fear. The frantic hunt for "strangers" exposes the desperate plight of Abuse living on borrowed time. The irrepressible search for Truth defies jail and faggot. The criminal impersonation of Truth is a tacit admission of its sovereignty. Horror is present in tragic abundance. But the nation "dances" and "sings," with a measure of the same grace which made Falide unique in *Zadig*. Misguided, grotesque, perverse as it often is, universal striving for fulfillment is inseparable from restless spirit and from the nostalgia of a divine homeland dimly remembered. Were proof needed of Voltaire's qualifications as a sage, his compassionate insight into the human comedy should suffice. Spirit glows warmly over his spectrum of the "fine picture." Maya herself has a share in divine reality. It is from her imperfect plane that pure aspiration must and does rise. The great ALL is perceptible in the midst of divisive carnal bondage. In essence if not in form, Voltaire might as well have written:

"Eva, j'aimerai tout dans les choses créees —"
(Alfred de Vigny, *La Maison du berger*).

("Eva, I shall love all among created things —")

One detail of the "fine picture" conveys glad tidings. Everyone is engaged in a frantic search for "pleasure." *Almost* no one finds happiness. A few persons do find it.

> " ' — I have seen Paris — it is chaotic, it is a rush in which everyone seeks pleasure, and in which almost no one finds it, at least as far as I can tell.' " (Ch. XXI, p. 205).

The "indiscernible community" — "a small number of inhabitants held in very low esteem" is alive, silently at work, preparing the day when "pleasure" — in its highest sense — will rebecome the birthright of all.

Candide is more "impatient" than ever "to see again the genuine Cunégonde." The devotion of the Seeker of Truth is undiminished by sad experience. It is as lasting as the wealth acquired in Eldorado. It can and does assist the bearer through the voyage of life. In spite of a vicious environment, in spite of the covetous designs of numerous thieves, the treasure somehow seems inexhaustible. One glimpse of the golden state of spirituality suffices to transform and transfigure an entire existence. Through the ebb and flow of spiritual relapse and gain, an all-important particle of the vision endures. The pupil of Pangloss, viewer of Eldorado, and lover of Truth will never renounce his quest. The same basic theme of Truth forever cherished once seen is exalted by esoteric writers . . . and by plain pure souls:

> "Can one have seen you and not see you again?"
> (*La Princesse de Babylone*, Ch. III).

> "Love that which will never be seen twice."
> (Alfred de Vigny, *La Maison du berger*).

> "When you've seen it, there's no going back."
> (*A former student of this writer.*)

Following a brief and disheartening glimpse of the English coast, Candide arrives in Venice where he has a long-awaited rendez-vous with Cunégonde. The expected meeting does not take place. The city of carnivals and illusory pleasure is the scene of another heartbreak for the young man. Maya greets him there also. "All is but illusion and calamity."

Paquette and Frère Giroflée belong to the general climate of unreality.

The girl is the tragic former sweetheart of Pangloss. Frère Giroflée is a florid, pseudo-monastic character and the current lover of Paquette. The strange couple conceals chronic misery behind a joint mask of ostentatious happiness.

310

Each character represents a human destiny ruined by perverted religion. The misfortunes of the girl began with her seduction by a monk who "had gone back to the source." The plight of Frère Giroflée is the result of forced commitment to monastic life. Paquette is as unhappy as a prostitute as the friar is wretched as a monk.

The venal sermons of the friar and the venal love of the girl point to the same basic prostitution of sacred values. The monk is subjected to the thievery of his superior. Paquette must surrender part of her earnings to various panders. The symbolic skirt of the prostitute has a symbolic counterpart in the robe which has been forced on her lover. The implied parallel between convent and brothel would not be out of place in the writings of Genêt. Tyranny, degraded values, and degraded creatures characterize both types of establishments.

Voltairian views of monasticism are well known. Convents are integral parts of the "infamous" which must be "crushed." The perfect spirituality of Eldorado is evidenced by one fact. No monastic brotherhood is needed or wanted there:

> " 'What! you have no monks who teach, who quarrel, who govern, who scheme and who send to the stake people who do not think as they do?' 'We would have to be insane,' said the elder." (Ch. XVIII, p. 193).

> " '— a monk in his capacity of monk, is good only to devour the substance of his fellow-countrymen.' "

> " 'I regard religious vows as a criminal assault against the country and against the self.' " (*L'Homme aux quarante écus, devenu pére, raisonne sur les moines*).

Similar condemnations abound in occult and esoteric writings.

Also voiced is the judgment of independent authors who cannot be accused of partiality to any form of religion. The following statement of Jacolliot — a person who had traveled extensively in the Orient — contrasts the monastic practices of East and West.

> "— this uncompromising enemy of priestcraft, monastic orders, and the clergy of every religion and every land — including Brahmans, lamas, and fakirs — is so struck with the contrast between the fact-supported cults of India and the empty pretence of Catholicism, that after describing the terrible self-tortures of the fakirs, in a burst of honest indignation, he thus gives vent to his feelings; 'Nevertheless, these fakirs, these mendicant Brahmans, have still something grand about them; when they flagellate themselves, when during the self-inflicted martyrdom the flesh is torn out by bits, the blood pours on the ground. But you (Catholic mendicants), what do you do today? You Gray Friars, Capuchins, Franciscans, who play at fakirs, with your knotted cords, your flints, your hair shirts, and your rose-water flagellations, your bare feet and your comical mor-

tifications — fanatics without faith, martyrs without tortures? Has not one the right to ask you, if it is to obey the law of God that you shut yourselves in behind thick walls, and thus escape the law of labor which weighs so heavily upon all other men? — Away, you are only beggars.' "
(*Isis Unveiled*, p. 585, Vol. 2).

The well-known hatred of Voltaire for monastic institutions is explained by the author himself on a socio-political basis. Monks and other members of the clergy are viewed as part of a tyrannical system cemented by "divine right." Not only do they "teach — quarrel, govern, and send to the stake people who do not think as they do." They also "devour the substance of their fellow-men." The money-madness of the Church is denounced in many Voltairian texts devoted to indulgences, dispensations, ecclesiastical taxes and other forms of financial vampirism. The traditional image of Voltaire is that of a pragmatist and pleasure-seeker. It is naturally opposed to the squandering of human resources and to mortification. It may be noted also that the mode of existence prevailing in the XVIIIth Century made the pursuit of suffering unnecessary for the average man. Life was "mortifying" enough to all but a lucky few, as *Candide* well shows. Martyrdom was readily available to the rare persons who craved it and to the many who did not. But the chief reason for Voltairian hatred of convents and related institutions probably lies in spiritual considerations which could not be exposed overtly at the time of writing.

Some types of "mortification" reflect a genuine spirituality stimulated by cults which are viewed by occultists as "fact-supported." The *Third Philosophical Letter* of Voltaire seems designed to encourage deep thought on the existence of such religions. The text is devoted to Quakers in general and to George Fox in particular. Reference is made to certain whippings which were apparently sought and savored by the recipients. The reader may conclude that Fox and his followers were all victims of "holy insanity" — to use approximately the words of Voltaire — without pondering the possible occult nature of the "disorder". But the reader may also compare the flagellations received by the Quaker with the kind of occult experimentation which made history in XVIIIth Century France and which is described in detail in *Isis Unveiled*.

The Voltairian report on George Fox is in part as follows:

"George Fox went, praising God, to the insane asylum, where one did not fail to carry out faithfully the verdict of the judge. Those who administered to him the punishment of the whip were quite surprised when he begged them to give him a few more lashes for the good of his soul. Those gentlemen did not fail to oblige; Fox had his double dose, for which he thanked them cordially. He began to preach to them; at first they laughed, then they listened; and, since enthusiasm is a contagious disease, several were persuaded, and those who had whipped him became his first disciples."

Mme Blavatsky reports as follows the activities of some "convulsionnaires."

"And now for the views of Dr. Figuier upon these remarkable and unquestionably historical phenomena. 'A Convulsionary bends back into an arc, her loins supported by the sharp of a peg,' quotes the learned author, from the *procès verbaux*. 'The pleasure that she begs for is to be pounded by a stone weighing fifty pounds, and suspended by a rope passing over a pulley fixed to he ceilling. The stone, being hoisted to its extreme height, falls with all its weight upon the patient's stomach, her back resting all the while on the sharp point of the peg. Montgeron and numerous other witnesses testified to the fact that neither the flesh nor the skin of the back were ever marked in the least, and that the girl, to show she suffered no pain whatever, kept crying out, 'Strike harder — harder!'

Jeanne Maulet, a girl of twenty, leaning with the back against a wall, received upon her stomach one hundred blows of a hammer weighing thirty pounds; the blows, administered by a very strong man, were so terrible that they shook the wall. To test the force of the blows, Montgeron tried them on the stone wall against which the girl was leaning. . . . He gets one of the instruments of the Jansenist healing, called the 'GRAND SECOURS.' 'At the twenty fifth blow,' he writes, 'the stone upon which I struck, which had been shaken by the preceding efforts, suddenly became loose and fell on the other side of the wall, making an aperture more than half a foot in size.' When the blows are struck with violence upon an iron drill held against the stomach of a Convulsionnaire (who, sometimes, is but a weak woman), 'it seems,' says Montgeron, 'as if it would penetrate through to the spine and rupture all the entrails under the force of the blows.' (vol. 1, p. 380) But, so far from that occurring the Convulsionnaire cries out, with an expression of perfect rapture in her face, 'Oh! how delightful! Oh!, that does me good! Courage, brother; strike twice as hard, if you can!' 'It now remains,' continues Dr. Figuier, 'to try to explain the strange phenomena which we have described.' " (*Isis Unveiled*, pp. 373-74, Vol. 1).

The "strange phenomena" in question are not regarded as great wonders by Adepts of magic, "especially in Siam and the East Indies, . . ." According to Mme Blavatsky such persons

"— are too familiar with the properties of the *akasa*, the mysterious life-fluid, to even regard the insensibility of the Convulsionnaires as a very great phenomenon. The astral fluid can be compressed about a person so as to form an elastic shell, absolutely non-penetrable by any physical object, however great the velocity with which it travels. In a word, this fluid can be made to equal and even excel in resisting-power, water and air." (*Isis Unveiled*, p. 379, Vol. I).

313

Akasic manipulation is often mentioned in literary texts and folklore. M. de Charlus frequents strange establishments where he receives merciless beatings. Courtial des Péreires has a similar weakness for the whip. The beautiful book of Gregorio López y Fuentes, *El Indio*, contains an Indian legend which is the story of a woman of bizarre or "contrary" temperament. The lady takes great pleasure from receiving blows which are never strong enough to suit her. The same person, when missing and feared drowned, is finally located — drowned — thirty leagues *upstream* from the site of her fall into a river. The active spirituality of the woman who "returns to the source" casts interesting light of her odd behavior.*

Such persons and characters as George Fox, M. de Charlus, and Courtial are usually diagnosed as "madmen." But the popular concept of insanity in modern "Westphalia" is as open to question as "the best of possible worlds" at the squalid bottom of an evolutionary curve. M. de Charlus and Courtial elude the probes of unaided psychiatry. They are powerful minds and live spirits. They pay the penalty incurred by persons who are ahead of their time.** Courtial has a head start of 35 years.

> "Qui n'a pas l'esprit de san age
> De son âge a tout le malheur."
> (*Letter of Voltaire* to Cideville, 1741).

> ("Whoever does not have the spirt of his era
> Of his era bears all the woe.")

The Western monastic blend of frustrated flesh and unsatisfied spirit is embodied in Frère Giroflée. The poverty, chastity, and asceticism which might be expected of him are his major phobias. Apparently convinced that "you live only once," and that nothing exists beyond matter, the monk is totally absorbed by the pleasures of food and sex. His sybaritic like-style is poles apart from the joyful rigors of live spirituality. The chubby, lecherous frair is unlikely to possess — or even conceive — those "clairvoyant powers" which depend "so much on the bodily prostration" of the practitioner.*** Such achievements as those of the "convulsionaires" are far beyond his grasp — unimpressive though they be. Frère Giroflée personifies a pathology of being which spares no spiritual faculty — however rudimentary it may be.

The primary grievance of esoteric writers against monastic life concerns the spiritual murder of persons committed to an allegedly spir-

*Ch. XIV.
**Death on the Installment Plan, pp. 328, Tr. Ralph Manheim.
***Isis Uneviled, p. 181, Vol. 1.

itual way of life. The famous novel of Diderot — *La Religieuse* — may some day be found to make sense in that unexpected light.

The misery which reigns in the convent is vividly described by Frère Giroflée:

> " 'Jealousy, discord, fury, inhabit the convent. It is true that I have preached a few bad sermons which brought me a little money, half of which is stolen from me by the prior; the rest of it is used by me to keep women; but, when I return to the monastery at night, I am ready to crush my head against the walls of the dormitory, and all my fellow-monks are likewise!" (Ch. XXIV, p. 222).

No direct comparison is made by Voltaire between the spiritual misery prevailing in Western convents and the spontaneous, joyful spirituality of heathenism. It is the task of the reader to bear in mind the free love of Knowledge and the natural togetherness of Man and Deity which reign in Pagan Eldorado. The general sense of the implied comparison comes close to the verdict of Jacolliot which is quoted by Mme Blavatsky.

Paquette and Frère Giroflée form a symbolic couple of Love and Knowledge debased by sick religion. Given a "fact-supported" doctrine; given a faith possessing the "lost key" to ancient Science, they might blossom spiritually. Such may be the reason why their names — which bring to mind two flowers — were chosen. *Paquette* resembles the French word "pâquerette" designating a small daisy which is a symbol of Easter or Resurrection.* Giroflée is the French equivalent of "stock."

The spiritual destitution of the couple seems beyond help. Paquette and Frère Giroflée receive from Candide a priceless gift which is part of the treasure brought from Eldorado. But the donation is unlikely to improve their prospects:

> "Candide gave two thousand piasters to Paquette and one thousand piasters to Frère Giroflée. 'I guarantee,' he said, 'that with that money they will be happy!' " — 'I don't believe that at all," said Martin: 'with those piasters you may make them still unhappier by far.' " (Ch. XXIV, pp. 222-23).

Victims of corrupt religion are apt to lose all sense of authentic value and to blindly squander spiritual opportunity.

A redeeming trait finally saves the grotesque and pathetic comple: willingness to break away from a wretched way of life. Frère Giroflée and Paquette eventually join the small community headed by Candide as the end of the story. The monk finds reasonable happiness as a useful carpenter. The possible allusion to Joseph does not suggest transcendental attainment. But the situation of the friar is improved. Paquette becomes proficient in the art of embroidery and contributes love-

A la Recherche du temps perdu, p. 126, Vol. I.

liness to the small establishment. Wasted manpower and undeveloped skill are allowed to produce. Most important of all, two human beings achieve a modest degree of self-knowledge and well-being. Little more can be expected for them in the spiritually blighted domain of "Westphalia."

The portrayal of Pococurante adds to the social cross-section contained in *Candide* the presence of the rich. As his name indicates, the Venetian lord has few or no cares. He has been spared the struggles and tragedies besetting other "passengers" of the vessel of life. Material wealth gives him security, leisure, and rare possessions. His palace is filled with priceless works of art and literature. But he derives little pleasure from his privileged status; only the dubious satisfaction of being chronically blasé. Intellectually and spiritually, the nobleman is poorer by far than one might expect him to be. Self-inflicted malnutrition prevails in the midst of superior substance. One field of excellence is open: self-gratification punctuated by reference to the first person:

"I like only that which suits my needs." (Ch. XXV, p. 255).

The rogues 'and victims' gallery depicted in preceding chapters of *Candide* is not unrelated to certain values. Even the corrupt sailor carousing on the ruins of Lisbon may some day make positive sense out of negative deeds. But the ego-gratifying vacuum cultivated and extrolled by its owner can only be sterile. Mind and spirit are closed to the teachings of commitment, experience, and recognized error. Systematic scorn is as damaging to its source as it is to its object.

Two complementary dormant treasures are present under unique conditions. One is human intelligence unimpeded by lack of time, wellbeing, or reference material. The other, an impressive esoteric cultural heritage, awaits exploration. One spark of spiritualized intellect would suffice to bring about a chain reaction of light were such a spark attainable. Vanity kills the crucial spark.

The requirements of esoteric study are listed in the chapter. Pococurante meets most of them.

The nobleman is aware of the reality of ecclesiastical thought-control:

"All over our Italy, people write only that which they do not think; those who inhabit the motherland of the Caesars and Anthonies dare not have one idea without the permission of a Jacobin friar." (Ch. XXV, p. 227).

Pococurante knows his classics. His critique of Homer and Milton is defensible. Homer is commented as follows:

" '—that endless repetition of fights which all resemble one another, those gods who always act to do nothing decisive in the end; that Helen who is the cause of the war and who is hardly a character of the play; that Troy which is besieged and not captured, all that caused me the most deadly boredom.' " (Ch. XXV, p. 255).

Milton does not fare much better:

" '— that obscure, bizarre, and disgusting poem, was scorned at birth; I now treat it as it was treated in its own homeland by the contemporaries. Besides, I say what I think, and care very little whether or not others think as I do.' Candide was distressed by those words; he respected Homer, he liked Milton a little." (Ch. XXV, p. 228).

Ability to think for oneself is proclaimed and demonstrated. Unlike the common herd of pre-conditioned "lettrés," Pococurante will neither salivate nor swoon upon hearing such magic words as *The Great Classics!*" There is virtue in such free thought, a virtue which is essential to esoteric reading. The nobleman is accordingly resistant to the formidable power of persuasion of critics. His freedom from such influence is a major asset, the critics either being blind or pretending to be.

One can easily speculate about possible results were Pococurante to ask himself a few simple questions and to establish a rapport between them. Could religious censorship and persecution similar to Italian thought-police be somehow related to the strange appearance of some texts? Did Homer and Milton find themselves compelled to cover their deep meaning? Did any truly great author ever write obscure, bizarre, and disgusting material for the sole sake of obscurity, bizarrerie and dirt?

Accurate perception remains isolated and therefore sterile. Unable to forswear the delights of contempt, Pococurante will not give esoteric writers the benefit of the doubt. He will continue to gloat over apparent shortcomings. He will remain "superior to everything he possesses." There lies the irony of his situation. The gifted nobleman will "possess" nothing. Po*cocu*rante will continue to be "cuckolded" — "cocu" — by his own vanity. He will continue to look blindly down on veiled versions of Universal Truth.*

The supper gathering Candide and six dethroned kings prolongs the illustration of Maya which dominates the European scene. Royalty fares little better than other actors of the drama of life. Transient glory, misery and make-believe characterize the assembly. The prominent themes of exile and masquerade; the substance and etymology of the word "car-

---

*Ramayana, source and origin of Homer's inspiration, *Isis Unveiled*, p. 278, Vol. II. Numerous quotations of Milton in *The Secret Doctrine*.

nival" point to "incarnation." The forced wanderings and imminent departures of royal characters suggest birth, death, and other vicissitudes of the voyage of life. Fall from exalted spheres evokes cyclic descent from spiritual planes to low regions of materiality. Life is a toilsome journey. Death in Venice — and elsewhere — is only one step on the rugged path.

Actively or passively — as usurpers or victims — all six kings have been involved in tragic intrigues. Esoteric study of each royal case history reveals a descending order of guilt and a rising order of preoccupation. The number of monarchs — six — suggests possible correspondence to six of the seven levels of consciousness from the lowest plane — the physical — to *Buddhi* — divine intuition, next to the highest.

The royal sequence may be summarized as follows: First and least scrupulous in Achmet who dethroned his brother, was subsequently dethroned himself, and who spends his retirement years in a seraglio. Lust for power and carnal lust are his chief interests in life. Next are Ivan and Charles Edouard who were cheated of their rights to the crown. While their pursuit of redress has involved countless innocents and caused abundant bloodshed, the initiative of their struggles can be traced to their respective dynasties. Extenuating circumstances are found in their cases. "Fate" has denied the claims of the fourth king who nevertheless bows to the decree of Providence. The fifth king lost his kingdom twice but remains serenely submitted to divine will. The sixth king has been forced to renounce elective royal status, retains no prestige or wealth and is in fact destitute. While his career seems to have been non-violent — a fact which sets him apart from his companions — he lacks any visible form of grandeur. Religious concern seems to be nil. The rising level of preoccupation noted among the first five kings seems to stop where Theodore begins.

The obsession of Achmet with thrones and harems is aggravated by blindness. The former king fails to realize that he is the most prominent and pathetic prisoner of the seraglio where he spends his golden years. Base appetites and lack of insight combine to designate him as the lowest possible plane of existence personified. Ivan and Charles Edouard view their past imprisonment honestly and realistically. But they do not perceive its continuation in their present plight. They remain prisoners of illusion. Some beginning of spiritual awareness exists in the next king under the passive form of resignation. Slight progress seems to mark the passage from each man to the next.

The story of the fifth king points to a significant rung of the spiritual scale:

"The fifth one said: 'I too am King of the Poles, I have lost my Kingdom twice; but Providence gave me another State in which I did more good than all the kings of the Sarmatians were ever able to do on the banks of the Vistula; I too resign myself to Providence, and I came to spend the carnival in Venice.'" (Ch. XXIV, p. 231).

The fifth king does not deplore his loss of earthly power. He shows active concern with the lot of others. Such traits clearly transcend the sterile personal regrets or blank indifference of his preceding colleagues. The ex-monarch is thankful for his God-given ability to "do good." The loss of his first kingdom seems to correspond to universal cyclic descent into materiality. The loss of the second kingdom may reflect subsequent estrangement from inferior planes of being. Having duly sojourned in the realm of Maya, having learned from the experience, the king has begun to accede to high spiritual spheres. Immaterial rewards have more than repaid him for the loss of his first and second earthly domains. The unspecified or "nameless" State — "un autre Etat" — conferred upon the fifth king by Providence — Karma — is irrelevant to terrestrial geography. The fifth "State" or plane of consciousness, *Manas*, is "the seat of intellect"* and the gateway to divine intuition in its higher aspect. Its role of important articulation is stressed by the "transition" of the second Polish King. It is also stressed in theosophical texts:

> " 'Follow the law of analogy' — the Masters teach. *Atma Buddhi* is dual and *Manas* is triple; inasmuch as the former has two aspects, and the letter three, *i.e.,* as a principle *per se*, which gravitates, in its higher aspect, to Atma-Buddhi, and follows, in its lower nature, *Kama* the seat of terrestrial and animal desires and passions.' " (*The Secret Doctrine* p. 254, Vol. II).

The next higher plane is that of *Buddhi* or *Buddhic Consciousness*. The essence of the sixth principle is best understood by "emphasizing the contrast between the laboriously acquired knowledge of the senses and mind (manas), and the intuitive omniscience of the Spiritual divine soul — Buddhi."** The latter distinction corresponds to the contrast which is made by Voltaire between lumbering "stagecoaches" and "the conveyances of up there."

The sixth King, a former sovereign of Corsica, seems to lack any trait — spiritual or other — likely to represent "intuitive omniscience" or anything divine.

> "It remained for the sixth monarch to speak: 'Gentlemen,' he said, 'I am not such a great lord as you; but after all, I have been king just

The Secret Doctrine, p. 378, Vol. II.
**The Secret Doctrine*, p. 279, Vol. II.

319

like another. I am Theodore, I was elected King of Corsica; I used to be called *Your Majesty,* and now I am hardly called *Sir.* I have had money and do not possess one coin; I have had two Secretaries of States, and I hardly have a valet; I have seen myself on a throne, and I have been in jail in London for a long time, on straw. I much fear being treated in like manner here, although I came as did your Majesties to spend the carnival in Venice." (Ch. XXVI, p. 232).

Theodore is mindful of the possibility of continued imprisonment. His awareness of Mayavic "jails" gives evidence of insight. His humilty is as genuine as his recognition of the "King" latent in every man. The exiled monarch has been "called" — élu" — or "elected." The religious connotation of the term points to mystical experience. The reduction of his title from "Your Majesty" to "barely Sir" reflects nearly total absorption of the Self into the Absolute or the "nameless" state. Destitution suggests liberation from materiality. The bed of straw brings to mind the biblical figure of Job which is fraught with meaning:

"The *Book of Job* is a complete representation of ancient initiation, and the trials which generally precede this grandest of all ceremonies." (*Isis Unveiled,* p. 494, Vol. 2).

Theodore does not mention the Deity or Providence. The Supreme Being is all the more conspicuous for the seeming absence. Grossly inadequate nomenclature yields to direct perception of Absolute Reality. "— the Initiates never use the epithet 'God' to designate the One and Secondless Principle in the Universe! —"* The *Ineffable Name,* prominently featured in occult writings, has powers which are accessible only to the enlightened few. The Corsican exile seems to be one such person.

The *ineffable* Name in the search for which so many kabalists — unacquainted with any Oriental or even European adept — vainly consume their knowledge and lives, dwells latent in the heart of every man." (*Isis Unveiled,* pp. 343-44, Vol. 2).

The King who once had two Secretaries of States and now barely claims one valet is symbolically removed from the plane of "satellites" and "servants." A spirituality of high order is suggested by the latter detail.

The presentation of Theodore is an excellent example of sudden "withdrawal" following several advances made to potential esoteric readers.

No great amount of imagination is required to surmise the possible meaning of the six kings. As was previously noted, the *exoteric* por-

---

Ibid., p. 555, Vol. II.

trayal of the first five royal exiles suggests a smoothly rising order of preoccupation. But the appearance of Theodore is calculated to discourage casual investigators. The ex-king corresponds exactly to the Western idea of pathetic "failure:" a man without money. A man who does not even try to conceal his loss of social prestige or wordly goods. In short, a welfare case. The reader is unlikely to connect the destitute ex-monarch with another royal beggar: Buddha. Several elements of esoteric algebra — "a small fund of philosophy" — must be known and applied to the text before the abyss separating material appearance from spiritual reality can be spanned. The warm-and-cold treatment given to new "contacts" by the Guermantes, the Cambremers, and "Legrandin" seems relevant to the royal assembly of Voltaire. The appearance of Theodore is as deceptive and "devoid of any expression of spirituality" as the exoteric "backside" of "Legrandin."

It may be noted briefly from the *Recherche* that "Legrandin" is very fond of a character named Theodore.*

Highest in the hierarchy of consciousness, the spiritual principle designated as *Atma* has no royal figure as a representative. Such an absence is symbolic of the removal of Atma from ordinary human attributes. It is noted in *Micromégas* that certain elements do not interpenetrate. They are connected with but distinct from lower levels of existence. Atma dwells far above the contingencies of incarnation. In the words of Mme Blavatsky, "Atma is no body, or shape, or anything."**

The ultimate plane is represented by the diamond given by Candide to Theodore. The stone has its origin in Eldorado. It is a particle of the universal spiritual treasure. The generous offering closes the cycle of individual progression. High attainment receives its legitimate reward from the long-lost and long-pursued common heritage. The reader is reminded of the "grain of sand" of Zadig. He is also reminded of the "poor" fisherman.

The inestimable worth of the gift is generally sensed — if not fully perceived. It is as impossible to evaluate instantly as the miraculous "catch" of the fisherman of *Zadig*:

> "The five kings listened to this speech with a noble compassion. Each of them gave twenty sequins to King Theodore to get clothes and shirts; Candide gave him a diamond worth two thousand sequins. 'Who can be,' said the five kings, 'this plain private citizen who is in a position to give one hundred times as much as each of us, and who does give it?'"
> (Ch. XXIV, p. 232).

---

*A la Recherche du temp perdu, p. 701, Vol. III.
**The Secret Doctrine, p. 245, Vol. I.

The final question is best answered in the light of the travels of Candide. The young hero carries the vision of a golden land unchartered by earthly maps. In spite of occasional weakness, he is and remains the lover of Truth, the man who "raised the veil." For the same reason he can give far more than may be reckoned in ordinary human terms. While other donors follow the scriptural injunction to clothe the naked, Candide alone can offer the supreme gift from the spiritual country "where nothing lacks." The fact that the compassionate hero may not fully realize the value of his gift confirms the validity of the precept: "Know Thyself!" which is specifically pertinent to Chapter XXVI. One may carry — and give — a spiritual treasure while remaining partially unaware of its worth:

> " 'There are, in any crowd,' thought Rivière, undistinguishable men, and who are prodigious messengers. And without knowing it themselves. Unless —" (Antoine de Saint-Exupéry, *Vol de Nuit*, Ch. IV).

The six Kings are personifications of six levels of consciousness. The highest principle — Atma — is significantly removed from the plane of incarnation. Correspondences are as follows:*

1.	Body (Sthula Sarira)	Achmet
2.	Prana (Life Essence)	Ivan
3.	Linga Sharira or Astral Body	Charles-Edouard
4.	Kama Rupa (Animal Soul)	First Polish King
5.	Human Soul, Mind (Manas)	Second Polish King
6.	Spiritual Soul (Buddhi)	Theodore
7.	Universal Spirit (Atma)	Diamond

The combination of numbers representing the value of gifts made to Theodore involves five donations of *20* sequins each. The diamond offered by Candide is worth 2000 sequins or *100* times more than the contribution of each king. The passage seems calculated to call attention to the numbers *2, 100* and *20* — "deux", "cent", "vingt." Voltaire may have wished to suggest the number which is stressed exoterically in *Micromégas* and in Chapter XVIII of Candide: *220*.

The "reverse side" of the "fine picture" sketched in the passages devoted to Paris is supplemented by the shadowy projection of Venice. Maya reigns in both cities. But Maya herself is inseparable from Spirit. The Parisian syndrome of frenzied nothingness veils an abundance of repressed and deflected spiritual yearning. Venice is similarly endowed. The litanies of Kings is exile suggest the exalted origin of Man. The diamond of Eldorado represents the source and destination of Being, the Alpha and Omega of the Great All and That which constitutes a link

---

*The Secret Doctrine. p. 596. Vol. II.

between them. The misguided yearning for greatness and pleasure which is evidenced by the political and sensuous ventures of Achmet shows a spark of tortured spirit to dwell on the very lowest plane of existence. The concerns of the other Kings reflect various modalities of the same Presence. Estranged as they are from their ethereal homeland, men do carry, in different amounts, a share of the universal heritage. In the midst of incarnate death they are in spiritual life.

The vertical section of Spirit which is suggested in the setting of Venice contracts with the horizontal, fresco-like description of Paris. But the common factor of more or less active spirituality weds into a cross-like pattern the Voltairian tale of two cities. The virtual image of the cross — a symbol of life and death, physical and spiritual, — "belongs" in the masterful presentation of the veiled yet real "fine picture." The esoteric conjunction of Paris and Venice transcends earthly Time and Space for those travelers who "drink" of the Spirit:

> " — all the travellers whom Candide met in the taverns which were on the way told him: 'We are going to Paris.' That general eagerness finally gave him the desire to see that capital; that did not represent too big a detour away from the road to Venice." (Ch. XXII, p. 207).

Candide, the lover of Truth, hoped to meet the beloved in Venice. Cunégonde has not arrived. But the young man has had "contact" with the septenary structure of the Self. The experience thus gained is necessary to probe the most commonplace mysteries of the septenary universe. The long-awaited reunion has been delayed. But the rendez-vous of Man and Truth in Venice has not been entirely missed.

A spectacular series of "rebirths" is recorded in Chapter XXVII. Candide is reunited with Pangloss and with the durable Jesuitic baron. Cacambo also reappears. The agencies of Maya and reincarnation are suggested with mock subtlety:

> " 'Is it a dream' said Candide;. 'Am I awake' Am I on that galley-slave-ship? Is that M. le baron whom I killed? Is that Master Pangloss whom I saw hanged?' " (Ch. XXVII, p. 235).

Pangloss and the baron have incurred the wrath of the authorities. The culprits are found by Candide toiling as galley-slaves. Unable to curb his homosexual tendencies, the baron has become involved with a young officer of the sultan's palace. Unable to control his romantic penchants, Pangloss has become involved with a beautiful woman. Sex — guilty knowledge — is a source of identical calamities for both men. But an important distinction is made by Pangloss. It is far less reprehensible "to place a bouquet back on the bosom of a woman" — and to take a long time doing it — than to be found stark naked with an icoglan.

323

The transgression of Pangloss is not only harmless but perfectly natural. Having as its goal the unveiling of the secrets of Life, and the "propagation of the species" it is the legitimate pursuit of Man. The perversion of corrupt ecclesiastical bodies is a crime against Nature and a crime against mankind. The pollution of society which is stressed at the beginning of *Candide* is indirectly called to attention once more.

The term used by Voltaire to designate the young officer of the sultan's household adds to the esoteric dimension of the passage. The vowel content of the rarely used word "*icoglan*" implicates IAO-Jehovah. The androgynous characterization of Jehovah is consistent with the following tenet of the Secret Doctrine:

> "The 'Divine Hermaphrodite' is then Brahma-Vâch-Virâj; and that of the Semites, or rather of the Jews, is Jehovah-Cain-Abel." (*The Secret Doctrine*, p. 126, Vol. II).

The perversion of the Jesuit is traced to a high source. Voltaire casts the Jehovic "Vice-God" into the role of a sex deviate. The unsual word "icoglan" conveys far more than humorous exoticism or fanciful "espièglerie."

The same "Divine Hermaphrodite" seems to be represented by Pozzo in the famous play of Samuel Beckett: *En Attendant Godot*. The relationship alleged to exist between the Jehovic God and Man made in His image is suggested as follows:

> "POZZO — (stopping). You are indeed human beings, however. (He puts on his glasses). As far as I can see (He removes his glasses). Of the same specie as I (He bursts out in an enormous fit of laughter). Of the same specie as Pozzo! Of divine origin!" (Act I).

Pozzo is the ruthless tormentor of "Lucky" — mankind, the slave of conspicuously non-existent "luck" or "chance." Vladimir and Estragon toy with the idea of re-baptizing "Pozzo." The names *Cain* and *Abel* are briefly considered. Their combination amounts to "Brahma-Vâch-Virâj" — or Jehovah. One may add that the faculties of Pozzo are on the decline in the second act. The tyrant is literally "at the end of his rope." The small bare tree of the first act — the tree of knowledge — has covered itself with leaves. The mysterious meaning of "Godot" may some day be understood as the long-awaited downfall of the "Vice-God" or the emergence of Eternal Truth.

The uneasy partnership of perverted religion and inhibited science is dramatized in Chapter XXVIII of *Candide*. Pangloss relates a strange adventure which ends in his "resurrection" from the dissecting table:

"A surgeon bought my body, carried me to his home, and dissected me. First of all he made on me a cross-shaped incision from the navel to the clavicle — the cross-shaped incision caused me to scream so loud that my surgeon fell over." (Ch. XXVIII, p. 237).

The incorrect certification of death is once more called to attention. The limited insights of exact science are questioned as is the concept of "exact" science itself. The surgeon has failed to detect the presence of a considerable remnant of life. The deep mystery of physical existence eludes the probe of the scalpel. The identity of views shared by Voltaire and by Mme Blavatsky can be inferred from the following passage:

"There are anatomists who uncovering to sight no indwelling spirit under the layers of muscles, the network of nerves, or the cineritious matter which they lift with the point of the scalpel, assert that man has no soul. Such are as purblind in sophistry as the student, who, confining his research to the cold letter of the Kabala, dares say it has no vivifying spirit. To see the true man who once inhabited the subject which lies before him, on the dissecting table, the surgeon must use other eyes than those of his body." (*Isis Unveiled*, p. 16, Vol. 1).

The cross-shaped incision is a clue to the esoteric content of the passage. The cross is symbolically related to ancient initiation rites.

"Symbol of the dual generative power, it was laid upon the breast of the initiate, after his 'new birth' was accomplished, and the Mystae had returned from their baptism at sea. It was a mystic sign that his spiritual birth had regenerated and united his astral soul with his divine spirit, and that he was ready to ascend in spirit to the blessed abode of light and glory — the Eleusinia." (*Isis Unveiled*, p. 254, Vol. 2).

The surgeon and his pious wife represent exact science and ecclesiastical dogma. Their union is not wholly harmonious. The divided couple is a far cry from Science-and-Religion-In-One. Panic and disagreement follow the "resurrection" of Pangloss, the embodiment of the united "twins." The pious wife calls for exorcism. Such a procedure would require the services of a priest. The intended ceremony would — if performed — cause a second auto-da-fé from which Pangloss could hardly hope to escape. The surgeon does not heed the recommendation of his wife. The woman representing the Church is much more frightened than is the man representing Science. The religious establishment has infinitely more to dread from the living reality of occult mastery than does the scientific world.

Interestingly, it is Pangloss, the "heretic," who can be revitalized by the dual symbol of Life and Christ. Official knowledge and official religion can only react with fear to the esoteric reality of the Cross. The occult is generally disturbing to the world of science. The true meaning of the teachings of Jesus is an understandable source of phobia to the Church.

The scientific segment of society proves capable of decent conduct. Having recovered from the initial shock, apparently touched by the plea of Pangloss. "Have mercy on me ," the surgeon decides against use of exorcism and gives every possible assistance to the master. Only one explanation is given for his action. He becomes "bolder."

Daring is required to resist the call to witch-hunts in "Westphalia." Another kind of courage is also needed: courage to use subjective faculties. The reader is reminded of the "bold" "reasoner" of *Micromégas* who measured the Saturnian and the title character. His method consisted of a "three plus one" technique related to the cross. The demonstration dealt a heavy blow to presumed holders of a monopoly on science. Pangloss renders the same service to the surgeon and his wife with a like method. The experiment seems conclusive where the husband is concerned. The physician quickly shows capacities for daring of his own.

Knowledge-and-Religion-In-One may not be unduly startling to the man of science. The surgeon may have found himself on the borders of metaphysics more than once. He may well have pondered the "heretical" beginnings of many significant developments of knowledge which were the "falsehoods" of one age and the recognized truths of the next. Whatever the case may be, scientific lucidity seems to recognize one fact. Little, if anything, can be lost in transition from necromantic exorcism to pure occult mastery.

The surgeon may have sensed the presence of Chrestos, the Higher Self, in the person of Pangloss and in the depths of his own being. The plea for humanity: "Have mercy on me!" has apparently been "heard." Jesus is said to have uttered similar words in the Garden of Gethsemane. The "great cry" born of the cross has found an echo in a scientific mind.

The kindly treatment accorded to Pangloss reflects long-suppressed and blissful rebellion against the tyrannical shrew of a wife: Theology. The woman is finally compelled to contribute to the care of the master. No generous change of heart seems to occur in her case. Her harried scientific "spouse" simply and gladly "puts her in her place."

The Voltairian version of the "Taming of the Shrew" bears esoteric resemblance to an episode of *Zadig*. The restitution of the five hundred ounces of "borrowed" silver and the "resurrection" of Pangloss seem to represent the same event which is repeatedly foretold in the trilogy composed of *Zadig, Candide,* and *L'Ingénu.* The revival of occult mastery personified by Pangloss probably points to the "mighty rush of facts" anticipated by Mme Blavatsky, a development implying return of the Primitive Wisdom-Religion. A humorous element of prophecy is discernible in the reactions of the surgeon and of his wife. Scholars are generally expected to weather the shock gracefully. Churches grudgingly bow to the inevitable.

A survey of adventures follows the reunion of Candide, Cacambo, and the baron. The general picture is somber. Slavery is the lot of all characters but one. The Western version of Truth — Cunégonde — and her senior counterpart — the old woman — are reported in bondage to a petty tyrant.

Institutional and incarnate slavery are repeatedly called to attention by the symbolic chain of convicts and by certain "chains of events." Salvation is stressed also. Release is bought with the diamond of Candide. Another wonder is performed by the spiritual treasure of Eldorado. The same immaterial assets which liberated Cunégonde from previous servitude buy her freedom from the latest owner. The old woman is released in like manner. Truth remains invincible as long as the diamond of superior vision and the treasure of Love are retained by Man.

The Voltairian concept of redemption differs from the Christian version of blood and whitewash — bleeding and enemas — which is mentioned at the beginning of *Candide.* The transaction involves Insight and Compassion or the eternal duality of Knowledge and Love. In a manner reminiscent of *Micromégas,* symbolic diamonds break "chains" of perception and being:

> " 'What a frightful chain of many calamities!' said Candide. 'But after all, I still have a few diamonds.' " (Ch. XXVIII, p. 234).

> "The chain of events of this universe has led you to our galley-slave-ship and — you redeemed us.' " (Ch. XXVIII, p. 238).

The optimism of Pangloss remains incorrigible:

> " 'Well, my dear Pangloss,' said Candide, 'when you were hanged, dissected, riddled with blows, and when you rowed in the galley-slave-ship, did you still think that all was going for the best?' — 'I am still of my first opinion,' replied Pangloss, 'for after all I am a philosopher, it is not proper that I should recant, it being impossible for Leibnitz to be wrong and pre-established harmony being besides the finest thing in the world, as well as solid and subtle matter.' " (Ch. XXVIII, p. 239).

Karma is evoked by means of a play on words. The French expression "roué de coups" suggests the relevance of a "wheel" — "roue."

The symbolism of chains — planetary and human — weighs heavily on the entire chapter. The supremacy of universal law is proclaimed. The "pre-established harmony," the system of worlds and monads sensed by the genius of an alleged non-initiate, Leibnitz,* — is beyond human affirmation or denial. The crucial and mysterious teamwork of Karma-Sutratma is perceived in the very depths of matter — "solid" — matter. The pervasive energy of Spirit is noted — "subtle" matter. The manifesto of Pangloss contains in compact form the basic elements of the Secret Doctrine.

The status of "philosopher" is claimed with sober pride. The word "philosopher" is often used by Voltaire to designate a believer in the Secret Doctrine — as is the word "reasoner." The unwillingness of the teacher to recant reflects far more than professional face-saving. The creed of Pangloss answers deeply rooted personal aspirations. But it is not the product of the cogitations of any one man. It is a revelation of boundless scope transmitted by an unbroken chain of divinely inspired minds. Rejection of such a perfect and durable monument would amount to absurd and reckless vanity. The stubbornness of Pangloss is an expression of deepest reverence.

> "It is useless to say that the system in question is no fancy of one or several isolated individuals. That it is the uninterrupted record covering thousands of generations of Seers whose respective experiences were made to test and to verify the traditions passed orally by one early race to another, of the teachings of higher and exalted beings, who watched over the childhood of Humanity." (*The Secret Doctrine*, p. 272-73, Vol. I).

The optimism of Pangloss is not unfounded. Within the framework of the master's faith, what is commonly regarded as "fact" belongs to the negative, illusory side of the Voltairian "fine picture." The diametrical opposition existing between popular concepts of "fact" and the occult significance of the term allows Voltaire to ring the death-knell of uneducated optimism while proclaiming glad tidings: the supremacy of universal harmony and the ultimately blissful destiny of Man.

> "— man was born for joy only; — he would not love pleasures passionately and continuously if he were not formed for them — the essence of human nature is to rejoice, and — all the rest is madness. That excellent moral system never was contradicted by anything but fact." (*La Princesse de Babylone*, Ch. I).

The Secret Doctrine, p. 596, Vol. II.

The spiritual nature of Voltairian "pleasure" may easily be inferred from two texts which confirm the substance of the *Discours sur la nature des plaisirs*. It is stated in *La Princesse de Babylone* that the essence of human nature is joy. *Micromégas* comes as close to defining the essence of all beings and things as Spirit as is esoterically possible. Joy or "pleasure" is therefore the equivalent of Spirit. The optimism of Pangloss and the puzzling "hedonism" of Voltaire are rooted in the same occult view of divine reality.

The second reunion of Candide with the baron is no more successful than the first. The suitor of Cunégonde is determined to marry his beloved. The Jesuit remains intractable on the subject of the proposed union. He will interpose himself between Man and Truth as long as he lives. The message is clear:

> " 'You can kill me again,' said the baron, 'but you will not marry my sister as long as I live.' " (Ch. XXIX, p. 240).

The threat of the Jesuit has a double-edged, prophetic quality which implies the possibility of his own removal.

The forgiveness of Candide — which has redeemed a suffering body — is powerless to redeem a non-existent soul. The story features a number of characters who return from apparent death. But the baron is the only one who can re-form a mortal shell disassembled by the sword. His singular ability to survive is identical to that of disembodied entities which are mentioned in *Isis Unveiled*. Such entities will "permit themselves to be perforated with bullets or the sword, or to be dismembered, and then instantly form themselves anew."* The utterance of the Jesuit: "You can kill me again, but you will not marry my sister as long as I live" may be interpreted in two ways. It may be read as the equivalent of the unadorned phrase: "Over my dead body!" It may also suggest that the existence of the baron is a shadowy one against which swords will not prevail. Voltaire seems to endorse the occult belief in soulless beings reportedly walking the earth in "empty" or borrowed bodies:

> 'Our present cycle is preeminently one of such soul-deaths. We elbow soulless men and women at every step in life." (*Isis Unveiled*, p. 369, Vol. II).

The spiritual mode of life of the troublesome Order is suggested to be as unnatural as its mode of birth. The final disposition which is made of the baron is significant. The nobleman is first returned to the galleys

---

Isis Unveiled, p. 359, Vol. I.

and eventually sent back to the Father General in Rome. The slave-ship and its symbolic chains point to need of corrective reincarnation. The Roman province of the Father General is practically represented as a spiritual junkyard.

Voltaire seems to have envisioned the longevity of the Company of Jesus. The Jesuit of *Candide* who has weathered the era of tumbrils and slit throats apparently expects to survive other setbacks. The liber-ating effect of the Revolution and the reactionary trends to follow were probably anticipated by Voltaire.

The removal of the Jesuit is one of many prophetic Voltairian pro-jections pointing to the eventual triumph of Truth. The impossible co-existence of Truth and oppression will be resolved by force if neces-sary. "Force" is on the side of Spirit with which it is synonymous on the esoteric plane. The tide of evolution works against tyrants. Voltaire and his esoteric brothers all look to the day of inevitably glory. "Rea-son" is the daughter of Time.

> "— as you do, gentlemen, I consider that Time ripens all things; through time do all things come into evidence; Time is the Father of Truth."
> (Rabelais, *Tiers Livre*, Ch. XL).

No "Congregation" or "Index" will prevail against the Daughter of Time:

> "Reason travels, little by little, from North to South, with her two close friends, Experience and Tolerance. Agriculture and Commerce accompany her. She presented herself in Italy, but the Congregation of the *Index* rejected her. All she was able to do was to send secretly a few of her agents, who do not fail to do some good. A few more years, and the country of the Scipios will no longer be that of ecclesiastical Harlequins.
>   She has from time to time some cruel enemies in France; but she has so many friends there that, of necessity, in the end, she will be prime minister there.
>   When she presented herself in Bavaria and Austria, she found two or three big and bewigged heads which looked at her with stupid and dazed eyes. They said to her, 'Madam, we have never heard of you; we do not know you.' 'Gentlemen,' she replied to them, 'with time you will know and love me. I am very well received in Berlin, Moscow, in Co-penhagen, in Stockholm. Quite some time ago, through the credit of Locke, Gordon, Trenchard, and milord Shaftesbury, and so many others, I have received my letters of citizenship in England. You will grant me some some day. I am the daughter of Time and I expect everything from my Father.'" (*L'Homme aux quarante ecus — Le Bon sens de M. André.*)

The same vindication of Time materialized as "Reason" is connected with the Proustian daughter of "Saint Loup:"

"I saw Gilberte advancing — I was surprised to see next to her a young girl about sixteen years old whose tall build measured that distance which I had refused to see. Colorless, imponderable time had, so that I might so to speak see and touch it, materialized in her — Meanwhile Mlle de Saint Loup was in front of me." (*A la Recherche du temps perdu*, p. 1031, Vol. III).

The "Westphalia" of *Candide* will not witness the advent of "Reason." The Gilbert of *Stello* and the "Gilberte" of Proust will come into being before the day of liberation arrives. Many years will pass before the Daughter of Time is duly "known" and "loved." Precarious and unglamorous survival is all that can be expected by Truth and her devotees in the time and space setting of *Candide*.

Unrelenting abuse has destroyed the original beauty of Truth. The thrill of spontaneous spirituality is stifled by disfigured dogma and punitive morality. Adulterated verities repel the most elevated souls. Candide has lost all desire to marry the pathetic victim of assorted tormentors. The eventual union of Man and Truth has the uninspiring quality of a forced marriage dictated by pity.

One aspect of the situation is ironically positive. Rebellion against tyrannical arrogance is a more powerful inducement to "marriage" than are the failing charms of Truth. The excesses of the Jesuit do more to unite the couple than can be done by the principals themselves. The reality of divine justice is perceptible in the wholesome revolt of the lover of Truth:

"Candide, in the bottom of his heart, had no desire to marry Cunégonde. But the extreme impertinence of the baron determined him to conclude the marriage, and Cunégonde pressed him so earnestly that he could not go back on his word. He consulted Pangloss, Martin, and the faithful Cacambo. Pangloss wrote a beautiful treatise through which he proved that the baron had no right at all over his sister, and that she could in accordance with all the laws of the Empire, marry Candide in left-handed fashion. (Ch. XXX, p. 240).

The situation may be settled by a "left-handed" arrangement involving common-law or "left-handed" spirituality, the purer variety of occult pursuit having been forced underground.

Life is less than blissful in the small community headed by Candide and Cunégonde. It is saddened by the constant proximity of strife and bloodshed. But the group is at least and at last spared direct involvement with surrounding madness. General conditions of life in the Iron Age require intercourse with Truth to be private and discreet.

Revelation is reluctant and scanty. The unfriendly dervish — a modern Western European mutation of Jesrad — supplies no such enlighten-

331

ment as did the angelic hermit of *Zadig*. The operation of Universal Law is hopelessly obscured on cosmic and individual planes. It is not even remotely suggested by the dervish that Karma does exist. The omnipresence of Spirit and the universal scale of analogy must be sensed in the silence and solitude of each human heart. The acquisition of occult knowledge is strongly discouraged. Such is the disheartening message conveyed by a rebuff and by a closed door:

> " 'With what are you meddling?' — 'I was entertaining the hope,' said Pangloss, 'of reasoning a little with you on effects and causes, on the best of possible worlds, on the origin of evil, on the nature of the soul and on pre-established harmony.' The dervish, hearing those words, slammed the door in their faces." (Ch. XXX, p. 243).
> " 'What must one do then?' said Pangloss. 'Be quiet,' said the dervish." (Ch. XXX, p. 243).

A few resources remain. Properly understood and obeyed, the exhortation to "silence" may produce Self-Knowledge and Knowledge of the Universe. Properly answered and heeded, the "great question" of action vs. inaction — "ne rien faire" — may lead to spiritual progress. The task of escaping the "lethargy" and "convulsions" of incarnate existence will be arduous in the setting of modern Europe. But the process will be aided by residence near Constantinople. The famous city remains the symbol of the Constantinian era, an age which saw the "throttling" of "the old religions in favor of" Christianity. But it is relatively close to the source of Knowledge. The wisdom of India is almost inaccessible. But one may settle for the gateway to the East until the advent of a more enlightened era.

A last, edifying glimpse of the Jehovic deity is afforded by the story. The latest owner of Cunégonde is none other than the biblical God. His esoteric identity is transparently veiled by an allusion to the historical figure of François Léopold Rakoczy. The Voltairian *Ragotski* once gained a small kingdom by means of rebellion. His unimpressive status of destitute usurper corresponds to the occult view of Jehovah as a third-rate mythological entity. His ill-gotten, shabby realm is the realm of slavery. Under his iron the rule Truth can do little more than exercise limited housekeeping talents. Cunégonde spends most of her time washing dishes and bowls and is eventually found by Candide as she places laundry on a series of clotheslines:

> "Cunégonde washes bowls on the shores of the Propontide, in the home of a prince who has very few bowls; she is a slave in the house of a former sovereign named Ragotski, to whom the Grand Turk gives three coins a day in his retreat." (Ch. XVIII, p. 233).

"They landed on the shore of the Propontide at the house of the prince of Transylvania. The first sight which they saw was Cunégonde and the old woman, who were spreading towels on strings in order to make them dry." (Ch. XXIX, p. 239).

The detersive essence of Christianity is stressed once more. The re-union of Man and Truth is a tragic and sublime caricature. Karma, represented by circular objects — dishes, bowls — is relegated to the dingy kitchen of the despot. The concept of Retribution is supplanted by obsessive and futile "purification." The splendid necklace of Sutrat-ma or "golden thread" is reduced to a collection of rags hanging from prosaic strings. The cyclic pattern of cosmic and individual existence is lost to human sight.

The destitution of the tyrant is a hopeful sign in a somber picture. Jehovah cannot compete with "Eldorado" where spiritual gold abounds and where spiritual and material slavery are inconceivable. One brief glimpse of the blessed "state" where nothing lacks has made Candide infinitely richer than the "Vice-God." Man has the ability to discover and develop his innate spiritual spark. The release of Truth can result. Even in spiritually blighted "Westphalia."

Man must toil with special dedication to "cultivate" his "garden" in the unfavorable setting of the bottom of a cycle.

"When man was placed in the Garden of Eden, he was placed there *ut operaretur eum,* in order that he might work there, which proves that man was not born to rest." (Ch. XXX, p. 244).

The latter biblical reference raises some questions about the true significance of the Garden of Eden where work was a primary goal from the first rather than the eventual punishment of "sin." The Voltairian garden is apparently not the same as the traditional playground of Adam and Eve. The reader is invited to go beyond the limits of biblical *Genesis* and to return to the source of Eden — and other things.

What is the raison d'être of man, struggling on his "little globe of mud?" What is the exact nature of the task assigned him? The reader is left to make necessary connections between a seemingly dull prospect — "doing nothing" — and the injunction to "work." Physical "inaction" — spiritual growth — is the most arduous enterprise open to Man. This is especially true in the time and space setting of modern Europe. "A great question" indeed in the words of Candide. Yet a question which does have an answer. "Man was born for joy only." "Man was placed" in the "Garden of Eden" in order that he might work there. There may thus be a connection between the Voltairian concepts of "joy" and "work."

The etymology of the word *Eden* — which can be traced to the Greek term meaning "pleasure" further tends to suggests the spiritual nature of Voltairian "work" and "hedonism." The etymology of the word "paradise" is also noteworthy. The Greek term "paradeisos" mean "garden." The terrestrial plot to be "cultivated" leads to heavenly "gardens of delight."

Celebrations of the grand labor abound in esoteric literature:

> "— behold the form of a man absorbed by some study — you will judge him not to live in the self, to be abstracted from the self by ecstasy, and will say that Socrates did not abuse the term, when he said philosophy was nothing but meditation of death." (Rabelais, *Tiers Livre*, Ch. XXXIX).

The state of abstraction from the lower self is attainable "not necessarily at death only, but during *Samadhi* or mystic trance."* The same quality of life achieved through "meditation of death" is suggested by Alfred de Vigny:

> "THE TWO PARTS OF MY LIFE. *The contemplation of beauty* in thought and in creation; and,
> *Action,* in which nothing pleases me except that which is passionate and beautiful.
> I was born to be a benedictine monk.
> The continuous, uninterrupted contemplation of any thing is a joy, and the natural state for me is abstraction.
> I was born abstracted, my Greek professor used to repeat to me: 'you are *abstracted* and *absent-minded*." (Diary, 1850).

The abstraction of Vigny and the predilection of Voltaire for "doing nothing" did not rule out action. Vigny pursued a military career, ran for office, and forced literary recognition when he was venomously received in the Académie Française. The Voltairian record of productivity and militancy is common knowledge. The cherished myth of the practical misfit scornfully called "egghead" — or even worse "mystic" — suffers, as it should, from their undeniable achievements. Such beings as Voltaire and Vigny could be most effective in dealing with the "real world." But their greater love never went to the realm of "the madding crowd's ignoble strife." The final chapter of *Candide,* the poetry and the *Diary* of Vigny are clear on one point. The majority of worldly pursuits are futile — if not dangerous. The area of politics is particularly disappointing and treacherous.

> " ' — I presume that in general, those who meddle with public affairs sometimes perish tragically, and that they deserve it.' " (Ch. XXX, p. 243).

---

*The Secret Doctrine, p. 569 fn., Vol. II.

"Public action is only secondary and I was born disenchanted with life, finding nothing in it worthy of attention, except contemplation and passion for beauty." (Alfred de Vigny, *Diary*, 1850).

The above-stated belief in the precedence of contemplation and "beauty" over "practical" and public affairs reflects more than the vagaries of an idealistic dreamer. Vigny — and his numerous esoteric brothers — saw little hope of meaningful socio-political progress until a sufficient number of minds began to understand the scheme of existence — "above" and "below." The day is virtually at hand when the "fictions" of such "dreamers" will prove surprisingly relevant to what we call "the real world."

"Thought alone, pure Thought, the inner exercise of ideas and their interplay, is for me a veritable joy — o meditation; meditation, o solitude! Bath of the soul, o rest and labor all in one; I listen to the harmonious steps of ideas through the spheres of all the worlds and in all the constellations of the past and the starry dreams of the future." (Alfred de Vigny, *Diary*, 1853).

The Talmudic "garden of delights," the difficult, rewarding domain to be cultivated by Candide, the ecstatic philosophies of Rabelais, Vigny, and others are all rooted in the same concept of "rest and labor all in one." The Edenic realm may be approached through study and meditation. Spiritual opportunity is not limited to the black arts. The "left-handed" or unlawful marriage of Man and Truth suggested by Pangloss may be consummated on highest planes:

"Instead of becoming a neophyte, and gradually obtaining his esoteric knowledge through a regular initiation, an *Adam*, or Man, uses his intuitional faculties and, prompted by the serpent (*Woman* and matter), tastes of the Tree of Knowledge — the esoteric or Secret Doctrine — unlawfully." (*The Secret Doctrine*, p. 202, Vol. II).

Human resourcefulness is expected to rise to the occasion.

The small, battered group headed by Candide and Cunégonde finally settles on a farm of modest size. Spiritual prospects are remarkably good. Truth — or "Reason" — does travel "little by little" in company with Agriculture and Commerce. The rural community enjoys a vivifying closeness to Nature. Peasant — or Pagan — influence is represented by Cacambo. Martin, the personification of Western skepticism, co-exists with the Pagan embodiment of Doubt. Metaphysical knowledge is available from Pangloss. Truth is at hand, disfigured, ill-humoured, but still loved. The proximity of a wise and serene elder is an additional source of enlightenment. "Commerce" of high character is bound to result. Last but not least, Knowledge is accompanied by Love and Compassion. Paquette and Frère Giroflée benefit from the kindness of their friends.

Various details suggest the spiritual dedication of the small group. Vegetarian fare seems to prevail in the household of Candide and in the home of the saintly neighbor. The prediction made in Eldorado seems to be fulfilled: "You will be served according to merit."

Cunégonde excels as a pastry-cook. The spiritual symbolism of pastry or bread may be traced to ancient rites:

> "The hierophant-initiator presented symbolically before the final *revelation* vine and bread to the candidate who had to eat and drink of both in token that the spirit was to quicken matter, *i.e.,* the divine wisdom was to enter into his body through what was to be revealed to him." (*Isis Unveiled*, p. 561, Vol. 2).

The care of linen — which is assigned to the old woman — seems to be related to the same spiritual concern. While the French word "linge" does not quite coincide with the term "lin," the importance of the latter fabric in religious rituals is suggested. As a traditional aristocrat in the hierarchy of fabrics, linen has a long history of participation in ancient mysteries. A special variety of the woven fiber was worn by Egyptian priests at ceremonies honoring Isis. The same linen-wearing priests — "linostoles" — are evoked in Chapter XI of *L'Ingénu*. Linen is pertinent to the esoteric identity of the old woman who was once symbolically betrothed to Egypt.

> "The linen of Egypt was famous throughout the world. The mummies are all wrapped in it and the linen is beautifully preserved. Pliny speaks of a certain garment sent 600 years B.C. by King Amasis to Lindus, every single thread of which was composed of 360 minor threads twisted together. Herodotus gives us (book i), in his account of Isis and the Mysteries performed in her honor, an idea of the beauty and 'admirable softness of the linen worn by the priests.' The latter wore shoes made of papyrus and garments of *fine linen*, because the goddess first taught the use of it and thus, besides being called *Isiaci,* or priests of Isis, they were also knonw as *Linigera,* or 'the linen-wearing.' This linen was spun and dyed in those brilliant and gorgeous colors, the secret of which is likewise now among the lost arts." (*Isis Unveiled*, p. 536, Vol. 1).

The indirect reference to linen may also be connected with a passage of St. John's *Revelations*. As was previously noted, the theme of *revelation* itself is linked to the symbolism of bread or pastry made by Cunégonde. The symbolic marriage of Candide and Cunégonde may easily be likened to the union defined in the following text. The same passage of the Secret Doctrine is relevant to the martyrdom of the old woman and of her successor.

" 'The Logos is passive Wisdom in Heaven and Conscious, Self-Active Wisdom on earth,' we are taught. It is the Marriage of 'Heavenly man' with the 'Virgin of the World' — Nature, as described in *Pymander;* the result of which in their progeny — immortal man. It is this which is called in St. John's Revelation the marriage of the lamb with his bride. (xix, 7) That 'wife' is now identified with the Church of Rome owing to the arbitrary interpretations of her votaries. But they seem to forget that her linen may be fine and white *outwardly* (like the 'whitened sepulchre'), but that the rottenness she is inwardly filled with, is not 'the righteousness of Saints' (v. 8, ibid), but rather the blood of the Saints she has 'slain upon the earth.' (Ch. xviii. 24)" (*The Secret Doctrine,* p. 231, Vol II).

The Babylon of *Revelations,* "The Great, the Mother of Harlots and Abominations of the Earth" is defined as follows by occultists:

" — *all and every exoteric* Churchianity, that which was the 'ceremonial magic' of old, with its terrible effects, and is now the harmless (because distorted) farce of ritualistic worship. The 'mystery' of the woman and of the beast, are the symbols of soul-killing Churchianity and of SUPERS-TITION." (*The Secret Doctrine,* p. 748, Vol. II).

Voltaire seems to hold the same esoteric view of "the Mother of Harlots and Abominations." But he tends to be more precise:

"—, certainly *Babylon* means *Rome.*"
(Voltaire, *Romans et Contes,* Pot-Pourri, XIII, p. 420, Ed. Bénac, Classiques Garnier).

The theme of *Revelations* which is introduced by symbolic bread and linen suggests the possibility of an intellectual and spiritual apocalypse. Such an event is likely to result from proper cultivation of the Voltairian "garden."
Esoteric "coffee" is also meaningful. The excellent beverage served in the home of the saintly neighbor of Candide emphatically does *not* came from two interesting lands:

" — his two daughters and his two sons offered to them — some Mocha coffee which was not mixed with the bad coffee from Batavia and the islands." (Ch. XXX, pp. 243-44).

It may be inferred from the meaningful nose of beautiful Almona — which is *not* like a Lebanese tower — that the countries from which the coffee comes *not* should receive attention. The origin of the coffee has little importance in itself. But the localities seem calculated to suggest submerged continents. Atlantis and Lemuria are once more brought to mind.

337

" 'Atlantis' is the Fourth Continent. It would be the first historical land, were the traditions of the ancients to receive more attention than they have hitherto. The famous island of Plato of that name was but a fragment of this great Continent." (*The Secret Doctrine*, p. 8, Vol. II).

Batavia is used again as a front for Lemuria, a sunken continent the existence of which was already recognized in the days of Mme Blavatsky.

"The third Continent, we propose to call 'Lemuria.' The name is an invention, or an idea, of Mr. P. L. Sclater, who asserted, between 1850 and 1860, on zoological grounds the actual existence, in prehistoric times, of a Continent which he showed to have extended from Madagascar to Ceylon and Sumatra. It included some portions of what is now Africa; but otherwise this gigantic Continent, which stretched from the Indian ocean to Australia, has now wholly disappeared beneath the waters of the Pacific, leaving here and there only some of its highland tops which are now islands." (*The Secret Doctrine*, p. 7, Vol. II).

The exoteric reader of *Candide* can only speculate on the nature of conversations connected with the origin of coffee. The esoteric reader can guess, Candide and his friends are in "good company" and may become "good company" themselves. The "good Moslem neighbor is proof of the fact that all the paths of men of good will lead to "Rome" — which is not the Vatican. The serene elder whose peaceful pursuits and "commercial" ventures reflect the ideal of Voltairian "gardening" seems to have preserved the primitive spiritual ardor of his faith, a faith which has "sadly degenerated"* in the case of many of his "correligionists" as *Candide* clearly shows. His presence and the presence of Pangloss tend to support occult belief in the continuity of a chain of spiritual pioneers. "— in what age were there no *Occultists* and no ADEPTS?" asks Mme Blavatsky.**

The existence of the elder and the survival of Pangloss in the midst of the Iron Age strongly suggest that the answer is NEVER.

Candide has lost the remainder of his treasure to pilfering "Jews" or Judaeo-Christians. But the symbolic wealth is no longer needed. The primary goals of Man in Search of Truth are being reached within the narrow limits of the "best of possible words." Virtue is practiced and there is daily commerce with "Mlle Cunégonde." The esoteric reader is reminded of an important axiom:

"There is nothing solid except virtue and the joy of seeing again Mlle Cunégonde."

Isis Unveiled, p. 575, Vol. 2.
**The Secret Doctrine*, p. 484, Vol. I.

"Instructed" optimism is Wisdom itself. Even and especially in an age of darkness.

> "Says a Persian proverb: 'The darker the sky is, the brighter the stars will shine.'" (*Isis Unveiled*, p. 64, Vol. I).

The esoteric architecture of *Candide* centers on the various sectarian mutilations of Truth. The history of Christianity is traced from the era of relative, original purity to the times in which Voltaire lived. The fate of the neo-Platonist School of Alexandria, the Reformation, the spread of Islam, and the Schism of the Orient form the background of an age of ultimate religious persecution. Jansenism and Jesuitry are represented as opposite poles of Christian spirituality. The positive pole itself leaves much to be desired. The History of sectarian division is supplemented by a prophetic glimpse into an age when the integral restoration of Truth is expected. The "resurrection" of Pangloss — Science and Religion in One — may point to our own era.

The esoteric geography of *Candide* follows the expansion of Christianity from Western Europe to the New World. A tidal wave of misery marks the passage of the conquering creed. Truth is martyred and degraded in the Americas. The "pox" is expected to eventually contaminate the Far East. But the irrepressible Love of Man In Search of Truth impels humanity to return toward the source. Candide — the allegorical "candidate" to perfection — carries his quest to the gateway to the East.

The first level of esoteric History and Geography is overshadowed — and dwarfed — by elements of occult philosophy dealing with planetary and human evolution. *Candide* is placed from the very beginning under the sign of materiality suggested by the 350 pounds of Mme la baronne. The separation of the sexes — which took place during the Fifth subcycle of the Third Race — foreshadows other forms of "sectarianism." The sailor of Chapter V and the ape-men of Chapter XVI call esoteric attention to the Fourth Race stage of Atlantean evolution. The birthplace of the wicked navigator points to the emplacement of Lemuria. The Peruvian locality of Eldorado serves as a link between the two submerged continents which were once connected with each other. The theme of periodic cataclysms alternately involving water and fire is introduced by the ocean storm and by the earthquake of Lisbon. Great "revolutions" or geological upheavals are evoked by the elderly resident of Eldorado. The occasional tilting of the axis of earth is a concealed element of Chapter XXI — disguised as the eternal war between hawks and doves. The relevance of submerged continents is reaffirmed in the final chapter. The cosmic and individual scheme of "necessity" underlies the entire story. The esoteric vista afforded by

Candide has vertiginous dimension in both Time and Space. The essence of Voltairian "optics" is the One Immaterial Reality which is symbolized by a titanic threshold. The portal of the palace of Eldorado beckons the reader beyond contingency.

> "Space and Time are One. Space and Tire are nameless, for they are the incognizable THAT; which can be sensed *only through its seven rays*." (*The Secret Doctrine*, p. 612, Vol. II).

The realm of squalor, division, and strife — our own Fifth Race — is characterized by crude terminology. Voltaire seems to endorse the occult view of our phase of evolution. *"We are at the bottom of a cycle and evidently in a transitory state"** The "bottom" is in evidence indeed. The well-aimed kick of the vengeful Lord, a kick still heard around the world, initiates a series of tribulations for mankind. Somewhat similarly, Paquette, Cunégonde and the old woman are launched on a course of wandering ordeals by sexual abuse. The phrase which may be politely translated as "twenty kicks in the rear" — vingt coups de pied au cul" — seems to phonetically suggest a *race* — "cula"** or phase of evolution. The omnipresent "behind" characteristic of *Candide* is a sad, logical reflection on the general level of concern corresponding to a nadir of spirituality. But the unmentionable anatomy has a vast potential of enlightenment. Careful study of the self and world; careful examination of certain texts may lead "behind" or beyond appearance into the realm of Truth. The "behind" of *Candide* and "Legrandin," the true "portal to being" of Samuel Beckett, vindicate a contention of occultists. Spirit — or Truth — may be found on the least exalted planes.

> "I apologize for returning again to this shameful orifice, it is my muse who requires it. Perhaps one must see there less the stigma which is named than the symbol of those stigmata which I conceal — One tends to underestimate it, in my opinion, that little hole, people call it that of the ass and affect to scorn it. But would it not be rather the true portal to being,—? Are these not significant things? History will judge. But I shall try nevertheless to make a little less room for it in the future. And that will be easy for me, for the future, let us skip it, is hardly uncertain at all. And as far as leaving aside the essential is concerned, I am a master of that art, I believe,—" (*Molloy*, p. 122, Ed. de Minuit).

Zadig in search of Isis-Astarté, Candide in search of Isis-Cunégonde, personify the eternal quest of Man for Truth. Neither Man nor Truth

---

*Isis Unveiled, p. 247, Vol. 1.
**Tod, *Annals of Rajasthan*, Vol. I, pp. 32-33, quoted in *Adyar* Edition of The Secret Doctrine.

can be denied. Their destiny is to be joined. But conditions of union differ vastly between the Ancient Pagan world and modern Western societies. The former environment exalts spiritual aspiration and related knowledge. The latter crushes them whenever possible. Pagan Truth retains her glorious beauty and vitality. The Western version of Truth — which is emptily sensuous at best — becomes a pathetic caricature. The "veil-lifting" of *Zadig* is a virtual guarantee of steady devotion to Truth. The corresponding experience in *Candide* is subject to severe doubt and spiritual setbacks. Revelation is markedly diminished in transition from Jesrad to the forbidding dervish. The cosmic awareness which enabled Zadig to find solace in the midst of despair is gone. It is relegated to the suspect pronouncements of Pangloss. The cyclic geometry of Evolution-Reincarnation is obscured. The circle of cosmic design and Retribution is concealed in the scullery of Jehovah. The necklace of Sutratma is all but impossible to discern in the piteous strings of the usurper's backyard. The end of the story of Zadig remains under the influence of a Golden Age. The conclusion of *Candide* finds benighted mankind deep in the Iron Age. Voltaire's awareness of the abysmal difference is expressed in *L'Homme aux quarante écus.*

> "I was counting in accordance with the records of the Golden Age, and one must count in accordance with the Iron Age." (*Entretien avec un géomètre*).

Doubt and unbelief flourish. They are represented by Cacambo and Martin. But doubt itself may lead to solid faith.

Human pleas for a Savior will not be heard for a long time. No new Savior can appear during the Kali Yuga.* "Every man for himself" is the uninspiring motto of physical and spiritual survival. Time alone can terminate the era of general degradation and base selfhood which has arrived — as predicted many centuries earlier:

> "The *Kali yuga* reigns now supreme in India, and it seems to coincide with that of the Western age. Anyhow, it is curious to see how prophetic in almost all things was the writer of Vishnu Purana when fortelling to Maitreya some of the dark influences and sins of this Kali Yug. For after saying that the 'barbarians' will be masters of the banks of the Indus, of Chandrabhaga and Kasmera, he adds:
> 'There will be contemporary monarchs, reigning over the earth — kings of churlish spirit, violent temper, and ever addicted to falsehood and wickedness. They will inflict death on women, children, and cows; they will seize upon the property of their subjects, and *be intent upon the wives of others;* they will be of unlimited power, their lives will be short,

---

The Secret Doctrine, p. 470, Vol. I.

their desires insatiable. . . . People of various countries intermingling with them, will follow their example; and the barbarians beings powerful (in India) in the patronage of the princes, while purer tribes are neglected, the people will perish (or, as the Commentator has it, 'The Mlechchas will be in the centre and the Aryas in the end.') Wealth and piety will decrease until the world will be wholly depraved. Property alone will confer rank; wealth will be the only source of devotion; passion will be the sole bond of union between the sexes; falsehood will be the only means of success in litigation; and women will be objects merely of sensual gratification. . . . *External types will be the only distinction of the several orders of life;* — a man if rich will be reputed pure; dishonesty (*anyaya*) will be the universal means of subsistence, weakness the cause of dependence, menace and presumption will be substituted for learning; liberality will be devotion; mutual assent, marriage; fine clothes, dignity. He who is the strongest will reign; the people, unable to bear the heavy burden, *Khara bhara* (the load of taxes) will take refuge among the valleys . . ." *(The Secret Doctrine,* p. 377, Vol. I).

The valor of protagonists — modern mankind and Truth — is severely tested and fully measured by the number and nature of obstacles placed between them. Hardship is at its worst. Merit at its best. The descending arc of evolution can go no lower. Comfort can be gained from the fact that the illegitimate oppressor — Jehovah — is in desperate straits. The acolytes of temporal and spiritual tyranny seem to sense approaching disaster. A new era is in sight — for the "instructed" at least. Such are likely reasons underlying the enthusiasm of Voltaire in an age which was less than golden:

> "Oh! the good era that our Iron Age is "
> (*Le Mondain*)

The alloy of pessimism and optimism which is the chief characteristic of *Candide* loses its puzzling quality in the light of the Secret Doctrine. The indestructible faith of Pangloss is no product of insanity or blindness. The "fine picture" does exist. The unbelievable teacher is a spokesman of Truth.

L'INGENU

Primitive Paganism and modern Christianity confront each other from the very beginning of the story. Brought by an English vessel, a young North American Indian suddenly and unexpectedly appears on the coast of France. The stranger is greeted by a puzzled French bourgeois family.

The scene is Lower Brittany, specifically the region of Saint Malo. The area is rich is legendary and adventurous heritage. Traditionally it is to France what Ireland is to England. The odyssey of Saint Dunstan who sailed a sea-worthy peak from the former land to the latter casts a hazy syncretic charm over the Celtic countryside. Magic and religion blend in the person of the legendary man. Faith does appear to move mountains. Magic and religion dwell in local folklore and in tangible monuments. Brittany is the land of menhirs, dolmens, granite calvaries, rocking stones, and korrigans or sprites. Magic and religion are fused in the background of Our Lady of the Mountain, the Church which supplies the French family with material and spiritual nourishment. The kindly head of the small clan is the Prior of Our Lady. Practical ventures are not excluded from regional tradition. Saint Malo once was a thriving den of sea-scouring pirates. Discovery and exploration belong to the heritage of the city. It was in Saint Malo that Jacques Cartier was born. It was from Saint Malo that his famous expedition sailed for the "New World."

The epic background of legend, magic, and history seems to be at variance with the flesh-and-blood, down-to-earth portrayal of the French family. The Kerkabons typify bourgeois Catholicism in latter-day "Westphalia." They are smugly comfortable — materially and otherwise —, fairly benevolent, and naively provincial. Heroic pursuits lie beyond their field. Legendary saints and mountains are least of their concerns. But the atmosphere in which they live remains under the spell of "Ar-mor" — the sea. Lost relatives — or "connections" — are remembered with the "New World." The tidy realm of the Kerkabons is not immune to vague yearning. Mentally as otherwise, it is a "terraqueous" domain of blurred memory and occasional dreaming. It is a climate of native sentimentality reminiscent of Marie de France. It is a kingdom of domestic realism worthy of eternal bourgeois codes and of a Meissonnier painting.

The Kerkabons represent — in multiple aspects — the ambivalence of the average Fifth Race man whose feet are said to be firmly planted on the ground but whose most vital roots are rather in the air.

The young man who strides ashore from a passing ship wears an aura of exotic adventure and sea-faring romance. The landing of the American brings the unknown into the mental *terra firma* of the European West. A comparable culture shock awaits the Indian. The meeting is a fruitful contact between primitive tradition and the ways of modern Europe. Without knowing it, the traveler has reached the land of his ancestors. The theme of the prodigal son come home and the suggestion of a closed cycle are present. The meaning of unsuspected backgrounds and kinships, is submitted to the alert reader.

Duality pervades the first chapter — and the entire story. Sea and land, mystery and "reality," Paganism and Christianity, primitive innocence and civilized "sophistication" are enhanced by contrast. Personified Adventure and middle-class euphoria Incarnate behold each other in mutual fascination and mutual disbelief. Parallel and opposite traits are added to cyclic hints. The same geometry eventually resolves itself in grand convergence and revelation of the Unknown.

The irruption of the young man on the peaceful scene is well explained by the conveyance of the ship. The Kerkabons see no reason to connect the English craft with a Savior or with a "vessel" of "flesh" suggesting incarnation. Nor are they prone to seek symbolic meaning in the leaping of the young stranger "over and beyond the heads" of his "companions." But near-prodigy is sensed in the startling arrival.

A male version of Venus has emerged from the sea. Several details suggest an androgynous being. Virility is attested by build and athletic performance:

> "A very well built young man, . . . sprang in one leap over the heads of his companions, and found himself facing mademoiselle." (Ch. I, p. 247).

The "very well built young man" is clearly not effeminate. But he has feminine features: long braided hair and "a peaches and cream complexion!" — "un teint de lis et de rose!" — His manner is described as "martial and gentle." Mars and Venus are in conjunction.

Such attributes are consistent with the allegory of Adam Kadmon, the first spiritual man, the predecessor of the second Adam or Adam of Dust. The symbolism of Adam Kadmon — male and female in one — is found on numerous planes of the Secret Doctrine. The same androgynous being appears in the text of *Genesis*. The septenary scheme of emanation to which it belongs has a counterpart in the seven days of biblical Creation.

"When the time for an active period had come, then was produced a natural expansion of this Divine essence from within outwardly, obedient to eternal and immutable law, and from this eternal and infinite light (which to us is darkness) was emitted a spiritual substance.' (Idra Suta: ii) This was the first Sephiroth, containing in herself the other nine Sephiroth, or intelligences. In their totality and unity they represent the archetipal man, Adam Kadmon, the *protogonos,* who in his individuality or unity is yet dual or bisexual, the Greek *Didumos,* for he is the prototype of all humanity." (*Isis Unveiled,* p. 213, Vol. 2).

"The whole Darwinian theory of natural selection is included in the first six chapters of the book of *Genesis.* The 'Man' of Chapter i is radically different from the 'Adam' of chapter ii, for the former was created 'male and female' — that is bisexual — and in the image of God; while the latter, according to verse seven, was formed of the dust of the ground, and became "a living soul" after the Lord God 'breathed into his nostrils the breath of life.' " (*Isis Unveiled,* p. 303, Vol. 1).

The full significance of what Christian "Creation" has divided* from the onset — the original oneness of male and female principles — has multiple reflections in occult philosophy and esoteric literature. As was previously noted, the Christian tradition leaves out of account the first spiritual Eve. Woman is degraded from the beginning to "simple humanity." The same oversight and the philosophy with which it is connected are commented as follows in the Secret Doctrine:

"According to the Kabala the *curse on man came with the formation of woman.*** The circle was separated from its diameter line. 'From the possession of the double principle in one, that is the Androgyne condition, the separation of the dual principle was made, presenting two opposites, whose destiny it was, for ever after, to seek reunion into the original *one* condition. The curse was this, viz.: that nature, impelling the search, evaded the desired result by the production of a new being, distinct from that reunion or oneness desired, by which the natural longing to recover a lost state was and is for ever being cheated. It is by this tantalizing process of a continued curse that Nature lives.' (*Vide 'Cross and Circle,'* Part II).

The same view of the traditional Christian Creation is suggested by the following passage of the Proustian *Recherche:*

"O grand attitudes of Man and Woman, in which seeks to unite, in the innocence of primitive days and with the humility of clay, what the Creation has divided." (*A la Recherche du temps perdu,* p. 79, Vol. III).

The evolutionary view of "Creation" and "Fall" — emanation and

---

*This is the view taken and adopted by all the Church Fathers, but it is not the real esoteric Teaching. The *curse* did not begin with the formation of either men or women, for their separation was a natural sequence of evolution, —" (*The Secret Doctrine,* p. 216, Vol. II).
**A la Recherche du temps perdu,* p. 79, Vol. III.

descent into materiality — is connected by Voltaire with the esoteric suggestion of "Fallen Angels." The "angelic" or immaterial ancestry of Man is introduced into the text through choice and repeated use of of the word "Angleterre." — "England". The voyage of the young hero of *L'Ingénu* has involved a stay in the latter country. Attention seems to be drawn to the anecdotal meaning of the term "land of angels" — "terre des anges". The same phonetic resemblance between the words "ange," "angel," and "Angle" which is said to have inspired a pun of Pope Gregory may have inspired the esoteric use of "England" which is made by Voltaire and by other writers.

> "According to tradition, here is the way in which Gregory, being still a monk, made plans to convert the Anglo-Saxons. 'One day when there was a market in Rome, Gregory, finding himself in the crowd, saw among the slaves for sale some young men with white complexions, and with graceful faces enhanced by beautiful hair. He asked from what country they had come; he was told that they came from Britain . . . and that they were Pagans. 'Alas!' said Gregory with a sigh, how grievous that men with such luminous faces should be submitted to the prince of darkness!' And he wished to know what the name of the nation was. He was told that they were called 'Angles.' 'That is an appropriate name,' he said, 'for they have the faces of *angels* and are meant to be companions of angels in heaven. And what is the name of the province where they were born?' — '*Deira*,' he was told. 'Very good,' he said, 'liberated from the wrath (*de ira*) of God, and destined to the mercy of Christ. And the King of the province, what is his name?' He was told that he was called *Aella*. 'Alleluia,' said Gregory, the praise of the God Creator must be sung in that country.' " (Bede, *Ecclesiastical History*, II, i).

The interpretive skills of Gregory and his bigoted views of Paganism were probably appreciated by Voltaire. *L'Ingénu* contains an illustration of the same missionary zeal.

Céline exploits the same esoteric possibilities of England in *Mort à Crédit*. Arrival in England is compared to arrival "in another world."* The family Jehovah himself tends to turn "explorer"** in the misty or ethereal setting — "between heaven and earth."*** The country is likened to a "kingdom of phantoms."**** The average Englishman is said to be " a cross between a pastor and a little boy."***** The latter element of the formula may represent an esoteric "child" or "initiate." The "mindless" schoolmates of Ferdinand are designated as "angels."****** The English language "is a kind of music, it comes from another planet."******* Such are but a few details suggesting the esoteric

---

**Death on the Installment Plan*, Ralph Manheim Tr., p. 126.
***Ibid.*, p. 128.
****Ibid.*, p. 129.
*****Ibid.*, p. 224.
******Ibid.*, p. 230.
*******Ibid.*, p. 231.
**** ****Ibid.*, p. 235.

meaning of the stay in England: return to a semi-ethereal mode of existence.

The predilection of Odette Swann for English expression seems to have the same spiritual significance.

The "angelic" or ethereal nature of the Voltairian Adam Kadmon corresponds to the transition from pure spirituality to material existence. The passage of the young man from water to land — the latter element representing solid materiality — is supplemented by the presence of a small detail: the bottle of Barbadoes water — presumably rhum or "spirit" carried by the young hero. No occultist will find anything but the deepest reverence in the merry suggestion of universal Genesis thus introduced:

"And the Spirit of God moved upon the face of the waters." (I, 2).

"Narayana moving on the (abstract) waters of Space, is transformed into the Waters of concrete substance moved by him, who now becomes the manifested WORD or Logos." (*The Secret Doctrine*, p. 7, Vol. I).

The Logos is identical with the androgynous Adam Kadmon. The Genesis — related aspect of the Voltairian story — which is also suggested by the word "Ingénu" — is supported by the said identity:

"The 'Heavenly Man' (Tetragrammaton) who is the Protogonos, Tikkoun, the firstborn from the passive deity and the first manifestation of that deity's shadow, is the universal form and idea, which engenders the manifested Logos, Adam Kadmon, or the four-lettered symbol, in the Kabala, of the *Universe itself,* also called the *second Logos.* The second springs from the first and develops the third triangle from the last of which (the lower host of Angels) MEN are generated." (*The Secret Doctrine*, p. 25, Vol. II).

The distance separating the country of origin of the young man — Canada — from Barbadoes represents a sizable segment of the Western Hemisphere. It may constitute a veiled reference to the sunken continent of Atlantis. Casual observations of the traveler reveal his keen interest in coast-lines and geographical data:

"— he had wanted to see how the coasts of France were made." (Ch. I, u. 248).

The question of "how the coasts of France we made" may involve geological formation as well as present structure The curiosity which impels the traveler to explore the surface of the planet Earth may extend to the history of the same planet.

The itinerary followed by the young Indian from Canada to England and finally to Brittany roughly coincides with the axis of another submerged continent the existence of which is affirmed in the Secret Doctrine. The Hyperborean Continent — of which Greenland and Spitzbergen are regarded as remnants — is believed to have once extended" — from Newfoundland nearly to the coast of France."*

The quaint legend of Saint Dunstan which forms the introduction to *L'Ingénu* has a concealed connection with the periodic emergence and submersion of continents. The legend is as follows:

> "One day saint Dunstan, of Irish nationality and a saint by profession, left Ireland on a small mountain which sailed toward the coasts of France, and arrived by means of that conveyance in the bay of Saint Malo. When he was ashore, he gave a blessing to his mountain, which made deep curtseys to him and which returned to Ireland following the same path as it had travelled to come." (Ch. I, p. 246).

The chief interest of the legend lies in its connection with *Meru*, the Mountain, esoterically the North pole.

> "Meru, the abode of the gods — was placed, as before explained, in the North Pole, while Pâtâla, the nether region, was supposed to lie in the South. As each symbol in esoteric philosophy has *seven* keys, geographically, *Meru* and *Pâtâla* have one significance, and represent localities; while astronomically, they have another, and mean 'the two poles,' which meaning ended by their being often rendered in *exoteric* sectarianism — the 'Mountain' and the 'Pit,' or Heaven and Hell. If we hold at present only to the astronomical and geographical significance, it may be found that the ancients knew the topography and nature of the Arctic and Antarctic regions better than any of our modern astronomers; they had reasons, and good ones for naming one the *'Mountain'* and the other the *'Pit.'* — The vast concave, that is for ever hidden from our sight and which surrounded the southern pole, being therefore called the PIT, while observing, toward the Northern pole that a certain circuit in the heavens always appeared above the horizon — they called it the Mountain. As Meru is the high abode of the Gods, these were said to *ascend* and *descend* periodically; by which (astronomically) the Zodiacal gods were meant, the passing of the original North Pole of the Earth to the South Pole of the heaven.' " (*The Secret Doctrine*, p. 357, Vol. II).

The word *Meru* is connected by occultists with the word *America*:

> "— the name of *America*, may one day be found more closely related to Meru, the sacred mount in the centre of the *seven* continents, according to the Hindu tradition, than to Americus Vespuccius, whose name by the bye, was never Americus at all, but Albericus, a trifling difference

The Secret Doctrine, p. 791, Vol. II.

not deemed worth mentioning till very lately by exact history." (*Isis Unveiled,* p. 591, Vol. 1).

The legend of Saint Dunstan adds to the esoteric themes of Genesis and transition from ethereal regions the theme of the "Mountain" — or pole — periodically "ascending" and "descending" from one cardinal point to the opposite other. The genesis of Earth and Man is suggested to form the concealed architecture of the adventures of the young American.

The similarity which exists between the terms "Amérique" and "Armorique" may lead one to wonder about a possible connection between the latter word and *Meru.* The obvious link is "Ar-Mor" which means "the sea." One may also surmise the existence of a linguistic tie between Pole and Ocean, the location of the latter being determined to a major degree by the stability or shifting of the former.

The relevance of the Pole to the Voltairian evocation of legend seems to be supported by the record of the actual saint. The historical personage was born near Glastonbury, England and was educated by Irish pilgrims. He was reprimanded for his excessive love of books. He was once accused of practicing the black arts. He eventually became abbot of Glastonbury.

The famous abbey is of deep interest to various writers — such as Michel Butor and John Michell. The richly meaningful design of the structure is linked to major geographical features of Earth and to certain sites receiving privileged amounts of magnetic currents. Voltaire may have mentioned the Saint for three reasons. To illustrate once more the occult view of Christianity built — literally and otherwise on "the mangled remains of the seven primitive churches" The fact that Christian sanctuaries, monasteries, and convents are almost invariably built on the former site of a sacred Pagan ground reflects more than a desire to rape and obliterate all things "heathen." It is also determined by a pragmatic desire to exploit special magnetic attributes once enjoyed by the dispossessed. Voltaire may have hinted at the crusading spirit of the historical Saint Dunstan who strove to uproot Paganism. The Prior of L'Ingénu — and more particularly the Abbé de Saint Yves — will prove worthy successors of the Saint where crusading is concerned. But their insight will not approach the science of their predecessor. Such a failing is consistent with the theme of evolutionary "fall" which is the Ariadne's thread of *L'Ingénu.* The story takes place during a phase of human "progress" in which the majority of priests have done more than their share of "falling." They have lost knowledge, the one redeeming trait they once had. Voltaire finally seems to have used Saint Dunstan and his connection with Glastonbury Abbey to further suggest the esoteric significance of "the Mountain" and the network of "dragon currents" or magnetic fields — well known to the Chinese — which criss-cross the Earth.

The global and cosmic background of human existence is a common concern of esoteric writers. A major function of *Micromégas* is to raise myopic eyes to the plane of the universe. The majority of men goes through life blind to the visible wonders of Cosmos. The loss of cosmic vision which prevails in *Candide* is an unmistakable sign that mankind is fumbling through "the bottom of a cycle." Céline has his own way — earthy in form, Voltairian in spirit — of castigating the blindness which reigns on our little "molehill:"

> "What's the sky to you? A hole, Ferdinand! One more hole!" (*Death on the Installment Plan*, Ralph Manheim Tr., p. 390).

> "What can it matter to you? You just drift along. You don't give a good goddam about the universal consequences that can flow from our most trifling acts, our most unforeseen thoughts. . . . It's no skin off your ass. . . . You're caulked . . . hermetically, sealed. . . . Nothing means anything to you. . . . Am I right? Nothing Eat! Drink! Sleep! Up there as cozy as you please. All warm and comfy on my couch. . . . You've got everything you want. . . . You wallow in well-being . . . the earth rolls on. . . . How? Why? A staggering miracle . . . — how it moves . . . the profound mystery of it . . . toward an infinite, unforeseeable goal . . . in a sky all scintillating with comets . . . all unknown . . . from one rotation to the next. . . . Each second is the culmination and also the prelude of an eternity of other miracles . . . of impenetrable wonders, thousands of them, Ferdinand! Millions! billions of trillions of years! . . . And you? What are you doing in the midst of this cosmogonic whirl? this vast sidereal wonder? Just tell me that! You eat! You fill your belly! You sleep! You don't give a damn. . . . That's right! Salad! Swiss cheese! Sapience! Turnips! Everything! You wallow in your own muck! You loll around, befouled! Glutted! Satisfied! You don't ask for anything more!" (*Death on the Installment Plan*, Ralph Manheim Tr., p. 357).

The recurring apocalyptic vision of Ferdinand — which is disguised as "delirium" — contains hints of planetary commotion and suddenly changed fauna. Sharks and wolves are "seen" in the Parisian region. The works of Velikowsky show that remnants of warm-climate animal life have been found in the Parisian Basin. Such were the crocodile bones studied by Cuvier.* Such were also the teeth and bones of "elephants, rhinoceroses, hippopotami — tigers (the teeth of which were 'larger' than those of the largest lion or Bengal 'tiger') — which were found in Yorkshire in 1823 by Geology Professor William Buckland, of the Uni-

---

*Immanuel Velikovsky, *Earth in Upheaval*, pp. 25-26.

versity of Oxford. The apocalyptic vision of Ferdinand which shows a rapid succession of animal species corresponding to warm and cold habitats is connected with the tilting of the axis of earth. It is an invitation to meditate on the possible fate of our globe — "from one rotation to the next."

Saint-Exupéry connects the importance of a certain "mountain" with geological change:

> "'Geographies,' said the geographer, 'are the most precious of all books. They never go out of fashion. It is very rare for a mountain to change places. It is very rare for an ocean to empty itself of its water. We write eternal things. What counts for us is the mountain. It does not change.'" (*The Little Prince*, Ch. XV).

The geographer of *The Little Prince* is far from ignorant. He knows that certain cataclysmic events are *rare*. But he knows that they *do* happen.

The geographical interest of the hero of *L'Ingénu* is connected at an early stage with the secret science of "explorers."

The esoteric interest of the Poles is more than symbolic. The claim of occult philosophy that "the only world of reality is the subjective" does "invert the poles" of Western thinking. This explains the esoteric significance of Proustian "inverts." The same fact is connected with the esoteric meaning of Voltairian "homosexuals" — left-handed though they be. But the interest of Arctic and Antarctic regions of our planet does not lie exclusively in the "dreamy," "fanciful" realms of metaphysics. The passage of *Micromégas* in which terrestrial life is revealed to space travelers contains "amusing" observations on the subject. The passengers of the ship discovered by the title character and by the Saturnian are "philosophers" returning from an expedition *under* the Arctic circle:

> "The newspapers said that their ship drifted ashore on the coasts of Bothnia and that their rescue was effected with some difficulty, but one never knows in this world the underside of the cards. I will tell the thing ingenuously as it occurred without injecting anything of my own, which is no small achievement for a historian."

The reliability of official news media is subjected to critical thought. The controlled ability of Micromégas to inject knowledge of his own is intriguing. The esoteric reader is reminded of a statement made more than once by Mme Blavatsky. According to that statement the printed version of the Secret Doctrine withholds far more than it gives out. What Micromégas could "give out" may concern occult tenets relative to the poles. Among them might be the view that "vast concaves" leading inside our hollow earth are concealed under polar ice. The emphatic use of the preposition *under* and the reference to the *under-side* of cards may suggest as much. The French word "cartes" which means "cards" also means "maps." The quoted passage of *Micromégas* gives rise to speculation which brings to mind — and tends to validate — the statement of Saint Exupéry. Some "geographies" may well be "the most precious of all books."

The mystery of human origin and destination is suggested by a startling confession of L'Ingénu. Asked who he is and where he is going, the young man replies that he does not know. Identity is expressed by tribe or nationality, not individuality. "I am a Huron." The hero seems to partake of the nameless state which represents impersonal and spiritual Being.

The arrival of the Huron in non-ethereal realms is attended by understandable culture shock. The Kerkabon family combines typical traits of modern middle-class Christianity. Subconscious ambivalence reigns, an attitude which can be expected of Fifth Race mankind. Spirit and Matter are in approximate equilibrium. Sensuality is general but controlled The head of the household personifies prevailing values. As the worthy resident of a Pantagruelic domain— the "pays de Cocagne" bordering on Normandy — the prior does honor to a fine table. But his indulgence is not excessive. He has had his share of amorous pleasure in his day. But age — perhaps wisdom — has subdued clamoring flesh. He is professionally addicted to the texts of Augustine. But he "amuses himself" with Rabelais. Rabelaisian interests may lead to rapid growth.

The womenfolk tend to combine religion and pleasure. Such an aspiration is legitimate, "pleasure" and spirituality being synonymous in the esoteric vocabulary. But the only religion known to them has degraded divine essence to the plane of materiality. They are accordingly and devoutly sensuous. Kindness and healthy curiosity are their redeeming traits.

The name of the Kerkabon family seems to reflect the smug yet genuine benevolence of the Church-affiliated gentry — "Good Church". It may be noted briefly that the name "Méséglise" which is connected with "Legrandrin" in the *Recherche* means the exact opposite. The Church is a major aspect of "the infamous" in the Voltairian system. The Proustian name which means "Bad Church" may therefore be regarded as an "inverted" "Good Church" if "Legrandin" has anything to do with Voltaire.

The Kerkabon clan is the "élément bien pensant" of modern Western Europe, the ultimate in sugar-coated ignorance, bigotry and provincialism. Such traits are promptly demonstrated by disarming comments.

352

The physical appearance of the young American elicits the following gem:

> " 'That big boy has a peaches and cream complexion! What a beautiful skin he has for a Huron!' " (Ch. I, p. 248).

Language is another source of priceless statements. The alleged beauty of the Huronian dialect strains the imagination of Mlle de Karkabon:

> " 'Is that possible?' exclaimed Mlle de Kerkabon. 'I had always thought that French was the most beautiful of all languages next to the dialect of Low Brittany.' " (Ch. I, p. 250).

Pity, as well as curiosity, is aroused by the stranger. Everyone laments the fact that the young man is an orphan. Cleverly concealed by the vivid — though concise — evocation of bourgeois *sensibilité* is the esoteric meaning of the passage:

> "The company was moved, and everybody repeated:
> *'Neither father, nor mother!'* "

The italicized wail of the Kerkabon family serves the esoteric needs of an important occult concept: the Anupadaka or "Parentless." Although it is often linked to the status of *Bodhisattva* or voluntary, altruistically motivated reincarnation, the state of *Anupadaka* is latent in every man. The "Parentless" state is also a "nameless" state.

> "*Atma* (our seventh principle) being identical with the universal Spirit, and man being one with it in his essence, what is then the Monad proper? It is that homogeneous spark which radiates in millions of rays from the primeval 'Seven': — of which seven further on. It is *the* EMANATING *spark from the* UNCREATED Ray — a mystery. In the esoteric, and even exoteric Buddhism of the North, Adi Buddha (*Chogoi dangpoi sangye*), the One unknown, without beginning or end, identical with Parabrahm and Ain-Soph, emits a bright ray from its darkness.
> This is the *Logos* (the first), or Vajradhara, the Supreme Buddha (also called *Dorjechang*). As the Lord of all Mysteries he cannot manifest, but sends into the world of manifestation his heart — the 'diamond heart,' Vajrasattva (*Dorjesempa*). This is the second logos of creation; from which emanate the seven (in the exoteric blind the five) Dhyani Buddhas, called the Anupadaka, 'the parentless.' These Buddhas are the primeval monads from the world of *incorporeal being,* the *Arupa* world, wherein the Intelligences (on that plane only) have neither shape nor name, in the exoteric system, but have their distinct seven names in esoteric philosophy." (*The Secret Doctrine,* p. 571, Vol. I).
> "The Occult Catechism contains the following questions and answers: *'What is it that ever is?' 'Space, the eternal Anupadaka.'* ' — even every

---

*"Meaning 'parentless.' "

353

Soul-endowed man also is an Anupadaka in a latent *state.*'" (*The Secret Doctrine*, p. 52, Vol. I).

The "Nameless" and "Parentless" state appears in many literary texts notably the works of Proust. Odette, the likely "Great O" of the probable Kalahamsa — the "Great Swan of Time" — is compared to "a young girl of good family, who no longer belonged to any family."* "Albertine," the beloved of Marcel, has "neither father nor mother."** Mme de Villeparisis, the libertine noblewoman, has "plunged into nothingness the greatest name in France."***

The appellation *L'Ingénu* reflects character traits demonstrated in the course of life, not an externally determined identity such as a family name. It is consistent with the suggested passage from a nameless, parentless state into material and personalized being.

> "'I have always been called L'Ingénu,' the Huron resumed, 'and I received confirmation of the name in England, because I always say naïvely what I think as I do all that I please.'" (Ch. I, p. 249).

The idea of "confirmation" is connected with the fact of informal — yet appropriate — "baptism." The identity of the young man seems to be fully known in ethereal "English" spheres. Such a fact tends to suggest a link to one of the "Intelligences" which "have neither shape nor name, in the exoteric system, but have their distinct seven names in esoteric philosophy." If such be the case, L'Ingénu belongs to exalted spiritual hierarchies. The "Parentless" Anupadaka of voluntary reincarnation is present in non-latent state.

The last part of the statement of the young man is a probable allusion to the famous "Do as you please" of the Abbaye of Thélème. Rather than sophisticated anarchy, the Rabelaisian injunction prescribes self-knowledge and self-discipline of a kind which has natural appeal to "well-born" persons. The importance of "birth" or Karmic antecedents is conveyed in the case of the young American by the word "naïvely" — "naïvement" — which has related etymology. The young hero will subsequently declare that he admires the works of Rabelais. Voltaire seems to indulge in the type of Rabelaisian allusion which has numerous counterparts in the writings of great "smugglers." Such is the chapter of *The Little Prince* in which an intriguing physician and "peddler of perfected pills" which slake "thirst" answers a question. Asked what one might do with fifty-three minutes saved, the medicine-man replies: "One does as one pleases with them."

A la Recherche du temps perdu, p. 77, Vol. I.
**Ibid.*, p. 48, Vol. III.
*** *Ibid.*, p. 294, Vol. II.

The Secret Doctrine records as follows the change which came over mankind as the Atlantean Fourth Race made its appearance on Earth. Various phases of the change seem to be reflected by traits of the Voltairian hero.

"— with the Fourth Race we reach the purely human period. Those who were hitherto semi-divine beings, self-imprisoned in bodies which were human only in appearance, became physiologically changed and took unto themselves wives who were entirely human and fair to look at, but in whom lower, more material, though sidereal, beings had incarnated. These beings in female forms (Lilith is the prototype of these in the Jewish tradition) are called in the esoteric accounts 'Khado' (Dakini in Sanskrit). Allegorical legends call the chief of these Liliths, (*Sangye Khado* (Buddha Dakini, in Sanskrit); all are credited with the art of 'walking in the air,' and the greatest *kindness to mortals*; but *no mind* — only animal instinct.

The worshippers were giants in stature; but they were giants in knowledge and learning, though it came to them more easily than it does to the men of our modern times. Their *Science* was innate in them. The Lemuro-Atlantean had no need of discovering and fixing in his memory that which his informing PRINCIPLE *knew* at the moment of his incarnation. Time alone, and the ever-growing obtuseness of the matter in which the *Principles* had clothed themselves, could, the one, weaken the memory of their pre-natal knowledge, the other, blunt and even extinguish every spark of the spiritual and divine in them. Therefore had they, from the first, — fallen victim to their animal natures and bred 'monsters.' — i.e., men of distinct varieties from themselves." (*The Secret Doctrine*, pp. 284-85, Vol. II).

The athletic ability of the young American has already been noted. The spectacular leap of the hero above and beyond the heads of his traveling companions is a likely remnant of "the art of walking in the air" which was once practiced by his "sidereal" ancestry. "Kindness to mortals" is demonstrated by generosity. A small talisman which is highly prized by the young man is given to the Kerkabons. Innate spiritual knowledge or instinctively accurate perception will become apparent in the course of the story. It will be found that the puzzling primitive has basically sound judgment — "il avait l'esprit juste".* The influence of a "mindless" heredity will be observed. It will be compensated by the presence of other faculties. The legacy of gigantic stature is dimly perceived by Mlle de Kerkabon who glowingly refers to L'Ingénu as "this big boy." The prevalence of instinct is obvious and readily admitted by the principal himself. The "clothing" of spiritual principles in matter is eventually represented by the acquisiton of a "coat of skin," the "fleshy body" of mankind, and by the "taking of a wife." Metaphysical con-

---

*Ch. VI.

sciousness is retained from a lingering spiritual heritage. It is symbolized by the bottle of "spirits" and by the talisman. It will become
manifest in the hero's reaction to Christian faith. The inverse relation-
existing between spiritual instinct and un-spiritualized intelligence will
be reflected throughout the story by waxing and waning trends of both
attributes. The progressive and retrogressive aspect of human evolution
which is expounded in the Secret Doctrine will be a central element of
L'Ingénu. The "Atlantean" hero and Western European Fifth Race mankind — the Kerkabons — will be affected by the same process operating
in opposite directions. Primitive spirituality will be enriched by the
growth of the intellect. A transmutation of Western rationality will take
place.

The American hero tells his story to the Kerkabons. He has had one
love only: an Indian mistress named Abacaba. The reversible quality
of her name suggests the cyclic pattern of Universal Law. Her description is a poetic evocation of Nature:

> "— reeds are not straighter, hermin is not whiter, sheep are less gentle,
> eagles less proud, and deer are not so light as was Abacaba." (Ch.
> I, p. 251).

Righteousness, purity, tenderness, dignity, and speed characterize the
maiden. Such traits are perceptual and ethical requirements of spirituality. The lightness or "speed" of deer suggests the agency of an
"informing PRINCIPLE" capable of immediate cognition. Intuition is
the sole remnant of primitive spirituality possessed by Fifth Race mankind.

The intuitive flash is often celebrated by esoteric writers who rely
on its work for the unveiling of their concealed message. The allegorical
Eva of Alfred de Vigny has the gift of soaring thought which is compared to the leaps of gazelles. The "Minotaur" of Shelley — alias JOHN
— perhaps *Revelations* — and JOHN BULL, the "English" common man
— can leap any gate in all Boeotia."*

The portrayal of Abacaba and the cyclic quality of her name point
to her esoteric identity: the occult concept of Nature or the Primitive
Wisdom-Religion.

The young man once helped Abacaba defeat her enemy: a poacher of
bullying disposition who belonged to the tribe of the Algonquins:

> " 'A badly brought up Algonquin, who lived a hundred leagues away,
> came to take her hare; I learned of it; I rushed over, I overcame the
> Algonquin with a blow of my club, I brought him bound and gagged
> to the feet of my beloved. The parents of Abacaba wanted to eat him;
> but I never had any taste for that kind of feast; I gave him his freedom

---

Oedipus Tyrannus.

356

and made a friend of him. Abacaba was so moved by my behavior that she preferred me to all her admirers." (Ch. I, p. 251).

The Indian maiden is a huntress. She may therefore be connected with Diana-Isis as may Cunégonde whose name is rooted in the concept of cynegetics. The vowel content of the word *Algonquin* suggests the veiled presence of IAO, the tyrannical and loutish "Vice-God" of Voltairian mythology. The "poaching" — stealing, plagiarising — tendencies of the villain and the expression "mal élevé" — ill-manered, badly brought up — suggest unmerited high status and usurpation of the rights of others. Such traits leave little doubt as to the veiled identity of the character. The scorned cannibalistic feast is a probable barb aimed at the Christian sacrament of communion. The "Algonquin" is an American extension of Itobad, the icoglan and Ragotski — not to mention the "Egyptian" and "Jew" of *Zadig* or the transparent "Lord" of Thunder-ten-tronckh.

The Algonquin is controlled with the aid of a club, a weapon suggesting Hercules. The latter name is later conferred upon the young hero. Surprisingly the subdued bully becomes the friend of the title character. The magnanimous conduct of the victor wins the favor of the beloved The resulting triangle — IAO, Abacaba-Truth, and Hercules — is brought into harmonious co-existence by the girl. The enlightening, unifying influence of Abacaba is consistent with her identity of Primitive Wisdom-Religion. The unexpected friendship seems to reflect Pagan awareness of the true essence of IAO, Bacchus, Saturn, and other equivalent mythological figures. Primitive insight does not allow the "badly brought up Algonquin" to be more than an inferior "Vice-God." The Ingénu deserves credit for an important revelation: IAO is only a second-rate and vulnerable figure. The alliance of Man and Truth suffices to expose him as such. As *Candide* clearly shows and as *L'Ingénu* will confirm — the same insight is hard to come by in the "Westphalian" sector of Fifth Race mankind.

The forgiving attitude of the young Indian may also be explained by other facts. Champions of Truth are ever reluctant to kill. The young man shows the same reverence of life as Zadig and Candide. His willingness to "forgive and forget" may also reflect his own state of purity and the lingering influence of the "mindless" race.

The encounter between Abacaba and the Algonquin grows out of pursuit of the same prey: a hare. The symbolic value of the animal connects the veiled substance of the episode with twin aspects of the same primitive tradition common to America and Egypt:

"Among the Algonquin Indians, the Great Hare is the animal-demiurge.

357

The myth was also known to the Egyptians." (J. E. Cirlot, *A Dictionary of Symbols*, Philosophical Library, New York, 1962).

The contested status of Demiurge — or Creative Logos — is understandably coveted by the "badly brought up Algonquin." The defeat suffered by the usurper at the hands of the young hero is one suggestion among many of the esoteric standing of the Ingénu.

The esoteric value of the hare probably lies also in its hybrid character. One variety of hare, the leporine, is of mixed origin. Its remarkable fertility tends to support a major tenet of the Secret Doctrine. The rule of sterility which is believed to apply to all mixed species is not universal. The alleged interbreeding of Atlanteans with animals may therefore be compatible with the continuity of the resulting race.

> "If men existed two million years ago, they must have been — just as the animals were — quite different physically and anatomically from what they have become; and they were nearer then to the type of pure mammalian animal than they are now. Anyhow, we learn that the animal world breeds strictly *inter se, i.e.,* in accordance with genus and species — only since the appearance *on this earth* of the Atlantean race. As demonstrated by the author of that able work, *Modern Science and Modern Thought*, this idea of the refusal to breed with another species, or that sterility is the only result of such breeding, 'appears to be a *prima facie* deduction rather than an absolute 'law' even now. He shows that 'different species, in fact, often breed together, as may be seen in the familiar instance of the horse and ass. It is true that in this case the mule is sterile . . . but this rule is not universal, and recently one new hybrid race, that of the leporine, or hare-rabbit, has been created which is perfectly fertile.'" (*The Secret Doctrine*, p. 287, Vol. II).

The esoteric function of the hare in *L'Ingénu* is in part that of a connecting link with the Atlantean phase of evolution, a phase *exoterically* surveyed in the chapter of *Candide* featuring the ape-men. The Ingénu will soon display bestial traits worthy of his gigantic ancestors as he descends into regions of deep materiality: *Low* Brittany. The hybrid character of the hare may also symbolize the outlook of Fifth Race mankind, an adjustment equally susceptible to the forces of matter and spirit. The dualism in question which is apparent in the psychology of the Kerkabons becomes increasingly apparent in the behavior of the young Indian as he plunges into materiality and "generation." The presence of the hare is also a reflection of the spiritual decline which befell Fourth Race and Fifth Race humanity. The Primitive Wisdom-Religion-Abacaba-and Jehovah — the "badly brought up Algonquin" — compete for dominance over mankind — the ambivalent and cowardly hare.

The appearance of the Indian Jehovah is quickly — and logically —

358

followed by the disappearance of Abacaba. Jehovah and Truth cannot visibly co-exist. The allegorical maiden is devoured by a beast — a likely precursor of the Beast of the Apocalypse, "soul-killing Churchianity" and "SUPERSTITION". Spirit enters a period of obscuration.

> " 'She would still love me if she had not been eaten by a bear.' " (Ch. I, pp. 251-52).

Following the evolutionary trend of descent into materiality, Abacaba or Primitive Wisdom, is eclipsed and forced to become more and more esoteric. The same process of "going underground" is recorded by Vigny in *La Maison du berger*. The Muse is prohibited from teaching "wisdom" — Science — when satyrs make their first appearance on the scene of evolution.

> "La muse a mérité les insolents sourires
> Et les soupçons moqueurs qu'éveille son aspect,
> Dès que son oeil chercha le regard des satyres,
> Sa parole trembla, son serment fut suspect;
> Il lui fut interdit d'enseigner la sagesse."

> ("The Muse has deserved the insolent smiles
> And the sneering suspicions aroused by her appearance,
> As soon as her eye sought the eye of satyrs,
> Her word quavered, her oath became suspect;
> She was prohibited from teaching wisdom.")

The same process of obscuration is allegorized in mythology:

> "The fable of Aristeus pursuing Eurydike into the woods where a serpent occasions her death, is a very plain allegory, which was in part explained at the earliest times. Aristeus is *brutal power,* pursuing Eurydike, the esoteric doctrine, into the woods, where the serpent (emblem of every sun-god, and worshipped under its grosser aspect even by the Jews) kills her; i.e., forces truth to become still more esoteric, and seek shelter in the underworld, which is not the hell of our theologians. Moreover, the fate of Orpheus, torn to pieces by the Bacchantes, is another allegory to show that the gross and popular rites are always more welcome than divine but simple truth, and proves the great difference that must have existed between the esoteric and the popular worship." (*Isis Unveiled*, pp. 129-30, Vol. 2).

The symbolism of spirit engulfed by a "beast" is conveyed by the first illustration of *The Little Prince*. An animal is about to be swallowed by a snake which has *seven* coils. The theme of "spirit strangled in the coils of matter"* is transparently rendered.

The Secret Doctrine, p. 377, Vol. II.

The bear which killed Abacaba is exterminated by the bereft lover who wears its hide as a coat:

> " 'I punished the bear, I wore its hide for a long time, but that did not console me.' " (Ch. I, p. 252).

Nothing can alleviate the sorrow of mankind as long as Truth is obscured.

The veiled significance of the "coat of skin" — which is given in a previous chapter — bears repeating:

> "The Chaldean Kabalists tell us that primeval man, who, contrary to the Darwinian theory was purer, wiser, and far more spiritual, as shown by the myths of the Scandinavian Bor, the Hindu Devatas, and the Mosaic 'Sons of God,' — in short of a far higher nature than the man of the present Adamic race — became despiritualized or tainted with matter, and then for the first time, was given the *fleshy body,* which is typified in *Genesis* in that profoundly significant verse: 'Unto Adam and to his wife did the Lord God *make coats of skin,* and clothed them.' (*Genesis,* iii, 2) Unless the commentators would make of the First Cause a *celestial tailor,* what else can the apparently absurd words mean, but that the spiritual man had reached, through the process of involution, that point where matter, predominating over and conquering spirit, had transformed him into the physical man, or the Second Adam, of the second chapter of *Genesis?*" (*Isis Unveiled,* p. 149, Vol. 1).

The tone of exasperated irony which pervades the above text would not be out of place in the writings of Voltaire. Literal or phallic interpretation of the Scriptures is attacked. Eurydike is indeed buried in darkness when such renditions as the myth of a *celestial tailor* prevail. Voltaire treats the same subject with his own brand of humor, noting allegory to be "popular in Canada" — or ethereal regions — and generally misunderstood elsewhere. The celestial tailor of Mme Blavatsky has a counterpart in *L'Ingénu.* Voltaire describes the feverish preparations made for the Christian baptism of the hero. The services of the most skilled tailor in Saint Malo are retained for the grand occasion. The vowel content of the words Sa*i*nt M*a*lo confirms previous suggestions that *Low* Brittany is the low point of the descending arc of evolution, a stage dominated by IAO-Jehovah.

The esoteric "coat of skin" is found in numerous literary texts. One attempt to shed the burdensome garment in described by Proust. The grandmother of Marcel is involved:

> "One day when she had been left alone one instant, I found her, standing up, in her nightgown, trying to open the window — We barely had time to seize my grand-mother, she waged against my mother an al-

most brutal struggle, then defeated, forcibly seated back into an arm-chair, she stopped willing, regretting, her face rebecame almost im-passible and she began to carefully remove the hair of fur which had been left on her nightgown by a coat thrown over her." (*A la Recherche du temps perdu*, p. 333, Vol. II).

Man has many coats of skin to wear and discard in the course of his voyage through "necessity." The fact is noted by Céline in the final lines of *Mort à Crédit*. "There's no shortage of overcoats." The kind, wise uncle of Ferdinand lavishes sage advice on his badly shaken nephew. The *Angelus* is part of a deceptively prosaic picture as is the "crocodile" — *Makara*, Capricorn.* Mankind is cautioned not to go through the "degrees" foolishly — "by mistake". The necessary "light" is there, within reach:

> "He covered me all up, he buried me under a pile of overcoats — I had all his bearskins on top of me. . . . I looked at the walls of the room. . . . They'd got smaller too. . . . It was the middle room, the one with the *Angelus* in it. . . .
> 'What do you think, you old crocodile? — the dear child! — The little treasure! — And me trying to explain —
> 'Don't take the stairs by mistake — The lamp is on the table — There's no shortage of coats.' " (*Death on the Installment Plan*, Ralph Manheim Tr.).

The descent of primeval man into materiality is eloquently dramatized in *L'Ingénu* by loss of occult heritage — talisman —, acquisition of a physical body — "coat of skin" —, acquisition of a name — separate be-ing —, acquisition of relatives — incarnation —, the "taking of a wife" . . . and conversion to Christianity.

The identity of the young man is revealed by the talisman given to the Kerkabons in a gesture of gratitude The hero proves to be the long-lost nephew of the benevolent family. The melodramatic element of the situation serves to veil the importance of a spiritual happening. Occult parentage is implied to exist between the Old World and the New. Two separated "generations" are reunited. A fusion of time and space marks the transfer of the magical object.

The Ingénu may not be fully aware of the value of the cherished pos-session. Innate spirituality tends to make him take for granted the precious talisman. The hero parts with the symbol of his occult heritage. The transaction initiates the gradual blunting of spirituality which marked the development of the Fourth Race and which is recorded by Mme Blavatsky in a text previously quoted.

The Secret Doctrine, p. 219, Vol. I.

" 'It is my most precious possession,' he said to them; 'I was assured that I would always be happy as long as I wore this little knicknack on my person, and I give it to you so that you may be happy always.' " (Ch. II, p. 253).

The power of talismans is recognized in *Isis Unveiled*:

"Apply a piece of iron to a magnet, and it becomes imbued with its subtile principle and capable of imparting it to other iron in its turn. It neither weighs more nor appears different from what it was before. And yet, one of the most subtile potencies of nature has entered into its substance. A talisman, in itself perhaps a worthless bit of metal, a scrap of paper, or a shred of any fabric, has nevertheless been imbued by the influence of that greatest of all magnets, the human will, with a potency for good or ill just as recognizable and as real in its effect as the subtile property which the iron acquired by contact with the physical magnet." (*Isis Unveiled*, p. 462, Vol. I).

A parallel is invited between the fetishes of the Negro of Surinam and the talisman of the Ingénu. The words of the money-minded mother of the slave come to mind: "My dear child, bless our fetishes, worship them always, they will make you live happy." The equivalence of spiritualty and joy is stated in each case. The fetishes of the black man are praised at a time when slavery begins. The talisman of the Ingénu is commended at a time when the bondage of mankind to false values nears its end.

The Kerkabons are touched by the tone of simple penetration of the donor. They are also amused. Such a naive endorsement of "superstition" is all that can be expected from a near-"savage." The shock of the encounter with the American is gratifyingly lessened by a feeling of racial and cultural superiority. The materialistic outlook of the French family does not allow its members to see more than "a small talisman" always worn "around the neck" of the stranger: "two small portraits" — of a man and woman — "rather poorly done, tied together by a very oily leather thong." The double medallion design is indeed a "most precious" "jewel" — identical to the COLLIER of Vigny's *Destinées*. The deceptive, drab object represents two circles: the cyclic pattern of cosmic evolution and the corresponding scheme of life on the human plane. The NECKLACE and the THREAD are received by modern Western mankind from a kinsman. The gift is indeed connected with a "New World" in the making, a world which has regained awareness of KARMA-SUTRATMA, the cornerstone of the Secret Doctrine. Any person truly possessed of that "jewel" can retain true happiness throughout the worst struggles of life. Such a person is blessed with "Happy Certainty" and "Trusting Hope."

The "oily" character of the "thong "or thread — suggestive of a certain "coat of skin" — brings to mind an early phase of human evolution designated as the era of the "sweat-born" in the Secret Doctrine. Another evolutionary hint is supplied by the combination of the "male and female" represented by the portraits. The reference to "grease" or "oil" also brings to mind "Chrestos" — the "anointed." The combination of sacred "oil, of a Christ-figure, and of a given "necklace" points to more than the transmission of knowledge. The "most precious" personal possession of one being — Karma — is surrendered for the sake of others. The gift is — among other things — the GREAT SACRIFICE: voluntary reincarnation.

One may gauge the full depth of esoteric humor characterizing the "rather poorly done" portraits. How can so many, such things be rendered — pictorially or otherwise!

The Kerkabons are unprepared to perceive the multiple meanings of the occasion. But the transmission of magic has an immediate result: the discovery of amazing "connections."

The talisman supplies a missing link in the mysterious chain of human parentage. A close tie is found to exist between a primitive world and representatives of Western European Fifth Race mankind. The dramatic discovery illustrates a major tenet of the Secret Doctrine. Certain data pertaining to the origin of Man — and Cosmos — can be obtained from occult science and from it only. The talisman — or symbol of secret lore — solves the enigma of the genealogy of modern Man.

"No greater riddle exists in science, no problem is more hopelessly insoluble, than the question: How old — even approximately — are the Sun and Moon, the Earth and Man? What does modern science know of the duration of the ages of the World, or even of the length of geological periods?

Nothing; *absolutely nothing.*

If one turns to science for chronological information, one is told by those who are straightforward and truthful, as for instance Mr. Pengelly, the eminent geologist, 'We do not know.' One will learn that, so far, no trustworthy numerical estimate of the ages of the world and man could be made, and that both geology and anthropology are at sea. Yet when a student of esoteric philosophy presumes to bring forward the teachings of Occult Science, he is at once sat upon. Why should this be so, since, when reduced to their own physical methods, the greatest scientists have failed to arrive even at an approximate agreement?" (*The Secret Doctrine,* p. 66, Vol. II).

"If the Pythagorean metempsychosis should be thoroughly explained and compared with the modern theory of evolution, it would be found to supply every 'missing link' in the chain of the latter. But who of our scientists would consent to lose his precious time over the vagaries of the ancients." (*Isis Unveiled,* p. 9, Vol. I).

"The mistaken theories of monogenesis, and the descent of man from

363

the mammals instead of the reverse are fatal to the completeness of evolution as taught in modern schools on Darwinian lines, and they will have to be abandoned in view of the insuperable difficulties which they encounter. Occult tradition — if the terms Science and Knowledge are denied in this particular to antiquity — can alone reconcile the inconsistencies and fill the gap." (*The Secret Doctrine*, p. 118, Vol. II).

The occult kinship esoterically disclosed in Chapter II involves a spectacular background of History and Geography. An allegory of Atlantis seems to have risen from the sea in the person of the young hero. The Atlantean continent is linked to Brittany by cultural ties. Atlantis and the Armoric peninsula share a common bond with Egypt. The Egyptian pyramids are believed to have been built by degenerate descendants of the last Atlanteans. The Egyptian Karnak is regarded by occultists as the "twin brother to the Carnac of Bretagne, the latter Carnac meaning the serpent's mount."* Various cyclopean ruins such as the *menhirs* of Brittany are regarded by occultists as remnants of subterranean dwellings once inhabited by the "divine instructors" of mankind.

> "— the Adepts or 'Wise' men of the three Races (the Third, Fourth, and the Fifth) dwelt in subterranean habitats, generally under some kind of pyramidal structure, if not actually under a pyramid. For such 'pyramids' existed in the four corners of the world and were never the monopoly of the land of the Pharaohs, though until found scattered all over the two Americas, under and over ground, beneath and amidst virgin forests, as in plain and vale, they were supposed to be the exclusive property of Egypt. If the true geometrically correct pyramids are no longer found in European regions, many of the supposed early *neolithic* caves, of the colossal triangular pyramidal and conical *menhirs* in the Morbihan, and Brittany generally; many of the Danish tumuli and even of the 'giant tombs' of Sardinia with their inseparable companions, the *nuraghi*, are so many more or less clumsy copies of the pyramids." (*The Secret Doctrine*, pp. 351-52, Vol. II).

The cultural tradition of Notre Dame de la Montagne — the habitat and the Church of the Kerkabons — combines a legendary Irish saint, the "Mountain" or North Pole, Brittany, and the Celtic heritage in general. The Nordic heritage is itself believed to have its origin in the Atlantean civilization. Europe is thought to be inhabited by descendants of "pure Atlanteans and 'Africo'-Atlantean" races.** The Celtic and Atlantean background of the Kerkabons is common to L'Ingénu and to his long-lost relatives. The relationship revealed by occult lore —

The Secret Doctrine, p. 380, Vol. II.
**Ibd.*, pp. 740-41, Vol. II.

the talisman — has staggering implications. Western European Fifth Race mankind has cultural ties with the entire world.

"The mystery veiling the origin and the religion of the Druids, is as great as that of their supposed fanes is to the modern Symbologist, but not to the initiated Occultists. Their priests were the descendents of the last Atlanteans, and what is known of them is sufficient to allow the inference that they were eastern priests akin to the Chaldeans and Indians, though little more. It may be inferred that they symbolized their deity as the Hindus do their Vishnu, as the Egyptians did their *Mystery God*, and as the builders of the Ohio Great-Serpent mound worshipped theirs — namely under the form of the 'mighty Serpent,' the emblem of the eternal deity TIME (the Hindu Kâlâ). Pliny called them the 'Magi of the Gauls and Britons.' But they were more than that. The author of *'Indian Antiquities'* finds much affinity between the Druids and the Brahmins of India. Dr. Borlase points to a close analogy between them and the Magi of Persia; others will see an identity between them and the Orphic priesthood of Thrace; simply because they were connected, in their esoteric teachings, with the universal Wisdom Religion, and thus presented affinities with the exoteric worship of all." (*The Secret Doctrine*, p. 756, Vol. II).

The geographical setting of *L'Ingénu* — the region of Saint Malo — seems to be the same as the coastal area celebrated — and shielded — by "Legrandin" in the *Recherche*. The Proustian Balbec is generally believed to represent Cabourg, a sea-side resort of Eastern Normandy which was visited by Proust. But the characterization of Balbec which is made by Legrandin seems to designate Brittany: "Balbec, the most ancient geological bone structure of our soil, truly Ar-Mor, the Sea, the end of the land."* The apparent conflict between the Pays d'Auge or coastal region of Eastern Normandy and Brittany may be resolved by a text of Anatole France, an author to whom exoteric reference is made by Legrandin in the same passage. *Penguin Island* begins with stories of legendary "auges de granit" — granite "troughs" — reported to have sailed to the bay of the Mont Saint Michel which is not far distant from Saint Malo. The reference to Anatole France may thus be an esoteric invitation to translate the "Pays d'Auge" as the Mont Saint Michel and Saint Malo area.

The reluctance of Legrandin to send eager explorers to Balbec becomes understandable if Balbec represents the esoteric domain of Legrandin-Voltaire. "No Balbec before fifty years, . . ."** says the puzzling engineer to young "Marcel" who wishes to visit the magical religion. The prohibition of Legrandin may be compared to the incorruptible attitude of "Mrs. Right-Time" — "Mme Bontemps". The ineluctable law which applies to the esoteric domain of Balbec also applies to the release of "Albertine"

---

*A la Recherche du temps perdu, p. 130, Vol. I.
**Ibid., p. 132, Vol. I.

whose secret — "inversion", esotericism — parallels the secret of "Saint Loup" — Vigny.

Legrandin is noted to have extensive knowledge of the "celestial geography of Low Normandy." The observation may concern the cosmogenetic element of *L'Ingénu*. The region of the Mont Saint Michel is found to have retained the cult of Odin which rivals — if it does not supplant — the cult of Christ.* The apparent opposition between both types of worship covers an esoteric equivalence. Odin is regarded by occultists as one of many Buddhas or "historical sages,"** in other words as a counterpart of Christ.

The etymology of the word *Balbec* is a subject of occasional speculation twice accompanied by reference to the esoteric brotherhood of the Templar Knights.*** The true meaning of *Balbec* is eventually perceived by "Marcel" in a vision of Ancient Egypt. Balbec becomes a mummy bathed in sunshine. The site of Thebes-*Karnak where Baal* was once venerated is evoked. The titanic ruins of Baalbek, Lebanon are also brought to mind. The resident of the Judaeo-Christian establishment — the "Grand Hotel" of Balbec — finds the cultural source of his own heritage in Egypt and in the East.

The syncretic background of Celtic regions which is noted by "Legrandin," Anatole France, and "Marcel" points to the same secret lore which is methodically woven into the fabric of *L'Ingénu*.

The reunion of long separated relatives prompts unorthodox thoughts on the sacredness of family ties. As was the case in the strange paternity suit featured in *Zadig*, blood connections are judged relatively unimportant in their biological aspect. They belong to the realm of incarnate illusion — Maya. Learning that he is the long-lost nephew of the prior of Notre Dame de la Montagne, the young hero is heard to voice unenthusiastic feelings: he might as well have the prior as an uncle as another man.

The clamorous joy of the Kerkabons is not fully shared by the Ingénu. It is quickly surmised by his new-found family that he may have a nostalgic longing for "England" — the "land of angels" or ethereal existence. The esoteric meaning of "England" is hardly suspected at first but the speculation does honor to the occasional insight of the family. The young American remains puzzling to the Kerkabons. He scorns beds to which he prefers a simple blanket and a floor. Spying through a symbolic keyhole, the Kerkabon women observe the sleep of their strange relative who lies "in the most beautiful posture in the world."

Ibid., p. 890, Vol. II.
**The Secret Doctrine*, p. 423, Vol. II.
****A la Recherche du temps perdu*, pp. 936, 1105, Vol. I.

Lingering spirituality makes furniture irrelevant to the ethereal creature.

The spiritual generation gap separating the Kerkabons from their nephew is manifest in their different modes of thanksgiving. The ways of the Indian are unconventional by "Westphalian" standards:

> "They went to give thanks to God in the Church of our Lady of the Mountain, while the Huron, with an air of indifference, amused himself by drinking in the house." (Ch. II, p. 255).

The esoteric significance of "drinking" and the Voltairian value of "amusement" cast merry lights on the passage. Appearances to the contrary, it is the unrefined and "indifferent" — or serene — "stranger" who partakes of the "spirit." No church or *Te Deum* are needed by the primitive; only the "house" or Temple constituted by Man himself.

> "The world needs no sectarain church, whether of Buddha, Jesus, Mahomet, Swedenborg, Calvin, or any other. There being but ONE Truth, man requires but one church — the Temple of God within walled in by matter but penetrable by any one who can find the way; the pure at heart see god." (*Isis Unveiled,* p. 635, Vol. 2).

The church-going of the Kerkabons is a matter of some irony. The syncretic quality of the name of their parish — Our Lady of the Mountain — combines the Virgin — a Christian mutation of Isis — and Paganism — the "Mountain" or North Pole. But the devout family would react with horror were anyone to disclose to them the Pagan origin of their creed. The estrangement of modern Western man from the source of his spiritual heritage is a common theme of esoteric writers which is dramatized in the humorous passage of Chapter II. So total is the related blindness of the average person that the symbolism of the Primitive Wisdom-Religion is experienced daily without recognition. The Christian separation of Temple and Inner Man blurs the vision of a major segment of Fifth Race humanity.

The same separation may explain why Proustian dreams envision "houses" and "churches" made one within the boundless vista of the ocean. The landlocked church of Balbec — hemmed in by solid materiality — must be viewed through the medium of Art — Elstir — to reveal its obscured Pagan beauty. The dreams of Marcel are realized in Venice, a city symbolically wedded to the sea where "houses" and "churches" are joined.

The same city is credited with the discovery of the Inner Man in *Candide.*

The educational background of the Huron is evaluated. It is quite limited. Asked if he has ever read any books, the young man replies

367

that he has some knowledge of the works of Rabelais and that he is familiar with certain writings of Shakespeare. Understandable delight is expressed — "he was quite pleased with them." ("il en était fort content.") The presence of the word *fort* suggests sensitivity to the spiritual message of Rabelais. The texts have been read in "English" — or esoteric — "translation." Similar enjoyment has been derived from the works of Shakespeare. The "informing PRINCIPLE" and 'innate Science" attributed to early human races seems to operate in the case of the primitive. The veiled material which will not be perceived by his allegorical relatives for some time is instantly clear to him.

> "First of all he was asked if he had ever read any books. He said that he had read Rabelais translated into English, and a few excerpts from Shakespeare which he knew by heart; that he had found those books at the home of the ship captain who had brought him from America to Plymouth, and that he was quite pleased with them. The bailli did not fail to interrogate him on those books. 'I confess to you,' said the Ingénu, 'that I thought I divined parts of them and that I did not understand the rest.'" (Ch. II, p. 256).

The exoteric aspect of Rabelaisian texts is naturally puzzling to the Ingénu. But the young man will soon learn the facts of life which prompt certain commentaries and which make certain veils necessary.

Limited as it seems to be, the educational background of the Ingénu has formidable potential. The intuitive nature of his insight compensates his apparent lack of knowledge. The sensitive reader goes straight to the core of obscure material. Few "Low Britons" are capable of so grasping even part of the message "smuggled" by Rabelais and Shakespeare. The inquisitive bailli — whose fiendish identity becomes more and more clear as the story progresses — knows that he is in the presence of an unusual person.

The uncle and the nephew have a common interest in Rabelaisian literature. The prior "amuses himself" with Rabelais when tired of Saint Augustine. Voltaire does not specify the type of amusement thus derived. But it is likely to grow from exoteric pornography. The priest is not reported to read Rabelais in "English" translation, a fact which tends to suggest dead-letter interpretation. The popular philosophy of "giving the devil his due" seems to be practiced by the prior. Saint Augustine is a professional must. Rabelais is a fair substitute for prohibited sex. The situation is not without irony. One man— a primitive — perceives the spiritual elevation of Rabelais. The other — a civilized and presumably learned representative of spirituality — sees mostly dirt. But Eros at its most phallic has symbolic power to lift earthly vision to the plane of "lofty contemplation." Eros — Love — will eventually wed the comprehension of the kindly prior and the insight of his sensitive nephew.

The descent of the Ingénu from ethereal "England" into the depths of *Low* Brittany is marked by loss of the "nameless" state. The significance of the loss is enhanced by the meaning of the name acquired. The new Christian is baptized Hercules.

> "The Adam Primus, or Kadmon, the Logos of the Jewish mystics, is the same as the Grecian Prometheus, who seeks to rival with the divine wisdom; he is also the Pymander of Hermes or the POWER OF THE THOUGHT DIVINE, in its most spiritual aspect, for he was less hypostasized by the Egyptians than the two former. Desiring to endow man with an immortal spirit, in order that by linking the trinity in one, he might gradually return to his primal spiritual state without losing his individuality, Prometheus fails in his attempt to steal the *divine* fire, and is sentenced to expiate his crime on Mount Kazbeck. Prometheus is also the Logos of the ancient Greeks, as well as Herakles." (*Isis Unveiled*, p. 298, Vol. 1).

Prometheus is also the personification of "suffering mankind."*

The sum of allegorical identities represented by the hero belongs to several planes of interpretation and existence. Hercules is the ordinary man — "suffering mankind" — going through the descending arc of evolution. The original "parentless" and "nameless" status of the young man may convey the suggestion of voluntary reincarnation or of the return to Earth of a perfected being. The theft of the "divine fire" stolen by Prometheus is consistent with a role previously connected with a major Voltairian character: the role of Instructor of Mankind. The Huron — whose tribal name evokes the French word meaning "circle" — "rond" — may thus be linked to the cyclic return of a temporarily obscured spiritual message. The male, cyclic counterpart of cyclic Abacaba is the transmitter of the doctrine previously forced underground by the Jehovic "Algonquin mal élevé."

The merry company gathered for the baptism enjoys socially acceptable ribaldry. The conversation assumes a racy quality consistent with phallic traits of Catholicism "that religion of sensualism par excellence." One might easily forget that the occasion is a spiritual one. The patron saint of the neophyte, the number and nature of his amorous exploits, are a choice subject of discussion. A learned Jesuit in attendance gives his professional version of the Labors of Hercules:

> "The name of Hercules had been given to the neophyte — The Jesuit who was very learned, told him that he was a saint who had performed twelve miracles. There was a thirteenth one which was worth all the others, but which could not properly be discussed by a Jesuit; that of having

---

The Secret Doctrine, p. 414, Vol. II.

changed fifty girls into women in one night. One wit in attendance commented the latter miracle with energy. All the ladies lowered their eyes and judged from the physique of the Ingénu that he was worthy of the saint whose name he bore." (Ch. IV, p. 263).

Christian looting of Pagan tradition is once more noted. Hercules is appropriated and digested by the omnivorous stomach of the Church. The demigod conveniently becomes "a saint who performed twelve miracles."

The "energetic" retort of the "wit in attendance" is not given in the text. But it can be surmised by "instructed" readers. The spirited guest is one of many "reasoners" lovingly featured in the works of esoteric writers. Such incorrigible "skeptics" are prone to sense — and voice — disturbing and beautiful truths. Two varieties of "learning" are personified in the confrontation: the secret science of the Church duly remodelled for consumption by the flock and the secret science of the layman.

The "saint" who descended to Hades and performed "twelve miracles" is the Pagan personification of the candidate facing the trials of initiation. His story was expurgated and re-cycled to become eventually the Apocryphal Gospel of Nicodemus. The latter gospel is regarded by occultists as a shameless example of clumsy falsification. The perceptible grin of Voltaire alluding to the "saint" and the spirited reaction of the learned layman seem to be aimed at the same target as are the following comments of Mme Blavatsky:

> "More than four centuries before the birth of Jesus, Aristophanes had written his immortal parody on the *Descent into Hell,* by Herakles. The chorus of the 'blessed ones,' the initiated, the Elysian Fields, the arrival of Bacchus (who is Iacchos — Iaho — and *Sabaoth*) with Herakles, their reception with lighted torches, emblems of *new life,* and RESURRECTION from darkness, death unto light, eternal LIFE; nothing that is found in the *Gospel of Nicodemus* is wanting in this poem:
>
>> 'Wake, burning torches . . . for thou comest
>> Shaking them in thy hand, Iacche,
>> Phosphoric star of the nightly rite!'
>
> But the Christians accept those *post-mortem* of their god, concocted from those of his Pagan predecessors, and derided by Aristophanes, four centuries before our era, *literally!"* (*Isis Unveiled,* p. 518, Vol. 2).
> "Comments are unnecessary. This *Gospel* closes with the words: 'In the name of the *Holy Trinity* (of which Nicodemus could know nothing yet) *thus ends the Acts of our Saviour Jesus Christ, which the emperor Theodosius the Great found at Jerusalem, in the hall of Pontius Pilate among the public records';* and which history purports to have been written in Hebrew by Nicodemus, *'the things being acted in the nineteenth*

year of Tiberius Caesar, emperor of the Romans and in the seventeenth year of the government of Herod the son of Herod, king of Galilee, to the eighth before the calends of April, etc., etc.,' It is the most barefaced imposture that was perpetrated after the era of pious forgeries opened with the first bishop of Rome, whoever he may have been. The clumsy forger seems to have known neither known or heard that the dogma of the Trinity was not propounded until 325 years later than this pretended date. Neither the *Old* nor the *New Testament* contains the word Trinity, nor anything that affords the slightest pretext for this doctrine (——) No explanation can palliate the putting forth of this spurious gospel as a divine revelation, for it was known from the first as a premeditated imposture. If the gospel has been declared apocryphal, nevertheless every one of the dogmas contained in it was and is still enforced upon the Christian world. And even the fact that itself is now repudiated, is no merit, *for the Church was shamed and forced into it."* (*Isis Unveiled,* p. 522, Vol. 2).

The veiled significance of the thirteenth labor of Hercules is probably connected with the advent of *Fifth* Race mankind. The number of women — fifty — suggests the latter correspondence. The night during which the exploit took place seems to represent a minor "Night of Brahma" or *pralaya* — an interval between sub-cycles of evolution. The mystical symbolism of "love" suggests that the "divine fire" of Prometheus-Hercules was indeed transmitted following a period of obscuration.

The Kerkabon women — who find L'Ingénu worthy of his mythological "patron saint" — do not know how right they are — on a plane still inconceivable to them. The stranger in their midst is a voluntary messenger of Herculean spirit. The Dhyani Buddhas emanated from the second Logos — Adam Kadmon, Hercules — "emanate or create from themselves, by virtue of Dhyana, celestial Selves — the *super*-human Bodhisattvas. These incarnating at the beginning of every human cycle on earth as mortal men, become occasionally, owing to their personal merit, Bodhisattvas among the Sons of Humanity, after which they may re-appear as *Manushi* (human) Buddhas."* The twelve Labors of Hercules which are viewed by occultists as the trials of the spiritual candidate have a fitting culmination in the thirteenth Labor mentioned in *L'Ingénu.* Greater love has no man than he who lays down True Life for the sake of his fellow-creature. The thirteenth "miracle" of Love *is* worth all the others.

The deep substance of the conversation explains the reserve of the Jesuit. Worldly members of the Order of Jesus are not usually reluctant to discuss worldly matters such as exoteric labors of love. But an ex-

---

*The Secret Doctrine, p. 571, Vol. I.

change bearing on the concepts of Karma, Sutratma, Adeptship and Bodhisattva is not calculated to promote the interests of their brotherhood. Nor is a debate on apocryphal gospels.

The literal story of defloration is savored by the majority of persons in attendance. The reaction of the Kerkabon clan is one of controlled prurience. Demure relish is evident on the part of the ladies. Early characterization of the women as "devout and pleasure-loving" is confirmed. The phallic turn of mind of the family is demonstrated by lowered eyes and lowered vision. The deep essence of the conversation is unperceived by most. Totally absorbed by the libertine quality of the subject, the Kerkabons are blind to the profound meaning of "libertine" thought. One may expect them — and the correligionists whom they represent — to swallow the Scriptures in literal, bawdy, and uncritical manner. One may also expect them to remain oblivious to occult forces acting under their very eyes. The tournament of secret lore opposing the Jesuit and the learned layman is such an occasion.

The abundance of esoteric meaning connected with mythological Hercules is a source of merriment to numerous writers. Herculean deeds are mentioned by Rabelais in Chapter XXVII of the *Tiers Livre*. It is observed that the demi-god is deceptive. "Il a menty, le paillard" — "he lied, the rake". M. Bergeret, a scholarly character created by Anatole France, is also fascinated by "Hercule Mélampyge." His profound rêverie — animated by heroic, silent laughter — is interrupted by a student "en mal de dissertation."

> " 'Do you think that Paul Louis Courier might be a good topic for a doctoral thesis? Because, as soon as I have passed the licence. . . .' "
> (*L'Anneau d'Amethyste*, Ch. **IV**).

Mr. Bergeret could easily suggested a few "good topics" of dissertation if discovery were truly welcome in the academic world.

Multiple suggestions of the esoteric status of Hercules are found in the first paragraph of Chapter II. The Voltairian hero is an "early riser."

The Kerkabons — Latter Day "Westphalians" — are esoteric or spiritual laggards. Their nephew is noted to have left the house at daybreak, to have traveled two or three leagues, and to have killed thirty pieces of game with single bullets when he meets the prior and his sister upon his return. The latter persons have just awakened and are taking a "walk" "in their small garden."

> "He had already travelled two or three leagues, he had killed thirty pieces of game with single bullets, when upon returning he found M. le prieur

of our Lady of the Mountain and his discreet sister, walking in their small garden. He offered them all his game and, pulling out of his shirt a sort of small talisman which he always wore around his neck, he begged them to accept it as a token of gratitude for their good reception." (Ch. II, p. 253).

The talisman is designated as "un petit brimborion" — "a small knick-nack." The word "brimborion" may constitute a phonetic reference to Orion or "brin d'Orion" — "bit or particle of or from Orion." The constellation of Orion—the Hunter — is astronomically and mythologically connected with Canis Major and Sirius, the Dog Star. The hunting expedition of the Ingénu returns him to the distant source of a starry realm. The garden of the Kerkabons is small in comparison.

The dizzy voyage through space is also a journey in Time. The two or three leagues probably represent the two or three Races of mankind preceding the Fifth Race, the latter segment of humanity being personified by the "sleeply," sluggish Kerkabons. The young man has spanned the enormous chronological distance separating the ethereal origin of mankind from its nethermost degree of materiality. A symbolic return to the source has been made to regions of immaterial being.

All three characters are materially situated within the setting of Fifth Race. But an important difference exists between the young man and his relatives. The "walks abroad" of the uncle and aunt cannot be compared with the spectacular excursion of Hercules. Such "walks" are confined to a "small garden" reminiscent of the "Park" of Thunder-ten-tronckh. Unlike their puzzling nephew, the Kerkabons are unaware of the occult scheme of life and, therefore, of their own spiritual origin. The remedy to their ignorance is offered as the talisman representing precious lore is given to them. The gift of Knowledge which is also a gift of Love will prove useful in the end.

Also given is the entire product of the hunt derived from the sortie of two or three "leagues." The "hunt" is a quest of Spirit comparable to the pursuits of Diana-Isis, Diana-Cunégonde and Diana-Abacaba. The likely reference to the biblical figure of Nimrod is another link to Atlantean races which are regarded by occultists as "prototypes" of the Nimrods."[*]

The Promethean role of Hercules is symbolized by the technique and the end result of the "hunt." The occult concept of Three-In-One is humorously represented by $3(0)$ or three pieces of game killed by *single* bullets. The Voltairian Hercules-Prometheus apparently desires "to endow man with an immortal spirit, in order that by linking the trinity

---

[*]*The Secret Doctrine*, p. 272, Vol. II.

in one, he might gradually return to his primal spiritual state without losing his individuality." A symbolic transmission of "Spiritual Fire" is made as the game killed by the "firearm" is offered. The product of the hunt, the talisman, and the shared bottle of "Spirit" or Barbadoes water are *three* deceptively different representations of the same one gift.

The esoteric concept of the "Three In One" is connected with the Sun. The Sun is also one of the many meanings of mythological Hercules.*

> "Rudimentary man, having been nursed by the 'air,' or the 'wind,' becomes the perfect man later on; when, with the development of 'Spiritual Fire,' the *noumenon* of the 'Three in One' within his Self, he acquires from his inner Self, or Instructor, the Wisdom of Self-Consciousness, which he does not possess in the beginning. Thus here again divine Spirit is symbolized by the Sun or Fire; divine Soul by Water and the Moon, both standing for the Father and Mother of *Pneuma,* human Soul, or Mind, symbolised by the Wind or air, for *Pneuma* means 'breath.' " (*The Secret Doctrine,* p. 113, Vol. II).

The importance of the Sun — physical and spiritual — is stressed in the same initial paragraph of Chapter II. Man and sun rise simultaneously as the cock crows according to "custom." The sun-God represented by Hercules is compared to less brilliant suns or states of spiritual consciousness:

> "The Ingénu, according to his custom, woke up at sunrise to the crowing of the rooster, which is called in England and in Huronia *the trumpet of daylight.* He was not like the good company languishing on an idle couch until the sun has travelled half of its course, which can neither sleep nor get up, which loses so many precious hours in that ambiguous state between life and death, and still complains that life is too short." (Ch. II, p. 253).

The esoteric meaning of a Day is that of a cycle of evolution, usually a Day of Brahma:

> "A 'Day' of Brahmâ equals 4,320,000,000 years, as also a Night of Brahmâ or the duration of Pralaya, after which a *new* SUN rises triumphantly over a new manvantara, for the septenary chain it illuminates." (*The Secret Doctrine,* pp. 655-56, Vol. I).

The cosmic symbolism of the egg is indirectly brought into the text by reference to the rooster.

> "The 'First Cause' had no name in the beginning. Later it was pictured in the fancy of the thinkers as an ever invisible, mysterious Bird hat

---

The Secret Doctrine, p. 44, Vol. II.

dropped an Egg into Chaos, which Egg became the Universe. Hence Brahm was called Kalahansa, 'the swan in (Space and) Time.' He became the 'Swan of Eternity,' who lays at the beginning of each Mahamanvantara a 'Golden Egg.' It typifies the Great Circle, or O, itself a symbol for the universe and its spherical bodies." (*The Secret Doctrine*, p. 359, Vol. I).

The number 4,320,000,000 contains — among other things — the numeral *4* in conjuntion with *3*. The occult theme of the quaternary evolving from the ternary — a theme which has already been found in the present study — seems to be embodied in the very schedule of the universe. The symbolism of *4* representing material creation is paralleled by the quaternary meaning of the cross. The cross, a graphic representation of *4*, may be directed downward to the plane of materiality and incarnation. It may also point upward to spiritual release. The "double cross" in question is a central element of *L'Ingénu*, an element which is embodied in the title itself. The hero whose descent into generation is traced will in due course, "develop his genius" or Spirit.

The same compounded esotericism seems to have inspired a great contemporary when he wrote the following verse:

"I, born of flesh and ghost, was neither
A ghost nor man, but mortal ghost.
And I was struck down by death's feather.
I was a mortal to the last
Long breath that carried to my father
The message of his dying christ.

You who bow down at cross and altar,
Remember me and pity Him
Who took my flesh and bone for armour
And doublecrossed my mother's womb."
(Dylan Thomas, *Before I knocked*).*

It may also be noted — in connection with solar symbolism — that the puzzling, bewitching rose of *The Little Prince* was "born" — made incarnate — "at the same time as the sun." The flower is Eternal Truth.

The conjunction of symbolic details found in the first paragraph of Chapter II suggests an allusion to initiation rites. The idle couch is one meaningful element of the passage.

" 'To crucify before (not against) the sun' is a phrase used of initiation. It comes from Egypt, and primarily from India. The enigma can be unriddled only by searching for its key in the Mysteries of Initiation.

---

*This text was called to the attention of the writer by one of her students.

The initiated adept, who had successfully passed through all the trials, was *attached,* not *nailed,* but *simply* tied on a couch in the form of a *tau* T (in Egypt) — plunged into a deep sleep (the 'Sleep of Siloam' it is called to this day among the Initiates in Asia Minor, in Syria, and even higher Egypt). He was allowed to remain in this state for three days and three nights, during which time his Spiritual Ego was said to confabulate with the 'gods,' descend into Hades, Amenti, or Pâtala (according to the country), and do works of charity to the invisible beings, whether souls of men or Elemental Spirits; his body remaining all the time in a temple crypt or subterranean cave. In Egypt, it was placed in the Sarcophagus in the King's Chamber of the Pyramid of Cheops, and carried during the night of the approaching third day to the entrance of a gallery, where at a certain hour, the beams of the rising Sun struck full on the face of the entranced candidate, who awoke to be initiated by Osiris, and Thoth the God of Wisdom.

Let the reader who doubts the statement consult the Hebrew originals before he denies. Let him turn to some most suggestive Egyptian *bas-reliefs...*Two God-Hierophants, one with the head of a hawk (the Sun), the other ibis-headed (Mercury, Thoth, the god of Wisdom and secret learning, the assessor of Osiris — Sun), are standing over the body of a candidate just initiated. They are in the act of pouring on his head a double stream of water (the water of life and new birth), which stream is interlaced in the shape of a cross and full of small ansated crosses. This is allegorical of the awakening of the candidate (now an Initiate), when the beams of the morning sun (Osiris) strike the crown on his head, (*his entranced body being placed on its wooden tau so as to receive the rays*). Then appeared the Hierophants — Initiators, and the sacramental words were pronounced, ostensibly, to the Sun-Osiris, addressed in reality to the Spirit Sun within, enlightening the newly-born man." (*The Secret Doctrine,* pp. 558-59, Vol. II).

The "good company" — which the Voltairian Hercules does not resemble — remains on an "idle couch" until the sun has covered one half of its course. The said portion of mankind does not meet the requirements of spiritual dedication. "Man was not born to rest"; Man was placed into his "small garden" so that he might "cultivate it." Spiritual laggards do not even realize that they have a "garden" to till. The "good company" in question will "awaken" and "rise" only when the arc of collective spiritual reascent is reached by Fifth Race mankind, esoterically when the Sun has passed mid-point in its "daily" course. No pioneers are found in that category. The same persons are prone to complain about the brevity of their sojourn on earth. They are unable to conceive life beyond physical existence. But they are destined to belong to the "good company" of the future.

The paragraph is also relevant to genuine "good company." Members of the latter collectivity are aware of evolutionary "days" and "nights" on all planes of existence. The small élite never loses sight of spiritual suns within or without the Self. The "indiscernible community" knows the true meaning of esoteric "inaction" or "idleness." No one needs tell its seekers where the action is. The most spectacular battles are those which are fought in the depths of the Inner Man. Authentic "good company" may also complain of the brevity of life. But it does so to deplore the limited progress which can be made in one existence. Perhaps also to regret that true "life" or spiritual experience is so threatened and so transient on earth. The idle couch and transcendental slumber of the second group have the warm approval of Voltaire.

Hercules occupies a unique position relatively to both sides. In the words of Voltaire he is *not like* the persons who lag spiritually. His primitive heritage and his apparent status of Bodhisattva make it impossible for him to be as they are. But he must live among them and labor under the trials and errors imposed by Karmic law.

Nor is the young man *like* authentic "good company." For he is an integral part of it. There also his position is unique. Having renounced Nirvâna for the sake of mankind, he is again traveling the "toilsome path" as are all mortals. But his sacrificial journey through Maya begins from the vantage point of previous perfection. The messenger is destined to achieve in one brief lifetime what less advanced travelers will accomplish at the term of multiple rebirths — "I learn very fast that which I want to learn," says the Huron. The esoteric equivalence of "speed" and spirituality is clearly perceptible in his case. The gigantic span of ages and "leagues" bridged by the hero fuses Time and Space into One reality. The contingencies of incarnate life co-exist with non-contingent Being. The ordinary human condition is enriched by a privileged amount and quality of vision.

The complex yet simple relationship existing between Hercules and the bulk of mankind is best outlined in geometric form flashing upon the inner eye. It is a system of forces of light and darkness — physical and spiritual — instinctive and intellectual; progressive and retrogressive; parallel and opposite; seemingly rectilinear, actually cyclic, involving meteoric speed and the unfolding of ages. The Voltairian hero is at one with suffering mankind by virtue of physical existence and infinite compassion. At the same time he is doubly *alone*: isolated from spiritually slow mortals; *alone* in unity with the Absolute.

The return to the source of the young hero, a journey through timeless, spaceless "leagues," is the essence of his bequest to men of good will. The precious gift is Knowledge and its twin aspiration to release " '— from all terrene concerns — a flight of the *alone* to the ALONE.' "*

---

*Porphyry quoted in *Isis Unveiled,* p. 413 Vol. 2.

The symbols found in the passage are standard tools of esoteric expression. The meaning of the crowing rooster is suggested in Rabelaisian writings. It is related to materiality. "Allegorical" wisdom worthy of "Pythagorean" use is said to come from immaterial regions "where the song of roosters is not heard."* The importance of timely drinking — or spiritual "awakening" — is called to attention in the Book of Gargantua.

The egg-related symbolism of cosmic — and literary — creation is used in the *Recherche*. The first production of Marcel is inspired by the shifting vision of three steeples later supplemented by the sight of three farms. The two suggested triangles representing spirituality and materiality — heaven and earth — suggest the interlocking triangles the combination of which is known as the Seal of Solomon. The emblem in question is relevant to "creation."

> "By the 'Six directions of Space' is here meant the 'Double Triangle,' the junction and blending together of pure Spirit and Matter, of the Arupa and the Rupa, of which the Triangles are a Symbol. This double Triangle is a sign of Vishnu, as it is Solomon's seal, and the Sri-Antara of the Brahmins." (*The Secret Doctrine*, p. 118, Vol. I).

The "blending together of pure Spirit and Matter" is supplemented by the presence of fowls and overtly represented by an egg. The meaning of discarded steeples and things hidden behind them is transparent. One may also note the prominence of the dual personality of the author. The page of which he "never thought again" is much in evidence.

> "I never thought of that page again, but at that moment, when, in the corner of the seat where the driver of the doctor habitually placed in a basket the poultry just bought by him at the marked of Martinville, I had completed my writings, I found myself so happy, I felt that it had so perfectly rid me of those steeples and of what they hid behind them, that, as if I had been a hen myself and had just laid an egg, I began to sing at the top of my voice." (*A la Recherche du temps perdu*, p. 182, Vol. I).

The dual personality of the Ingénu is dimly sensed by the Kerkabons. Innate spirituality is a mixed blessing in a society dominated by "steeples" and well-meaning priors. It is a source of confusion and fear to long-time residents of materiality. Practical effects of the divine spark cannot be ignored. The unusual assets and the startling "deficits" of the young man become disturbingly clear as he is prepared for Christian baptism.

---

*Quart, Livre, LXXX.

"The Ingénu had an excellent memory. The solidity of a Low Brittany constitution, fortified by the climate of Canada, had made his head so strong that, when one knocked on it, he hardly felt it; and, when one made an imprint on it, nothing was erased; he had never forgotten anything. His thought process was all the quicker and clearer as, his childhood not having been loaded with the useless and silly things which weigh upon ours, things entered into his brains without a cloud. The prior finally resolved to have him read the New Testament." (Ch. III, p. 257).

Hard-headedness does not suggest great intelligence. Memory, while phenomenal, seems mechanical. Lack of culture seems to be the main asset of the young man. The general picture seems unimpressive.

"The Canadian" origin of the Ingénu suggests snowy wastelands symbolizing purity. The *fortifying* influence of the same background is linked to the esoteric concept of "force," "strength" or spirituality. The solidity of organs which is connected with *Low* Brittany seems to represent a vigor of less ethereal character. The specific reference to "organs" tends to confirm previous suggestions of the raw materiality prevailing in "Saint Malo." The physiological turn of the allusion is comparable to the quality of the oath uttered by the wicked sailor of *Candide*: "Head and blood " — an expression calculated to suggest the evolutionary descent of man into materiality and the acquisition of a "coat of skin."

The Canadian background of the young man may also have been intended to convey the occult view of the age of two continents. The Secret Doctrine teaches that the so-called "New World" is actually older than the "Old."* The primitive, "Huronian" culture which has been a way of life to Hercules is far more ancient than the Christian European background of the Kerkabons.

Voltaire may also have had in mind the Hindu scientist *Kanada* — one of the earliest atomists of Antiquity whose teachings somewhat resemble the monadic theory of Leibnitz.** The field of study of Kanada deals with primeval matter and Aether, two subjects which are relevant to the process of "generation" undergone by the Ingénu. The monadic aspect of Kanadian lore is also relevant to "generation" or incarnation.

The combined influences of Canada and Low Brittany produce a mixture of spiritual and carnal traits. Matter and Spirit seem to be as evenly balanced as they are balanced in the make-up of Fifth Race mankind. The young man has acquired a major characteristic of his relatives. The process of his assimilation by Western European society

*The Secret Doctrine, p. 407 fn., Vol. II.
**Ibid., p. 495, Vol. I.

seems to be complete. But the Huron benefits from huge cultural gaps which will never be filled.

The primitive has not been exposed to "useless" or "silly" teachings. Voltaire seems to subscribe to the view of an Arabian sage which is heartily endorsed by Mme Blavatsky.

> " '— remember, O my beloved, that the light of Allah's truth will often penetrate much easier an empty head, than one that is so crammed with learning that many a silver ray is crowded out for want of space; —' " (*Isis Unveiled*, p. 43, Vol. 1).

The same belief is conveyed by the well-known formula of Montaigne commending "a well-made rather than a well-filled head."

The "usefulness" of Huronian culture needs no other proof than the reaction of Hercules to Shakespearean and Rabelaisian texts. Freedom from educational brainwashing can have wondrous effect where certain "clouds" or "veils" are concerned.

The benefits of hard-headedness result from the absence of the intellect. Such benefits are almost inconceivable to the average Western European person who regards the intellect as the highest faculty of Man. But the "deficit" of the Ingénu is more than compensated by the innate knowledge of his "Informing Principle." The lingering influence of primeval "mindlessness" should not be confused with stupidity. Voltaire leaves no room for doubt where the soundness of the hero's faculties it concerned: "Il avait l'esprit juste."

Physical blows are hardly felt by the hard-headed Ingénu. The enviable ability to resist external pressure is noted. The supremacy of mind — or spirit — over matter is suggested. The young man seems to possess a remnant of the immunity to pain which characterized the first Races of men. "—the first Root Race, the 'Shadows' of the Progenitors, could not be injured, or destroyed by death."* The same belief is conveyed under cover of sad irony in the *Poem on the Disaster of Lisbon*.

The phenomenal memory of Hercules may represent far more than the automatic response of a mental robot:

> "— theopneusty, when in full sway, results for the high Adept in a full recollection of everything seen, heard, or sensed." (*The Secret Doctrine*, p. 79, Vol. V, *Adyar* Edition).

The same faculty sheds light on a startling statement of Vigny: "I was born with such a memory that I have forgotten nothing of what

---

The Secret Doctrine, p. 138, Vol. II.

has been said to me since I have been on earth."* The power of retention of M. de Charlus — who knows Balzac by heart — probably has no other source. The stress which is placed by Proust on the superiority of total recall over "the memory of the intelligence" is rooted in the same belief that every man is potentially omniscient.

The mental handicaps of Hercules do not resist esoteric examination. The spiritual legacy of the First Races of mankind is partially retained by the young man. Seeming deficits are valuable protections against frequently irrational pressures of Western "rationality." The cultural vacuum detected in the young man is a blessing in transparent disguise. The acquisition of intellectual faculties will take place in due course of evolution as the predominance of Spirit decreases. It will take place under privileged conditions.

The indignation of the young man is aroused by the story of Caïph and Pilate and by their role in the trial of Christ.

> "The prior finally resolved to have him read the New Testament. The Ingénu devoured it with great pleasure; but, not knowing in what time or in what country all the adventures related in that book had happened he did not doubt that the scene was in Low Brittany, and he swore that he would cut off the nose and ears of Caïph and Pilate if he ever met those ruffians." (Ch. III, p. 257).

The fervent desire to punish the culprits is cooled by certain revelations. Hercules is told that the misdeeds in question took place in a distant land, a long time before his birth. But the "error" of the primitive is made of unerring recognition of Christ by Chrestos. The spontaneous identification of one sacrificial figure with another dissolves the Mayavic illusion of Time and Space. The instinctive affinity of Chrestos — the Higher Self in every man — with the Savior has the same effect of transcendence. The uneducated Huron is also quick to surmise that Saviors might be crucified were they to appear again in Low Brittany. The "mistakes" of the Ingénu are manifestations of lingering superior insight immune to the Mayavic contingencies of earthly Time and Space.

"Mindlessness" reacts with natural "pleasure" to the esoteric material of the New Testament. The message of *Revelations* and Universal Love has strong appeal.

Hercules is informed that Caïph and Plato died "approximately sixteen hundred and ninety years" before his time. The latter computation is challenged in the Cluny edition of *L'Ingénu* in which the following comment is made:

Diary, 1847.

381

"Voltaire appears to forget that his prior and his Huron live in 1689; he has 'those people' die toward the date of birth of Christ, whom they saw put on the cross."

"Zadig — Voltaire — who did not pride himself upon being a good poet" — is taken to task for being a poor mathematician. The "erroneous" chronology of Hercules may be a valuable clue to the genuine nature of the "mistake" of Voltaire. The writer of the footnote affixed to the Cluny edition takes for granted the accuracy of orthodox tradition relative to the birthdate of Christ and the adherence of Voltaire to the same tradition. Which is taking a great deal for granted. Occultists categorically reject the Church chronology of the biography of Jesus:

> "Everyone knows that the real time and year of the birth of Jesus are totally unknown." (*The Secret Doctrine*, p. 653, Vol. I).

The orthodox chronology of the birth and life of Jesus is believed to have been contrived by clumsy looters of Pagan knowledge. The occult teaching according to which a Day of Brahma lasting 4,320,-000,000 years is followed by a Night of Brahma of like duration and the related belief in the existence of a new sun assigned to each new planetary chain is said to have "penetrated into Palestine and Europe centuries before the Christian era." It is said to have been "present in the minds of the Mosaic Jews, who based upon it their small cycle, though it received full expression only through the Christian chronologers of the Bible, who adopted it, as also the 25th of December, the day on which all the *solar* gods were said to have been incarnated. What wonder, then, that the Messiah was *made* to be born 'the *lunar* year of the world, 4,320'? The 'Son of Righteousness and *Salvation*' had once more arisen and had dispelled *pralayic* darkness of chaos and *non-being* on the plane of our objective litle globe and chain. Once the subject of the adoration was settled upon, it was easy to make the supposed events of his birth, life, and death, fit in with the Zodiacal exigencies and old traditions, though they had to be somewhat re-modelled for the occasion."*

The length of the life of Christ and his age at the time when his teachings began remain subjects of controversy:

> Ecclesiastical history assures us that Christ's ministry was but of three years' duration. There is a decided discrepancy on this point between the first three synoptics and the fourth gospel; but it was left for Irenaeus to show to Christian posterity that so early as A.D. 180 — the probable

---

The Secret Doctrine, p. 656, Vol. I.

time when this Father wrote his works against heresies — even such pillars of the Church as himself either knew nothing certain about it, or deliberately lied and falsified dates to support their own views. So anxious was the worthy Father to meet every possible objection against his plans, that no falsehood, no sophistry, was too much for him. How are we to understand the following, and who is the falsifier in this case? The argument of Ptolemaeus was that Jesus was too young to have taught anything of much importance; adding that 'Christ preached for one year only, and then suffered in the twelvth month.' In this Ptolemaeus was very little at variance with the gospels. But Irenaeus, carried by his object far beyond the limits of prudence, from a mere discrepancy between one and three years, makes it *ten* and even twenty years 'Destroying his (Christ's) whole work, and *robbing him of that age* which is *both necessary* and more honorable than any other; that more advanced age, I mean, during which also, as a teacher, he excelled all others.' And then, having no certain date to furnish, he throws himself back on *tradition*, and claims that Christ had preached for over TEN years! (book ii, c., 22, pp. 4-5) In another place he makes Jesus fifty years old." (*Isis Unveiled*, p. 305, Vol. 2).

"Says the Codex: 'John, son of the Aba Saba-Zacharia, conceived by his mother *Anasabet* in her hundredth year, had baptized for *forty-two years* when Jesus Messias came to the Jordan to be baptized with John's baptism. . . . But he will *pervert* John's doctrine, changing the baptism of the Jordan and perverting the sayings of justice.'" (Codex Nazareus, vol. i, p. 109, '*Sod, the Son of the Man*.' XXIV).

The above passage of the *Codex* is commented as follows by Mme Blavatsky:

"The statement, if reliable, would show that Jesus was between fifty and sixty years old when baptized; for the Gospels make him but a few months younger than John. The kabalists say that Jesus was over forty years old when first appearing at the gates of Jerusalem. The present copy of the 'Codex Nazareus' is dated in the year 1042, but Dunlap finds in Irenaeus (2nd Century) quotations from and ample references to this book. The basis of the material common to Irenaeus and the 'Codex Nazareus' must be at least as early as the first century, 'says the author in his preface to *Sod, the Son of the Man*, p.1'" (*Isis Unveiled*, p. 135, Vol. 2)

The chronological "error" of Voltaire tends to cast doubt on the orthodox view of the birthdate of Christ, a mystery which is a common concern of esoteric writers. A discreet but significant allusion to the "hidden life of Jesus" appears in the *Diary* of Vigny. "Jesus Christ had, from twelve to thirty years, an unknown life; what the clergy calls his hidden life. There would be a great ideal work to do on that life. One would have to try to imagine what could be thought and experienced by the Man-God feeling his godliness growing within him." One may note that the observation of Vigny was made in 1843, the year of his Way to Damascus. There is a rare quality of humor about the thoughts of the imaginative poet speculating on the experience of a blossoming "Chrestos."

Related observations are found in the writings of Flaubert. The main characters of *Bouvard and Pécuchet* make interesting discoveries. "— dates are not always authentic. They learned from a manual to be used in colleges that the birth of Jesus must be moved back five years earlier than it is placed ordinarily."*

The revelatory value of the question of the birthdate of Christ is comparable to that of the question of Peter having or not having been in Rome. Any text either facing or skirting such issues deserves to be examined in the light of the Secret Doctrine.

The descent of the Ingénu into regions of base materiality is marked by a series of experiences with debased Christian sacraments. Cannibalistic communion having already been rejected, the Voltairian survey of empty or perverted rites continues.

The crime denounced in the *Codex*: "changing the baptism of the Jordan" is a common grievance of Talmudists, occultists, and Voltaire. It is one aspect of a systematic process of sterilization and falsification which is illustrated in *Zadig* by the symbolic diversion of the Waters of Life. The occult view of the history of baptism stresses one belief. The sacrament was perverted by the successors of Christ, not by Christ himself:

> "The baptism was changed from *water* to that of the Holy Ghost, undoubtedly in consequence of the ever-dominant idea of the Fathers to institute a reform, and make the Christians distinct from St. John's Nazarenes, the Nabatheans and Ebionites, in order to make room for the new dogmas. Not only do the Synoptics tell us that Jesus was baptizing the same as John, but John's own disciples complained of it, though surely Jesus cannot be accused of following a purely Bacchic rite. The parenthesis in verse 2d of John, iv, '— though Jesus himself baptized not,' is so clumsy as to show upon its face that it is an interpolation. Matthew makes John say that he that should come after him would not baptize them with water' but with the *Holy Ghost* and fire.' Mark, Luke, and John corroborate these words. Water, fire, and spirit, or Holy Ghost, have all their origin in India, as we will show.
>
> ___
>
> Verily the disciples who wrote the Codex Nazareus were right. Only it is not Jesus himself, but those who came after him, and who concocted the *Bible* to suit themselves, that 'perverted John's doctrine, *changed* the baptism of the Jordan, and perverted the sayings of justice.' " (*Isis Unveiled*, pp. 135-36, Vol. 2).

___

*Ch. IV.

The complicated question of baptismal history and variable baptismal rites seems to be unknown to the Kerkabons. But their naïve nephew displays surprising knowledge of unorthodox rites. The following response rewards the proselyting efforts of Mlle Saint Yves:

> "'Ah! anything you want, Miss, anything you order; baptism by water, baptism by fire; baptism by blood; there is nothing I can refuse you." (Ch. IV, p. 262).

The reluctant convert is swayed into acceptance of a suspect sacrament by the power of sublimated seduction. The natural charm of Mlle Saint Yves, her appealing glances, and the touch of her hand dissolve strong and well-grounded misgivings. All is temporarily forgotten but physical attraction. The sexual drive of incarnate existence becomes increasingly strong as the evolutionary descent to material planes follows its course. Also noted is the sensuous appeal of Catholicism which works wonders in the recruitment of the flock.

Baptisms by water and fire — the latter element symbolizing the Holy Ghost — are no startling novelties. Baptism by blood might raise certain questions if interpreted literally. But Hercules is not repelled:

> "In India and Central Asia, he (the Candidate) was bound on a lathe, and when his body had become like that of one dead (entranced), he was carried into the crypt. Then the Hierophant kept watch over him 'guiding the apparitional soul (astral body) from this world of Samsara (or delusion) to the *nether* kingdoms, from which, if successful, he had the right of releasing seven suffering souls' (Elementaries). Clothed with his Anandamayakosha, the body of bliss, the Srotapana remainded there where we have no right to follow him, and upon returning — received the *Word*, with or without the 'heart's blood' of the Hierophant.

> Only in truth the Hierophant was never killed — neither in India nor elsewhere, the murder being simply feigned — unless the Initiator had chosen the Initiate for his successor and had decided to pass to him the last and supreme WORD, after which he had to die — only one man in a nation having the right to know that word. Many are those grand Initiates who have thus passed out of the world's sight, disappearing as mysteriously from the sight of men as Moses from the top of Mount Pisgah (*Nebo*, oracular Wisdom), after he had laid his hands upon Joshua, who thus became 'full of the spirit of wisdom, i.e., initiated.

> But he died, he was not killed. For killing, if really done, would be-belong to black, not to divine Magic. It is the transmission of light, rather than a transfer of life, of life spiritual and divine, and it is the shedding of Wisdom, not of blood. But the uninitiated inventors of theological Christianity took the allegorical language *à la lettre;* and instituted a dogma, the crude, misunderstood expression of which horrifies and repels the spiritual 'heathen.'" (*The Secret Doctrine*, pp. 271, 72, Vol. V, *Adyar* Edition).

The serenity of the Ingénu facing the possibility of a bloody rite reflects the blinding effect of his love for Mlle Saint Yves. The double-edged quality of the "blinding" process will become apparent in due course of the story when the esoteric identity of Saint Yves becomes perceptible. In the words of Anatole France which have already been quoted, physical love will prove its ability "to naturally rise to celestial thoughts."

The young primitive has also retained sufficient insight to see beyond the facade of exoteric symbolism. The veil surrounding religious rites offers no more resistance to his innate knowledge than does the exoteric surface of literary works or sacred Scriptures.

The literal, perverted approach to religious symbols and rites is a major concern of occultists and esoteric writers. In the words of Mme Blavatsky, "If the alleged founder of the Christian religion is now, after a lapse of nineteen centuries, preached — more or less unsuccessfully however — in every corner of the globe, we are at liberty to think that the doctrines attributed to him would astonish and dismay him more than anyone else."* The "heretical" Christ portrayed by Vigny in *Le Mont des oliviers* voices the same "dismay" — if not the same astonishment. The Savior foretells the phallic, criminal abuse to which his message will be subjected:

> "Père, oh! si j'ai rempli mon douloureux message,
> Si j'ai caché le Dieu sous la face du sage
> Du sacrifice humain si j'ai changé le prix,
> Pour l'offrande des corps recevant les esprits.
> Substituant partout aux choses le symbole,
> Le parole au combat, comme au trésor l'obole,
> Aux flots rouges du sang les flots vermeils du vin,
> Aux membres de la chair le pain blanc sans levain;
> Si j'ai coupé les temps en deux parts, l'une esclave
> Et l'autre libre; — au nom du passé que je lave,
> Par le sang de mon corps qui souffre et va finir,
> Versons-en la moitié pour laver l'avenir!
> Père libérateur! jette aujourd'hui d'avance,
> La moitié de ce sang d'amour et d'innocence
> Sur la tête de ceux qui viendront en disant:
> 'Il est permis pour tous de tuer l'innocent.'
> Nous savons qu'il naîtra, dans le lointain des âges,
> Des dominateurs durs escortés de faux sages
> Qui troubleront l'esprit de chaque nation
> En donnant un faux sens à ma rédemption.
> — Hélas! je parle encor, que déjà ma parole
> Est tournée en poison dans chaque parabole;
> Eloigne ce calice impur et plus amer

*The Secret Doctrine, p. 305, Vol. II.

Que le fiel, ou l'absinthe, ou les eaux de la mer.
Les verges qui viendront, la couronne d'épines,
Les clous des mains, la lance au fond de ma poitrine,
Entin toute la croix qui se dresse et m'attend,
N'ont rien, oh! père, oh! rien qui m'épouvante autant!

("Father, oh! if I have fulfilled my painful mission,
If I concealed the God under the face of the sage
If I have changed the value of human sacrifice
For the offering of bodies receiving the spirits,
Substituting everywhere to things the symbol,
Word to battle, and alms to treasure,
To the red flow of blood the crimson flow of wine;
To the limbs of the flesh the white unleavened bread;
If I cut the times in two parts — one a slave,
And the other free; — in the name of the past which I cleanse,
By the blood of my suffering and doomed body,
Let us pour half of it to cleanse the future!
Liberating father! cast today in advance
Half of that blood of love and innocence
Onto the hands of those who will come and will say:
'It is just to slay the innocent for the sake of all.'
There will be born — we know — in the distant ages
Harsh tyrants escorted by false sages
Who will confuse the mind of every nation
By giving a false sense to my redemption.
— Alas! as I still speak, already my word
Is turned into poison in every parable;
Remove that impure chalice, more bitter
Than gall, or absinth, or the ocean brine.
The whips which will come, the crown of thorns,
The nails in the hands, the spear sunk into my chest,
In short the whole cross which stands awaiting me,
Have nothing, o Father, which so horrifies me.")

The ultimate horror of the crucifixion is a crucified message used to maintain a sinister industry of oppression, torture, murder, and mutilation of Truth.

"Verily the Grand Martyr has remained thenceforward, and for eighteen centuries, the Victim crucified daily far more cruelly by his clerical disciples and lay followers than he ever could have been by his allegorical enemies." (*The Secret Doctrine*, p. 84, Vol. V, *Adyar* Edition).

The nephew of the Kerkabons senses the influence of "false sages," poisoned dogma and empty ritual. The young man initially refuses to be baptized in church. Formalistic religion is symbolized by the stagnant waters of baptismal founts. The primitive seeks and finds a body of living water. The esoteric interest of the "small river Rance" may well lie in the idea of spirituality gone rancid — "rance" — or sour.

387

The bishop and his showy cortège are left waiting while the distraught Kerkabons search for the elusive neophyte. The fugitive is finally found by his women relatives.

> "Elles se promenaient tristement le long des saules et des roseaux qui bordent la petite rivière de Rance, lorsqu'elles apercurent au milieu de la rivière une grande figure assez blanche, les deux mains croisées sur la poitrine. Elles jetèrent un grand cri et se détournèrent. Mais, la curiosité l'emportant bientôt sur toute autre considération, elles se coulèrent doucement entre les roseaux, et, quand elles furent bien sûres de n'être point vues, elles voulurent voir de quoi il s'agissait." (Ch. III, p. 260).

> "They were walking sadly along the willows and reeds which line the banks of the small river Rance, when they saw in the middle of the river a tall and fairly white figure with both hands crossed on the chest. They let out a great cry and looked away. But, curiosity soon overcoming any other consideration, they slipped gently between the reeds, and, when they were quite sure of not being seen, they wished to see what was taking place.")

The primitive is impelled to seek the true source of Knowledge and Being in Nature. But his goal cannot be achieved in the unfavorable setting of modern Western Europe. The spritual wayfarer yearning for the harvest of grace of initiation will have to settle for an empty ritual. Baptism is powerless to impart the desired purity of Sciences and Ethics. The suit of armor of Zadig — representing the spiritual Mastery of Antiquity — was white. The frustrated candidate to Wisdom can only be "fairly white" in the environment of Low Brittany.

Christian baptism is found wanting in many respects. The transmission of Science effected at ancient initiation rites is out of question in the case of exoteric infants and otherwise unprepared persons. In the words of Voltaire, "— the matter was not the same for a tall Huron who was twenty-two years old as it was for a child who is regenerated without knowing it." The doctrinal background of Christian baptism combines non-existent knowledge and non-existent love. The sacrament is a means of individual salvation rather than an opportunity to serve mankind. The original cleansing must be sustained in later life by a redemption which is no more than therapeutic use of innocent blood. Salvation is restricted to those who receive the one and only form of prescribed rite. The majority of mankind which is non-Christian is doomed to eternal flames for lack of orthodox baptism. The English — who do not practice the same religion as do the Kerkabons — are thought to be irretrievably damned. The twin myths of races either "chosen" or "cursed" on a self-serving basis of selectivity is a base aspect of the Christian heritage connected with baptism. The "heretical" English are briskly labeled and processed by the sister of the prior:

388

" 'Certainly they are the accursed of God; and we will capture Jamaica and Virginia from them before long.' " (Ch. II, p. 256).

A dubious benefit of baptism is the automatic delivery of the "regenerated" soul to an endless tug-of-war between a cruel God and a cruel Devil. The inquisitive bailli — whose fiendish identity is transparently suggested from the very beginning of the story — becomes the inquisitorial shadow of the hapless neophyte. It is soon observed by a nonplussed Mlle de Kerkabon that her nephew seems "to have the devil in him since he received baptism."

Pagan and Christian values are sharply contrasted in the episode opposing initiation to baptism. The hero faces the Kerkabon family alone. Individual conviction resists a conspiracy of mellow but deadly proselytes. The Kingdom within the Self defies socio-religious conformity. Religious carousing confronts pure spiritual yearning. The inevitable "grand gueuleton" and the inevitable dirty jokes are exposed to true light by the departure of Hercules and by his search for genuine spirituality. The young man is no puritan. Nor does he need to be to know something is wrong. The vanity of the Kerkabon family, gleefully turning a sacrament into a socio-religious superproduction geared to sectarian and personal propaganda, blindly faces Pagan innocence. Pagan purity cannot even be conceived by the smug and ignorant group. A formidable barrier stands between them and the "fairly white figure" or the would-be initiate, a figure sketched with sober — yet vibrant — reverence. It is not by chance that the complacent family is reduced to impotent voyeurism and spying. The unfathomable "stranger" in their midst can only be viewed through symbolic media: the keyhole of a closed door and the "veil" formed by a curtain of reeds.

The cultural barrier is not hopelessly impregnable. Hearts find a way to vistas which are beyond reach of brains. The deficits of the Kerkabons in general and of the women in particular are compensated by invaluable curiosity and by ability to *feel*. A dormant spark of divine consciousness is briefly awakened by the startling sight of the neophyte. The talisman or spiritual gift of the young Pagan seems to work a wonder. The glimpse of the candidate lost in contemplation is a crucial experience for Mlle de Kerkabon and Mlle Saint Yves. It is the beginning of a movement of spiritual rebirth not only for individuals but for Fifth Race mankind. Apparently sensitive to the unique quality of the vision, the women refrain from impulsive and hastly intrusion. Wholesome instinct and wholesome curiosity prompt them to respect the solitude of the seeker and to observe silently for a while. The first gleam of intuitive cognition and the first positive response to the unknown form the seed of spectacular future growth.

The reality of Chrestos — the Higher Self — is dimly yet strongly perceived. The cruciform incision of Pangloss has a poignant counterpart on the body of a latter-day witness. The presence of the eternal symbol is manifest in the hands crossed on the breast of the neophyte. The echo of an unforgettable "great cry" is heard once more — as it had been heard in Candide. But it is no longer heard by a lone scientist. It is voiced by the Kerkabon women, "uninstructed" proxies of Fifth Race mankind.

The symbolism of the sun completes the picture of devoutly sought initiation. The surrounding willow-leaves are regarded by occultists as reservoirs of "solar vital energy."* The Pagan concept of the spiritual sun, the true meaning of the crucifixion merge into long-lost ONENESS.

The passage is a poem in prose worthy of study from the metrical standpoint. Sadness is reflected in the pre-romantic tone and rhythm of the first sentence. Sudden, startling perception explodes in the words "when they saw." Oblivion to all but the heart-rending vision pervades the "great cry" and the averted eyes. The short sentence floats suspended in a non-sensory world. Return to earthly consciousness is traced by gradual deceleration of the last clauses. The swelling waves of briefly transcended materiality close in on the women. The complex esoteric beauty of the cross of the Ingénu defies dissection — as does the corresponding beauty of the cross of Pangloss. The passage may be counted among inspired pages in which the "familiar" ground of spirited expression "does the walking for" the writer.**

Kinship and physical attraction remain important in the relationship of Hercules with the women. But carnal bonds are gradually reinforced by superior spiritual ties. Love joins and inspires profoundly alien destinies. As the primitive surrenders part of his innate spirituality to surrounding Christian values, he falls prey to bestial aspects of instinct. But the necessary experience is rich in teachings. The young man learns to overcome and renounce animal traits of the Lower Self. Knowledge and reason favor rather than impede superior development. As the women dimly respond to the inspiring Pagan presence, they begin to break away from the stifling influence of social convention and truncated dogma. To their pragmatic control of everyday experience is added a spark of intuitive consciousness born of contact with pure spirituality. The conflict between ideal and rationality ceases. Only the superior aspects of instinct and reason remain in joint harmony.

The fact that the young man is "found" by the women is deeply

---

*The Secret Doctrine, pp. 557-58, Vol. II.
**A la Recherche du temps perdu, p. 115, Vol. I.

meaningful. Feminine sensitivity and intuition are first to respond to the mysterious presence. Saint *Yves* and the allegorical *Eva* of Vigny seem to share more than phonetic resemblance.

> " 'C'est à toi qu'il convient d'ouïr les grandes plaintes
> Que l'humanité triste exhale sourdement."
> (*La Maison du berger — Ta Eva*).
> ("It is by you that it is fitting that be heard
> The great complaints uttered in undertone by mankind.")

Voltaire lays the groundwork for the concealed identity of Mlle Saint Yves at an early stage of the story. The girl is reported to be "tender," "quick," and "good" or "wise." The French adjective "sage" conveys a dual meaning of goodness and wisdom or knowledge, an interesting fusion of Science and Ethics. The natural vivaciousness of Mlle Saint Yves is charmingly subdued by a "veil" of reserve.

> (" — s'il lui échappait un regard, un mot, un geste, une pensée, elle enveloppait tout cela d'un voile de pudeur infiniment aimable. Elle était tendre, vive, et sage." (Ch. V, p. 263).

> (" — if she ever failed to suppress a glance, a word, a gesture, a thought, she enveloped all that in an infinitely charming veil of reserve. She was tender, quick, and good.")

Intellectual and emotional alertness are present though culturally repressed. Their combination will require little help to produce superior insight. The adjective "tender" suggests the nature of the divine spark of Love which will ignite spiritual consciousness. The same adjective is used in a very special sense in the final chapter of *L'Ingénu*: to convey the idea of limited or beginning spiritual awareness or the idea of a novitiate. The attractive "veil" or reserve which dims and controls ability to "love" gradually becomes the "veil" of self-conscious, active spirituality.

Abacaba and Saint Yves share certain common traits. The righteousness of the Indian maiden was evoked by the straight beauty of reeds. The same quality is manifest in the "wisdom" or "goodness" of the European girl. The purity and dignity of the Indian maiden which were symbolized by the hermin and the eagle have civilized counterparts in the reserve of the young Bretonne. The gentleness or loving disposition of one woman has a correspondence in the "tenderness" of the other. Modified as they seem to be in transit from Pagan America to Christian French bourgeoisie, the basic qualities of both women are the same. Saint Yves is the likely Western European reincarnation of the Primitive-Wisdom-Religion. The occult doctrine which has long been restricted to "underground" or esoteric planes begins a process of re-emergence.

391

The awakening of spiritual "Self-Consciousness" is recorded in Saint Yves. Having persuaded Hercules to receive Christian baptism, the heroine feels "her triumph" although she does not yet perceive all its implications. The effect of her victory seems partially destructive for it is reflected by the spiritual loss of the young man. But the temporary "loss" is "necessary" to a vast scheme of individual and collective evolution. It is virtually cancelled by the relationship linking the couple as complementary parts of the same unit. One effect of the victory of Saint Yves is a new if vague awareness of personal power. Dormant Truth comes to life in the heart of an important representative of Fifth Race European mankind.

Correspondence is implied between Hercules-Adam-Kadmon and "Sophia" — "Wisdom" — Saint Yves, the feminine component of the bisexual human prototype. The spiritual Eve symbolicaly reborn through contact with Pagan spirituality is the same figure which is zealously left out of Christian Scriptures. The inferior version of Eva or Sophia — Missouf-and the "Eve of Dust" — are no longer sole representatives of wronged womanhood.

The girl is the cultural product of "Westphalia" and "Low Brittany." She is a natural and active proselyte of the only faith known to her. The "Eve of Dust" which is very much alive in Saint Yves instinctively mixes sex drives and religion. But the spiritual Eva — or Sophia — within her, blissfully ignorant of her contrived theological "fault" or "fall," is invincibly drawn to noble aspects of the baffling Pagan presence of Hercules.

The romance of Spiritual Adam and Spiritual Eve is not favored by the power structure of "Low Brittany." The growing love of the couple finds numerous obstacles in its path. The mellow surface of general benevolence is quickly shattered when the mutual attraction between Man and Truth is perceived.

Reckless "love" is a problem in itself. Acquired in the process of materialization, stimulated by semi-subtle religious aphrodisia, the bestial drives of Hercules require external curbs and prove self-defeating. The amorous hero fails to see the importance of any considerations other than mutually agreeable mating. The Kerkabons barely prevent him from raping the beloved. Such behavior reflects litle credit on the noble savage. But the Ingénu has done no more than follow the natural impulse of "generation." Having acquired the symbolic "coat of skin," Man proceeds with the logical sequel: the "taking of a wife." The conduct of the young man is condemned by civilized morality. But it is comparable to the original innocence of biblical Adam and Eve.

The ways of the young hero are not recommended in the social setting of modern Western Europe. But they do not suffer unduly from thoughtful comparison with the ways of "Low Brittany." The reprimands of the abbot produce a retort which is difficult to refute:

> "The abbot tried to prove to him that positive law had to have total precedence, and that, without the conventions reached between men, the law of nature would almost always be nothing but natural banditry. 'One must have,' he said to him 'lawyers, priests, witnesses, contracts, dispensations.' The Ingénu replied to this with the observation which has always been made by savages: 'You must then be very dishonest people, since so many precautions are necessary among you.' " (Ch. VI, p. 267).

One fact is undeniable. "Without the conventions reached between men, the law of nature would almost always be nothing but natural banditry." It is a sad but inevitable reflection on the "best of possible worlds" struggling at the bottom of an evolutionary curve that the said world cannot have the sublime anarchy of Eldorado or preach the "Fay ce que voudras" to the masses. The earth must become "another earth" before laws and conventions can be discarded and full freedom can be allowed to the perfect purity of each individual. Voltaire naturally recognizes the "necessity" of certain controls in social settings such as those of "Westphalia" and "Low Brittany." The arbitrary basis and outrageous abuse of many laws and customs aroused his just wrath. But he does not object to sensible, ethical codes. Such codes — incidentally — were few in his time and remain few to this day.

The rest of the homily of the abbot is open to criticism. The matter of *why* things are so is shunned by the apostle of positive thinking. "Such a question, if asked, would involve evolutionary considerations fatal to dogma. The true "rationale" of Western morality might emerge. The morass or arbitrary and contradictory precepts would be exposed for what it is: a system of "conventions," not a fact-based extension of solid values reflecting the order of the universe. The inquiry might reveal that the alleged basis of Western morality — the Ten Commandments — antedated Moses by many centuries. That elementary precepts such as "Thou shalt not kill" and "Thou shalt not steal" are turned into a daily farce by sanctimounious pillars of society. That the difference may not be great between the dreaded anarchy and the *unnatural* banditry which prevails.

Partial truths are stated by the abbot with unintended candor. Morality has much to do with the vested interests of a swarm of parasites. The "good" of society and true general well-being are different things. Marriage has become a device subordinated to the maintenance of the political and social status quo. Money — the unfailing pass-key to institutional enigmas — must not be diverted from those who possess it. Legal protection of property — a basically sound goal in the case of property acquired honestly — is used to avert the dangerous redress of re-distributed wealth. Superflous and greedy bureaucracies must be maintained. Religious pen-pushers naturally claim the lion's share of matrimonial fleecings. Dispensations of all kinds are a lucrative sideline of the Church. Voltaire points out — and L'Ingénu soon discovers — that it is a grievous sin to sleep with one's cousin or god-mother without approval of the Pope. The same act can be sanctified for a consideration. Such a practice would have a crude name in non-ecclesiastical spheres. The same practice provides the Altar with tentacular control over many lives.

The form of Western marriage which prevailed in the days of Voltaire was a business transaction geared to the benefit of parents and husbands of bartered brides. Such a custom could easily raise two questions: Is "savage" rape worse than legalized rape arranged over the counter? Is civilized banditry better than natural banditry? The matter will soon be settled in general manner. Hercules will discover that Western societies are run by "refined rogues."

The apologist of "positive law" is either confused or lying. Little is positive in Western morality or in its countless "Thou Shalt Nots!" The "moral" system is rooted in wobbly religious dogma and staunch worship of the Lower Self. Personal and collective ethics based on fear and negotiable whitewash can hardly be called "positive." It is not safe to compare such a graveyard of values with the innocence of the primitive. The Pagan world described in *Zadig* promoted and glorified knowledge and good deeds even in its period of decline. Modern Western law "shamefully" limits itself "to punishing crimes."*

The negative orientation of Western society points to appalling fundamental hypocrisy. Love, a natural and positive aspiration of Man, is caught in a tight network of stifling customs and rules contrived by power-crazed and money-mad fiends. The noble objectives of goodness and happiness to be attained by the principal parties — and the principal parties themselves — are almost forgotten. The inversion of sacred values which pervades the Western world could not be more patent. The negative outlook of civilized societies invites edifying conclusions. All is subordinated to the glory and profit of parasitic bodies. One more question would arise were real issues squarely faced. What would become of the power structure and of its malignant ramifications if

---

La Princesse de Babylone, Ch. V.

sin, crime, and other evils suddenly disappeared? What would become of the massive labor force thriving on their prudent control? The reader is left to imagine a non-doctrinal "tremendous crash."

The esoteric value of "love" adds interesting dimension to papal management of "marriage" through dispensation and thought-control. Spiritual yearning is robbed of its vital core of knowledge and freedom. It is ruthlessly codified in the interest of clerical monopolies. The union of Man and Truth is one risk which the Church cannot afford to take. The Ingénu will soon discover that the papacy has excellent reasons for strictly supervising the natural "love between boys and girls."

Even "Wesphalian" marriage combines business and pleasure. But the sacrament of confession totally lacks inducement. The ritual has the distinction of being baseless and distasteful. Only one authority can be found in support of its practice.

> "The Ingénu still had in his pocket the book which his uncle had given him. He did not find that a single apostle had gone to confession, and that made him very rebellious. The prior silenced him by showing to him, in the epistle of Saint James the Minor, these words which grieve heretics so much: 'Confess your sins to one another.'" (Ch. III, pp. 258-59.

The personal interpretation of the Scriptures is viewed as sacrilegious. Hercules is practically labeled "heretic" because of his weakness for independent thought. The concept of "heresy" raises one question. Who are the true "heretics," those who truncate and falsify eternal verities or those who try to find fragments of Truth in the Scriptures? Voltaire generally shows that the quarries of inquisitors and proselytes are closer to original truth than are their executioners and evangelists. There lies the cardinal sin. Mutilated and adulterated as they are, the Scriptures still contain illuminating material for those who read between the lines. Personal exegesis cannot be tolerated. The Pope is not alone in wishing to control the marriage of Man and Truth. All levels of the Church are intent on the same pursuit. The tyrannical arrogance of the usually kind prior is a sympton of weak dogma and institutional fear.

The injunction of Saint James the Minor seems clear. But practice is far removed from precept. If general mutual confession was ever intended among priests, compliance is not evident. As far as Hercules can see, compliance is restricted to an exclusive — if not hypothetical —group. The sacrament has become the layman's affliction to be endured at the discretion of the Church.

The alleged goal of the ritual is not achieved. Rather than repentance of sins confession produces a feeling of outrage and a flare-up of violence. Having reluctantly confessed himself, Hercules proceeds to enforce the cited reciprocity of the sacrament. The episode turns into a brawl in which the physically subdued priest finds himself under the knee of the enraged "penitent." The Pagan view of confession which is dramatized by Voltaire is as critical as the corresponding opinion of occultists:

> "When a Buddhist monk becomes guilty (which does not happen once in a century perhaps) of criminal conversation, he has neither a congregation of tender-hearted members, whom he can move to tears by an eloquent confession of his guilt, nor a Jesus, on whose overburdened, long-suffering bosom are flung, as in a common Christian dust-box, all the impurities of the race. No Buddhist transgressor can comfort himself with visions of a Vatican, within whose sin-encompassing walls black is turned into white, murderers into sinless saints, and golden or silvery lotions can be bought at the confessional to cleanse the tardy penitent of greater or lesser offenses against God and man." (*Isis Unveiled*, p. 321, Vol. 2).

Karmic justice is not swayed by the probes or effusions of the confessional. Genuine spirituality scorns "loopholes."

The worthlessness of confession is tacitly recognized by the Kerkabon family. The glory of effecting a spectacular conversion overrides all other considerations such as the questionable state of grace of new recruit. There is no shortage of theologians generally willing to bend the rules for the sake of the good cause. The case of Hercules is no exception. It is suggested by some that confession may not be required after all since "baptism takes care of everything."

The act of the "penitent" forcing the confessor to his knees reduces the monk to his rightful status of fellow-sinner. The kneeling position itself seems to be deemed worthy of the representative of spiritual abjection. The kneeling position is regarded as idolatrous in the Secret Doctrine and was once condemned as such by a council of the Church. It is symptomatic of a creed which specializes in degrading all aspects of divine essence. Mme Blavatsky makes the following comment on certain traits of Christianity, a faith which is often "as idolatrous and pagan as any other religion:"

> "And that, notwithstanding the formal prohibition of the great Church Council of Elyrus, in A.D. 303, when it was declared that 'the form of God, which is immaterial and invisible, shall not be limited by figure and shape.' In 1692, the council of Constantinople had similarly prohibited 'to paint or represent Jesus *as a lamb*,' as also 'to bow the knee in praying, as it is the act of idolatry.' But the council of Nicaea (787) brought this idolatry back, while that of Rome (883) excommunicated John, the Patriarch of Constantinople, for his showing himself a declared enemy of image worship." (*The Secret Doctrine*, p. 279, Vol II).

The same reverent dislike of image-worship is demonstrated by a Proustian free soul: the duchess of Guermantes. The great lady is a reliable "invert" who never fails to take a stake a stand diametrically opposed to received opinion.* Her reaction to certain indignities is connected with "Voltairian" feeling. The "although" which appears in the following passage is a "because" in disguise:

> "— all heads had turned in her direction at a concert given on Holy Friday where, although a Voltairian, she had not remained because she found it indecent that Christ be put onstage." (*A la Recherche du temps perdu*, p. 447, Vol. II).

Confession amounts to extortion of many secrets by confessors. No one knows better than priests that knowledge is power. The practice of confession is another aspect of tentacular control over society. The gloomy "dust-box" or confessional can easily serve the needs of a spiritual — and temporal — Gestapo.

The same sacrament is conducive to criminal mesmerism. Some effects of the ritual belong to the realm of sorcery and irresponsible hypnotism. Such cases as those of Louis Gaufridi — a XVIIth Century Provencal priest — and Father Girard — an XVIIIth Century Jesuit — are well-known. The mass of precedents which was examined during the trial of Father Girard shows left-handed practices to be frequent products of the confessional.**

Hercules seems aware of occult forces which may be used during confession. The precise description of the Huron subduing the prone confessor with his knee seems significant. The forcibly obtained "mea culpa" or breast-beating is performed by a person other than the unwilling penitent. The compounded absurdity of irrelevant atonement is stressed. The lower limb — a common symbol of gross materiality — is substituted to the right hand which is associated with white magic or superior faculties. The confessing monk is designated as "the adversary party" to the procedure. The word "adversary" has fiendish connotations. The course of Retribution will not be affected by the forced penance of the monk. But a certain type of poetic justice is at work. Retaliation is as appropriate in nature as it is in intensity. Tainted magic is countered by means of corresponding defensive weapons.

Dubious scriptural bases, irrelevance to divine justice, questionable practitioners, and occasional black magic are chief distinctions of a major Christian sacrament.

A la Recherche du temps perdu, p. 469, Vol. II.
**Isis Unveiled*, p. 633, Vol. II.

Hercules is surprisingly eager to submit to circumcision, a step which seems to be advocated by the Scriptures. His desire to undergo the operation is all the more puzzling — exoterically — in view of his instinctive revolt against confession. But the apparent inconsistency can be explained.

Scriptural authority seems abundant. The young man is sensitive to the alleged safety of numbers:

> "At last grace operated; the Ingénu promised to become a Christian; he did not doubt that he must begin with being circumcised; 'For,' he said, 'I do not see in the book which I was made to read a single character who was not, therefore it is obvious that I must make the sacrifice of my foreskin; the sooner the better.'" (Ch. III, p. 258).

The ordinary man in Hercules falls into common error: literal and phallic interpretation of the Scriptures. "Spirituality" concentrates on a certain management of the physical body. The emphasis on kneeling and breast-beating which is a major trait of confession has a counterpart in the sacrifice of an anatomical feature.

The spiritual pioneer concealed within Hercules is not deceived. His insistence on circumcision has two useful results. The Kerkabon family is cornered into recognition of the absurd. The family is also forced to admit that the word of the Scriptures is conveniently ignored by Christians whenever such disregard is expedient.

The supremacy of spirit over matter also explains the attitude of Hercules. Physical submission to authority is felt to be of less moment than spiritual injury such as might be sustained in the confessional. The young man is guided by the pure logic of superior dedication. The primitive maintains allegiance to the non-physical realm of his origin.

The Kerkabons react with horror to the prospect of circumcision. The practice belongs to the barbaric realms of distant lands and times, not to the peak of civilization represented by Low Brittany. Catholic sensuality rebels. The prisoners of deep materiality view with dismay any alteration of the Lower Self.

Hercules is persuaded to renounce the operation. He is told that circumcision is "no longer in fashion." The statement of the prior invites interesting conclusions on the elasticity of Christian precepts. The iron-clad principle of Scriptural Authority suffers some damage as a result of the conversation.

The law prescribing circumcision was abrogated by an initiate: St. Paul. The contrasting figures of Peter and Paul are indirectly evoked by the reported "change of fashion." Corresponding to Peter are the temporal, materialistic aspects of Christianity and the foundation of obtuse harshness which is retained from the Old Testament. Corresponding to Paul are the mystical tradition of the East, the true message of Christ, and an enlightening influence.

> "The erudite author of *Supernatural Religion* assiduously endeavors to prove that by *Simon Magus* we must understand the apostle Paul, whose Epistles were secretly as well as openly calumniated by Peter, and charged with containing 'dysnoëtic learning.' The Apostle of the Gentiles was brave, outspoken, sincere, and very learned; the apostle of Circumcision, cowardly, cautious, *insincere,* and very ignorant. That Paul had been, partially, at least, if not completely, initiated into the theurgic mysteries, admits of little doubt." (*Isis Unveiled*, p. 89 Vol. II).

The first contact of Hercules with Christianity is marked by conflict and confusion. Insoluble differences exist between the Old and the New Testaments. The embarrassing question asked in the XIXth Century by Mme Blavatsky is relevant to doctrinal "new fashions." "Are we required to believe and worship a Deity who contradicts himself every few hundred years?" Papal personalities are indirectly brought to mind with less than infallible attributes. Pontifical hassles invite sad thoughts on the alleged unity of the "universal" Church.

The Papacy itself is critically examined. Finding himself in need of a dispensation to marry Mlle Saint Yves — who is his godmother — Hercules is informed of the existence and function of the Pope. His first reaction is naively enthusiastic but short-lived.

> " 'Who can be,' he said, 'that charming man who favors with such kindness the love between boys and girls? I want to go and speak to him right away.' "
> They explained to him what the Pope was, and the Ingénu was even more surprised than before. 'There is not one single word about that in your book, my dear uncle, I have travelled, I know the sea; we are here on the coast of the Ocean, and I would leave Mlle de Saint Yves to go and ask permission to love her from a man who lives near the Mediterranean, four hundred leagues from here, and whose language I do not understand? That is ridiculous nonsense." (Ch. V, p. 266).

The central element of the passage is the esoteric meaning of "Love:" spirituality. It is supplemented by the symbolism of land and sea representing the material and the spiritual worlds respectively. The knowledge of the sea which is claimed by the hero suggests knowledge of sunken continents and periodically tilting planetary axes. The same lore implies familiarity with the voyage of life through multiple rebirths. Also implied is awareness of the unfathomable human deep. The Mediterranean, etymologically and otherwise related to the "middle" or "cen-

ter" of the land is opposed to the spiritual essence of oceans of reincarnation and occult knowledge. The young man has no desire to leave
"the coast of the Ocean," a choice base of operations for fearless explorers, a site which remains connected with original wisdom and the
mystery of human origin. Landlocked authority does not appeal to con-
noisseurs of boundless horizons. Instinct warns the primitive against
total estrangement from the familiar heritage of the sea.

The Pope is emphatically designated as a "man" or ordinary being.
The myth of divine inspiration or infallibility is subjected to doubt.
The question of *what* the Pope is invites speculation on a sub-human
plane. The Pope is also denounced as a usurper and spiritual upstart.
The distance of *four* hundred leagues separating Hercules from Rome is
a probable allusion to those races of mankind which precede the fifth.

The fund of stolen lore which forms the stock-in-trade of the Church
belong to the legacy of four sub-cycles of evolution. But the orthodox
interpretation of *Genesis* dwarfs the history of Man and Earth to a
mere four thousand years before Christ. The Voltairian hero and Savior
who spans several races and knows the "sea" has reason to reflect on
unbridgeable gaps represented by *four* thousand leagues.

> "The Book of Enoch, — is a *résumé,* a compound of the main features
> of the History of the Third, Fourth and Fifth Races; — Perhaps St.
> Augustine was quite right in saying that the Church rejected the BOOK
> OF ENOCH out of her canon owing to its too great antiquity, *ob
> nimiam antiquitatem.** There was no room for the events noticed in it
> within the limit of the 4004 years B.C. assigned to the *world* from its
> 'creation!' " (*The Secret Doctrine,* p. 535, Vol. II).

The *four* thousand leagues may also be intended to suggest the scope
of secret records of human history. "Eastern Initiates maintain that they
have preserved records of the racial development and of events of universal import ever since the beginning of the *Fourth Race.*"**

The symbolic gap of four thousand leagues may account for the
existence of a linguistic barrier between Hercules and the Pope. The
messenger of Primitive Wisdom-Religion and the successor of ignorant
Saint Peter do not speak the same language. The disparity of knowledge separating Huron from Pope makes communication difficult at best.
Were he a legitimate spokesman of Truth, the pontiff would be an
Adept of the highest degree. But he is the mere custodian of a temporal structure deprived of the key to ancient Science; he is only the
latest human brace of an "imaginary stilt:" apostolic succession. Both

---

City of God, I xv, ch. xiii.
**The Secret Doctrine,* p. 646, Vol. I.

400

Pope and Church are accordingly insecure and despotic. The perceptive lover of Truth senses the threatening debility of the religious establishment and of its Chief Executive. No man endowed with a live spirit can do business with such a clearing-house. The "parentless" Ingénu needs no papal "father figure."

The Pope is unqualified to preside over the courtship of young "lovers." The mystical destiny of Man is best fulfilled without professional go-betweens. Panurge, Hercules, the sages of Eldorado and occultists all agree. The shortcomings of the Church are not merely those of incompetence. The successor of Saint Peter and those who serve him are bent on one pursuit: systematic sabotage of the free quest for sacred Love or Truth.

Financial aspects of the dispensation are not stressed. The young hero may not even conceive that spirituality and money can and do mix in some societies. Whatever the case may be, money is a secondary consideration. In this instance as in the case of confession and circumcision, material hardship is felt to be less injurious than spiritual duress.

No one ever opposed material oppression more courageously than Voltaire. General extortion, abusive taxation, arbitrary imprisonment, torture and pseudo-legal killing were consistently denounced by him in word and deed. The famous cases of Calas, Sirven, and La Barre give ample proof of the importance which he attached to deprived, tormented, and wilfully destroyed flesh. But he never lost sight of the ultimate goal of such crimes: aggravated assault on human spirit. The section of the *Dictionnaire Philosophique* which is devoted to *Torture* condemns the subject practice as an imitation of Jehovic tyranny, a "crime of lèse-majesté divine and human." The biblical God and his executioners have the same quarry and use the same methods. The "infamous" cannot survive without degrading the Deity or the human reflection of divine essence. The supremacy of Spirit is ironically manifest in one fact. Spirit is the eternal target of temporal abuse. "Behavior modification" is but a new name for most ancient arts.

All esoteric writers are naturally and supremely concerned with the depraved handling of human Spirit. Vigny is most articulate:

> "Personally, if some old utensils of barbaric times were absolutely necessary to political men, I would rather see them refurbish, restore, bring on the scene and put to use the racks and tools of Torture. For they would at least soil only the body and not the soul of the creature of God. They might cause suffering flesh to speak, but the scream of nerves and bones under pincers is less vile than the cold sale of a head over a counter, and there never was yet a name which was inscribed lower than the name of: JUDAS." (*Diary*, 1837).

Vigny did not favor a return to torture chambers. No more vibrant condemnation of physical cruelty could possibly be found than the controlled yet passionate description of the martyrdom of Urbain Grandier in *Cinq-Mars*. Few if any names could be found which are "incribed lower" than is the name of LACTANCE in the same novel. Voltaire and his fellow-"smugglers" attack the insidious spiritual crime which cloaks itself in non-violence if not benevolence. Having a lesser degree of visibility, such a crime is more profitable to its authors than maimings and auto-da-fés which are conducive to disgust and general revolt. Sugarcoated spiritual meddling may not even be recognized as such by those who practice it.

The Kerkabon family is a semi-conscious instrument of such spiritual wrong-doing. No physical or mental duress is used or needed to convert Hercules to Christianity. In all respects but one — susceptibility to charm — the young man has remarkable sales resistance to Christian faith. But the sweet conspiracy of kindly "bons vivants" is more dangerous to spiritual integrity than any conceivable form of physical hardship.

The Kerkabons personify "nice" and blind missionary zeal ensnaring innocent victims whose primitive spiritual awareness is superior to their own. Voltaire's concern with the religious aspect of the white man's guilt is clearly voiced in *La Princesse de Babylone*. The story of a Far Eastern King is told:

> "He was the most fair-minded, the most polite, and the wisest monarch on earth. It was he, who first plowed a small field with his imperial hands to make agriculture respectable to his people. He first established prizes for virtue. The laws, everywhere else, were shamefully limited to punishing crimes. This emperor had just expelled from his States a troop of foreign priests who had come from the most remote part of the West, in the insane hope of forcing all China to think as they did, and who, under the pretext of disseminating truths, had already acquired wealth and honors. He had told them, as he expelled them, these very words, which are recorded in the annals of the Empire:
>
>> 'You could cause as much harm here as you have elsewhere; you came to preach dogmas of intolerance to the most tolerant nation on earth. I am sending you back in order not to ever have to punish you. You will be led honorably to my borders; you will be supplied with everything necessary to return to the limits of the hemisphere from which you came. Go in peace if you can be in peace, and return no more.'" (Ch. V).

The "pox" has only bleak prospects in positively oriented societies. Such collectivities know the value of preventive isolation. The sacred value of human life is also recognized. One may compare the treatment

402

accorded heretics in one hemisphere with the corresponding witch-hunts of the Western Garden of Eden.

One element of the above text — the idea of forcing others to think as one does — bears a striking resemblance of meaning and expression to the briefing of a director of Jesuitic missions operating in the Far East. Cited in *Isis Unveiled* are instructions of M. de la Loubère to his subordinates. It was the opinion of the said director that doctrinal changes should be used, in case of need, to make Christian faith attractive to Oriental converts. Such extensive alterations were required as to make the conquering creed unrecognizable. The attitude of the Jesuit is basically identical to the occasional "flexibility" of the proselyting Kerkabons. M. de la Loubère expressed himself as follows:

> " 'These examples are sufficient to show with what precautions it is necessary to prepare the minds of the Orientals to think as we do, and not to be offended with most of the articles of the Christian faith.'
> And what, we ask, is left to preach? With no Savior, no atonement, no crucifixion for human sin, no Gospel, no eternal damnation to tell them of, and no miracles to display, what remained for the Jesuits to spread among the Siamese but the dust of the Pagan sanctuaries with which to blind their eyes? The sarcasm is biting indeed. The morality to which these poor heathen are made to adhere by their ancestral faith is so pure, that Christianity has to be stripped of every distinguishing mark before its priests can venture to offer it for their examination. A religion that cannot be trusted to the scrutiny of an unsophisticated people who are patterns of filial piety, of honest dealing, of deep reverence for God and an instinctive horror of profaning His majesty, must indeed be founded upon error. That it is so, our century is discovering little by little." (*Isis Unveiled*, pp. 578-79, Vol. 2).

The same type of chameleon strategy was prescribed by Gregory the Great to Saint Augustine when the conversion of Pagan Anglo-Saxons was being planned.

> " 'Tell Augustine that about which I long reflected with respect to the Angles; to-wit that one must carefully refrain from destroying the temples of the idols of that nation; that one must destroy only the idols which are there; that one must make holy water with which to sprinkle those temples, put altars and relics in them. If those temples are well built, it is necessary that they be transferred from the cult of the demons to the service of the true God, for the people, when they see that their own temples are not destroyed, will go more willingly to customary places to worship the true God. And since, in that country, they observe the custom of immolating oxen as a sacrifice to the demons, one must make that custom serve some religious solemnity: for instance on the day of dedication or on the feast day of holy martyrs whose relics they have, they may make huts of foliage around the Church . . . and instead of immolating their animals to the devil, they

may sacrifice them in the honor of God and give thanks after becoming satiated to the donor of all things — for it is absolutely impossible to change hardened minds: when one wishes to arrive at the
peak of a mountain, one climbs step by step, one does not rise by leaps
and bounds." (Bede, *Ecclesiastical History*, I, 30).

The passage of *The Princess of Babylon* which is quoted above may
have been inspired by the instructions of Gregory and M. de la Loubère.
Voltaire must have been impressed by such briefings which tend to
promote apostolic success, safety, good working conditions, and the
acquisition of real estate.

Blind and static euphoria is the deadliest attribute of perverted Truth
in the chronological setting of *L'Ingénu*. The inquisitors of *Candide* are
not confused about their own motives. Nor are the impersonators of
Cunégonde. But the European portion of Latter-Day-Fifth Race mankind
residing in "Low Brittany" has comfortably settled in a spiritual vacuum
in the bosom and with the blessing of a deceptively "Good Church." The
Kerkabons sincerely believe themselves dedicated to the "good cause"
which they equate with Christian affiliation and proselytism. They are
unable to grasp the superior essence of the stranger in their midst until
a certain "turn of the wheel" of evolution takes place. Western society
is blindly complacent and superficially kind. Such is the probable reason why no counterpart to the ambivalence of Cacambo is found in
L'Ingénu. Such may also be reason why the "True Story" is tinged
with flesh-and-blood realism, a trait sharply contrasting with the shadowy
— Goya-like quality of *Candide*. Persecution still exists. But it has learned
to wear a mask of benevolent good cheer. Blindness is general. Materiality and materialism reign supreme.

Ordination is next on the list of Christian practices and sacraments
reviewed by Voltaire. Hercules is offered the security and prestige of
a position in the Church. The offer made by his benevolent uncle is
prompted by genuine kindness. But good intentions are not matched by
the quality of the proposed status. The well-meaning prior is the unwitting spokesmen of a sad truth. Correspondence is strongly suggested
to exist between a *low* spiritual plane and the fact of being a *Christian*.

> " 'Heavens be praised, my dear nephew, that you have the honor of
> being a Christian and a Low Breton!' " (Ch. V, p. 264).

Peril lurks in the very kindliness of the offer. The hero is in danger
of being absorbed by the establishment of debased verity. Only one
step separates the status of spiritual victim from that of active instrument of truncated truth. As was previously suggested, the Kerkabon

404

family itself falls into the category of such victims and instruments.

Hercules refuses to give up his marriage plans thus disqualifying himself from the priesthood. His decision is prompted by love rather than recognition of true danger. The hero is approaching a short phase of his life during which superior vision will be almost entirely neutralized by forces of darkness. The young lover perceives no conflict between ordination and courtship. But the two cannot be reconciled in "Low Brittany." The dilemma is especially thorny on the esoteric plane of mystical union. Although the feat was actually performed in spectacular cases — of which Rabelais is only one — it is difficult to be at the same time a churchman and a devotee of Truth. The love of eternal verities is a sure and mighty guide to the outside of the Church. It is the apparent destiny of Hercules to be so guided. The young man is rescued from the priesthood by undying devotion to the woman who will emerge as UNVEILED TRUTH.

The obnoxious presence of the inquisitive bailli completes the survey of Catholicism. The personage appears at an early stage of the story in a manner which suggests him to be a permanent fixture of life in Low Brittany. The bailli does not fail to attend the baptismal feast of Hercules or to ply the new convert with questions. The Huron is quick to sense the concealed identity of the unattractive guest who comes as close to being the devil as is humanly possible.

> "The Huron reacted heatedly; he drank a great deal to the health of his godmother. 'If I had been baptized by your hand, he said, I feel that the cold water which was poured on my bun of hair would have scalded me.' The bailli found that excessively poetic, not knowing how familiar allegory is in Canada." (Ch. IV, pp. 262-63).

The bailli is described as "the greatest questioner in the province" and as an incurable pursuer of "strangers." The word *questioner* brings to mind two aspects of the activities of Inquisitors: the act of obtaining desired information and the technique used to obtain it. The term *question* was at one time the equivalent of "torture." The word "province" brings to mind the Provincial Delegates of certain religious orders whose work did not differ greatly from the work of Inquisitors. The Voltairian pursuer of "strangers" or heretics clerly belongs to fiendish hosts. The reference of the Ingénu to scalding water, the "heat" of his response to the probes of the bailli, the need of a spiritual antidote represented by abundant "drinking," and the phonetic resemblance between the words "bailli" and "bouilli" — "boiled" — are clues to the identity of the character. The popular French expression "aller" or "envoyer" "au diable bouilli" — "to go" or "to send to the boiling devil"

—may have determined the choice of the word "bailli." The inquisitive guest combines perversity with a remarkable flair for the "familiar" or the realm of things occult. His total personality suggests a predilection for black magic. While his knowledge of "poetry" and "allegory" is limited, his recognition of pure spirituality represented by the Huron is immediate and unerring.

The encounter of the Ingénu with the devil adds interesting dimension to the Heraklean descend into Hell which is suggested in Chapter IV of the story. The presence of the Fiend seems to constitute a reference to a specific passage of the Gospel of Nicodemus which is a masterpiece of bungled plagiarism.

> "Then begins a turmoil in Hell which has been graphically described by Homer, Hesiod, and their interpreter, Preller, in his account of the Astronomical Hercules *Invictus,* and his festivals at Tyre, Tarsus, and Sardis. Having been initiated in the Attic Eleusinia, the Pagan god descends into Hades and, 'when he entered the nether world he spread such terror among the dead that all of them fled!' (Preller, ii. p. 154). The same words are repeated in *Nicodemus.* Follows a scene of confusion, horror and lamenting. Perceiving that the battle is lost, the Prince of Hell turns tail and prudently chooses to side with the strongest. He against whom, according to Jude and Peter, even the Archangel Michael 'durst not bring a railing accusation before the Lord,' is now shamefully treated by his ex-ally and friend, the 'Prince of Hell,' Poor Satan is abused and reviled for all his crimes both by devils and saints; while the *Prince* is openly rewarded for his treachery. Addressing him, the King of Glory says thus: 'Beelzebub, the Prince of Hell, Satan the Prince shall now be subject to thy dominion *forever, in the room of Adam* and his righteous sons, who are mine. . . . Come to me, all ye my saints, who were *created in my image,* who *were condemned by the tree of the forbidden fruit,* and *by the Devil and death.* Live now *by the wood of my cross;* the Devil, the prince of this world is overcome (?) and *Death is conquered.'* Then the Lord takes hold of Adam by his right hand, of David by the left, and *'ascends from Hell, fol-lowed by all the saints,'* Enoch and Elias, and by the 'holy thief.'"

> "The pious author, perhaps through an oversight, omits to complete the cavalcade, by bringing up the rear with the penitent dragon of Simon Stylites and the converted wolf of St. Francis, wagging their tails and shedding tears of joy!" (*Isis Unveiled,* p. 517, Vol. 2).

A great vertical distance lies between the Pagan descent of the Initiate into the nether world and the Heraklean descent remodelled by Nicodemus. The former voyage is the crowning achievement of Knowledge and desire to serve. The gathering described by Nicodemus is as enlightened, harmonious, and altruistic as a political convention. If any platforms are evolved by its swarm of stage-struck mediocrities, they are based on the propositions that might makes right and Knowledge is damnable. Satan himself is degraded. Debasement could not be more

406

complete. The "Fall" of Man from spiritual to material regions is reflected by the fall of religion from Paganism to Christianity. The Heraclean legend mentioned by Voltaire is an eloquent example of mistreated Pagan wisdom. The quality of Knowledge and Ethics underlying the original tradition is dragged down to the lowest possible level by Christian plagiarists.

The Ingénu discovers the reverse side of a benevolent picture. Satanic reality lurks everywhere. The ways and deeds of the bailli are sinister previews of things to come. Hercules will not witness auto-da-fés such as those of *Candide*. But he will see the results of Huguenot persecution. The fate of harassed "strangers" will show that the era of darkness is far from over. The young man will personally experience the efficiency of jailers who specialize in spiritual repression. As he becomes estranged from the symbolic ocean of his latest voyage, as he leaves the Kerkabons — who respond unconsciously to the temperate climate of the sea — as he plunges ever deeper into the symbolic materiality of land, he will face the sad fact of a social bedlam made up of "refined rogues."

Alienation from former friends inevitably follows exposure to the "pox." Membership in the "Good Church" leads to rejection of purer forms of faith. Hercules soon finds himself fighting the "English." The fact is indicative of radically altered values. Wholesome dislike of the devilish bailli and related works fails to protect the young hero against general, contagious madness. Critical faculties seem non-existent. Intuitive perception seems lost. While his reception on the "enemy" vessel shows peaceful — if not friendly — intent on the part of the "English," Hercules remains insensitive to evidence of continued good will. Aroused by rumors, borrowed anger, and blind passion, the young man initiates hostilities against his former companions. The result is bloody strife, blindness and divisiveness at their worst. In a word: Maya.

The irresistible power of the stampeding human herd is a sad commentary on "Westphalia" or "Low Brittany." The spectacle of surrounding lunacy should suffice to enlighten the young man. But the brutish impact of "what everyone else is doing" becomes unquestioned "motivation" and unquestioned "normalcy." The "Low Briton" joins a raving, lynching mob. It would be difficult to sink lower. The esoteric component of the young man which is mankind struggles madly in darkness. The superior being who comes "from another world"* must experience and overcome the benighted condition of ordinary humanity.

Estrangement from the source of "Spiritual Fire" — the "Three In One"

---

*Ch. X.

— is stressed by a small detail. The young hero now carries a *two-shot* rifle. The weapon is used to shoot birds: "winged" or spiritual beings.

Hercules finds a well-filled purse which produces more greed than satisfaction. Yearning to receive money and prestige, the young man decides to go to Versailles. Urged by relatives and friends to seek rewards for his services against the "English," he undertakes to go to court and present a plea to the King.

One redeeming motive determines his decision: love of Mlle Saint Yves who has been imprisoned in a convent. The fiery suitor is ready to go to any length to secure her release. The new Christian is again saved from spiritual death by undying devotion to Truth.

> "He wanted to go and set the convent on fire, to either kidnap his beloved, or to burn himself with her." (Ch. Vi, p. 269).

The mystical ardor of Hercules prolongs the faithful tradition of Zadig and Candide. Devotion to Truth remains unaffected by occasional weakness. Man is impelled to fulfill his destiny of all-consuming divine love. Alfred de Vigny may have had in mind the Voltairian couple when he wrote the following lines:

> "Le pur enthousiasme est craint des faibles âmes
> Qui ne sauraient porter son ardeur ni son poids.
> Pourquoi le fuir? — La vie est double dans les flammes."
> *La Maison du berger* — A Eva).

> ("Pure enhusiasm is feared by weak souls
> Which cannot bear either its ardor or its weight.
> Why elude it? — Life is double in the flames.")

The esoteric identity of Saint Yves is called to the attention of the reader. The devotion of the Ingénu to Saint Yves inspires the following words:

> "I shall see the King, I shall make the truth known to him; it is impossible not to surrender to that truth when one perceives it. I shall return soon to marry Mlle Saint-Yves." (Ch. VIIII, p. 274).

The passionate statement of the Ingénu is comparable to a corresponding passage of *Candide*. The lover of Cunégonde is "too pure to betray the truth." Hercules seeks redress on behalf of betrayed Truth. Through choice and repetition, the words of the hero beg the reader to make the necessary esoteric connection between the prisoner and oppressed Truth.

The dedication of Voltaire to the spiritual quest of mankind and his commitment to the Secret Doctrine explode in the discreet yet vibrant *credo*: "It is impossible not to surrender to that truth when one perceives it."

It may be noted in passing that the allegorical figure of Truth — a woman imprisoned in a convent — seems to have a counterpart in a poem of Shelley: *Epipsychidion,* a text dedicated to the "noble and unfortunate Lady, Emilia V........, now imprisoned in the convent· of ...."

Religious persecution is the logical companion of the imprisonment of Truth. The plight of the Huguenots is next in the review of "Christian" practice. Common sense as well as decency is outraged by *dragonnades* and forced emigration. The victims represent a vast amount and rare quality of talent forever lost to France. Blunder is added to crime.

Deep affinities exist between Hercules and the Huguenots. The young man owes to a Protestant the knowledge of French which he acquired in Canada. The symbolic tie represented by language is suggestive of benefit derived from heretical contact. In spite of their doctrinal and political vagaries, religious dissenters have something to offer to objective minds. Their fundamental aspiration — return to the source of knowledge — has the interest and respectful sympathy of Voltaire.

The banishment of the victims bears symbolic relevance to the plight of mankind estranged through "necessity" from its spiritual cradle. The quotation of Virgil's melodious lines embraces the entire human family:

> "Nos dulcia linquimus arva,
> Nos patriam fugimus."

The Voltairian reference to conversions effected by the dragons conveys concentrated esoteric irony. The value of "conversions" extorted by brute force is dubious. The dual significance of the French word "dragon" — which covers "dragons" as well as "dragoons" — adds unsuspected dimension to the passage. The esoteric meaning of "dragons" or mythical monsters is as follows:

> "As will be found more than once as we proceed, the 'Serpent' and 'Dragon' were the names given to the 'Wise Ones,' the initiated adepts of olden times." (*The Secret Doctrine,* p. 404, Vol. I).

One may note in retrospect —without surprise — that the name of the shrewd and loyal friend of Zadig, *Cador,* is the anagrama of "Draco," the Latin word for "dragon." Such a person is a fitting "companion" for the title character who "was as wise as one can be, for he sought to live with wise men."

Dragonnades may result in conversions totally unintended by persec-

409

utors. Spiritual backlash may lead beyond Protestantism in the path of "heresy." It may indeed lead all the way "to the source." Resistance to oppression may produce a small but significant number of initiates. Such a tiny minority — dedicated and powerful — may become an agent of divine justice. Such a development seems to reflect the Voltairian view of Karmic Retribution.

Proustian literature contains an amusing reference to the esoteric concept of "dragons." M. de Charlus — a notorious "invert" — is bewitched by dragoons — or dragons. In the judgment of the puzzling nobleman, a dragon can be "something very beautiful."*

The arrival of the Ingénu on the grand scene of Versailles is effected in a strange conveyance. The small covered coach used by the traveller is designated as a "chamber pot." Voltaire may have used the prosaic detail to express a dim view of courtly splendor, an illustration of Maya difficult to surpass. Such a view seems consistent with the arrival of the young hero at the palace kitchens. The seamy side of the royal "fine picture" does exist and is exposed. A barb may have been intended with respect to primitive or non-existent sanitation. The splendid edifice of Versailles was notoriously lacking in such conveniences in the days of Louis XIV. The monarch himself is known to have gone through life virtually untouched by baths. The Huron is better equipped than the Sun King. The fact that one meaning of mythological Hercules is the Sun adds to the irony of the latter suggestion. The chamber pot may represent in part an oblique reference to corresponding utensils made of silver and gold by the residents of Thomas More's *Utopia*. Similar views of material gold are held by the Voltairian residents of Eldorado. The weaponry value of loaded chamber-pots is demonstrated in Chapter III of *Candide*. Such a missile is hurled at the title character by a Protestant lady filled with sectarian zeal. The implied equivalence leaves litle to imagination. Voltaire also mentions "la guerre des pots de chambre" in *Le Siècle de Louis XIV*. The reference to chamber pots may be calculated to suggest any or all of the above interpretations. Most probable is an allusion to biological aspects of incarnation. The Huron is brought to Mayavic depths of superficial grandeur and barely concealed filth by symbolic "wheels" of evolution which are connected with the lowest plane of being. "Inter faeces urinamque nascimur." Or, in the words of Voltaire, "the immortal soul" of Man "is born and lodged between urine and something worse."** The carriage of the In-

---

A la Recherche du temps perdu, p. 778, Vol. III.
**Mariage de l'Homme aux quarante écus.*

génu is a far cry from "the conveyances of up there." Hercules is in the depths of "generation" or materiality.

Limited vision is logically connected with low planes of existence. Royal underlings prove as inaccessible as their royal master. Perplexity is voiced by the hero:

" 'Est-ce-que tout le monde est invisible dans ce pays-ci?' "

(" 'Is everyone invisible in this country?' ")

The theme of an invisible world is woven into the question. The French expression "tout le monde" — "everybody" — lends itself to a play on words as it may be translated literally as "the whole world." Cosmic vision is lacking in low spheres of Being. The observation applies to the fifth sub-cycle of human evolution in general and to the royal court of France in particular.

The same factor of lacking or partial insight is connected with humorous scenes. The adventures of Hercules have a comical aspect in the general reaction to his appearance and manner. Some street characters mistake him for a great lord traveling incognito. The designation of "great lord" is socially inaccurate. But it is correct from the esoteric standpoint. The equivalence of "Lords" is given in the Secret Doctrine. "Lords" constitute a hierarchy which has extensions on all planes of Genesis from the plane of archetypal Creative Powers to the plane of the Higher Self in every human being. "Lords" of the "Dazzling Face" are adepts "of the White Magic."* The occult concept of "Lord" fits the dual personality of the hero: a voluntarily reincarnated being endowed with superior vision yet partaking of the trials and errors of ordinary human condition. It is also consistent with the evolutionary aspect of the Huron who is the embodiment of "round" or cyclic patterns of existence. The presumed identity of the Ingénu carries the common esoteric distinction of being wrong in one sense and correct in others.

Those persons who do not suspect the presence of a disguised grandee are inclined to regard the Ingénu as the buffoon of the King. The impact of indefinible distinction is dimly felt. Directly or indirectly, greatness is associated with the mysterious traveler. The popular tendency to equate the unknown and the foolish is also noted.

The occult concept of "Kings" is another element of the Theogony of Creation:

---

*The Secret Doctrine, p. 427, Vol. II.

"They are sometimes seven, sometimes ten, when they become prajâ-pati, the 'Lord of Beings'; then, they rebecome the *seven* and the *fourteen* Manus, as the representatives of the seven and fourteen cycles of Existence ('Days of Brahmâ); thus answering to the seven *AEons*, when at the end of the first stage of Evolution they are transformed into the seven stellar Rishis, the Saptarishis; while their human doubles appear as heroes, Kings, and Sages on this earth." (*The Secret Doctrine*, p. 442, Vol. I).

It will be remembered at this point that the size of "Micromégas" is given in "royal" footage — "pieds de roi." — The suggested rank of "King" is a significant aspect of the true stature of the Titan.

The early rising and the mythological personality of the Voltairian hero reflect the occult concept of a "King." The former trait is connected with evolutionary cycles or "Days of Brahmâ." The latter status is that of a "Hero" or demi-god. The "Sage" who is not exoterically apparent in the Ingénu is authentic on the esoteric plane. The traveler who came "from another world" may well be connected with a community of "Sages of this earth." He may therefore be labeled as the "buffoon" or mock — "human" — "double" of a "King." A startling autobiographical hint is offered by Voltaire: According to the *Epître Dédicatoire à la Sultane Sheraa*, it was a "sage" who "amused himself" by writing *Zadig*.

The speculations of street-corner oracles do not lack merit. The unsophisticated by-standers are very close to truth. Much is unknown — or occult — about the young man who travels "incognito." The inquisitive company displays imagination and a commendable desire to look beyond appearance. Such traits are prized by "Lords" and "Kings." Voltaire suggests that the adventures — or avataras — of the Ingénu might be studied with profit by readers willing to use the same faculties. The passage may be compared to the episode of *Zadig* in which a naïve fisherman fails to ask the name of his Savior. The exoteric reader who smiles at the "simple-minded" character is unaware of an important fact. The target of the Voltairian grin conveyed by the passage is the reader himself. Similar "bait" is used in Chapter VIII of *L'Ingénu*.

The curiosity of by-standers featured in Chapter VIII reflects an important phase of human evolution. Mankind seems to have entered a stage of development in which the ordinary man dimly senses vital truths. The "Era of Suspicion" has begun.

The imprisonment of Hercules is ordered by well-informed representatives of the Throne and Altar. The long arm of the confessor of the King — Père de la Chaise — is involved in the arrest — as are the bailli and a jesuitic spy. The meaningful team formed by the latter persons implies the agency of a kind of satanism which is not limited to political affairs. The word "spy" belongs to the same plane of esoteric significance as do the terms "bandits," "guards," "satellites," "familiars," and "servants." The vigilant authorities have a good grasp of the convictions of their victim. The young man is in subversive sympathy with "heretics." He is known to want to "burn convents and kidnap girls." The perceptive power structure knows what that means.

Voltaire shows once more that free thought and free expression cannot be tolerated by a despotic régime. The involvement of Jesuitry with the black arts is once more noted. The material prison to which the Ingénu is committed represents more than the actual site of his confinement. Society in general is viewed as a jail where the noblest aspirations of Man are suppressed. Lovers of Truth — and Truth itself — are unwelcome in man-made Maya.

The symbolic prison of incarnation is rich in seeming paradox. Under certain conditions the "dungeon" is the scene of a sublime metamorphosis. The curse of forced solitude becomes a spiritual blessing. The bondage of separate existence yields to the loneliness of Man at one with the Absolute. Darkness becomes true light. Anguish is felt but spirit is uncrushed. The transcended Lower Self recedes to become the chrysalis of divine essence. Personal suffering produces selflessness. Mankind finds its raison d'être and the key to the mystery of human condition in the soaring flight of Spirit beyond the confining "coat of skin."

Common misfortune creates instant bonds between Hercules and his cellmate, a jansenist named Gordon. Wisdom will be attained through joint efforts of the two prisoners. The dedicated lover of Saint Yves contributes intuitive spirituality and instinctive mystical devotion. Gordon contributes formal knowledge, experience in the dungeon of incarnate life, and compassion. The total fund of insight and love represented by the two captives meets all requirements of transcendental progress.

Selflessness is demonstrated by both men. The first greeting of Gordon to the hero is as follows:

> "I shall always forget myself to lighten your torments in the infernal abyss where we are plunged. Let us worship Providence which led us there, let us suffer in peace, and let us hope.'" (Ch. X, p. 278).

A certain "infernal abyss" is suggested to be on earth. The statement of the unorthodox Jansenist echoes the occult view of Hell:

> "—, tradition shows the celestial *Yogis* offering themselves as voluntary victims in order to redeem Humanity — created god-like and perfect at first — and to endow him with human affections and aspirations. To do this they had to give up their natural status and, descending on our

413

globe, take up their abode on it for the whole cycle of the Mahayuga, thus exchanging their impersonal individualities for individual personalities — the bliss of sidereal existence for the curse of terrestrial life. This voluntary sacrifice of the Fiery Angels, whose nature was *Knowledge* and *Love,* was construed by the exoteric theologies into a statement that shows 'the rebel angels hurled down from heaven into the darkness of Hell' — our Earth." (*The Secret Doctrine,* p. 246, Vol. II).

The equivalence of Earth and Hell which is virtually established by Gordon contains the seeds of the occult definition of "voluntary sacrifice." The new friend of Hercules seems to dimly sense the spiritual status of his cellmate. The remote closeness of Jansenism to Truth — a theme frequently conveyed in the works of Voltaire — is noted once again.

Awareness of universal suffering is enhanced — not diminished — by personal hardship. The prisoners "did not dare complain when all was suffering."

The selflessness of Hercules is generated in part by thoughts of those who love him:

"He pitied those who loved him far more than he pitied himself." (Ch. X, p. 282).

The true nature of mystical love is revealed to Gordon by Hercules. The legitimate and divine aspiration of Man is no longer tainted with guilt:

""He had regarded love before only as a sin of which one accuses oneself in confession. He learned to know it as a feeling as noble as it is tender, which can raise the soul as well as weaken it, and which can even produce virtues sometimes." (Ch. XIV, p. 295).

The agony and mystery of human condition are regarded in identical light by all esoteric writers. The question of "Why the soul is confined in its feeble prison" is evoked by Christ in *Le Mont des oliviers.* The same eternal enigma is pondered in the *Diary* of Vigny:

"It is true that you do not know why you are a prisoner or the reason of your punishment; but you know beyond any doubt what your penalty will be: suffering in prison, death afterwards.
Do not think of the judge, or of the trial of which you will always be ignorant, but only of thanking the unknown jailer who frequently grants you joys worthy of heavens." (*Diary* 1832).

Joyful harvests are reaped by Hercules and Gordon. Reading, meditation, exchanged knowledge, friendship and love turn incarceration into a bearable plight. "A noble, grateful, and sensitive soul can live happy" in its prison of flesh.* Hercules and Gordon are such souls.

> "Thus days, weeks and months went by; and he would have thought himself happy in the sojourn of despair had he not loved." (Ch. X, p. 283).

The apparent conflict between love and captive happiness is dissolved on the esoteric plane. It is *because of* love of mankind and Truth that the Ingénu finds solace in the dungeon of incarnate life. The conditional form of the verb "would have thought" leaves room for the expression of conscious happiness.

Progress seems difficult and slow. Age-old questions such as the destiny of Man and the nature of Good and Evil seem to remain unresolved. But the apparent confusion of the two captives is belied by esoteric substance:

> "La conversation roula sur la Providence, sur les lettres de cachet, et sur l'art de ne pas succomber aux disgrâces auxquelles tout homme est exposé dans ce monde. 'Il y a deux ans que je suis ici,' dit le vieillard, 'sans autre consolation que moi-même et les livres; je n'ai pas eu un moment de mauvaise humeur.'" (Ch. X, p. 279).

> ("The conversation bore upon Providence, on *lettres de cachet*, and upon the art of withstanding the misfortunes which befall every man in this world. 'I have been here for two years,' said the old man, 'without any other consolation than myself and books: I never had one moment of ill temper.'")

The cyclic design of Providence — Karma — is suggested by the verb "rouler" — "to roll". The prisoners have knowledge of the general scheme of evolution. The *Huron* — who personifies among other things the shape of the Great Circle — imparts to the Jansenist the Karmic lore desperately needed by Port Royal. Jansenism is no longer marred by the absence of a crucial doctrinal "missing link:" Free Will-Retribution-In-One. The "Oreillons" of the new era no longer lack the "resources" of the Primitive Wisdom-Religion.

The discussion on *lettres de cachet* has enlightening potential. Such exoteric letters or orders of arbitrary imprisonment command the concern of all persons sensitive to injustice. But esoteric *lettres de cachet* are equally interesting. Such "letters" or literary works bearing the seal —"cachet" — of occult inspiration — the snake in a circle — have power to release mankind from material and mental tyranny. Their ultimate function is to destroy the Bastilles in which suffering bodies and spirits of

*Ch. XIX.

415

the Judaeo-Christian world are deprived, poisoned, and crushed. Hercules is naturally well equipped to derive full benefit from such "letters" and to make their benefit available to others. His intuitive ability to "read" esoteric texts is not limited to Shakespeare, Rabelais, or the New Testament. The meager fund of reading of the hero is enriched in the course of imprisonment. The scope of his "explorations" broadens accordingly. The guidance and the culture of Gordon are added to the spiritual insight of the primitive. Under such conditions the study of "sealed letters" can only produce spectacular results. Mankind enters an era in which the separated twins of intuition and analytical reasoning collaborate harmoniously and creatively. The age of "experimental faith" begins. The "transmutation of the intelligence" is at work.

The research team composed of Hercules and Gordon parallels the corresponding group composed of Candide, Cacambo and Martin. The latter two characters who represent two forms of Doubt in *Candide* have no counterpart in *L'Ingénu*. Doubt is on the decline in the evolutionary setting of "Low Brittany." Such a decrease of skepticism is not all to the good. It is a sign of smug, vacuous euphoria where the majority of men are concerned. But the lessening influence of Doubt is positively meaningful in the case of spiritually alert persons. In spite of occasional failing, Hercules, the Pagan primitive, maintains allegiance to spirituality. Gordon, the embodiment of Western European culture is a religious person as well as a scholar. The divine spark is alive in each allegorical aspect of Man-In-Search-Of-Truth. Such a fact suggests the beginning of an era in which mankind is ready to rediscover the concrete realities of spiritual life.

The symbolism of the dungeon in which learning is acquired implies a parallel between material and mental prisons. Within the general context of the story the latter element of *L'Ingénu* tends to convey a belief shared by occultists. Little progress is expected on the plane of sociopolitical "jails" as long as true Knowledge remains inaccessible to the majority of minds. Voltaire seems to endorse the view that the Secret Doctrine alone contains the key to all world problems.*

The recorded development of the intelligence belongs to the collective evolutionary curve underlying *L'Ingénu*. As was previously noted, the mind was acquired and gradually enriched as man began to "recede from the center of light, acquiring at every new and lower sphere of being . . . a more solid physical form and losing a portion of his divine faculties." The esoteric component of Hercules representing ordinary mankind follows the necessary pattern of general evolution. In-

*The Secret Doctrine, p. 341, Vol. I.

416

nate spirituality decreases as the predominance of the intellect begins to be felt. The evolutionary loss of divine faculties is the esoteric synonym of physical "generation." The esoteric component of Hercules which is a superior being voluntarily reincarnated submits to the same aspect of Universal Law. But he experiences and overcomes the limitations of matter within the brief confines of one earthly life.

Further metaphysical discussions are reported. The following statements are made:

"'We are the machines of Providence.'" Ch. X, p. 280).

"'If I thought something, it would be that we are under the power of the Eternal Being, like the stars and the elements; that it does all within us, that we are small wheels of the immense machine of which it is the soul; that it acts through general laws and not through particular designs; that alone seems to me to be intelligible, all the rest is for me an abyss of darkness.'" (Ch. X, p. 281).

The passage contains a typical Voltairian rejection of the Jehovic God and a profession of faith in an Unknowable Supreme Being designated as the divine "soul" of the Universe. "General laws" are opposed to personal designs such as might be formed by the biblical "Vice-God." While the First Cause "does all within" Man, the human status of "small" — karmic — "wheel" implies the reality of free will. Belief is expressed in universal harmony. Man is surmised to receive the same influences as "the stars and the elements." The Hermetic axiom "As above, so below" seems to apply to the entire cosmic scheme which may be inferred to consist of "wheels" — planetary chains and cycles — of varying spatial and temporal dimension. The limitations of the unaided intellect are twice suggested. The expression "If I thought something" tends to place the source of enlightened thinking in a subjective realm. Numerous mysteries are hinted to lie beyond the realm of the intellect. The analogies which exist between Man and Cosmos are among them. The general probability of their presence is alone "intelligible." Their dynamic mechanism — Karma is unknowable. An immaterial yet vital connecting thread is virtually presumed to course through all planes of existence from the highest to the lowest. The "unintelligible" thread is likely to be Spirit. In view of its tightly woven esoteric content, the passage can well afford to proclaim ignorance with respect to "all the rest."

Voltairian professions of ignorance should be taken with a grain of salt. But the final sentence of the above quotation reflects a view commonly expressed by esoteric and occult writers. Man must evolve beyond the plane of "this earth" before he can aspire to absolute knowledge of all things. As Voltaire himself pointed out in *Micromégas*, "One never knows the underside of the cards in this world." As was previously noted, Mme Blavatsky makes a similar statement in connection with the Kabalistic tradition:

> "Its adepts are few; but these heirs elect of the sages who first discovered 'the starry truths which shone on the great Shemaïa of the Chaldean lore' have solved the 'absolute' and are now resting from their grand labor. They cannot go beyond that which is given to mortals of this earth to know; and no one, not even these elect can trespass beyond the line drawn by the finger of the Divinity itself." (*Isis Unveiled*, p. 17, Vol. 1).

The ostentatious "ignorance" of Voltaire — the "infidel" — is commented by Mme Blavatsky with every appearance of a knowing smile:

> "Voltaire, the greatest of 'infidels' of the eighteenth century, used to say that if there were no God, people would have to invent one. . . . Voltaire becomes, toward the end of his life, Pythagorical, and concludes by saying: 'I have consumed forty years of my pilgrimage . . . seeking the philosopher's stone called truth. I have consulted all the adepts of antiquity, Epicurus and Augustine, Plato and Malebranche, and I still remain in ignorance. . . . All that I have been able to obtain by comparing and combining the system of Plato, of the tutor of Alexander, Pythagoras, and the Orientals is this: *Chance is a word void of sense*. The world is arranged according to mathematical laws. (*Dictionaire Philosophique*, Art. Philosophie, quoted in *Isis Unveiled*, pp. 268-69, Vol. 1).

The notorious "infidel" suggests the existence of a connection between the mathematical laws which underlie the Universe and their "necessary" Unknowable Principle. Divine Intelligence is manifest in Cosmos. It is inept to explain Divine Intelligence by chance and absurdity. The reasoning of Voltaire amounts to a demonstration of the existence of God.

The Pythagorean concept of the Universe evolving in accordance with mathematical laws is frequently called to attention in the works of Voltaire. The Platonic axiom: "God geometrizes," the awareness of omnipresent proportion stressed in *Micromégas*, and the pre-established harmony dear to Pangloss belong to the same philosophy. The popular tendency to separate terrestrial from divine mathematics does not exist in the Secret Doctrine. Voltaire and his numerous fellow-"smugglers" share the view of "Nature" upheld by the *mathematikoi* and *physikoi* of Antiquity. But the popular separation is a useful means of esoteric concealment.

The veiled identity of Saint Yves is reaffirmed. The young hero frequently speaks of his love:

"He spoke as often of his beloved Saint Yves as he spoke of ethics and metaphysics." (Ch. XIV, p. 295).

The thinly veiled esoteric equation is comparable to a passage of *Candide*. "Nothing exists except virtue and the joy of again seeing Mlle Cunégonde." The tendency of the exoteric reader to view as different things knowledge and ethics is exploited in each case to conceal the identity of allegorical Truth. Saint Yves, love, ethics, and metaphysics constitute One Reality.

The apparent standstill of intellectual and spiritual growth covers actual gains. Retrogressive and progressive forces of evolution are at work. Animal instinct, a sensualized remnant of primitive spirituality, recedes. The elevated aspect of spirit becomes dominant. Hercules soon recognizes that he has changed "from a brute into a man." The cold, analytical element of "reason" decreases. "Reason" expands to embrace intuitive consciousness. The Jansenist is converted to the philosophy of mystical love.

The evolution of the Ingénu is revealed by non-physical yearning for "Saint Yves."

"The more purified his feelings became, the more he loved." (Ch. XIV, p. 295).

The evolution of Gordon could easily be summarized by a few "conflicting" lines of *La Bouteille à la mer*. The limited scope of "exact" science has been transcended. The Jansenist has gained access to the "divine elixir" of spiritualized knowledge.

"Calculs de la science, ô décevantes fables! . . ."

("Reckonings of science, o disappointing (or "deceptive") fables!")

"Quel est cet élixir, Pêcheur, c'est la science,
C'est l'élixir divin que boivent les esprits, —
Trésor de la pensée et de l'expérience; —"

("What is this elixir, Fisherman it is science,
It is the divine elixir drunk by the spirits, —
Treasure of thought and experience: — ")

Gordon combines scholarly and religious "experience" with the "divine elixir" supplied by the Ingénu. The "Barbadoes water" or Spirit shared by the wayfarer with Fifth Race mankind takes effect. The Voltairian aspect of a timeless "Bottle to the Sea" has "reached port." A truly Herculean labor is celebrated with humorous and profound reverence:

419

"Finally, ultimate prodigy, a Huron was converting a Jansenist." (Ch. XIV, p. 295).

The conversion of a Christian by a *Huron* personifying Karma amounts to re-discovery of the cyclic scheme of the Universe. The salvation wrought by Promethean Hercules points to re-discovery of Pagan knowledge by modern Fifth Race mankind. The era of Prometheus Unbound begins. The true meaning of the word "conversion" is the essence of the episode. Voltaire seems to anticipate the definition given by Saint Exupéry: "To convert is always to release."*

The age of the Ingénu suggests chronological precision of prophetic nature. "Suffering Mankind" — Prometheus Hercules — is 22 years old at the time of his baptism. The significant number 220 seems to be called to esoteric attention. The trial of "Micromégas" which lasted 220 years may be over. The same "trial" may coincide with an important "turn of the wheel" in the history of Western mankind.

The event may be connected with the name of the Jansenist. *Gordon* may have been calculated to suggest a doctrinal "Gordian knot" which can only be removed by heroic measures. The "excellent sword of knowledge" may be involved in the task.

The Ingénu becomes an "Instructor of Mankind" comparable — if not identical — to "Zadig." Mythological Hercules represents on a certain plane "the magnetic light which, when having made its way through the 'opened eye of heaven,' enters into the regions of our planet and thus becomes the Creator." The demigod is also connected with the Avataras of Saviors and with the spiritual effort of Man Redeemed by the Higher Self:

> "In ancient symbolism it was always the SUN (though the Spiritual, not the visible, Sun was meant), that was supposed to send forth the chief Saviors and Avatars. Hence the connecting link between the Buddhas, the Avatars, and so many other incarnations of the highest SEVEN. The closer the approach to one's *Prototype*, 'in Heaven,' the better for the mortal whose personality was chosen, by his own *personal* deity (the seventh principle), as its terrestrial abode. For, with every effort of will toward purification and unity with that 'Self-god,' one of the lower rays breaks and the spiritual entity of man is drawn higher and ever higher to the ray that supersedes the first, until, from ray to ray, the inner man is drawn into the one and highest beam of the Parent-Sun." (*The Secret Doctrine*, pp. 638-39, Vol. I).

Hercules is a Savior in disguise, a "fisher" or a "creator" of men.

Flight to Arras, Ch. XXVII.
**Isis Unveiled*, p. 131, Vol. 1.

His voyage from "another world" into "the regions of our planet" is intended to help Man rise closer to his "prototype in Heaven." One being descends that others may rise. True light is transmitted to mankind at the price of a sojourn in darkness. The sacrifice of voluntary reincarnation is "measured" in the following passage. But it is not measurable in ordinary human terms:

> "'Qu'il est dur,' disait-il, 'de ne commencer à connaître le Ciel que lorsqu'on me ravit le droit de le contempler! Jupiter et Saturne roulent dans ces espaces immenses; des millions de soleils éclairent des milliards de mondes; et, dans le coin de la terre où je suis jeté, il se trouve des êtres qui me privent moi être voyant et pensant, de tous ces mondes où ma vue pourrait atteindre et de celui où Dieu m'a fait naître! La lumière faite pour tout l'univers est perdue pour moi.'" (Ch. XI, p. 286).

> (" 'How hard it is,' he said, 'to barely begin to know Heaven when I am robbed of the right to behold it! Jupiter and Saturn roll in immense spaces; millions of suns light billions of worlds; and, in the corner of earth where I am cast, there are creatures who deprive me, a seeing and sentient being, of all those worlds where my vision could reach and of that in which God caused me to be born! The light which is made for the entire universe is lost to me.'")

The complaint of the exoteric prisoner is clear. The lament of the voluntary exile from heavenly regions is also perceptible. The first sentence invites speculation. Hercules seems to recognize that he has taken for granted the sight of starry skies until he was imprisoned, a common enough attitude for an average person. The same sentence may convey the idea of having been in "Heaven" — known Nirvâna — for a brief period of time prior to arrival on earth. The expressions: "I am robbed of the right to behold it" — Heaven — and "there are creatures who deprive me — of all those worlds" seem incompatible with the meaning of voluntary reincarnations. But the *right* to remain in celestial spheres is opposed by the very selflessness which brought release from the chain of rebirth. The indefinite pronoun "on" — a favorite tool of French esoteric writers* — may therefore be read as "I." The creatures who deprive the young man of heavenly bliss are suffering men whose anguish cannot be ignored. The sensitivity of the hero to human misery is the cause of exile. The Nirvanic quality of the previous condition is also suggested by two words. The verb "ravir" which means "to rob" also means "to give bliss." The verb "contempler" — to "behold" — also means "to practice spiritual contemplation." The total formula of bliss-

---

*A la Recherche du temps perdu, p. 792, Vol. III.

ful contemplation is the exact equivalent of "blissful omniscience," an expression which defines Nirvânâ. The concept of Aristotlean *"privation"* is the frequent companion of Maya in occult and esoteric writings. It is suggested by the expression: "deprive me". Such a deprivation is clearly consistent with the loss of cosmic vision lamented by Hercules. The "forced" removal of the hero from the homeland where God "caused him to be born" brings to mind voluntary removal from the spiritual Alpha and Omega of the Great Circle of Necessity. "Force," "will," and spirit are synonymous on the plane of non-contingent existence. Hercules has been impelled to come to earth by his "strength" or spirituality. His symbolic descent will have a parallel in the "fall" of Saint Yves who "will succumb out of virtue" — or "strength" — at a later stage of the story. The cosmic vision claimed by Hercules also suggests voluntary reincarnation. It is doubtful that the ordinary human eye — or a powerful telescope — can reveal the "millions of suns" or the "billions of worlds" now lost to his sight. The "inaccessible light" made for "the entire universe" is also meaningful. Voltaire seem to have deliberately avoided the light shining for *all men*. The vision claimed by the hero is the privilege of perfection.

The component part of Hercules which is "suffering mankind" may be compared to the blind man of occult philosophy for whom the visible world "exists in its privation, and is a reality for the spiritual senses."* The cosmic vision of Humanity survives in dimly remembered, latent state.

Zadig and the Ingénu retain universal insight in the midst of terrestrial blindness. The durable quality of their vision reflects in part their status of Savior. No such asset is granted to Man in Search of Truth within the setting of *Candide*. "Westphalia" corresponds to an all-time low in spiritual and cosmic awareness. No Savior other than the Higher Self can be awaited during such a phase of human evolution. Cosmic blindness is inevitable when the cyclic scheme of the Universe is obscured and when allegorical Truth is "enslaved." No passage is devoted to contemplation of the stars — in privation or otherwise — within the dismal environment of *Candide*. The rebirth of cosmic awareness which takes place in *L'Ingénu* marks a significant "turn of the wheel" of evolution. Humanity senses — in privation — the importance of its place in the universal scheme of existence. Positive cosmic consciousness is bound to follow. Mankind ceases to journey through the stars unseeing — as if the galaxies were, in the words of Céline, "raindrops in May."

Isis Unveiled, p. 157, Vol. 2.

The Hu*ron* represents a major "turn of the wheel." He is part of a cosmic impulse initiating and sustaining the course of cyclic evolution. He is a Savior who restores a legacy of cosmic knowledge to "suffering mankind." He is part of "suffering mankind" itself gradually unveiling the mystery of its own existence and the meaning of its own destiny.

The "turn of the wheel" is a standard element of esoteric literature. It is used in *L'Homme aux quarante écus* to celebrate the approaching spiritual rebirth of Fifth Race men of good will. It is used by Vigny in *Stello* to illustrate the mysterious work of Karma during the French Revolution. It is prominent in *Paris* — a poem and city in which the joint presence of a Furnace and Wheel — Christian Hell and Karma — is expected to produce an intellectual and spiritual apocalypse. It is present — on several planes of meaning — in *La Maison du berger*. It makes frequent appearances in the poetry of Shelley. It is featured in La *Bête Humaine*. It may be found in the Proustian *Recherche* beyond the priceless veil of the "tortillard d'intérêt local." ("rickety winding little train")

It may be noted briefly that the Proustian "tortillard" is used by "Marcel," his "love," "Saint Loup," and a mysterious Russian great lady who may be Mme Blavatsky in disguise. The small train — or portion of a cycle — brings together literary figures representing a span of several centuries. The "tortillard" serves the same function as does the convergence of Time and Space which underlies *L'Ingénu*. The same extra-temporal projection is represented in *Zadig* by the restitution of "borrowed silver" and by the miraculous catch of the fisherman. It is dramatized in *Candide* by the discovery of the Septenary Self and by the resurrection of the Primitive Wisdom-Religion allegorized as Pangloss. It is a refracted aggregate of symbols in *L'Ingénu*. The sharing of "spirits," the gift of magic, the product of a timeless hunt are fused into a crucial transmission of light.

"Such is he course of Nature under the sway of KARMIC LAW: of the ever present and the ever-becoming Nature. For, in the words of a Sage, known only to a few Occultists: — 'THE PRESENT IS THE CHILD OF THE PAST: THE FUTURE, THE BEGOTTEN OF THE PRESENT. AND YET! O PRESENT MOMENT! KNOWEST THOU NOT THAT THOU HAST NO PARENT, NOR CANST THOU HAVE A CHILD; THAT THOU ART EVER BEGETTING BUT THYSELF? BEFORE THOU HAST EVEN BEGUN TO SAY 'I AM THE PROGENY OF THE DEPARTED MOMENT, THE CHILD OF THE PAST,' THOU HAST BECOME THAT PAST ITSELF. BEFORE THOU UTTEREST THE LAST SYLLABLE, BEHOLD! THOU ART NO MORE THE PRESENT BUT VERILY THAT FUTURE. THUS, ARE THE PAST, THE PRESENT, AND THE FUTURE,

THE EVER-LIVING TRINITY IN ONE — THE MAHAMAYA OF
THE ABSOLUTE IS." (*The Secret Doctrine*, p. 446, Vol. II).

"What is, of all things in the world, the longest and the shortest, the
quickest and the slowest, the most divisible and the most far-reaching,
the most neglected and the most regretted, without which nothing can
materialize, which devours all that is small and vivifies all that is great?"
(*Zadig, Les Enigmes*).

The evolutionary waning of "what is small" and the parallel growth
of "what is great" is the Ariadne's thread of the Voltairian trilogy represented by *Zadig, Candide,* and *L'Ingénu*. It is within the modern
setting of the story of Prometheus-Hercules that "suffering mankind"
rediscovers true greatness.

The turning point is stressed by the active role of Saint Yves. Astarté
and Cunégonde are found by their respective lovers joyfully but passively. Saint Yves comes to the rescue of her devotee. Mankind is released from its prison of darkness by the intervention of Truth. The
heroine pays the supreme price to liberate her allegorical worshipper.
Prostitution and death *is* the price.

The ultimate expression of Love, the Great Sacrifice of voluntary
reincarnation, is personified by the young hero. Love is the universal,
allmighthy force which brings together the messenger from outer spheres,
the kindly Kerkabons, and the selfless Jansenist. The divine gift is received by all persons prepared to receive it. Several curves of evolution meet at one tangential point where Love and Knowledge are fused.
Within the wide, slow curve of Fifth Race progress, there flashes — with
meteoric speed — the elliptical arc of Herculean descent. Contact is followed by a collective surge toward superior knowledge or spirituality.

Prostitution is incarnation or a measure of spiritual death. The
passionate sacrifice of Saint Yves suggests the voluntary reincarnation
of a great spiritual leader of mankind. As was previously noted, Mme
Blavatsky wrote that her generation lived on the eve of a general spiritual rebirth. Vigny similarly announced the advent of a new era
heralded by a divine messenger — "quelque forme animée" — "some
animated form"—, a messenger who was to lead the "human family to
its end"* or destiny. Shelley also seems to foretell the coming of a
crucial figure at the end of *Prometheus Unbound*. The question of a
possible historical identity of Saint Yves will be examined in a subsequent chapter.

Similar concerns with the progress and "end" of the human family

---

*Paris.

prompt Hercules to write observations on ancient history. The essay is based on presumed analogies between nations and individuals:

> "I imagine that the nations were like me for a long time, that they acquired learning only at a very late stage, that for centuries they were preoccupied only with the present moment which was flowing by, very little with the past, and never with the future." (Ch. XI, p. 284).

The text begins with the vague outline of an ego-centric theory of evolution. The proverbial candor of "children" and primitives colors the hypothesis: "I imagine that the nations were like me for a long time." But the puerility of Hercules is only apparent. The young man seems to subscribe to the Hermetic axiom: "As above, so below." It is speculated that nations are ruled by the same Universal Law which rules individuals. Such a belief is stated in the Secret Doctrine:

> "— no nation or nations, can escape their Karmic fate any more than units and individuals do." (*The Secret Doctrine*, p. 675, Vol. I).

The esoteric meaning of the word "nation" is that of a Root Race* Such a significance is consistent with the probable etymology of Hercules — *cula*, race — which has already been noted. It is also compatible with the Sun-related cosmogenetic aspect of the mythological demi-god.

The first sentence is an equation in which the concealed identity of the hero is the unknown. Nations are surmised to have evolved in the same manner as the young man. Who or what is the young man? The equivalence of Hercules and evolving — or "suffering" — mankind may easily be inferred.

The exoteric comparison between age-old nations and an ephemereal mortal contains a flaw of either form or substance. Exoteric Hercules cannot claim to have developed over a period of "centuries." But the evolutionary personification of Man and the reincarnating spirit of the individual are entitled to the claim. The calculated gaucherie of expression tends to suggest the veiled identity of the "Huron."

The esoteric concept of "nations" or "races" is relevant to *L'Ingénu* on a specific plane of occult history. The war between descendents of the Atlanteans and the Aryan races is designated in *Critias* as the "war of the nations."

> "'First of all,' we read in 'Critias' that 'one must remember that 9,000 years have elapsed *since war of the nations,* which lived above and outside the Pillars of Hercules, and those which peopled the lands on this side.' — They of Plato's day, the initiated writers, at any rate,

---

The Secret Doctrine, pp. 394-95, Vol. II.

meant by a millennium, not a thousand but 100,000 years — Thus, when saying 9,000 years, the Initiates will read 900,000 years, during which space of time — i.e., from the first appearance of the Aryan race, when the Pliocene portions of the once great Atlantis began gradually sinking and other continents to appear on the surface, down to the final disappearance of Plato's small island of Atlantis, the Aryan races had never ceased to fight with the descendants of the first giant races. This war lasted until nearly the close of the age which preceded the Kali Yug, and was the Mahabhâratean war so famous in Indian History." (*The Secret Doctrine*, pp. 394-95, Vol. II).

The war recorded by Plato has a non-violent counterpart in the confrontation of Hercules with the Kerkabons. The "big boy" is the heir apparent of Atlantean giants. His European connections also have Atlantean origins. The relatives of the hero are of Aryan, Celtic lineage which is itself of Atlantean ancestry. But they are unaware of the pre-historical aspect of their own background prior to the arrival of the Ingénu. The symbolic reunion of ethnic groups and familial bonds which takes place in Chapter II is an esoteric re-discovery of Atlantean ties by modern Firth Race mankind. Voltaire seems to predict a development which is anticipated in the Secret Doctrine:

> "We are but beginning to understand the past; one hundred years ago the world knew nothing of Pompeii or Herculanum; nothing of the lingual tie that binds together the Indo-European nations; nothing of the significance of the vast volume of inscriptions upon the tombs and temples of Egypt; nothing of the meaning of the arrow-headed inscription of Babylon; nothing of the marvelous civilizations revealed in the remains of Yucatan Mexico, and Peru. We are on the threshold. Scientific investigation is advancing with giant strides. Who shall say that one hundred years from now, the great museums of the world may not be adorned with gems, statues, arms, and implements from Atlantis, while the libraries of the world shall contain translations of its inscriptions, throwing new light upon all the past history of the human race, and all the great problems which now perplex the thinkers of to-day." (*The Secret Doctrine*, p. 793, Vol. II).

The theme of an exoteric "war of the nations" is often used to convey the esoteric view of a future apocalypse. The novel of Saint Exupéry, *Flight to Arras*, is a case in point. Marcel Proust seems to have utilized World War I to project his own expectation of an imminent "turn of the wheel." The atmosphere of Paris in wartime — a cosmopolitan Babylon delightful to "eclectic" "inverts" — is that of an impending upheaval. The situation is dominated by "aviators" — winged men or spiritual beings of the future. The feverish capital is compared to Pompei and Herculaneum. Numerous details point to an esoteric tribute to the *Paris* of Vigny, a poem in which a "volcano caused its mountain to

426

explode." A tribute to a second Sage seems to be veiled by the following allusion to "Hercules:"

> "As for Paris, it was not founded by Hercules as was Herculanum. But how many similarities impress themselves upon us! And that insight which is given us is not of our era, all eras have possessed it." (*A la Recherche due temps perdu,* pp. 805-06, Vol. III).

Proust seems to conceal in his description of Paris "at war" a dual allusion to Vigny, Voltaire, and to an ancient form of Wisdom transmitted through the ages. The suggested parallel is comparable to a joint reference to a "necklace" and "trial" which is made in another part of the *Recherche.* Voltaire, Proust — and many others — seem to connect an approaching "apocalypse" with a sudden explosion of esoteric literature.

> "Pour jeter en éclats la magique fournaise,
> Il suffira toujours du caillou d'un enfant."
> (Alfred de Vigny, *La Maison du berger*).

> "To blow into fragments the magical furnace,
> The small rock of a child will ever suffice."

Comparative thoughts are induced by the travels of L'Ingénu. Canada lacks monuments which are found in abundance in other parts of the world. Could such a lack of vestiges of the past suggest an immaterial origin of Man?

> " 'I have travelled over five or six hundred leagues of Canada, I did not find one single monument there; no one in that country knows anything of what his great-grandfather did. Would that not be the natural state of man?" (Ch. XI, p. 284).

The five or six hundred "leagues" covered by the young man represent the enormous time span leading back to human origin — "*five or six Races.* The absence of monuments and the seeming absence of flesh-and-blood relatives are noted. The findings of Hercules reflect basic tenets of the Secret Doctrine:

> "— the first two races of men were too ethereal and phantom-like in their constitution, organism, and *shape,* even to be called physical men — this is one of the reasons why their relics can never be expected to be exhumed among other fossils." (*The Secret Doctrine,* p. 289, Vol. II).

As was previously noted, "the Secret Doctrine claims for man —

427

a variety of modes of procreation before humanity fell into the ordinary method of generation." The mystery of primeval human ancestry cannot be solved with the aid of modern genealogy or anthropology.

An immaterial mode of life is suggested to have once prevailed in "Canada." The "natural — native or original — "state" of Man cannot be studied — or conceived — in terms of fossils, monuments, or family trees. The speculation of Hercules is compatible with the occult view that America, not Europe, is the authentic Old World. It is also consistent with the tradition of the Hyperborean Continent, a land mass believed to have been inhabited by a race of astral or ethereal constitution.

Hercules compares various civilizations. European countries seem to be more advanced than the native land of the essayist. But the same countries are filled with "refined rogues." Puzzlement follows. Uncivilized Indians are noted to have no beards. The hero wonders whether the bearded —or beardless — state may be connected with various stages of human progress. The writer is more confused than ever. The ancient and brilliant civilization of China was produced by beardless men. The theory seems untenable.

A false assumption is to blame for the perplexity of the young man. Europeans are not necessarily more civilized than unsophisticated Indians or sophisticated Chinese. The quality of civilization may not be measurable on the sole basis of material achievement. The matter of ethical orientation may be chief criterion of genuine superiority.

The concealed Sage within Hercules invites alert readers to check their premises. The myth of "the finest castle in the world" is offered to critical study.

The amusing considerations of the hero have serious evolutionary implications. The appearance of beards — more generally hair — corresponds to a specific stage of the materialization of Man. The growth of hair is believed to have followed the atrophy of the Third Eye and the resulting loss of spiritual insight.

> " ' — *When the Fourth* (Race) *arrived at its middle age, the inner vision had to be awakened, and acquired by artificial stimuli, the process of which was known to the old sages. . . . The third eye, likewise, getting gradually* PETRIFIED, *soon disappeared. The double-faced became the one-faced, and the eye was drawn deep into the head and is now buried under the hair."* The third eye is dead and acts no longer; but it has left behind a witness to its existence. This witness is now the PINEAL GLAND." (*The Secret Doctrine*, pp. 294-95, Vol. II).

The occult tenet enunciated above may account for an interesting aspect of the philosophy of Descartes. As was previously noted, the Cartesian theory of the soul is presented in *Micromégas* in deceptively humorous fashion.

> "It is well known, (and also regarded as a fiction now, by those who have ceased to believe in the existence of an immortal principle in man), that Descartes saw in the pineal gland the *Seat of the Soul.* Although it is joined to every part of the body, he said, there is one special portion of it in which the Soul exercises its functions more specially than in any other. And, as neither the heart, nor yet the brain could be that 'special' locality, he concluded that it was that little gland tied to the brain, yet having an action independent of it, as it could easily be put into a kind of swinging motion 'by the animal Spirits' which cross the cavities of the skull in every sense.'
> Unscientific as this may appear in our day of exact learning, Descartes was yet far nearer the occult truth than is any Haeckel. For the pineal gland, as shown, is far more connected with Soul and Spirit than with the physiological senses of man. If the old 'eye' of man is now atrophied, it is a proof that, as in the lower animal, it has once been active; for nature never creates the smallest, the most insignificant form without some definite purpose and use. It was an *active* organ, we say, at that stage of evolution when the spiritual element in man reigned supreme over the hardly nascent intellectual and psychic elements." (*The Secret Doctrine,* p. 298, Vol. II).

The spiritual function of the pineal gland is humorously hinted by a physician-writer: Céline. Skillful use of the word *Epiphany,* which means to *shine upon,* connects the small gland with a realm of non-physical radiance — "Thou hast poured by radiance over me!"

> " 'Put your wretched thoughts in order, Ferdinand! That's where to begin. Not with grotesque, material, negative, obscene substitutions, but with the essential, that's what I'm getting at. Are you going to assault the brain, correct it, scrape it, mutilate it, force it to comply with an assortment of stupid rules? carve it up geometrically? recompose it according to the rules of your excruciating idiocy? . . . Arrange it in slices? like an Epiphany cake? . . . with a prize in the middle." (*Death on the Installment Plan,* R. Manheim Tr. p. 339).

The passionate outpouring of Courtial des Péreires is identical in substance to a major article of faith of occultists and esoteric writers. The mystery of the human mind does not yield to material or intellectual scalpels. The specialist in brain research must "use other eyes than those of his body."

The beard theory of the Ingénu has a bearing on the hero himself. The young man has "a small amount of beard." The fact is duly noted by the Kerkabons at an early stage of the story. The small growth of beard of the presumed "Indian" is eventually regarded as proof of European ancestry. It is also the esoteric symbol of a transitional state between the ethereal condition of original mankind and the physical condition of modern Western Man. The absence of beard which is a common trait of Indians and Chinese may symbolize a remnant of spirituality lost to Europeans.

The occult concept of "hair" is also connected with the mythological rendition of anthropogenesis. The hair of Brahma parts symbolically to divide mankind into Races:

> " 'Thirteen curls of hair exist on the one side and on the other of the skull' — *i.e.,* six on one and six on the other, the thirteenth being also the fourteenth, as it is male-female, 'and through them commenceth the division of the hair' (the division of things, Mankind, and Races)." (*The Secret Doctrine,* p. 625, Vol. II).

The genesis or "division" or "things, Mankind, and Races" belongs to the essence of *L'Ingénu.*

The tradition of ancient China is admired by the young writer. It is unmarred by the presence of supernatural events or characters. Such a simplicity contrasts with the fabulous mythological heritage claimed by Western nations.

> " 'The ancient chroniclers of French History, who are not very ancient, trace the origin of the French to a Francus, son of Hector. The Romans claim to be descendents of a Phrygian although there is not in their language a single word having the least connection with the Phrygian language." (Ch. XI, p. 284).

Such legends do deserve careful examination. The fantastic genealogy claimed by Frenchmen and Romans points to the Illiad and, beyond Greece, to Oriental tradition. A great deal might be learned from a return to the latter source.

> "Is it not barely possible that even the *Ramayana* itself, the famous epic poem, is but the original of Homer's *Iliad,* as it was suggested some years ago? The beautiful Paris, carrying off Helen, looks very much like Ravana, king of the giants, eloping with Sita, Rama's wife? The Trojan war is a counterpart of the *Ramayana* war, moreover, Heredotus assures us that the Trojan heroes and gods date in Greece only from the days of the Iliad." (*Isis Unveiled,* p. 566, Vol. 1).

Hercules notes — with some skepticism — that gods are said to have inhabited various portions of Earth at various times. Such reports may easily be explained by the esoteric concept of *Gods:*

"Eminent men were called gods by the ancients. The deification of moral men and suppositious gods is no more a proof against their monotheism than the monument-building of modern Christians who erect statues to their heroes, is proof of their polytheism." (*Isis Unveiled*, p. 24, Vol. 1).

Mythological devils are said to have inhabited Scythian regions in the distant past. Such stories have their explanation also. The Arctic regions were once regarded as the site of Hell:

"The secret books inform us that the climate has changed in those regions more than once since the first men inhabited those now almost inaccessible latitudes. They were a paradise before they became hell; the dark Hades of the Greeks and the cold realm of Shades where the Scandinavian Hel, the goddess Queen of the country of the dead, 'holds sway deep down in Helheim and Niflheim.'" (*The Secret Doctrine*, pp. 773-74, Vol. II).

History appeals to the young man. No other area of human knowledge seems more likely to satisfy his curiosity which is especially keen in the realm of human progress. The conscientious documentation of Thucydides is compared to the legendary reporting of previous chroniclers. The young writer seems to take a dim view of mythical, supernatural "events."

"I see before Thucydides, only novels similar to those such as *Amadis,* and far less amusing. There are everywhere apparitions, oracles, prodigies, magic spells, metamorphoses, interpreted dreams, and which build the destinies of the greatest empires and of the smallest States; here beasts which speak, there beasts which are worshipped, gods transformed into men and men transformed into gods. Ah! if we must have fables, let those fables at least be the expression of truth! I like the fables of philosophers, I laugh at those of children, and I hate those of impostors." (Ch. XI, p. 285).

The admirer of Rabelais is naturally attracted by the fables of "philosophers" or "children." The "necessity" of "fables" is virtually defined as an esoteric function. Fables must be vehicles of Truth. Truth cannot be transmitted without veils.

The frequent equivalence of "myth," "fable," and Truth is stated and commented as follows in the Secret Doctrine:

"It has been often remarked by observant writers, that the 'origin of nearly every popular myth and legend could be traced invariably to a fact in Nature.'

In these fantastic creations of an exuberant subjectivism, there is always an element of the objective and real. The imagination of the

431

masses, disorderly and ill-regulated as it may be, could never have conceived and fabricated *ex nihilo* so many monstrous figures, such a wealth of extraordinary tales, had it not had, to serve it as a central nucleus, those floating reminiscences, obscure and vague, which unite the broken links of the chain of time to form with them the mysterious, dream foundation of our collective consciousness.

The evidence for the Cyclopes — a race of giants — will be pointed out in forthcoming Sections, in the Cyclopean remnants, so called to this day. An indication that, during its evolution and before the final adjustment of the human organism — which became perfect and symmetrical only in the Fifth Race — the early Fourth Race may have been three-eyed, without having necessarily a third eye in the middle of the brow, like the legendary Cyclops, is also furnished by Science." (*The Secret Doctrine*, p. 294, Vol. II).

"—, each age had its unbelieving Thomases. Did they ever succeed in checking the progress of truth? No more than the ignorant bigots who sat in judgment over Galileo checked the progress of the earth's rotation. No exposures whatever are able to vitally affect the stability or instability of a belief which humanity inherited from the first races of men, those, who — if we can believe in the evolution of spiritual man as in that of the physical one — had the great truth from the lips of their ancestors, the *gods of their fathers,*' that were on the other side of the flood.' The identity of the Bible with the legends of the Hindu sacred books and the cosmogonies of other nations, must be demonstrated at some future day. *The fables of the mythopoeic ages will be found to have but allegorized the greatest truths of geology and anthropology.* It is in these ridiculously expressed fables that science will have to look for her 'missing links.' " (*Isis Unveiled*, pp. 121-22, Vol. 1).

The essay of Hercules invites certain parallels between Indian and Far Eastern races. The absence or near-absence of beard which is a common trait of Indians and Chinese suggests the possibility of an ethnic tie between both races. The powerful attraction exerted by the Chinese culture on the Huron may constitute another hint of common racial background. The existence of such a connection is substantiated in the Secret Doctrine. The "red Indians and the Mongolians" are regarded as descendants of the same original stock.

"Esotericism now classes these seven variations, with their four great divisions, into only *three* distinct primeval races — as it does not take into consideration the First Race, which had neither type nor colour, and hardly an objective, though colossal form. The evolution of these races, their formation and development, went *pari passu* and on parallel lines with the evolution, formation, and development of three geological strata, from which the human complexion was as much derived as it was determined by the climates of those zones. It names three great divisions, namely, the RED-YELLOW, the BLACK, and the BROWN-WHITE. The Aryan races, for instance, now varying from dark brown, almost black, red-brown-yellow, down to the whitest creamy colour, are yet all of one and the same stock — the Fifth Root-Race — and

432

spring from one single progenitor, called in Hindu *exotericism* by the generic name of Vaivasvata Manu; the latter, remember, being that generic personage, the Sage, who is said to have lived over 18,000,000 years ago, and also 850,000 years ago — at the time of the sinking of the last remnants of the great continent of Atlantis, and who is said to live even *now* in his mankind. The light yellow is the colour of the first SOLID human race, which appeared after the middle of the Third Root Race (*after its fall* into generation — as just explained), bringing on the final changes. For, it is only at that period that the last transformation took place, which brought forth man as he is now, 'Siva' gradually transforming that portion of Humanity which became 'black with sin' into *red-yellow* (the red Indians and the Mongolians being the descendants of these) and finally into brown-white races — which now, together with the yellow races, form the great bulk of Humanity. The allegory in *Linga Purâna* is curious, as showing the great ethnological knowledge of the ancients." (*The Secret Doctrine,* pp. 249-50, Vol. II).

The essay of Hercules serves several esoteric functions. The rejection of the supernatural is an effective "blind" placed in the path of the casual researcher. The popular mind equates the occult and the supernatural. The reader must know that "there are no miracles"; he must have "a small fund of philosophy" in order to perceive the concealed substance of the text.

The essay tends to stimulate critical thoughts on mythological and fabulous traditions. How and why can such bizarre tales circulate in every part of the world? How does one explain their basic identity of themes? A provocative effort is made to suggest the existence of an important connection between "myths," "fables," and Universal Truth.

The essay contains in hypothetical, compact form basic tenets of occult philosophy. The theme of evolution is exoterically apparent. The existence of anthropological knowledge reaching beyond the Aryan "side of the flood" is suggested. The esoteric outline of the human pilgrimage through "fall" and re-ascent is traced in a few words: "gods transformed into men and men transformed into gods." The occult teaching relative to the Oneness of Time dominates the beginning of the text. It is applicable to the trilogy written by a certain Sage, a sequence which has a triumphant culmination in *L'Ingénu*.

The essay lays the groundwork for a deceptively negative profession of faith concealed in a dialogue between Hercules and Gordon:

"'Any sect seems to be the rallying point of error. Tell me if there are sects in geometry.' —'No, my dear child,' said the good Gordon to him with a sigh; 'all men agree on truth when it is demonstrated, but they are too divided on obscure verities.' — 'Call them obscure falsehoods. If there had been a single truth concealed in your accumulated arguments which have been repeated again and again for so many centuries, it would have been discovered no doubt; and the universe would have agreed at least on that one point. If that truth were necessary as the sun is necessary to earth, it would be shining forth like the sun. It is an absurdity, it is an outrage against mankind, it is a crime against the infinite and Supreme Being to say: 'There is one truth essential to man and God has concealed it!' " (Ch. XIV, pp. 293-94).

Sectarianism — the dismemberment of Truth — is recognized as the source of all error and ignorance. It is a "necessary" or inevitable manifestation of Maya — divisiveness — which prevails when spirituality is at an all-time low. The natural process of fragmentation of Truth has been carried to unnatural extremes by some human beings. If "the one truth essential to man" must remain "concealed," the blame must lie to a certain extent with ignorant and criminal minds. Such minds are themselves "necessary" products of evolutionary conditions specific to a dark age. "Obscure" or esoteric verities must remain underground until the repercussion of a certain "turn of the wheel" is felt. They must maintain the appearance of "obscure falsehoods" while the "obscure falsehoods" of superstition eclipse them in the popular mind.

The existence of a Deity is proclaimed. The "infinite Being" is no anthropomorphic tormentor of men. The consistency of geometry is noted. The divine network connecting its Source and its manifest extensions may be inferred to lie in the realm of "obscure" or hidden verities. "Suffering mankind" senses the existence of an "essential truth" in privation. "Suffering mankind" senses that "God geometrizes." There exists a "single truth hidden in the accumulated arguments which have been repeated again and again" for many centuries. It *has* been "discovered" but remains inaccessible to all but a few men. It *is* "as necessary as the Sun is to the Earth." The "necessary" connection between Sun and Earth — "Hercules-Spirit" and the manifest Universe — is the raison d'être and the evolutionary harvest of *L'Ingénu*. Truth is therefore as brilliant as the Sun. In the words of her immortal Lover, "It is impossible not to surrender to that truth when one perceives it."

The crucial "when" is approaching for a sizable portion of mankind. The exposure of fraudulent scriptures will take place in a final chapter of the story. The unveiling of other "scriptures" or "letters" patiently transmitted through the ages will occur. A conspiracy of falsehood will be defeated by a conspiracy of Truth.

In the meantime the terrestrial brilliance of the Primitive Wisdom-Religion remains clouded and contingent on a trinity of minds. The elements of the collective trinity are listed in the essay of Hercules. "Philosophers" constitute a tiny minority capable of discerning — and transmitting — "the one truth essential to man" under a veil of symbols and allegories. The majority of the human family is composed of "slow risers" or exoteric "children." Such "children" carry the seeds of the esoteric "children" of the future. A broad spectrum of development is represented by this group. Many of its members stagnate intellectually and spiritually. Others are active confederates of the cardinal sinners of the third group: the "impostors."

The impostors are dedicated to the suppression of Truth. The joint efforts of gullible exoteric "children" and conscious impostors produce toxic dogma and bloody practice:

> "'Minds can only be enlightened by the flames of the stake, and truth could not possibly shine forth through its own light.'" (Ch. XI, p. 285).

The flames of the stake do have an enlightening aspect. Litlle insight is needed to perceive their meaning. Any spiritual structure which must resort to them is weak and desperate. Truth "does shine forth through its own light" as long as there are human beings who defy the faggot for her sake. Truth does require mystical "flames" to survive in the midst of oppressed mankind. The exponents of ruthless orthodoxy are unwitting spokesmen of profound verities, a fact which explains the presence of authenticating italics.

The Kerkabon family belongs to the category of exoteric "children." Fifth Race mankind is "necessarily" deprived of spiritual light within the time and space setting of "Low Brittany." Contact with the Primitive Wisdom-Religion personified by Hercules opens an inspiring phase of their pilgrimage through life.

Hercules partakes of the spiritually amphibious nature of the Savior — Oannes-Vishnu, the "Fish-Man". He is a "philosopher" or an esoteric "child" who shares the incarnate condition of "suffering mankind." His Promethean gift of "divine fire" tends to establish contact between two planes of existence. The transmission of Herculean "magic" has power to transfigure the lives of many men. Hercules is a mystical matchmaker between the ordinary person and the Higher Self. The severance of Chrestos — or Christ — from the human tabernacle is a major falsification wrought by Christian dogma which has brought abject hopelessness to mankind. The separation of Man from his divine essence may explain the following observation made by Vigny in his *Diary* of 1834: "The religion of Christ is a religion of despair —." The same forced removal of "Jesus-Christ" from the human "brow" and from the human "heart" is denounced in *Paris*. Alienation from the Self is also noted by Voltaire in the *Poem on the Disaster of Lisbon*: "Man, estranged from the Self, is unknown to Man." The gift of Prometheus-Hercules to Fifth Race mankind restores the true potency of Christ to its rightful place: the inmost dwelling in every "soul-endowed man."

Mythological Hercules is Logos. His spiritual function is differentiated on two planes of existence:

> " 'The Logos is passive Wisdom in Heaven and conscious, Self-Active Wisdom on Hearth,' we are taught." (*The Secret Doctrine*, p. 231, Vol. II).

The incarnate component of the Voltairian Logos is clearly conscious and "Self-Active" as it strives to give the "divine fire" to mankind. The feminine component of Hercules — Saint Yes — proves equally "conscious" and "Self-Active" under the influence of her celestial counterpart.

The sensuous, culturally shallow young person of the beginning of the story responds to Divine Love. Wishing to find and to liberate her devotee, the allegory of Truth plans and completes a hazardous journey to Versailles. The fact and manner of her departure from Low Brittany give proof of insight, self-knowledge, and determination. The powerful obstacles of culture, temperament, and training which tend to oppose her act are overcome by devotion. The Pagan influence of Hercules has destroyed spiritual inhibition. It has also destroyed the illusion of sectarian barriers:

> "She was no longer the simple girl whose provincial training had narrowed the thinking." (Ch. XVIII, p. 303).

The expanding horizons of modern Western mankind reflect the Promethean influence of Paganism — the "Huron." Residents of "the finest castle in the world" become aware of its limitations. Gordon, the spiritually inclined scholar, has made the rewarding transition from "provincial" and gloomy Jansenism to radiant faith. He will be followed by numerous others.

The mode of expression used by Voltaire seems to invite another connection with Pascal, the genial but spiritually deprived author of the "*Provinciales.*" The same expression may bring to mind sectarian religious bodies which have "provincials" in their hierarchies. The Jesuits and the Franciscans have representatives so designated. The broadening outlook of allegorized Truth gradually transcending "provincialism" marks the beginning of collective emancipation from established religion. Generally achieved is a departure from divisiveness or Maya at its worst. The ultra-nationalistic "blinders" or "Westphalians" or "Low Britons" are being slowly discarded.

436

The imprisonment of Hercules is paralleled by the imprisonment of Saint Yves. As was previously noted, the girl is temporarily confined to a convent. The feminine counterpart of "Suffering Mankind" learns a great deal during her forced residence in her own "dungeon." Numerous novels are read *in secret*. The insight derived from books finds "useful" application in the escape of the captive and in her planning of the trip to Versailles. More than a loose connection seems to exist between the literary interests of Saint Yves and her mode of travel. The heroine travels on horseback. Pegasus is involved. The passionate "verse" previously written by the devotee of Truth will "reach" the beloved. Literature plays an important role in the release of "Suffering Mankind."

The importance of "letters" remains crucial after the arrival of the heroine in Versailles. The major mystery to be solved is the sudden disappearance of Hercules. Nothing has been heard of the young man for more than a year. The story of his imprisonment is revealed by a writing person or clerk. The man of "letters" — "plumitif" — deplores the fact that he too is a prisoner of the power structure who cannot "do good" to others. His power is strictly limited to "causing harm sometimes." But his sensitivity to the magical charm of allegorized Truth is an important link in the chain of events leading to the liberation of "Suffering Mankind." The spirited Love of Saint Yves succeeds where less ardent inquiries had failed. The Promethean hero is found. The Savior — and his "divine fire" — are captives in an esoteric "dungeon."

Several planes of captivity are involved. "Suffering Mankind" is oppressed materially, intellectually, and spiritually. Hercules is a voluntary prisoner of incarnation who renounced the "bliss of sidereal existence" for the sake of Humanity. He is a captive teacher and writer, a prisoner who must imprison his message. The teachings which constitute his terrestrial raison d'être are disguised beneath an amusing surface of "tales," or "fables." But the message can stimulate thoughts on human and cosmic evolution. It can also suggest that "fables" are "emblems of Truth."

The plight of the captive hero confined to the Bastille — a fortress where Voltaire was once detained — is a transparent autobiographical allusion. But it is from the "subjective," esoteric aspects of "imprisonment" that the most important and startling biographical insights may be derived. The DAG or Savior of *Zadig* has a worthy "successor" in Voltairian Hercules. The titanic figure of the "Instructor of Mankind" which dominates the esoteric plane of *Zadig, Micromégas,* and *L'Ingénu* is no "fable." It is probably Voltaire Himself.

The theme of "captive" esoteric substance is sumptuously allegorized as "Albertine," the beloved and the rejected "work" of the Proustian

Recherche. The ruthless cross-examination to which the girl is subjected by her lover tends to detect — and remove — any objectively perceptible sign of inversion. "The prisoner" — or captive substance — desperately yearns to be out in the open. Her rebellious opening of symbolic "windows" is a catastrophic omen. The beloved is in danger of being "seen" by the physical senses and the unaided intellect. The "Prisoner" who becomes the "Fugitive" is automatically destroyed in her esoteric function. For, in the words of Proust, "Albertine is capable of anything except of confessing" her true nature. The release of the allegorical "work" of Marcel must comply with the requirements of incorruptible Mrs. "Right-Time" — Mme Bontemps — or be deferred until a specific portion of the current cycle has run its course. The premature escape of the girl is accordingly followed by her destruction. Carried by a runaway horse — Pegasus, literary inspiration — the love of Marcel is thrown against a tree — of Knowledge. The requirements of evolution are finally met at the end of the *Recherche.* The "daughter" of "Gilberte" and "Saint Loup" becomes the materialization of the necessary time span which the passionate author had long "refused to see." "Gilberte" and her "reincarnation," "Albertine" come into being as the "daughter" of "Saint Loup." The appearance of the girl is the long awaited release of captive esoteric substance transmitted by numerous writers over a period of several centuries. It is the triumph of previously unattainable *Liberty.* It is the realization of an ideal embodied in two transparent anagrams: the names of *Gilberte* and *Albertine.* The liberation achieved in due course of time is not irrelevant to the Voltairian liberation of "Suffering Mankind."

> "Ainsi la destinée conduisait à Paris presque tout ce canton de la Basse-Bretagne.") (Ch. XIII p. 291).

> ("Thus Destiny led to Paris almost this entire subdivision of Low Brittany.")

The release of the Voltairian Ingénu is bought from a powerful dignitary: Mr. M. de Saint Pouange. The price demanded by the official is the prostitution of Saint Yves.

The portrayal of the seducer is generally regarded as an allusion to the Comte de Saint Florentin. But the phonetic quality of the name "Saint Pouange," the family kindship of the character with Louvois, and the personality of the admirer of the heroine may well designate Philippe Emmanuel de Coulange. If one may paraphrase the Voltairian expression relative to Missouf, Saint Pousange resembles "the portrait made to us" by Saint Simon of Emmanuel de Coulange. The name of the seducer may constitute a reference to the prominent "bon vivant" of the court of the Sun King. But the main esoteric interest of Saint Pouange does not seem to lie in a connection with any historical "personage."

The official belongs to the category of exoteric "children." He has sufficient influence to open doors of material prisons. But he is himself the captive of a mayavic seraglio comparable to the residence of Achmet. Physical lust and lust for power are his chief interests in life. In spite of obvious defects, the seducer is not entirely corrupt. His first response to Saint Yves is not altogether lecherous. The pleas of the heroine are heard with emotion:

"Saint Pouange felt moved." (Ch. XV, p. 296).

The appeal of Truth is sufficiently strong to be felt by a person of minimal decency. Saint Pouange is capable of such dim recognition.

The conscience of the official is not wholly dead. The shame which he represses as he prepares the degradation of Saint Yves is a sign of innate decency. The end of the story reports his genuine change of heart and his deep remorse. Combined with a particle of instinctive goodness, his dedication to false values identifies him as the average person. As his name indicates, he is neither "angel" nor "beast": — "peu ange," Voltaire may have had in mind a famous thought of Pascal which is commented on in the *Lettres Philosophiques* when he selected his name.

"L'homme n'est ni ange ni bête."

("Man is neither angel nor beast.")

Saint Pouange represents the ambivalent consciousness of Fifth Race mankind, a segment of Humanity equally susceptible to the opposite attractions of Spirit and Matter. He is a slow "riser" or exoteric "child." He will not fully comprehend the consequences of his act or the general meaning of events until such developments are clear to all men.

The name of the official contains the three vowels which suggest the name of IAO. Saint Pouange belongs to the hierarchy of major and lesser Jehovahs which controls Western societies. As the perceptive "plumitif" well notes, such executive potentates do — and define — "Good an Evil." Their course of action is generally designed to maintain a status quo based on the Judaeo-Christian mystique of phallic "might" as right. Such persons are reliable panders of superior essence to mediocrity. More or less directly and consciously, they are tools of the prostitution of sacred values. Their promotion of the Jehovic syndrome is cloaked beneath a verbal barrage of benevolence if not Morality. Voltaire appears to have "seen" a poorly liberalized, stubbornly patriarchal society of the future in which Jehovic despotism relies more and more on mealy-mouthed propaganda.

The prostitution of Saint Yves is planned and implemented by a bigoted woman working in close cooperation with a Jesuit. The grotesquerie of the entremetteuse is entertaining. But the effect of her endeavors is less amusing. It is with the support of the blind, mentally passive, and zealously base flock composed of such creatures that temporal and spiritual evil remains in power. Totally absorbed by her copy of the *Christian Pedagogue,* an orthodox booster of orthodox "virtue," the bigot seems oblivious to the involvement of Truth and to the criminal nature of her own acts. No great contradiction is implied between the pious propaganda which is her daily bread and the prostitution of Truth in the name of Christ. The sarcasm conveyed by Voltaire is biting and sad. Swallowing and following the "fables" and directives of "impostors," the woman is an active contributor to the degradation of sacred values. With total lack of feeling other than obtuse delight she receives the symbolic diamonds representing the price of prostituted Truth. It is fitting that the tainted gems should be hers in the end. Their history of human suffering cannot sway her greed. Their spiritual significance is lost on her dense mind. Lack of heart and lack of vision are distinguishing traits of this tool of "impostors."

The devout woman is an able civic worker who thrives on ego-boosting, lucrative intrigue. Her pious pretense of "caring" for others carries psychological fringe-benefits; a synthetic aura of Christian saintliness, the prestige of efficiency and social know-how, and the glamorous pedestal of the modern Lady Bountiful. There are also tangible gains; costly diamonds.

The case history of the "friend" of Saint Yves has complex sociological implications. The wonder-worker is an enthusiastic pillar of the status quo, the only kind of system she is able to conceive. There would, after all, be no raison d'être for social engineers such as she in a less blighted and corrupt community. The lady is a valuable "token" of the alleged benevolence of society and a champion of its fundamental falsehoods. It is with the help of her many peers that politics and History are shaped on less than exalted planes. It is under their influence that the leadership of "provinces" and "armies" is supplied. The exhortations of the entremetteuse to Saint Yves contain an interesting element of autobiography:

> " '—I must confess to you that, had I been as difficult as you are, my husband would not have the benefit of the small position from which

he earns his living; he knows it, and, far from being angry, he sees in me his benefactress, and he regards himself as my creature. Do you think that all those who have led the provinces, or even the armies, owed their honors and their fortune to their sole services? There are some who owe this to the ladies their wives. The dignities of war have been solicited by love; and the position was given to the husband of the fairest.' " (Ch. XVII, p. 301).

The facade of happy success is belied by another statement:

" 'We poor women always need to be led by a man.' " (Ch. XV, p. 298).

The effect of the Judaeo-Christian feminine mystique is perceptible in the slyly domineering, falsely submissive attitude of the devout woman. The schemer knows well enough that a great deal of "leading" is the work of persons such as she. But she also knows — and resents — the fact that womanly power must not manifest itself openly. The words "we poor women" convey no small amount of compounded irony. The subordination of one sex to the other is recognized as fact. Suppressed rancor finds compensation in shady manipulation of others. The feminine aptitude to influence important events from the bedroom is a mere substitute for direct involvement. The fact that the husband of the devout woman "regards himself" as her "creature" fills her with a sorely needed sense of personal power. The friend of Saint Yves unconsciously "gets even" with the terrestrial subdelegate of Jehovah; the husband designated by society as her lord and master. Her rebellion is unconsciously directed at the Supreme Father-Husband Figure: the biblical god whose might she emulates on her own limited and sordid plane of "creation." The leering, hypocritical submission of the devout woman to the prevailing state of affairs is typical of the culturally throttled, therefore castrating female.

The modern counterpart of Missouf avenges her thwarted aspiration to transcendence by undermining — if possible destroying — every other transcendence within reach. The transcendence of her husband has been liquidated. The transcendence of another woman — Saint Yves — is intolerable and must perish. It is a painful reminder of what the Higher Self might have been. The falsely resigned "beaten woman" of the modern Western world is the natural enemy of Saint Yves. The prisoner of immanence and the legalized demi-mondaine leaves no stone unturned until the free agency and the purity of the heroine are reduced to a plan of degradation resembling her own. Voltaire appears to have "seen" the modern woman who proclaims her delight in second-class status and who denies any wish to be "liberated." Were such a person as happy as she pretends to be, she would be content to live — and let live her liberated sisters. Her inability to tolerate feminine transcendence is a dead giveaway.

The tormented Self of the devout woman finds expression on the esoteric plane of various statements. The lady is the unconscious spokesman of many truths belonging to the forbidden domain of transcendence. The leadership of esoteric "provinces" and "armies" does involve ecclesiastical orders governed by "provincials." It is indeed dependent on spiritual "arms." The entremetteuse is correct in saying that "fortunes" are contingent upon labors of "love" or mysticism. Esoteric "fortune" — Karma — is ever determined by spiritual Eros. The lady is also correct in saying that the consent of Saint Yves to prostitution will earn the approval of all. The resulting liberation of "Suffering Mankind" will eventually dwarf the importance of personal scruples and personal sacrifice. That is not to say that the end to be gained justifies any and all means. But that is to say that esoteric "prostitution" may represent a noble act. The statement bemoaning the condition of "poor women" is allegorically valid. Divine Intuition is often represented as Spiritual Eve while the coldly rational intellect is represented as male. The observation of the devout woman is identical in esoteric substance to the veiled tenor of two lines of *La Maison du berger,* a poem dedicated to *Eva.* It is also identical to a passage of *L'Ingénu* which deals with "taming."

> " 'We poor women always need to be led by a man.' "
> (*L'Ingénu,* Ch. XV, p. 298).

> "Your thought has leaps like those of the gazelles
> But could not proceed without guide or support."
> (*La Maison du berger*).

> "One must admit that God created women only to tame men."
> (*L'Ingénu,* Ch. XIII).

The "taming" in which the devout woman excels is performed on an inferior plane of "love." The higher level of "taming" involves contact with a brotherhood of superior minds and spirits who all wish to be "tamed." According to Saint Exupéry, "to tame" means "to create ties" — to make intellectual and intuitive connections. Such a "taming" process requires that Reason — the logical "guide" and "support" mentioned by Vigny — and Spirit — the "leaps of the gazelles" be fused in sensitive, creative harmony. Such is one of the meanings of the mystical "marriage" so often celebrated by esoteric writers. The modern "Missouf" or devout woman is incapable of attaining or of conceiving

442

such a "love." She can only sense and hate the compelling, disturbing presence of the divine spark in modern Eva or Sophia: Saint Yves.

The misery of the devout woman may be traced to the suppression of transcendence which affects the bulk of the Judaeo-Christian world and which is especially severe in the case of women. It may also be traced to the contrived separation of Reason and Spirit which is another bane of modern Fifth Race mankind. The separated "twins" are reduced to deformed, withered versions of their superior essence. "Reason" becomes a social "realism" which glorifies externals at the expense of true Reality — intrinsic value, genuine merit. The same "realism" denies the reality of the Higher Self which cannot be ignored with impunity by any human being. Restless Spirit seeks solace in the misery of others. Positive relief is sought from outside help, in this case from the guidance of a Jesuit. The supreme irony of the plight of the devout woman lies in her attempts to obtain consolation from the religious structure which is the doctrinal source of her misery. The cornered spiritual market described in *Candide* is still in business. Merchants of "pox" remain merchants of palliatives if not of cures.

The masterful psychological sketch of the devout woman supplies a significant glimpse of a society dedicated to crushing the initiative and transcendence of the individual. The society in question cloaks its shaky deeds in a garb of benevolence. The devout woman suffers from a severe case of thunderbolt envy. The disease — which is by no means limited to females — might, if faced honestly, shed more light on the ailments and needs of a sick community than does its dwarfed and distorted Freudian version.

It may finally be noted that the devout woman strikingly resembles various portraits of Mme de Maintenon which may be found in the works of Saint Simon, Mme de Sévigné, and Diderot. Her predilection for intrigue and Jesuitic guidance, her interest in pedagogy, and her autobiographical glorification of bartered love all suggest a spirited barb aimed at the royal consort who earned the unanimous aversion of "good company."

The involvement of Saint Yves with exoteric "children" such as Saint Pouange and the devout woman is closely linked to her dealings with "impostors." The latter persons are efficient and many. The abbé de Saint Yves seeks a lettre de cachet against his sister. Some attempts are made to marry the heroine to the son of the devilish bailli. The projected union is naturally abhorrent to the allegory of Truth. The fiendish plan is cleverly foiled by the girl. The end of the story finds the bailli beating a hasty retreat to his unnamed yet easily identified *province.*

Father Tout à Tous is a prominent "impostor" and a specialist in Jesuitic casuistry. As his name indicates — "All to all" — he is a versatile repairman of guilty conscience. Prostitution is assured of his blessing as long as it is calculated to help the "good cause." No moral enormity is too great for his "accommodating" soul. The elasticity of his ethics is demonstrated when he learns the identity of the would-be seducer: powerful Saint Pouange. The man whom he had just pronounced "an abominable sinner" is instantly transformed into a misunderstood paragon of virtue. The accuser is instantly transformed into an unsavory trouble-maker. The homily of Father Tout à Tous to recalcitrant Saint Yves is a masterpiece of professional sophistry. The all-purpose confessor has an impressive répertoire of useful authorities ready for all occasions. His argument leans heavily on the teachings of Augustine, a saint who is no favorite of Voltaire or of other esoteric writers.

An interesting maxim, set off by italics, is inserted in his pious discourse:

"'Where there is nothing, the king loses its rights.'"

The exoteric surface of the statement refers to murderous taxation. A semi-esoteric interpretation may be made: There is no possible escape on earth from the exactions of the mighty. A thoroughly esoteric reading is also possible: Where Maya or materiality ends, earthly sovereignties lose all their powers. One may note that the various planes of interpretation are separated only by an almost imperceptible hairbreadth. The fact in suggestive of Jesuitic slyness in manipulation of esoteric and occult material.

The only alternative to prostitution which is offered to Saint Yves is the abandonment of imprisoned "Suffering Mankind." Such a prospect is unthinkable to the heroine. The Jesuit who protects the reputation and the interests of Saint Pouange could probably prevail upon the official to effect the desired liberation on a gratuitous basis. But the prostitution of Truth is essential to his own survival. The supreme power over the fates of Saint Yves and Hercules rests with the Father. Suffering Mankind and Truth will not be united if he can prevent it. The esoteric reader is reminded of the threat made by the Jesuitic baron and brother of Cunégonde "You can kill me again but you will not marry my sister as long as I live." The modern churchman is no more liberal where the crucial "marriage" is concerned than his predecessor.

Surrounded by such enemies, Saint Yves can only succumb. But her "fall" is a symbolic triumph of spirituality.

Truth IS "above and below" in the Absolute, on all planes of existence. Truth lives in more or less latent form in every human heart. The "prostitution" of Saint Yves serves to promote the union of Eternal Verities with their nascent, fragmentary human reflection. The evolution of the heroine from sensuality and "provincialism" to mystical love and universal values marks the beginning of a spiritual rebirth for Fifth Race mankind. The integral concept of Truth for which Humanity is yearning will not come from earthly planes. The terrestrial powers which try to rule the destinies of men insist on its the continued prostitution. Drastic steps are made "necessary" by the inexorable progress of the wheel of evolution and by frantic efforts of counter-evolutionaries. The spiritual release of "Suffering Mankind" requires the sacrificial descent to earth of a special emissary. The gift brought by the "visitor" will be the general framework of the Secret Doctrine. It will supply a solid foundation to veiled particles of Truth which have been "smuggled" to the modern age from time immemorial. The gift of the "stranger" to "Suffering Mankind" will be the gift of UNVEILED TRUTH.

The prostitution of Saint Yves is an act of submission to materiality or voluntary reincarnation. It is courageously decided upon by a perfected being who renounces its right to "blissful omniscience" in order to respond to the spiritual awakening of mankind. The name and the personality of the seducer — Saint Pouange — convey the idea of limited ethereality. "Saint Yves" is symbolically prostituted to matter. As the title of Chapter XVI suggests, the girl "succumbs out of virtue," the latter word being used in the etymological sense of "strength" — esoterically "spirit". The veiled nature of the sacrifice of the heroine is suggested by the idea of cruel "necessity." It is also suggested by the word "désastre" — "disaster". The French term "astre" means "star." The prefix "des" may be translated as "estrangement from." The "disaster" of Saint Yves amounts to exile from the bliss of sideral existence. The melodramatic surface of the following passage covers the esoteric reality of "a fate worse than death" which can only be endured out of love of mankind.

> "She had no other resource than resolving to think only of the Ingénu while the cruel man would ruthlessly enjoy the necessity to which she was reduced." (Ch. XVII, p. 303).

Fulfillment is unlikely for the hapless "Saint Pouange." The "resource" used by the victim grants him the use and "enjoyment" of a vacated shell more than ever dedicated to its True Love. The esoteric reader is reminded of the unsuccessful rapist of *Candide*. The supremacy of "mind" over matter shines forth. A physical body may be raped. Spirit is incorruptible by definition.

The true meaning of the "prostitution" of Saint Yves is gratefully acknowledged by "Suffering Mankind." Saint Yves is hailed as an "angel who broke the chains" of her love. She is greeted as a "divine being descended from Heaven" in order to aid the captive. The "fall" of the Voltairian angel of mercy bears more than surface resemblance to the sacrifice of *Eloa* which is celebrated by Vigny. A suggestive reference to Eloa is also made by Proust in connection with a mysterious Russian great lady: "Princess Sherbatoff." Voltaire, Vigny, and Proust may all designate the same "messenger."

The role of "saving angel" played by Saint Yves brings to mind the fisherman featured in *Zadig*. "The fellow" in question recognized and hailed a Savior in the same capacity of "saving angel." The Babylonian "Instructor of Mankind" has a modern feminine counterpart in *L'Ingénu*. The transcendent role of woman is a sign of changing times.

The resistance of Saint Yves to the prospect of prostitution is the occasion of a typical Voltairian commentary on the degradation of sacred values:

> "She viewed with horror that practice of selling the misfortune and the happiness of men." (Ch. XVIII, p. 306).

The fate of *men* — perhaps mankind — is at stake. The presence of the plural tends to suggest the collective dimension of the esoteric "love affair". The removal of spiritual middlemen is devoutly wished. It is the common long-range goal of Instructors of Mankind. Christ, Rabelais, and Voltaire — to name but a few "smugglers" — agree on the adulterous influence of power-crazed, greedy spiritual merchants. Such persons are determined to pollute — and if possible to destroy — the spirituality which is the natural heritage and the rightful aspiration of Man. The money-lenders despised by Christ, the adulterous monk looming in the oracle received by Panurge, and the procurers of Truth portrayed by Voltaire have a common interest in the same unholy "commerce." The modern social system represented by the executive: Saint Pouange and by established religion — the Jesuit — depends upon the prostitution of Truth for its survival. The revulsion of Saint Yves may be summarized in a few famous words: "Crush the infamous!"

Gordon is released — as is Hercules — by the sacrifice of the heroine. The misery of a stranger is not overlooked by the girl. There are indeed no strangers for the personification of highest Love. The abnegation of Divine Truth incarnate does not restrict or measure its benefits to a privileged few.

The liberation of Gordon marks an important event in the history of

446

human Knowledge. The spiritually inclined scholar leaves his "prison." He will have ample opportunity to use his unique background of learning for the benefit of human progress. The impressive fund of formal knowledge of Gordon has been vastly enriched by the secret lore acquired from Hercules — a personified "turn of the wheel." The former Jansenist has been converted from belief in the flames of Hell to faith in the cyclic work of evolution. His example will be followed by others who will make the same transition from the Christian Furnace to the Wheel of Karma. The sum of intellectual and spiritual assets possessed by "Gordon" is likely to supply the Ariadne's thread required for some "explorations." The spiritually inclined scholar will be equipped as he must be for the making of certain "discoveries." Such persons as the relatives of Saint Yves who lack the required preparation will not be so fortunate. Paris — the symbol of modern Western civilization — will remain for them a maze with no exit.

> "— when they had arrived in Paris, they found themselves lost as if in a vast maze without thread and without exit. Their fortune was unimpressive; they needed carriages every day to go in search of discovery, and they discovered nothing." (Ch. XIII, p. 288).

The Parisian "maze of iniquities"* — perhaps "inequities" or conflicting values — may eventually reveal a soluble nature. Illuminating equivalences may be found in due course of Time:

> " 'Vois-je une Roue ardente, ou bien une Fournaise?' "

> " 'Do I see an ardent Wheel, or else a Furnace?' "

> Que jetteras-tu donc dans ton moule d'acier?
> Ton ouvrage est sans forme, et se pétrit encore
> Sous la main nouvrière et le marteau sonore;
> Il s'étend, se resserre, et s'engloutit souvent
> Dans le jeu des ressorts et du travail savant, — ' "

> (" '— What are you doing, Paris, in your ardent forge?
> What will you cast into your steel mold?
> Your work is formless and still being shaped
> Under the toiling hand and the echoing hammer;
> It stretches, tightens, and often is engulfed
> By the interplay of coils and of learned labor."
> (Alfred de Vigny, *Paris*).

The reunion of Man and Truth is marked by the usual loss of sensory consciousness which is also reported in *Zadig* and *Candide* at the time of the "lifting of the veil."

---

*Ch. XVII, p. 301.

"The two lovers see each other and both faint."
(Ch. XVIII, p. 304).

There is no apparent raising of the symbolic veil. But the departure from customary ritual is more than a concession to modern dress. Truth is no longer concealed from those who seek her. The same process of evolution which led her underground causes her to emerge from age-old secrecy. The "Huron" or "turn of the wheel" has performed "necessary" work. Primitive Pagan Truth — Abacaba — is restored to visible life in the person of a modern successor: Saint Yves. The general outline of the Primitive Wisdom-Religion or Secret Doctrine becomes accessible to non-initiates. Voltaire seems to have foretold the era of UNVEILED TRUTH which was heralded and implemented in the XIXth Century by Mme Blavatsky.

> "— the Eternal Night was in and behind all, and we pass from what we see to that which is invisible to the eye of sense. Our fervent wish has been to show true souls how they may lift aside the curtain, and, in the brightness of that Night made Day, look with undazzled gaze upon the UNVEILED TRUTH." (*Isis Unveiled*, p. 640, Vol. 2).

The same transition from "the eye of sense" to non-sensory perception is noted by Voltaire. The long-awaited reunion of Mankind and Unveiled Truth is marked by the use of a new kind of communication. Words become inadequate to express certain things. Ordinary language is transcended:

> "The two lovers conversed by means of glances which expressed all the sentiments with which they were penetrated." (Ch. XIX, p. 307).

The mystical "penetration" defined by C. G. Jung operates. Direct cognition supplements and supersedes the operation of the unaided intellect. The era of transcendental "conveyances of up there" has arrived.

The same development is unanimously predicted by occult and esoteric writers. The vindication of the Secret Doctrine which is forecast by Mme Blavatsky for the end of the XXth Century implies the re-discovery of a sixth sense. The new sense — and the third eye — are "seen" as they return in the apocalyptic vision of *La Nausée*. Intuitive "flights" — represented by esoteric "aviation" — and non-sensory communication — disguised as "wireless' exchange — are linked to the announcements of two surprising "marriages" or connections in the *Recherche*. One of the "grooms" is "Saint-Loup." The other is a relative of "Legrandin." The far-reaching repercussions of the amazing engagements are noted with typical esoteric humor:

448

"Ces fiançailles excitèrent de vifs commentaires dans les mondes les plus différents." (*A la Recherche du temps perdu*, p. 662, Vol. III).

("Those engagements gave rise to the liveliest commentaries in the most diverse spheres.")

The physical death of Saint Yves which marks the final portion of *L'Ingénu* contrasts with the apparent longevity of Astarté, the old woman, and Cunégonde. The extinction of the allegory of Truth seems to be a poor omen for the dawning era of enlightenment. But physical death carries positive symbolism. It is accession to True Life. The Truth of the latter half of the Fifth Race becomes too purified from materialistic dross to retain her divisive mortal shell. The process of emancipation from sectarianism and "provincialism" is paralleled by the "death" of the exoteric crust of certain scriptures — literary and other. Such a "death" is the ultimate goal of all esoteric writers. It is the revelation of the soul and spirit which are the core and the raison d'être of their works. The transition is noted by Voltaire in a few simple words which are the very definition of material involution and of mysticism:

"Her soul was killing her body." (Ch. XXX, p. 313).

The same dissolution of an exoteric shell "devoutly to be wished" by all "smugglers" is evoked in various texts. The "howls" which are expected to accompany "death" in the following passage of *Comment c'est* may not be those of the author. The lack of answer which is repeatedly stressed — "pas de réponse" — suggests irrefutable facts:

"alors ça peut changer pas de réponse finir pas de réponse je pourrais suffoquer pas de réponse m'engloutir pas de réponse plus souiller la boue pas de réponse le noir pas de réponse plus troubler le silence pas de réponse crever pas de réponse CREVER hurlements JE POURRAIS CREVER hurlemens JE VAIS CREVER hurlements bon." (Samuel Beckett, *Comment c'est*, p. 177, Editions de Minuit).

("Then it can change no answer end no answer I might suffocate no answer be engulfed no answer no more soil the mud no answer the darkness no answer no more disturb the silence no answer CROAK no answer CROAK howls I MIGHT CROAK howls I AM GOING TO CROAK howls good.")

"— ma carapace de monstre autour de moi pourrira." (Samuel Beckett, *L'Innommable*, p. 77, Editions de Minuit).

("— my monstrous shell around me will putrefy.")

The fact that the same process is a matter of "words, voices" and hidden architectures — or skeletons — is also stressed:

"—, rigidité cadavérique, dégagement de l'ossature, ça devrait suffire. C'est que c'est une question de mots, de voix il ne faut pas l'oublier,— " (Samuel Beckett, *L'Innommable*, p. 199, Editions de Minuit).

(" — cadaverous rigidity, extraction of the skeleton, that should suffice. The fact of it is that it is a matter of words, of voices, one must not forget that — ")

The same meaning of "death" is made crystal clear by Saint Exupéry:

"Death is a great thing. It is a new network of connections with the ideas, the objects, the habits of the dead person. It is a new arrangement of the world. Nothing has changed in appearance, but everything is changed. The pages of the book are the same, but the meaning of the book is different." (Antoine de Saint-Exupéry, *Flight to Arras*, Ch. II).

The physical death of Saint Yves represents — among other things — the beginning of the end of sectarian bodies. It is basically equivalent to the statement of Mme Blavatsky which has already been quoted: "A few centuries more, and there will linger no sectarian beliefs in any of the great religions of humanity. Brahmanism and Buddhism, Christianity and Mohammedanism will all disappear before the mighty rush of *facts*."

Vigny seems to have expected the same "mighty rush of *facts*" to restore the supremacy of THE UNIVERSAL WRIT — the Secret Doctrine:

"Ton règne est arrivé, PUR ESPRIT, roi du monde!
Quand ton aile d'azur dans la nuit nous surprit,
Déesse de nos moeurs, la guerre vagabonde
Régnait sur nos aïeux. Aujourd'hui c'est l'ECRIT,
L'ECRIT UNIVERSEL, parfois impérissable,
Que tu graves au marbre ou traînes sur le sable,
Colombe au bec d'airain! VISIBLE SAINT ESPRIT!"
(Alfred de Vigny, *L'Esprit pur*).

("Your reign has arrived, PURE SPIRIT, king of the world!
When your azure wing in the darkness surprised us,
Goddess of our ways, the vagrant war
Reigned over our forefathers. Nowadays it is the WRIT,
THE UNIVERSAL WRIT, at times imperishable,
Which you engrave on marble or trace on the sand,
Dove with the bronze beak! VISIBLE HOLY SPIRIT!")

The physical "death" of Truth marks the beginning of a spiritualizing trend on the human plane of evolution. Mankind enters the reascending phase of its long pilgrimage. The Ingénu undergoes a process of "generation" which has spiritual "regeneration" as its ultimate outcome. As the title of Chapter XI indicates, the Ingénu "develops his genius" or Spirit. The average human being evolves from the status of "brute" into the status of "Man."

The physical death of Truth has cosmic manifestations. Involution begins. Having reached and completed a phase dominated by dense materiality, the universe slowly becomes more ethereal. The change affects all kingdoms of Nature — from minerals to humans. The physical constitution of all creatures is gradually modified in a process of adaptation to new conditions of existence.

> "The elements, whether simple or compound, could not have remained the same since the commencement of the evolution of our chain. Everything in the Universe progresses steadily in the Great Cycle, while incessantly going up and down in the smaller cycles. Nature is never stationary during manvantara, as it is ever *becoming,* not simply *being;* and mineral, vegetable, and human life are always adapting their organisms to the then reigning Elements, and therefore those Elements were then fitted for them, as they are now for the life of our present humanity. It will only be in the next, or fifth Round that the fifth Element, *Ether* — the gross body of Akâsa, if it can be called even that — will, by becoming a familiar fact of Nature to all men, as air is familiar to us now, cease to be as at present hypothetical, —" (*The Secret Doctrine,* pp. 257-58, Vol. I).

The same belief in the future visibility of Ether, a development expected in the Fifth Round, is reflected in the *Recherche,* a work in which the plane of subtle matter receives abundant coverage. Rivebelle, a site the name of which means "beautiful shore" — is the region where the astral body can "travel" during sleep and where — in the words of Paracelsus — it can soar " 'to its parents, and hold converse with the stars.' "* The stars themselves are regarded as "images of gods"** or as images of perfected beings in the Secret Doctrine. "Marcel" takes numerous "trips" to "Rivebelle," a "place of aerial pleasure superimposed on the other, and more intoxicating."*** The "crutches of reasoning"**** are left far behind by the daring "explorer." The tables of of the "restaurant" of Rivebelle "like so many planets" resemble ancient allegories.***** The "trips" of Marcel involve close "converse" with "Saint Loup" acting as a guide and as a generous giver of "drinks." Port wine is consumed — Porto perhaps "Oporto". The "nourishment" absorbed in "Rivebelle" turns Marcel into a "being whose supreme joy

---

*Iis Unveild, p. 179, Vol. 1.
**Ibid., p. xxi, Vol. 1.
***A la Rcherche du temps perdu, p. 812, Vol. I.
****Ibid., p. 815, Vol. I.
*****Ibid., p. 810, Vol. I.

would be to meet Legrandin with whom" he "had just conversed in a dream."* The ethereal realm where Proust confabulates with allegories of Vigny and Voltaire may be seen under certain conditions:

> " 'Mais en effet,' dis-je, 'd'habitude, de Balbec, on ne voit pas cette côte, et on ne l'entend pas non plus. Il faut que le temps ait changé et ait doublement élargi l'horizon.' " (A la Recherche du temps perdu, p. 823, Vol. II).

> (" 'But precisely,' I said, 'usually, from Balbec, one does not see that coast, and one does not hear it either. It is necessary that the weather be changed and that it have doubly broadened the horizon.' ")

The visibility of "Rivebelle" depends on a necessary change of weather — "temps", a word which also means "time". The sidereal realm cannot be "heard" — a word which also means "understood" — or even conceived under generally prevailing conditions specific to a certain age. The atmosphere of the "place of aerial pleasure" is compared to the atmosphere of "oriental tales."** The latter writings may embrace Far Eastern Scriptures as well as Voltairian short stories. One cannot expect their message to be generally "heard" at all times. The occult belief according to which there is no sound without Ether*** may finally be noted. The Proustian assertion that Ether may literally be heard is valid.

The "crutches" of reasoning may shed light on the strange moving habits of a character created by Beckett. Molloy tries to combine — with limited success — the use of bicycle "wheels" — cyclic evolution — with the presence of "crutches." As one might easily predict, progress is hampered rather than aided by the cumbersome "supports."

The death of Saint Yves is a source of speculation on the mysterious work of the human body. How does one die of grief as does the heroine who cannot survive her loss of "virtue?" What unknown connection between mind and matter may exist which makes such a death possible? Voltaire seems to rely on the reader to supply the answer.

> "La maladie devint mortelle en deux jours. Le cerveau qu'on croit le siège de l'entendement fut attaqué aussi violemment que le coeur, qui est, dit-on, le siège des passions.
> Quelle mécanique incompréhensible a soumis les organes au sentiment et à la pensée? Comment une seule idée douloureuse dérange-t-elle le cours du sang, et comment le sang à son tour porte-t-il ses irrégularités dans l'entendement humain? Quel est ce fluide inconnu et dont l'exis-

---

*Ibid., p. 820, Vol. I.
**The Secret Doctrine, p. 536, Vol. I.
***A la Recherche du temps perdu, p. 820, Vol. I.

tence est certaine, qui, plus prompt, plus actif que la lumière, vole en moins d'un clin d'oeil dans tous les canaux de la vie, produit les sensations, la mémoire, la tristesse ou la joie, la raison ou le vertige, rappelle avec horreur ce qu' on voudrait oublier, et fait d'un animal pensant, ou un objet d'admiration ou un sujet de pitié et de larmes?" (Ch. XX, pp. 313-14).

("The illness became fatal in two days. The brain, which is believed to be the seat of comprehension, was attacked as violently as the heart, which is said to be the seat of passions.

What incomprehensible mechanism has submitted the organs to feeling and to thought? How does one single painful idea disturb the course of the blood, and how does blood in its turn carry its irregularities into human comprehension? What is that unknown fluid, the existence of which is certain, which, quicker, more active than light, flies in less than a wink into all the channels of life, produce sensations, memory, sadness or joy, reason or disorder, recalls with horror what one would like to forget, and turns a thinking animal either into an object of admiration or into a subject of pity and tears.")

Orthodox answers to the final question are virtually ruled out by the mode of expression. The "unknown" — perhaps "occult" — and the "certain" seem to be one and the same. The adjective "incomprehensible" places speculation beyond the realms of the unaided intellect or the bounds of "exact science." Accepted localizations of the unknown mechanism are subjected to doubt. Brains are "believed" to constitute the site of comprehension. The heart is "said" to harbor passions. Emphatic reference to the "single painful idea" which is the cause of death points to the standard system of esoteric expression, the case of spirit vs. matter being commonly styled as "ideas" vs. flesh. The obvious "force" of the "single idea" is the power of life and death. The "speed" which is a major characteristic of the "unknown fluid" is synonymous with "force." The unknown mechanism is Spirit.

Blood and the "unknown fluid" are juxtaposed yet represented as distinct from each other. The mysterious relationship presumed to exist between the two vehicles of life is rooted in the system of "good philosophers who reason by analogy." The Secret Doctrine teaches that the circulation of the blood obeys the same laws as cosmic pulsation.

"—, there is a regular circulation of the vital fluid throughout our system, of which the Sun is the heart — the same as the circulation of the blood in the human body — during the manvantaric solar period, or life, the Sun contracting as rhythmically at every return of it, as the human heart does. Only, instead of performing the round in a second or so, it takes the solar blood ten of its years, and a whole year to pass through its *auricles* and *ventricles* before it washes the lungs and passes thence to the great veins and arteries of the system.

This, Science will not deny, since Astronomy knows of the fixed cycle of eleven years when the number of solar spots increases, *which is due to the contraction* of the Solar HEART. The universe (our world in this case) breathes, just as man and every living creature, plant, and even mineral does upon the earth; and as our globe itself breathes every twenty-four hours. Could the human heart be made luminous, and the living and throbbing organ be made visible, so as to have it reflected upon a screen, such as used by the astronomers in their lectures — say for the moon — then every one would see the Sun-spot phenomenon repeated every second — due to its contraction and the rushing of the blood." (*The Secret Doctrine,* pp. 541-42, Vol. I).

The law of analogy is suggested by the style of Voltaire. The presence of the words "in its turn" conveys the idea of parallel cyclic processes on physical and non-physical planes. The fact that the Huronian Hercules of Voltaire represents Logos, the Sun, and a "turn of the wheel" adds cosmic dimension to the ailment of Saint Yves. The fatal grief of the girl is caused by the existence of Hercules, the lover she was forced to "betray." The mysterious "mechanism" or "unknown fluid" which has the power of life and death is the spiritual impulse pervading, maintaining, and changing the universe.

"Fohat, then, is the personified electric vital power, the transcendental binding Unity of all Cosmic Energies, on the unseen as on the manifest planes, the action of which resembles — on an immense scale — that of a living Force created by WILL, in those phenomena where the seemingly subjective acts on the seemingly objective and propels it to action. Fohat is not only the living Symbol and Container of that Force, but is looked upon by the Occultists as an Entity — the forces he acts upon being cosmic, human and terrestrial, and exercising their influence on all those planes respectively. On the earthly plane his influence is felt: the magnetic and active force generated by the strong desire of the magnetizer. On the Cosmic, it is present in the constructive power that carries out, in the formation of things — from the planetary system down to the glow-worm and simple daisy — the plan in the mind of nature, or in the Divine Thought, with regard to the development and growth of that special thing. He is, metaphysically, the objectivised thought of the gods; the 'Word made flesh,' on a lower scale, and the messenger of Cosmic and human ideations: the active force in Universal Life. In his secondary aspect, Fohat is the Solar Energy, the electric vital fluid, and the preserving fourth principle, the animal Soul of Nature, so to say, or — Electricity." (*The Secret Doctrine,* pp. 111-12, Vol. I).

The origin of "sensations, memory, sadness" and "joy, reason or disorder" is given out as follows in the Secret Doctrine:

This 'mystery' or the origin of the LIFE ESSENCE, Occultism locates in the same centre as the nucleus of *prima materia* (for they are one) of our Solar system.

'The Sun is the heart of the Solar World (System) and its brain is hidden behind the (visible) Sun. From thence, sensation is radiated into every nerve-centre of the great body, and the waves of the life-essence flow into each artery and vein. . . . The planets are its limbs and pulses. . . .' (Commentary)
—Occult philosophy denies that the Sun is a globe in combustion, but defines it simply as a world, a glowing sphere, the *real* Sun being hidden behind, and the visible being only its reflection, its *shell.*" (*The Secret Doctrine,* pp. 540-41, Vol I).

The identity of the mysterious "mechanism" connecting mind and matter is abundantly suggested by rejection of physical localization and by the esoteric equivalence linking Hercules and the Sun. The riddle offered by Voltaire to the reader of *L'Ingénu* hardly constitutes a question at all. The "unknown fluid" is Spirit.

"By whatsoever name the physicians may call the energizing principle in matter is of no account; it is a subtile something apart from the matter itself; and, as it escapes their detection, it must be something beside matter." (*Isis Unveiled,* p. 340, Vol. 1).

The commentary on the death of Saint Yves is a Voltairian poem in prose. The flash, the whirlwind, the crescendo and dizzy speed of coursing Spirit dwell in the few lines which constitute a rhythmical embodiment of the "unknown fluid" itself. The answer to the enigma of the mysterious "mechanism" may be found in the alchemy of the Verb if the reader merely "listens."

Chapter XX contains one of several Voltairian commentaries on the inadequacy of exact science in general and medicine in particular. Thanks to the conflicting ministrations of two doctors, the illness of Saint Yves becomes fatal in two days. The youth and previous health of the heroine invite edifying conclusions on the competence of both medical men. Each physician is primarily concerned with his own image. The patient is secondary at best. The medical men are found wanting in knowledge and ethics.

The death of Saint Yves is a source of meditation on the brotherhood of mortal creatures. All are doomed to material destruction. Such is "the fate of all animals." The parallel between man and beast is qualified by a distinction favoring an aspect of animal instinct. Animal stoicism at the time of death is unmatched by human beings. The substance of the passage announces *La Mort du loup:*

"Let others try to praise the spectacular deaths of those who enter into destruction without feeling; it is the fate of all animals. We only die with indifference as they do when age or illness has made us similar to them through blunting of our organic faculties." (Ch. XX, p. 317).

455

" 'H́élas!' ai-je pensé, 'malgré ce grand nom d'Hommes,
Que j'ai honte de nous, débiles que nous sommes!
Comment on doit quitter la vie et tous ses maux,
C'est vous qui le savez, sublimes animaux!
A voir ce que l'on fut sur terre et ce qu'on laisse,
Seul le silence est grand; tout le reste est faiblesse.' "
(Alfred de Vigny, *La Mort du loup*).

" 'Alas!' I thought, 'in spite of that great name of Men,
How ashamed I am of us weak creatures that we are!
How one must leave life and all its woes,
You are the ones who know that, sublime animals!
To see what one was on earth and what one leaves,
Alone silence is great; all the rest is weakness; — ' "

Saint Yves dies without ostentatious stoicism. Any display of super-human courage would be suspect in the ultimate test· of frailty and strength:

" 'Tu as du bon venin? Tu es sûr de ne pas me faire souffrir longtemps?' "
(*The Little Prince*, Ch. XXVI).

"' You have some good venom? You are certain that you will not make me suffer too long?' "

"Whoever suffered a great loss has great regrets; if he suppresses them it is because he carries vanity into the very arms of death." (Ch. XX, p. 317).

The lack of vanity of Saint Yves is significant on two esoteric planes. The sacrificial descent of a carrier of UNVEILED TRUTH and the spiritual rise of Fifth Race mankind are both involved. The dividing line of Maya — illusion, "vanity" — which dominates the passage as an element of "transition" is the hinge separating and joining two poles of existence: the material and the immaterial. The symbolic border is transcended in two opposite directions by two aspects of the same impulse brought about by a crucial "turn of the wheel." The spiritual readiness of Fifth Race mankind calls forth a messenger of UNVEILED TRUTH. The messenger suffers the "great loss" of spirituality inherent to Bodhisattva. Mankind undergoes a great trial of intellectual and spiritual evolution which will eventually be reflected on the physical plane. The agony of incarnation is as rending to the voluntary victim as is transcendence of the material level to the ordinary man. The "fall" and "rise" of "Saint Yves" are two aspects of the same important event unanimously predicted by occultists and esoteric writers.

The goal of the sacrificial descent is ever the same for the spiritual leaders of all times:

456

"Quand les Dieux veulent bien s'abattre sur les mondes,
Ils n'y doivent laisser que des traces profondes;
Et, si j'ai mis le pied sur ce globe incomplet,
Dont le gémissement sans repos m'appelait,
C'était pour y laisser deux Anges à ma place
De qui la race humaine aurait baisé la trace,
La Certitude heureuse et l'Espoir confiant."
(Alfred de Vigny, Le Mont des oliviers).

("When the Gods are willing to be felled onto worlds,
They must leave there only profound marks;
And, if I set foot on this incomplete globe
The moaning of which unceasingly called me,
It was to leave there two Angels in my place
Of whom the human race would have kissed the footsteps,
Happy Certainty and trusting Hope.")

The expectation of success is ever the same also. The theme of mankind finally redeemed through its own efforts is found in the texts of all esoteric writers:

"L'or pur doit surnager, et sa gloire est certaine;"
(Alfred de Vigny, La Bouteille à la mer).

("Pure gold must stay afloat, and its glory is certain."

"Le rideau s'est levé devant mes yeux débiles,
La lumière s'est faite, et j'ai vu ses splendeurs;
J'ai compris nos destins par ces ombres mobiles
Qui se peignaient en noir sur de vives couleurs.
Ces feux, de ta pensée étaient les lueurs pures,
Ces ombres, du passé les magiques figures;
J'ai tressailli de joie en voyant nos grandeurs.
Il est donc vrai que l'homme est monté par lui-même
Jusqu'aux sommets glacés de sa vaste raison,
Qu'il peut y vivre en paix et sonder l'horizon.
Il sait que l'univers l'écrase et le dévore;
Plus grand que l'univers qu'il juge et qui l'ignore,
Le berger a lui-même éclairé sa maison."
(Alfred de Vigny, La Maison du berger — Réponse d'Eva).

("The curtain has risen in front of my weak eyes,
There was light, and I saw its splendors;
I understood our destinies through those flitting shadows
Which outlined themselves in black on a background of bright colors.
Those fires, of your thought were the pure gleams,
Those shadows, of the past were the magical figures;
I thrilled with joy as I saw our grandeurs.
So it is true that man has risen through his own efforts
All the way to the icy peaks of his vast reason,
That he can live there in peace and probe the horizon.

He knows that the universe crushes and devours him;
Greater than the universe which he judges and which scorns him,
The shepherd has himself brought light into his house.")
(*Reply of Eva*).

The behavior of Saint Yves at the time of "death" conveys suggestions of initiation rites. "Vanity" — Maya — is not "carried" by the girl "into the very arms of death." Maya accompanies the candidate to initiation to the very threshhold of True Being but goes no further. Such is the meaning of certain aspects of Pagan initiation rites representing a last symbolic voyage in the realm of inferior consciousness. The simplicity of the heroine denotes a sound approach to universal mysteries. Humanity enters a new phase of its development with adequate understanding of the event. The warning issued by spiritual masters of all times and humorously echoed by Céline seems to be "heard" and heeded: "Don't take the stairs — "degrees" — by mistake."

Initiation is also suggested by the cause of the death of Saint Yves. One exclamation of the girl — later repeated and set off by italics — is the echo of an occult precept:

> " 'Ah! madam,' she said to the deadly friend, 'you have destroyed me! you give me death.' " (Ch. XIX, p. 308).

> "Her lover had his heart too full of what she had done for him, he loved her too much to allow the adventure of the diamonds to make a strong imprint on his heart. But these words which he had perceived only to well: *'You give me death!'* still frightened him secretly and ruined his joy." (Ch. XIX, p. 311).

> " 'This is a secret which gives death; close thy mouth lest thou shouldst reveal to the vulgar; compress thy brain lest something should escape from it and fall outside.' "

> " — the *Agrushada Parikshai* says explicitly, 'Every initiate, to whatever degree he may belong, who reveals the great sacred formula, must be put to death.' " (*Isis Unveiled*, p. 40, Vol. 2).

The undue disclosure of secret knowledge entails death for the culprit. Saint Pouange, a grossly unqualified candidate to the Mystery of Life, has had "commerce" with Saint Yves. His illicit access to Truth spells the doom of the source of revelation.

The death of the girl has predictable effect on the hero. Hercules is overwhelmed with grief. The bereft lover is suspected of suicidal schemes. Friends and relatives watch him closely. The young man is finally persuaded to go on living. The convincing arguments of Gordon are interestingly defined in terms of what they are *not*:

458

"Gordon carefully refrained from unfolding to him those dull clichés through which attempts are made to prove that it is not permitted to use one's freedom to cease to exist when one exists wretchedly, that one must not leave one's house when one can no longer stand to stay in it, that man is on earth like a soldier on duty; as if it mattered to the Being of beings that the collection of a few particles of matter be in one place or another; invalid reasons which a firm and thoughtful despair disdains to heed, and to which Cato replied only with a blow of the knife." (Ch. XX, pp. 317-18).

Life can be sufficiently grim to turn any person into a potential suicide. The text conveys understanding and even sympathy. The reader is reminded of the fisherman of *Zadig*. The old woman of *Candide* and her frequent wish for death also come to mind.

The stale arguments usually invoked against suicide seem to be ridiculed. But they are not invalid on the esoteric plane of thought. "Man is on earth like a soldier on duty." The same view is essentially expressed in *Candide*: "Man was not born to rest." Man is on earth to fulfill a part of his spiritual destiny — "ut operaretur eum." Other considerations which cannot be presented openly underlie the passage. Life is more than physical existence. It cannot be rejected by escape from the physical body. Abandonment of the karmic burden is impossible and damaging to the Eternal Ego when attempted. Retribution takes dreadful forms in cases of suicide and other avoidable violent death. It is not indifferent — in an impersonal way — to the Being of beings that the aggregate of a few particles of matter be in one place or another. The Great All is sensitive to the smallest disturbance of universal harmony. Matter is materialized spirit and the vehicle of a very special spark in the case of human life. Voltaire understandably shuns exoteric reference to soul and spirit.

Christian belief is nowhere mentioned in the arguments of Gordon. But it seems to be suggested by the words "thoughtful — despair," a phrase which tends to evoke the Pascalian "thinking reed" and the Voltairian view of jansenistic spirituality. Gordon, the former Jansenist and recent convert to Karmic belief, is likely to scorn the arbitrary surface of the Jehovic "Thou shalt not." But he is certain to endorse its occult implications. The total expression: "thoughtful and firm despair" opposes to baseless sermons the reality of spiritual "strength" or knowledge. Such knowledge is likely to embrace occult views of disembodied souls or tormented entities produced by suicide. The destruction of the physical Self is therefore unthinkable for reasons which have little to with "worn out clichés." Such is the probable reason why the reader is treated to arguments *not* used. It is also doubtful that Hercules — the embodiment of cosmic and individual "turns of the wheel"; —

the successful proselyte of Karmic philosophy — needs any such teachings from his own pupil.

Voltaire's reference to the death of Cato seems to sanction the suicide of the famous Roman if not suicide in general. The story of the illustrious statesman is that of a person of simple manner, great courage, and high ethics. Cato was handicapped in political life by his refusal to buy votes. The virtuous and learned Roman took his own life in order to avoid death at the hands of the soldiers of Caesar. His last night on earth was spent reading the writings of Plato on the immortality of the soul. Added to the impressive background of the great Pagan the phrase "invalid reasons" suggests a special case.

The case of the Voltairian Hercules is also irrevelant to "worn out clichés." It is suggested to represent another special situation. A provocative question is asked by the hero: "Do you think there is anyone on earth who has the right and the power to keep me from ending my life?" The alleged absence of any such earthly power tends to place the existence of the young man beyond ordinary jurisdiction. Such an idea is consistent with the esoteric personality of the traveler who came from "another world." Voluntary reincarnation is dedicated to a precise mission which is the chief determinant of physical "life" and "death." The suffering which no outsider has the right to prolong is the sojourn in the limbo of incarnate illusion.

Relief comes to Hercules in the form of symbolic "death" to materiality or initiation. The young man makes the transition which he vainly sought to achieve in the waters of the Rance. The Adam Kadmon component of suffering mankind follows the path toward wich he guided Spiritual Eve. The perils and rigors of the happening are suggested by numerous details and significant words. Hercules is "without arms." He is "watched closely" as is every neophyte.

> "Subjective communication with the human, god-like spirit of those who have preceded us to the silent land of bliss, is in India divided into three categories. Under the spiritual training of a *guru* or sannyasi, the vatou (disciple or neophyte) begins to *feel* them. Were he not under the immediate guidance of an adept, he would be controlled by the invisibles, and utterly at their mercy, for among those subjective influences he is unable to discern the good from the bad. Happy the sensitive who is sure of the purity of his spiritual atmosphere!" (*Isis Unveiled*, p. 115, Vol. 2).

The travail of spiritual birth is described by Voltaire:

> "Le morne et terrible silence de l'Ingénu, ses yeux sombres, ses lèvres tremblantes, les frémissements de son corps portaient dans l'âme de

tous ceux qui le regardaient ce mélange de compassion et d'effroi qui enchaine toutes les puissances de l'âme, qui exclut tout discours, et qui ne se manifeste que par mots entrecoupés. L'hôtesse et sa famille étaient accourues; on tremblait de son désespoir, on le gardait à vue, on observait tous ses mouvements. Déjà le corps glacé de la belle Saint Yves avait été porté dans une salle basse, loin des yeux de son amant, qui semblait la chercher encore, quoiqu'il me fût plus en état de rien voir."

Au milieu de ce spectacle de la mort, tandis que le corps est exposé à la porte de la maison, que deux prêtres á côté d'un bénitier récitent des prières d'un air distrait, que des passants jettent quelques gouttes d'eau bénite sur la bière par cisiveté, que d'autres poursuivent leur chemin avec indifférence, que les parents pleurent et qu'un amant est prêt à s'arracher la vie, le Saint Pouange arrive avec l'amie de Versailles." (Ch. XX, p. 318).

("The grim and terrible silence of the Ingénu, his dark eyes, his trembling lips, the shivering of his body carried into the soul of all those who watched him that mixture of compassion and fear which joins as if in a chain all the powers of the soul, which excludes all speech, and which manifests itself only through halting words. The hostess and her family had come rushing; one trembled over his despair, one kept him closely watched, one observed all his movements. Already the icy body of beautiful Saint Yves had been carried into a low room, far from the eyes of her lover, who seemed to search for her still, although he no longer was capable of seeing anything."

In the midst of this spectacle of death, while the body is on display at the door of the house, while two priests next to a holy water basin recite prayers absent-mindedly, while passers-by throw a few drops of holy water on the bier idly, while others go on their way with indifference, while relatives weep and a lover is ready to wrest life from himself, the Saint Pouange arrives with his woman friend from Versailles.")

Silence, trembling, temporary loss of sight and sensory perception are present. The common factors of all Ways to Damascus and "liftings of the veil" attend the occasion. Ordinary language fails. It is powerless to convey the rush of new sensations. All the "powers of the soul" are summoned. The spiritual gains acquired in the course of a long chain of rebirths are all needed to perform the arduous task. The combination of the verb "enchaîne" with the said powers suggests the immaterial harvest reaped from many lives. Compassion is felt by the observers. Knowledge is manifest in the fear of the by-standers who are aware of the true nature of the occasion. The body of Saint-Yves, now resting in a crypt — "salle basse" — now displayed by the symbolic threshhold, brings to mind the initiate of Ancient Egypt lying on a Tau-shaped couch in the depths of a pyramid. As was previously noted, the candidate was eventually brought out to receive the light of the rising sun. The "rising sun" is the chief participant in the action described by

Voltaire. It is represented by Hercules — "Suffering Mankind" — and by his rise or emergence from a state of dim spirituality. While the body and the soul involved are those of two exoterically different persons, Adam-Kadmon and Sophia-Eve are only two different aspects of the same "Heavenly Man." The separation is itself symbolic. The mystical marriage implies divorce from earthly shells and earthly values. The "spectable of death" or deceptive veil of spiritual birth is overlooked and misunderstood by the majority of "passers-by." Few if any wonder for whom the bell tolls. Few if any conceive the reality of the rite of carnal release or wonder if it will materialize in their own destinies. The holy water and absent-minded prayers dispensed by the priests and by the strangers constitute a sad commentary on established religion. Compassion is absent. Insight is nil.

The miserly drops of spiritual stagnation would burn sacerdotal fingers were the priests to understand the true nature of proceedings. The Waters of Life are being imparted to the Lover of Truth — Mankind — *inside the house.* The "house" is the only temple worthy of the name: the tabernacle represented by each human being. The days of lucrative supremacy are over for spiritual middlemen.

The grief of the hero serves to convey an important tenet of occult philosophy:

> "Les âmes fortes ont des sentiments bien plus violents que les autres quand elles sont tendres." (Ch. XX, p. 317).

> ("Strong souls have far more violent feelings than do others when they are tender.")

"Strength" is connected with "tenderness" or sensitivity. The esoteric equivalence of "strength," knowledge and spirituality is added to mystical Love. Within the general context of the passage devoted to the "powers of the soul," the word "tender," when used in the sense of "new" or youthful — with the popular connoctation of "tender age" — in French "âge tendre" — suggests the status of a novice or neophyte. The exoteric statement of a well-known psychological fact conceals the warning issued to those who pursue secret knowledge. For better or for worse, all latent human energy released in occult experimentation is drastically intensified at the time of first contact with the invisible world. Hercules proves to be as "tender," — also "quick and wise" — as his feminine counterpart or mystical component: Saint Yves

> "There is a strange law in Occultism which has been ascertained and proven by thousands of years of experience; nor has it failed to de-

462

monstrate itself, almost in every case, during the years that the Theosophical Society has been in existence. As soon as anyone pledges himself as a "probationer," certain occult effects ensue. Of these the first is the *throwing outward* of everything latent in the nature of man; his faults, habits, qualities or subdued desires, whether good or bad, or indifferent. For instance, if a man be vain or a sensualist, or ambitious, whether by atavism or Karmic heirloom, those vices are sure to break out, even if he has hitherto successfully concealed and repressed them. They will come to the front irrepressibly, and he will have to fight a hundred times harder than before, until he kills all such tendencies in himself.

On the other hand, if he be good, generous, chaste and abstemious, or has any virtue hitherto latent and concealed in him, it will work its way out as irrepressibly as the rest. Thus a civilized man who hates to be considered a saint, and therefore assumes a mask, will not be able to conceal his true nature, whether base or noble.

THIS IS AN IMMUTABLE LAW IN THE DOMAIN OF THE OCCULT.

Its action is the more marked the more earnest and sincere the desire of the candidate, and the more deeply he has felt the reality and importance of his pledge." *The Secret Doctrine — Adyar Edition, —* p. 417, Vol. V).

The initiation of "Suffering Mankind" marks the release of previously inhibted and suppressed spirituality.

The transcended regions of incarnate illusion are subjects of final irony. In the midst of general confusion a message is received from court. The "servant" of the King's confessor sends a casually regretful message concerning the imprisonment of the hero. The letter contains an invitation to the royal palace for the prior, Hercules, and Gordon.

"Il écrivait à l'abbé de la Montagne, que *Sa Révérence était informée des aventures de son neveu, que sa prison n'était qu'une méprise, que ces petites disgrâces arrivaient fréquemment, qu'il ne fallait pas y faire attention. . . ."* (Ch. XX, p. 315).

("He had written to the abbé de la Montagne that *His Reverence was informed of the adventures of his nephew, that his imprisonment was only an error, that those small misfortunes frequently happened, and that one should not pay attention to them."*)

The boundless arrogance of the mighty speaks for itself on the exoteric plane. The misery and the persecution endured by Suffering Mankind over a period of centuries are shrugged off as matters of no consequence.

Esoteric validity underlies the text of the letter. The prison of flesh

463

or incarnation is only "an error" or an aspect of Maya. The "dungeon" forced on mankind by perverse beings is also an "error." It is a criminal blunder which is about to reap its just retribution. The Mayavic or illusive nature of the prison is undeniable. Human ability to transcended its "chains" has demonstrated itself. The preposterous exoteric appeasement relative to "small misfortunes" to which "one should not pay attention" is the esoteric prolongation of certain words of the old woman: "Those things are trivia and not worth mentioning." The "All is well" of Pangloss is echoed indirectly by unexpected spokesmen. The evolutionary outlook of occult philosophy is implicitly made part of orthodox "scriptures."

The esoteric validity of the letter seems to be intended by the ecclesiastical writer. The Church which can no longer withhold important knowledge from mankind decides to make the best possible adjustment to the new state of affairs. The omnivorous structure which turned Pagan Hercules into a Catholic saint is not above an attempt to assimilate a minimal dose of Maya. Voltaire seems to have anticipated the XXth Century era of "new theologians" and the frantic efforts of such persons to be on the rigth side of inevitable developments. Their task is a difficult one. The concept of Maya does not allow itself to be digested in isolation from related beliefs. Pantheism, cyclic evolution, Karma and reincarnation must be swallowed also bitter pills though they be. The remedy sought by sick spiritual structures has deadly potential for their dogma and for their existence.

The invitation to court receives the response which it deserves. Suffering Mankind may no longer be pacified or seduced with crumbs of political charisma. The letter from the "servant" or the King's confessor is torn to pieces and thrown into the face of the messenger. Fraudulent writings or "Scriptures" boomerang on impostors. The five hundred ounces of "silver" "borrowed" in ancient times demand and receive explanation.

The general commotion is described as follows:

> "The prior having read the letter aloud, his nephew, who was furious, mastering his anger for a moment, said nothing to be bearer; but turning toward the companion of his misfortunes, asked him what he thought of that style. Gordon replied to him: 'So that is the way men are treated like apes! They are beaten and then made to dance.' The Ingénu, recovering his true nature, which always returns in the great movements of the soul, tore the letter to pieces, and threw them at the nose of the messenger. 'Here is my reply.' His uncle, terrified, thought he could see thunder and twenty letters de cachet falling upon him. He quickly went to write and to excuse, as well as he could, what he was mistaking for the wild impulse of a young man, and what was actually the expression of a great soul." (Ch. XX, p. 316).

Two opposite conceptions of the Deity confront each other in the passage. The dreaded thunderbolt suggests the revenge of the anthropomorphic Jehovic God. The "expression of a great soul" is a manifestation of the "Great Soul of the Universe," the immaterial, Unknowable Deity of occult philosophy. The "Vice-God" is a figment of timorous imagination. The "Great Soul" is a forceful reality made manifest by the spirited stand of liberated mankind.

The expression "Grèat Soul" is the translation of the word *mahatma* which designates the "diamond-souled," the "Parentless" or the status of advanced beings whose "whole personality is merged in their compound sixth and seventh principles — or Atma-Buddhi." As was previously noted, "every Soul-endowed man is an Anupadaka — 'Parentless' — in a latent state." The spirited response of Hercules to contemptible attempts of appeasement demonstrates two facts. Suffering Mankind does have the potential of a "Great Soul." The potential in question is self-conscious and growing.

The esoteric aspect of Promethean Hercules which corresponds to the instructor of Mankind" or donor of "Divine Fire" is a full-fledged "Great Soul." The perfected being concealed in a human shell has performed his mission. His gift of spirit — "rhum" — magic — a talisman — and knowledge — evolutionary studies written in the dungeon of the Bastille and in the jail of incarnation — has borne fruit. The identity of a specific "Great Soul" is hinted: Voltaire himself.

The involvement of the author of *L'Ingénu* and of his writings seems to be supported by the reference to "lettres de cachet." As was previously noted, such "sealed letters" represent esoteric literature. The allusion to the thunder of Jehovah — a *dual*; male and female deity* — serves to convey the idea of 2. The *20* lettres de cachet complete the numeral which is often suggested by Voltaire in provocative contexts and which is openly featured in *Micromégas*. The "trial" of a specific "Great Soul" — Micromégas-Voltaire — a procedure which lasted *220* years seems to be involved.

The coming together of the universal Great Soul and of the now conscious Great Soul in ordinary man is the crux of *L'Ingénu*. Mankind rediscovers the Alpha and Omega of Being. Mankind has a rendezvous with its own "small voice." The site of the meeting is the Well of Knowledge.

> " 'It is strange,' I said to the little prince, 'everything is ready: the pulley, the bucket and the rope. . . .
> He laughed, touched the rope, worked the pulley. And the pulley

---

The Secret Doctrine, p. 18 Vol. I.

moaned as moans an old weathervane when the wind has been asleep
a long time.

—'You hear,' said the little prince, 'we are awakening this well and
it sings. . . .' " (*Le Petit Prince,* Ch. XXV).

The final chapter of *L'Ingénu* records the simultaneous occurrence of
two important events. the emergence of esoteric literature and the rejection of fraudulent religious scriptures. A cause-effect relationship is suggested to link both developments.

A similar synchronization may be noted in the second act of *Waiting for Godot.* Jehovic power declines as the Tree of Knowledge acquires leaves. Pozzo-Abel-Cain-Jehovah perceives that he is in trouble.
The faithfully awaited rendez-vous of Man and Truth does not materialize within the exoteric limits of the play. But its possibility continues
to exist for a future date. The mystery represented by the significance
of Godot may be solved by combining the idea of the divine — "God"
— the concept of a cyclic "force" of emanation and evolution represented
by the letter *o.* Cheated, baffled mankind has never stopped "waiting
for Godot."

> "Vladimir — We are not saints, but we are at the rendez-vous. How
> many people can say the same thing?
> Estragon — Masses of them.
> Vladimir — You think so?
> Estragon — I don't know.
> Vladimir — That's possible.
> Pozzo — Help!"

Pozzo begs for help which he is willing to buy. The equivalence of
money and time —which is established by a popular proverb — is also
suggested in the first Act of the play by a routine involving a watch.
The plea for assistance is a request for a reprieve — probably of a
few years:

> 'Pozzo — Help, I will give you money!
> Estragon — How much?
> Pozzo — One hundred francs.
> Estragon — That is not enough.
> ———
> Pozzo — Two hundred!
> Vladimir — Someone is coming."

The Jehovic father figure of *Death on the Installment Plan* is likewise
desperate. New methods of handling "letters" make his writing — or
scriptural — skills obsolete. The rising level of general education threat-
ens his means of existence. The "cabals" of ambitious young "clerks"

holding advanced "degrees" can only cause his downfall. The mediocre position which he has held in a "fire insurance" company *"for two and twenty consecutive years"** is imperiled by new trends or by evolution.

The horoscope of Jehovah is ever the same in esoteric writings. The Vice-God is slated to vanish at the end of Kali Yuga.**

Mankind ceases to deserve the name of "Ingénu" or "Candide" in the sense of "simple-minded one." But the meaning of inspired candor remains. The spiritual "candidate" to perfection becomes conscious of his own existence in the common man. Voltaire notes with wry amusement the long-overdue tribute paid by a professional "Christian" to Chrestos:

> "The abbé de Saint Yves almost knelt before the Ingénu who was no longer the *ingénu*." (Ch. XIX, p. 307).

The vain attempt to appease long-abused mankind shows that the wheel of evolution *has* turned. A general degree of sensitive intelligence begins to prevail. It is damaging to the conglomerate of sectarian and social structures which have conspired for centuries to blind, exploit, and oppress the average man. The "bold" response of Hercules to the message from court would have been suicidal in the age of *Candide*. It can no longer be squelched in the age of L'Ingénu. The era of forced servility to the Throne-Altar compound — or its Latter Day mutations — is over.

The declining fortune of the villainous bailli — or devil — is a heartening sign of the times. Spiritual terror is replaced by love and insight. The doom of the fiend is sealed.

No character is forgotten in the closing chapter. Having despatched the hateful bailli to his legitimate domain, Voltaire reports on the fate of the devout woman, Father Tout à Tous, and other members of the supporting cast. Gratification comes to all in forms dearest to their hearts. The gazette-like passage enumerating various delights — from gastronomy to ownership of dimonds and books — suggests the bliss of Devachanic sleep, a pleasurable repose reflecting dominant desires of the life last ended. Symbols of human aspiration and error seem to be uniformly sublimated into joy. The new motto of Gordon: *"Misfortune serves a purpose"* is suggested to apply to all types of human experience — or "fortune" — the sordid and criminal not excluded.

Hercules, Saint Yves and Gordon clearly outdistance all others on the path of Knowledge and True Being. The Sage concealed in L'Ingénu

---

*Words set off in special print in the original French text. (Letter from "Auguste").
**The Secret Doctrine, p. 420, Vol. II.

becomes "an excellent officer." He is noted to be "at the same time a warrior and a fearless philosopher." The emphasis placed on the expression "at the same time" seems intended to suggest the esoteric significance of spiritual "arms." The function of the word "and" is to fuse — not separate — the "warrior" and the "fearless philosopher." It is observed that the "officer" in question "has appeared in Paris under another name." The identity of the captive writer of captive substance who once found himself in the Bastille is offered to the imagination of the reader.

Mankind learns to "cultivate" its "garden," or, in the words of the Saturnian of *Micromégas*, to "propagate" the human "species." It is on earth "like a soldier on duty." The meaning of the "duty" inherent to "generation" begins to be grasped. It is a task of intellectual and spiritual "regeneration" which must be carried out during countless "passages" through the realm of materiality. It is the timeless labor of the candidate to perfection.

> "— the passage entrance and the sarcophagus in the King's chamber meant regeneration — not generation. (*The Secret Doctrine*, p. 470, Vol. II).

> "Qu'importe oubli, morsure, injustice insensée,
> Glaces et tourbillons de notre traversée?
> Sur la pierre des morts croît l'arbre de grandeur."
> (Alfred de Vigny, *La Bouteille à la mer*).

> ("What matter oblivion, barbs, insane injustice,
> The floes and eddies of our crossing?
> On the rock of the dead grows the tree of grandeur.")

The Panglossian "great goal of Nature" is the One Reality which must be sought through "generation" or material existence on physical, intellectual and spiritual planes. The "great goal" is the conquest of the Absolute, the immaterial "country where nothing lacks." For, in the words of Candide and Cacambo, "— it is absolutely necessary that there be one."* The awakened "genius" of the Ingénu perceives the meaning of the scheme of life. All must return to "the country where all is well" at the end of the Grand Cycle of Necessity. Armed with understanding of its own destiny, mankind is on its way to the remote goal of "perfection." "Another earth" is in the making.

L'Ingénu completes the trilogy begun in *Zadig* and continued in *Candide*, a sequence supplemented by the commentary of *Micromégas* on the fragmentary status of human knowledge. The decline and obscura-

---

Candide, Ch. XVII, p. 191.

tion of Pagan Truth which are reported in the first two stories — and which have a counterpart in the "death" of Abacaba — are followed in *L'Ingénu* by the rediscovery and vindication of the Universal Writ. The latter developments are announced in several prophetic episodes of *Zadig* and *Candide*. The restitution of "borrowed silver," the comparative tactics of Almona, the catch of the dazzled fisherman, the encounter with the six Kings and the "resurrection" of Pangloss all point to the same "turn of the wheel" which is personified by Hercules. The theme of redress eventually gained by mistreated Truth underlies the entire trilogy. The same theme seems to be stressed by the "amusing" reference to the "trial" of Micromégas.

The story describes a social system wary of visible abuse such as the practice of auto-da-fés. But the general surface of benevolence does not resist thoughtful examination. "Heretics" continue to be persecuted. Intellectual and spiritual free enterprise carries stiff penalties. The prostitution of sacred values goes on. Materialism and mediocrity reign supreme. The "pox" has expanded its treater of operations to the entire world. It has virtually destroyed the critical and sensitive faculties of the average Western man who plays the role of unwitting acessory to many crimes as well as the role of unconscious victim. The relative well-being enjoyed by the "Kerkabons" is the privilege of "right-thinking" persons. The family of "bons vivants" is an active element of the "Good Church." Those persons who do not fit into the same system are less fortunate. The mystique of the "finest castle in the world" continues to prevail whether the vengeful Lord of Thunder-ten-tronckh be dead or not. Western mankind tends to regard itself as the one chosen race. "Heretics" naturally belong to the "accursed race." Divine Reality is eclipsed by a social "realism" which is allergic to intrinsic values. Frustrated spirit seeks solace in compensatory exercise of power. The power "to do good" is scorned. Society is a hierarchy of major and lesser Jehovahs — male and female — who seek ultimate fulfillment in their vaunted ability to regard other persons as their own "creatures." Society is in the grip of an insidious yet unsubtle Jehovic syndrome.

Such is the realm of false well-being and false enlightenment which is visited by L'Ingénu. The very falsehood of it all bears fruit. The era of suspicion begins. Western mankind senses its "privation." It is ready for the "turn of the wheel."

The role played by the "Huron" — a representative of the New World — in the evolution of mankind seems to reflect an article of faith of the Secret Doctrine. It is anticipated that America will be the cradle of a new race characterized by a high degree of spirituality:

469

"Since the beginning of the Atlantean Race many million years have passed, yet we find the last of the Atlantaans, still mixed up with the Aryan element, 11,000 years ago. This shows the enormous overlapping of one race over the race which succeeds it, though in characters and external type the elder loses its characteristics, and assumes the new features of the younger race. This is proved in all the formations of mixed human races. Now, Occult philosophy teaches that even now, under our very eyes, the new Race and Races are preparing to be formed, and that it is in America that the transformation will take place, and has already silently commenced.

— Mankind will not grow again into giant bodies as in the case of the Lemurians and the Atlanteans; because while the evolution of the Fourth Race led the latter down to the very bottom of materiality in its physical development, the present Race is on its ascending arc; and the Sixth will be rapidly growing out of its bonds of matter, and even of flesh.

Thus it is the mankind of the New world — one by far the senior of our Old one, a fact men had also forgotten — of *Pâtâla* (the Antipodes, or the Nether World, as America is called in India), whose mission and Karma it is, to sow the seeds for a forthcoming, grander and far more glorious Race than any of those we know of at present." (*The Secret Doctrine*, pp. 444-46, Vol. II).

L'Ingénu deals primarily with a modern phase of Fifth Race evolution. But the subject segment of time is situated within the framework of occult genesis. Human lineage is traced, spanning the era of ethereal men, bi-sexual mankind, Atlantean giants, and recorded history down to the late XVIIth Century. The latter period which is an esoteric blind for Voltaire's own times serves as a basis of projection into the future. The era of UNVEILED TRUTH and the hidden meaning of the death of Saint Yves seem to involve the XIXth Century and the publication of the Secret Doctrine. The gradual disappearance of sectarianism seems to involve our own times. The story is overshadowed by "the great goal of Nature": the distant yet "necessary" universal Nirvâna. The veiled scope of the Voltairian trilogy in general and of *L'Ingénu* in particular is as timeless as the path from the Alpha to the Omega of Being.

The story follows the pattern of a Cycle unfolding under the sign of *Meru*, the shifting "Mountain" or North Pole. The terrestrial focus of cyclic activity is the reunion of several sets of "separated twins." The omnipresence of Spirit in Matter is rediscovered in an era which seems to correspond to the atomic age. The "microcosm" finds its place within a far greater world. Man is no longer divorced in his own mind from the divine reality of which he carries potencies within himself. Mankind begins to grasp what is scientific in metaphysics and metaphysical in science. Rationality and intuition are found to be inseparable from each other. The source of Christianity is traced to ancient Paganism

470

and to the genuine message of Christ. The oneness of transcendental Knowledge and Ethics can no longer be regarded as a pious dream. It is gradually recognized as imperious reality.

The date July 15, 1698 which is in conjunction with "the Mountain" at the beginning of *L'Ingénu* should probably be connected with the intellectual and spiritual "shifting of poles" which forms the hidden core of the story. *Meru*, America, is deeply involved in the "turn of the wheel."

The veiled structure of the Voltairian "True Story" is a spectacular convergence of evolutionary curves embodying and transcending earthly concepts of Time and Space. We are told by Plato that "God geometrizes." So does Voltaire.

NUMBERS

The Voltairian trilogy devoted to Man in Search of Truth contains an abundance of significant numbers. *Candide* and *L'Ingénu* deserve special numerological notice.

The lover of Cunégonde is situated within the perspective of occult evolution in Chapter II. His height — 5'5" — suggests that he represents the Fifth Race. The illicit "walk" or "trip" of Candide which is savagely punished by military justice is an abortive attempt to return to the source — and destination — of Being. It is viewed with the same disfavor as the abortive attempt to "raise the veil" which marks the beginning of the story. The presence of 5 which points to the Fifth Race also suggests the date when the Age of Iron — or Kali Yuga — is believed to have begun. Mme Blavatsky once wrote that the "Black Age" had begun "about 5,000 years" before her time. Says the writer of the Secret Doctrine, "In about nine years hence, the first cycle of the first five millenniums, that began with the great cycle of the Kali Yuga will end."* The probable reference of Voltaire to the Kali Yuga — an era which he mentions by name in *Le Mondain* — is consistent with the evolutionary setting of *Candide*: an age of evil and strife such as can be expected at the "bottom" of a cycle.

The forbidden "walk" of Candide is shorter than the corresponding excursion of Hercules in Chapter II of *L'Ingénu*. The lover of the woman who will emerge as UNVEILED TRUTH freely travels 2 or 3 leagues. The lover of abused and mutilated Truth is caught before he has covered 2 leagues. The seemingly slight difference reflects a short but important segment of the evolutionary curve. The longer "trip" of Hercules is consistent with an approaching period of spiritual rebirth during which the horizons of mankind are markedly broadened. It is consistent with the meaningful "turn of the wheel" which is the specific raison d'être of *L'Ingénu*.

The spirited "trip" of Hercules brings him back to the Second Race — ethereal being — if one allows it the maximum of *3 leagues*. The forced "run" of Candide brings him to the "Third Race." The distance actually covered does not seem to exceed the limits of the era of Atlantean giants. The relevance of Atlantean giants is also suggested by the

---

*The Morning of the Magicians, p. 206.

size of the recruiters. The young hero is caught by 4 soldiers whose height is 6' — a titanic stature in the eyes of Candide. The combination of 4 and tall build seems calculated to bring to mind Fourth Race Atlantean giants. The "Bulgarians" of *Candide* are — among other things — transparent targets of anti-Prussian satire. The Germanic and Atlantean aspects of the "Walk" of Candide are subtly connected. Voltaire seems to call esoteric attention to the link which is said to exist between Nordic Aryan races and the sunken continent of Atlantis, a link which is also suggested to exist in *L'Ingénu*. It is interesting to note that the same racial tie which is stressed in occult teachings eventually became part of the Nazi mystique tortuously evolved by Horbiger, the Moses of Hitlerism. Rauschning, a prominent Nazi once spoke as follows: " 'At bottom, every German has one foot in Atlantis.' "*

Candide is given a "choice" between 36 vicious beatings and 12 lead bullets in the head. It soon becomes apparent that the Panglossian "effect" of each procedure is the same loss of the same "coat of skin." The esoteric equivalence of 36 and 12 and the three-to-one relationship existing between both numbers suggests the concept of Three in One which has numerous meanings in occult philosophy including the Oneness of Time. The latter theme is illustrated in the passage by an interesting use of tenses.

> "He followed his urge, one fine spring day, to go for a walk, walking straight ahead, believing that it was a privilege of the human specie, as of the animal specie, to use its legs for its pleasure. He had not covered two leagues when four other heroes who were six feet tall reach him, bind him, lead him into a dungeon. He was asked juridically which he preferred of being whipped thirty-six times by the whole regiment or of receiving all at once twelve lead bullets in the brains. He protested in vain that wills are free, and that he wanted neither alternative, he had to choose; he determined, by virtue of the gift of God which is named liberty, to pass thirty-six times through the sticks; he weathered two walks. The regiment was made up of two thousand men; that made him four thousand blows from sticks, which, from the nape of the neck all the way to his posterior, exposed the muscles and the nerves. As they were getting ready for the third race, Candide. unable to stand any more, asked as a favor that they have the kindness of crushing his skull; he obtained this favor; he has a blinding strip placed on his eyes, he is made to kneel. The King of the Bulgarians passes in that moment asks about the crime of the patient; and, as that King had a great genius, he understood, through all that he learned about Candide, that he was a young metaphysician very ignorant of things of the world, and he granted him his grace with a

*The Morning of the Magicians, p. 206.

473

clemency which will be praised in all the newspapers and in all centuries."

The story is first reported in the past or perfect, the tense of narration. The dramatic impact of the passage of the King and the preparations for execution are related in the present. The imperfect is also used. It is finally predicted that the clemency of the King will be praised forever and ever. Past, present, and future are all fused in the meaningful incident. Voltaire seems to suggest that even a doomed "trip" may reveal the Oneness of Time. The fact that Time is represented as Space announces the immaterial compound of which the palace of Eldorado is made.

The emphatic presence of the number 36 seems calculated to suggest the 360 degrees of a circle or the cycle of "necessity" which is a major element of Voltairian writings in general and of *Candide* in particular. Within the perspective of the Grand Cycle the terrestrial concept of Time is virtually abolished. The theme of "necessity" is present. Candide is first placed into a "dungeon" symbolizing the "dungeon" of flesh. The only possible "escape" contemplated by the authorities leads to the firing squad or to loss of one's skin. No alternative is offered between a purely vegetative existence and no existence at all. The occult concept of "necessity" becomes the Judaeo-Christian concept of "punishment." Such myths are edifying commentaries on prevailing "Westphalian" dogma. The briefly glimpsed Oneness of Time and the cyclic scheme of the Universe belong to the realm of spiritual free enterprise which can be fatal to "Westphalian" powers. Such insights — or "good trips" — must be suppressed. Cyclic vision must be "blindfolded" and "killed" in the physical person of the "patient." It is regarded as an illness which may be regrettably contagious. The *few* circular bowls relegated to the kitchen of Jehovah in a final chapter of *Candide* reflect the same determination to conceal the cyclic design of the Universe.

The esoteric symbolism of the cross which is suggested by 2 and 4 — 2000 men and 4000 blows — seems to have the same function as does the presence of the crucifix in the story of the wicked sailor. The theme of evolutionary descent into materiality which is woven into the text — beginning with the 350 lbs. of Mme la baronne — is also conveyed by one meaning of the cross:

"The Cross within a circle symbolizes pure Pantheism; when the Cross was left uninscribed, it became phallic." (*The Secret Doctrine*, p. 5, Vol. I).

The suggested presence of the cross uninscribed is consistent with the obsessive phallicism of the era depicted in *Candide*.

The reception of Candide and Cacambo at the inn of Eldorado contains another suggestion of the cross — *and* circle — as well as an abundance of numbers. The occasion is described as follows:

"Aussitôt, deux garçons et deux filles de l'hôtellerie, vêtus de drap d'or, et les cheveux noués avec des rubans, les invitent à se mettre à la table de l'hôte. On servit quatre potages garnis chacun de deux perroquets, un contour bouilli qui pesait deux cent livres, deux singes rôtis d'un goût excellent, trois cents colibris dans un plat, et six cents oiseaux-mouches dans un autre; des ragoûts exquis, des pâtisseries délicieuses; le tout dans des plats d'une espèce de cristal de roche. Les garçons et les filles de l'hôtellerie versaient plusieurs liqueurs faites de canne de sucre." (Ch. XVIII, p. 190).

("Immediately, two boys and two girls of the inn, wearing cloth of gold, and having their hair tied with ribbons, invite them to sit at the table with the host. Four soups were served which all contained two parrots, one boiled condor weighing two hundred pounds, two roasted monkeys having an excellent flavor, three hundred humming birds in a dish, and six hundred colibris in another; some exquisite stews, delicious pastries; all of it on platters made of a sort of rock crystal. The boys and girls of the inn poured several liquors made out of sugar-cane.")

The even balance of the sexes is illustrated by the presence of 2 boys and 2 girls wearing identical attire. The relevance of Adam-Kadmon, the bi-sexual prototype of mankind, is suggested. It is consistent with the return to the source represented by the "trip" to Eldorado. The symbolism of the cross is again suggested by the numbers 2 and 4. The word "contour" — exoterically designating a condor — means a rounded outline or circle. The combination of cross and circle may be connected with: 1) physical and spiritual birth; 2) "Pure Pantheism;" and 3) Material man as he exists in his present form pictured against the background of his spiritual origin itself represented by a circle:

"— if the Deity, and his universe, and the stellar bodies are to be conceived as spheroidal, this shape would be archetypal man's. As his enveloping shell grew heavier, there came the necessity for limbs, and limbs sprouted. If we fancy a man with arms and legs naturally extended at the same angle, by backing him against the circle that symbolizes his prior shape as spirit, we would have the very figure described by Plato: the cross within a circle." (*Isis Unveiled*, p. 469, Vol. 2).

The evolutionary connection between limbs and a more or less materialized condition of existence is established at the beginning of *Candide*. The hero's ability to "walk" — with legs and otherwise — is affected by three runs or "races." The wicked sailor gone berserk on the ruins of Lisbon boasts of his demonstrated ability to "walk" on the cross. The desecration of the crucifix which he has committed 4 times links him to the black magic for which certain groups of Fourth Race Atlanteans are notorious. "Limbs" or physical attributes are suggested by "Head" and "blood" in the case of the sailor. The hybrid creatures of Chapter XVI are connected with the same stage of human development. They are designated as "one-*quarter* men." Their ability to chase "two stark-naked girls who were running lightly on the edge of the meadow" gives ample proof of the fitness of their "limbs." The meadow where the strange episode takes place contains several streams which *cross* one another. In summary, the combination of cross and "contour" is related to the gradual process of human materialization various stages of which are insistently suggested in the writings of Voltaire.

The reference to parrots — speaking and winged creatures — is a probable allusion to the allegorical "winged" ancestry of Mankind of the first two Races. The reference to monkeys corresponds to the stage of Atlantean bestiality which produced hybrid species. The joint presence of the "contour" or circle and of "winged" or ethereal creatures seems calculated to bring to mind the virtually immaterial beings which preceded the middle of the Third Race. It may also suggest a far greater cycle than a Race. The presence of the number *3* — "three hundred huming-birds" may be linked to the Third *Round*, the period during which various types of animal life originated:

> "The amphibia, birds, reptiles, fishes, etc., are the results of the Third Round — " (*The Secret Doctrine*, p. 684, Vol. II).

Number *3* may further suggest the period of 300,000,000 years which saw the development of mineral and vegetable existence, an epoch which preceded the appearance of animal life. The number *6* — "six hundred colibris" — yields the number 18 when multiplied by its companion *3*. The product of 18 may have been calculated to call esoteric attention to the age of physical man. The Secret Doctrine teaches that the first physical men made their appearance on earth 18,000,000 years ago.

> "The Secret Doctrine maintains that, — physical Humanity has existed upon it (our globe) for the last 18,000,000 years. This period was preceded by 300,000,000 years of the mineral and vegetable development." (*The Secret Doctrine*, p. 149, Vol. II).

The relevance of minerals seems to be suggested by vessels made of "rock crystal." The connection with vegetal life seems to be made through the cereals which are necessary to obtain flour and "pastries" and through reference to "sugar-cane." Voltaire seems to call esoteric attention to an entire Manvantara and to the evolution of all forms of life. It is logical that such an immense vista should by opened to those who travel near the "source" while aborted "trips" undertaken in "Westphalia" barely cover 2 leagues or Races.

It may be noted in passing that the reference to "rock crystal" and "liquor" carries meaningful esoteric substance. As was previously noted, a rock may represent an Interpreter of the Secret Doctrine. Crystal is a common symbol of "the vision and purity of the JUST."* Liquor is obviously "spirit." Transcendental knowledge and vision are linked to the immense revelation of a Day of Brahma.

The preparation of the boiled "contour" involves fire and water. An allusion to cyclic recurrence of fire and water-connected cataclysms is likely. Such a hint seems to be supported by the report of "great revolutions" witnessed by a resident of Eldorado. Historical "revolutions" such as the invasion of the New World by the Spaniards serve as an esoteric front for more ancient upheavals. The same occult concept of Deluge and Ecyprosis is linked in Chapter V of *Candide* to the earthquake of Lisbon.

The four different soups which are served to the travelers may correspond to the four ages of Mankind which preceded our own era or Kali yug. A passage of *Manu* (book i) defines the four ages in terms of the decreasing longevity of mankind:

> " 'In the first age, neither sickness nor suffering were known. Men lived for centuries.'
> This was in the Krita or Satya-yug.
> 'The Krita-yug is the type of justice. The *bull* which stands firm on its four legs is its image;. man adheres to truth, and evil does not as yet direct his actions.' But in each of the following ages primitive human life loses one-fourth of its duration, that is to say, in Treta-yug man lives 300, in Dwapara-yug 200, and in Kali yug, or our own age, but 100 years, generally, at the most." (*Isis Unveiled*, p.. 467-68, Vol 2).

The importance of longevity is stressed by the age of a resident of Eldorado who is 172 years old. The four soups which are served to Candide and Cacambo may constitute an allusion to the 4 ages and to the one-fourth loss of longevity which marked the arrival of each new age. The 300 huming-birds may correspond to the average life expectancy in Treta-yug: 300 years. The 2 monkeys and the one bird weighing 200 lbs may suggest the 200 years of life assigned to Man

---

*Alfred de Vigny, *Les Oracles*.

in Dwapara-yug. The 1 "contour" which is prominently heavy or material may represent the bottom of a cycle and the life expectancy of 100 years which is regarded as an approximate maximum for modern mankind.

The joint presence of 300 "colibris" and 600 "oiseaux-mouches" suggests a correspondence between Third and Six Race mankind. Such a connection may be intended to reflect the occult view according to which: "—we are approaching the time when the pendulum of evolution will direct its swing decidedly upwards, bringing Humanity on a parallel line with the primitive third Root-Race in Spirituality." The synonymous essence of the words "colibri" and "oiseau-mouche" tends to support the correspondence. According to the Larousse Dictionary, the former term is the generic name for the latter "humming-bird." The artificial separation of similar types of creatures suggests the future recovery of a lost "winged" status. The period of time elapsing between the Third and the Sixth Race is an era of illusory division or dense Mayavic darkness during which the oneness of spiritual essence is lost to the sight of men.

The same juxtaposition of 300 and 600 suggests a relationship of one-half such as the approximate equilibrium between matter and spirit prevailing in our present sub-cycle. The same proportion of one-half may designate the half-way point of the present Fifth Race reached by modern mankind.

The product of 3 by 6 may also suggest the 180 degrees represented by the sum of the angles of a triangle. As was previously noted, the triangle is rich in occult symbolism. The equilateral triangle suggested by 6 — 60 degrees — is related to the "consubstantiality of the (manifested) Spirit, matter, and the Universe."* Such a meaning is compatible with the esoteric significance of the supper in which "spirit" is served and every kingdom of Nature is represented. The equilateral triangle is a commonly used representation of the higher faculties of Man: Manas, Buddhi, and Atma which are known collectively as the Upper Triad. The same superior attributes of Man find their highest expression in the spiritual land of Eldorado, the realm of "blissful omniscience."

The repetition of 2 and the suggestion of an equilateral triangle point to the Double Triangle commonly known as the Seal of Solomon. As was noted in a previous chapter, one triangle descends into matter, the world of Form or "Rupa." The other rises toward spirituality, the "Formless" or Arupa. The Double Triangle also symbolizes the periodic

---

*The Secret Doctrine, p. 614, Vol. I.

inversion of the poles and the resulting upheavals in continental structures.* The theme of "fall" and "rise" is consistent with the general evolutionary picture concealed in *Candide*. The "great revolutions" are clearly relevant to Chapter XVIII.

The suggested Seal of Solomon has a mutilated counterpart in the description of the auto-da-fé featured in Chapter VI. The paper miter placed on the head of Candide is decorated with inverted flames. The flames which appear on the miter of Pangloss are upright. The Double Triangle is present on two different persons or in disassembled form. The divorce is symbolic of an age in which spirituality and "the real world" are poles apart in the conception of men. It is also meaningful where the spiritual status of the heroes is concerned. Candide — ordinary Man in Search of Truth — has a spark of spiritual fire. But his "fire" tends to be forced down by personal weakness and by persecution. Pangloss — the adept — is spiritually unaffected by general trends. The symbolic flames of the master are directed — stubbornly — upwards as are his optimistic pronouncements: "All is well." "All is for the best." One may also note that the devils which adorn the miter of Candide are "unarmed." Corresponding devils on the couvre-chef of Pangloss are equipped with claws and tails. Voltaire seems to court a comparison between the suggested consubstantiality of Spirit and Matter which underlies the chapters devoted to Eldorado and their status of artificially separated "twins" in "Westphalia."

The conversation of Candide and Cacambo with the elderly resident of Eldorado contains a meaningful number. The new friend of the travelers is 172 years old. His longevity situates him beyond the beginning of Kali Yuga, the present age of mankind. His age seems calculated to bring to mind the length of Satya-yug. It is also equal to the length of a *sandhi* "or the time when day and night border on each other, morning and evening twilight:"

> "The Satya-yug and Buddhistic cycles of chronology would make a mathematician stand aghast at the array of ciphers. The Mahakalpa embraces an untold number of periods far back in the antediluvian ages. Their system comprises a kalpa or grand period of 4,320,000,000 years, which they divided into four lesser yugas, running as follows:

1st — Satya yug	1,728,000	years
2nd — Treta yug	1,296,000	,,
3rd — Dvapa yug	864,000	,,
4th — Kali yug	432,000	,,

Total 4,320,000

Ibid., pp. 359-60, Vol. II.

which makes one divine age of Maha-yug; seventy-one Maha yugs makes 306,720,000 years, to which is added a sandhi (or the time when day and night border on each other, morning and evening twilight), equal to a Satya-yug, 1,728,000, make a manvantara of 308,448,000 years; fourteen manvantaras make 4,318,272,000 years; to which must be added a sandhi to begin the kalpa, 1,728,000 years, making the kalpa or grand period of 4,320,000,000 of years." (*Isis Unveiled*, pp. 31-32, Vol. 1).

The age of the elder corresponds esoterically to the duration of a sandhi or interval linking the present Kali Yug to the preceding period (Dvapa yug). The father of the sage is known to have witnessed "great revolutions." The numerical attributes of the new friend of Candide and Cacambo suggest that his parent represents the age preceding the "sandhi" or 1,728,000 years or Dvapa yug. The latter period is said to have lasted 864,000 years. The "great revolution" witnessed by the father of the elderly man is therefore likely to be one of the several sinkings of Atlantis, an event which took place 850,000 years ago.*

The conversation with the aged Peruvian contains a reference to the occult concept of the ternary supplemented by the quaternary a concept which is also suggested in *Micromégas*. Overt enumeration of 2,3 and 4 amounts to designation of the One Supreme Being.

" 'Do you worship only one God?' said Cacambo, who always served as the interpreter of the doubts of Candide. 'Apparently,' said the old man 'there are neither two, nor three, nor four.' "

"The mystic Decad (of Pythagoras) 1 plus 2 plus 3 plus 4 $= 10$ is a way of expressing this idea. The One is God; the Two matter; the Three, combining Monad and Duad and partaking of the nature of both is the phenomenal world; the Tetrad, or form of perfection, expresses the emptiness of all, and the Decad, or sum of all, involves the entire cosmos." (*Isis Unveiled*, p. xvi, Vol. 1).

Divine Unity is also stressed by a profusion of precious materials and stones found at the residence of the elderly man. The door is *only* silver. The walls are *only* gold. The antechamber is set with *mere* rubies and emeralds. The house is described as "quite simple." "— but the order in which all" is arranged adequately "compensates "that extreme simplicity." The label of "simplicity" must be read esoterically to be fully savored. *All* is simple and harmonious in spite — or because — of seeming wealth and diversity — because All is One.

Numbers are many in the brief description of the trip to the royal palace.

The Secret Doctrine, p. 332, Vol. II.

"Après cette longue conversation, le bon vieillard fit atteler un carosse à six moutons, et donna douze de ses domestiques aux deux voyageurs pour les conduire à la cour. Candide et Cacambo montent en carrosse; les six moutons volaient, et en moins de quatre heures on arriva au palais du roi situé à un bout de la capitale." (Ch. XVIII, p. 193).

("After this long conversation, the kindly elder had six sheep harnessed to a coach, and gave twelve of his servants to the two travellers to take them to court Candide and Cacambo get into the coach, the six sheep were flying, and in less than four hours the palace of the King located at one end of the capital is reached.")

The 6 sheep and their collective ability to "fly" seem to represent the five lower planes of human consciousness which are vehicles of Divine Intuition: Buddhi, the sixth principle. Their animal or matter-connected nature contains in latent form the spiritual energies which can become manifest as "the conveyances of up there." Such energies are necessarily released and used in the spiritual country of Eldorado. The seventh or highest principle — Atma — will be the portal of the royal palace, the symbolic Gate to the Highest. It will be made of an unknowable or immaterial substance. It will be reached through the path of ecstasy:

"Candide hearing these statements remained in ecstasy and thought within himself: 'This is quite different from Westphalia and from the castle of his lordship the baron: had our friend Pangloss seen Eldorado, he would not have said that the castle of Thunder-ten-tronckh was what is best on earth: there is no doubt about it one must travel.'" (Ch. XVIII, p. 193).

The connected — yet separated — presentation of the lower 6 principles and of the Highest is identical to the relationship linking the 6 monarchs of Chapter XXVI and the "diamond" brought from Eldorado. Atma is indissolubly bound to the human individual. But it is exempt from encasement in matter.

The prominence of 6 may also be connected with the idea of a voyage through Time leading to the advanced state of spirituality which is expected to prevail in the Sixth Race. The idea of spatial travel is fused with the number of time units required to cover a certain distance: 4 hours or less. The passage describing the trip to the royal palace is characterized by the same fluid use of tenses which marked a less pleasant and a less fruitful excursion: the attempted "walk abroad" of Candide. The perfect, the imperfect and the present are used. The future also appears in the concurrent dialogue. The King is expected to receive the travelers in a manner "which will not displease" them. The trip which

481

takes less than 4 hours — perhaps covering the time span of 3 Races — suggests once again a departure from material realms achieved with the aid of "speedy" conveyances fusing Time and Space. Voltaire seems to stress again the evolutionary gap separating the Third from the Sixth Race or the essential identity of 300 colibris and 600 oiseaux-mouches. The evolutionary meaning of the passage appears to be supported by the symbolism of the "harness" — or "yoke", "collar, "necklace" — representing Karma. The "wheels" which may be presumed to propel the "fllying" coach are also significant.

The importance of 6 is also suggested by the relationship existing between 2 travelers and 12 servants. The esoteric equivalence of the latter word suggests another reminder of the septenary constitution of Man — and Cosmos. Each "traveller" or eternal Spirit Atma — is assigned six subordinates as he performs his pilgrimage through incarnation. The numbers 6 and 12 are also associated with the chronology of Cosmos in the Secret Doctrine.

> "It was taught in the *inner* temples that this visible universe of spirit and matter is but the concrete image of the ideal abstraction; it was built on the model of the first DIVINE IDEA. Thus our universe existed from Eternity in a latent state. The soul animating this purely spiritual universe is the central sun, the highest deity itself. It was not the *One* who built the concrete form of the idea, but the first-begotten; and as it was constructed on the geometrical figure of the dodecahedron, the first begotten 'was pleased to employ twelve thousand years in its creation.'
>
> The latter number is expressed in the Tyrrhenian cosmogony, which shows man created in the sixth millennium. This agrees with the Egyptian theory of 6,000 'years' and with the Hebrew computation. But it is the exoteric form of it. The *secret* computation explains that the 'twelve thousand and the 6,000 years' are YEARS OF BRAHMA — one Day of Brahma being equal to 4,320,000,000 years." (*The Secret Doctrine*, p. 340, Vol. I).

The relevance of 24 is suggested by the combination of 2 and 12. The importance of 12 will also be stressed in the report of the reception at the royal palace. Voltaire may have wished to place the regions of Eldorado under the 12 signs of the Zodiac within the 12,000 year-exoteric framework of occult tradition. The suggested number 24 may then point to the 24,000 years thought to be required by each revolution of the great "wheel."* The connection which is made by Pythagoras between the Zodiac and the "music of the spheres."** seems to be made

---

The Secret Doctrine, p. 347, Vol. V, *Adyar Edition*.
**The Secret Doctrine*, p. 601, Vol. II.

by Voltaire also. "A very pleasant music" is heard at the inn. 2000 musicians perform at the royal palace. The 12 servants who serve as guides during the voyage through Time and Space probably represent — among other things — the 12 sectors of the Zodiac. As was previously noted, the word "guides" carries the esoteric meaning of "planets" and "Zodiacal signs."*

The portal of the royal palace — an improved version of the "pearly gates" — is full of mathematical interest:

> "The portal was two hundred and twenty feet high and one hundred feet wide."

The significance of 220 will be shown to be prophetic in a subsequent chapter of the present study. It is therefore connected with Time. The construction "material" of the monument is indescribable:

> "— it is impossible to express what its building material was."

Exoteric description of the material involved is clearly out of question. The immaterial essence of the portal cannot be revealed without serious damage to esotericism. Another consideration may be taken into account. The average Western mind finds it difficult to conceive an imponderable substance.

Time is a likely component of the symbolic "threshhold" the Kingdom of Perfection is entered at the term of a long, hazardous voyage. Space is represented by precise dimensions. The cosmic plane of "blissful omniscience" is situated where earthly time and space have been transcended and fused as they are in the astronomical concept of light years.

The portal is 100 feet wide. The presence of the multiple of 10 is another probable reference to the Pythagorean Decad representing the entire cosmos. The same number may have been intended to bring to mind the numeral 10,000 which is related to certain "great revolutions." Occult philosophy teaches that the displacement of ocean beds takes place every decimillennium.** The number 10,000 is embodied in the very structure of the portal. A relationship of 5 to 11 exists between the dimensions of the rectangle. The surface of the entrance is 22,000 sq. ft. Five elevenths of 22,000 amount to 10,000.

The divine essence which prevails in the royal palace is suggested by the lack of reference to "windows." The castle of Thunder-ten-tronckh

---

*The Secret Doctrine, p. 332, Vol. V, Adyar Edition.
**Isis Unveiled, p. 31, Vol. 1.

and its sensory outlook have been left far behind. The supremacy of *inner lights* seems absolute.

The reception at the royal palace is characterized by symmetry:

"Twenty beautiful girls of the guard received Candide and Cacambo upon their descent from the coach, led them to the baths, dressed them in robes made out of humming-bird down fabric, whereupon the Grand men officers and the Grand women officers of the crown led them to the apartment of His Majesty, between two rows of one thousand musicians each, according to ordinary custom. When they came near the throne room, Cacambo asked a Grand Officer how one should proceed in order to salute His Majesty; whether one threw oneself to the ground on one's knees or belly; whether one placed one's hands on one's head or one's behind; whether one licked the dust of the room; in short what the ritual was. The custom,' said the Grand Officer, 'is to embrace the King and to kiss him on both sides.'"

The presence of 2 and 20 seems calculated to stress again 220.

The spiritual country of Eldorado is the realm of Love as well as Knowledge. The ceremony of introduction to the King is one detail among many showing conclusively that the country in question is "worth more than Westphalia." The more or less ridiculous rituals of self-abasement prevailing in less exalted spheres such as the French court suffer in comparison. The protocol of Eldorado combines universal love and universal dignity.

Eldorado is the immaterial land of transcended "necessity." The arrival at the royal palace naturally coincides with release from the Karmic "wheels" of the "coach." It is marked by a rite of purification or symbolic "bath." The substance of which the robes are made comes from former "winged" or spiritual creatures. The various parts of the "coat of skin" which are enumerated by Cacambo play no part on the grand occasion. The importance of the physical body is dwarfed by the supremacy of spiritual attributes. The ceremony of homage to the "crown" is a probable allusion to the esoteric concept of *Kether* which represents the Upper Triad.*

The total number of kisses to be received by the King is 4. The esoteric combination of 3 — the "Crown" — and 4 seems to reflect the septenary view of Man, Cosmos, and Matters. The "kisses" themselves suggest an allusion to the symbolism used by Alchemists:

"— all the matter of the Universe, when analyzed by science to its ultimates, can be reduced to four elements only — carbon oxygen,

---

The Secret Doctrine, p. 592, Vol. II.

nitrogen, and hydrogen: and — the three primaries, the noumenoi of the four, or graduated Spirit or Force, have remained a *terra incognita* and mere speculations, names, to exact Science. Her servants must believe in and study first the primary causes, before they can hope to fathom the nature and acquaint themselves with the potentialities of the effects. Thus, while the men of Western learning had, and still have, the four, or matter to toy with, the Eastern Occultists and their disciples, the great alchemists the world over, have the whole septenate to study from. As those Alchemists have it: — 'When the Three and the Four kiss each other, the Quaternary joins its middle nature with that of the Triangle,' (or Triad, i.e., the face of one of its plane surfaces becoming the middle face of the other), and 'becomes a cube; then only does it (the cube unfolded) become the vehicle and the number of LIFE, the Father-Mother SEVEN.'" *The Secret Doctrine,* pp. 592-93, Vol. II).

The "kissing" or 3 and 4 fits into the esoteric reality of Eldorado. The "consubstantiality of the (manifested) Spirit, matter, and the "Universe" which is suggested in another part of the chapter is involved. The septenary structure of Man and Cosmos is likewise embraced by the all-embracing "kiss" of the Crown.

The emphasis placed on 2 seems to oppose the characteristic of oneness which is stressed in the chapter and which is inherent to the realm of True Being. The duad is a Pythagorean representation of Matter. But the dividing line between Candide and Cacambo which is esoterically non-existent tends to be further blurred by the unifying force of the "Crown." The 2 sides of the royal face — probably Matter and Spirit — are external aspects of the same profound unity. They are also reminiscent of the mythological God Janus whose two faces gaze simultaneously on the past and the future. The latter variety of second sight is inherent to the spiritual consciousness represented by Eldorado, a state in which the Oneness of Time is repeatedly suggested. The equal participation of the sexes which is demonstrated by the agency of men and women "Grand Officers" is consistent with the plane of spiritual achievement of "Crown" or Upper Triad which is sexless. The same balance is suggestive of the "Heavenly Man." It is only on inferior planes of differentiated matter that one of the male-female components predominates. The two groups of musicians may be inferred to produce unison or harmony. In summary the surface dualism of the passage covers an element of solid unity.

The departure from Eldorado requires an extraordinary machine. The device is built in 15 days by 3,000 "good physicists." The division of 3,000 by 15 yields 200. The cost of the machine is 20,000,000 pounds. "Fifteen days" is the commonly used French expression for "2 weeks." The final passage of the chapter seems designed to draw further attention to 2 in general and *220* in particular.

485

The separation of Candide from the "King" or "Crown" reflects the difficulty encountered by the average "Westphalian" in gaining permanent access to high spiritual planes. The "Kingdom of Heaven" which is "within" can only be envisioned in transient experience. As Voltaire noted in the *Poem on the Disaster of Lisbon*, "Man foreign to the Self by man is ignored."

The estrangement from the King seems to have another significance. As was previously noted, the word "King" can convey the meaning of a "Sage on earth." The separation of the average Western Man from a "Sage" — such as the "ancient" one who amused himself by writing *Zadig* and *Candide* — appears to be linked to the number 220. The brief stay in Eldorado suggests — among other things — that the divine reality of a great message is dimly sensed. But the intuitive perception of Western man is too vague, fitful, and repressed for a full revelation or genuine "lifting of the veil." The texts of a specific "writer whose works Christendom cannot read"* will not be fully understood by the average "Westphalian" for some time. The "trial" of a certain author which lasted 220 years seems to be involved.

The importance of 220 is suggested on the exoteric surfaces of *Micromégas* and *Candide*. The number represents the duration of a "trial" in the former story and the height of a portal in the latter. The total formula is that of a Time-Space compound. Numerous esoteric allusion to the same number may be found in the trilogy. Their appearance seems to generally coincide with the presence of certain themes.

The unveiling of Astarté by Zadig seems to be connected with the intriguing number. Astarté resumes speaking "20 times." The number of protagonists which is 2 is tressed by the expression "both" — "tous deux." The basic meaning of the "lifting of the veil" implies a varying degree of freedom from the perceptual bonds of matter.

The same combination of 2 and 20 appears with some insistence in the story of the old woman. The companions of the heroine — and the heroine herself — are guarded by 2 black eunuchs and by 20 soldiers at the time of the siege of Azov. The 20 janissaries and the 2 eunuchs are mentioned twice within the same paragraph. The captivity of the women is marked by partial "release" from "matter" — amputation of one buttock. It is ended by an imperfect liberation. The heroine and her companions fall into the hands of less barbaric masters. The basic themes of the episode are oppression and partial liberation.

As was previously noted, the supper with the 6 Kings contains suggestions of 220. 20 sequins are given to the destitute monarch. Candide

---

Romans de Voltaire, Livre de Poche Ed., Preface by Roger Peyrefitte.

gives a diamond worth 2000 sequins. His donation is observed to be worth 100 times more than that of the others. The basic themes of the episode are the bondage of material misery and the release which may be attained with the aid of a spiritual "diamond."

The report on the misfortunes of Pangloss and of the Jesuitic baron toiling as galley-slaves contains a reference to 100 blows administered on the soles of the feet of each man. Also mentioned is the daily punishment of 20 blows. The themes of material slavery — "chains" of incarnation; "vessels" of flesh — and redemption are clearly combined. In the words of Pangloss: " '— we were receiving 20 lashes of the whip per day when the chain of events of this universe led you into our galley-slave ship, and when you redeemed us.' "

The Ingénu is 22 years old when he reaches the nether depths of materiality — "Low Brittany." The release from carnal bondage which he has earned is laid aside for the sake of mankind. A Savior enters the "dungeon" of flesh in order to aid the liberation of others. The arrival of the hero virtually coincides with an emotion-packed event. The talisman which reveals important "connections" is passed from person to person "20 times per *second*." The symbol of magic and occult lore which will play an important role in the liberation of "Suffering Mankind" is transmitted from Pagan to Christians under the numerical sign of 220 and under the aegis of Time. General emancipation from tyranny is eventually achieved under the same signs. The wrath of a *dual* Jehovic God — or establishment — is feared. 20 "lettres de cachet" may be issued against the "rebel." Other "letters" of esoteric nature may be involved.

The suggested importance of 220 is consistently connected by Voltaire with the theme of oppression endured by "Suffering Mankind" and with the theme of eventual liberation.

The Voltairian Eldorado represents vision at its peak. The symbolic summit— or "threshold" — in question has a concrete pyramidal focus: the relationship between 5 and 11 embodied in the portal of the royal palace. As final revisions are being made to the present work, a most admirable book has been published under the title *The View Over Atlantis.** The author notes the following:

> "We have now considered the six stages of the Great Pyramid and seen how at its apex the dimensions of the earth were condensed into 5 cubic inches of gold."

---

* *The View Over Atlantis,* John Michell, Bantam Books, 1969.

The following observation is also made by John Michell with reference to a series of numbers the most important one of which is 220:

> "The numbers quoted above are all related in a mathematical series to the characteristic Pyramid numbers, 5, 8, and 11."

The mystery of Egyptian pyramids has been and remains a source of fascination to mathematicians, astronomers, and other scientists. It is an accepted fact that the location and proportions of the gigantic structures bear relationships to the distribution of terrestrial land masses and to the general appointment of our universe. Voltaire seems to have entrusted the same element of knowledge to his own "pyramid" as did the descendants of Fourth Race Atlanteans to their own monument.

It is noted by John Michell that Galileo correctly estimated the dimension of the orbit of our planet as being equal to 220 diameters of the Sun. The numbers 5 (one-half of the Pythagorean Decad) and 11 are stressed by the famous "heretic:"

> "'The diameter of the sun is 11 semi-diameters of the earth, and the diameter of the grand orb (the earth's orbit around the sun) contains 2,416 of these same semi-diameters — so that the diameter of the said orb contains the sun's diameter 220 times very near.'"

John Michell comments as follows:

> "The extraordinary thing about this passage is that while the conclusion is correct in that the diameter of the earth's orbit is about 220 times the diameter of the sun, the figures by which it is reached are quite wrong. In view of this and of other inaccurate figures which he gives earlier, it is remarkable that Galileo could have arrived at the correct figure of 220 for the multiple by which the diameter of the earth's orbit is greater than the diameter of the sun."

We can only speculate on the errors of Galileo which may have been deliberate precautions — or deliberate hints. Whatever the case may be, the number 220 which is an essential element of cosmic architecture is consistently brought to attention by Voltaire as it is stressed by Galileo. The same number is connected by the author of *Candide* with a meaningful stage of evolution of our "little globe of mud." "As above, so below."

Numbers contained in Chapters XVI and XVIII of *Candide* situate mankind within the general scheme of cosmic evolution. Major and lesser cycles and periods — kalpas, yugas, and Root Races — are represented as are the four Kingdoms of Nature: the mineral, vegetal, animal and human. The septenary structure of Cosmos and Man is suggested. Esoteric reference is made to periodic cataclysms or "great revolutions." The trip to the royal citadel of spirituality spans a major portion of human evolution from "winged" or ethereal being to present-day materiality. Allusions to the Sixth Race extend the scope of concealed substance into the distant —yet "next-scheduled"—future. A major element of cosmic architecture receives form in "stone."

Bearing in mind the allegation of occultists that the most arcane secrets of secret lore are represented mathematically, we can only speculate on the full extent of knowledge which may some day be found to lie beyond the surface of Voltairian numbers. Or on the realms of staggering insight where that "threshold" may lead us.

LE MONDAIN

Joy pervades the poem from the very first line. The "good old days" are not regretted. The Golden Age is not mourned. The Garden of Eden holds few — if any — seductions for one privileged to live in modern times.

"Regrettera qui veut le bon vieux temps
Et l'âge d'or, et le règne d'Astrée,
Et les beaux jours de Saturne et de Rhée,
Et le jardin de nos premiers parents:
Moi je rends grâce à la nature sage
Qui pour mon bien, m'a fait naître en cet âge
Tant décrié par nos tristes frondeurs:
Ce temps profane est tout fait pour mes moeurs."

("Let them who wish regret the good old days
And the golden age, and the reign of Astraea,
And the heyday of Saturn and Rhea
And the garden of our first parents:
I give thanks to wise Nature
Which, for my own good, caused me to be born in this age
So descried by our gloomy fault-finders:
This profane era is just right for my ways.")

Belief in progress is the core of occult philosophy which holds that Nature never works backwards. No mind intent on the occult scheme of cosmic development and human destiny can wish to retrograde. The general advancement of mankind is the chief concern of "good company." What Voltaire was to write in the *Poem on the Disaster of Lisbon* as a matter of individual observation applies on collective planes: "No one would wish to be reborn" or to retrace the painful steps of past experience. Having traversed a phase of deep materiality, Fifth Race mankind is approaching a rising segment of its evolutionary curve. It is logical that its great Instructors yearn for the next Golden Age rather than the last. It is natural that they wish to leave behind the era of spiritual stagnation and general misery and to long for better days.

Traditional versions of mythological and biblical tales are lumped together and subjected to the same exoteric irreverence. But the mockery is double-edged. Saturn is an equivalent of Jehovah. Rhaea personifies materiality.* Astraea represents the debasement of mankind which accompanies the end of each golden age.** Voltaire is unlikely to mourn eras dominated by such figures. The occult view of the "garden of our first parents" is geographically precise. But the attitude of Voltaire toward such locations is unaffected by knowledge of their past splendors. Little nostalgia should be felt for the "Garden" or Adi-Varsha of the first Races, a region eventually transformed into a "frozen white corpse" or icy wasteland.**** The Eden of central Asia and the Gan-Eden of the Middle East.**** have also turned into deserts..

As for the biblical real estate briefly and precariously occupied by Adam and Eve, the character of the wrathful landlord and the existence of better realms speak for themselves in *Candide* and in other writings of Voltaire. The survey of more or less mythical gardens leads to one conclusion. Mankind should not wallow in sterile longing for the irretrievable past. Mankind should use the teachings of the past in order to "cultivate the garden" of the present and in order to prepare the garden of the future.

The apology of well-being and luxury which constitutes a major part of the poem is not incompatible with spiritual interests. A needlessly suffering body is hardly ever transcended. The Secret Doctrine advocates liberation from base self-indulgence. But it recognizes the importance of basic human needs. A minimum of physical comfort is required by the average man before he can turn his sights to high planes of attainment. Culture is a frequent product of material well-being. Spiritual awakening is the occasional product of culture. The pragmatic side of Voltaire and the comparative knowledge of "Westphalia" which pervades his works cannot fail to perceive or stress that spiritual leaven has litle chance to operate in the absence of bread.

Rank materialism itself may bear amazing fruit. The bulk of mankind must experience the emptiness of mere physical comfort before it can feel a need of more rewarding things. If the Arbogads, Pococurantes, and Saint Pouanges of this world have any prospect of true happiness, it is because of the irrepressible demand of Spirit which cannot be met on any material plane. The dregs of sensuous gratification and wealth are known to have produced a few Ways to Damascus. Under proper conditions material excess itself may play a role in the spiritual growth of Man. In that area as in others, "there is no evil out of which some good" may "not come."

---

*The Secret Doctrine, p. 269, Vol. II.
**Ibid., p. 785, Vol. II.
***Ibid., p. 201, Vol. II.
****Ibid., p. 202, Vol. II.

Poverty is the chief prop of all forms of oppression. A general measure of plenty is a liberating force and an effective foe of the "infamous." As Alfred de Vigny noted in his Diary, the masses cannot ask themselves or anyone else subversive questions when all their time and energies are consumed in bare survival. The very faculty of conceiving such questions is vulnerable to the murderous force of material misery and ignorance.

Love of luxury is the material expression of a search for beauty. The acquisition of material forms of beauty may be no more than a pursuit of status symbols. But the impact of Beauty and Truth — which are reflections of the same Reality — may work wonders where all else fails.

The rising standard of living celebrated in *Le Mondain* may have interesting by-products. Exoteric "commerce" implies an exchange which may transcend earthly goods. Esoteric "commerce" with various planes of consciousness may result from pragmatic commercial ventures. The case of Sétoc, the merchant who discovers the meaning of a truly "great fortune" needs not be unique. Exoteric imports from far-away lands tend to arouse interest in their country of origin. The resulting knowledge of foreign cultures may prove illuminating. It is from comparative study of world civilizations that Truth is bound to emerge.

> "Il est bien doux pour mon coeur très immonde
> De voir ici l'abondance à la ronde,
> Mère des arts et des heureux travaux,
> Nous apporter, de sa source féconde,
> Et des besoins et des plaisirs nouveaux.
> L'or de la terre et les trésors de l'onde,
> Leurs habitants et les peuples de l'air,
> Tout sert au luxe, aux plaisirs de ce monde,
> Oh! le bon temps que ce siècle de fer!
> Le superflu, chose très nécessaire,
> A réuni l'un et l'autre hemisphère.
> Voyez-vous pas ces agiles vaisseaux
> Qui du Texel, de Londres, de Bordeaux,
> S'en vont chercher, par un heureux échange
> Ces nouveaux biens, nés aux sources du Gange.
> Tandis qu'au loin vainqueurs des musulmans,
> Nos vins de France enivrent les sultans!"

> ("It is very sweet for my base heart
> To see here abundance all around,
> Mother of arts and of happy labors
> Bringing to us, from her fruitful source
> New needs as well as new pleasures.
> The gold of earth and the treasures of the waves,
> Their inhabitants and the population of the air,
> All serves luxury and the pleasures of this world.

Oh! what a good era our Iron age is!
The superfluous, a most necessary thing,
Has united one hemisphere with the other.
Do you not see those speedy ships
Which, from Texel, from London, from Bordeaux,
Sail off to seek, in happy exchange,
Those new goods, born of the springs of Ganges,
While afar, having overcome the Moslems,
Our French wines intoxicate the sultans!")

An important esoteric equation is virtually given in the above passage. "New needs" are connected with "new pleasures." "Necessity" and joy are suggested to be one. The dynamic principle of evolution or "necessity" is Spirit. It is the dimly felt, restless dweller within Fifth Race man which demands more or less clearly defined fulfillment. The fusion of "pleasure" and "necessity" which is celebrated by Voltaire marks a phase of evolution in which mankind rediscovers the spiritual sense of "joy" and the spiritual essence of destiny. The esoteric equivalence of "pleasure" and "need" is consistent with other expressions of Panglossian optimism. "Pleasures lead to God." "Man was born for joy only."

The golden harvest to be gained on *earth* is clearly defined in *Candide* as spiritual "gold." "The populations of the air" "— winged" or spiritual beings — are logically connected with the "commercial" stirrings of men. The treasures of the ocean become accessible to many men. The ocean of occult knowledge, the ocean of reincarnation, and the undreamed wealth dormant in the human deep are evoked. The symbolism of the fish is present. "Fishers of men" or " Saviors" are at work. The entire Western world seeks the "goods" from the "springs of Ganges."

An intellectual and spiritual "return to the source" is in the making. East and West are bound to "meet." "Vessels" of flesh develop "speed." The dissemination of intoxicating "wine" or "spirit" is involved. There lies the positive value of the grim Kali Yuga. The modern age is destined to witness changes which prepare the Golden Age to come.

Voltaire evokes the origin of Man:

"Quand la nature était dans son enfance
Nos bons aïeux vivaient dans l'ignorance,
Ne connaissant ni le *tien*, ni le *mien*,
Qu'auraient-ils pu connaître. Ils n'avaient rien;
Ils étaient nus, et c'est chose très claire
Que qui n'a rien n'a nul partage à faire.
Sobres étaient. Ah! je le crois encor;
Martialo n'est point du siècle d'or.
D'un bon vin frais ou la mousse ou la sève
Ne gratta point le triste gosier d'Eve;
La soie et l'or ne brillaient pas chez eux.
Admirez-vous pour cela nos aïeux?

493

Il leur manquait l'industrie et l'aisance;
Est-ce vertu? C'était pure ignorance,
Quel idiot, s'il avait eu pour lors
Quelque bon lit, aurait couché dehors?"

("When Nature was in its infancy
Our good forefathers lived in ignorance
Knowing neither *mine*, nor *thine*,
What could they have known? they had nothing:
Naked were they, and it is perfectly clear
That he who has nothing has no sharing to do.
Temperance did they practice. Ah! I do believe
That Martialo does not belong to the Golden Age.
Of a good wine the foam or nectar
Never tickled the sad throat of Eve;
Silk and gold did not shine among them.
Do you admire our forefathers for that?
They lacked industry and well-being
Is that virtue? It was pure ignorance
And what idiot, had he then possessed
Some good bed would have slept out of doors?")

The destitution of original mankind may easily be explained by the
"infancy" of "Nature." The esoteric value of the word "infancy" tends
to place the entire passage within the immaterial realm of First and
Second Race humanity. The absence of "mine" and "thine" connects
the "ignorant" primitives with a mode of ethereal existence foreign to
the bondage of separate being. The first Races were so immaterial as to
need *no-thing*. It was not until the process of division and differentiation
which accompanied the "fall" into matter reached a certain stage that
the twin slaveries of ownership — to have or not to have — acquired
any meaning. Lack of property and lack of clothes suggest that our
"good forefathers" had not yet acquired the divisive "coat of skin"
which is the corollary of Mayavic sub-cycles. Temperance was inherent
to their mode of existence. Ethereal creatures needed no "wine." The
absence of physical bodies took care of beverages. "Spirit" was the
very essence of life. Our first parents had as much use for beds as they
had for the knowledge of Martialo, the author of a famous cook-book.
The reference to beds may be compared to the moving passage of
L'Ingénu in which the new arrival from ethereal spheres scorns furniture
and goes to sleep on the floor wrapped in a mere blanket "in the most
beautiful posture in the world."

"Pure ignorance" was "pure" indeed. It was the condition of creatures
untainted by gross matter. It was the intellectual vacuum of beings
whose all-embracing Informing Principles functioned with instant and
infallible accuracy. The question: "What could they have known?" is

asked with tongue in cheek. Such beings knew plenty which we — the prisoners of incarnation and cold reason — can hardly conceive. The line: "Is that virtue? It was pure ignorance" conceals a profound answer. "Virtue" or "strength" equals "spirit" or "pure ignorance."

The deceptive passage is followed by an enthusiastic description of the luxurious and refined way of life of an XVIIIth Century "honnête homme." The importance of Art is stressed. The works of great painters may be found in privileged homes. The vista which may be admired from the "windows" of certain drawing-rooms transcends the scope of sensory consciousness:

> "De ce salon je vois par la fenêtre,
> Dans des jardins, des myrtes en berceaux;
> Je vois jaillir les bondissantes eaux. . . ."

> ("From this drawing-room I see through the window,
> Within gardens, some myrtle trained into arbors;
> I see the bouncing water spring forth. . . .")

The well "cultivated" "gardens" combine the symbolism of death, life, and ever-renewed Being. Myrtle is often associated with the nether world of ancient mythology. A famous sonnet written by Ronsard contains a much-commented reference to "myrtle-like" shadows." — "les ombres myrteux." The word "berceau" which means "arbor" also means "cradle." The eternal surge of the water of Life rising and falling is noted. The brief glimpse of the "garden" embraces Siva the Destroyer, and Vishnu the Preserver furthering the common goal of evolution. It may be noted in passing that the "windows" used by Voltarian transcend the scope of the five senses which is the pride of Thunder-ten-tronckh.

The poem ends with an ironic reference to the author of *Télémaque.*

> "Or maintenant, Monsieur du Télemaque,
> Vantez-nous bien votre Ithaque,
> Votre Salente, et vos murs malheureux,
> Où vos Crétois, tristement vertueux,
> Pauvres d'effets et riches d'abstinence,
> Manquent de tout pour avoir l'abonance:
> J'admire fort votre style flatteur
> Et votre prose, encore qu'un peu traînante;
> Mais mon ami, je consens de grand coeur
> D'être fessé dans vos murs de Salente,
> Si je vais là pour chercher mon bonheur.
> Et vous, jardin de ce premier bonhomme,
> Jardin fameux par le diable et la pomme,
> C'est bien en vain que, par l'orgueil séduits,

495

Huet, Calmet, dans leur savante audace,
Du paradis ont recherché la place:
Le paradis terrestre est où je suis."

("Well, now, M. du Télémaque
Do boast to us of your little Ithaca,
Of your Salente of your woeful ramparts
Where your Cretans, sadly virtuous
Poor in possessions and rich in detachment,
Lack everything to have abundance:
I much admire your flattering style
And your prose, somewhat sluggish though it be:
But my friend, I wholeheartedly consent
To be spanked under your walls of Salente,
If I go here to search for my happiness.
And you, garden of that first fellow,
Garden made famous by the devil and the apple,
It is in vain, that overpowered by pride,
Huet, Calmet, in their learned daring,
Of paradise have sought the location.
Earthly paradise is where I am.")

Voltaire has no need of any fictitious paradise born of the imagination of any writer. He has no wish to retreat to the version of Utopia conceived by Fénelon — though he understands it well. His conception of genuine happiness leads a long way from the biblical Garden of Eden. It is found in a symbolic land of spiritual "gold." It is a radiance which may transfigure the Earth. It is a radiance which *is* and which is not of this world.

The reference to the "base heart" of Voltaire is heavy with meaning. The French adjective "immonde" is untranslatable in its etymological sense. The startling word is usually rendered in English as "filthy." It is composed of the negative prefix *in* or *im* end of the term meaning "world" — "monde". The exoteric irony conveyed by the unexpected epithet serves to veil a major clue to the deep sense of the poem. The heart of Voltaire *is* dedicated to *"wordly"* or cosmic concerns. The true nature of his preoccupations is essentially spiritual or *"unworldly."*

It may be noted briefly that the same strong adjective is used by Marcel Proust to characterize M. de Charlus and Rachel.*

The deceptive flippancy of *Le Mondain* veils a timeless teaching: "The Kingdoms of Heaven is within you."

The poem is an exquisite esoteric prank and a choice bait thrown at pathological detractors. Voltaire naturally knew what accusations of superficiality and materialism would greet his undetected "thanksgiv-

---

*A la Recheche du temps perdu, pp. 280-1001, Vol. III.

ing." Trigger-happy critics did not let him down. The exoteric surface proved a gold-mine to "gloomy fault-finders." The genuine "gold" went unseen. The deceptive tone of the text served its dual purpose of concealment and poetic justice.

The poem is a Voltarian *Magnificat*. Mystical joy — not hedonism — is the key to *Le Mondain*.

POEME SUR LE DESASTRE
DE LISBONNE

The famous commentary on the earthquake of Lisbon bears the alternate title of *Examination of this Axiom: All is Well.* The exoteric surface of the text seems to ring the death knell of Voltairian optimism.

That all is not well is strongly suggested by the very form of the poem. The size of the preface and the volume of notes written by the author in order to either clarify or veil deep meaning suggest the delicate nature of the work represented by the text. Voltaire was to comment on a horrible event yet to somehow transmit a gleam of hope reflected from the unmentionable Secret Doctrine. In the absence of convenient spokesmen such as may be brought into a short story, Voltaire found himself facing a particularly thorny problem inherent to the form of poetry: how to say enough without saying too much.

The preface draws attention to false conclusions which are frequently drawn from Pope's *Essay on Man,* a text admired by Voltaire which contains the axiom under discussion. Emphasis is placed on the ease with which certain writings can be misinterpreted. The relative ease with which the same writings can be understood is conversely implied and overtly stressed:

> "Il y a toujours un sens dans lequel on peut condamner un écrit, et un sens dans lequel on peut l'approuver. Il serait bien plus raisonnable de ne faire attention qu'aux beautés utiles d'un ouvrage."

> ("There is always one sense in which one may condemn a text, and one sense in which one may approve of it. It would be much more reasonable to pay attention to the useful beauties of a written work only.")

The statement brings to mind the "pious lie" once in fashion among the Ancients, a lie which might prove "useful" to the moderns. The transparent esoteric bait contained in *Candide* is announced by the allusion to the "useful beauties" of certain texts.

The preface — and the poem proper — contain numerous elements of esoteric symbolism such as the symbolism of "chains," "wheels" and wheel-related terms. The words "necessary" and "necessarily" are frequently and emphatically used.

> "Si un homme mangé par les bêtse féroces fait le bien de ces bêtes et contribue à l'ordre du monde, si les malheurs de tous les particuliers

ne sont que la suite de cet ordre général et nécessaire, nous ne sommes donc que des roues qui servent à faire jouer la grande machine; nous ne sommes pas plus précieux aux yeux de DIEU que les animaux qui nous dévorent."

("If a man eaten by wild beasts contributes to the well-being of those beasts and contributes to the order of the world, if the tragedies suffered by all individuals are only the result of that general and necessary order, we therefore are mere wheels used to propel the great machine; we are no more precious in the eyes of GOD than the animals which devour us.")

The concept of an unknowable and impersonal Causeless Cause manifest in the inexorable work of countless "wheels" is linked to the cosmic scheme of "necessity." The "eyes" of the anthropomorphic Deity which are believed to supervise human destinies seen indifferent or closed to the suffering of men. It is suggested by Voltaire — as it is suggested by all esoteric writers — that such a "Vice-God" is a myth. The essential force of Nature knows no favorites and no "souffre-douleur."

"Je sens passer sur moi la comédie humaine
Qui cherche en vain au ciel ses muets spectateurs."
(Alfred de Vigny, *La Maison du berger*).

("I feel passing over me the human comedy
Which seeks in vain for mute spectators in Heaven.")

The "delicate" substance of Pope's *Essay on Man* elicits the following comment:

"— l'ouvrage ayant été traduit par des hommes dignes de le traduire, a triomphé d'autant plus de critiques qu'elles roulaient sur des matières plus délicates."

("— the work having been translated by men worthy of translating it, has overcome critiques all the more as they dealt with delicate matters.")

The above praise of translators may well be double-edged. It seems impossible to know with absolute certainty whether "men worthy of translating" should be read as "men worthy of traducing" certain works. If the latter suggestion is intended by Voltaire, the success of the said translations may be explained by the blurring of esoteric substance — "delicate matters," — a blurring caused by ignorance or deliberate intent. It is also conceivable that the praise of translators is sincere. Whatever the case may be, attention is called to the "delicate" nature of certain writings which "revolve" around certain subjects. The reader of the *Poem on the Disaster of Lisbon* should be prepared to approach the text with caution.

Another writer is the subject of double-edged comments:

> "Bayle, le plus grand dialecticien qui ait jamais écrit, n'a fait qu'apprendre à douter, et — il se combat lui-même."

> ("Bayle, the greatest dialectician ever to write, only learned to doubt — and he is at variance with himself.")

Bayle is mentioned in the works of Mme Blavatsky with perceptible sympathy and with "Voltairian" verve:

> "Bayle shows, by numerous instances, that whenever it was proved that several bodies of the same saint, or three heads of him, or three arms (as in the case of Augustine) were said to exist in different places, and that they could not well be all authentic, the cool and invariable answer of the Church was that they were all genuine; for 'God had multiplied and miraculously reproduced them for the greater glory of his Holy Church!" (*Isis Unveiled,* p. 72, Vol. 2).

The assertion that Bayle "only learned to doubt" is understandable in the above case. That Voltaire exploited the dual meaning of the French verb "apprendre" — "to learn" and also "to teach" — is likely. The sentence may be read to mean that Bayle only taught to doubt. Honest doubt is necessary to the acquisition of true knowledge when true knowledge is suppressed and must go underground. Doubt is fervently courted by esoteric writers where the deceptive appearance of their texts is concerned. The apparent success of Bayle in arousing skepticism seems to have the approval of Voltaire.

The apparent inconsistency of Bayle who "is at variance with himself," "fights himself," or "contradicts himself" may reflect the use of a typical esoteric device. As was previously noted, the reader who faces a glaring contradiction may choose one of two paths. He may conclude that the mind of the great author is regrettably muddled and that the great author is not so great after all. Or he may concentrate on a rigorous definition of contradictory terms. The internal "combats" of Bayle do not necessarily reflect mental confusion. The word "combat" is often used to designate spiritual battles.

The "contradictions" of Cicero are noted with ostentatious candor:

> "Et ce qu'il y a de plus étrange, c'est que Cicéron finit son livre *de la nature des Dieux* san réfuter de telles assertions. Il soutient en cent endroits la mortalité de l'âme dans ses Tusculanes, après avoir soutenu son immortalité."

500

("And, strangest of all, Cicero ends his book *on the nature of the Gods,* without refuting such assertions. He maintains in a hundred places the mortality of the soul in his Tusculanes, after having maintained its immortality.")

Cicero probably mentioned in turn the perisprit — or astral soul or astral body — which is mortal and the Spirit which is incorruptible. The contradiction is easily resolved by "a small fund of philosophy" and by a determination to define certain terms. The enlightening potential of esoteric "contradiction" is further suggested within the text of the *Poem on the Disaster of Lisbon*:

"O mélange étonnant de contrariétés!"

("O, amazing mixture of contradictions!")

The preface ends with an "afterthought" presented under the form of a postscriptum. The reader is urged not to mistake what the author refutes for what he submits. It is difficult to imagine a more provocative warning:

"— il faut distinguer les objections que se fait un auteur de ses réponses aux objections, et ne pas prendre ce qu'il réfute pour ce qu'il accepte."

("— one must distinguish the objections made to himself by an author from his answers to objections and one must not mistake what he refutes for what he accepts.")

Marcel Proust was to express similar ideas on certain works of art more genuinely alive than what "we falsely call life." The surface of such works must be "painfully deciphered" and often "read in reverse."*

The structure of the poem justifies the warning. The text is built on a series of questions and objections. An imaginary interlocutor who may be presumed to be the reader compensates for the absence of a "useful" or deceptive spokesman such as Pangloss. The simulated exchange deserves attentive examination:

"Direz-vous en voyant cet amas de victimes
DIEU s'est vengé, leur mort est le prix de leurs crimes?

Demandez aux mourants dans ce séjour d'effroi
Si c'est l'orgueil qui crie: O Ciel secourez-moi;
O Ciel ayez pitié de l'humaine misère!

Tout est bien, dites-vous, et tout est nécessaire.
Quoi! l'univers entier, sans ce gouffre infernal,

---

*A la Recherche du temps perdu, p. 896, Vol. III.

Sans engloutir Lisbonne, eut-il été plus mal?
Etes-vous assuré que la cause éternelle,
Qui fait tout, qui sait tout, qui créa tout pour elle,
Ne pouvait nous jeter dans ces tristes climats
Sans former des volcans allumés sous nos pas?
Borneriez-vous ainsi la suprême puissance,
Lui défendriez vous d'exercer sa clémence?

Les tristes habitants de ces bords désolés,
Dans l'horreur des tourments seraient-ils consolés,
Si quelqu'un leur disait: *Tombez, mourez tranquilles*:
Pour le bonheur du monde on détruit vos asiles;
D'autres mains vont bâtir vos palais embrasés,
D'autres peuples naîtront de vos murs écrasés;
Le Nord va s'enrichir de vos pertes fatales;
Tous vos maux sont un bien dans les lois générales;
DIEU *vous voit du même oeil que les vils vermisseaux,*
Dont vous serez la proie au fond de vos tombeaux,
A des infortunés quel horrible langage!
Cruels à mes douleurs n'ajoutez point l'outrage."

("Will you say as you see the heaps of victims
GOD avenged himself, their death is the price of their crimes?

Ask the dying in this sojourn of terror,
If it is pride which screams: O Heaven help me;
O Heaven have mercy on human misery!

All is well, you say, and all is necessary.
What! would the entire universe, without this infernal abyss,
Without the destruction of Lisbon, have fared worse?
Are you assured that the eternal cause,
Which does all, which knows all, which created all for itself,
Could not cast us under those sad climates
Without forming volcanoes lit under our feet?
Would you so limit the supreme power,
Would you forbid it from exercising its clemency?
Would the tragic dwellers of these sad shores
Be consoled if in the horror of their torments
They were told: *Fall, die serenely,*
For the happiness of the world your shelters are destroyed;
Other hands will build your flaming palaces
Other nations will be born in your crushed walls:
The North will grow richer from your fatal losses;
All your tragedies are good within the general scheme;
GOD *sees you with the same eye as the vile worms*
Of which you will be preys at the bottom of your graves.
To the unfortunate, what a horrible speech!
Cruel ones, to my grief, do not add insult.")

Common sense and compassion reject such ineffective and callous "consolations." But the passage contains several tenets of occult faith which are stressed by italics.

The Secret Doctrine rejects the concept of a personal God enforcing his supremacy through personal revenge. The statement "GOD avenged himself" would constitute —if made — an insult to mankind and an outrage to the Supreme Being. The comment "Their death is the price of their crime" may reflect the work of inscrutable karmic justice. But the human mind is not equal to the task of probing *that* one mystery. Hardship may be the result of previous misdeeds. Hardship may also be the privileged test of high spiritual attainment. Whatever the case may be, indifference or complacency in the face of the suffering of others calls for its own retribution. Civilizations are fated to rise and fall in accordance with cyclic law. Cataclysms mark the end and the beginning of many cycles. Minor upheavals — such as earthquakes — play a part in the inexorable unfolding of evolution.

Human "pride" seems to be the source of the eternal lament of mankind: "O Heaven help me! / O Heaven have mercy on human misery!" The word "orgueil" which approximates the meaning of "vanity," "illusion," Maya, conveys the occult view of the age-old outcry of mankind. Such a supplication is prompted by anguish rather than "pride." But it is also the product of Mayavic lack of insight. Cataclysmic occurrence is not viewed by the Supreme Being as spectator sport. Karmic justice is not mollified by prayer or beseeching posture. Universal Law cannot abdicate its own essence to perform miracles for individuals or collectivities.

The validity of the passage stressed by italics is best left untold to the majority of persons. Most human beings are unprepared for such revelation. Such is the probable meaning of the word "infortuné" which seems calculated to evoke a "Fortune" or Karmic stage of development as yet unrelieved by knowledge of cyclic evolution. Few minds are capable of accepting that kind of science with serenity. Those which are able to do so need no such expostulations as are contained in the passage.

"The eternal cause" — a transparent mutation of the First or Causeless Cause — seems to possess human or anthropomorphic traits. It is represented as an "eternal craftsman" endowed with hands.

> "L'éternel artisan n'a-t-il pas dans ses mains
> Des moyens infinis tout prêts your ses desseins?"

> ("Does not the eternal craftsman have in his hands
> Infinite powers all ready to carry out his designs?)

Two possibilities of interpretation are present. The Deity may be

503

anthropomorphic in which case the divine hands resemble the physical hands of Man. Or the Deity may be immaterial in which case the divine hands are purely symbolic. Similar possibilities exist in connection with the "designs" of the Deity. Such "designs" may reflect the personal decisions—or whims—of the biblical "Vice-God." Or they may reflect the impersonal, immutable, and rational scheme of Universal Law and its Causeless Cause. The latter probability seems to be supported by the presence of the expression: "eternal cause." It is also suggested by the word "craftsman"—"artisan"—which may be connected with the "Masonic" concept of the "Craft" and with related views of the Supreme Being. While numerous shades of freemasonry do exist, the purer forms of the "Craft" are based on belief in an impersonal, immaterial deity. In summary the margin of interpretation offered by the passage seems to prepare the esoteric distinction which will be made more than once in the course of the poem between the biblical GOD and the First Cause.

The question of whether or not man *could* have been placed in an environment unmarred by volcanoes tends to reject the concept of an allegedly merciful biblical God. A personal God who could forego cataclysms but would fail to do so would be open the charges of inhumanity or neglect. The question of divine clemency is raised in the passage: "Would you so limit the supreme power? / Would you forbid it from exercising its clemency?" The suggested negative answer seems to rule out the existence of a divine power susceptible to alteration of its own divine essence. The concept of a cruel and weak Deity whose omnipotence can be swayed, limited—perhaps even created—by Man is left to speak for itself in the mind of the reader. The matter of occasional divine clemency—or favoritism— in clearly settled in the final lines of the poem. The authentic Divinity cannot be "limited" in any way. It is designated as "Sole Unlimited Being." The impersonal power which rules the Universe *cannot* alter the course of a scheme of life in which men and erupting volcanoes come into occasional contact. The passage announces a profound "platitude" of the unborn Pangloss: "For, if there is a volcano in Lisbon, it could not be elsewhere. For it is impossible that things not be where they are. For all is well."

Rejection of the biblical GOD is also suggested in the following lines:

"God sees you with the same eye as the vile worms
Of which you will be preys at the bottom of your graves."

The First Cause is unlikely to have or need physical eyes. While the general symbolism of the eye—and hand—of God should be taken

504

into account, the reference of Voltaire to divine physical organs and limbs seem to coincide with references to Jehovah. Such a correspondence is consistent with the occult view of the "Vice-God" or crude understudy of the Supreme Being. The GOD of all capital letters is not authenticated by esoterically meaningful italics. The irrational third-rate potency of world mythology may be surmised to have the same regard for human beings and for worms.

Universal Law is impartial where physical man and worms are concerned. This is not to say that man and worm have the same rank in the hierarchy of Being.

> "The occult doctrine — teaches a cyclic, never varying law in nature, the latter having no personal, 'special design,' but acting on a uniform plan that prevails through the whole manvantaric period and deals with the land worms as it deals with man. Neither the one nor the other have sought to come into being, hence both are under the same evolutionary law, and both have to progress according to Karmic law. Both have started from the same neutral centre of Life and both have to re-emerge into it at the consummation of the cycle." (*The Secret Doctrine*, p. 261, Vol. II).

It is suggested in notes that the legitimate First Cause is more discriminating — if less personal — than the biblical GOD. Voltaire draws attention to the extreme diversity prevailing in Creation:

> "— il peut donc y avoir des intervalles immenses entre les êtres sensibles, comme entre les insensibles."

> ("— there may thus exist immense gaps between tangible, as between intangible beings.")

The exoteric biblical GOD who fails to measure such "immense gaps" as the abyss separating man from worm is not likely to represent the Voltairian concept of "divine intelligence."

The dual meaning of the words "sensibles" and "insensibles" — "tangible and intangible" — is exploited. The "sensible" forms of existence are those which are accessible to the physical senses. Material and immaterial planes of being are contrasted to one another as well as embraced by the unifying cosmic vision of Voltaire. The idea of sensitivity is present also. Spiritual responsiveness to divine reality is reflected on the scale of more or less immaterial existence. Voltaire may also wish to contrast the genuine sensitivity of the Great All to the one-way sensitivity of the Jehovic GOD. The 'Great All' which he mentions in the course of the poem — "le Grand Tout" — reacts impersonally to any disturbance of its smallest part. The biblical GOD is explosively sensitive to human slight — fancied or real. But he is insensitive where human misery is concerned. Human sensitivity — limited though it be — seems vastly superior of the compassion of which the allegedly merciful "Vice-God" is capable:

> "Je désire ardemment, sans offenser mon maître,
> Que ce gouffre enflammé de soufre et de salpêtre
> Eût allumé ces feux dans le fond des déserts.
> Je respecte mon Dieu, mais j'aime l'univers.
> Quand l'homme ose gémir d'un fléau si terrible,
> Il n'est point orgueilleux, hélas! il est sensible."

> ("I humbly wish, without offending my master,
> That this blazing abyss of sulphur and saltpeter
> Had been ignited in remotest deserts.
> I respect my God, but I love the universe;
> When man dares complain of such a dreadful scourge,
> He is not presumptuous, alas, he is perceptive.")

The work of volcanoes clearly belongs to the realm of material imperfection. It is suggested that the genuine Supreme Being could not set "hand" to such a creation, a thought which coincides exactly with the view of occultists. The God "respected" by Voltaire seems to be distinct from the personal GOD who has the same regard for men and for worms. The name of the "respected" God has only one capital letter.

> "It is to avoid such anthropomorphic conceptions that the Initiates never use the epithet 'God' to designate the One and Secondless Principle in the Universe; and that — faithful in this to the oldest traditions of the Secret Doctrine the world over — they deny that such imperfect and often not very clean work could ever be produced by Absolute Perfection." (*The Secret Doctrine*, p. 555, Vol. II).

The "blazing abyss" mentioned in the passage may represent more than natural "fires" or volcanoes. It is reminiscent of the intercontinental "fault" discussed in *Candide*. The joint obsessions of original sin, eternal damnation, and the stake are probable targets of Voltaire. If such fiery doctrine and practices must exist, they should be restricted to deserts where they would die a natural death for lack of physical and spiritual victims. The "dreadful scourge" of which man "dares complain" seems to be the familiar formula of faggot and "pox,"

The word "saltpeter" — "salpêtre" — was probably used to express a dim view of Christian dogma and persecution. The substance known as saltpeter has explosive properties well suited to characterize the explosive Jehovic God. The word *Petra* may be connected with Peter, the alleged founder of the Church and with the idea of an Interpreter of the Secret Doctrine. The first part of the word is derived from *salt* — in French "sel" — and therefore conveys the idea of bitterness. The total meaning of the word *saltpeter* suggests an Interpreter of the Secret Doctrine named Peter who became a human symbol of the Church. The interpretive role played by the said Church consisted of building a "new" doctrine "on the mangled remains" of the Primitive Wisdom-Religion. The resulting creed is *bitter* or conducive to despair. It is based on worship and fear of explosive Brute Force.

The "blazing abyss of sulphur and saltpeter" refers to the action of natural forces and to the practices of unnatural religion.

It is shown in *Candide* that auto-da-fés are ineffective cures for cataclysms. It is even demonstrated that auto-da-fés are occasionally followed by cataclysms. The reader is at liberty to establish a Panglossian cause-effect relationship between the burning of "heretics" and certain catastrophies. It is suggested in the poem as it is suggested in *Candide* that collective Karma is at work in Lisbon.

The line containing the reference to the "respected" God constitutes an interesting example of esoteric subtlety and dualism. The exoteric reader has little reason to notice that the God in question has only one capital letter in his name. The eloquent distinction between "respect" and "love" is a revealing commentary on the Deity of orthodox Christians, the only God exoterically apparent in the passage. The separation suggested to exist between the same God and the universe is also eloquent. The concept of a transcendent Deity removed from his own Creation yet emotionally and brutally involved with it is offered to the judgment of the reader. The esoteric level of the line seems to deal with the personal God which is more or less active in every man. Such a "God" — Chrestos, the Higher Self — is prized or "respected" as the remote reflection of the Unknowable. But it is not worshipped for the Supreme Being alone is worshipped. Nor is it *loved* for it is both Love and Self. The words "my God" may also be interpreted as "my conception of God," a conception designated as the "Great All" in subsequent lines. Within such a context the concessive meaning of the word "but" dissolves. The divine principle in Man is "respected" *because* of conscious co-essence of "All" — the Universe — and Self.

The expression "without offending my master" may suggest a *master, guru,* or spiritual guide as well as the Ultimate Master or Unknowable Principle.

The few words sound vague, flat and gratuitous on the esoteric plane. One may explain their awkward quality by need of a rhyme for the word "saltpeter." "Zadig did not pride himself upon being a good poet." But another explanation may be given on the esoteric plane. Voltaire expresses reverent understanding of the Ultimate Master. Such insight can only heighten his compassion for ignorant, baffled human victims of Natural Law. Compassion is the live force and the raison d'être of the *Poem on the Disaster of Lisbon.*

The last two lines of the stanza contain a predictable conclusion. Man is neither presumptuous nor deluded when he questions the existence of certain evils. He is admirably "perceptive." The surface of dutiful resignation conceals the ever-present: "Crush the infamous!"

The impersonal divine Unity which is insistently suggested to supersede the biblical GOD is exalted in the next line. The "Vice-God" is left out of the picture. There remains only the Great All and its reverent human reflection:

"Je me suis du grand *Tout* qu'une faible partie; —"

("I am only a feeble part of the great *All;* — "

The esoteric value of "weakness" which is conveyed by the word "feeble" amounts to the meaning of "incarnate." The bland adjective prepares startling autobiographical suggestions which are made in a final passage of the poem.

Suspect awkwardness marks speculations on the origin of Evil.

"De l'Etre Tout-Parfait le mal ne pouvait naître.
Il ne vient pas d'autrui puisque DIEU seul est maître."

("Evil could not originate with the All-Perfect-Being
It does not come from another since GOD alone is master.")

Evil is the sum of woes inherent to materiality or "weakness." Voltaire seems to deny — as does Mme Blavatsky — that "such imperfect and often not very clean work could ever be produced by Absolute Perfection."

The joint presence of "il" — "it" — representing Evil — and "autrui" — meaning "another, one's fellow-man" — added to the presence of the All-Perfect-Being and to the presence of GOD weighs heavily and clumsily on the two lines. It is exoterically apparent that the antecedent of "il" is Evil but the text requires laborious digestion from attentive readers on the exoteric plane itself. The French word "autrui" is seldom if ever disconnected from other human existence. It never serves to represent the allegedly unique and divine Christian GOD. It is absurd to link the word in question to the exoteric All-Perfect-Being which seems to be the Jehovic GOD. It is nonsensical to link the term to the esoteric concept of the All-Perfect-Being which is Impersonality Itself. Alertness is clearly in order in the face of such ostentatious clumsiness. The second line may easily the interpreted as follows: Evil comes from no other principle than GOD — the "Westphalian" spouse of deepest material-ity — since the latter GOD alone is master — in the modern Western world. Such an interpretation is consistent with the preceding line which has clearly disqualified the All-Perfect-Being as a possible source of evil. It is also consistent with the concealed message of preceding stanzas. Irreductible opposition between the All-Perfect-Being and the "Vice-God" is clear. The Perfection of the Great All — l'Etre-*Tout*-*Parfait* — cannot be a source of evil. The GOD of all capital letters and less than capital character can be and is such a baneful influence.

So conscious was Voltaire of the gaucherie of his style and so eager to make it a subject of thought that he attached an explanatory note to the word "autrui:" "That is to say from another principle." Creation of the ambiguous line and addition of the impish note must have been sweet sorrow.

The fifth stanza begins with an impassioned protest:

> "Non, ne présentez plus à mon coeur agité
> Ces immuables lois de la nécessité,
> Cette chaîne des corps, des esprits et des mondes.
> O rêves de savans, o chimères profondes!
> DIEU tient en main la chaîne et n'est point enchaîné.
> Par son choix bienfaisant tout est déterminé."

> ("No, do not offer again to my suffering heart
> Those immutable laws of necessity,
> That chain of bodies, spirits, and worlds.
> O dreams of scholars, o profound myths!
> GOD holds the chain in hand and is not chained himself;
> By his benevolent choice all is determined.")

The passage seems to reject a metaphysical system of "bodies," "spirits," and "worlds" resembling the cosmic outlines of the Secret Doctrine. But a wide margin of possibilities exists between rejection and actual meaning. The esoteric reader can only be amused by the design of of-fering metaphysical lore to Voltaire. The futility of such an attempt is suggested by Voltaire himself. The cosmic system which seems to be rejected is characterized by the author in a corresponding note both in terms of what it is and in terms of what it is not. The warning which is given at the end of the preface to the poem applies at this point. "One must distinguish the objections made to himself by an author from his answers to objections, and one must not mistake what he refutes for what he accepts." The continuous emphasis which is placed by Voltaire on "necessity," "chains," and "spirits" is likely to represent what the writer "accepts." Inspired "dreams" and profound "myths" do exist which are vehicles of truth. The apparent opposition between the uselessness of "chimeras" or "myths" and their quality of depth is inherent to the nature of allegory. Esoteric concealment is most effective in the midst of exoteric "futility." It is most "useful" as a dual-purpose veil-and-bait in the midst of vehement denegation. A favorite trick of the typical esoteric creation — such as Proustian "Albertine" — is an indignant denial of any tendency resembling "inversion." The emphatically negative stanza of the poem has the quality of a dead give-away to the esoteric reader. The nonsensical concept of a personal GOD holding mankind in chains — such as the shackles of ignorance — and acting through benevolent choice is the "chimera" which the author rejects. The passage represents in part a preview of *L'Ingénu.* Voltaire treats with passionate scorn the proposition that "There is a truth essential to man and God has concealed it."

The same passage of the poem is often compared with a stanza of the *Destinies* of Vigny. No comparison is more legitimate or far-reaching when the full extent of affinities linking both writers is perceived:

> "Oh! dans quel désespoir nous sommes encor tous!
> Vous avez élargi le COLLIER qui nous lie,
> Mais qui donc tient la chaîne — Ah! Dieu juste, est-ce vous?"

Stressed by unexpected all-capital letters — which are difficult to explain exoterically — the word COLLIER is the key to the philosophy of Vigny. Within it are fused basic elements of the Secret Doctrine: the occult concept of a "chain" of worlds, the circle of Karma, the "yoke" or bondage of incarnation, the "yoke" or union of mysticism, and the Necklace or Golden thread of Sutratma-Reincarnation. The word is placed in a deceptive context of anguished ignorance. Man seems to ask an awesome question to which there is no answer. The answer is concealed in the capitalized word. Voltaire supplies the solution of the same eternal riddle of Destiny on the esoteric plane of his text as does Vigny. The combination of "necessity" — a concept implying the presence of a circle — "chains," "spirits," and "worlds" amounts to a typical admixture of esoteric algebra symbolically representing basic tenets of the Secret Doctrine.

The last lines of poetry written by Vigny in *L'Esprit pur* beg posterity to be "attentive" to his *Destinies.* The *Poem on the Disaster of Lisbon* contains a kindred verse in which Voltaire refers to the difficulty of making himself "clear in thick darkness." The preface and notes which are added to the same poem constitute a comparable plea for the right kind of "attention."

One may finally note in connection with the Voltairian "chain" held

510

in the "hand" of GOD that the GOD of all-capital letters is connected with special print and with a physical attribute. The author seems to be consistent in drawing attention to the same anthropomorphic deity by means of the same technique throughout the text.

Voltaire comments on the abyss separating human condition and human aspiration. Optimism is not supported by fact. But the illusory nature of material "fact" does not necessarily alter the invisible reality of a "fine picture."

> "Vous criez *tout est bien* d'une voix lamentable:
> L'Univers vous dément, et votre propre coeur
> Cent fois de votre esprit a réfuté l'erreur."

> ("You shout *all is well,* in a piteous voice:
> The universe belies you, and your own heart
> A hundred times has refuted the error of your mind.")

The joint presence of "heart" and "mind" contains kaleidoscopic possibilities. The French word "esprit" which means "wit" and "mind" also means "spirit." As was previously noted, the triple significance of the term is a frequent and "useful" tool of esoteric French writers. The slippery quality of popular concepts of "heart" and "mind" is the object of occasional Voltairian irony such as the quip previously noted in *Micromégas*. The heart which is usually regarded as the seat of passions is a poor instrument of metaphysical insight in that capacity. But the "heart" is connected with the "small voice" or spiritual intuition in esoteric writings.* The byzantine esoteric possibilities which are present in the passage may be mastered with the help of the verb "has refuted." The prefatory warning of Voltaire seems to apply again. If such be the case the teachings of Mayavic facts recorded by the intellect become the "error." The authenticating value of italics used to stress the axiom *all is well* tends to support the latter interpretation.

The apparent conflict between "heart" and "mind" may be a clue in itself. As long as the "separated twins" remain inimical to each other, no enlightenment can be given to eternal riddles such as *"all is well."* It is only on the plane of Divine Wisdom that the two are in harmonious conjunction and that *all is well* is valid.

The relationship between body and mind is briefly mentioned. The physical shell of Man is said to have no thinking faculty of its own:

> "Il n'a point la parole, il n'a point la pensée."

> ("It has no word, it has no thought.")

---

*The Secret Doctrine, p. 280, Vol. I.

511

The reader can only conclude that the superior faculties of Man are localized in non-physical realms. Such a belief is consistent with previously found suggestions of an "unknown fluid" irrigating and linking body and mind. The physical ability to communicate by "word" may be surmised to have an unnamed immaterial source — such as the Logos or Verbum of occult philosophy. Human suffering and evil stem from the limitations of material existence — which are examined in further detail in a subsequent part of the poem. Such views of superior faculties thwarted by the "impediments of matter" are in complete harmony with parallel tenets of the Secret Doctrine.

Merchants of materialistic doctrines who would reduce latent gods to the status of mere physical creatures are taken to task:

"Tristes calculateurs des misères humaines,
Ne me consolez point, vous aigrissez mes peines;
Et je ne vois en vous que l'effort impuissant
D'un fier infortuné qui feint d'être content."

("Sad exploiters of human miseries
Do not console me, you intensify my grief;
And I perceive in you only the impotent striving
Of a proud unfortunate feigning contentment.")

The "vanity" of certain individuals has far-reaching effects which plague entire societies. Countless human beings are doomed to material and spiritual anguish by "vain" or false doctrines. The related exploitation of "human miseries" is a most abhorrent evil in a word fraught with evil. The "infamous" is composed of Mayavic "money-changers" who thrive on the oppression of mankind. Most revolting is the mask commonly worn by powers of tyranny acting under the guise of "consolation."

Voltaire speculates on the possible meaning of human destiny:

'Ou l'homme est né coupable, et DIEU punit sa race,
Ou ce maître absolu de l'être et de l'espace,
Sans courroux, sans pitié, tranquille, indifférent,
De ses premiers décrets suit l'éternel torrent;
Ou la matière informe, à son maître rebelle,
Porte en soi des défauts *nécessaires* comme elle;
Ou bien DIEU nous éprouve, et ce séjour mortel
N'est qu'un pasage étroit vers un monde éternel.
Nous essuyons ici des douleurs passagères.
Le trépas est un bien qui finit nos misères.
Mais quand nous sortirons de ce passage affreux,
Qui de nous prétendra mériter d'être heureux."

("Either man was born guilty, and GOD punishes his race,
Or that absolute master of being and space,

Without wrath, without pity, serene, indifferent,
Of its first decrees follows the eternal torrent;
Or amorphous matter, rebelling against its master;
Carries within itself defects which are *necessary* as it is;
Or GOD tests us, and this mortal sojourn
Is only one narrow passage toward an eternal world.
We experience transient pains on earth,
Death is a blessing which ends our miseries.
But when we shall emerge from these fearsome straits,
Who among us will claim to deserve happiness?")

The ambiguous wording of the first line results in competition between GOD and man for antecedence to the possessive "his" — "sa". While it is unlikely that GOD punishes his own race or essence, the bizarre interpretation may have been courted by Voltaire. Such a hypothesis consigns the said GOD to the realm of the absurd, a distinct possibility in Voltairian thought. The orthodox interpretation of original sin and resulting punishment is hardly more rational. A GOD who manages to be at the same time merciful, vengeful, and jealous eternally chastises billions of innocents for the sin committed by two problematic ancestors.

The personal GOD may be testing his human creatures. A single appearance on earth entails eternal reward or eternal punishment. The gambling odds determining the quality of life eternal are those of being or not being in a state of grace at the right time. The testing GOD is obviously not the author of all things revered by "Micromégas," a Supreme Being who causes proportion to rule the universe.

The impersonal, rational power enacting unknown "first decrees" — the Eternal Cause of Voltaire — is identical to the First Cause of occult philosophy. The "serene, indifferent — absolute master of being and space" is offered to the judgment of the reader in contrast to the punishing and irrational GOD.

Matter may carry defects inherent to its nature. The rebellion of matter against its unnamed master places the said master in immaterial realms. Such a Voltairian proposition is identical to the view of the antagonism of spirit and matter which is a basic element of the Secret Doctrine. The origin of both Good and Evil lies in the struggle of the two poles of existence:

"Everywhere the speculations of the Kabalists treat of Evil as a FORCE, which is antagonistic, but at the same time essential, to Good, as giving it vitality and existence, which it could never have otherwise." (*The Secret Doctrine*, p. 413, Vol. I).

"In human nature, evil denotes only the polarity of matter and Spirit, a struggle for life between the two manifested Principles in Space and

Time, which principles are one, *per se,* inasmuch they are rooted in the Absolute. In Kosmos, the equilibrium must be preserved. The operations of the two contraries produce harmony, like the centripetal and centrifugal forces, which are necessary to each other — mutually interdependent — 'in order that both should live.' If one is arrested, the action of the other will become immediately self-destructive." (*The Secret Doctrine,* p. 416, Vol. I).

The stress placed by Voltaire on the word *necessary* connects the entire passage with the circle of necessity and with the Secret Doctrine. The crucial equivalence of necessity and materiality is openly given in the meaningful line.

Our "mortal sojourn" may be "only one passage" on the path to an eternal world. The word "one" — "n'est qu'un passage" — allows for the possibility of many "passages" on earth. The significant indefinite article which coincides in French with the form of the numeral "one" seems calculated to prepare a subsequent observation on rebirth.

The last three lines of the stanza contain an interesting ambiguity. The "fearsome straits" may represent incarnate life. Such a meaning is consistent with the previously stated view — also held by Occultists — that death is a blessing. But the "fearsome straits" or passage may also represent Devachan, a concept unknown to the majority of Westerners who therefore tend to regard the hereafter as a terrifying mystery. The emergence from the said "passage" then becomes reincarnation and, in a few cases, Nirvâna. The connection between "merit" and "happiness" which is made in the final line applies to rebirth as it does to Nirvâna. Merit is the determining factor of spirituality gained at every step of the voyage of life. Spirituality itself is the equivalent of happiness in the Voltairian and in the occult system.

The rich stanza is designed to produce a critical comparative survey of the Jehovic GOD and of the impersonal First Cause. It is intended to show that evil is a "necessary" attribute of matter. It is calculated to suggest the existence of Karma and the reality of reincarnation.

A God once visited earth. His divinity seems to be attested by the absence of all-capital letters.

"Un Dieu vint consoler notre race affligée;
Il visita la terre, et ne l'a point changée!
Un sophiste arrogant nous dit qu'il ne l'a pu.
'Il le pouvait,' dit l'autre, 'et ne l'a point voulu.'"

("A God came to console our afflicted race;
He visited the earth and did not change it!
An arrogant sophist tells us that he could not do so.
'He could have,' says another, 'and did not will to do so.'")

The sacrifice of Christ has brought little relief to mankind. The "arrogant sophist" denouncing the alleged helplessness of the Savior is partially correct. The phase of human evolution during which Jesus lived did not permit a full revelation of Truth. No force on earth or above can produce any changes in violation of Universal Law. The second speaker is correct also. Christ was an embodiment of highest spirituality therefore a man of considerable power. His refusal to disregard the law of evolution was one aspect of his wisdom. The amusing debate — strangely situated within a sad context — suggests that numerous controversies of like nature are products of ignorance, illusion, divisive thinking or Maya.

"Ignorance" is the subject of further comments:

> Je ne conçois pas plus comment tout serait bien!
> Je suis comme un docteur, hélas! Je ne sais rien."

> ("I can no more conceive how all would be well;
> I am like a doctor, alas! I know nothing.")

The conditional may suggest that all *is* well. The hypothetical axiom is not set off by authenticating italics. The affirmative form seems valid. "All" and "no-thing" are the same in the esoteric system. Knowing "no-thing" may therefore amount to knowing a great deal. The unflattering view of certain "doctors" or scholars which is held by Voltaire leaves ample room for insights gained from other sources. The profession of ignorance should be taken with the same esoteric skepticism as other Voltairian statements of like nature.

A comparison is made between the "winged men" of Plato and modern-day mankind:

> "Platon dit qu'autrefois l'homme avait eu des ailes,
> Un corps impénétrable aux atteintes mortelles;
> La douleur, le trépas, n'approchaient point de lui.
> De cet état brillant qu'il diffère aujourd'hui!"

> ("Plato says that formerly man had had wings,
> A body impenetrable to fatal blows:
> Neither pain nor death could approach him.
> From that brilliant state how he differs today!")

The "winged" beings of Plato are the men of the first "age" to whom — according to the book of *Manu* — "neither sickness nor suffering were known."

> "The *Phaedrus* of Plato displays all that man once was and that which he may yet become again. 'Before man's spirit sank into sensuality and was embodied with it through the loss of his wings, he lived among

the gods in the airy (spiritual) world where everything is true and pure.' "
(*Isis Unveiled*, pp. 344-45, Vol. 2).

The wistfulness which accompanies the reference to "winged men" is made of nostalgia, not disbelief. The loss of "wings" lamented by Voltaire reflects the loss of omniscience enjoyed by our "winged" ancestors. The existence of a truth "as necessary to the earth as the sun" is unknown to the majority of modern mankind. The primeval "brilliance" or Informing Principle no longer exists to reveal the truth which has gone underground. But the "conveyances of up there" or intuitive faculties have not entirely disappeared. The realm of the "true and pure" which belongs to the distant past may also belong to the distant future.

The same loss of "wings" is sadly pertinent to the reading of esoteric texts such as the *Poem on the Disaster of Lisbon*.

The limited scope of human intelligence is surveyed:

"Que peut donc de l'esprit la plus vaste étendue?
Rien: le livre du sort se ferme à notre vue.
L'Homme étranger à soi de l'homme est ignoré.
Qui suis-je, où suis-je, où vais-je, et d'où suis-je tiré?
Atomes tourmentés sur cet amas de boue,
Que la mort engloutit et dont le sort se joue;
Mais atomes pensans, atomes dont les yeux
Guidés par la pensée ont mesuré les cieux:
Au sein de l'Infini nous élançons notre être,
Sans pouvoir un moment nous voir et nous connaître."

("What can the broadest scope of mind achieve?
Nothing: the book of the fate closes to our sight.
Man foreign to the self by man is unknown.
What am I, where am I, where am I going, and whence do I come?
Tormented atoms on this globe of mud,
Swallowed by death and toys of fate;
But thinking atoms, atoms whose eyes
Guided by thought have measured heavens;
Into infinity our being soars,
Without being able to see and know ourselves for one moment")

The first two lines seem to convey a pessimistic message condensed in an emphatic *Nothing*. But the stress subsequently placed on "thought" and the dualism of mind-spirit — "esprit" — present two sets of possibilities. The combination of intellect and "scope" — étendue" — is reminiscent of passages of *Micromégas* which have already been quoted in which "thought" is defined as "the true life of the spirits" and in which "thinking beings" are said to be "non-spatial" — "sans étendue." The spatial mind which collects and classifies the sensory data of materiality can do nothing to open the book of fate. But man is endowed with faculties which

have enabled him to measure heavens and with aspirations geared to Infinity. The existence and the nature of superior human vision are suggested by the word "atoms." As was previously noted, the Secret Doctrine teaches that the atom is the most metaphysical object on our plane of life. The "eyes" of thinking human "atoms" are those of transcendental insight. The importance of Self-Knowledge is stressed twice. It is through that generally neglected domain that the book of fate may be approached. Man the microcosm in the macrocosm must learn to know himself before he can unveil the mystery of lives far less complex than his own. The last line of the stanza contains a suggestion of the enduring force of truth. Man may not "see" or "know" himself "for one moment." The esoteric reader is reminded of a passage of *The Princess of Babylon* in which the allegory of Truth is addressed in these words: "Can one have seen you and not see you again?"

The stanza is a fine example of pessimistic exoteric material susceptible to transfiguration. Taken in their esoteric sense the key words "esprit," "étendue," and "rien" — "no-thing" — shed serene light on a deceptive passage. Liberated from "the impediments of matter" the superior faculties of man are virtually boundless. Spirit can achieve the omniscience of true "being and nothingness."

The compelling beauty of the stanza belongs to a timeless commonwealth of pure greatness. The melody of Racinian elegy dwells in the verse: "Qui suis-je, où suis-je, où vais-je, et d'où suis-je tiré?" The spirit of Pascal throbs in the evocation of "thinking atoms" capable of measuring the heavens. The finale of *L'Esprit pur* — a flight of ultimate release captured by a poetic Beethoven — is announced in the Voltairian vision of Man soaring toward Infinity. The stanza featuring the mysterious yet accessible "closed book" thrills with movements and tones which may help us perceive "the end of things."

Voltaire designates physical existence as the realm of fear. Fear of death is equalled by fear of life:

"Nul ne voudrait mourir; nul ne voudrait renaître."
("No one would wish to die; no one would wish to be reborn.")

The verb "renaître" which conveys in unveiled form the idea of reincarnation is the subject of a note:

"On trouve difficilement une personne qui voulût recommencer la même carrière qu'elle a courue, et repasser par les mêmes evénements."
("It is difficult to find a person willing to retrace the same course which has been travelled, and to go through the same events.")

The special notice received by the significant verb — "to be reborn" — is an esoteric wink. The device used to force the attention of the reader

517

is similar to the humorous treatment of the word "autrui" in a preceding passage. The exoteric meaning of the line is sufficiently clear to make the addition of the note esoterically suspect.

Rare, transient pleasures lighten the burden of life:

> "Quelquefois dans nos jours consacrés aux douleurs
> Par la main du plaisir nous essuyons nos pleurs."
> ('Sometimes in our days doomed to grief
> With the hand of pleasure we wipe away our tears."

The esoteric significance of the word "pleasure" is given by Voltaire in the *Cinquième Discours sur la Nature du plaisir*:

> "Il faut que l'on soit homme afin d'être chrétien,
> Je suis homme, et d'un DIEU je chéris la clémence.
> Mortels! venez à lui, mais par reconnaissance.
> La nature attentive à remplir vos désirs
> Nous appelle à ce DIEU par la voix des plaisirs."

> ("One must be a man in order to be a christian,
> I am a man, and of a GOD I prize the clemency.
> Mortals! do come to him, but out of gratefulness.
> Nature, attentive to fulfill your desires,
> Calls you to that GOD through the voice of pleasures.")

Voltaire refers to "the science of Man" in *L'Ingénu*. The science in question must be conceived and pursued — if not mastered — before the message of Christ can assume full significance. The occult meaning of "Christ" embraces Chrestos, the Higher Self, the principle which must be awakened if "the science of man" is to be grasped at all. The eternal message of great spiritual leaders underlies the stanza: "O Man, Know Thyself!" The Kingdom of Heaven is within you."

One may note that the combination of terms "christian" and "a GOD" tends to designate Christ as one master among others.

The substance of the stanza is consistent with numerous scattered expressions of Voltairian optimism some of which have already been quoted: "— man is born for joy only." "— a noble, grateful and sensitive soul can live happy." The antagonism alleged to exist between joy and faith is rejected. It is a criminal fabrication of "speculators in human miseries." True happiness is next to godliness. The irrepressible longing for joy which impels every man to seek fulfillment is proof of the existence of Spirit. Nature did not create such a powerful yearning without providing for its satisfaction. Nirvanic bliss is the ultimate destiny of every human being. Foretastes of Absolute Bliss are attainable on earth. The concept of "pleasures" leading to GOD which is presented in the *Cinquième Dis-*

518

cours is applicable to all Voltairian writings. "True happiness" is defined as the "true life of the spirits" in chapter VII of *Micromégas*. The human ability to "wipe away" "tears" "with the hand of pleasure" which is recognized in the *Poem on the Disaster of Lisbon* is stressed in like manner by all esoteric writers. Man is occasionally granted "joys worthy of heaven" during his passage in the dungeon of incarnation.*

The final stanza of the commentary on the disaster of Lisbon begins — and ends — with references to "hope:"

> "Un jour tout sera bien, voilà notre espérance;
> *Tout est bien aujourd'hui,* voilà l'illusion.
> Les sages me trompaient, et DIEU seul a raison.
> Humble dans mes soupirs, soumis dans ma souffrance,
> Je ne m'élève point contre la Providence
> Sur un ton moins lugubre on me vit autrefois
> Chanter des doux plaisirs les séduisantes lois,
> D'autres temps, d'autres moeurs; instruit par la vicillesse,
> Des humains égarés partageant la failblesse,
> Dans une épaisse nuit cherchant à m'éclairer,
> Je ne sais que souffrir, et non pas murmurer."

> ("Some day all will be well, that is our hope;
> *All is well today,* that is the illusion.
> The sages were deceiving me, and GOD alone is right.
> Humble in my sighs, submissive in my suffering,
> I no longer rise against Providence.
> In less lugubrious tones I was seen once
> Celebrating the lovely laws of sweet pleasures,
> Of other times, other mores; instructed by age,
> Of benighted mankind sharing the weakness,
> In thick darkness seeking to find my way,
> I can only suffer, not complain.")

General hope of fulfillment should focus on the future. Untainted joy is not of this earth. While the axiom *"All is well"* is valid within the evolutionary perspective of the Secret Doctrine, the insight represented by the said doctrine is available to a few men only. As Voltaire states in *Memnon,* "the arrangement of the entire universe" must be conceived before the truth of the Panglossian refrain can be seriously considered. All seems and is far from well on the plane of existence of countless persons who do not have the "resources" of Voltaire. The author wisely refuses to assume the burden of guilt inherent to promotion of uninstructed, doomed optimism.

The hemistich "that is the illusion" deserves careful examination. The

---

*Alfred de Vigny, *Diary*, 1832.

presence of the word "All" adds to the complexity of the passage. The Panglossian axiom is incorrect if the word "All" is taken in its popular sense of "everything." It is valid if the word "All" is taken in its esoteric sense of "Great All" or cosmic perspective of Divine Wisdom. The significance of the word "illusion" may be applied to the word "illusion" itself in which case the illusory character of *All is well dissolves*. Voltaire may well have used the Mayavic power of "illusion" to court an inversion of the poles of exoteric appearance and esoteric reality.

The next line is isolated by punctuation:

"The sages were deceiving me, and GOD alone is right."

It is therefore "daring" to connect the verse with the "illusion" immediately preceding. Such a connection would imply that sages do not deceive and that GOD alone is wrong. In spite of the presence of punctuation and *because* of the Voltairian view of "daring," the proximity of terms does not seem totally innocent. Sages are prone to mislead in order to transmit veiled truths, a fact well known to Voltaire. GOD alone, GOD removed from the universe, conflicts with the Great All and with the All-Perfect-Being celebrated a few stanza earlier. The myth of a solitary GOD jealously hoarding Truth is regarded by the author as an outrage against Man and Deity. The illusive characteristic stressed by Voltaire seems to apply to the line last quoted.

One may note that the future-oriented statement "Some day all will be well" is not stressed by italics while the axiom "*All is well today*" is so endorsed. The perfection of Universal Law knows no such contingency as earthly time.

The remainder of the stanza contains a profession of humility and submission to the decrees of Providence, an attitude not entirely borne out by the general surface of the poem. The apparent contradiction is resolved by the esoteric equivalence of Karma and Providence. The creator of Jesrad is unlikely to "argue against what must be worshipped."

The parallels of opposite direction implied by the words "submitted" — "soumis" — and "I do not rise" suggest downward and upward motion respectively. Startling as the question may seem, it is appropriate to wonder if the word "submitted" conveys the idea of voluntary descent into matter or voluntary reincarnation. Such a theme is compatible with the statement: "I do not rise," an observation which does not rule out ability to "rise" but which seems to reflect a choice. It may be remembered at this point that Saint Yves "yields" out of "virtue" or "succumbs out of virtue" — "elle succombe par vertu". The verb "succomber" contains the same basic prefix as does the past participle "soumis". Virtue in the ety-

cours is applicable to all Voltairian writings. "True happiness" is defined as the "true life of the spirits" in chapter VII of *Micromégas*. The human ability to "wipe away" "tears" "with the hand of pleasure" which is recognized in the *Poem on the Disaster of Lisbon* is stressed in like manner by all esoteric writers. Man is occasionally granted "joys worthy of heaven" during his passage in the dungeon of incarnation.*

The final stanza of the commentary on the disaster of Lisbon begins — and ends — with references to "hope:"

"Un jour tout sera bien, voilà notre espérance;
Tout est bien aujourd'hui, voilà l'illusion.
Les sages me trompaient, et DIEU seul a raison.
Humble dans mes soupirs, soumis dans ma souffrance,
Je ne m'élève point contre la Providence
Sur un ton moins lugubre on me vit autrefois
Chanter des doux plaisirs les séduisantes lois,
D'autres temps, d'autres moeurs; instruit par la vicillesse,
Des humains égarés partageant la failblesse,
Dans une épaisse nuit cherchant à m'éclairer,
Je ne sais que souffrir, et non pas murmurer."

("Some day all will be well, that is our hope;
All is well today, that is the illusion.
The sages were deceiving me, and GOD alone is right.
Humble in my sighs, submissive in my suffering,
I no longer rise against Providence.
In less lugubrious tones I was seen once
Celebrating the lovely laws of sweet pleasures,
Of other times, other mores; instructed by age,
Of benighted mankind sharing the weakness,
In thick darkness seeking to find my way,
I can only suffer, not complain.")

General hope of fulfillment should focus on the future. Untainted joy is not of this earth. While the axiom *"All is well"* is valid within the evolutionary perspective of the Secret Doctrine, the insight represented by the said doctrine is available to a few men only. As Voltaire states in *Memnon,* "the arrangement of the entire universe" must be conceived before the truth of the Panglossian refrain can be seriously considered. All seems and is far from well on the plane of existence of countless persons who do not have the "resources" of Voltaire. The author wisely refuses to assume the burden of guilt inherent to promotion of uninstructed, doomed optimism.

The hemistich "that is the illusion" deserves careful examination. The

---

*Alfred de Vigny, *Diary*, 1832.

presence of the word "All" adds to the complexity of the passage. The Panglossian axiom is incorrect if the word "All" is taken in its popular sense of "everything." It is valid if the word "All" is taken in its esoteric sense of "Great All" or cosmic perspective of Divine Wisdom. The significance of the word "illusion" may be applied to the word "illusion" itself in which case the illusory character of *All is well dissolves.* Voltaire may well have used the Mayavic power of "illusion" to court an inversion of the poles of exoteric appearance and esoteric reality.

The next line is isolated by punctuation:

"The sages were deceiving me, and GOD alone is right."

It is therefore "daring" to connect the verse with the "illusion" immediately preceding. Such a connection would imply that sages do not deceive and that GOD alone is wrong. In spite of the presence of punctuation and *because* of the Voltairian view of "daring," the proximity of terms does not seem totally innocent. Sages are prone to mislead in order to transmit veiled truths, a fact well known to Voltaire. GOD alone, GOD removed from the universe, conflicts with the Great All and with the All-Perfect-Being celebrated a few stanza earlier. The myth of a solitary GOD jealously hoarding Truth is regarded by the author as an outrage against Man and Deity. The illusive characteristic stressed by Voltaire seems to apply to the line last quoted.

One may note that the future-oriented statement "Some day all will be well" is not stressed by italics while the axiom *"All is well today"* is so endorsed. The perfection of Universal Law knows no such contingency as earthly time.

The remainder of the stanza contains a profession of humility and submission to the decrees of Providence, an attitude not entirely borne out by the general surface of the poem. The apparent contradiction is resolved by the esoteric equivalence of Karma and Providence. The creator of Jesrad is unlikely to "argue against what must be worshipped."

The parallels of opposite direction implied by the words "submitted" — "soumis" — and "I do not rise" suggest downward and upward motion respectively. Startling as the question may seem, it is appropriate to wonder if the word "submitted" conveys the idea of voluntary descent into matter or voluntary reincarnation. Such a theme is compatible with the statement: "I do not rise," an observation which does not rule out ability to "rise" but which seems to reflect a choice. It may be remembered at this point that Saint Yves "yields" out of "virtue" or "succumbs out of virtue" — "elle succombe par vertu". The verb "succomber" contains the same basic prefix as does the past participle "soumis". Virtue in the etymological sense is "strength" or esoteric spirituality. The same theme of voluntary prostitution to matter seems to be connected with the experience of Saint Yves and with the autobiographical comment of Voltaire.

The "Great Sacrifice" entails submission to Karma during the voluntary return to materiality. The statement: "I do not rise against Providence" — Karma — is a seemingly tenuous yet meaningful clue to Bodhisattva. It is supported by numerous other suggestions scattered in the writings of Voltaire.

Voltaire's use of the possessive adjective *my* in the phrase: "in my suffering" may have been intended to stress personal decision. The phonetic quality of the expression "soumis dans ma souffrance" is debatable. Voltaire's ability to write harmonious verse is not. The hemistich might easily have read: "soumis à la souffrance," a change which would relieve a certain heaviness without major alteration of exoteric meaning. In view of the proximity of the subject pronoun "je" — "I" — few if any — exoteric readers would ask the question: "Whose suffering?" The words "submitted to" which amount esoterically to "having descended into *my* suffering" have the further effect of limiting resignation to Voltaire's own cross. The scope of infinite compassion seems to be locked in the one short word. Selection of the first-person possessive adjective may have been prompted by four considerations: 1) use of discordant words calculated to awake the critical faculties and the curiosity of the reader; 2) exploitation of unwieldly sounds which are made to convey the sensation of a heavy burden — the "burden" of life incarnate; 3) desire to record esoterically as astonishing autobiographical fact; 4) need to explain such a decision in the light of love of mankind.

Another line of the same stanza suggests the same line of interpretation:

"Of benighted mankind sharing the weakness —"

Esoteric "weakness" represents limited spirituality or incarnation. The question of "why the soul is bound in its feeble — or weak — prison,"* a question raised by Vigny — comes very close to stating the equivalence. The Voltairian "sharing" of "human weakness" — probably prompted by spiritual "strength" — suggests voluntary reincarnation.

The eternal search for Truth — or light — is mentioned in the line:

"In thick darkness seeking to find my way."

The passage may be translated as "seeking" to find light." The dual

---

*Alfred de Vigny, *Le Mont des oliviers.*

521

essence of many French reflexive verbs such as "s'éclairer" makes full and simultaneous English translation impossible. The verb may equally well mean "to find light" or "to make oneself clear." Voltaire apparently wished to summarize the purpose of his mission on earth in those words. It is difficult to deny that he "tried to make" himself "clear in thick darkness."

The occult concept of the GREAT SACRIFICE may be relevant to Voltaire:

> "The 'BEING' just referred to, which has to remain nameless, is the *Tree* from which, in subsequent ages, all the great *historically* known Sages and Hierophants, such as the Rishi Kapila, Hermes, Enoch, Orpheus, etc., etc., have branched off. As objective *man,* he is the mysterious (to the profane — the ever invisible) yet present Personage about whom legends are rife in the East, especially among the Occultists and the students of the Sacred Science. It is he who changes form, yet remains ever the same. And it is he again who holds spiritual sway over the *initiated* Adepts throughout the whole world. He is, as said, the 'nameless One' who has so many names, and yet whose names and whose very nature are unknown. He is *the* 'Initiator,' called the 'GREAT SACRIFICE.' For, sitting at the threshhold of LIGHT, he looks into it from within the circle of Darkness, which he will not cross; nor will he quit his post till the last day of this life-cycle. Why does he sit by the fountain of primeval Wisdom, of which he drinks no longer, as he has naught to learn which he does not know — aye, neither on this Earth, nor in its heaven? Because the lonely, sore-footed pilgrims on their way back to their *home* are never sure to the last moment of not losing their way in this limitless desert of illusion and matter called Earth-Life. Because he would fain show the way to that region of freedom and light, from which he is a voluntary exile himself, to every prisoner who has succeded in liberating himself from the bonds of flesh and illusion. Because, in short, he has sacrificed himself for the sake of mankind, though but a few Elect may profit by the GREAT SACRIFICE." (*The Secret Doctrine,* pp. 207-208, Vol. I).

The Great Sacrifice "who has so many names and yet whose names and whose very nature are unknown" seems to recur in Voltairian writings. Zadig is DAG, a Savior in disguise and an Instructor — or Initiator — of Mankind. Candide takes place in an era not favorable to Saviors. But the absence of such a figure is partially compensated by the "nameless" presence of the author himself and by the presence of Pangloss. L'Ingénu is the story of a celestial messenger carrying the timeless legacy of Truth to modern mankind. The "nameless" Promethean hero who becomes "Hercules" eventually reappears in Paris "under another name" which may be the true one. The question of powers controlling his life, a question raised by the "prisoner" himself — may have its answer in the text quoted above: "— nor will he quit his post till the last day of this life-cycle."

The sacrificial BEING "sitting at the threshhold of LIGHT" and looking "into it from within the circle of Darkness" may have a great deal in common with the writer who "shares the weakness" of "benighted mankind." Such a Being may be connected with the literary beacon who sought to "make himself clear" also in the midst of "darkness."

The poem *Voyage à Berlin* contains the following remark: "Were I a true traveller —" — "Si j'étais un vrai voyageur". The observation may refer to secret political missions perhaps even to occult involvements connected with the trip to Prussia. It may also signify that the entire journey of Voltaire on our "small globe of mud" was no ordinary jaunt. Voluntary reincarnation seems to be the only alternative to regular "travel."

Micromégas suggests the same possibility from the very first lines:

> "Dans une de ces planètes qui tournent autour de l'étoile nommée Sirius, il y avait un jeune homme de beaucoup d'esprit que j'ai eu l'honneur de connaître dans le dernier voyage qu'il fit sur notre petite fourmillière;—" (Ch. I, p. 107).

> ("On one of those planets which revolve around the star named Sirius, there was a young man of great wit (or "spirit") whom I had the honor of knowing during the last trip which he made to our little anthill.")

The spirited "animal from Sirius" — who also appears in *Memnon* — seems to have been a close acquaintance of Voltaire.

The interesting technique used to verify the measurements of "Micromégas" involves a *tree* planted in an unmentionable part of his Excellency's anatomy. The subject of the experiment is required to "lie down" for, "had he remained standing, his head would have been too far above the clouds." The sysmbolism of downward motion suggests incarnation. The symbolism of "clouds," "smoke," or "veils" is a standard tool of scriptural and other esoteric expression. The meaning of a celestial "voice" such as that of the Sirian — a voice which must be softened to be "heard" — seems clear. The head which would normally be beyond human vision or understanding needs little interpretive comment. The act of "lying down" which is performed on request — yet voluntarily and graciously — shows sensitivity to human need, an attitude which is the virtual definition of Bodhisattva. The "amusing" passage contains an astounding element of autobiography. The occult message of Voltaire never could have reached mankind had it not been made temporarily captive in books. It was necessary to its transmission that a sacrificial descent to earth be consented.

The measuring procedure involves a degree of "infamy" to which less dedicated beings would object. The surface buffoonery conceals the occult symbolism of the cross — the physical *birth* of one designed to aid the spiritual *birth* of others. The anatomical involvement of a nether pole of being represents the depths of materiality.

> "The crucifix was an instrument of torture, and utterly common among Romans, as it was unknown among Semitic nations. It was called the 'Tree of Infamy.' It is but later that it was adopted as a Christian symbol; but, during the first two decades, the apostles looked upon it with horror." (*Isis Unveiled*, p. 255, Vol. 2).

The co-essence of "cross," "tree of infamy" and "tree of life" tends to confirm the symbolism of incarnation which is suggested in *Micromégas*. The intellectual and spiritual giant submitting to the cross of birth or tree of infamy seems to be Voltaire himself. He is "measured" — or judged by physical characteristics or exoteric externals. He is eventually found to be "a young man" 120,000 ft. high — "cent vingt mille pieds de roi." His stature — which is suggested to be "royal" — cannot be denied. But his true essence eludes the majority of "measures."

The Titan named "Micromégas" may well belong to the *Tree* of "great *historically* known Sages."

The *Recherche* seems to confirm the suggestions of voluntary reincarnation which are found in the autobiographical comments of Voltaire. The name of M. "Legrandin" is indicative of greatness — "grand, tall, great." The ending of the name may constitute a phonetic reference to the last syllable of the word "mondain." The "worldly" character is "worldly" to a cosmic degree. What lies behind the name and its mysterious wearer is suggested by Proust in the following terms:

> "Avant d'arriver chez Saint-Loup, qui devait m'attendre devant sa porte, je rencontrai Legrandin, que nous avions perdu de vue depuis Combray et qui, tout grisonnant maintenant, avait gardé son air jeune et candide, Il s'arrêta.
>
> —'Ah! vous voila,' me dit-il, 'homme chic, et en redingote encore! Voilà une livrée dont mon indépendance ne s'accommoderait pas. Il est vrai que vous devez être un mondain, faire des visites! Pour aller rêver comme je le fais devant quelque tombe à demi-détruite, ma lavallière et mon veston ne sont pas déplacés. Pendant que vous irez à quelque *five o'clock,* votre vieil ami sera plus heureux que vous, car seul dans un faubourg, il regardera monter dans le ciel violet la lune rose. La vérité est que je n'appartiens guère à cette terre où je me sens si exilé; il faut toute la force de la loi de gravitation pour m'y maintenir et que je ne m'évade pas dans une autre sphère. Je suis d'une autre planète. Adieu, ne prenez pas en mauvaise part la vieille franchise du paysan de la Vivonne qui est aussi resté le paysan du Danube." (*A la Recherche du temps perdu*, p. 154, Vol. II).

> ("Before arriving at the home of Saint-Loup, who was to wait for me in front of his door, I met Legrandin, of whom we had lost sight since

Combray and who, all gray now, had kept his youthful and candid look. He stopped.

—'Ah! there you are,' he said to me, 'smart-looking man, and in a frock-coat yet! That is a livery which my independence would find it hard to take. It is true that you must be a worldly socialite, that you must make calls. To go and dream as I do in front of a half-destroyed grave, my loose necktie and my jacket are not out of place. While you are going to some tea, your old friend will be happier than you, for alone in a remote district of the town, he will be watching the pink moon rising in the purple sky. The truth is that I hardly belong to this earth where I feel so much in exile; it takes all the force of the law of gravity to maintain me there and to keep me from escaping to another sphere. I am of another planet. Farewell, do not take amiss the old-fashioned frankness of the peasant of the Vivonne who has also remained the peasant of the Danube.' ")

The admitted nostalgia of "Legrandin" for "another planet" is supplemented by significant symbolic details scattered in the *Recherche*. The "loose necktie" suggests the privileged Karma of voluntary reincarnation. The plain jacket or coat — which strangely belies the exoteric appearance of "snobbery" — is the plain "coat of skin" worn by common men. It is the garb of a person who takes little interest in earthly "garments" or physical bodies. It is the mark of a being who cares even less for "smart-looking clothes." The half-destroyed grave mentioned by the puzzling engineer may represent a return from the "beyond." It may also convey an allusion to the ancient tomb mentioned in the *Voyage à Berlin*. Voltaire observes that the sight of the monument brings ecstasy to certain viewers. The same grave seems to be the object of an allusion in another passage of the *Recherche*. It is noted that an old "archaelogist" weeps in front of Assyrian ruins located in the area of Berlin and Postdam.* The sensitive connoisseur may be Voltaire. Françoise, the shrewd "servant," is aware of the degree of devotion of which "Legrandin" is capable. The engineer would rather give up his own "couch" and "lie down on earth" than abandon a fellow-"invert:"

> " 'Petite, si jamais vous êtes dans la peine, allez vers ce Monsieur. Il coucherait plutôt par terre et vous donnerait son lit.' " (*A la Recherche du temps perdu*, p. 701, Vol. III).

> " 'Little one, if you are ever in grief, go to that gentleman. He would rather lie down on the earth (or "on the ground") and give you his bed.' ")

The willingness of "Legrandin" to "lie down on earth" is the subject of numerous esoteric allusions made by fellow — "smugglers" of the

---

A la Recherche du temps perdu, pp. 526-27, Vol. II.

Secret Doctrine. Vigny refers to "Vole-à-terre" — "flight — to earth" — in a passage of *Stello* which will be quoted in a subsequent chapter.

The *Poem on the Disaster of Lisbon* contains a fantastic element of Voltairian autobiography. Comparable material is found in the writings of various esoteric authors. Vigny gave the date of his Way to Damascus as 1843 using a reference of *L'Esprit pur* — a poem written in 1863 — to his "twenty years of silence." Proust consigned his spiritual "genealogy" to the strange utterances of two minor characters of the *Recherche*. Voltaire did no more than follow the practice of other "deceivers" who were all driven by the same love of mankind.

The *Poem on the Disaster of Lisbon* contains another element of autobiography. More transparent — and less startling — is an allusion to *Le Mondain*.

> "Sur un ton moins lugubre on me vit autrefois
> Chanter des doux plaisirs les séduisantes lois.
> D'autres temps, d'autre moeurs:—")

> ("On a less lugubrious tone I was seen once
> Celebrating the lovely laws of sweet pleasures,
> Of other times, other mores;—")

Youthful hedonism and optimism seem to be rejected. But the previous celebration of "pleasure" which forms the essence of *Le Mondain* is not without parallel in the *Poem on the Disaster of Lisbon*. Voltaire acknowledges the value of "pleasures" occasionally granted to suffering mankind. "Other times, other mores" seems to finalize the divorce between the tragic now and the merry then. But the same period of human evolution is evoked in both texts. The long-lost days of the "winged men" of Plato represent the era which is celebrated esoterically in *Le Mondain*.

The importance of Time is also stressed by reference to "age." The "instruction" or insight which has been gained by the author has brought wisdom. But wisdom merely confirms the conviction of youth. The "unworldly" writer of *Le Mondain* gave thanks to Providence for the privilege of living in modern times. Modern times were designated as "the Iron Age." The voluntary exile of the subsequent poem does "not rise against Providence." The period in which he lives is not entirely deprived of hope. The comparison of esoteric material found in each text does not reveal any difference. The few years of earthly time which have elapsed from one writing to the next do not succeed in blurring the timeless identity of inspiration. The same basic view of "pleasure" — or spirituality, a pursuit which entails obedience to certain "laws" — and the same evolutionary perspective underlie both works. The reference to "a less lugubrious tone" is an invitation to look beyond appearance. *Le Mondain* and the *Poem on the Disaster of Lisbon* are variations on identical themes.

The last lines of the poem contrast contingency, misery, or illusion and divine reality. The comparison seems calculated to help the reader distinguish between what the author "refutes" and what he "accepts." The "unique, unlimited being" which dominates the last stanza is not the biblical GOD. The final word supports the contention of a great writer mentioned in the preface: "Hope springs eternal."

> "Un calife autrefois à son heure dernière,
> Au Dieu qu'il adorait dit pour toute prière:
> 'Je t'apporte, ô seul roi, seul être illimité,
> Tout ce que tu n'as pas dans ton immensité,
> Les défauts, les regrets, les maux, et l'ignorance.'
> Mais il pouvait encore ajouter *l'espérance.*"

> ("A caliph once said in his last hour
> To the God he worshipped as his whole prayer:
> 'I bring you, o unique king, unique unlimited Being,
> That which you do not have in your immensity,
> Imperfection, regret, misfortune ignorance.'
> But he could also have added: "hope.")

Voltaire suggests in appended notes that certain "resources" exist which "—destroy doubt and put certainty in its place." The author seems to anticipate the line of *Le Mont des oliviers* which has already been quoted: "Evil and Doubt! With one word I can pulverize them." Vigny, Voltaire —and many others—hold identical views on the existence of knowledge capable of endowing mankind with "Happy Certainty and Trusting Hope."[*] The findings of the "arrogant sophist" and the findings of "the other" inquirer featured in the *Poem on the Disaster of Lisbon* are jointly correct in the philosophy of both writers. The Word of Jesus could have changed the earth had evolutionary conditions been ripe for general enlightenment in his times. Such was not the case in the days of Christ, in the days of Voltaire, or even in the days of Vigny. But the mission of spiritual leaders is ever the same. One "set foot on this atrophied globe."[**] Another came to "our small globe of mud." A third made a sublime contribution to a timeless Bottle to the Sea. "Happy Certainty and Hope" were their intended gifts to the men of the future.

The Poem on the *Disaster of Lisbon* is an esoteric batlefield between the biblical GOD and the impersonal Supreme Being of occult philosophy.

---

[*]Alfred de Vigny, *Le Mont des oliviers.*
[**]Alfred de Vigny, *Le Mont des Oliviers.*

Jehovah is symbolically omitted, therefore discarded, in the final lines. The "unique, unlimited Being" stands victorious at the end of the confrontation. The suggested twilight of the false GOD and the decline of related Judaeo-Christian ignorance explain the final emphasis on "hope." The existence of messengers who strive to make themselves "clear" "in thick darkness" supports optimistic views. The capacity of "human atoms" to yearn for "infinity" and to "measure heavens" may some day "measure" other things including the entire esoteric bequest of Voltaire.

Nowhere in his monumental works does Voltaire seem to have suffered more from inability to speak openly. The vibrant ease and clarity which normally characterize his style are tortured and obscured. Warnings and explanations are needed and given. Several hints are offered of the concealed genesis of certain "failures" of form.

The esoteric substance of the poem is consistent with the veiled substance of other Voltairian texts. Evolution of the author toward pessimism is belied by the concealed message. The same melodic theme of the "music of the spheres" which is found in *Zadig, Micromégas, L'Ingénu* and *Le Mondain* is simply transposed from a blissful tone into a somber minor key.

WHAT IS IN A NAME?
(VOLTAIRE)

The accepted Genesis of the name VOLTAIRE is open to question. It is generally stated in literary manuals that the name originated on the maternal side of the philosopher's family. Some explanation is given of how the transmutation from Arouet l(e) j(eune) took place. While the raw material in question does yield the famous *nom de plume,* a few operations other than the anagrammatic process described are needed to obtain the chosen name. Certain letters must be substituted to others. The involved sleight of hand is not inscrutable. But it is bizarre. Most important of all, it fails to show why the end product was selected in the first place.

The rich meaning conveyed by proper names created by the author himself, the esoteric character of Voltairian thought and the philosopher's denial of the existence of chance all invite speculation. There is reason to wonder what IS in the famous name.

The following ideas may have influenced the choice of VOLTAIRE:

Vole terre. ("Voler" — "to fly," "terre" — "earth") The earth flies" or rotates through space: 1) exoterically in accordance with the laws of the heliocentric system; 2) esoterically in accordance with the occult view of Universal Law. Such considerations, if they were involved in the choice of the name, may also represent an allusion to Galileo, a human symbol of persecuted and vindicated knowledge.

Volte terre. ("Volte" — "turn," "terre" — "earth") Again the rotation of earth. Possible allusion to the periodical tilting of the axis of earth which is mentioned esoterically in *L'Ingénu.* Subversion of terrestrial political, intellectual, and spiritual status quo. Anticipation of the Great Revolution. Anticipation of a second — perhaps greater by far — "Revolution" prepared by Voltaire. The latter development seems to have been expected to take place in our times.

Vult terre. (Old French form of "vouloir" — "to want," "terre" — "earth") Desire to conquer the earth; determination to convert mankind to a better social, political, intellectual, and spiritual orientation than that prevailing in Voltaire own times.

Vult taire. (Old French form of "vouloir" — "to want," "taire" — "to hush, to be or keep quiet") Desire to pursue and advocate spiritual development through "instructed" silence or discovery of the Higher Self. Occut exploration in general. Observance of discretion or esoteric necessity.

Vol (à) terre. "Voler" — "to steal," "terre" — "earth") Theft from earth regarded as a symbol of materiality. Mission intended to reduce the prevalence of materialistic creeds and pursuits on earth.

Vol (à) terre. ("Vol" — "flight," action of flying, "terre" — "earth") Symbolic ability to "fly" or to use "the conveyances of up there" in the acquisition of knowledge. A faculty which Voltaire possessed to the highest degree and which he advocated to others. Voltaire's downward flight to earth or voluntary reincarnation.

The ironic presence of the three vowels representing IAO may have been intended to supplement the silence-connected interpretation. Desire to "hush" or silence forever Jehovah and his "thunder." Determination to cure related ailments which plague XVIIIth Century — and more modern — societies.

We may never know which — if any or all — of the above ideas were on the mind of the Sage when he selected the name. But we may turn to secret brothers of Voltaire who seem to have certain views on the matter.

Voltaire is mentioned openly in the Proustian *Recherche*. Brichot, a scholarly character possessed of encyclopaedic knowledge — seldom fails to mention "M. de Voltaire" with emphatic irony. Various traits and activities of the professor suggest the probable esoteric identity of Diderot. The irony which is aroused in the scholar whenever "M. de Voltaire" is mentioned seems to be of double-edged variety. The famous name and the aristocratic *de* are probably used in earnest, indeed with a reverence worthy of the *Rêve de d'Alembert*:

> "Mlle de l'Espinasse — A quoi rêvez-vous?
> Bordeu — A propos de Voltaire.
> Mlle de l'Espinasse — Eh bien?
> Bordeu — Je rêve à la manière dont se font les grands hommes.
> Mlle de l'Espinasse — Et comment se font-ils?
> Bordeu — Comment? La sensibilité . . ."

> ("Mlle de l'Espinasse — What are you dreaming of?
> Bordeu — of Voltaire.
> Mlle de l'Espinasse — Well?
> Bordeu — I dream of the manner in which great men are made.
> Mlle de l'Espinasse — And how are they made?
> Bordeu — How? Sensitivity . . ."

"Sensitivity" is connected with a Voltairian "descent" in another work of Diderot:

"Si vous rendez de Voltaire moíns sensible à la critique, il ne saura plus descendre dans l'âme de Mérope, il me vous touchera plus." (*Le Neveu de Rameau*, p. 405, Ed. Garnier).

("If you make de Voltaire less sensitive to criticism, he will no longer be able to descend into the soul of Mérope; he will no longer touch you.")

The name of the title character of *Mérope* — a tragedy written by Voltaire — is derived from a Greek word meaning "mortal" or "man." ("*mérops, méropos*".) The same word is noted to convey the esoteric significance of "daughter of Atlantis" in the Secret Doctrine.* The deep sense of the passage last quoted may be as follows: Voltaire was able to "descend" into a "mortal soul" — the human condition — by choice. The "sensitivity" which impelled him to do so seems to be sensitivity to human need. "Criticism" is then of non-literary character. It is the legitimate grievance of men who, in the words of *Candide*, could "complain a little about what takes place — in physical and moral domains." It is the "perceptiveness" recognized by Voltaire in the *poem on the Disaster of Lisbon*. "When man dares complain of such a dreadful scourge, / He is not presumptuous, alas, he is perceptive." ("sensible"). Diderot seems to salute the sensitivity of Voltaire to human misery, a quality which prompted the "great man" to share the condition of ordinary mortals. The Voltairian "descent" is judged necessary to "touch" or "reach" human beings — or to bring a certain message to mankind.

"Legrandin" is accused of claiming a "false title." The intriguing character — whose "candid," "ingenuous," and "worldly" traits are noted in various parts of the *Recherche* — wishes to be known as the Count of Méséglise. The controversial status proves legitimate in the end. The deceptive "snob" is truly "noble." The question of what is in a name seems to be settled where the "Count of Méséglise" is concerned. The rare elevation of "Legrandin" is expected to gain universal recognition in due course of time:

"Tout autre titre faux eût donné moins d'ennuis aux Guermantes. Mais l'aristocratie sait les assumer, et bien d'autres encore, du moment qu'un mariage jugé utile, à quelque point de vue que ce soit, est en jeu. Couvert par le duc de Guermantes, Legrandin fut pour une partie de cette géné-ration-là et sera pour la totalité de celle qui la suivra, le véritable comte de Méséglise." (*A la Recherche du temps perdu*, p. 672, Vol. III).

("Any other false title would have caused less trouble to the Guermantes. But the aristocracy knows how to assume them, and many others yet, as long as a marriage considered useful, from any point of view

---

The Secret Doctrine, p. 768, Vol. II.

531

whatsoever, is at stake. Shielded by the duke de Guermantes, Legrandin was for a part of that generation, and will be for the entirety of the following one, the true Count of Méséglise.")

Vigny did not fail to give recognition to Voltaire the man or to *Voltaire* the name. Voltaire the man receives the following tribute in the *Diary* of 1840:

> 'Voltaire avait cette faculté double et si rare de la méditation et de l'improvisation dans la conversation."
>
> ("Voltaire had that faculty — double and so rare — of meditation and improvisation in conversation.")

Voltaire the name receives notice in *Stello*. One of the major characters of the story is Gilbert — the probable source of the Proustian name "Gilberte." The hero is a gifted poet condemned to die in destitution by an ignorant and vicious society. Gilbert commits suicide by swallowing a meaningful *key*. In a chapter entitled *Demi-Folie* — "half-madness' — the dying, delirious young man utters the following, "incoherent" words:

> " — il ouvrit les yeux. 'Un rat!' cria-t-il — 'Un lapin! Je jure sur l'Evangile que c'est un lapin — C'est Voltaire! C'est Vol-à-terre! — Oh! le joli jeu de mots! N'est-ce-pas? Hein mon cher seigneur — il est gentil, mon jeu de mots? — Il n'y a pas un libraire qui veuille me le payer un sou —'" (*Stello* 8, Demi-Folie).
>
> ("— he opened his eyes. 'A rat! he screamed — 'A rabbit! I swear on the Gospel that it is a rabbit — It is Voltaire! It is Vol-à-terre! — Oh! the lovely pun! Isn't that right? Nay, my lord — it is sweet, my pun? There is not a single publisher willing to give me one cent for it —' ")

Diderot seems to have understood — and revered — the willingness of "M. de Voltaire" to share the weakness of benighted mankind. Proust pays tribute to the greatness of a true "nobleman;" "Legrandin." Vigny suggests a connection between the name of the Sage of Ferney and a "flight to earth" or voluntary reincarnation.

What IS in the name of the great man is the boundless love of the ultimate sacrifice. It is the esoteric concept of VOLONTAIRE.

FRATERNAL "CASTIGATION"

Alfred de Vigny refers to Voltaire in Section II of *La Maison du berger*. The allusion seems to convey little praise. Along with co-defendants Anacreon and Horace, Voltaire is found guilty of contributing to the delinquency of Poetry.

To Vigny — as to all esoteric writers — poetry is far more than a melodious outpouring of imagery and sound. As was previously noted, the author of *Les Destinées* indicated in his *Diary* the existence of a key word to the "poetic enigma" of his verse. With gentle irony the same author notes in the same *Diary* the popular tendency to view poetry as "the daughter of a lovely whim:"

> —"on regarde la poésie comme toujours menteuse et fille d'un gentil caprice." (*Journal,* 1843).

> ("— Poetry is regarded as always deceptive and as the daughter of a lovely whim.")

The Muse is deceptive indeed. She is a weaver of spells and veils. But her status of esoteric accomplice serves a precise body of Truth. Poetry is "poetised Truth."

Vigny traces the evolution or "Fall" or Poetry which parallels the evolution of Man:

> "La Muse a mérité les insolents sourires
> Et les soupçons moqueurs qu'éveille son aspect.
> Dès que son oeil chercha le regard des satyres,
> Sa parole trembla, son serment fut suspect;
> Il lui fut interdit d'enseigner la sagesse.
> Au passant du chemin elle criait: 'Largesse!'
> Le passant lui donna sans crainte et sans respect."

> ("The Muse has deserved the insolent smiles
> And the mocking skepticism aroused by her appearance.
> As soon as her eye sought the eye of satyrs,
> Her word grew tremulous, her oath was suspect;
> She was prohibited from teaching wisdom.
> To the passer-by on his way she shouted: Largess!
> The passer-by gave to her without fear or respect.")

The reference to satyrs links the "Fall" of poetry to Fourth Race bestiality. Eurydike becomes esoteric through cyclic "necessity." Her in-

533

creasing inability to "teach wisdom" — science — is reflected by the "smiles" and "mocking suspicion" of the majority. Smiles of different character are elicited from rare esoteric readers.

> "Ah! fille sans pudeur, fille du Saint Orphée,
> Que n'as-tu conservé ta belle gravité!
> Tu n'irais pas ainsi, d'une voix étouffée,
> Chanter aux carrefours impurs de la cité;
> Tu n'aurais pas collé sur le coin de ta bouche
> Le coquet madrigal, piquant comme une mouche
> Et, près de ton oeil bleu, l'équivoque effronté."

> ("Ah! brazen woman, daughter of Saint Orpheus,
> Why did you not preserve your beautiful gravity!
> You would not thus go, in a hoarse voice,
> Singing on the impure street-corners of the city:
> You would not have glued on the corner of your mouth
> The flirtatious madrigal, piquant as a beauty-spot
> And near your blue eye the impudent ambiguous leer.")

The reference to "Saint Orpheus" provocatively combines sainthood and Paganism. The figure of Poetry is situated within the realm of esoteric allegory. The "depth" or "weight" ("gravité") which has been lost is the substance of occult lore conveyed by Orphism and comparable doctrines. But the loss is partially compensated by esoteric "ambiguity." Poetry has followed the general descent into materiality, sensuality, and phallicism. Naked Truth has lost her original *innocence* and acquired a questionable "coat of skin" or veil. But her transcendental insight remains accessible to those who can probe beyond the surface. The "blue eye" of the Muse is akin to the vision of beautiful Falide. It is connected with the watchfulness of the "blue-eyed angel" presiding over the spiritual progress of mankind which is mentioned in a subsequent stanza.

Modern technology is symbolized by a monstrous locomotive. It must be subordinated to lofty spiritual aims if mankind is to be saved from an apocalypse of its own making.

> "Oui, si l'ange aux yeux bleus ne veille sur sa route,
> Et le glaive à la main ne plane et la défend,
> S'il n'a compté les coups du levier, s'il n'écoute
> Chaque tour de la roue en son cours triomphant,
> S'il n'a l'oeil sur les eaux et la main sur la braise,
> Pour jeter en éclats la magique fournaise,
> If suffira toujours du caillou d'un enfant."

> ("Yes, if the blue-eyed angel does not watch over its course,
> And with a sword in hand does not hover protectively,
> If it did not count the thrusts of the lever, if it does not listen,

534

To each turn of the wheel in its triumphant course,
If it does not keep an eye on the waters or a hand on the coals,
To blow into fragments the magical furnace,
The small rock of a child will ever suffice.")

The crucial importance of Time symbolized by a number of "thrusts" of a "lever" is connected with the evolutionary process. The cosmic energy of Karma is present in the invincible "turn of the wheel." The occult view of periodic cataclysms connected with fire and water — the "coals," the "water" — is stressed. Modern mankind courts disaster if it fails to "listen" to the teachings of Karma-Evolution. The materialistic civilization of the West is likened to a sorcerer's apprentice in the next stanza. "Man has climbed too soon on the iron bull." "No one is master of the bellowing dragon" evolved by materialistic science. The "sword of knowledge" and the ethical orientation suggested by the "blue-eyed" angel" are indispensable to the *material* survival of mankind.

The catastrophic potential of modern civilization is only the reverse side of a "fine picture." The technological juggernaut is inseparable from a cultural foundation of undreamed potency. Literature is such a "magical furnace." The esoteric "rock" of an esoteric "child" can release its hidden might.

The stanza condemning Voltaire describes a scene of debauchery. An unnamed dirty old man — generally believed to be Anacréon —, Horace and Voltaire are found guilty of the same crime. They have contributed to the degradation of Poetry:

"Tu tombas dès l'enfance, et, dans la folle Grèce,
Un vieillard, t'enivrant de son baiser jaloux,
Releva le premier ta robe de prêtresse,
Et, parmi les garçons, t'assit sur ses genoux.
De ce baiser mordant ton front porte la trace;
Tu chantas en buvant dans les banquets d'Horace,
Et Voltaire à la cour te traîna devant nous."

("You fell in your very infancy, and, in demented Greece,
An elder, intoxicating you with his jealous kiss,
Was first to raise your priestly robe,
And, among young men, seated you on his knee.
Of his mordant kiss your brow carries the trace;
You sang and drank in the banquets of Horace,
And Voltaire to court dragged you under our eyes.")

The *Classiques Larousse* edition of the poetry of Vigny identifies the elderly culprit as Anacréon. Commendable "objectivity" is displayed toward the accused. The footnote reads as follows:

535

"Le poète Anacréon, pour lequel Vigny est injuste (comme pour Horace et Voltaire.")

("The poet Anacreon, toward whom Vigny is unjust — as he is unjust toward Horace and Voltaire.")

The defense seems full of good intentions. But it is unnecessary. Anacréon, Horace, and Voltaire have "drunk" of the "spirit" and "raised the veil" of the priestess. The "reprimand" is a fraternal accolade.

Numerous examples of fraternal "castigation" can be cited. Voltaire once wrote about the works of Shakespeare that he had never seen so many gems under so much filth. No better definition of a certain type of esotericism could possibly be given. Rabelais and Céline are cases in point. Dirt is a most effective veil which has the power to absorb all faculties of an unsuspecting reader. Voltaire also commented that Rabelais never wrote anything without being drunk. The person who can ask himself: "Drunk on what?" — "spirit" perhaps — can understand the true nature of the "criticism" of Voltaire and the true nature of Rabelaisian writings. Voltaire was once labeled as a "materialist" by Mme Blavatsky. The person who can ponder the Voltairian concept of matter offered in *Micromégas* is likely to find interesting things.

The final reference of Vigny to Voltaire the court poet is also "amusing." The author of *La Maison du berger* and the author of *L'Ingénu* seem to agree on one point. The court of France represents a pole of utmost degradation. The last line of the deceptive stanza is a probable allusion to the prostitution of Truth-Saint-Yves and to the parallel "descent" of "Vol-à-terre" into a "dungeon" of flesh.

Double-edged criticism is as typical of esoteric technique as double-edged praise. Careful disguise of secret sympathy is essential to esoteric concealment. Esotericism would have died long ago had fraternal admiration of one "smuggler" for another been allowed to transpire. It is noted in the Proustian *Recherche* that occasional "rosserie" aimed at fellow "inverts" is an excellent form of collective camouflage.

We have much to learn from a certain type of literary invective which amounts to the recognition of a Masonic grip. When we do learn, we will realize how many of the greatest beings ever to grace the earth with their presence and writings are laughing in their graves. We will discover new dimensions of Cosmos and Self. We will find literary constellations of undreamed splendor glowing and winking in blissful complicity. We will then possess "stars which know how to laugh."*

---

*Antoine de Saint Exupéry, *Le Petit Prince,* Ch. XXVI.

PROPHECY

Occult philosophy teaches that prophetic insight is a natural attribute of advanced spirituality. The person who transcends the perceptual bonds of matter enjoys unhampered vision embracing eternity.

"The Arhan, though he can see the Past, the Present, and the Future, is not yet the highest Initiate; —" (*The Secret Doctrine*, p. 206, Vol. I).

Superior vision has access to ethereal planes of being where prototypes of all forms of existence — past, present, and future — may be "seen:"

"Everything that *is, was,* and *will be,* eternally is, even the countless forms, which are finite and perishable only in their objective, not in their *ideal* Form. They existed as Ideas, in the Eternity, and when they pass away, will exist as reflections. Neither the form of man, nor that of any animal, plant or stone has ever been *created,* and it is only on this plane of ours that it commenced 'becoming,' *i.e.,* objectivising into its present materiality, or expanding *from within outwards,* from the most sublimated and supersensuous essence into its grossest appearance. Therefore our human forms have existed in the Eternity as astral or ethereal prototypes; according to which models, the Spiritual Beings (or Gods) whose duty it was to bring them into objective being and terrestrial life, evolved the protoplasmic forms of the future *Egos* from *their own essence.*" (*The Secret Doctrine*, p. 282, Vol. I).

"— ancient as well as modern wisdom, vaticination and science, agree on corroborating the claims of the kabalists. It is on the indestructible tablets of the astral light that is stamped the impression of every thought we think, and every act we perform; and that future events — effects of long-forgotten causes — are already delineated as a vivid picture for the eye of the seer and prophet to follow." (*Isis Unveiled*, p. 178, Vol. 1).

The productions of numerous great artists and other creators are believed to originate from planes of ethereal forms:

"As God creates, so man can create. Given a certain intensity of will, and the shapes created by the mind become subjective. Hallucinations, they are called, although to their creator they are real as any visible object is to any one else. Given a more intense and intelligent concentration of this will, and the form becomes concrete, visible, objective; the man has learned the secret of secrets, he is a MAGICIAN.

537

The materialist should not object to this logic, for he regards thought as matter. Conceding it to be so, the cunning mechanism contrived by the inventor; the fairy scenes born in the poet's brain; the gorgeous painting limned by the artist's fancy; the peerless statue chiselled in ether by the sculptor; the palaces and castles built in air by the architect — all these, though invisible and subjective, must exist, for they are matter, shaped and moulded. Who shall say, then that there are not some men of such imperial will as to be able to drag these air-drawn fancies into view, enveloped in the hard casing of gross substance to make them tangible? (*Isis Unveiled*, p. 62, Vol. 1).

The Proustian concept of Art is rooted in the same belief. Inspired music is a product of the exploration of "the invisible:"

"Swann was therefore not wrong in thinking that the motif of the sonata really did exist. Certainly human from that standpoint, yet it belonged to an order of supernatural creations which we have never seen but which in spite of that we recognize with delight when some explorer of the invisible succeeds in capturing one, in bringing it from the divine world to which he has access to shine a few instants above curs. That is what Vinteuil had done for the little motif." (*A la Recherche du temps perdu*, pp. 350-51, Vol. I).

Some paintings have their origin in the same world of ethereal forms. The striking resemblance which exists between Odette and the Zephora of a Renaissance fresco is a valuable esoteric hint of the identity of the "demi-mondaine." Biblical Zephora or Zipporah — "the shining" — "is one of the personified Occult Sciences —".* The equivalence sheds interesting light on the companion of the Great Swan of Time partially allegorized in its "Jewish" or Judaeo-Christian segment. But the reference of Proust to the fresco and to other paintings plays another esoteric role. The clairvoyance of artists painting from models yet *unborn* is suggested. Some portraits such as a work of Giorgione — which is tantalizingly mentioned by Proust, Rilke, and Beckett — will some day prove beyond doubt the reality of Ether. Voltaire and Vigny were painted with remarkable accuracy in the XVIth Century.

It is only natural that great spiritual seekers of all times should have taken interest in their successors whether artistic or literary. Numerous indications of their interest may be found in literature. The name *Volateran* appears in the controversial *Cinquième Livre* of Rabelais. Commentators generally connect it with Raphael Maffei de Volterra who lived in the XVth Century. But it is logically conceivable to the esoteric researcher that Rabelais referred to Voltaire. The name "Volateran" appears on a list of scholars and explorers — including Jacques Cartier — who are

The Secret Doctrine, p. 465 fn., Vol. II.

dedicated to a secret enterprise, "hidden behind a piece of tapestry, on the sly, writing beautiful jobs, and all from Hearsay."* — Oral teachings. The common task of such "good company" involves the "trade" of "witness," "drinking," and "the sparing of truth." Rabelais may also have "seen" the creation and the person of Proust whose name appears in Ch. XXVIII of the *Quart Livre*. "Marcel" may have referred to that possibility when he noted that "Cottard" could name him** and when he reported the words of "Albertine:" "Cottard saw us."*** One may finally note that the name *Saint-Exupère* is mentioned several times in the writings of Anatole France.****

The ability of born seers to gaze into Ether is accompanied — in the case of Initiates — by knowledge of evolutionary cycles and related mathematics. As was previously noted, the prevision of certain events is no more attributable to prophecy or seership than is the astronomical prediction of an eclipse. Such a belief is suggested by Sartre. The narrator of *La Nausée* — who claims that he can probe beyond surfaces and that he can "*see* the future," — supports his assertion in logical manner. Watching the slow walk of an old woman along a deserted street, he estimates time and distance so as to predict every phase of the woman's progress. The combination of motion, minutes and meters is "time, time laid bare." Sartre may try to tell us that time and space are one and that what is called prophecy is a question of mathematics. If so, he tells us the same thing as the Secret Doctrine.

The ability to see the future — through seership, mathematics or both — is alleged to exist by numerous great minds. Plato makes the following comment on derided prophecy:

> "'Me too' says he in his *Eutyphron*, 'When I say anything in the public assembly concerning divine things, and *predict to them* what is going to happen, they ridicule as mad; and although *nothing that I have predicted has proved untrue*, yet they envy all such men as we are. However, we ought not to heed, but pursue our own way.'" (*Isis Unveiled*, p. 16, Vol. 2).

Vigny claims prophetic insight for Paris — and probably for himself:

> — si la force divine
> Est en ceux dont l'esprit sent, prévoit et devine,
> Elle est ici."
> (*Paris*).

Cinquièue Livre, XXX.
**A la Recherche du temps perdu*, p. 869, Vol. II.
***Ibid.*, p. 1098, Vol. II.
****L'Anneau d'amethyste — Le Mannequin d'osier —.

<pre>
("   — if the divine strength
Is in those whose spirit feels, foresees and divines,
It is here.")
</pre>

Voltaire has a humorous observation on the "trade" of the prophet:

"— there is a lot to be said for the trade of the prophet, the proof of it is that a thousand people dabble in it." *(Le Taureau blanc,* Ch. VI.)

The unorthodox knowledge possessed by Voltaire on Lebanese ruins, secret cities, and officially unknown Martian moons belongs to the Secret Doctrine and may not be due to seership or prophecy. But it is suggested by various elements of Voltairian writings that the sage anticipated certain events which took place after his death.

The vision of slaughtered servants, noblemen and priests heaped in a tumbril which appears in Chapter XV of *Candide* seems to be a preview of the Great Revolution. The spectacle of surrounding butchery witnessed by the main characters of the same story in the final chapter includes "neatly stuffed heads" carried to a "Sublime Gate" possibly connected with the guillotine. The word "empaillées" — derived from "paille" — "straw" — suggests esoterically "placed" or "dropped into straw." The heads of victims of the Terror fell into a basket containing straw.

"On voyait des têtes proprement empaillées qu'on allait présenter à la Sublime Porte. Ces spectacles faisaient redoubler les dissertations.—" (Ch. XXX, p. 241).

("They saw neatly stuffed heads which were being carried to the Sublime Gate. Those sights caused discussions to redouble.")

The combination of things "seen" and "redoubling" discussions may have been intended to suggest prophetic "double vue" or "second sight." The end of the story takes place in the vicinity of Constantinople. Warning is given about the dangers of political life. The combination of geography and warning may have been intended to call attention to a tragic figure who was to receive passionate attention from Vigny. André Chénier, a well-known poet whose story is told in *Stello,* was born in Constantinople. He was an active supporter of the French Revolution who died on the guillotine in the bloodbath immediately preceding the fall of Robespierre.

Modern views of the origin of species seem to have been anticipated by Voltaire. The portion of *Candide* which is devoted to the ape-men or "Oreillons" conveys esoteric messages relative to the bestiality of Fourth Race mankind and to the theological "missing link" of Karma, the "resource" crucially wanting in Jansenism. The suggestions of a "missing link" which are found in Chapter XVI do not seem to be limited to religious dogma or to be unique in the works of Voltaire. Gordon — a former Jansenist — observes in *L'Ingénu* that "men are treated like apes,—" It is noted in *L'Homme aux quarante écus* that a certain theory situates the origin of human life in the sea. A book is mentioned in the same passage according to which "the race of men was the bastard branch of a race of baboons." The report is immediately followed by an ironic comment: "I would as soon descend from a fish as from an ape." Voltaire may have foretold the theories of Darwinism.

The same passage contains speculations on the formation of mountains. It is alleged by a certain "Taliamed" that the sedimentations of seas formed the Alps, the Taurus, and the mountains of America. The absence of fossilized shells from American mountains is used by the opposition to prove the theory invalid. "Taliamed" is unshaken by the argument. *Shells will be found* some day on the mountains of America:

> " 'Vous savez qu'il n'y a aucune coquille dans les montagnes d'Amérique. Il faut que ce ne soit pas vous qui ayez crée cet hémisphère, et que vous vous soyez contenté de former l'ancien monde: c'est bien assez.
> —Monsieur, Monsieur, si on n'a pas découvert de coquilles sur les montagnes d'Amérique, *on en découvrira*.
> —Monsieur, c'est parler en créateur qui sait son secret et qui est sûr de son fait.' "

> (" '—You know that there is no shell whatsoever in the mountains of America. It must be that it was not you who created that hemisphere, and that you contented yourself with forming the old world: that is quite enough.
> —Sir, Sir, if no shells have been discovered on the mountains of America, *some will be discovered*.
> —Sir, that is speaking as a creator who knows his secret and who is sure of his fact.' ")

The theory of "Taliamed" is now vindicated by modern findings. Marine limestone and shells of various types *have* been discovered "in the mountains of America."

The skeptical irony pervading the passage last quoted conveys useful esoteric teachings. The general tenor of the chapter to which the text belongs tends to ridicule the controversial theory. But the title of the same chapter — *New Pains Occasioned by New Systems* — seems to invite second thoughts. The stress which is placed on the certainty of Taliamed — "a creator who knows his secret and who is sure of his fact" — is calculated to arrest serious esoteric attention. The italics which accompany the prediction have similar effect. The warning contained in the preface

541

of the *Poem on the Disaster of Lisbon* appears to apply. The reader seems to be begged not to mistake what the author refutes for what he accepts.

The following semi-prophetic passage of *The Secret Doctrine* seems to deserve the same kind of skeptical attention:

> "GIANTS! CIVILIZATIONS, AND SUBMERGED CONTENTS TRACED IN HISTORY
>
> When statements such as are comprised in the above heading are brought forward, the writer is, of course, expected to furnish *historical* instead of *legendary* evidence in support of such claims. Is this possible? Yes; for evidence of this nature is plentiful, and has simply to be collected and brought together to become overwhelming in the eyes of the unprejudiced.
>
> Once the sagacious student gets hold of the guiding thread he may find it out for himself. We give *facts* and show landmarks; let the wayfarer follow then, *What is given here is amply sufficient for THIS century.*
>
> In a letter to Voltaire, Bailly finds it quite natural that the sympathies of the 'grand old invalid of Ferney' should be attracted to the 'representatives of knowledge and wisdom, the Brahmans of India.' He then adds a curious statement. 'But,' he says, 'your Brahmans are very young in comparison with their ancient instructors.'"

A footnote is inserted at this point with reference to a passage of Voltaire's *Lettres sur l'Atlantide*. Part of the footnote is as follows:

> "Neither Voltaire nor Bailly, however, knew anything of the Secret Doctrine of the east." (*The Secret Doctrine*, p. 742, Vol. II).

The sweeping, undocumented substance of the footnote is suspiciously atypical of Mme Blavatsky. The exhortation to the "sagacious student" to "find out for himself" and to "get hold of the guiding thread" is provocative. The "sagacious" student needs only be "bold" enough to turn his attention to Voltaire to come face to face with "overwhelming" material. The double stress placed on information *sufficient for THIS century* raises interesting questions about the next century. Such questions are partially answered in the following lines:

> "The day when much, if not all, of that which is given here from the archaic records, will be found correct, is not far distant." (*The Secret Doctrine*, p. 423, Vol. II).

> "It is only in the XXth century that portions, if not the whole, of the present work will be vindicated." (*The Secret Doctrine*, p. 442).

The quotation is closely followed by a reference to Voltaire:

> "We bide our time. Even the famous 'Ezour-Veda' of the last century, considered by Voltaire 'the most precious gift from the East to the West,' and by Max Müller, 'about the silliest book that can be read,' is not

altogether without facts and truths in it." (*The Secret Doctrine*, p. 442, Vol. II).

Voltaire may have inspired in part a meaningful passage of *Isis Unveiled* in which Memnon the statue is mentioned. The statue may represent an esoteric blind for *Memnon* the story — a text which will be examined at the end of the present chapter. If such be the case, Voltaire is once more connected with vindication of the Secret Doctrine and with an important "unveiling:"

> "The cold, stony lips of the once vocal Memnon, and of these hardy sphinxes, keep their secrets well. Who will unseal them? Who of our modern, materialistic dwarfs and unbelieving Sadducees will dare to lift the VEIL of ISIS?" (*Isis Unveiled*, p. 573, Vol. 1).

The following text may apply to the footnote denying that "Voltaire — knew anything of the Secret Doctrine of the East:"

> "— those of us who pretend to teach others more ignorant than ourselves — are all liable to err. Thus mistakes have been made in 'Isis Unveiled,' 'Esoteric Buddhism,' in 'Man,' in 'Magic: White and Black' etc., etc., and more than one mistake is likely to be found in the present work. This cannot be helped." (*The Secret Doctrine*, p. 640, Vol. II).

"Mistakes" which "cannot be helped" may perhaps be translated as "necessary mistakes" or "blinds."

The references of Mme Blavatsky to Voltaire are sufficiently numerous and intriguing to explain the necessity of a strong "blind" such as the footnote. As was previously noted, the Sage is mentioned with a perceptible smile as a great "infidel." His view of the nature of the soul is quoted approvingly. The expected vindication of the Secret Doctrine is occasionally predicted in texts marked by the "chance" appearance of his name. The denegation of Mme Blavatsky is comparable to the unconvincing protests of Proustian "Albertine," which are designed to guard her secret and the secret of other "inverts."

We can only speculate on the manner in which our century was determined as the time of emergence of occult verities. The matter probably belongs to the realm of carefully guarded secrets connected with occult astronomy and mathematics. We may wonder if the designated period is in any way linked to the "acceptable year" of the Book of Isaiah.* As was previously suggested, the "acceptable year" may itself be represented in the Proustian *Recherche* by "Mme Bontemps."

The *Recherche* contains numerous elements or prophecy. Albertine is

---

Issiah, Luke, Ch. IV, v. 19.

the allegory of a work which "Marcel" passionately wants to write — a work based on the parallel secrets of Albertine and "Saint Loup." The "necessary" time span which the narrator has long "refused to see" finally materializes as the "daughter" of "Saint Loup" — Vigny. The statement of "Saint Loup": "I am the first one"* nears its day of vindication. "A concealed jewel is found again.'** The jewel probably represents the NECKLACE of the *Destinées*. "Marcel" finds that his turn to write has come at last. The mantle of the prophet — symbolized by a shawl — has been passed from Vigny to Proust.*** The construction of the Proustian "cathedral" — a work which is also compared to a dress or "veil" — is about to begin. The monumental structure will not be devoted exclusively to one person such as "Bergotte" — Anatole France — or "Saint Loup." It will glorify a host of inspired writers similarly dedicated to the same One Truth. The exoteric facade of the "cathedral" is expected to stand at least forty years. A secret "carefully buried" over a period of forty years will then come to light.****

> "— chaque fois que quelqu'un regarde les choses d'une façon un peu nouvelle, les quatre quarts des gens ne voient goutte à ce qu'on leur montre. Il faut au moins quarante ans pour qu'ils arrivent à distinguer." (*A la Recherche du temps perdu*, p. 552, Vol. II).

> ("— every time someone looks at things in a slightly new way, the four-fourths of people see nothing of what is being shown to them. One has to wait at least forty years before they manage to perceive.")

The waiting period of "at least forty years" designates our era as the time of emergence of the esoteric message of the *Recherche*. The same approximate date is judged suitable for a "trip" to Balbec, an experience ardently desired by adolescent "Marcel." The poetic region seems to be regarded by "Legrandin" as his private preserve for a certain time at least. "No Balbec before fifty years!" warns the puzzling engineer. The beautiful — and forbidden — area vaunted by "Legrandin" is compared to the site of *L'Ingénu* — "the territory between Normandy and Brittany" — which it may represent. The "necessary" time span which "Marcel" tends to refuse to "see" applies to the symbolic domain of "Legrandin" as it applies to the lost "necklace" of Vigny.

The "concealed jewel" "buried" in the *Destinies* is represented in the *Recherche* by the sumptuous NECKLACE which is the intended gift of

---

A la Recherche du temps perdu, p. 702, Vol. III.
**Ibid.*, p. 625, Vol. II.
***Ibid.*, p. 412, Vol. II.
****Ibid.*, p. 209, Vol. III.

"Saint Loup" to "Rachel." It is likened — through proximity — to a "trial" which may be the "trial" of *Micromégas*. The jewel is connected with matters of "cosmic importance."* A similar "necklace" is mentioned in *L'Ingénu*.

The person and the work of Vigny may have been "seen" by Voltaire. The emergence of UNVEILED TRUTH which is the major esoteric development of *L'Ingénu* results in part from the sharing of "spirits" brought from Barbados by Hercules. The flask of liquor which has traveled from the Caribbean area to Europe is a Voltairian "bottle to the sea." The "adventuress" of Vigny seems to be anticipated:

"Seule dans l'Océan, seule toujours! — Perdue
Comme un point invisible en un mouvant désert,
L'aventurière passe errant dans l'étendue,
Et voit tel cap secret qui n'est pas découvert."

("Alone in the Ocean, alone ever! — Lost
Like an invisible point in a moving desert,
The adventuress passes wandering in space,
And sees an occasional secret cape yet undiscovered.")

"Un soir enfin, les vents qui soufflent des Florides
L'entraînent vers la France et ses bords pluvieux."

("One evening at last, the winds blowing from the Floridas
Carry it toward France and its rainy shores.")

The plural designation of "Floridas" may embrace a wider area than does the modern name of the peninsula and State. The plural may reflect a vague geographical concept. Ponce de Leon discovered Florida while searching for "Bimini" — "a fabulous island believed to contain a marvellous fountain or spring whose waters would restore to old men their youth, or, at least had wonderful curative powers."** While Barbados is located in the Eastern sector of the Caribbean, the general area designated by Voltaire as "les Barbades" and by Vigny as "Les Florides" may be regarded as the same semi-mythical, magical region. The two "bottles to the sea" — or individual aspects of a collective message — follow the same general transatlantic course.

The conversion of the Voltairian *Huron* — Karma personified — may represent among other things a reference to the poem of Vigny entitled *Paris*. The "divining force" which is said to be "here" in the latter text may refer not only to the prophetic vision of the writer but also to

Ibid., pp. 278-79, Vol. II.
**Encyclopaedia Brittanica*, Florida.

the discovery potential of the work itself. *Paris* contains provocative esoteric "bait." Is the City of Lights a Wheel? Or is it a Furnace? The moderately "instructed" reader who can ponder the transparent karmic symbolism of the wheel and the equally transparent allusion to the Christian Inferno may discover the entire esoteric message of Vigny. Esoteric understanding of Vigny may lead to the unveiling of the immense field of esoteric literature. The person who thinks that he has discovered *one* esoteric writer when he understands Vigny is in for a surprise. He will eventually realize that Vigny is only one "smuggler" among many. One might compare his prospects to the experience of Proustian "Marcel" detecting the amazing presence of one "invert" only to find that "inverts" are to be found everywhere. Voltaire suggests as much. The dazzled fisherman of *Zadig* does not realize at first the extent of his "catch." (Nor does the fisherman of the *Bottle to the sea*). Saint Yves feels "her triumph" when she "converts" the H*uron*. But she does "not perceive all its implications." As was previously suggested in the present work, one esoteric aspect of Saint *Yves* seems to be identical to the allegorical *Eva* of to be *La Maison du berger*. It is the intuitive faculty capable of "hearing" the veiled message of great literature.

Voltaire may allude specifically to *Paris* in connection with a certain discovery. The well-meaning element of the Kerkabon family tries to locate and to release the allegory of Suffering Mankind imprisoned in a "dungeon." But the Kerkabons are "lost" in the "labyrinth" or "maze" of Paris. The "resources" of the unsuccessful explorers are not equal to the task. Paris the city — perhaps *Paris* the poem — can only be searched with "wheels." All prospects of "discovery" to be made in *Paris* are doomed by an apparent absence of Karmic knowledge:

> "Finally the brother and the sister left; but, when they had arrived in Paris, they found themselves lost as if they had been in a vast maze without thread and without exit. Their fortune was meager, they needed carriages every day in order to go in search of discovery, and they discovered nothing."

The absence of "guiding thread" — esoteric awareness in general and knowledge of Sutratma in particular — is combined with the idea of unavailable "wheels" and with the idea of an insufficient "fortune" — "Karma" — or degree of evolutionary readiness. Also present is the idea of "going around in circles." The total esoteric formula is equivalent to the NECKLACE of Vigny's *Destinies*, the symbolic cornerstone of occult philosophy and "the key to our poetic enigma." The probability of a Voltairian allusion to the *Destinies* added to an allusion to *Paris* is also suggested in the following words:

546

"Ainsi la destinée conduisait à Paris presque tout ce canton de la Basse-Bretagne."

("Thus destiny was leading to Paris almost the whole subdivision of Low-Brittany.")

Proust seems to point to the vast discovery potential of the works of Vigny when he reports the passionate statement of "Saint Loup:" I am the first one." The proud words are connected with a type of person who does not believe herself capable of "love." The writings of Vigny *are* capable of "awakening" the intuitive person.

One may note that the generous revelations of Jesrad — the hermit portrayed in *Zadig* — have their source in a *Book of Destinies*. Vigny once planned an anthology so designated and wrote the crucial poem known as *Les Destinées*.

Logical as the conclusion may be that Vigny took certain cues from Voltaire and that no prophecy was involved on the part of the Sage of Ferney, it may not be insane to conceive the reverse possibility.

It is observed at the beginning of *L'Ingénu* that "Low Brittany" is sadly deprived of vineyards — "vignes. The symbolism of "deprivation" and lacking "spirit" is clear. The fact that the precious commodity is supplied by the "bottle to the sea" of a "converted" Huron also seems meaningful. The name of Vigny lends itself to a play on words involving the term "vigne." The lacking "vignes" the absence of which is remedied by a transmission of "spirit" may point to the illuminating potential of the writings of Vigny — or, in the words of Proust, to "the first one."

The wanderings and the arrival in "port" of the *Bottle to the sea* seem to be predicted by Vigny with remarkable precision in the poem itself. The symbolic flask launched into the Ocean of Time, Space, Existence, and Secret Knowledge, is shown drifting in the vicinity of Australia. The proximity of the latter land mass is suggested by the conjunction of "the Pacific sea," the "tropics," and the "sarigue," an animal found in Australia. The bottle is sighted by a passing vessel. Small boats are lowered in an effort to retrieve "the adventuress." But adverse forces intervene. The attempt is abandoned. The "divine elixir" which has long waited for "summer to change its destinies" continues to be tossed on the surface of the ocean.

L'Orientalisme d'Alfred de Vigny is the work of an Australian woman, Vera A. Summer. The study was published in 1930. Even more than the chosen topic, the mode of treatment of texts examined suggests an author who sensed — if she did not actually perceive — the presence of a veiled message. Vigny may have foreseen that his symbolic *Destinies* would come close to being "changed" — interpreted esoterically — by Vera *Summer*. The *Destinies* were eventually "changed" by a non-initiate in the summer of 1968.

It may be briefly noted that Australians have a prominent place in the cosmopolitan friendships formed by "Saint Loup" during the apocalyptic years of "Word War I."*

One may also note that Vigny expected the opposition of "obstinate ice" to the progress of the "bottle." Little prophetic ability was needed on that score.

The final stanza of *L'Esprit pur* — the testamentary poem of Vigny — conveys more than a vague expression of hope of full understanding:

> "Jeune postérité d'un vivant qui vous aime!
> Mes traits dans vos regards ne sont pas effacés;
> Je peux en ce miroir *me connaître moi-même*,
> Juge toujours nouveau de nos travaux passés;
> Flots d'amis renaissants! Puissent mes Destinées
> Vous amener à moi de dix en dix années,
> Attentifs à mon oeuvre, et pour moi c'est assez!"

> ("Young posterity of a living man who loves you!
> My features in your eyes are not erased;
> I can in this mirror *know myself,*
> Ever-new judge of our past labors:
> Waves of ever-reborn friends! May my Destinies
> Bring you to me from ten to ten years,
> Attentive to my work, and for me that's enough!")

The unveiling of the concealed message of Vigny seems to be expected within a period vaguely designated by the words: "from ten to ten years." The expression seems numerically meaningless. Phonetically, however, it yields the combined figures of ten, one hundred, and ten — "dix," "cent," "dix" — or a total of 120 years. The poem containing "the key word to our poetic enigma" is specifically mentioned — "mes Destinées." Hope is expressed that the text in question will produce esoteric contact — "bring you to me" — between posterity and the author. The waiting period connected with the *Destinies* — written in 1849 — will last 120 years. Vigny seems to have expected his "Bottle to the sea" to become accessible to the general public in 1969.

It is probably not by chance that the line featuring the "ten to ten years" is line No. 69 of the poem.

The figure 120 makes numerous appearances in the works of esoteric

---

Ibid., p. 789, Vol. III.

writers — as does the 220 of Voltaire. Proust notes that "the elect" emerge "every ten years in their genuine form as if the past did not exist."[*] Battles of words which involve certain doctrines are said to be renewed "from ten to ten years."[**] A somewhat surprising engagement — or "connection" — reported to Marcel involves a dowry of 120,000,000 francs. The proverbial equivalence of time and money suggests an allusion to the 120 years conveyed by *L'Esprit pur*. The latter impression tends to be confirmed by the fact that the impending "marriage" is that of "Saint Loup." The height of esoteric exhuberance is reached in a passage of the *Recherche* which teems with the symbolism of "music," flight, elevation, energy, silence, and Mystery-brand aircraft endowed with 120 horsepower. The musical "phrases" of *Tristan* are compared to material vehicles capable of soaring into the sky:

> "— birds resembling not the swan of Lohengrin, but that airplane which I had seen in Balbec converting its energy into elevation, hovering over the waters of the sea, and losing itself in the sky. Perhaps, like the birds which rise the highest, which fly the fastest, have a more powerful wing, was it necessary to have those truly material machines to explore infinity, some of those one hundred and twenty horsepower brand Mystery on which, however, no matter how high one sails, one is slightly prevented from savoring the silence of space by the powerful hum of the engine." (*A la Recherche du temps perdu,* p. 162, Vol. III).

The above text seems to convey — among other things — an allusion to two poems of Vigny, one of which is *Paris*, which are labeled *Elevations* by Vigny himself. The prosaic "horsepower" — literary inspiration — mentioned by Proust seems to have the same "elevating" function as the "wholly terrestrial imagery" of Vigny:

> "I have named these poems (*Les Amants de Montmorency and Paris*) *Elévations,* because all must start from wholly terrestrial imagery to rise to views of a more divine nature and to allow — as far as that is possible — the soul which will follow me into superior regions, to take it on earth and to place it at the feet of God." (*Letter of Vigny to Mlle Camille Maunoir*).

Vigny seems to have designed — and expected — his *Elévations* to lead the ordinary reader into "superior regions."

The important mission of Mme Blavatsky seems to have been foretold by a number of esoteric writers. It was not until the works of Mme Blavatsky were published that the general outline of the Secret Doctrine

---

[*]*A la Recherche du temps perdu,* p. 964, Vol. III.
[**]*Ibid.,* p. 893, Vol. III.

became accessible to the general public. The books of Mme Blavatsky are indispensable tools of the comparative task facing the esoteric researcher. It was inevitable that esoteric writers should take ardent interest in the crucial messenger of UNVEILED TRUTH. Voltaire, Shelley, and Vigny seem to have used their prophetic insight to announce the mission of a great spiritual leader.

It is suggested by Mme Blavatsky herself that her passage on earth was the result of voluntary reincarnation. A moving autobiographical note is attached to *Isis Unveiled*. The text is entitled *My Books*. The writer professes to be no more than a transmitter of Knowledge. The date of the author's death — May 8, 1891* — the "price" paid by her, and the symbolism of the "string" — or thread of reincarnation — should all be noted:

> "Nothing of that have I invented, but have simply given it out as I have been taught; or as quoted by me in *The Secret Doctrine* (Vol. I, p. ixlvi) from Montaigne: "I have here made only a nosegay of culled flowers, and have brought nothing of my own but the string that ties them."

> "Is any one of my helpers prepared to say that I have not paid the full price for the string?" (*April* 27, 1891, *My Books*, p. 53).

Voltaire was well qualified to grasp the value of the sacrifice of voluntary reincarnation. His portrayal of Latter-Day Saint Yves, a being who submits to the prostitution of incarnate existence in order to save Suffering Mankind, is in part a tribute to the standard-bearer of UNVEILED TRUTH.

The final portion of *Prometheus Unbound* features a strange "infant" — esoterically an initiate. The baby is seen at the confluence of two streams suggesting various sets of "separated twins" finally joined again. The "dear" — expensive, even tragic — "disunion" which has long estranged the two branches ends where the "infant" appears. "The Mother of the Months" — the moon or Isis — is "borne" / "by ebbing light into her western cave." An "aery veil" is mentioned. The strange infant is suggested to be sexless — spiritual — by a neutral mode of expression: Shelley refers to "Its countenance." The "winged infant, white" has "limbs" which "gleam white." Spirituality and incarnation are suggested. The islet where the baby is "seen" is an "isle of lovely grief" — a symbol of mystical love and unlimited love of mankind. It is surrounded by an icy landscape evoking the idea of purity. The frozen, gleaming scenery

---

*c.f. "May 8, the day of celebration of victory" — Samuel Beckett, *Comment C'est*.

may also constitute an allusion to Russia, the native land of Mme Blavatsky. The verb forms "rushes," and "rushing" — which are esoteric vehicles of "speed" or spirituality — may have been intended to suggest that country. The said forms appear in the poem with interesting frequency. The general symbolism of the poem and of the passage seems to combine the liberation of Suffering Mankind — Prometheus — Isis, a veil, the Western world, the incarnation of a spiritual being, and Russia. *Prometheus Unbound* was published in 1820.

Paris was written by Vigny in 1831, the year of birth of Mme Blavatsky. The poem seems to announce a new era ushered by an a "animated form" or important incarnate figure. The poem features an abundance of fire and sun, the presence of an ominous "rock" or boulder, and a universal synthesis of cultures. The general atmosphere is that of an impending intellectual and spiritual apoclypse. The incarnate force which is expected to "lead the human family to its goal" is insistently connected with the sun, *Helios*, and with PTR, the "rock" or esoteric "interpreter" of the Secret Doctrine. The name of *Helena Petro*vna Blavatsky may be suggested. The coincidence of dates linking the year of birth of Mme Blavatsky and the writing of the poem is also intriguing.

One of the earliest productions of Vigny, a poem written in 1821, is outwardly devoted to the cause of Greek independence. But esoteric reading reveals the content of many symbols. Among them are "separated twins," a soul rising and falling like a dove, "another Greece" which is "Parentless," an invisible gold necklace, rebirth, and Judaic spoliation. Reference is made to the "prophetic head" of the heroine. The poem —which is entitled *Helena* — is designated by Vigny as the "adventure" — perhaps avatar or reincarnation — of a young Greek woman ravished or, in the strange word of Vigny "cossacked" — "cosa'quée" by the Turks. It is observed by Vigny in a corresponding portion of his *Diary* that the majority of readers reacted only to the aspect of the text which militates in favor of the Greek cause. Little or no interest was taken in the "cossacked" victim who seems to be regarded as crucial by the author. "Helena" may have a concealed dimension connected with Russia and with the esoteric theme of "prostitution" or incarnation.

Eloa was written by Vigny in 1823. The exoteric surface of the poem tells the story of a "fallen angel" who yields to the temptation of Satan. The esoteric substance of the text deals with voluntary reincarnation. The name of the angel — Eloa — seems to be connected with the occult concept of the Androgynous Eloha which is an element of the hierarchy of creative powers.* Satan himself belong to the same hierarchy. The

---

*The Secret Doctrine, p. 70, Vol. III — Adyar Edition —.

androgynous nature of the Angel created by Vigny is suggested by the expression: "Une Ange." The general portrayal of Satan reflects the occult view of the reverse side of God: *Satan est Deus Inversus.** The theme of voluntary reincarnation is introduced into the text by the symbolism of a wounded eagle and by the parallel "falls" of Satan and Eloa. The mission of the celestial creature who is "strong from birth" is that of a "consoling spirit." The conjunction of "strength," "birth" and "fall" is identical to the characterization of Voltairian "Saint Yves:" "She succumbs out of virtue."

Eloa contains a line which is quoted by Marcel Proust in an interesting context:

> " 'Toi seule me parus ce qu'on cherche toujours,—"
> (*A la Recherche du temps perdu*, p. 878, Vol. II).
>
> " 'You alone seemed to me what one always seeks,—")

The quotation is used in connection with Princess Sherbatoff, a mysterious Russian great lady of questionable — and questioned — background. The Princess seems to represent the popular image of Mme Blavatsky: a woman revered by a few deluded devotees and suspect to the majority of others. The falsely ironic connection made between the Princess and the Eloa of Vigny tends to confirm the presumed prophetic value of *Eloa*, a poem written several years before the birth of Mme Blavatsky. The appearance of the same Princess on the "tortillard d'intérêt local" — "rickety litle winding train" — arouses the curiosity of the narrator of the *Recherche*. "Marcel" is quick to conclude that the strange lady must be "a madam on a trip" — "une maquerelle en voyage."** "Her face, her manners proclaimed it." The priceless irony of Proust conveys the idea of a symbolic "fish" — or Savior — prosaically designated as a "mackerel" on a "trip." The "trip" is effected by means of Karmic "wheels." The esoteric symbolism of prostitution is present. The Princess is elsewhere noted to live "rather by self-imposed rule than by a necessity to which one submits."*** She is regarded by those who venerate her as the incarnation of an "ideal" which has long been thought "inaccessible."**** The latter observation is immediately preceded by an "exoteric" allusion to "M. de Voltaire." The suggestive proximity which

---

*Ibid., p. 411-24, Vol. I — Verbatim Edition —.
**Ibid., p. 878, Vol. II.
***Ibid., p. 877, Vol. II.
****A la Recherche du temps perdu, p. 859, Vol. II.

courts a connection between Princess and Sage makes plenty of sense to the esoteric reader. As does the connection with the Eloa of Vigny.

The Proustian allusion to *Eloa* suggests recognition of esoteric material present in the early works of Vigny. It is generally noted by critics that the author took interest in Far Eastern philosophy toward the end of his life. But the admission is based on exoteric material found in the *Diary* and in the correspondence of the poet. It is a recording of the obvious which leaves concealed substance untapped. Esoteric reading clearly shows that the "smuggler" was active at an early stage. In the words of Proust, the startling "new orientation" — or "inversion" of "Saint Loup" had its origin in youth.*

Mme Blavatsky predicts the vindication of the Secret Doctrine for the second half of the XXth Century. Vigny and Proust expect the emergence of their veiled message during the same period. Did Voltaire make any comparable forecast?

Memnon or *Human Wisdom — La Sagesse Humaine —* was published in 1749. The title character is a fairly typical human being — unfortunate and baffled — who receives the visit of an ethereal creature. Memnon is warned against the futility of seeking absolute wisdom on earth. But the messenger resolves openly what may be termed the major Voltairian "paradox." Memnon is told in substance that Panglossian optimism is valid *if* one considers "the arrangement of the entire universe."

The celestial visitor from Sirius has six wings out of seven possible attributes. His status of near-perfection is noted. Information is given on his world of origin. Superior to Man though they be, Sirians remain slightly removed from Absolute Wisdom. A brief sketch is made of planetary chains. Cosmos is designed to reflect various planes of attainment. The crucial equivalence of "wisdom" and "pleasure" is affirmed. "One has less wisdom and pleasure in the second (globe) than in the first, and so forth all the way to the last globe where everyone is totally insane." The location of "our little anthill" as determined by the genie coincides with the theosophical estimate. According to the Sirian, our planet comes close to being the Insane Asylum of the Universe. In the opinion of occultists, our world is only" — one remove higher than Asiah, the fourth and lowest world, in which dwell the grossest and most material beings."**

The curiosity of Memnon is intense. The ethereal status of the visitor is almost impossible to conceive. Typical mental blocks of the average Westerner are noted with exquisite humor. What kind of existence is pos-

---

*A la Recherche du temps perdu, p. 680, Vol. III.
**Isis Unveiled, p. 210, Vol. 2.

sible without a physical body? What can the pursuit of happiness signify in the absence of Food and Sex?

The gentle spirit states the nature of his occupations:

> "Memnon lui dit alors: 'Monseigneur, sans femme et sans dîner, à quoi passez-vous votre temps?' — 'A veiller,' dit le génie, 'sur les autres globes qui nous sont confiés et je viens pour te consoler.' "

> ("Memnon then said to him: 'Your Lordship, without a wife and without a dinner, how do you spend your time?' — 'Keeping watch,' said the genie, 'over other globes which are entrusted to us and I have come to console you.' ")

The function of the genie is that of a "Son of Light." The "Sons of Light" of occult philosophy belong to the hierarchy of divine intelligences which supervise the emanation and the maintenance of the universe. The ethereal creature of *Memnon* is a "Creator" comparable to the Taliamed of *L'Homme aux quarante écus*, a being who will eventually prove to "know his secret" and to be "sure of his fact." The task of the "Sons of Light" is closely connected with the activity of the "never resting Breaths." "Centres of Forces at first, the invisible sparks of primordial atoms differentiate into molecules, and become Suns — passing gradually into objectivity — gaseous, radiant, cosmic, the one 'Whirlwind' (or motion) finally giving the impulse to the form, and the initial motion, regulated and sustained by the never-resting Breaths — the Dhyan Chohans."* The Sons of Light are also called the "Heavenly Snails:"

> "The 'Breath of all the 'seven' is said to be Bhâskara (light-making), because they (the planets) were all comets and suns in their origin. They evolve into Manvantaric life from primeval Chaos (now the noumenon of irresolvable nebulae) by aggregation and accumulation of the primary differentiations of the eternal matter, according to the beautiful expression in the Commentary, 'Thus, the Sons of Light clothed themselves in the fabric of Darkness.' They are called allegorically 'the Heavenly Snails,' on account of their (to us) formless INTELLIGENCES inhabiting unseen their starry and planetary homes, and, so to speak, carrying them as the snails do along with themselves in their revolution." (*The Secret Doctrine*, p. 103, Vol. I).

The concept of "Sons of Light" clad in "the Fabric of Darkness" is reminiscent of a line of the *Poem on the Disaster of Lisbon*:

> "Dans une épaisse nuit cherchant à m'éclairer, —"

The occult biography of Voltaire which is suggested in many of his

---

The Secret Doctrine, p. 103, Vol. I.

writings has a counterpart in *Memnon*. One aspect of the mission of the Sage is characterized by a typical esoteric understatement: the gift of the visitor to Suffering Mankind is a message of "consolation."

Sirius and snails are both mentioned in *Micromégas*. The title character of the latter story comes from the same celestial regions as does the ethereal being of *Memnon*. "Micromégas" has had difficulties caused by a book of which he is the author.

> "Vers les quatre cent cinquante ans, au sortir de l'enfance, il disséqua beaucoup de ces petits insectes qui n'ont pas cent pieds de diamètre, et qui se dérobent aux miscroscopes ordinaires; il en composa un livre curieux, mais qui lui valut quelques affaires. Le muphti de son pays, grand vétillard et fort ignorant, trouva dans son livre des propositions suspectes, malsonnantes, téméraires, hérétiques, sentant l'héresie, et le poursuivit vivement; il s'agissait de savoir si la forme substantielle des puces de Sirius était de même nature que celle des colimaçons. Micromégas se défendit avec esprit; il mit les femmes de son côté; le procès dura deux cent vingt ans. Enfin le muphti fit condamner le livre par des jurisconsultes qui ne l'avaient pas lu, et l'auteur eut ordre de ne paraître à la cour de huit cent années."

> ("When he was approximately four hundred and fifty years old, barely emerging from infancy, he dissected many of those small insects which are not one hundred feet in diameter, and which elude ordinary microscopes; he made on them a very curious book, but which caused him some trouble. The mufti of his country, a great quibbler and mightily ignorant man, found in his book some suspect premises which were offensive, summary, heretical, smacking of heresy, and prosecuted him briskly; it was a matter of knowing if the substantial form of Sirian fleas was of same nature as that of snails. Micromégas defended himself with wit, he put the women on his side; the trial lasted two hundred and twenty years. Finally the mufti had the book condemned by lawmen who had not read it, and the author was ordered not to appear at court for eight hundred years.")

The passage deserves special notice from the standpoint of esoteric expression. The consecrated formula of condemnation: "heretical, smacking of heresy" admirably conveys the helpless and powerless style of the Church representative. The word "téméraire" also belongs to the verbal armory of Catholic fulmination. The "boldness" implied by its substance is a highly prized quality in occult philosophy. The intended venom is a spectacular compliment which can easily turn against its users. Voltaire needed only quote documented anathema to achieve instant humor. There is great beauty also in the double antithesis: "grand vétillard et fort ignorant." "Trivia," the concerns of "quibblers," are incompatible with greatness. Esoteric "force" is incompatible with ignorance. The high priest representing the Church has a self-destructing quality which may be expected to play a role in the outcome of the "trial." The final condemnation issued by lawmen who have not "read" — perhaps understood — the book leaves room for vindication by other examiners. The support of women which is obtained by the defense is not negligible. Final banishment is no hardship. The Voltairian view of "court" is that of a place of ill-repute. The contention that the persecuted writer defended himself with "wit" or "spirit" can easily be believed in view of the life and works of "Micromégas."

The chief interest of the expressive passage lies in the nature of the controversial book. It is "a matter of knowing if the substantial form of Sirian fleas" is "of the same nature as that of snails." The question is resolved in the affirmative by an authority: the "Heavenly Snail" visiting Memnon:

"On our small planet everyone is equal."

If all is equal in Sirian regions, the substantial form of Sirian fleas equals the substantial form of Heavenly Snails which do exist on that star. *Memnon* is the work covertly mentioned in *Micromégas*. The "Sirian" is Voltaire himself.

The approximate age of Voltaire at the time of writing *Memnon* is suggested by the preposition "vers," by the long life expectancy of the author, and by an esoteric zero. The magical number *two hundred and twenty* — which is repeatedly connected by the Sage with the prolonged enslavement and the eventual liberation of mankind — belongs to the era of UNVEILED TRUTH. It is exposed in radiant nudity.

The "trial" of the condemned, misunderstood, and symbolic writing representing the entire production of Voltaire, a procedure lasting two hundred and twenty years, point to the interest of a simple addition. *Memnon* was written in 1749. The trial ends in 1969.

Voltaire does seem to have expected his occult testament to become accessible to the general public in 1969.

The present chapter will have no conclusion.

CONCLUSIONS

VOLTAIRE

Voltaire is anything but "passé." In spirit if not otherwise, Voltaire is alive and well. In the light of the veiled bequest which adds dizzying dimensions to the rich exoteric surface of his writings, the Sage is more inspiring and newsworthy than ever: timeless as the Secret Doctrine, contemporary as current events.

The exoteric teachings of Voltaire are not irrelevant to our age. Relatively little has changed since the XVIIIth Century. Human nature remains as Voltaire described it: sordid through "necessity," yet potentially divine. The iniquities denounced in *Candide* and *L'Ingénu* have stubborn prolongations in our present environment. The exploitation of the many by the few is more lucrative and more sophisticated than ever. General poverty is markedly less severe in Western countries than it once was. But the relative and precarious well-being of the average man is used as a tranquillizer, a pacifier, and as an agent of tentacular control. The Jehovic God may be dead. But he is ably replaced. The System giveth and the System taketh away. Power remains allergic to certain truths. Some boats may not be rocked. "Heretics" of various kinds are no longer burnt at the stake. But they can be and are efficiently starved to death. Adulterated "learning" and computerized inquisitions threaten the integrity of every thinking man. The modern separation of Church and States is little more than a reassuring myth. Bargain-basement evangelists and organized bigots call the tunes to which numerous institutions dance. The freedom of the press and the freedom of publication leave much to be desired. "Squealing" passes as evidence and is rewarded in court. The underlying rationale is not far removed from XVIIIth Century racks. Lettres de cachet are no longer known by that name. But that is academic to victims of artificially prolonged imprisonment. "Heroic butchery" has steadily continued in "Wesphalian" and Far Eastern Lidices. Jehovic thunderbolts and Jehovic brimstone are emulated by guns and napalm. Sectarianism remains conducive to slaughter. The right and left-foot advocates of Ireland communicate with bombs. The bandits of Pizarro whose feats are evoked in Candide have worthy successors in modern America. The genocide of Indians goes on to this day in Brazil. *Te Deums* are no longer sung to celebrate massacres. But the mystique of muscle and blood still prevails. It is a staple of the daily diet consumed daily by millions — deodorized and cellophane-wrapped — from television screens. The degradation of the old woman is a preview of Treblinka. The Negro of Surinam mourning his lost soul is the ancestor of Malcolm X. The Old Testament is still invoked to support the oppression of "inferiors" of the wrong color and sex.

"The infamous" still rules. It is all the more pernicious for its "Christian" and "democratic" camouflage. Although pushers of 1984 would like us to judge it so, Voltairian thought on socio-political questions can hardly be termed obsolete on the basis of spectacular progress. Nothing incidentally, would have more pleased the Sage than such obsolescence had it been attainable or attained in our age.

It is easy to see why the exoteric message of the author of *Candide* has been — and continues to be — the target of many sneers. Such commentaries as those of the Sage are distressingly applicable to our era of false enlightenment. Voltaire is too close for comfort.

The positive inspiration of the grand iconoclast cannot be grasped through study of his exoteric message alone. The humanitarian concern which made him despise and oppose material oppression fails to go back to the source of his hatred of "the infamous." It is in the realm of spiritual values that genuine understanding of Voltaire must be sought. It is in the theft, the mutilation and the distortion of Pagan knowledge and in the resultant chronic poisoning of entire societies that the root of his indignation may be found. It is only in the light of his love for everything true and pure that his denunciation of falsehood and corruption may be judged with competence. It is in the same light that his scorn of "Christian" dogma and practice may be seen as what it is: reverence of Life, Christ, and Chrestos. Voltaire belongs to a timeless brotherhood of great souls which never were content to dabble in symptoms of evil and misery but which relentlessly point to the spiritual source. They conceive no compromise where none should be conceived. They care enough to want only the best for themselves and their suffering fellow-creatures.

Charges levelled at Voltaire by numerous critics are now exposed as groundless. His defects were mostly in the eyes of beholders.

No one more readily recognized — or tried to alleviate — the misery of human condition. No one had fuller awareness of the weight of the cross of birth. It was that awareness which prompted him to celebrate and promote material progress as one small step toward superior fulfillment. It was the same awareness which apparently led him to forsake "the silent land of bliss" out of love of mankind.

558

No one had more exalted reverence for the Supreme Being. No one felt more contempt or hatred for its cruel caricature. No one understood better faith or mysticism. If "understanding" was involved, it was the understanding of direct experience. Far from being "deeply irreligious," Voltaire was one of the most ardent believers ever to live. His creed was no postulate, speculation, or lip-service. It was a freely embraced and revently transmitted bequest. Far from being "vague," Voltaire's faith in eternal life grew out of solid metaphysical and spiritual bases.

No one ever criticized institutions less "partially." Voltaire viewed all things — including politics — from a cosmic, evolutionary vantage point. If his attacks against the establishment have appeared fragmentary, fragmentary perception is to blame. If he "failed to enunciate the true social problem" — which usually remains undefined by his critics — it was because he could not write openly and because certain issues have no instant solution on earth. Voltaire cannot be accused of socio-political inertia. His courageous militancy speaks louder than the sneers of his commentators. In the light of his secret conviction, his positive legacy outweighs subversion by far. No one visibly engaged in undermining ever worked to build so much.

Voltaire is often accused of superficiality. The exoteric component of his works alone calls for indignant rebuttal of the charge. As for the concealed message, it is so vast and deep as to pulverize such claims.

Contradiction does abound in Voltairian writings — as it does in Voltairian biography. It is typical of esoteric authors and occultists who frequently use paradox as a decoy and as a stimulant. As Saint Exupéry once noted, "flowers" are "contradictory" until they are understood.

One anecdote contains a fine illustration of what may be called the Voltairian perception gap. To the acute puzzlement of a critic, the alleged miscreant and arch-iconoclast is regarded as a saint:

> "Toward the end of his life, this glory of Voltaire turns into idolatry. Mme Suard came to Ferney in 1775. One cannot imagine the reverence with which this twenty-year old young woman approached Voltaire. 'Never,' she said, 'could the raptures of Saint Theresa surpass those which I experienced upon seeing that great man.' She is a believer facing her God. Before leaving, she asked him for his blessing." (Lanson et Truffau, *Histoire de la Littérature Française,* Hachette, 1932, pp. 395-96).

The "great man" was well understood by Mme Suard.

Numerous biographical questions should be raised. The notorious love of Voltaire for the theater is one of them.

"Zadig did not pride himself upon being a good poet." The statement seems to contradict the orthodox view of "Zadig." Did Voltaire really think that his best production were versified tragedies? He seems to have believed that he would owe immortality to his plays, a fact commonly noted by critics with varying degrees of irony. Such expectations may reflect a dim view of popular taste rather than poor judgment on the part of the author. Voltaire may have felt that popularity is the reward of the worst attributes of a writer — an opinion shared by various literary personalities including Alfred de Vigny. Certain statements of Voltaire raise the question of what the theater really meant to him. Who knew better than he that the world is a stage? What better front could have been used for secret pursuits than the dazzling hedonism generally associated in the popular mind with the theater?

A passage of *Candide* may shed light on the matter:

> "They then talked about tragedies; the lady asked why there were tragedies which were performed sometimes, and which could not be read. The man of taste explained very well how a play might present some interest and have almost no merit." (Ch. XXII, p. 211).

Tragedies which "cannot be read" call for explanations. The statement that a play "might present some interest and have almost no merit" is intriguing. The exoteric reader is left to speculate on the possible nature of "clarifications" given by the "man of taste." The question is easily resolved by the "instructed" person: Absent or near-absent merit is literary. "Interest" is esoteric.

Diderot understood Voltaire and admired him accordingly. A passage of the *Rêve de d'Alembert* which has already been quoted pays tribute to "the great man." It is closely followed by an interesting portrait: "The great man is master of his sensitivity and of his entire being "in the midst of the greatest dangers."

> "— nothing of what can serve his designs, promote his goal, will elude him; he will be difficult to surprise; he will be forty-five years old; he will be a great king, a great minister, a great political man, a great artist, above all a great comedian, a great philosopher, a great poet, a great musician, a great doctor; he will reign over himself and over all that surrounds him — he will have . . . liberated himself from all the tyrannies of this world. Men of maudlin or insane temperament are on stage, he is in the pit; it is he who is the sage."

The "great man" who "will have liberated himself from all the tyrannies of this world" tends to confirm other suggestions of voluntary reincarnation such as the suggestive word "parterre" — "pit" — and the previously mentioned "descent" into a mortal soul. It is also hinted that the stage used for tragedies "served" the "designs" of a "great comedian" named Voltaire. The genuine "great man" remains concealed, esoteric or: "in the pit."

There is reason to doubt that the cumbersome trappings of classical tragedy represent the literary ideal of Voltaire. The dividing line between the atmosphere of classical tragedy and the climate of the "roman larmoyant" is a thin one resting primarily on the flair of the author. It is somehow difficult to imagine Voltaire writing: "Qu'entends-je?" — or other swooning exclamations which are standard tools of tragic language — with what is commonly called a straight face. The grandiloquent, emotional outpourings which appear in tragedies are basically the same which he mocks in his prose, especially in *Candide.* The fundamental rhythm of the alexandrin — the John Philip Souza of poetry — requires genial levitation to rise beyond the plane of soporific plodding. It is only the alchemy of the verb, skilfully caught and tooled by masters, which has given it wings. Voltaire admired the works of such great writers as Corneille and Racine who performed prodigies with its earthbound cadenza. But his admiration did not necessarily extend to the rigid form and rules governing their chosen genre. The tangible, communicable delight with which Voltaire handles prose suggests otherwise.

Voltaire the critic deserves esoteric examination. The appreciation of English literature which is expressed in his *XVIIIth Philosophical Letter* is an interesting example of specialized recognition. Voltaire did not fail to perceive that English literature is fraught with the inspiration of the Secret Doctrine. The defects of form which are noted in various English texts do not dim his awareness of "amazing gleams of light" scattered against a general background of "darkness." No one was better equipped than the Sage to understand the efforts of those who tried to make themselves "clear" "in thick darkness." The elevating power of English expression is praised. "The stilts of figurative style upon which the English language is propped, do lift the spirit very high." The "stylistic" inspiration of numerous works is traced to the Hebraic tradition and to "Asiatic bombast." The kabalistic and Oriental influence is suggested to account for many things. The general evaluation of English literature which is made by Voltaire conveys smiling recognition of uninhibited — if concealed — Spirit:

> "The poetic genius of the English resembles until now a luxuriant tree planted by nature, casting its thousand branches at random and growing unevenly and with strength; it dies if you wish to force its nature and to trim it into a tree such as those of the gardens of Marly."

The same "strength" and the same Tree of Knowledge may explain the puzzling admiration of Voltaire for such a work as Pope's *Essay on Man.*

In summary, we should expect the esoteric viewpoint to color the likes and dislikes of Voltaire the critic

We may need to revise our view of the private life of Voltaire. "Smugglers" are camouflage experts where their activities are concerned. No better shield for their secret pursuits has ever been devised than the appearance of a reckless love life. The average Western mind — which is culturally conditioned to prize dirt — is happy when finding it and rarely stops to search beyond. Voltaire enunciated this truth when he wrote the first chapter of *Candide*. The screen behind which the hero and the girl try to experiment is not a piece of furniture. It is eroticism itself. The autobiographical comments of Mme Blavatsky on the attitude of her relatives and associates are equally edifying on that score:

> "Had I been a common p— they would have preferred it to my studying occultism —
>
> I shall tell everything I did, for the twenty years and more that I laughed at the *qu'en dira-t-on?*, and covered up all traces of what I was *really* occupied in; i.e., the *sciences occultes,* for the sake of my family and relations, who would at that time have cursed me. I will tell how from my eighteenth year I tried to get people to talk about me, and say that this man and that was my lover, and *hundreds* of them." (*Personal Memoirs of H.P. Blavatsky,* compiled by Mary K. Kneff, p. 173. The Theosophical Publishing House, Wheaton, Ill:, USA, 1967).

One should note briefly that the mysterious Russian great lady created by Proust is remarkably successful in creating such a false impression. As previously noted, "Marcel" mistakes the Princess Sherbatoff for the owner of a house of ill fame at the time of their first meeting.

The true nature of the famous relationship between Voltaire and Mme du Châtelet may be startlingly opposed to traditional reports. The official story is as follows. Voltaire is believed to have been the lover of Mme du Châtelet during his time of residence in her castle at Cirey. "Mme du Châtelet supervises his production: she prudently puts under lock and key the works which could again endanger her great man — She herself has a laboratory, makes experiments, studies Newton."*

Several questions are in order. What was the exact nature of the lady's keen interest in science? What experiments took place in the laboratory? Was alchemy involved? Were the theater and the publicized love affair complementary parts of a deceptive screen? What prompted the obsessive fear of Mme du Châtelet that Voltaire might compromise himself? What could have been more dangerous than his well-known, explosive

---

*Lanson et Truffau, *Histoire de la Littérature Française,* p. 392.

socio-political views? Which aspect of the love affair would have been more disastrous if exposed: reality or fiction?

If we speculate on such matters, we do not seem to be alone. The puzzling vision of "Legrandin" sensuously bowing and scraping in front of a neighboring "châtelaine" may well express Proustian doubt of conventional Voltairian biographies. Proust made it abundantly clear in *Contre Sainte Beuve* that official biographies should be read with caution and that it is in the *works* of great writers that biographical truth itself should be sought. The question of what Mme du Châtelet and Voltaire might have meant to each other is briefly and subtly raised in the *Recherche*. "Brichot" is reported to enjoy a social status which seems to him "the equivalent of what might have been in the home of Mme du Châtelet the person whom he always called — with the impishness and the satisfaction of a man of literary culture: 'M. de Voltaire.'"*

The allusions of Diderot, Proust — and others — to the theater and to the love life of Voltaire point to an amazing biographical "backside." If the concepts of adeptship and voluntary reincarnation have any relevance to the Sage, it is unlikely that the "great man" needed sex to "amuse himself."

Other activities of Voltaire invite speculation. What was the real object of his stay at the Prussian court? Did he really embark on his trip to Postdam with puerile illusions about the "philosopher and warrior," the "Solomon of the North?" Voltaire had spectacular mastery of double-edged compliments. The suspicious combination of "philosopher and warrior" — which has substance in esoteric terms — invites reflection in the case of Frederick. So does the name Solomon, a monarch of mythical and allegorical character.** The glowing reference to the "Solomon of the North" may conceal the unflattering label of the "Nobody of the North." There is reason to surmise that the Prussian King was approached with perfect lucidity by his famous guest.

We may soon discover the concealed reality of the fantastic life of Voltaire. Numerous areas of occult biography await the exploration of daring researchers. Truth is likely to be found in esoteric particles scattered throughout the monumental works of the Sage.

---

*A la Recherche du temps perdu, pp. 976-77, Vol. II.
**Isis Unveiled, p. 391, Vol. 2.

LITERATURE IN GENERAL

Were esoteric literature confined to a few exceptional writers, or even a single case, it would deserve painstaking research. Far from being so restricted, the literary presence of the Secret Doctrine is the sea around us. It is found in the works of the most "unlikely" poets, novelists, playwrights, and philosophers. No single age from which we have inherited any texts is without its dedicated "smugglers." As much as an interpretation of Voltaire, the present work proffers a literary domino theory.

Because of the community of views and techniques existing among them, esoteric writers can be identified when one of them is understood. It is our privilege to live at the time when the expected fall of one mask entails the fall of numerous others.

Literary transmitters of the Secret Doctrine did not hesitate to mutilate their own images in order to pass on the torch. Rabelais disguised himself as a purveyor of buffoonery and dirt. Voltaire invited judgments of atheism, materialism, hedonism, superficiality, and snobbery. Vigny courted labels of aloofness, misogyny, morbid pessimism, and aristocratic arrogance. Céline, Proust, and "Saint Genêt, comédien et martyr," may have chosen the most despised masks of all. Many are the geniuses who vied with one another in disfiguring themselves for the sake of the same cause. The intensity of their conviction seems to have made the sacrifice relatively light. Such dedicated lovers of Truth and Suffering Mankind are not unduly concerned with their doubly mortal image. *We* should be concerned.

We have a twofold duty. Our commitment to knowledge demands that we seek literary truth to the fullest extent possible. Fairness requires that we strip of their veils the authentic and magnificent figures of numerous writers. It was their hope and belief that the task would be performed in our times.

The identity of persons engaged in the work matters little. We should do well to remember the lesson of *The Little Prince*. Knowledge should be judged on its own merits, not by the "clothes" worn by the "explorer." As long as we preoccupy ourselves with externals we will remain blind and will deserve to be. In the face of horizons embraced by esoteric literature, any researcher of sound mind can only feel insignificant. But there is joy in that kind of insignificance. The enterprise is vast enough to supply with happy toil a small army of "insects" of the Proustian specie. Whether or not the researchers believe in the Secret Doctrine should be irrelevant. The question which must be asked of each "suspect" writer is simply this: "Did you or did you nor use your texts to veil and transmit the substance of the Universal Writ?" The job must be done. Because of its nature; because of sacrifices gladly consented by so many, the work deserves all the reverence of which we are capable.

Certain facts should be remembered.

"A small fund of philosophy" is indispensable. Esoteric study is comparative. It is a matter of knowing whether or not Element SD is present in Literary Work X. It is clearly absurd to pass judgment on the question without knowing what SD is. The esoteric researcher must have read — and assimilated to the best of his ability — *The Key to Theosophy, Isis Unveiled*, and *The Secret Doctrine*. Such books supply the necessary knowledge to the average person. To the very sensitive and to the initiate, they probably yield much more. The day may come when such readings may be required for literature courses.

Volumes could be written on esoteric technique. It is doubtful, however, that such books will be needed. Literary transmitters of the Secret Doctrine conceal needed guidance material in their works. Rabelais gives many lessons on the art of grasping "the substantial marrow." The *Recherche* is an esoteric manual difficult to surpass. "Albertine," the "work" of Marcel, is an expert user of all means of concealment. The occasional clumsiness of her wiles is in itself a precious source of insight. The Proustian emphasis on idiosyncracies of language, etymology, names of persons and places, most of all on the plasticity of Time is a valuable aid to the esoteric reader. There is hardly an esoteric trick used in the *Recherche* which is not called to attention somewhere in the text. We must realize that many observations made in esoteric writings apply primarily to the writings themselves.

There is a great deal to be learned from psychological outlines sketched by esoteric writers. The ultimate target of such studies is likely to be the reader himself. The lack of curiosity of the fisherman of *Zadig* is an invitation to wonder about the identity of the hero. The speculations aroused in by-standers by the appearance and behavior of the Ingénu have the same purpose. The literary broadcasts of Bloch convey a personal hint to the typical Judaeo-Christian reader and scholar. Much could be learned by the young pedant from the names, titles, and words which he smugly drops in a vain display of superficial knowledge. The "Bhagavat" and the Delphic oracle might introduce him to undreamed domains were he to see in their existence more than the making of his personal prestige. One of the most useful messages conveyed by esoteric writers may be summarized in these words: O Reader, Know Thyself.*

The person who can perceive and heed the subtle directives of esoteric writers finds certain barriers miraculously shattered. The text which he studies ceases to be puzzling. Numerous contradictions dissolve. The fact that the author may have lived centuries ago in a distant land becomes irrelevant. The contingencies of Maya vanish under the probe of the Higher Self. There is a direct, true contact between the best of the reader and the best of the writer. The author who may have "died" in 1778 or in 1863 is suddenly ALIVE. The reader experiences the true significance of LIVING. The eternal Oneness of That which IS becomes Fact. The esoteric writer claims that Time and Space and death as we know them are mere effects of incarnate illusion. The esoteric writer proves his point.

The human mind is a mysterious machine which can travel and explore while its owner is asleep. Proust gives us numerous hints of what can be glimpsed in dreams and in the intermediate state between wakefulness and slumber. The great ambition of young Marcel is to converse with "Legrandin" in dreams. There is reason to believe that the ambition was fulfilled. The trips of Marcel to the ethereal regions of Rivebelle are made in the company of "Saint Loup." Some of the greatest rewards of intercourse with "Albertine" result from the slumbers of the "Great Goddess of Time," the "work" of Marcel. The researcher who learns to "swim" in the special element of esoteric literature may perform his most illuminating "readings" during sleeping hours. It is almost useless to try to convey the reality of the experience to a person unacquainted with it. It is even more useless to tell the seasoned traveler that such an experience does not exist. The Proustian emphasis on various states of consciousness is focused on a crucial concept of occult philosophy: Maya. It is a transparent invitation to meditate. Where is reality? Where is illusion? The same emphasis is an exhortation addressed to us. We must not fear to use all our faculties. We must not understimate our own ability to "travel."

Nothing happens by chance in the works of esoteric writers. Small details of expression are usually significant. Their understated "usefulness" bears repeating.

Special print such as italics and unexpected capital letters should arrest our attention. Their presence is a sign of important veiled material. Vigny capitalized the COLLAR or NECKLACE of *Les Destinées* in order to stress the key-word of his "poetic enigma." Voltaire made frequent use of italics to stimulate critical thoughts on hidden substance. The priceless *"Ni père ni mère"* of *L'Ingénu* which conceals the occult concept of

---

*A la Recherche du temps perdu, (p. 90, Vol. I).

"Parentlessness" is an example of such usage. The *Poem on the Disaster of Lisbon* teems with meaningful italics. The same poem exploits the difference between the anthropomorphic GOD of all capital letters and the Unlimited Being reflected in the personal God or Chrestos of every man.

Phonetic similarities are often used to convey hidden substance. The "ten to ten years" of Vigny which actually represent one hundred and twenty years constitute an example of such usage. The Voltairian Arbogad is an inverted Dagobert. The Proustian character named M. de Vallenères may be an inverted Gérard de Nerval.* Slight phonetic modifications are often called to attention. Zadig is intensely surprised when he sees the last two letters of his name. DAG, the Savior, has lost its A and has acquired an I. Proust gives the example of *Simonet* and *Simonnet* in the apparent hope that the difference will be remembered in connection with other names. Oriane — the duchess of Guermantes — may be a modified *Ariane* or *Ariadne* endowed with an illuminating "golden thread." A verbal "gem" of Françoise — the transformation of *envergure* into *enverjure* — suggests the interest of a similar alteration of *Guermantes*. The prestigious name may be the combination of the "germ" of all living things and of the stressed syllable *antes*.** Which conveys the idea of anteriority or of a beginning. Such a possibility is consistent with the many suggestions of genesis — such as the symbolism of the egg — which are present in *Swann's Way*. It is also consistent with the importance of the Great Swan of Time.

The significance of proper names is often illuminating. Much can be surmised from the names of Voltairian characters. The same fact seems to apply to the works of esoteric writers in general. Many identities can be established in the joint lights of character traits and names. Such is the case of M. de Norpois. The dignified magistrate is observed "au retrait" more than once. He is regarded as "a pest" — perhaps a plague — a word which may represent an allusion to the plague of Bordeaux. His use of the verb "savoir" is a likely reference to the famous: "Que sais-je?" His name — which is reminiscent of "Nord" and "Pole" — may be linked esoterically to *Meru*, the Mountain — esoterically the North Pole —, in French "la Montagne."

Hidden identities are often suggested by juxtaposition. The truth and the rose which are mentioned in one breath in Chapter XXI of *The Little Prince* are one and the same. The oneness of the Good and of the Beautiful is expressed in the same manner in Chapter XIV of the same book.

---

*A la Recherche du temps perdu, p. 189, Vol. II.
**Ibid., p. 171, Vol. I.

The identity of "Cottard" is hinted in the *Recherche* by suggestive passages featuring such details as "le quart d'heure de Rabelais."*

> " 'J'entends bien,' répondit Brichot, 'que, pour parler comme maître François Rabelais, vous voulez dire que je suis moult sorbonagre, sorbonicole et sorboniforme.' — 'Le quart d'heure de Rabelais,' interrompit le docteur Cottard avec un air non plus the doute, mais de spirituelle assurance." (*A la Recherche du temps perdu*, p. 1051, Vol. II).

> ("I do understand, replied Brichot, that, to use the words of Master François Rabelais, you mean that I am very sorbonizing, sorboni-cultural, and sorbonimorph. 'The quarter of an hour or Rabelais,' interrupted Dr. Cottard with no longer an air of doubt, but of witty assurance.")

The probable identity of another Proustian character is also suggested by proximity. The portrait of Prince Von Faffenheim contains a brief reference to Goethe.**

The peculiarities of language are exploited by esoteric writers. The French pronoun "on" should often be read as "je" if Marcel Proust must be believed. Words with multiple meanings are fine transmitters of deep substance. The triple potency of the French term "esprit" is rarely wasted. The dual meaning of "le temps" — the "weather" and "time" — is useful to Marcel Proust. The cheap "puns" of some Proustian characters are far more "amusing" than they seem to be. The playing on words of Vigny can reveal the autobiographical dimension of *La Flûte*. The "sea of deceptive stars" — a "drama" — is *Stello*. The "sails" or "veils" under which the book "sank" are esoteric devices. The "lack of knowledge" which caused the popular work to fail is the deficiency of the public, not that of the author. The "newspaper" which helped the writer survive difficult moments is a "diary."

Etymology clarifies many mysteries. The short stories of Voltaire give evidence of the fact. Proust places heavy stress on the origin of words. Warning is given against inadequate and biased interpretations. The etymologies of Brichot — the encyclopaedic mind — are opposed to the etymologies of the priest who is blinded by hatred of Paganism.

The importance of numbers — often disguised by the presence or the absence of esoteric zeros — should be kept in mind. M. de Charlus, the esoteric spirit par excellence, has interesting thoughts on the "swelling" of certain numbers representing statistics of "inversion." We should es-

---

A la Recherche du temps perdu, p. 200, Vol. I.
**Ibid.*, p. 256, Vol. II.

pecially note that numbers are meaningful in relation to Rounds and Races.*

Peculiarities of style and errors of substance call for study. The crippled poetry of "Zadig"—which has actual counterparts in the poetry of Voltaire—is occasionally designed to stimulate critical thoughts. The desired reaction may produce rewarding questions: How or why did a great writer create indigestible verse? How did he make certain mistakes? Why did he contradict himself? The presence of defects of form may be explained by hints of the author: "Zadig did not pride himself upon being a good poet." "Language is a source of misunderstanding."** What is lacking in letters is sincerity."**** An apparent lack of logic such as the Rabelaisian failure to maintain the original size of giants may point to the gradual "dwarfing" of mankind in the course of evolution. An inconsistency such as that of Vigny scorning Science in one stanza and celebrating Science a few lines later may point to two different kinds of knowledge. A major "oversight" such as dead characters suddenly brought back to life may point to reincarnation.

We need to pay attention to material absurdity. The eighth stanza of *La Maison du berger* seems designed to attract such notice. Eva is invited to a tryst in the rolling house of the shepherd. The "tryst" actually is a mystical communion with the poet. Eva is told that ultimate heights are not beyond reach of her mind or vision. The cabin of the shepherd is described as follows:

> "Elle va doucement avec ses quatre roues,
> Son toit n'est pas plus haut que ton front et tes yeux;—"

> ("It goes gently with its four wheels,
> Its roof is no higher than your brow or your eyes;—"

With due respect to poetic license and to the possibility of human oversight, a prosaic thought should come to mind. Unless Eva is an eight-foot Amazon, the place leaves much to be desired for exoteric love-making. The "tryst" must be symbolic. The problem of lacking head-room seems to be noted in the *Recherche*. The military subordinates of "Saint Loup" merrily discuss the high head-gear and the agility of their dashing officer.**** The two sheep of Candide which carry an impossible exoteric load serve the same interpretive purpose. The amount of wealth which they

---

A la Recherche du temps perdu, p. 298, Vol. III.
**The Little Prince*, Ch. XXI.
****Alfred de Vigny*, Diary, 1835.
*****A la Recherche du temps perdu*, pp. 93-94, Vol. II.

carry and which exceeds all the riches of the King of Spain suggest immaterial or spiritual treasures. Material absurdity is often calculated to guide our thoughts to the appropriate symbolic plane.

"Afterthoughts" and casual style should not be allowed to slip by. It is often in the midst of false relaxation that high intensity dwells. The "drifting" observations made by Vigny in the *Diary* of 1849 on the role of Destiny point to "the word of our poetic enimga." The "amusing" side remarks of Voltaire on "pious lies which might be useful" to the moderns point to the crucial identity of Cunégonde and to the explosive potential of the unimpressive word "useful."

We should be prudent in our interpretation of such terms as "seem," "appear," "thinking," "believing," "imagining," "like," "as if," etc. They are frequent vehicles of truth stated in ironic contexts. We must be skeptical of skepticism itself.

Helpful equivalences are generously given by esoteric writers. We must learn to recognize and apply them in algebraic spirit. We should ask ourselves whom — or what — the *Son of Man* may address when he calls: "Father!" in *Le Mont des oliviers*. We should take note of the childish belief of young Marcel which makes of Combray "the extreme limit of Christendom."* We should bear in mind the value of "inversion" which is given by a "lesbian." To see her and her companion indulge in their favorite pasttime is to see them "read."** We must learn to heed such clues as the grotesque statement of "Cottard" about his wife which suggests that the exoteric Mme Cottard is an esoteric man: "That wife of mine, he is jealous."***

We must resist the divisive, fragmentary perception which is a common product of misunderstood allegory. Numerous characters are mere aspects of things and beings. Cacambo is the doubting principle of Candide which is instinctive, primitive, and Pagan. Martin is the element of Candide which is intellectual, skeptical, European and which has "traveled." "Albertine," the duchess of Guermantes, and other Proustian characters are said to have several faces. "Mars and Venus were only the Strength and the Beauty of Jupiter."**** adds the *Recherche*. The clue is a valuable one to Proustian mythology. We may reflect with profit on the relationship existing between Marcel and the "little gang" of girls. It is the connection of an author with a journalistic corps.***** We must heed the statement of the writer according to which the suppres-

---

*A la Recherche du temps perdu, p. 114, Vol. I.
**Ibid., p. 161, Vol. I.
***Ibd., p. 922, Vol. II.
****Ibid., p. 686, Vol. II.
*****Ibid., p. 180, Vol. III.

sion of "real characters might represent a decisive step toward perfection."*

We must bear in mind the frequent dualism of the esoteric writer. The "average" "smuggler" is a being combining superior vision with the perception of ordinary mortals. He is at one with Suffering Mankind by virtue of human condition and boundless compassion. But his insight isolates him from less advanced persons. The resulting contradiction between two different viewpoints is an effective means of esoteric concealment.

Esoteric texts must be "tamed" in the manner suggested by Saint-Exupéry. "To tame" means "to create ties" or to make connections.* The connections must be made on a symbolic plane. When Vigny invites a certain Traveller—with a capital T or in French V—to ascend a certain Tower—with a capital T—, we should raise our vision beyond the Tower of Notre Dame or the Tower of Montmartre no matter what the predictable footnote may have to say. When we read *La Bouteille à la mer*, we may benefit slightly by knowing that Vigny loved the sea and that his maternal grand-father was a high-ranking naval officer. But the key to the "poetic enigma" of the author will never be found in such information. We must not be side-tracked by pedestrian footnotes.

Desirable as it is, coldly factual erudition can be the worst possible enemy of esoteric insight. The detailed reporting of events which represents its ultimate form is essentially opposed to symbolic flights and panoramic vision. The obsessive pursuit of erudition can stifle sensitivity to veiled substance. In the words of Marcel Proust, "We waste a precious time on an absurd track and we brush against Truth without knowing it."** Erudition may be a "flight" from "our own life"—or from "reality."*

We need to be less literal in our approach to symbolism than we generally tend to be. The current popularity of sexual interpretation has a legitimate basis. Sexual symbols abound in literary texts. But the researcher who does not rise beyond their plane is doomed to miss esoteric substance. The metaphysical meaning of sex is a crucial element of esoteric expression which can only be grasped in the realm of metaphysics. The Rabelaisian plea which is quoted in the present work and which appears in the midst of a pornographic text cannot be stressed too much: "I beg of you, do raise your minds above terrestrial thought, in lofty contemplation of the wonders of Nature."

All is fish to the symbolic net of esoteric writers. The most prosaic

Ibid., p. 85, Vol. I.
**A la Recherche du temps perdu*, p. 100, Vol. III.
***Ibid.*, p. 890, Vol. III.

571

beings, situations, and objects are humorously absorbed in their store-house of timeless mythology. The Voltairian use of rifles representing more or less dynamic spiritual "fire" is a good example of eclectic technique. The Huron who "amuses himself" by "drinking in the house" suggests little spirituality on the exoteric plane. Proust uses telegraphy to symbolize intuition. The mythological wheel of the bicycle of Albertine is as significant as the segment of evolution represented by the "tortillard d'intérêt local." Proustian aviators are explorers who know how to use "the conveyances of up there." "Flight" candidates who do not qualify usually try to enter the Académic Française!* We must learn to consider the symbolic possibilities of all aspects of life — the down-to-earth and the contemporary included.

What is true of symbolism applies to allegory. Spirit is present on all levels. Allegorical personages often wear strange "coats of skin." A character of *La Bête Humaine* — Flore — is a simple, if not simple-minded woman of gigantic proportions and great physical strength. Zola repeatedly describes her as "virgin and warlike." The transparent reference to Athena identifies the mutation of the Greek Goddess of Wisdom muscle-bound and stultified in an age of materialistic dullness. The sizable gap separating her original status from her modern degradation may be compared to the change suffered by Cunégonde and by other Voltairian allegories of Truth. We must not be surprised to find in existential literature a dog-headed young man briefly glimpsed in a café, a modern counterpart of Anubis. We must be prepared to meet Jehovah trying to learn to type on an American machine in *Death on the Installment Plan.*

We need to be more literal than we usually are in the face of startling statements. Such statements are often meant to be read literally. The tablets of Zadig "spoke." A statue "spoke" to Moabdar and caused him to become insane. Occult beliefs too staggering to be readily accepted by the average Westerner are their own best veils.

The plane of "lofty contemplation" which we are invited to explore is the realm of non-contingency. Mayavic "facts of life" such as sex, terrestrial Time and Space, and, in general sensory illusion, do not apply to the domain which lies beyond the veil. Men may be changed into women and vice versa, a fact which is illustrated in the *Recherche.* "La Molé" — esoterically Count Molé — represents such a case of inversion. The sex of esoteric "Mme Cottard" is suggested by her husband. The "lady" *methodically* carrying "des cartes" and slumbering in a heated room can easily be identified as a famous philosopher when certain clues are heeded. "Male" characters who speak to serpents may be esoteric

---

Ibid., p. 854, Vol. III.

mutations of eternal Eve. Earthly Space is frequently transcended. No major detour is involved in substituting Paris to Venice in *Candide*. The same two cities are connected in the *Recherche*. The Balbec of Low Normandy — which bears a relation to the Lebanese Baalbek — is a point of departure for "other worlds" represented by "Rivebelle" where matter is not "the same" as the matter of terrestrial regions.* The plasticity of Time alternately compressed and expanded is often illustrated. The theme of eventual vindication of Truth — an event expected in our own era — is present in the anterior settings of *Zadig, Candide* and *Micromégas*. Prophecy told in the past tense is commonly found in the Scriptures and in esoteric literature.** The restitution of "borrowed silver," the resurrection of Pangloss, the trial of Micromégas, and the corresponding final episode of *L'Ingénu* belong to that prophetic type of storytelling — as do the final chapters of the *Recherche*. An unorthodox view of time is required to make of Descartes the physical consort of Rabelais. But the two "smugglers" of the same Secret Doctrine can easily be regarded as esoteric "good companions." The figure of an Alfred de Vigny who dies on a World War I battlefield is bound to arouse skepticism. But the concealed identity of the poet whose mortal — and exoteric — shell is destroyed in a symbolic apocalypse or "war of the nations" can be supported. The holocaust of a World War is an ideal "blind" for the intellectual and spiritual upheaval which is predicted by all esoteric writers. Saint Exupéry makes similar use of World War II in *Flight to Arras*. We must learn to question and transcend the conventional framework of what is commonly regarded as reality if we are ever to use the conveyances of up there."*** The reality of material planes is likely to be no more than "the waste-product of experience."****

We should be aware of references and themes commonly found in the works of esoteric writers. Allusions to Pythagoras, Plato, Porphyry, Jamblichus, Plotinus, Apollonius of Tyana, Plutarch, Julian, and Hypathia do not suffice to support the claim that a certain author is esoteric. But they greatly increase the possibility of his being esoteric. Speculation on the birthdate of Christ, the presence of Peter in Rome, and the role of the said apostle in the foundation of the Church are usually meaningful.

The emblem of esoteric literature is the snake, dragon, or reptile biting its own tail or the "snake in a circle." It is generally found in the final portion of a text which is usually written toward the end of an

---

*A la Recherche du temps perdu, p. 398, Vol. II.
**The Secret Doctrine, p. 100, Vol. II.
***A la Recherche du temps perdu, p. 159, Vol. I.
****Ibid., p. 890, Vol. III.

author's career. While its presence may seem to be a minor detail, it is the distinctive sign or "precious seal" used by many senders of timeless Bottles to the sea.

We must be prepared to study fantastic areas of biography. Voltaire regarded his passage on earth as a voluntary reincarnation. Several passages of his short stories suggest that he had come to earth from the region of Sirus. Vigny celebrates his approaching release from the chain of rebirth in *L'Esprit pur*. The date of his Way to Damascus is virtually given in the same poem. The "twenty years of silence" point to the mystical experience of the "beggar" of *La Flûte*. The Self-Knowledge claimed by the author is said to extend to "past labors" — esoterically past lives. It is consistent with the status of a perfected being ready to "break the chain" of reincarnation. The *Diary* of the poet contains a hint of what one past life might have been. Vigny expresses admiration for Emperor Julian in the following terms: "If metempsychosis exists, I was that man!"* Vigny did believe in metempsychosis — rather transmigration. The conclusion to be drawn seems clear. The memory of the imperial initiate who tried to stem the tide of expanding Christianity is revered by Occultists. The famous Pagan who was eventually called "the Apostate" because, in the words of Mme Blavatsky, he refused to become one,** is the subject of a work of Vigny: *Daphué*. Vigny strongly suggests that he was the reincarnation of Julian.

The esoteric writer is — in the words of Proust — a "proud lord" who paints himself "in caricature, in the evening, as a peddler of clothes"*** — or veils. It is our duty to try to learn in what manner and to what degree the "proud lord" calumniates himself.

The biographies of Vigny usually mention a bevy of mistresses. Most famous among them is Marie Dorval, an actress for whom Vigny wrote poetry and a play. The true nature of the publicized liaison may be gathered from the *Recherche* and from the vibrant beauty of verse dedicated to Marie by her friend. "Saint Loup" is in the words of Proust "a perfect comedian,"**** a person who must conceal "perfection." The young man flaunts various paramours. The women are convenient means of concealment for his genuine vice: "inversion." Some conversations held by "Saint Loup" and "Rachel" concern literature, a "necklace," and a "trial" — exoterically the Dreyfus case. The latter cause célèbre is assimilated to a literary trial elsewhere in the *Recherche*.***** The poetry

---

*Diary, 1833.
**The Secret Doctrine, p. 334, Vol. V. — Adyar Edition —.
***A la Recherche du temps perdu, p. 924, Vol. III.
****Ibid., p. 176, Vol. II.
*****Ibid., p. 245, Vol. III.

dedicated by Vigny to Marie Dorval is filled with esoteric inspiration. The poet refers to himself as *"the visit,"* and *"the stranger."** The text which he will share with the beloved will serve as a pretense. "— It is another book which I shall unfold." Were we not so culturally prejudiced against our own subjective instinct, the beauty of the verse would suffice to make us doubt that Vigny dedicated such lofty vibrance to a cheap tramp. There is a splendid study to be made of the Proustian counterpart of Marie: "Rachel quand du seigneur," a study which will explode the tawdriness of official legend. Marie Dorval seems to have belonged to an impressive lineage of theatrical persons — such as Adrienne Lecouvreur — who "thought" — and acted — "very nobly."

Proustian biography should be re-examined. The homosexual fame of Proust was probably contrived by the author himself. André Maurois was not deceived when he wrote his preface to the *Recherche*. The snake in a circle which appears in the second part of the text is as significant as the general commentary. Maurois carefully defines the problem of Proust as a "moral" one. That "Proust may be "immoral" — in exoteric appearance perhaps — and may "suffer" accordingly is granted. But the charge of "amorality" is rejected. A wide margin of possibilities is allowed by such words.

Simone de Beauvoir reports that a mutual friend of Jean-Paul Sartre and herself once brought astounding, unspecified news on the sex life of Marcel Proust.** We may either conclude that the "secret of Polichinelle" represented by Proustian inversion was news to Jean-Paul Sartre and to Mme de Beauvoir. Or we may conclude that the much — publicised homosexuality of Proust is a myth.

The substance of *Contre Sainte Beuve* is applicable to Proust himself. We are more likely to discover biographical truth in the writings of the author than we are to discover it anywhere else. The bizarre ravings of Céleste and Gineste Albaret — and their significant names — are revealing. The mantle of the prophet passed by "Saint Loup" to "Marcel" is also significant. "The odd genius" of Céleste speaks as follows:

> "— she used to approach me with these words: 'Divine being from heaven deposed on a bed!' I used to say: 'But, now Céleste, why 'Divine being from heaven?' — 'Oh! if you believe that you have something in common with those who travel on our vile earth, you are quite mistaken!' — 'But why 'deposed' on a bed? you see very well that I am lying down.' — 'You never lie down. Did one ever see anyone lying like that? You came to land there. Your pajamas which are all white

---

Le Livre.
**La Force de l'Age, p. 642, Livre de Poche edition.

right now, along with the movements of your neck, make you look like a dove.' " (*A la Recherche du temps perdu*, p. 18, Vol. III).

The importance of ethics cannot be over-emphasized. Petty gloating over the minor faults of a writer is the death of esoteric insight. The "shortcomings" or "good company" are frequently designed to test the critical and ethical attitude of the reader. The researcher who dreams of making a big name for himself by showing that Voltaire — for instance — was not so great after all may well become an academic pontiff laden with honors and grants. But he will stay blind to the divine message concealed in the texts. He will miss an experience which is worth far more than all the professional sugar-plums in the world. Mechanical idol-worship is just as fatal to genuine understanding of esoteric works as is mechanical contempt. The person who decides to eulogize a writer because it is the thing to do — or for any other reason connected with the researcher's image — dooms himself to the same blindness as does the pathological fault-finder. Literary "good company" cares little for our lower selves except to help us transcend them. Literary "good company" appeals to what is best in us.

Literary "good company" tries to show that Knowledge should be approached for its own sake; that spiritual faculties do exist which are indispensable to esoteric exploration. Literary "good company" tells us that the invisible world accessible to those who use appropriate "conveyances" is no myth. Literary "good company" proves its point.

What is the nature of special faculties needed by the esoteric researcher? The answer lies in the Voltairian "conveyances of up there," in the "leaps of gazelles" of Vigny, in the airborne flights and telegraphic messages of Proust. The answer is intuition. It is possessed by us all to some degree. It is our task to recognize its importance and to cultivate it. It is not unusual to see it assert itself in the classroom and elsewhere. But it is sadly uncommon to see it heeded.

Every person who loves literature has had the same experience. A text suddenly proves puzzling in strange, magnetic fashion. Something is sensed. The fascinating and rebellious "something" resists superficial explanation. Freud may be called to the rescue but somehow fails to help. Sexual imagery clarifies so much and no more. The weird and potent feeling is usually forgotten after a few vain attempts at understanding. The "small fund of philosophy" necessary to genuine insight is lacking. The formidable weight of orthodox authority exerts itself. There are, after all, many books on library shelves which are the work of experts on the text in question. Were there anything special to know on the subject, such commentators would have found it.

576

We must never reject intuition summarily no matter how bizarre or unfounded it may seem. The divine flash is not rootless. It grows from the intensity of forgotten past experience. The Secret Doctrine teaches that it is the frequent product of a previous life. Its connection with fact is not apparent. But it is there nevertheless. Intuition is no wild, irrational hunch. Intuition of the right type can always be methodically supported in the course of subsequent examination. Hours, weeks, even years may go by before one may look back and joyfully recognize the perfect accuracy of the first forceful impression. Vigny tells us that the "leaps of gazelles" must be and are companions of reason. Shelley proclaims in *Oedipus Tyrannus* that the mount which "can leap any gate in Boetia" will not "throw" its rider. We may soon find in the course of previously inconceivable studies intuition to be the most rational thing in the world.

> "Alone the impression, however tenuous its subtance may seem, howeever elusive its trace, is a criterion of truth, and because of that alone deserves to be apprehended by the mind (or spirit) for it is alone capable, if the mind (or spirit) knows how to extract that truth, to bring it to greater perfection and to give it a pure joy." (*A la Recherche du temps perdu*, p. 800, Vol. III).

The apparent looseness of the intuitive approach is more than compensated by the solid quality of unveiled material. "This absence of a logical and necessary connection — more than facts reported, is the sign of truth"* says Proust. Not only is the esoteric message consistent within the works of a given writer but it is admirably consistent in a massive amount of great literature written through the ages. We must try to develop "the eye of the great searcher,"** a vision undaunted by "flights" and panoramic surveys.

We must learn to use all our powers of perception. There is sweet irony in one aspect of the message now disclosed. We are warned against our occasional tendency to underrate our own faculties and ourselves.

The predictable clamor for external evidence which is sure to come was anticipated and answered a long time ago by esoteric writers. Those authors who dedicated themselves to the transmission of the occult message; those who "betrayed" accepted norms of living and writing, can hardly be expected to leave behind convenient papers stating that they did so. Vigny states in his *Diary* that it is useless to look for the documents of his spiritual "trial." Proust gives a similar warning.

> " 's'il ne fallait condamner que les gens qui signent un papier où ils

---

A la Recherche du temps perdu, p. 96, Vol. III.
**A la Recherche du temps perdu*, p. 861, Vol. I.

déclarent 'j'ai trahi,' on ne punirait jamais le crime de trahison.' " (*A la Recherche du temps perdu*, p. 728, Vol. III).

("'— if one had to condemn only those who sign a paper in which they declared 'I have betrayed,' the crime of betrayal would never be punished.' ")

The etymology of the verb "trahir" — "to betray" — implies the idea of "going over to the other side" which can also be conveyed in French by the expression "passer outre" — "to go beyond." The latter phrase is commonly used by esoteric writers — such as Rabelais — in the sense of "going beyond matter" or "lifting the veil."

We are warned against other perils of esoteric research. Unflattering labels are apt to be earned by daring explorers. The exposure of literary "inversion" — individual and collective — is expected to produce a vitriolic outcry. But there is hope of acceptance in the future.

" 'Three out of ten!' exclaimed Brichot. 'If I reversed the proportion, I still would have to multiply by one hundred the number of culprits. If it is as you say, baron, and if you are not mistaken, let us admit then that you are one of those rare seers of a truth which no one suspects around them. Three out of ten! But be careful, less fortunate than those historians who will be vindicated by posterity, baron, if you wished to present to posterity the picture which you say, posterity might find it hard to take. It judges on the basis of documents only and would want to examine your dossier. And since no document would come to authenticate this type of collective phenomena which the only persons in the know are too interested in keeping in the dark, there would be great indignation in the camp of fine souls and you would be regarded categorically as a slanderer or as a fool.' " (*A la Recherche du temps perdu*, pp. 298-99, Vol. III).

We are told by literary transmitters of the Secret Doctrine that conventional external evidence does not exist where their occult persuasion is concerned. Ordinary documentation has no place in the subjective approach which is repeatedly prescribed by the authors themselves. If "objectivity" must sanctify all research, we may display more of it by heeding the directives of esoteric writers than by ignoring them.

Sainte Beuve, the famous critic, represents one example of "objectively" induced blindness. The commentator was sufficiently sensitive to react from time to the vibrance of the poetry of Vigny. His inspired comments on a few chosen lines could easily endear him to esoteric readers. But his general attitude is one of petty fault-finding and blind contempt. No one can blame the well-known critic for his apparent lack of a "small fund of philosophy." Western scholarship does not encourage familiarity with the Secret Doctrine. Many are the otherwise learned persons who do not even know that the Secret Doctrine exists. We can only regret that Sainte Beuve — and many others — fumbled in, around, and through esoteric gems unseeing. Proust probably had in mind the famous commentator when he created the character of Bloch, the Judaeo-Christian or Western scholar.

That Count Molé "fixed" Vigny in his reception speech at the Académie Française is a well-known fact of literary history. The matter is briefly mentioned in the esoteric salon of the duchess of Guermantes. The feelings of the "witty" — or "spiritual" — family are expressed by M. de Charlus. "La Molé" — whose historical prototype curtly declined an explanatory interview with Vigny — is unfit to be received in "good company." The magic of symbolic melody and the inspiration of *The Flute* do not stand a chance in the presence of such a person.

> " 'Had you invited the Molé, everything would have flopped. It would have been the small adversary droplet, neutralizing, which makes a philter powerless. The electricity would have gone out, the cakes would not have arrived on time, the orangeade would have given the colic to everybody. She was the right person not to have around. At her name alone, as in a fantasy, no sound would have come out of the brass instruments, the flute and oboe would have suddenly lost their voice — '
> — Countess Molé was not equal to the extraordinary reputation of intelligence which she enjoyed, and which made one think of those actors or novelists of mediocre caliber who at certain times have the status of genius, either because of the mediocrity of their colleagues, among whom no superior artist can show what true talent is, or because of the mediocrity of the public, which, were there an extraordinary individuality, would be incapable of understanding it. In the case of Mme Molé, it is preferable if not entirely accurate, to content oneself with the first explanation." (*A la Recherche du temps perdu*, p. 276, Vol. III).

Extraordinary beings who celebrate their impending release from "chains" of rebirth — as does Vigny in *L'Esprit pur* — can expect little insight from unenlightened critics who will not be enlightened. The ignorance of the public — which is shared by "La Molé" — seems to convey an allusion to the "drama of deceptive stars" — *Stello* — which, in the words of its author, "sank under its veils." Whatever the case may be, the Academician who "fixed" Vigny is ably "fixed" by Proust.

At the risk of being accused of intellectual arrogance, we must learn to question the awesome authority of prestigious critics. Many are those who cannot — or will not — perceive esoteric truth.

Daring is necessary to use subjective faculties and unorthodox evidence. Daring is required to resist the powerful influence of numerous critics. Daring of another kind is important also. It is best defined in the light of orthodox critiques such as typical commentaries on Rabelais.

It is often said of the father of *Gargantua* and *Pantagruel* that his chief intent was to arouse clear, frank, Gallic laughter; that satire and social critiques are present in his work but that they are part and parcel of a vein of simple humor also found in medieval fabliaux. In short, that Rabelais should not be regarded as a theoretician of reform.

> "Rabelais — accepts the order of things existing in his times. He is satisfied with it. He is not among those who dream of reorganizing society, particularly at the price of a revolution." (*Oeuvres complètes, Rabelais*, Classiques Garnier, p. xxxi).

Medieval humor does have genuine, and delightful, prolongations in the works of Rabelais. Medieval writers do not practice overt rabble-rousing. Nor does the Priest of Meudon. Rabelais was too intelligent to provoke doomed uprisings or useless bloodshed. Like Voltaire, and for the same reasons, he viewed political evolution within the framework of a vaster process. But his vitriolic attacks against a corrupt clergy are not intended as mere recreation. Such indictments cannot address themselves to the Church alone for Church, monarchy, and die-hard feudalism are indissolubly wedded. Rabelaisian laughter was not meant to dissolve into nothingness. It was designed to leave a deep, lasting mark which would eventually — centuries later — contribute to change. The poem entitled *Fanfreluches antidotées, trouvées en un monument antique* seems to contain a prophecy of the Great Revolution.

The critics often deplore the difficulties of Rabelaisian texts "which present only the interest of a rattle of obscure words."* It is observed in connection with Rabelaisian obscenity that "one would gladly do without certain pages."** The task of understanding Rabelais would indeed be easier in the absence of "obscure" and coarse passages. But the "substantificque moelle" would probably suffer from such removal.

We would do well to ask ourselves a few questions. If Rabelaisian verve is frequently medieval, what is "medieval verve?" We are usually told that it is made of good, clear, frank, Gallic laughter; tinged here and there with a bit of satire — that is conceded — but all meant in jolly, Campfire Girl spirit. XIXth Century critics once traced the inspiration of many fabliaux to the Far East, particularly to India. The fact is difficult to overlook in manuals of literature. But — as is generally stressed — Joseph Bédier took care of that. The final encyclical bull is a label of "contes à faire rire." Nothing is ever said about karmic symbolism or other such unfortunate substance.

Oeuvres complètes, Rabelais, Classiques Garnier, p. xxxi.
**Ibid.*

Yet it is there quite frequently. It is not by chance that Voltaire drew inspiration from *L'Ange et l'ermite* when he wrote *Zadig*. The significant wheel which constitutes a part of the name Jes*rad* is mentioned in the fabliau.

> "Things go with this life as they go for a turning wheel, which never remains still."

The corpse of a man killed unjustly is found by the angel and by the hermit of the medieval fabliau. The foul odor of the decaying body is noted. The angel buries the dead man without being distressed by the powerful miasma. The relative unimportance of physical death and physical corruption is suggested. One word which appears in the burial episode should arrest attention. What is the possible interest of the violent death of the person killed *unjustly?* Does a man killed "unjustly" emit a worse physical stench than one who dies in bed? Does the stench perhaps represent the torment of the soul hovering near mortal remains because of the unnatural severance from its body? We should remember in this connection that the unnamed specific organ of women which is mentioned by Rabelais causes its Dionysiac owners to be markedly sensitive to "odors." Should we overlook the presence of the word "unjustly" in the fabliau? Should we conveniently dismiss it as an example of charming medieval naïveté? If we must conduct studies on the subject of *naiveté* — which is a good idea — we would do well to begin with our own.

A cortège of glamorous nobles is encountered by the two characters. The angel cannot bear the perfumed foulness of their moral decay. A subversive sense of values is stressed by contrast. A convent is burnt in pre-Voltairian fashion because the monks have strayed from their spiritual duty and become corrupt. The Throne remains invisible. But the Castle and the Altar are represented as "infamous" and treated accordingly. Yet we are suavely told by various critics that no socio-political intent is present:

> "No satire, said we, at least, no satire in the primary intent of the authors; satire may exist, occasionally; it does not partake of the essence of the fabliau. The period, besides, which suffers from abuse, as does any other, is on the whole, a peaceful and prosperous era; the joy of life explodes in our fabliaux and the laughter of the XIIIth Century France is frank laughter, without hard feelings or afterthought. Our authors certainly have no such thought in their heads as reforming the status quo." (*Fabliaux et contes choisis du Moyen Age*, Librairie Hatier, série des *Classiques pour tous*, Notice).

If medieval "joie de vivre" somehow did exist, which is probable, it must have had little to do with the socio-political state of affairs. We should ask for whom — or for what — the period was "prosperous" and happy. History has the answer. "In the twelvth and thirteenth centuries, the Church enjoys incomparable power. It has become a veritable organized monarchy with its own finances, its bureaucratic hierarchy, its central government and its allmighty sovereign, the Pope. To make itself respected, it has at its disposal some spiritual weapons: excommunication and interdict — The Church, however, has its rebels, the heretics. It combats them mercilessly with steel and fire. Against the most dreaded heretics, the Albigeois, Innocent III preaches a crusade (1208) and Gregory IX founds the Inquisition."* The beauties of feudalism and the splendors of the Albigensian Crusade are too well known to need description here. The "happy" period witnessed the reign of "Saint" Louis, a King whose piety continues to receive fulsome praise "in all the newspapers of all centuries." Saint Louis was addicted to the spirited looting and to the pious gore of the Crusades, a weakness which caused his death. Joinville reports the defense of Christian faith which was once advocated by the saintly King: "— the laymen — when they hear evil spoken of Christian law, must only rise in its defense sword in hand sinking the sword into the belly of the opposing party as far as it will go." The same holy man once ordered the burning of the nose and lips of a Parisian bourgeois who had been found guilty of blasphemy. Saint Louis hated the Jews, coveted their wealth, and distinguished himself by creating the climate — if not the precedent — which led to the burning of Templar Knights under Philip IV. The general level of peace, prosperity, joy — and the beautiful lack of "hard feelings" — which prevailed in XIIIth Century France can easily be inferred form the chronic rash of savagely suppressed "jacqueries." It may indeed be inferred with a minimum of historical knowledge. We need only turn to those contemporary utopias with which we are familiar to vividly imagine the Great Society of XIIIth Century peasants. Let the reader believe — if he can — that the "medieval verve" of the "contes à faire rire" and its Rabelaisian reflection convey no feeling of socio-political outrage.

The phobic fear of uncomfortable parallels which may be drawn between societies of the past and our own Western system seems to inspire a large number of critics and commentators. Such is the probable reason why Voltaire has been and continues to be the target of many sneers. The subversive nature of many Voltairian ideas is often blamed on

*Malet Isaac, *Le Moyen Age jusqu'à la Guerre de Cent Ans*, p. 295.

Voltaire — not on the corruption and abuse which cried out for subversion in his day. It is hinted — if not actually said — that Voltaire suffered from some congenital compulsion to attack all forms of authority. The obscene iniquity of powers involved cannot be completely ignored. But it can be and often is whitewashed in a thousand little ways. It is observed that one should be philosophical and accept evil gracefully — in "objective" spirit so to speak. Scornful reference is made to such writings as "those pamphlets which, in the name of philosophical and religious tolerance, were undermining the monarchy of Louis XIV."* Voltaire emerges from such commentaries as *the* troublemaker to whom limited attention should be paid. No innuendo or assertion is too base or too false as long as it serves "the good cause" of tarnishing his character. Insinuations are made about his mental balance. *Lagarde et Michard* designate Voltaire as "the scatter-brained young man" — "le jeune écervelé." Much is made of the alleged "snobbery" which caused him to feel equal to the aristocracy. MM. Lanson and Truffau have the following comment on the success of Voltaire the court poet and on the infamous beating which he suffered at the hands of the lackeys of the Chevalier de Rohan: "His head swells a little; he allows himself to think that he is in his natural place in the aristocratic world where he is tolerated because of his wit; he becomes familiar, impertinent."** The subsequent thrashing seems to have the approval of the writers who feel that Voltaire was guilty of "presumption" — "outrecuidance." Nothing is said of the initial arrogance of the Chevalier de Rohan toward "that bourgeois who does not even have a name." Or of the magnificent retort which brought about the beating: "My name, I am starting it, and you are finishing yours!"

Those of us who are not dazzled blind by the smug, authoritative tone of Desgranges et al., will be eternally grateful to Voltaire, and to other courageous writers who "undermined" the Ancien Régime. We do not "identify" with the Chevalier de Rohan or with his aristocratic peers. MM. Lanson and Truffau are strange cheerleaders of the nobility with their plebeian names. It is doubtful that we, or the gentlemen in question, should have come within miles of court — except perhaps as lackeys — had we lived in the XVIIIth Century. We do not choose to forget this. We do not regard Voltaire — at any stage of his life or on any plane of his writings — as an "écervelé." We would welcome with delight a few "écervelés" of his kind were they to bless our falsely enlightened era with their presence. We note with amusement that the Chevalier the

---

*CH. M. Des Granges, *Histoire Illustrée de la Littérature Française*, p. 583.
**G. Lanson et P.Truffau, *Histoire de la Littérature Française*, p. 391.

Rohan was unwittingly correct in placing the label of "namelessness" on Voltaire. Also that MM. Lanson and Truffau were partially right in questioning the propriety of Voltaire's appearance at court. Neither the Chevalier nor the latter persons seem to have known what they had in front of them in person or in writing. But we do know and draw one conclusion. Had Voltaire been "only" what he appeared to be, he would have been infinitely too good to rub elbows with such a gold-plated ruffian as the Chevalier de Rohan.

The root of scurrilous attacks directed at Voltaire and at other courageous writers is the fear of displeasing insecure and irascible political authority. The literary commentator — who is himself in a position of relative authority — all too often tends to steer his course by the wishes of the fountainhead of Power. The pollution of Power is seldom brought up frontally. It is easy enough to seem "liberal" and "progressive" by floating between two levels of editorial waters not too far from the surface. One may even seem brilliant at small cost in that way. One may note — and piously deplore — the evils of another age as long as the pretense is maintained that they have no prolongation in our own. It is professionally healthy to pay lip service to "the finest castle in the world" which has nothing in common with barbaric, dim-witted Dark Ages. It is professionally sound to avoid theological matters as well. The exoteric surface of such politically inspired writings as those of Voltaire calls for more objectivity than it usually gets. We must therefore be prepared to challenge the accepted opinions of "Men of letters and various *authorities* who hide their belief in deference to popular prejudice." More than anything else in the study of esoteric literature we may need professional and political courage. Simone de Beauvoir was admirably perceptive when she wrote the following words:

> " — to make discoveries the essential is not to perceive here and there gleams of light which others do not suspect, but to rush toward them, not giving a damn about anything else." (*La Force de l'Age*, Ch. I, p. 149, Livre de Poche Edition)

If Truth-seeking be subversive, let us subvert.

We must face the fact that the last thing to be wanted by many persons is Truth. What applied to the era of Diogenes continues to apply in our own. The modern carrier of light — however modest that light may be — has a hard time finding MEN:

> " 'Men? There are, I believe, six or seven.' " (*The Little Prince*, Ch. XVIII).

584

" 'I am looking for men,' said the little prince. —
— 'Men,' said the fox, 'they have rifles and they hunt. That is quite a
nuisance! They also raise chickens. That is their only interest. Are you
looking for chickens?' " (*The Little Prince*, Ch. XXI).

" — we cannot help admiring once more the profound knowledge of
human nature which dictated to Mr. Sergeant Cox the following words,
delivered in the same address as before alluded to: 'There is no more
fatal fallacy than that truth will prevail by its own force, that it has only
to be seen to be embraced. In fact the desire for truth exists in very
few minds, and the capacity to discern it in fewer still. When men say
that they are seeking the truth, they mean that they are looking for
evidence to support some prejudice or prepossession. Their beliefs are
moulded to their wishes. They see all, and more than all, that seems
to tell for that which they desire; they are blind as bats to whatever
tells against them. The scientists are no more exempt from this common
failing than are others." (*Isis Unveiled*, p. 615, Vol. 1).

It is easy to predict what the reaction of many to esoteric literature
will be if the exoteric surface of writings is itself too close for comfort. There are many reasons why the formidable powder-keg of Western literature has been kept under wraps. Those reasons will not cease
to exist overnight.

Persons convinced of their inherent godliness are not easily manipulated commercially, religiously, politically, or otherwise. A huge segment of Western economies rests on exploitation of popular belief that
"you live only once." Such a belief is threatened. Allmighty commer-
cialism stands to lose a great deal if materialistic values are rejected
by many persons. Unprovoked and undeclared wars may prove difficult — if not impossible — to foist on a nation if the concept of Karma
— collective and personal — takes hold in many minds. Artificially maintained wealth feeding on artificially maintained poverty will suffer if
the philosophy of the Secret Doctrine ever spreads. Churches are unlikely
to thrive on the esoteric reading of *Revelations* or on the veiled content
of other "scriptures." Babylon, the "harlot" of power-mad, money-mad
sectarianism, may well have had its day. Babylon is unlikely to "fall"
with good grace.

The academic world itself is not without its own jealous Vaticans
ever ready to ostracize at the drop of a style-sheet. The case of the
astronomer of *The Little Prince* is not based on fiction. Many scholars
care more about the garb of discovery than about discovery itself.
Fanatical objectivists are strangely fond of externals. It is deemed
unfortunate when new findings look Pagan, occult, ancient, and non-
Western. Discoverers are subject to many unwritten laws. They must
not "drink" of anything resembling "spirit." They must not "see double"

or use "second sight." They must belong to the right professional guilds which hold royal monopolies on knowledge and discovery. The fact that a discoverer may be a woman is the ultimate outrage to right-thinking Judaeo-Christian hearts. The unfailing battle-cry of male chauvinism continues to be: "When did a woman discover anything big?" It is insufferable to have it kicked out the window.

The possession of advanced degrees is no guarantee of immunity from vicious professional attack. Ignaz Philip Semmelweiss, *M.D.*, was persecuted by his superior Johann Klein and by the majority of his medical colleagues for having discovered the cause of puerperal fever. The fever turned XIXth Century maternity hospitals into torture chambers and charnel houses where mothers and infants died from septicemia. The mortality rate went as high as 100% at Iena, Prussia. Ignaz Philip Semmelweiss, the man who put a stop to wholesale killings, the man who offered to give away his discovery so that the slaughter might cease, was branded by his colleagues as "the fool of Budapest."

Should we be tempted to believe that such practices no longer have currency in our age, we would do well to consider the case of Immanuel Velikovsky. The author of *Worlds in Collision and Earth in Upheaval* wears impressive scientific "clothes." Immanuel Velikovsky studied natural sciences at the University of Edinburgh, history, law and medicine (M.D.) in Moscow, biology in Berlin, the workings of the brain in Zurich, and psychoanalysis in Vienna."* Such a background did not protect him against the base maneuvers of certain "academic councils." The following story of suppression is told by the author himself:

> "In that issue (of the *American Behavioral Scientist*), sponsored by a group of eminent men in scholarship and public affairs, is also told the story of reception — or rejection — of this book, coupled with efforts toward its suppression; it was actually successfully suppressed while in the hands of its first publisher, who had to give it up, though a No. 1 national bestseller, under the exerted boycott of all this publisher's textbooks by certain groups organized for that purpose in some of the academic councils of the country." (*Words in Collision*, Preface to paperback edition, p. 9).

This story of suppression did not happen in a comfortably distant age. It happened in the year of grace 1950. There are, unfortunately, many Johann Kleins in the scholarly world, Quislings to the cause of Knowledge and Progress which they claim to represent. The well-named Klein specimen is familiar quarante to esoteric writers. "He would have, if he

---

*Foreword, *Worlds in Collision*, I. Velikovsky, Dell Pub. Co., 1967.

586

could have, annihilated the circulation of the blood, because another man had discovered it"* says Voltaire. The emergence of esoteric literature is as unlikely to please such a person as the discovery of the cause of puerperal fever and the tilting of the axis of Earth.

No good purpose would be served by pretending to believe that teaching institutions are always truth-seeking bodies or free agents. The mere fact that academic freedom remains controversial is sadly eloquent. Western systems tolerate but do not like "eggheads." The popular concept of education is that of a cannery dedicated to the production of money-making, money-yielding vegetables. The educated finished product must not rock the Judaeo-Christian Ark. No profession is as unprotected or prostituted as that of the teacher. Not only does the dullest, most ignorant layman think of himself as an education expert. He is given the power to control a process of which he has not the slightest conception. He is encouraged to hate the intellectual — for the wrong reasons — : not because intellectual commitment to Knowledge is lukewarm but because it is too ardent for his taste. The intellectual is a choice outlet for various frustrations. One needs only read the daily newspapers to see him reviled at every turn and made into a convenient scapegoat. It is easier — and it seems safer — to blame the intellectual than the evil which he rightfully condemns. It is easier — and more gratifying — to hate the intellectual than it is to become one. Many persons fall for the propaganda which cleverly shunts resentment from its logical circuit and which is reminiscent of years of infamy. To those who remember the Thirties in Nazi Germany, there is a somberly familiar ring to certain sneers and diatribes. We cannot expect modern inquisitors or their followers to welcome a development which jolts the narrow conception of the world in which they have a material and psychological stake.

When they are not doomed to slow death by financial destitution, schools, colleges, and universities are kept in a state of monetary prostitution to local governmental bodies, special interests, and nervous, misinformed communities. Whether or not such institutions of learning desire to propagate truth has little positive bearing on pressures placed upon them. While the nationalization of education tends to lessen the crushing force of provincial bigotry, the example of France shows it to be no guarantee of total liberation. There remain desires and ways to keep the powder-keg of Knowledge under wraps. Stendhal, Balzac, Proust, Gabriel Chevallier, and Marcel Aymé — to name but a few

---

*L'Homme aux quarante écus — Mariage de l'Homme aux quarante écus —.

587

writers — stress an interesting fact which is symptomatic of a general climate affecting public education. Whether our own XXth Century or other periods be involved, one does not enter the Académie Française without tacit approval of the still powerful clergy. The Church continues to influence literary acclaim and the related diffusion of knowledge. The fact amounts to tacit recognition of the latent power of literature. The scholar most likely to succeed in "Westphalia" is masterfully described by Sartre. The human well of science is symbolically "dead." His memory and his example are glorified by a statue which enhances — among other things — the importance of the "right clothes." The sacred enclosure where the great man is enshrined is effectively barred to "cars" — karmic wheels — by heavy "chains" of man-made slavery. The papers from which the academic bronze god has drawn his substance are symbolically "crushed" in his "heavy hand." The main function of Impétraz — in life and in death — is that of a Defender of the Faith exalting and guarding the supreme Principle of Authority: the Jehovic father figure which he ably represents:

> "Those ladies in black, who come to walk their dogs, glide under the arcades, along the walls. They seldom venture into the full light, but they cast sidelong girlish glances, furtive and satisfied, upon the statue of Gustave Impétraz. They probably do not know the name of that bronze giant, but they do see, from his frock-coat and from his top hat, that he was a member of fine society. He holds his hat in the left hand and places the right hand on a stack of papers: it is a little as if their grandfather were there, on that pedestal, cast in bronze. They do not need to look at him very long to understand that he thought as they do, exactly as they do, on all subjects. He has placed his authority and his immense erudition drawn from the papers which his heavy hand crushes at the service of their small, narrow, and solid ideas. The ladies in black feel relieved, they can go quietly about their household tasks, walk their dog: the holy ideas, the fine ideas which they hold from their fathers, they no longer have the responsibility of defending them; a man of bronze has made himself their guardian." (*La Nausée*).

The academic prostitute and vigilante described by Sartre is contrasted to the Autodidacte. The Self-Taught Man pursues knowledge in accordance with a strange alphabetical method. His spare time is spent in the library where he reads every publication available to him. Many years will be required before the project is completed from A to Z. The Self-Taught Man remains under the influence of intellectual clichés which blind the average Westerner and which arouse violent reactions in Roquentin. But his dedication of Knowledge has the respect of the narrator. Unimpressive, pathetic as he seems, the *Self-Taught Man* has a far better chance of discovering the Alpha and Omega of many things than do the students of officially approved Impétraz. It is not by chance that he is an "invert." It is not by chance that he is lynched in the end.

The learned scholar who might be the "Interpreter" of a grand message usually chooses the path of least resistance to power. He becomes the "*Impétraz*" or agent of the house allegedly built by Peter. His chosen course has the merit of practicality. Few persons have the vocation of martyrdom. Few persons can resist the temptation of comfortable prestige which rewards academic docility. The result is an old story:

> "Of late there has been a touching accord between philologists holding high official positions, and missionaries from heathen lands. Prudence before truth when the latter endangers our sinecures! Besides, how easy to compromise with conscience. A state religion is a prop of government; all State religions are 'exploded humbugs,' therefore, since one is as good, or rather as bad, as another, *the* State religion may as well be supported. Such is the diplomacy of official Science." (*Isis Unveiled*, p. 529, Vol. II).

The same political cowardice is clearly visible in numerous teaching institutions of the United States. Many are the private schools and colleges allegedly independent from any Church yet officially connected with some sectarian denomination of other. Such "private" schools have recently become insatiable eaters of federal funds granted by a government which claims to guard the separation of Church and State. The same government is officially committed not to ever subsidize any form of bigotry. One might expect such federally aided schools to observe certain standards of academic performance and academic freedom. One might expect the government to see that its grants are properly used. Alas! The small "private" college is all too often subjected to the sacrosanct dictatorship of a few Babbitts and priests. Any attempt to question the fundamental conflict of interests afflicting such establishment is treated as sacrilegious.

The prototype of the federally aided small "private" school is well described by Sinclair Lewis. One of its chief distinctions is a strong pi*a*no department. Another is a shorthand program undoubtedly dealing in abbreviated "scriptures." The ultimate pride of the institution is an athletic team. (The glorious era of the wrestler and of the football coach is in full swing.) The establishment is described within its "progressive" background: the city of Nautilus complete with manure-spreaders, corn-products, and College:

> "Nautilus manufactures steel windmills, agricultural implements, including the celebrated Daisy Manure Spreader, and such corn-products as Maize Mealies, the renowned breakfast-food. It makes brick, it sells

589

groceries wholesale, and it is the headquarters of the Cornbelt Co-operative Insurance Company.

One of its smallest but oldest industries is Mugford Christian College, which has two hundred and seventeen students, and sixteen instructors, of whom eleven are ministers of the Church of Christ. The well-known Dr. Tom Bissex is football coach, health director, and professor of hygiene, chemistry, physics, French, and German. Its shorthand and piano departments are known afar beyond the limits of Nautilus, and once, though that was some years ago, Mugford held the Grinnell College baseball team down to a score of eleven to five. It has never been disgraced by squabbles over teaching evolutionary biology — it never has thought of teaching biology at all." (Sinclair Lewis, *Arrowsmith,* Chapter 19).

The freedom enjoyed by State institutions of higher learning is just as relative. No one and nothing can elude the long arm of certain Powers. Sinclair Lewis is perceptive where the identity of those Powers is concerned.

The typical State University is molded into an image satisfactory to banking, industry, and Churches:

"The Regents were the supreme rulers of the University; they were bankers and manufacturers and pastors of large churches to them even the president was humble. Nothing gave them more interesting thrills than the dissecting-room of the medical school. The preachers spoke morally of the effect of alcohol on paupers, and the bankers of the disrespect for savings — accounts which is always to be seen in the kind of men who insist on becoming cadavers." (*Arrowsmith,* Chapter 3).

The trinitarian concentration of power represented by money, industry, and Churches which is noted by Lewis has increased at an appalling rate since the twenties. The growth of supergiant conglomerates overshadowing the entire planet virtually makes convertible terms of money, industry, and related dogma. The Jehovic syndrome is not limited to material greed. It is a reckless craving for power which cannot abide to see anyone or anything remain free. The sacred prerogative of privacy is all but gone. Obscurity itself is a shelter no more. Intellectual and spiritual privacy somehow survive here and there in varying degrees. But they are increasingly threatened by the Allmighty Gods controlling the media, the schools, the publication and the diffusion of knowledge. Publishing houses tend to be more and more frequently swallowed by giant, diversified corporations. We may wonder what avenues of free expression will soon remain or even remain now.

We are told — and should be able to see — that the political powers ruling our lives do not favor the use of "alcohol" — by the masses. The implied commentary of Sinclair Lewis is one echo of the collective message transmitted by many great minds, a message masterfully understated by Saint Exupéry. The Judaeo-Christian system is a "businessman." The Judaeo-Christian "businessman" is "not useful to the stars."

It is hoped that the dedicated element of the intellectual community will rise to a difficult occasion. It is hoped that students of the near future will not be forced to go behind the barn or the garage to discover esoteric embodiments of literary, human, or cosmic facts of life. Any institution of learning which says in essence: "You shall know the Truth — if you must — and keep your mouth shut" raises serious questions about its raison d'être. Any society which condones the suppression of knowledge at a time when knowledge is more necessary than ever buries its own freedom and gambles with its own existence.

The study of *foreign* esoteric Literature will not depend exclusively on our abilities or attitudes. The quality of translations used is obviously important. The virtuosity of esoteric writers playing on every conceivable nuance of etymological and other meaning can seldom be fully rendered by the most conscientious translator. We must bear in mind the considerable loss which is inevitably suffered in the process of translation. We must also be aware of less innocent failures.

The Harbrace paperbound edition of *The Little Prince* contains several inaccuracies. The expression "little fellow" which is almost a refrain in the original text becomes "small person" in Chapter II and "little prince" in Ch. XXVI. Such a departure from literal meaning has little importance. But other deviations result in positive distortion. The sentence: "Tu auras, toi, des étoiles qui savent rire!" becomes in translation: "You — only you — will have stars that can laugh!" The stressed pronoun "toi" or reinforced "you" has no equivalent in English and is difficult to render. The presence of *only* in the translation is therefore understandable. But the restrictive essence of the adverb is added. It is sufficient to obscure and distort the allegorical, collective value of the pilot who represents in part modern Western mankind, its materialism and its pride in machines. The recovery of lost — or impounded — cosmic knowledge seems limited to one man while the said knowledge becomes accessible to the totality of mankind in the original text. The june-bug mentioned by the "businessman" of Chapter XIII becomes a "giddy goose" in translation. The june-bug may have been intended to suggest the Egyptian scarabeus which is a symbol of "immortality" and "reincarnations of the liberated soul."* Its connection with the number 22 — a disturbance having been caused by the insect 22 years earlier — may constitute an

The Secret Doctrine, p. 552, Vol. II).

591

esoteric reference to the significant number 220. The symbolic creature indirectly linked to Voltaire is understandably "disturbing" to the Judaeo-Christian "businessman." The change into a "silly goose" is regrettable. The baobabs of Chapter V — probable "trees of knowledge" — are said to be "as big as churches" in the original text. The reader is at liberty to think that they are even bigger than churches. The comparison is eloquent. The same baobabs become "as big as castles" in translation. An important esoteric theme is lost in the process. One wonders why. The Little Prince claims that he once saw 43 sunsets in one day. The number 43 — which transparently suggests 4,320,000,000 years or a Year of Brahma — becomes 44 in translation. The idea of having witnessed an entire cycle of existence is destroyed. The change of 43 into 44 is difficult to excuse.

English-speaking students of Sartrian texts are likely to read the translation of *La Nausée* which is the work of Lloyd Alexander.* Interesting discrepancies exist in the translated version. The nightmarish vision of Roquentin which is described in the final pages of the book may be read in different ways. It may be viewed as the hallucination of an exhausted or unstable mind craving change, any kind of change, for the sole sake of change. It may be read as the vision of future mankind driven insane by a crushing sense of despair and futility. It may be regarded as the expression of fear of a scientific disaster which will produce monstrosities. It may finally be seen as the symbolic vision of the intellectual and spiritual apocalypse which esoteric writers seem to predict for the end of our century.

The change has tragic impact on many unprepared persons. The discovery of the existence of a sixth sense and the discovery of the dimension which the sixth sense reveals causes "hundred of suicides." But the reality of the new development belies appearance. Intellectual and spiritual values are involved. The chunk of dust-gathering, bleeding meat which is seen rolling and tumbling on a street suggests an accurate view of the flesh — "from dust to dust." A horrified mother suddenly discovers "a third eye, a laughing eye" — "un troisième oeil, un oeil rieur apparaîtra" — on the cheek of her child. The shocking return of the third eye is a sign of restored and increasing spirituality. Clothing unexpectedly becomes alive, an indication that nothing is dead in Nature. The human tongue — or language — suddenly develops countless ramifications which cause it to resemble a centipede and to terrify its owner. The staggering dimension of the Word becomes manifest. A man suddenly wakes up one morning in a forest of male organs which are being slowly destroyed by

---

New Directions publications, 1964.

birds. The phallic symbol of materiality yields to "winged" or spiritual beings.

The report of the discovery of the new sense is followed by a remark: Rien que cela; mais pour peu que cela dure quelque temps, il y aura des suicides par centaines." — "Nothing more than that; but assuming that it lasts for some time, this change will cause suicides by the hundreds." The passage is translated as follows by Lloyd Alexander: "Nothing more than that; but for the little time it lasts, there will be hundred of suicides." The French expression "pour peu que" is not easy to translate into English. But the difficulty does not justify the change from a development which *may* last a while into a development which *does* or *will* last a little while. The change which is esoterically suggested will not last *a little time*. It will be the beginning of an evolutionary trend destined to follow its course over a period of centuries. The apparent inability of the translator to do justice to "pour peu que" results in an important alteration of meaning. The possibility of a lasting change is lost in the process.

The word "third" is left out of the expression "third eye." It is easy to grasp the damaging effect of the omission. Many persons who know little about occult science have heard of the third eye which is often mentioned in the lyrics of contemporary songs. Such persons might conduct fruitful research based on the presence of the "third eye" were the phrase not mutilated. The oversight of the translator takes care of that.

Most amazing of all, the forest of male organs becomes a forest of "birch trees" under magic wand of Mr. Alexander. Important symbols are destroyed in the process.

Other types of mishandling are obstacles to the esoteric study of texts. Certain translations of Baudelaire and Saint Exupéry shift individual words and expressions from place to place. The extent of the shift may be such that chapter numbers no longer coincide in the original and in the translation. Such is the case of *Pilote de Guerre* the very title of which is altered. A few things are removed here and there. A few apocryphal remarks are inserted. One is appalled by the cavalier handling of texts which are treated as so much stuffed sausage. The order of presentation of certain writings may also be damaging to esoteric awareness. A paperback translation of Voltaire presents *Candide* first, *Zadig* second, and *L'Ingénu* last. Such a disregard of exoteric chronology itself tends to break the spine of the crucial sequence represented by the fate of Truth in various eras of human evolution.

We have enough mangled, distorted scriptures of ancient origin without adding to them the works of the moderns. Exoteric readers are entitled to accurate translations. Esoteric researchers can have no use for "arrangements" which turn the fruit of Knowledge into sterile marmalade.

The esoteric explorer should work from original texts written in a language which he knows thoroughly. He should be familiar with the origin, the history, and the many nuances of words. He should sense — for instance — beyond the modern meaning of the adjective "navrant" — "pitiful" — the ancient significance of "wounding." He would then *read* the comment of Barbey d'Aurevilly on the *heartbreaking* beauty which is Vigny: "— rien de si beau et de si navrant que ce livre — depuis Pascal!"

A probable result of the emergence of esoteric literature will be a healthy regard for the Humanities in general and language study in particular. The intrinsic value of language — which could hardly be questioned in an era of genuine enlightenment — will impose itself. It will no longer be a matter of what anyone puts into space. It will be a simple matter of pure, inspired common sense. It will be an awareness that "language is a perpetual Orphic song," the immortal vehicle of universal vibrations emanated form the Word Itself. "There is nothing dead in Nature" says the Secret Doctrine. We may even find through close acquaintance with our own tongue that there is no "dead" language.

There has been an amazing tendency of late to regard the Humanities as "irrelevant" and to treat them as "parents pauvres" of the academic community. Literature, History, and Philosophy have been viewed as lovely frills which have little bearing on the needs of "the real world." Budgetary cuts and budgetary death-warrants have followed. Unless it be admitted that modern societies are not made of men, one may ask how the Humanities or Sciences of Man coul ever be "irrelevant" to modern societies. The popular idea of "relevance" seems to focus on material objects and products. The Humanist does not usually have at his professional fingertips any reassuring paraphernalia of consumer-goods, testtubes, or machines — in short any convincing proof of productivity. — He therefore tends to be regarded as a useless, unrealistic loafer. His head is believed to drift in a hazy and suspect "ivory tower." His feet are said to lack the ultimate virtue of being "on the ground." The gist of the label of "metaphysician, very ignorant of things of this world" is stubbornly glued to the Humanist in the popular mind.

One might stress that the relative degree of well-being and freedom now enjoyed by many Westerners is due in large part to humanistic "dreamers" such as Voltaire, Zola, and Upton Sinclair who sat in their "ivory tower" to write certain books. One might argue that many such Humanists were singularly successful in the "real world" as social militants, political reformers, and businessmen. One might submit that esoteric metaphysicians such as Voltaire are unsurpassed in the art of keeping intellectual "feet on the ground." They are in fact the only ones who know where the ground is. One might note that every conceivable convenience, gadget, and machine allegedly representing "the real world" had its terrestrial origin in the much-descried "ivory tower" of a human skull. One might state that the ethical and productive "ivory tower" needs be relevant to nothing but itself. One might suggest that society make *itself* "relevant" to the knowledge which it does have.

Were the Humanities *only* what most of us have believed them to be, we would need them now more than ever as an antidote to our perilous, junk-ridden state. But they are much more. There is reason to believe that Literature is a gold-mine of concealed scientific knowledge. Norman Mailer speculates that it may have "more to offer on the nature of the universe than the cyclotron."* His statement is echoed by an interesting number of great contemporaries — scientific and other — . Who can tell what lies beyond the "obscure rattle" of Rabelaisian words? Who can probe the full extent of Voltairian esotericism particularly where astronomy is concerned? Hindu scriptures are known to contain closely guarded secrets which may be extracted through the study of metrics and numerology. It is possible — if not likely — that many Western texts with which we are familiar veil scientific lore of considerable importance which is accessible through similar techniques. The subtleties of language, the "vagaries" of mythology, the "frills" of literature, and the "daydreams" of metaphysics are about to receive respectful attention from scientific quarters.

We are culturally encouraged to believe that there is little left to be discovered about ourselves and our world. Such a view reflects the lingering psychology wedded to belief in a geocentric universe. It is also consistent with the Darwinian concept of linear evolution from the ape which makes of the present human specie the crowning glory of the universe. We are actually barely beginning to scratch the surface of what there is to learn. The emergence of esoteric material and the likely surge of interest in the Secret Doctrine will give novel, powerful impetus to all areas of study. New depths will be sought in ever deeper specialization. But specialization will be more and more geared to a gigantic synthesis. Literary scholars will seek astronomical, mathematical, anthropological, and other knowledge as they seldom sought it before. Scientists may well turn to Literature in order to extract and to evaluate the scientific meaning of texts. No area of learning will be viewed as a closed vase. The sky is no limit where the scope of future achievement is concerned.

Religious repercussions will be deep. Many Christians will dislike the fact of their left-handed Pagan genealogy. They have been taught —

Cannibals and Christians, Dell Publishing Co., Inc., p. 67.

and continue to be taught — that Paganism is ignorance, superstition, and the Devil itself. Some will be hurt by the devastating exposure of the genesis of their creed. There is no faithful, tactful way of interpreting the esoteric message of Voltaire — or of other esoteric writers. Their verdict is a unanimous broadside of contempt aimed at the same perversion of Truth. Their denunciation of falsehood and unnecessary, related misery grows out of pure love of Truth and Mankind. The genesis of holiness and of causticity is easy to trace in their thought. Sheer, legitimate disgust is a great maker of saints. Were it possible to be tactful in the face of certain evils, tact should bear another name. One can only hope that the following passage of *Isis Unveiled* — which applies to the message of all greeat "smugglers" — will be pondered in the right spirit:

> "Were it possible, we would keep this work out of the hands of many Christians whom its perusal would not benefit, and for whom it was not written. We allude to those whose faith in their respective churches is pure and sincere, and those whose sinless lives reflect the glorious example of that Prophet of Nazareth, by whose mouth the spirit of truth spake to humanity. Such there have been at all times. History preserves the names of many as heroes, philosophers, philanthropists, martyrs, and holy men and women; but how many more have lived and died, unknown but to their intimate acquaintances, unblessed but by their humble beneficiaries! These have ennobled Christianity, but would have shed the same lustre upon any other faith they might have professed — for they were higher than their creed."

> "An analysis of religious beliefs in general, this volume is in particular directed against theological Christianity, the chief opponent of free thought. It contains not one word against the pure teachings of Jesus but unsparingly denounces their debasement into pernicious ecclesiastical systems that are ruinous to man's faith in his immortality and his God, and subversive of all moral restraint." (Preface to Part II, *Isis Unveiled*, pp. iii-iv, Vol. 2).

It may safely be predicted that some persons will regard esoteric and related studies as a "threat to Western civilization." One might ask such vigilantes to define what they mean by the latter phrase — some special interests and other Vaticans perhaps —. One might refer them to the distinction which is carefully made by Saint Exupéry between "the bric-à-brac of another age" — termed a "*saloperie*"* — "dastardly filth" — and "the true civilization which we betray through our ignorance."**

Many Western fetishes will suffer. The bulk of XXth Century "West-

Flight to Arras, Ch. X.
**Ibid.*, Ch. XXVII.

phalia" will resent the fact that it is not "the finest castle in the world." Modern sensitivities and racist egos will be hurt. We have been led to regard other civilizations as infantile and barbaric when we regard them as civilizations at all. We have been encouraged to think of ourselves as the quintessence of evolution. We may as well face it. It is not so. We should take comfort from the knowledge that there are higher planes of achievement and happiness awaiting us than the status of scared, greedy, power-crazed "insects devouring one another on a small globe of mud."

Esoteric research will probably lead to contact with "the indiscernible community." Higher levels of esotericism are accessible to initiates only. The day— if it ever comes in our age — when "scholars" and "good company" communicate on an open basis may prove more significant to the progress of mankind than all possible landings of rocketry in outer space.

Voltaire predicts the general behavior of "scholars" in the episode featuring the "resurrection" of Ancient Knowledge — Pangloss — . The man of science is expected to weather the shock gracefully. Proust describes in some detail the first impact of the same event on the world of letters.

Rachel, the former mistress of "Saint Loup," recites "well-known poetry" — possibly that of Vigny — in a strange, new manner. The unorthodox or esoteric rendition is punctuated by pauses symbolizing emphasis on "silence." The audience is taken by surprise. Embarrassment prevails. The majority of squirming listeners decide to wait and see. The situation is compared to a formal dinner in which the guests are confronted by unfamiliar silverware. Startled glances dart back and forth in search of a clue to the fitting response. Well-timed approval is expressed by the allmighty duchess of Guermantes. The performance turns into a triumph. Bloch — the opportunistic Western scholar — becomes effusive.

The first acclaim reflects conformity rather than conviction. But "conversions" do take place. The evolution of "Bloch" is particularly interesting. The reaction of the young scholar to the literary work of "Marcel" has been a vague, prudent noise-making suggestive of similar involvement — just in case. But his overall attitude prior to the triumph of Rachel may be summarized in three words: sneer, scuttle, and "pump." Sneering and scuttling are manifestations of envy. "Pumping" is a professional investment. There might — after all — be something worth stealing in the unorthodox venture. The "copiateur"* is at work. The

---

*A la Recherche du temps perdu, p. 1034, Vol. III.

sensational success of esoteric interpretation is the signal of spectacular commitment. Finding that the moment has come, the young scholar decides to ride the crest of the new wave. Any stranger would swear that Bloch was "in the know" all along and that he was sole engineer of the entire development.

Simone de Beauvior anticipates a need for stout hearts. Proust anticipates a need for strong stomachs.

The final note is optimistic. "Legrandin" — who previously despised "Bloch" — relents toward the young man. The Judaeo-Christian scholar has acquired some insight and refined his ethics. He may soon join "good company." The forgiveness of the Sage reflects his expectation of changing times. The scholarly world has never lacked a number of pure souls capable of instant, selfless response to the Good and the Beautiful. Some of its members have long sensed the presence of a hidden message in Literature. The learned community warms up to the splendid work to be done and begins to love it as it should be loved: for its own sake.

Literary sectarianism fades. Superficial attributes are transcended. Among them is the deceptive multiplicity of "movements" and "schools." The profound unity of great works is perceived beyond the Mayavic veil of countless "isms."

> "I felt that I would not have to bother with the various literary theories which had troubled me at one time." (*A la Recherche du temps perdu*, p. 881, Vol. III).

The specific production of "Marcel" is but one stone in an impressive edifice built by a timeless brotherhood of great souls:

> "The reality to be expressed resided, I now understood it, not in the appearance of the subject, but at a depth where that appearance mattered little." (*A la Recherche du temps perdu*, p. 882, Vol. III).

The veiled unity of Literature is a reflection of the Great All and an echo of the harmony of the spheres. The Proustian vision of "the United States of the entire earth"* is the Diamond-Hearted radiance beamed through Logos, Time, and Space by a galaxy of divine intelligences bent on the same "One Great Work": "a single sonata, a single faith."**

What is Literature? It is "a vase containing all things." A gold-mine of secret knowledge. A hot line to ineffable Beyonds. A sublime conspiracy of Truth designed to end an age of darkness.

A la Recherche du temps perdu, p. 321, Vol. III.
**Ibid.*, pp. 1034-35, Vol. III.

HISTORY

History is bound to benefit by the unveiling of esoteric texts.

Occult science is as old as Man. Ancient History can hardly be studied without awareness of Pagan belief in the invisible world. Ancient Egypt, Greece, and Chaldea are inseparable from their mythologies and mysteries. India is a notorious source of secret lore. The Christian era has its share of occult tradition and related events. Some of the early popes were initiates. Many prominent figures are known to have practiced magic. Robert d'Artois tried to cast a spell on the King of France in 1333. The persecution of the Albigeois and of the Templar Knights can easily be traced in part to their esoteric backgrounds. Catherine de Medicis was the instigator of sinister rites which are described in *Isis Unveiled*. Mme. de Montespan was implicated in the famous affair of the Poisons. Her acolyte, La Voisin, was no mere pharmacist. The name of Rasputin is known to almost everyone. The judicial archives of Europe — those of the modern era included — feature many cases from which reference to sorcery could not be omitted in spite of the obvious distaste and skepticism of recording authorities. Hitler is known to have had mediumnic trances. The Nazi mystique was inspired by a strange occult doctrine. We should not be surprised at the consistent bearing of secret sciences on History. It is logical for men interested in the acquisition and maintenance of power to seek all available weapons likely to promote their aims. The offensive and defensive potency of spiritual "arms" is involved in a large number of historical episodes many of which are partially or totally unknown.

There is reason to believe that few — if any — truncated or slanted chapters of History went unnoticed or unrectified by esoteric writers. The full meaning of numerous allusions and portrayals may some day prove enlightening. What did Voltaire mean when he wrote in *L'Ingénu* that Richelieu and Mazarin "had their guards"?* Voltaire may have suggested what Vigny confirms in *Cinq Mars* where Richelieu is concerned: that the Cardinal exerted occult influence over the King of France while being himself similarly manipulated by Père Joseph. What did Voltaire mean in his description of the mysterious death of Charles XII when he referred to Siquier as a man of "leadership and execution?" Eso-

---

*Ch. *XIX*.

teric reading of the *History of Charles XII* may some day reveal that Charles was "executed" by Siquier under strange circumstances involving occult experimentation by the Swedish King. What did Proust mean when he caused one of his characters — Mme de Villeparisis — to deplore the "mésalliance" of the House of France with the Medicis? * Probably more than a barb aimed at aristocratic snobbery. Proust seems to have been aware — as are other esoteric writers — of the rare degree of evil reached by the enterprising Italian family. What is the full basis of the unanimous dislike of esoteric writers for Mme de Maintenon? Her involvement with the Jesuits perhaps? Such are but a few of the questions which may soon be answered by the study of esoteric texts.

One historical event is studied in the present chapter in the light of corresponding esoteric texts.

Shelley's tragedy in two acts, *"Oedipus Tyrannus,"* is generally regarded as a commentary on the marital troubles of George IV and Queen Caroline. Bearing in mind the fact that a transparent allusion frequently covers a less transparent one, we may wonder if a different chapter of English History is not the veiled subject of the work of Shelley.

Similarities exist between the trial of Caroline and the trial of Anne Boleyn. The charge of adultery is the same. The use of "rigged" or at least "technically augmented" procedures is frequently noted by historians in the case of Anne. It is also believed by a few persons that the manner in which the trial of Caroline was conducted was less than honest.

The title character of the work of Shelley — "Swellfoot" — fits the medical history of Henry VIII who suffered from a chronic leg ulcer. The fact that "Swellfoot" may be translated as "Oedipus" further tends to connect the trial covered by Shelley with Anne Boleyn and to eliminate Queen Caroline. The second wife of Henry VIII was charged not only with adulterous intercourse — at a time when she was recovering from childbirth and painful complications of childbirth — but also with incest allegedly involving her brother. The Greek tragedy of Oedipus is a story of incest. No charge of incest was ever brought against Queen Caroline.

The following statement is reported to have been made by Anne Boleyn to her judges:

> "Something that Lady Wingfield said to my discredit was mentioned. My lords, Lady Wingfield has been dead and gone to her account these many years; whatever she said is hearsay, and by English law hearsay is not evidence. I mention these things because they are samples of the evidence brought against me, and reasonable men, if there are flaws

---

*A la Recherche du temps perdu, p. 199, Vol. II.

in a sample of cloth, suspect the whole roll and scrutinise it with especial care. . . I am not asking you for mercy, mercy is for the condemned. For justice I do beg, that being the prerogative of the King's most humble subject."

Similar emphasis on "law" and "flaw" is found in the tragedy of Shelley. The identity of terms and substance seems calculated to favor a connection between the apparent trial of Caroline and the esoteric trial of Anne:

"Semichorus I

A law!

Semichorus II

A flaw!"

A statement of Purganax, the master-mind of the trial, seems to further connect the text with Anne Boleyn:

"I have rehearsed the entire scene
With an ox-bladder and some ditchwater
On Lady P------; it cannot fail."

Anne Boleyn received the title of Marchioness of Pembroke and was known as "Lady Pembroke" shortly before her marriage to Henry. The precedent value of the allusion to Anne seems to be an esoetric "nudge" among several others.

The strange name bestowed by Shelley on the accused Queen — "Iona Taurina" — seems equally significant. A certain amount of phonetic resemblance exists between "Iona" and "Anne." The word "Taurina" which suggests Taurus, or a bull probably represents another clue to the martyr whose maiden name was originally spelled *Bullen*.

The nature of charges brought against Caroline — or Anne — is the subject of much speculation.

"A Boar (interrupting —)   What!
Does anyone accuse her of?
Purganax.   Why, no one
Makes *any* positive accusations; — but
There were hints dropped, and so the privy wizards
Conceived that it became them to advise
His Majesty to investigate their truth; —
Nor for his own sake; he could be content
To let his wife play any pranks she pleased,. .
If, by that suffrance, *he* could please the Pigs;
But then he fears the morals of the Swine,
The Sows especially, and what effect
It might produce upon the purity and
Religion of the rising generation

Of Sucking-Pigs, if it could be suspected
That Queen Iona —
First Boar

(A pause)
Well, go on; we long
To hear what she can possibly have done."

The influence of official "wizards" or priests is clearly involved in the trial. The religion of unborn generations is admittedly at stake. The emancipation of the female is most dreaded. The validity of the charge of adultery is virtually exploded. The Queen could and would be allowed to "play any pranks she pleased" were she not guilty of an unnamable crime. The true nature of her offenses must not be suspected by the masses. The latter statement rules out a sexual crime, the charge of adultery having been public knowledge both in the case of Caroline and in the case of Anne. The true reason of the liquidation remains unrevealed:

"*Purganax.* —
A woman guilty of — we all know what."

It is difficult to imagine how the sexual misconduct of either Queen could have had the profound effect described on the morals and religion of Swine — current and to come. Royal debauchery was no great novelty in the XIXth Century. Nor did it originate in the Renaissance. The populace had been used to such sport from time immemorial and was not likely to react in dramatic manner.

The Queen is vindicated in the end. The manipulated trial which aroused the skepticism of the masses themselves turns to the disadvantage of instigators. The Green Bag filled with "ditch-water" —the "mudslinging" directed at the Queen — is snatched by the intended victim from the hands of Purganax "with a loud laugh of triumph." The "liquor" which was to be poured over the Queen's head is emptied over "SWELLFOOT and his whole Court, who are instantly changed into a number of filthy and ugly animals, and rush out of the Temple." The intended quarry becomes the "hunter" or the accuser:

"*Iona Taurina.* Come, let us hunt these ugly badgers down,
These stinking foxes, these devouring otters,
These hares, these wolves, these anything but men —
‾‾‾‾‾‾
Give them no law (are they not beasts of blood?)
But such as they gave you.")

A final barb is directed at fiendish cohorts which "have the Devil behind them:"

> "Tallyho! tallyho!
> Through pond, ditch, and slough,
> Wind them and find them,
>   Like the Devil behind them,
> Tallyho! tallyho!"

Truth will be vindicated with the help of popular tradition personified by "John Bull," the ordinary man. The memory of the tainted trial will not fade from collective consciousness. Intuitive perception will operate to re-establish facts and to draw conclusions. The "English" nationality of the avenger suggests a force of "angelic" or spiritual nature.

> *Minotaur.* I am the Ionian Minotaur, the mightiest,
> Of all Europa's taurine progeny —
> I am the old traditional Man-Bull;
> And from my ancestors having been Ionian,
> I am called Ion, which, by interpretation,
> Is JOHN; in plain Theban, that is to say,
> My name's JOHN BULL; I am a famous hunter,
> And can leap any gate in all Boeotia,
> Even the palings of the royal park,
> Or double ditch about the new enclosures;
> And if your Majesty will design to mount me,
> At least till you have hunted down your game,
> I will not throw you."

The amusing lesson on interpretation suggests among other revelations of truth — likely to affect Iona — the Book of John and corresponding "apocalypse." The Bull which is a symbol of "strength" also represents Aryan Races* — an occult belief which seems to be echoed by the allusion of Shelley to "Europa." The expected vindication is connected with popular tradition, strength or spirituality, the "leaps" of intuition. Western mankind, and with an "apocalypse."

The *Recherche* seems to contain an allusion to the Theban component of *Oedipus Tyrannus.* A certain "Mme de Thèbes" is mentioned by "Saint Loup" with intriguing irony. Her unexplained appearance in the text is linked to the importance of intuitive perception. The latter fact suggests a reference to a non-allegorical personage — an authoress named Mme de Thèbes — whose production surveys such relevant aspects of occult science as the lines and the magical powers of the hand. But other elements of the text seem calculated to bring to mind *La Maison du berger* and the tragedy of Shelley. The force which "can leap any gate in all Boeotia" is strikingly similar to "the leaps of the gazelles" of Vigny. "Marcel," the listener of "Saint Loup," is casually and unaccountably

---

The Secret Doctrine, p. 533, Vol. II.

called a "young pig" in the same discourse. Allusion to the Pigs and Sows representing the masses in *Oedipus Tyrannus* is probable. Saint Loup speaks as follows:

> " 'It is the flair, the divining ability of the Mme de Thèbes variety — you understand me — which tilts the scales for the great general as for the great physician.' " (*A la Recherche du temps perdu*, p. 114, Vol. II).

Evolution is represented by "the van of Change" in the tragedy of Shelley. Evolution and Karma are one and the same. Revenge is scorned. Hope is expressed that the materially and spiritually "famished" multitude will not follow "paths of blood" upon "awakening." The advent of Liberty must mark the break of a vicious circle of hatred.

> LIBERTY.   O Famine!
> I charge thee! when thou wake the multitude,
> Thou lead them not upon the paths of blood.
> The earth did never mean her foison
> For those who crown life's cup with poison
> Of fanatic rage and meaningless revenge —
> — But for those radiant spirits, who are still
> The standard-bearers in the van of Change."

The suggested designation of "Iona Taurina" as a "standard-bearer in the van of Change" seems to rule out the apparent exoteric connection between the wronged Queen and Queen Caroline. The wife of George IV can hardly be regarded in such light. Anne Boleyn — the known protectress of "heretics" and the "innocent" of esoteric writers — fits the label.

Tribute is paid to Anne in the writings of many great men. She is designated as "an angel" in a play of Shakespeare. The same passage of the same play suggests her to have been a treasure comparable to the riches of "all the Indies:"

> 2 *Gent.* Sir, as I have a soul, she is an angel;
> Our king has all the Indies in his arms,
> And more and richer, when he strains that lady:
> I cannot blame his conscience."
> (Shakespeare, *King Henry VIII*, Act, Iv., Scene I).

The overworked "conscience" of Henry which allegedly caused him to discard his first wife and to commit many atrocities was correct in one sense. The "consciousness" — if not "conscience" of the King seems to have vaguely felt the spirituality of Anne.

The Queen seems to be celebrated in other works of Shelley:

> "Death is no foe to Virtue; earth has seen
> Love's brightest roses on the scaffold bloom,

604

Mingling with Freedom's fadeless laurels there,
And presaging the truth of visioned bliss.
Are there not hopes within thee, which this scene
Of linked and gradual being has confirmed?
Whose stingings bade thy heart look further still,
When, to the moonlight walk by Henry led,
Sweetly and sadly thou didst talk of death."
(Percy B. Shelley, *Queen Mab*, VIII, The Fairy).

"GOD prosper, speed, and save,
God raise from England's grave
  Her murdered Queen!
Pave with swift victory
The steps of Liberty,
Whom Britons own to be
  Inmortal Queen."
(Percy B. Shelley, *A New National Anthem*).

The heroine of *Oedipus Tyrannus* is guilty of one crime:

"A loud cry from the PIGS. 'She is innocent! most innocent!' "

Anne Boleyn probably was an esoteric "innocent" — or initiate.

A similar version of the life of Anne seems to be given in a contemporary biographical novel, *The Concubine,* which is the work of Norah Lofts. The elevated, compassionate insight of the author deals alike with all characters — villains included. The vibrant objectivity of the writer is a tangible — if subjective — hallmark of "smugglers" of the Secret Doctrine. Among other signs of esoteric substance are the number 220 and the snake in a circle.

The veiled substance of the novel is as follows. Anne was a convert to the Secret Doctrine who came under the influence of the Wisdom-Religion in early youth, probably during her stay at the court of France. While Marguerite de Navarre is nowhere mentioned, an interesting parallel might be made between the mystical protectress of French "heretics" and the somewhat similar role eventually played in England by Anne. From the time of her return home, the future Queen began to play the part of an ordinary, vain, pleasure-seeking, ambitious girl. The general tenor of the book and the last message sent by Anne to Henry suggest that she died a martyr:

" 'Tell him,' Anne said slowly and distinctly, 'that I commend me to him and thank him for so constantly advancing me: from a private gentlewoman he made me a marchioness, from marchioness a queen; and now, having no further honour to bestow upon me, he gives me the crown of martyrdom.' "

The message is far from contrite. The progression from "private gen-

605

tlewoman" to "martyr" is outlined with a subtle sarcasm which somehow clings to Henry. The deep substance of the words of Anne may be compared to axiom quoted by Voltaire: "Où il n'y a rien, le roi perd ses droits."

Royal inability to impart further honors and further torment is noted with satisfaction. Escape from earthly tyrannies seems to have considerable appeal. The sentence: "I commend me to him" may be a reminder of inevitable Karmic retribution.

Many passages of the novel suggest that the "charm" of Anne had a deeper source than physical or intellectual allurement. The beauty or lack of beauty of the girl is a debated point. According to Norah Lofts, Anne was not pretty. She was "beautiful." The essence of her beauty was mostly non-physical. References are made to her "elusive and bewildering charm,"* to her "curious, far-seeing look" suggesting that "some part of her sight was always directed at some far-spread vista seen by her alone."** The emphasis placed on the compelling beauty of her eyes by more or less perceptive or friendly commentators is an interesting point of agreement:

> "He looked at her and noticed her eyes for the first time. Beautiful, wonderful eyes, looking at him with apparent candour, but behind the candour there was depth of mystery, and secrecy and understanding, and something else, a distant-seeing look, as though she saw more, knew more. . ." (*The Concubine*, p. 123).

> " '(Anne) — in fact has nothing but the English king's great appetite and her eyes, which are black and beautiful and take great effect.' " (Quoted in the Encyclopaedia Britannica, *Anne Boleyn*).

The intelligence of Anne was of a sort potentially dangerous to others as well as herself "which Henry had always, though sometimes unconsciously, resented in her: the ability to strip a thing down to its bones."*** The faculty of raising veils —political and other — which remains perilous to its owner in our own era-could not be welcome in the XVIth Century least of all in a woman.

The "charm" which attracted Henry was eventually used to "justify" the rejection and the condemnation of Anne. " '— the King has said to somebody in great confidence — that he had made his marriage seduced by witchcraft, and for that reason he considered it null;—' "**** The charge of witchcraft which Henry considered using against Anne belongs

---

*Norah Lofts, *The Concubine*, Pocket Books, Inc, New York, N.Y., 1963., p. 105.
**Ibid., p. 106.
***Ibid., p. 363.
****Ibid., p. 281.

606

to official History. What is conveniently called "witchcraft" may have been a knowledge and vision capable of laying bare certain fallacies regarded as essential to the preservation of the status quo. Shelley and Norah Lofts seem to agree on the authentic reason which caused the execution of Anne. Her ability to expose certain lies was too dangerous to the system to be allowed to exist. Least of all to *spread*:

> "It had been but a point of policy
> To keep Iona and the Swine apart."
> (*Oedipus Tyrannus*).

The question of why Anne Boleyn *had* to be executed is seldom asked by historians. It seems to be satisfactorily answered by Henry's obsessive desire for a male heir and by his wish to marry Jane Seymour. The threat posed to the dynasty by the prospect of illegitimate offspring is accepted as a valid reason for the disposal of Anne. But the crucial matter of whether or not she was guilty as charged remains a mystery to this day.

The Queen is reported to have implied that the true cause of her trial was not the cause officially invoked. Her last speech to her judges includes the following words:

> " 'I am willing to believe that you have sufficient reasons for what you have done, but they must be other than those which have been produced in court, for I am clear of all the offences which you then laid to my charge." (*The Concubine*, p. 334).

Unless we admit that Anne was guilty until proven innocent, we should keep an open mind on the possible nature of "other" "sufficient reasons."

The sympathetic attitude of Anne toward the Reformation may have involved far more than the partial "return to the source" represented by Protestantism. If such was the case, could Henry, who had alienated himself from Rome and who needed the support of the Anglican Church, afford the risk of a wife dedicated to the Secret Doctrine and to the protection of its believers? Could the influence of her creed have sapped the fundations of the English "Ancien Régime?" Shelley seems to answer the question in the affirmative. The combination of forces inimical to the Queen include established religion, the Throne, Mammon — in short what is designated by Shelley as "the settled Swellfoot system."

The system must be preserved at all costs. One of its basic requirements is the continued fertility of the average "famished" Pig. One must be born every minute — to consume and be taxed. Other traits of "Beotia" are cited. Among them is missionary zeal "To teach the other nations how to live:"

> *"Purganax.* Grant me your patience, Gentlemen and Boars,
> Ye, by whose patience under public burthens
> The glorious constitution of these sties
> Subsists, and shall subsist. The Lean-Pig rates
> Grow with the growing populace of Swine,
> The taxes, that true source of Piggishness
> (How can I find a more appropriate term
> To include religion, morals, peace, and plenty,
> And all that fit Boeotia as a nation
> To teach the other nations how to live?),
> Increase with Piggishness itself; — "

"Temporary" "state necessity" is invoked to justify austerity measures reducing the fare of famished multitudes from regular hogwash to water and straw. The same "state necessity" seems to demand the trial of the Queen. The populace may take comfort from vague hopes of singing to-morrows. Above all from knowledge that law and order will prevail.

> "That is — it is a state-necessity —
> Temporary, of course. Those impious Pigs,
> Who, by frequent squeaks, have dared impugn
> The settled Swellfoot system, or to make
> Irreverent mockery of the genuflexions
> Inculcated by the arch-priest, have been whipped
> Into a loyal and an orthodox whine."

Surrounded by such enemies, the Queen can only be destroyed:

> *"Swellfoot.* — Off with her head!"

The portrait of Anne which is usually conveyed by official history stresses her vanity, greed, and reckless ambition. It is not always noted that the girl resisted the advances of Henry during a period of nine years, a feat of no mean significance if one considers the power and the disposition of the love-sick King. Her wish to remove herself from court is not always mentioned. Such a desire seems to belie ambitious personal design. Much is made of the story of Catherine's jewels which Anne is said to have wanted and obtained after the disgrace of her predecessor. But the official version of the affair is regarded in some quarters as propaganda designed to discredit Anne. Catherine chose to believe that the royal order to part with the jewels had been prompted by "the concubine." History generally echoes her belief. But Harry Norris who had been despatched to receive the jewels felt otherwise. " '—they'll say that she asked for the Queen's jewels — it is not so. There is no woman alive who cares less for trappings and trivialities.' "* The courage of Anne as she

---

*Norah Lofts, *The Concubine,* p. 210.

faced the block is usually recognized. But its full extent — and source — can only be surmised from testimonies not always given:

> "'I have seen men and also women executed, and they have been in great sorrow, but to my knowledge, this lady hath much joy and pleasure in death.'" (Sir William Kingston in a letter to Cromwell)
> 'No person ever showed greater willingness to die.'" (The Spanish Ambassador in a letter to Charles V).

The *Encyclopaedia Britannica* renders a fairly typical opinion of the validity of charges brought against Anne:

> "Anne's guilt remains unproved. She protested her innocence to her jailer and made no confession on the scaffold. Yet, despite her universal unpopularity and the king's weariness of her, it hardly seems likely that two grand juries, a petty jury and a tribunal of nearly all the lay peers of England should have passed sentence of guilt quite contrary to the evidence — which they had before them and which we do not possess — and that such a sentence should have been concurred in by her own uncle and father."

The official view that so many judges could hardly be wrong seems based on the assumption that there is safety in numbers. Such an assumption may be sound in the case of free men. But the peers and other persons who pronounced Anne guilty cannot be so regarded. Henry had practically served notice that he would regard any verdict of "innocent" as treason. The fact that traitors died a horrible death was well known. The evidence "which we do not possess" remains an undeniable mystery. But the considerable amount of evidence we know of was grossly contrived, easily refuted by Anne, and virtually demolished by the simple logic of street people. The fact that the father of the accused pronounced her guilty loses strength in the light of his character. Sir Thomas Boleyn had encouraged the prostitution of Anne's elder sister — Mary — to the King and benefited thereby. His only regret was that Mary had not derived maximum profit from her love affair with Henry. His behavior toward Anne was dictated by the same considerations of personal design. Sir Thomas used his daughters as pawns which could and did serve his ambitions. Sir Thomas consistently played the role of Pontius Pilate when his daughters fell from royal favor. The uncle of Anne — Norfolk — was equally willing to pander to the passions of Henry and to save his own neck by sacrificing the neck of his niece. It is elementary to examine the character of "witnesses" in any important affair. We should question the reliability of calculating and terrorized judges be they peers, fathers, or uncles. We might also wonder why such comments as that of the Lord Mayor of London on the trial of Anne are generally overlooked:

609

"I could not observe anything in the proceeding against her, but that they were resolved to make an occasion to get rid of her." (The Lord Mayor of London, who was present at the trial).

One could easily conclude from the reading of the *Encyclopaedia Britanica* that the editors never heard of what is called "kangaroo courts," or that such institutions, which blight modern dictatorships in distant countries, were invented in our objective age. One might also conclude that ANY organized anarchy or perverted simulacrum of justice is preferable to the one unthinkable crime: questioning the Principle of Authority. Better by far sacrifice one head and the very concept of Justice than rock the Ark so manfully staffed by priests, Kings, fathers, uncles, and peers!

"Swellfoot systems" of all ages have one trait in common. They seek to perpetuate themselves in the name of all that is holy, in short in the name of "civilization." What is actually meant by the latter word should often be read as a special interests such as the Pentagon, U. S. Steel, Sears and Roebuck, or the Vatican. In the admirable words of Pauwels and Bergier, "Civilizations is a conspiracy — Modern life is a silent compact of comfortable folk to keep up pretenses. And it will succeed till the day comes when there is another compact to strip them bare."*

The "van of Change" is naturally unpopular with "Swellfoot systems" which tend to regard any *meaningful* progress as subversive. Whether they seek a return to the message of Buddha and Christ or faithful compliance with their Constitution, such "impious Pigs" as dare "squeak" are promptly classified and treated as "radicals." The human symptoms of traceable ailments are conveniently regarded as the cause of all evil. Such a transfer of guilt is a luxury which modern mankind can no longer afford. The Man of the Atomic Age has reached a point of his evolution where nothing short of a thorough "return to the source" of crises will save him. The quality of life — with which we are rightfully concerned — will become academic is Life is no more. Physical survival is at stake. The quality of life is unlikely to improve as long as certain values prevail where the Quality of Authority is concerned.

It is because of unquestioning submission to ANY KIND of Authority that History is — in the words of Voltaire — "a long catalog of murders" such as the execution of Anne Boleyn. It is out of the same submission that the gas chambers of Auschwitz and the torture chambers of the Third Reich were made. It is to the same unquestioning acceptance of "evidence which we do not possess" that we owe current warfare in the Far East and the existence of political butchers elsewhere. It is to the same unwillingness to know, to think, and to judge that we owe the rationale of

---

The Morning of the Magicians, p. 94.

modern elections: the admitted "selling" not of men but "images." It is to the same unquestioning attitude that mankind may owe an environmental disaster or one atom bomb too many some day.

The ability to criticize the Quality of human Power ruling our lives is not subversive in itself. We are told that it is the right and the duty of every citizen of Western Democracies. But it is labeled "subversive" whenever the said Powers are shown to have betrayed their mandate. In other words when unwelcome truths are told. We should question the value of a Principle of Authority which is afraid of the depths of our own literature and of the reality of our own History. We should wonder where true subversion lies. Whether it is the crime of persons who wish to live by the law of evolution? Or whether it is the act of those who would sabotage if not stop its course? The time may have come to determine where the greater peril lies to true civilization: in discriminating knowledge? or in sheepish ignorance?

The filtering process known as modern news management might easily be classified as "occult science." If the word "occult" means "hidden," the news media of the contemporary West should rank high in some hierarchies. The background of History now in the making is not alone committed to frequent secrecy. Some important developments of contemporary science are treated as skeletons in closets. Following the first low-altitude flight of Ranger IX over the moon, the *Figaro Littéraire* reported the presence of unexpected geometrical patterns on photographs of the lunar surface. The patterns — which were said to include checkerboard designs — were of a kind which could only have been made by intelligent beings. The article stated that the amazing data had been withheld from the American public for fear of a general panic. We may wonder what other facts may likewise be concealed in the same spirit of paternalistic over-protection. We may doubt the assumption that the American public would "panic" so easily. We may even speculate as to who or what is likely to "panic" when a major scientific development supports the Secret Doctrine. We may also wonder what machinery is at work when the privilege of exploring space is restricted to test-pilots and when eager scientists are consistently barred from becoming astronauts. The public which financially supports the acquisition of knowledge in general and space exploration in particular is entitled to know what is discovered on the moon — and elsewhere. It is better prepared by far to receive elements of scientific truth than news manipulators seem to believe. Some of its members would welcome such articles as that of the *Figaro Littéraire* on the front page of their daily newspaper. Some would welcome a televised reporting of moon exploration more enriching than

611

the performance which they do get: a mixture of Billy Graham and Dick and Jane.

If we must have *Genesis* thrown in with moon-landings, let us have Genesis all the way. Let us transcend the "cut and re-cut" version or "coupé superfétatoire" scorned by M. de Charlus. Let us not fear to study a doctrine which may hold the answers to questions asked by Man through the ages. Let us not fear the dizzying vistas of Time, Space and Beyond which it offers. Let us not fear to face the possibility that previous civilizations may have been far more brilliant than our own in some respects. Let us not dwarf the timelessness of our own heritage.

> "History itself is dealt with by the so-called historians as unscrupulously as legendary lore — While Materialists deny everything in the universe, save matter, Archaeologists are trying to dwarf Antiquity, and seek to destroy every claim to ancient Wisdom by tampering with Chronology. Our present-day Orientalists and Historical writers are to ancient History that which the white ants are to the buildings in India. More dangerous even than those termites, the modern Archaeologists — the 'authorities' of the future in the matter of Universal History — are preparing for the History of past nations the fate of certain edifices in tropical countries: 'History will tumble down and break into atoms in the lap of the twentieth century, devoured to its foundations by her annalists,' said Michelet. Very soon, indeed, under their combined efforts, it will share the fate of those ruined cities in both Americas, which lie deeply buried under impassable virgin forests. Historical facts will remain as concealed from view by the inextricable jungles of modern hypotheses, denials, and scepticism." (*The Secret Doctrine*, pp. 675-76, Vol. II).

The pessimistic view of Mme Blavatsky is compensated by an important fact. The Law of Evolution is on the side of Truth:

> "But very happily *actual* History repeats herself, for she proceeds, like everything else, in cycles; and dead facts and events deliberately drowned in the sea of modern scepticism will ascend once more and reappear on the surface . . ." (*The Secret Doctrine*, pp. 675-76, Vol. II).

The re-emergence of various historical facts which is expected by occultists and esoteric writers will depend on the same approach as will the discovery of integral literary truth. The objective value of some subjective faculties and the corresponding worth of non-material facts will have to be recognized. The limitations of "the plane of events, which in themselves are nothing"* will have to be faced. The hidden background of many developments will prove more meaningful and more enlightening than the face of developments themselves.

A la Recherche du temps perdu, p. 754, Vol. III.

> "Bloch thought that political truth can be approximately reconstructed by the most lucid brains, but he imagined, as do the masses, that it resides always, undeniable and material, in the secret file of the President of the Republic and of the Prime Minister, who communicate it to the ministers. Yet, even when political truth involves documents, it is rare for them to have more than the value of a radiological negative where the ordinary man thinks that the illness of the patient is inscribed in all letters, whereas, in fact, this negative supplies a simple element of appreciation combined with many others on which the reasoning of the physician will operate and from which he will draw his diagnosis. Thus, political truth, when one approaches informed men and when one believes it is reached, vanishes." (*A la Recherche du temps perdu*, pp. 241-42, Vol. II).

The Proustian view of the "negative" aspect of "fact," the Voltairian view of the reverse side of the "fine picture," and the exhortation of Vigny to seek historical truth "beyond what is seen"* all have their root in the same belief that events are only "the waste product of experience." The total experience is alone capable of conveying truth. It is inseparable from subjective factors which tend to become amazingly objective when certain veils are lifted. History is one gateway among others to a great Book of Fate embracing the awesome depths of the individual and collective unconscious. The Book in question — which is instinctively dreaded by the majority of Westerners — is the common base of History, Literature, Art, and of all other areas of human Knowledge.

> "As for the inner book of unknown signs (protruding, it seemed, which my attention, as it explored my unconscious, sought, bumped, outlined, as does a probing diver), for the reading of which no one could help me with any rule, that reading consisted in an act of creation in which no one can substitute to or collaborate with us. Thus how many shrink from writing it! How many tasks does one not assume in order to avoid that one! Each event, be it the Dreyfus case, be it the war, had supplied other excuses to writers to avoid that one book; — " (*A la Recherche du temps perdu*, p. 879, Vol. III).

One may note in passing what a major clue to the *Recherche* is given by the author in the above passage. What is the "Dreyfus case?" What is "the war?" One may also note that the Proustian concept of History, while paying due respect to the contingent domain of "facts" never loses touch with the realm of non-contingency, "other laws," or "Truth."

> "The Muse who gathered all that the higher Muses of philosophy and art have rejected, all that which is not founded on truth, all that which is only contingent but also reveals other laws: is History!" (*A la Recherche du temps perdu*, p. 675, Vol. III).

---

*Alfred de Vigny, *Cinq-Mars* (*Réflexions sur la Vérité dans l'Art*).

If M. de Charlus is correct, the historians of the future will not shirk the study of "inversion." They will be vindicated. Their work will be guided by a fundamental tenet of the Secret Doctrine:

> "It needs but the right perception of things objective to discover that the only world of reality is the subjective."

If the expectation of Mme Blavatsky is correct, the re-emergence of certain historical facts will soon take place. The dwarfed chronology of Antiquity will be re-examined. The area of study pertaining to modern times will benefit. Many distortions, if not falsehoods, will be exposed — as will corresponding Truths. Historians will bear in mind the new dimension of certain facts with which they are already familiar. International mythologies will be questioned from new angles. All countries say the same thing at certain times. All have God and right on their side for the same alleged reasons. A certain "Germanophilia" akin to the attitude of M. de Charlus will be useful. It will be based upon unerring recognition of "germane" or analogous aspects of historical fables. It will be inspired by awareness of "germane" elements in diverse cultures and by a feeling of "germaneness" or universal brotherhood.

Individual history will receive like attention. Whitewash jobs will be questioned particularly where *intent* is concerned. The sainthood of Louis IX may suffer. The allegation often made in encyclopaedias and manuals that Calvin, the man who deliberately schemed the burning of Servetus and of many others, was a good person on the whole will not stand. The related intimation that Torquemada did little more than use techniques already employed by civil courts of his times and that he was no monster will not hold. The shameful slurs often aimed at greatness will become fully and edifyingly understandable. It will be difficult to make the public swallow such enormities as the sneers commonly directed at Voltaire. The public will see why some commentators insist that the Sage who gave so much for the progress and happiness of mankind was a rather pernicious influence all in all. The public will draw certain conclusions.

The task facing historians is immense. The story of Anne Boleyn is only one case in point.

How many truncated, slanted, buried events are there? How many whitewash jobs? How many GREEN BAGS?

PHILOSOPHY

The area of Knowledge designated as Philosophy is least likely to be wanting where the presence of the Secret Doctrine is concerned.

It is hinted on the esoteric plane of *Micromégas* that each philosophical system briefly and humorously mentioned — the Thomistic creed excluded — contains elements of truth. The seemingly closed vase represented by each philosophy may bear studying in the light of One nameless Doctrine. We should follow in exploratory spirit the suggestion of the Sage.

The task will probably be as extensive as the corresponding work in Literature and History. The present chapter is therefore limited to a few suggestions.

Many a philosopher outlined a near-perfect system only to stop as if faced by an impassable wall. Many a philosopher built a near-perfect structure only to allow a signal weakness to mar the edifice. Many philosophical texts are obscure. Such "walls," "weakness," and difficulties of comprehension may — in many cases — be esoteric veils and baits.

Descartes is generally regarded as Rationality itself. Such a view is legitimate. But we may have a narrow idea of the Cartesian concept of "rationality" or "reason." The Cartesian theory of "animal spirits" the belief in a soul which must "go to school" to regain lost knowledge, the emphasis placed on the pineal gland — or residue of the Third Eye — may all be reflections of the Secret Doctrine. It is said in *The Morning of the Magicians* that Descartes would probably reject "Cartesian" philosophy were he alive in our age. It is conceivable that Louis Pauwels and Jacques Bergier — who flatly label Rabelais as an initiate — recognize the presence of the Secret Doctrine in Cartesian thought. Their speculation may represent a dim view of our insight. Descartes might indeed repudiate what we have made of his philosophy were he to return. The warning given by Joyce is also provocative: "Sink deep or touch not the Cartesian spring."* Bearing in mind the possible presence of the Primitive Wisdom-Religion in Cartesian texts, we may benefit greatly from such hints.

Spinoza is usually regarded as difficult. Will Durant makes the following comment on the *Ethics*:

---

*Quoted in *Samuel Beckett,* William York Tindall, Columbia Essays on *Modern Writers,* Columbia University Press, 1964.

"Read the book not all at once, but in small portions at many sittings. And having finished it, consider that you have but begun to understand it." (*The Story of Philosophy, The Lives and Opinions of the Greater Philosophers*, Simon and Schuster, New York, 1953, p. 130).

It is noted, however, that the maze of the *Ethics* is not impossible to explore. A certain approach is reported to exist which leaves not "a single line" "obscure:"

"One need not say, with Jacobi's enthusiastic exaggeration that 'no one has understood Spinoza to whom a single line of the *Ethics* remains obscure.' " (p. 130).

The key to the *Ethics* — and to the entire philosophy of Spinoza — may well lie in a strange place. Poverty once led the famous thinker to make an observation which is reported as follows in the work of Will Durant:

"And he would say sometimes, to the people of the house, that he was like the serpent who forms a circle with his tail in his mouth; to denote that he had nothing left at the year's end." (p. 121).

The snake in a circle may explain the surprising ease with which the works of Spinoza are "read" by some persons.

Sartrian thought may not be unrelated to the same snake. The narrator of *La Nausée* notes the futility of trying to "catch time by the tail."* The feeling of being "at the bottom of time" which is expressed more than once suggests the cyclic design of Time or Eternity. Hence the snake in a circle. Several Sartrian propositions may reflect basic tenets of occult philosophy. The "en soi" and "pour soi" may be akin to the atomic theory of Leibnitz which closely resembles the occult view: Every atom in the Universe has the potentiality of self-consciousness in it, and is, like the Monads of Leibnitz, a Universe in itself, and for itself."** The emphasis placed on Responsibility may correspond to Karma. Man the Builder of the Self- and his implied Self-Knowledge — may correspond to the ageless "Know Thyself!" or to the Voltairian concept of the "science of man." The importance of "commitment" practically postulates "spirit" of some kind. The stress placed on Human Solidarity may not be foreign to the Oriental view of Universal Oneness. "Hell is other people" may refer to the bondage of separate being. The loneliness and the frequent absurdity of human condition may represent Maya. Being *and* Nothingness seem to be one and the same, the word "Nothingness" being taken in the esoteric sense. (Simone de Beauvoir confesses an occasional "weakness" for the "calm indifference in which being equals nothingness."***) The Sartrian definition of existence could have been

---

The Nausea, New Directions, p. 40.
**The Secret Doctrine*, p. 107, Vol. I.
***Mémoires d'une jeune fille rangée*, Livre de Poche, p. 383.

written by Mme Blavatsky: "Existence is an imperfection."* It may also be noted that the definition of "sin" which is given by Simone de Beauvoir comes remarkably close to the Aristotlean concept of "privation" which is the frequent companion of Maya in esoteric texts: "Sin is the gaping void of God."**

The well-known proposition that "existence precedes essence" is meaningfully compatible with the feeling of being "at the bottom of time." In other words with the idea of living in an era which tends to reduce spirituality and essential truth to their smallest expression. One must go through existence before spirit or essence may be reborn. The famous Sartrian axiom may be basically identical to the Panglossian refrain according to which "all is for the best" *evolutionary conditions considered.*

Stripped as it is of objectively visible elements of occult philosophy, Sartrian existentialism can inspire XXth Century mankind at a time when established faiths are increasingly questioned while the bulk of mankind remains incompletely prepared for a conscious "return to the source." The visible surface of Sartrian philosophy seems to have been designed for a transitional age of restless unbelief.

Specific passages of the writings of Sartre tend to confirm general speculation on the presence of esoteric material. The initial part of *Les Mots* — the autobiographical work of the author — describes the days of boyhood and the constant role-playing of the dutiful, narcissistic child growing up in a world of dutiful, narcissistic adults. Deceit is prolonged into mature years and materialized in writing:

> "One writes for one's neighbors or for God. I decided to write for God with the purpose of saving my neighbors. I wanted gratitude and not readers. Scorn corrupted my generosity. During the period in which I was protecting female orphans, I had already begun to get rid of them by sending them into hiding. As a writer, my manner did not change: before saving mankind, I would start by blindfolding it; only then would I turn against the black, swift little henchmen, against words; when my new orphan dared untie the blindfold, I would be far away. Saved by a lone deed, at first she would not notice, shining on a shelf in the National Library, the brand new little volume that bore by name." (*The Words — Writing* — Fawcett Publications, Inc., pp. 112-113).

The same "blindfolding" process seems to be contemplated at the the end of *La Nausée*. The question of how the narrator's existence may be justified is answered by the writing of "a book" which is virtually admitted to be esoteric:

---

*The Nausea, New Directions, p. 101.

617

"It would have to be a book: I do not know how to do anything else. But not a History book — another kind of book. I do not know too well what kind — but one would have to guess, behind the printed words, behind the pages, something which would not exist, which would be above existence — a time would come when the book would be written, when it would be behind me, and I think that a little of its clarity might fall over my past."

The mission of the author is to aid the "unblinding" of mankind. It is openly designated as the mission of a savior. It will be accomplished through deception. Sartre might as well have written the observation of "Albertine" which states the raison d'être of all esoteric works: "When I lie to you, it is always out of love for you."

The name of the narrator of *Nausea* — Roquentin — suggests a "rock" or esoteric interpreter. The meaning of his reunion with his aging mistress — Anny — may therefore be symbolic. The sadness of the meeting which follows many years of physical separation is compensated by the existence of enduring closeness. Common concerns have continued to be shared during the period of physical estrangement. Fetishes of dubious value have been discarded by the woman. Anny compares Roquentin to a roadmarker suggesting solidity as well as a significant point on a highway or "path:"

"You are a roadmarker, she said, a roadmarker on the edge of a road. You explain imperturbably and you will explain all your life that Melun is twenty-seven kilometers from here and Montargis forty-two. That is why I need you so much."

The "road which is connected with "need" or "necessity" may be the course of human evolution. The "rock" or "Interpreter" seems to be regarded as a source of strength and as a guide.

The mistress of Roquentin may represent the esoteric equivalent of the "blind orphan" of *Les Mots*. Her enduring closeness to the narrator, her evolution and growing insight suggest the allegorical identity of XXth Century mankind. The time of her "unblinding" has not yet come, a fact which seems consistent with the statement made in *Les Mots*: "— I would be far away." But the long-awaited day is coming "by degrees" for the narrator and his love. The final pages of *Nausea* seem to convey the same veiled belief as the second act of *Waiting for Godot*. The apparent futility of "waiting" covers the reality of an approaching event. The imminent "unblinding" of "Anny" — an act which will be performed by the "blind orphan" herself — seems to be one esoteric version among many of the same development: "The shepherd has himself brought light into his house."

"I can no longer remember how I came. By way of the Dautry stairway, no doubt; have I really climbed one by one its one hundred and ten steps? What is still more difficult to imagine perhaps, is that, in a little while, I will descend them — I will be able, as I raise my head, to see the windows of those houses which are so near light up. From afar."

The pessimistic surface of the last lines of the book may cover a song of joy. The nature of coming "rain" may be inferred from fragments of the Tree of Knowledge to which "light" is added:

"Night falls. On the second floor of Hotel Printania two windows have just lit up. The yard of the New Station strongly smells of damp wood: to-morrow it will rain on Bouville."

The Sartrian combination of "blind orphan" and "Anny" is suggestive. The author may have courted a connection between the heroine of the well-known comic strip: Little Orphan Annie and the "woman" of La Nausée The references which are made to the eyes of Anny may be calculated to suggest the strange eyes of the comic strip figure. Anny has "eyes without expression."* Her statement that she has "changed up to and including the whites of" her "eyes"** arouses deep emotion in her lover who ceases to "look for a departed Anny." The possibility of an intended linkage between "Anny" and Annie may also be suggested by the observation: "Nothing that exists can be comic."*** If such be the design of the author, the use of a comic strip character is of the same order of expression as the exoteric emphasis placed on the rag-time melody *Some of these days — "*. The tune is a source of happiness, a manifestation of true reality, the child of "necessity," "the event which so many notes have prepared, dying in order that it might be born," and the irrefutable proof that *something has happened."****

As final revisions are made to the present work, the comic strip *Little Orphan Annie* has ceased to appear in American newspapers. The weekly feature which was regularly accompanied by quotations from the writings of great authors may have served its purpose. One of the last issues showed the "blind orphan" riding the white winged horse Pegasus, the symbol of literary inspiration. The feeling of "mission accomplished" which follows the reunion of "Anny and "Roquentin" in *La Nausée* may have had an unsuspected counterpart in the end of the famous comic strip.

*Nausea, New Dir., p. 155.
**Ibid., p. 143.
***Ibid., p. 128.
****Ibid., p. 22.

It is believed by some persons that a certain amount of esoteric material is conveyed by newspaper advertising and other down-to-earth media. It is therefore conceivable that comic strips are occasional vehicles of hidden substance:

> "The general theory of information and semantics proves fairly conclusively that it is possible to draw up texts which have a double, triple or quadruple meaning. There are Chinese texts in which seven meanings are enclosed one within the other. One of the heroes is in Van Vogt's *In Pursuit of the Slans* discovers the existence of other mutants by reading the newspapers and deciphering apparently inoffensive articles. A similar network of communication in our own Press and literature, etc., is quite conceivable. *The New York Herald Tribune* published on 15th March, 1958, an analysis from its London correspondent of a series of advertisements appearing in the Personal column of the *Times*. These messages had attracted the attention of professional cryptographers and the police in various countries; because they obviously had a hidden meaning. But this meaning was never deciphered. There are, no doubt, other still less decipherable means of communication. Who knows but that some fourth-rate novel, or some technical textbook, or some apparently obscure philosophical work is not a secret vehicle for complex studies and messages addressed to higher intelligences, as different from our own as we are from the great apes." (*The Morning of the Magicians*, pp. 411-12).

The much-bandied phrases "Sartrian thought," "Sartrian existentialism" may be reducible to a few simple words: the "unblinding" of a "blind orphan:" ourselves. Which is saying quite a bit. There are many great lessons to be learned from the eclectism of great minds. We may wonder accordingly how much science is concealed in "science-fiction." We may also speculate on the possible tenor of a certain type of "detective story" which is more than a detective story if Michel Butor is to be believed.* Spirit may be found on all planes of existence — comic strips included. "Roadmarkers," "guides," or — in the words of Saint-Exupéry — "stars which know how to laugh" are no myths.

We may soon find the same unfettered concept of "Reason" to underlie the systems of many philosophers. Voltaire, a thinker least likely to be suspected of occult inspiration, has long deceived all but a few persons. One fact is now clear, however. If we must scoff at the Secret Doctrine, we may no longer do so on the basis of "Voltairian" feeling. The next question to arise is that of other philosophical "smugglers" still undetected. We may soon find that Voltaire took no liberties with the meaning of the word "philosophy" when he referred to a certain "small fund." . . of the Secret Doctrine.

Passing Time, Ch. 4, Part I.

THE SECRET DOCTRINE
IS IT TRUTH?

Time will be required to reveal the full implications of the esoteric presence in Literature. Several categories of persons will be involved in the process.

To a small minority the reflection of the Wisdom-Religion in Literature will not be news. Little needs to be said about "good company." The majority of the public will probably — and understandably — recoil from a fact so startling and heavy with significance. Some persons will deny or summarily dismiss evidence. Various aspects of esoteric literature will be regarded as "subjective interpretation" or "coincidence." The latter word — a well tested formula of "exorcism" — will be used with sufficient frequency to change its meaning. No more needs to be said about voluntary blindness which has been aptly commented from Antiquity to Christ and M. de Charlus: *Oculos habent et non vident!* To a great number of persons endowed with the precious faculties of curiosity and independent thought, the emergence of esoteric literature will give occasion to ask a crucial question: Is the Secret Doctrine Truth?

To judge the Universal Writ in what is usually called "objective" manner would require phenomenal knowledge. No branch of human learning is unrelated to secret lore. Literature, philosophy, theology, history, psychology, psychiatry, criminology, medicine, anthropology, geology and mathematics are among fields which have counterparts in the Secret Doctrine. It is doubtful that any ordinary human mind is equipped to test the validity of occult science in all domains without external help. The average inquirer can only compare those elements of knowledge which he does posess with corresponding tenets of the Secret Doctrine. In the face of horizons so surveyed individual learning assumes its true dimension: that of a drop in an ocean.

Our attitude in facing the question is as important as knowledge itself. We may be helped in our search by remembering certain facts. The "indiscernible community" has a significant trait. Firm in its belief that collective and individual Man embraces Truth when ready, the said community seeks no converts. Nor does it ask anyone to believe on blind faith. Blind faith and superstition are its worst enemies. It is the expectation of "good company" that our critical faculties will be exercised honestly and fully. We are not required to abdicate common sense, reason, or doubt. We are asked to cultivate them in purest form. We are asked to be skeptical of illusion and acceptant of evidence.

We are asked to revise our thinking about the "natural" and the "supernatural." — "There are no miracles." But there are countless wonders. — The task is a difficult one for the average Westerner. We may reflect, however, on the many "solid truths" of science, religion, and politics which have been exploded in the course of recorded history. We need not look back in time to find many examples of collective fallacies manufactured daily and eagerly swallowed. It is as difficult to accept some of them as it is to believe in levitation or animated tablets. We may reflect that minds such as those of Plato, Rabelais, Voltaire, Shelley, Vigny, and Proust, to mention but a few, were unlikely to proclaim the existence of the invisible world without testing. Voltaire cunningly informs us that "Micromégas was on the spot." Vigny states that "the invisible is real" and that the concealed wisdom of Poetry is a "treasure of Thought and Experience." Proust declares Truth too staggering to be generally accepted in his age. Such statements point to more than abstract speculation. The apparent ability of literary "good company" to announce future events with chronological and other precision should invite deep thought. If such expression may be used, the conspiracy of genius which we face is unlikely to have toiled as it did for the mere sake of "pulling our leg."

Proust writes that certain "lies" have a way of becoming truths in due course of time.* "The truths of to-day are the falsehoods of yesterday." writes Mme Blavatsky. And vice-versa:

> "According to the ordinary course of affairs, a few generations pass away, and then there comes a period when these very truths are looked upon as commonplace facts, and a little later there comes another period in which they are declared to be necessary, and even the dullest intellect wonders how they could ever have been denied." (H. T. Buckle, *History of Civilization*, Vol. I, p. 256, quoted in *The Secret Doctrine*, p. 298, Vol. I).

We must bear in mind the mutability of all human things — human knowledge included.

The day may come when the endemic allergy of our times to certain ideas will cause much head-shaking. Certain questions will be asked — and answered — . What is so dreadful about a doctrine which proclaims the dignity of Man? Is not that what our democratic system is about?

---

*A la Recherche du temps perdu, p. 461, Vol. III.

What is so dreadful about a doctrine which glorifies the divine spark in Man? Is not that what our religious structures are about? What is so dreadful about a doctrine which promotes unhampered acquisition of Knowledge? Is not that what our institutions of higher learning are about?

Practical considerations demand an open-minded survey of the Secret Doctrine. The most apathetic and skeptical person can hardly be indifferent to the possibility of being buried alive. The occurrence of premature burial may not be ruled out by the recent advances of medical science. No professional pre-conception or sensitivity should carry weight in the face of such a possibility. The occult view of the death process should be thoroughly studied. Various aspects of medicine might benefit from related research. The Secret Doctrine is likely to have discreet devotees in all professional élites. Rabelais, Céline, and Jung are bound to have a few heirs. The time has come for such physicians to make themselves heard.

It is possible to be "buried alive" in more than one way. Professional persons dealing with psychology have the power to ordain tragic "funerals." Inspiring, compassionate work is often performed by such practitioners. But there is little protection against those who play God with the identities and fates of others. Nor is there much protection against well-meaning ignorance. Human beings are diagnosed, manipulated, and remodeled without appeal in the name of Science. There is hardly a man, woman, or child who does not fall into some neat pathological category and cannot be handled accordingly. The very absence of pathology tends to be regarded as suspect. There is a frightening tendency to label as "mentally sick" anything or anyone deviating from the unquestioned Norm; anything or anyone not understood. One shudders to think of the human mind and spirit dissected, classified, and processed on the basis of the behavior of pigeons and rats. One shudders to think of persons committed to mental institutions on the basis of what may be minimal insight.

The amount of irreparable harm which can be committed in the name of Science should open our eyes and minds to the necessity of a reassessment of knowledge in general — psychology and psychiatry in particular. What right do we have to refuse to investigate the possibility that the occult view of psychology may be correct? What right do we have to ignore positive findings if such findings are — or already were — made?

The indiscriminate Science-worship which is promoted by modern societies can be as damaging to mankind as superstition — which it often resembles — . The words of Professor Hiram Corson which were uttered during the last century remain sadly true in our day: " ' — instead of a Religious Papacy, we are in danger of being brought under a Scientific Papacy — we are in fact already brought under such a Papacy — " * The conclusion of Professor Corson may still be legitimate: Scientists " 'should 're-examine their stock in trade, so that we may make sure how far the stock of bullion in the cellar — on the faith of whose existence so much paper has been circulating — is really the solid gold of Truth.' " *

The spectacular advance of scientific knowledge which has been realized in our own century does not invalidate the above-quoted remarks. The same concern is voiced by contemporaries:

> "Science is, of course, the only true religion Americans still have left; like all religions it is worshipped abjectly by those who know it least. Beautiful women, literary people, social planners, editorial writers, presidents, politicians, and a sprinkling of illiterates do not know that science is most exact in those regions where it has progressed into the secrets of the universe about as far as the precision and exactitude of English spelling have advanced us into the secret lore of meaning. Which is to say: a distance. But not a great distance. Where science is exact, it is vastly insignificant; where it is significant it is open-ended, not certain, prey to reasoning by analogy, torn by debate, sustained by darkest mystery, and when all is said about as scientific as literary criticism. Be it understood between us that science possesses no secure idea of what is electricity, time, space, and the structure of the atom." (Norman Mailer, *Cannibals and Christians*, Dell Publishing Co., Inc., 1967, p. 67).

There is hardly a man, woman, or child alive in the Western world who has not been affected — directly or otherwise — by the theories of Freud. Some good has come from the removal of certain tabus which followed the diffusion of Freudian ideas. But the extent to which such benefits are cancelled — or exceeded — by harm can hardly be estimated. Countless persons who look to the purely physical aspects of sex and to sexuality for the ultimate good in life are doomed to disillusion. Countless persons needlessly cultivate toxic anxiety wondering whether or not they are in a Freudian state of grace: "sexually adequate." Countless mothers vacillate between fear of creating overdependency or Oedipal attachment and fear of "rejecting" a child. The house that Freud built is no longer immune to scientific attack. But the majority of victims — who do not know this — continue to torment themselves and others over manufactured dilemmas. Such persons might be helped — or crushed — were they to realize that the entire Freudian structure overshadowing their existence rests on the phobic withdrawal of one man:

> "It is said that Freud had an almost pathologic fear of metaphysics. According to Jung Freud was appalled by the occult implications he en-

---

*Quoted in Isis Unveiled, pp. 403-04, Vol. I.

countered in his exploration of the human psyche. Probing ever deeper into the mysteries of the unconscious regions he heard whispers — perhaps from that unseen world William James talked about — and they frightened him.

Freud confessed to him said Jung, 'that it was necessary to make a dogma of his sexual theory because this was the sole bulwark of reason against a possible outburst of the black flood of occultism.' " (William Braden, *The Private Sea — LSD and the Search for God,* Ch. XI, p. 143, Bentam Books).

If Freud was "appalled by the occult implications he encountered," we have a right to be even more appalled by the dishonest origin and glib merchandising of his theory. We also have the right to ask one question: How many other such "gospels" are now being foisted upon us in the name of Science? How many other prisons with invisible bars?

Parallel thoughts are unavoidable in connection with criminology. The understanding and the prevention of crime might be greatly aided by the contribution of Occult Science were the said contribution studied objectively. In the face of increasingly gruesome statistics what right have we to summarily reject any possible source of insight?

A secondary outgrowth of crime legally perpetrated in the modern West is suavely known as "behavior modification." The basic idea of burning — or "converting" — people who do not think — or behave — "as we do" is an ancient one. It is the common inspiration of oppressors of all times. The old passion for remodeling the bodies, the minds, and the spirits of others is far from dead. What should happen to no guinea-pig or other lab animal is inflicted upon human beings under the aegis of Public Weal and Science in mental and penal institutions. Various forms of "psycho-technology" ranging from the administration of drugs to limbic surgery are used. The rationale and performance of such activities do not essentially differ from those of practices condemned at the Nuremberg trial. The apathy of the public is cultivated by general silence and occasional propaganda. The victims are, after all, deviants or criminals. All is well with society in general and "Medical Facilities" in particular.

Certain questions should be raised with respect to deviance and crime. Is not the ultimate deviance that which scorns Natural Law to brutally violate the sanctuary of the human mind? Is not the ultimate crime that of all-mighty, drug-pushing, scalpel-happy, admittedly fumbling *experimenters?* Is it not also the indifference of the average man preferring not to think and not to know — much as others once ignored the overpowering stench of nearby crematoria? Is it not the unwillingness of the same average man to conceive that Science-and-Politics-In-One can do wrong? Is it not his inability to ask whose behavior might bear

625

"modifying?" Is it not his reluctance to surmise that no one is safe and his own brain may be next?

The scientific threat to our minds can only be countered by a powerful combination of Knowledge and Ethics. The scientifically programmed cretinization of mankind is least likely to succeed in a world where "the science of Man" prevails. What right have we to spurn without examination what may be our sole bulwark against the black flood of scientific vampirism?

Drug addiction is a problem of stolen frontiers. An honest look at our society can easily explain why some persons turn to drugs. Raised on the myth of the "finest castle in the world" and grand opportunity, many spirited beings find stone age mentalities and closed doors at every turn. Wealth and power strive to maintain on the muddy, mercantile plane of provincial soap-opera the same yearning mankind which should — and could — be reaching for the stars. Disastrous as it often is, drug addiction is a sign of the search for true meaning in life. Our stolen frontiers exist. They are as boundless as Man and Cosmos. They are within grasp. What do we fear most? The possibility of "bad trips" experienced by many? Or the possibility of "good trips" which we are meant to take? What right have we to shed crocodile tears or to compute sadistic sentences as long as the pure "trips" of mind and spirit — which can destroy addiction at its source — remain the forbidden fruit?

Much of the turmoil of our times grows out of repressed and suppressed spirit. More than ever in the course of our recorded history, "necessity" and spirituality are inseparable. Such is the message of esoteric literature in general and of The Little Prince in particular. Mankind — the passenger and pilot of a stranded aircraft — must re-discover what is lacking from its "machine." Mankind has a rendez-vous with its own "small voice." The "missing part" is Spirit. The site of the meeting is the Well of Knowledge.

Our continued "drinking" of physical life — in short our survival — is more than ever dependent on Spirit. Because of the nature of recent developments, we have unparalleled opportunity to destroy ourselves. Whether we consider the materially and otherwise famished millions who will not starve with good grace, the waste of irreplaceable resources, planned obsolescence, ecology, the population bomb, cloning, or the atom, we will ever stumble into the same wall which is that of our own vision, motivation, or spirit. Are we sufficiently "daring" to go back to that source? What do we most want out of life? What is the meaning of life? What can we do to maintain life? Such questions can no longer be ignored whether we be concerned with idealism or bare survival. We have reached a point where idealism and bare survival practically coincide whether we like it or not. The war between "sheep" and "flowers" — the importance of which no "grown up" will ever understand — is no mere poetic fancy. It is — among other things — the very real network of hidden natural forces with which we are increasingly tampering. The warning of Saint-Exupéry is not unique. Shelley urges "Boeotia" to "choose reform" in *Oedipus Tyrannus*. Vigny enjoins the mighty to take heed. Sartre exhorts us all to prevent the possible physical disasters of our own making which may result from abdication of our superior faculties:

> *"Et nunc, Reges mundi, nunc intelligite!"* (Alfred de Vigny, *Les Oracles*).

> " 'What have you done with your science? What have you done with your humanism? Where is your dignity of thinking reed?' " (Jean-Paul Sartre, *La Nausée*).

Spirit is less than ever a beautiful Sunday frill, some vague something in books or speeches. It is "useful." It is "necessary." It is our only chance.

Our Western world has long suffered from inability to define its terms and from inability to "go back to the source." We can no longer afford to palliate evil with loosely used words or to pursue false glamor and false benefit dabbling with symptoms. We must carry our search for the source of our troubles all the way. The source may be traced through the negative orientation of the Jehovic syndrome reflected on all planes of our society: a power to look *down*, strike *down*, keep *down*. It may ultimately be found in the greed and apathy which condone the supremacy of such a power. It lies in an area which defies external legislation: the innermost Self. We can expect little relief to our current crises until a fact-based system of ethics guides a sufficient number of hearts and minds. Such a system seems to be offered by the Secret Doctrine. We could do worse than give it serious thought. We are told that Occult Science — still holds the Key to all the world problems."* What right have we to spurn without examination a body of knowledge which may offer so much?

The words "spirit," "spiritual," and "spiritual values" do not have good press in our times. They are frequently connected with the idea of quackery. They show up with monotonous and phony regularity in official speeches which practice belies. They tend to be identified with the posturing hypocrisy which bleeds a brother all week and goes to Church on Sunday. The instinctive distrust which will probably be felt

---

The Secret Doctrine, p. 341, Vol. I.

by many sensitive souls is understandable. Time and study will be needed to restore the positive radiance of the Word.

The Secret Doctrine and its multiple reflections have more to offer than relief to problems and fears. The acquisition of what Voltaire called "the science of man" is a labor of joy. Marcel Proust recognized the unique quality of the undertaking when he despaired of making it tangible to the majority of readers. "Can one ever hope to transmit to the reader a pleasure which one has not felt?"* The experience represented by the esoteric concept of "pleasure" is non-transferable. Each man must earn the joy of discovering his innermost essence and its relation to the world. Such is the reason why no one can presume to answer the title question of this final chapter for another person. It is the privilege and duty of each individual to examine the possibility that the *Secret Doctrine* may be Truth.

Our universe is infinitely more exciting than most of us tend to realize. Cosmic consciousness begins at home: in our own minds. But its fruit is not limited to the realm of abstract ideas. Proust probably meant to be read literally when he suggested that our names may not be unknown in Cassiopea, Venus, or other "far out" regions.** Contemporary science is alert to the same possibility:

> "Radio-telescopes receive waves emitted ten thousand million light years ago and modulated in such a way as to resemble messages. The astronomer John Krauss, of the University of Ohio claims to have captured signals coming from Venus on June 2, 1956. Other signals from Jupiter, it is alleged, were received at the Princeton Institute." (*The Morning of the Magicians*, p. 185).

What we regard as "far out" may actually be "far in." We are privileged to live in a fantistic era of transition which is destined to bring home the oneness of certain "dreams" and reality:

> "As Teilhard de Chardin has stated, only the fantastic is likely to be true at the cosmic level. We believe that human phenomena must also be measured against the cosmic scale. The thinkers of antiquity said this. Our modern world, with its planetary rockets and its efforts to contact other intelligent beings, is saying it." (*The Morning of the Magicians*, Preface).

Numerous writers agree that our era faces a spectacular turning point in human evolution. The symbolic apocalypse envisioned in the *Recherche* is a "stellar and celestial" "bomb" launched toward us."*** The same

---

*A la Recherche du temps perdu, p. 855, Vol. III.
**Ibid., p. 378, Vol. II.
***Ibid., p. 802, Vol. III.

event is contemplated by Sartre: "It can happen any time, perhaps right now: the omens are present.* D. H. Lawrence has similar tidings:

> "'There's movement in the sky. The World is going to change again. They're throwing something to us from the distance, and we're going to have it, whether we want it or not.'" (D. H. Lawrence, St. Mawr).

The impending revolution of knowledge which is forecast by many writers will involve a return to the source of ancient lore and a giant forward step. It is noted in *The Morning of the Magicians* that studies recently made by Banach and Tarski in the field of advanced mathematics have produced conclusions "which resemble to an hallucinating degree the powers claimed by Hindu experts in the Samadhi technique."** Parallel developments are reported in other fields of knowledge. A cycle of particular importance seems to be closing. We are back with the "musikoi" and "mathematikoi" of Antiquity. We are re-discovering their scientific assets which may be profitably combined with the gains of intervening centuries. The same trend of timeless fusion is expected to open many doors.

> "At their present farthest limits physics, biology, mathematics touch on certain traditional concepts: certain aspects of esotericism, visions of the Cosmos, of the relation between energy and matter. Modern science, once freed from conformism, is seen to have ideas to exchange with the magicians, alchemists and wonder-workers of antiquity. A revolution is taking place before our eyes — the unexpected remarriage of reason, at the summit of its victories, and intuition. For the really attentive observer the problems facing contemporary intelligence are no longer problems of progress. The concept of progress has been dead for some years now. Today it is a question of change of state, of a transmutation. From this point of view those concerned with the domain of the interior life and its realities are in step with the pioneering savants who are preparing the birth of a world that will have nothing in common with our present world of laborious transition in which we have to live for just a little while longer." (*The Morning of the Magicians,* pp. xxii-xxiii).

> "Maybe we are living at a time when the near future speaks the same language as the distant past." (*The Morning of the Magicians,* p. 414).

In preparing ourselves for the coming new age we can hardly do better than study the works of great "smugglers." Most of us have barely begun to scratch the surface of literary texts. The surface is rich and deserves our love. But the veiled message has a beauty and a scope which defy words. We must explore its grand integrity.

---

*Nausea, New Dir., pp. 158-59.
**The Morning of the Magicians, p. 393.

Man is by definition "man-asic." He is a thinking being. His mind has equal access to orthodox rationality and to the esoteric realm of "Reason." Unless we wish to renounce our claim to human dignity, we must face the coming test of expanding horizons with hope and courage. The "trial" which "lasted two hundred and twenty years" is more than the trial of Voltaire. It is our own.

The task will require a "daring" which is admirably defined by a great contemporary scientist. One may question the chronology offered by Dr. Velikovsky where some cosmic upheavals are concerned. One may not accept his literal interpretation of certain terms. One may regret his lack of reference to *The Secret Doctrine*. But one can only welcome his general contribution to Knowledge. One can only applaud the quality of spirit which he knows how to practice as well as advocate:

> "— science today, as in the days of Newton, lies before us as a great uncharted ocean, and we have not yet sailed very far from the coat of ignorance. In the study of the human soul we have learned only a few mechanisms of behavior as directed from the subconscious mind, but we do not know what thinking is or what memory is. And in biology we do not know what life is. The age of basic discoveries is not yet at its end, and you are not latecomers, for whom no fundamentals are left to discover. As I see so many of you today, I visualize some of you, ten or twenty or thirty years from now, as fortunate discoverers, those of you who posses inquisitive and challenging minds, the will to persist, and an urge to store knowledge. Don't be afraid to face facts, and never lose your ability to ask the questions: Why? and How? Be in this like a child.
>
> Don't be afraid of ridicule: think of the history of all great discoveries. I quote Alfred North Whitehead:
> 'If you have had your attention directed to the novelties of thought in your own lifetime, you will have observed that almost all really new ideas have a certain aspect of foolishness when they are first produced.' "

Therefore dare.

And should even the great ones of your age try to discourage you, think of the greatest scientist of antiquity, Archimedes, who jeered at the theory of Aristarchus, twenty-five years his senior, that the earth revolves around the sun. Untruth in science may live for centuries, and you may not see yourself vindicated, but dare.
Don't persist in your idea if the facts are against it; but do persist if you see facts gathering on your side. It may be that even the strongest opposition, that of figures, will crumble before the facts. The greatest mathematician who ever walked on these shores, Simon Newcomb, proved in 1903, that a flying machine carrying a pilot is a mathematical impossibility. In the same year of 1903 the Wright brothers, without mathematics, but by a fact, proved him wrong.

All fruitful ideas have been conceived in the minds of the non-conformists, for whom the known was still unknown, and who often went back to begin where others passed by, sure of their way. The truth of today was the heresy of yesterday.

Imagination coupled with skepticism, and an ability to wonder — if you possess these — bountiful nature will hand you some of the secrets out of her inexhaustible store. The pleasure you will experience in discovering truth will repay you for your work; don't expect other compensation, because it may not come. Yet dare."

The "forest" of *Macbeth* is on the move. The "Bottle to the sea" has reached port. The "trial" which lasted 220 years is ended. "Godot" is no myth. The Saints — the true ones — are marching in. They bear such noble names as Rabelais, Voltaire, Vigny, and Proust. They count on our capacity for vision and courage.

The final *allegro* of *L'Esprit pur* may be heard reverberating in many forms and places. One such echo of the same grand *Marseillaise* is a song of merry solemnity. We may do worse than ponder its true depth:

"All you *need* is *love!"*

If we can laugh at ourselves for having been so blind so long, if we can recognize and cultivate the divine spark within, if we can take delight in literary study and general exploration unlimited, we may receive the gift which great minds and spirits wish us to possess. It is a message of life, goodness, unity, hope and joy. There is reason to suspect that it is the message of Truth.

Our world could use it.

Science and the Modern World (New York, 1925), Chapter III. (*Earth in Upheaval*, pp. 278-79).

BIBLIOGRAPHY

The Key to Theosophy, H.P. Blavatsky, first simplified Adyar edition by Clara M. Codd, The Theosophical Publishing House, Adyar, Madras, India, 1953.

Isis Unveiled, H. P. Blavatsky, The Theosophical University Press, Pasadena, California, 1963.

The Secret Doctrine, H. P. Blavatsky, The Theosophical University Press, Pasadena, California, 1963.

The Secret Doctrine, H. P. Blavatsky, The Theosophical Publishing House, (Adyar Edition), 1962.

La Sorcellerie des Campagnes, Charles Lancelin, Librairie Henri Durville, 36 Avenue Mozart, Paris, 16e.

Histoire Illustrée de la Littérature Française des Origines à 1930, Ch. -M. Des Granges, quatorzième edition, Paris, Hatier, 8 Rue d'Assas, 1937.

Manuel Illustré d'Histoire de la Littérature Française Des origines à l'époque contemporaine, G. Lanson et P. Truffau, quatrième edition, Librairie Hachette, 79, Boulevard Saint Germain, Paris 1932.

Romans de Voltaire, Présentés par Roger Peyrefitte, Le Livre de Poche Edition, Editions Gallimard et Librairie Générale Française, 1961.

Voltaire, Romans et Contes, Editions de H. Bénac, Garnier Classics, Paris Book Center, New York, 1960.

Candide, L'Ingénu, L'Homme aux 40 écus, par Voltaire, Bibliothèque de Cluny, texte établi et présenté par Pierre Grimal, Librairie Armand Colin, Paris, 1957.

A la Recherche du temps perdu, texte établi et présenté par Pierre Clarac et André Ferré, Bibliothèque de la Pléiade, Gallimard, Paris, 1954.

Death on the Installment Plan, Louis-Ferdinand Céline, Translated by Ralph Manheim, Signet, 1966.

The Morning of the Magicians, Louis Pauwels and Jacques Bergier, Avon Books, a division of the Hearst Corporation, 959 Eight Avenue, New York, N. Y. 10079, 1968.

Rabelais, Oeuvres Complètes, Editions Garnier Frères, 6 rue des Saint-Pères, Paris, 1962.